...lear and authoritative ...
private international law, a complex a... ...
now appears in a revised and fully updated ...

The English conflict of laws is a body of rules whose
is to assist an English court in deciding a case which conta... a
foreign element.

In this new third edition, the chapters on tort, jurisdiction
and staying of actions have been almost entirely rewritten. The
chapter on the Brussels and Lugano Conventions has been recast
and expanded. The growing influence of European Union law
on UK private international law is evident in this new edition,
which will be a valuable text for students and practitioners
alike.

J. G. COLLIER is a Fellow of Trinity Hall and Lecturer in
Law at the University of Cambridge.

Conflict of Laws

J. G. Collier

Fellow of Trinity Hall and Lecturer in Law, University of Cambridge

Third edition

CAMBRIDGE
UNIVERSITY PRESS

PUBLISHED BY THE PRESS SYNDICATE OF THE UNIVERSITY OF CAMBRIDGE
The Pitt Building, Trumpington Street, Cambridge, United Kingdom

CAMBRIDGE UNIVERSITY PRESS
The Edinburgh Building, Cambridge CB2 2RU, UK
40 West 20th Street, New York NY 10011-4211, USA
10 Stamford Road, Oakleigh, VIC 3166, Australia
Ruiz de Alarcón 13, 28014 Madrid, Spain
Dock House, The Waterfront, Cape Town 8001, South Africa

http://www.cambridge.org

First published 1987 © Cambridge University Press 1987
Second edition 1994 © Cambridge University Press 1994
Reprinted 1996
Third edition 2001 © Cambridge University Press 2001

Printed in the United Kingdom at the University Press, Cambridge

Set in 10/12pt Plantin [GC]

A catalogue record for this book is available from the British Library

Library of Congress Cataloguing in Publication data
Collier, John G. (John Greenwood)
Conflict of laws / J.G. Collier. – 3rd ed.
    p.   cm.
Includes bibliographical references and index.
ISBN 0 521 78260 0 (hb) – ISBN 0 521 78781 5 (pb.)
1. Conflict of laws – Great Britain.   I. Title.

KD680.C65   2001
340.9′0941 – dc21

ISBN 0 521 78260 0 hardback
ISBN 0 521 78781 5 paperback

Contents

Preface	*page* vii
Table of statutes	viii
Table of cases	xxiv

Part I: General principles — 1

1	Introduction	3
2	Characteristics of the English conflict of laws	8
3	Choice of law rules	11
4	Proof of foreign law	33
5	Domicile and residence	37
6	Substance and procedure	60

Part II: Jurisdiction and foreign judgments — 69

7	Jurisdiction of the English courts	71
8	Staying of English actions and restraint of foreign proceedings	84
9	Foreign judgments	109
10	Jurisdiction and judgments in the European Union and EFTA	131
11	Arbitration	179

Part III: Law of obligations — 187

| 12 | Contract | 189 |
| 13 | Tort | 220 |

Part IV: Property and succession   241

14   Property *inter vivos*   243

15   Succession   268

16   Matrimonial property relations   277

17   Trusts   286

Part V: Family law   293

18   Marriage   295

19   Matrimonial causes   319

20   Children   334

Part VI: Exclusion of foreign laws   359

21   Public policy   361

Part VII: Theoretical considerations   375

22   Reasons for and basis of the conflict of laws   377

23   Public international law and the conflict of laws   386

Index   395

Preface to the third edition

In the preface to the second edition I said that the conflict of laws had undergone very substantial changes in the six years since the book first appeared in 1987. More changes have meant that the chapters on tort, jurisdiction and staying of actions have been almost entirely rewritten and that on the Brussels and Lugano Conventions has again been recast and expanded. The influence of the European Union on our private international law is now considerable and looks likely to increase.

I am grateful once more to my colleagues and the students in the Cambridge Law Faculty for discussions with them. I am particularly indebted to Dr Pippa Rogerson for dealing with chapter 8 for me; much of that chapter is really hers. Once more I am very glad to thank Mrs Carol Dowling, who has, with the utmost efficiency, typed and retyped everything I have written for this edition, as she did last time.

I have tried to state the law as it stood on 1 March 2001.

Table of statutes

1677   Statute of Frauds (29 Car. 2 c. 3) s. 4   67
1772   Royal Marriages Act (12 Geo. 3 c. 11)   309
1837   Wills Act (7 Will. 4 & 1 Vict. c. 26)   272
        s. 9   273
        s. 18   273
1859   British Law Ascertainment Act (22 & 23 Vict. c. 63)   34
1861   Wills Act (24 & 25 Vict. c. 114)   272
1868   Judgments Extension Act (31 & 32 Vict. c. 54)   128
1882   Bills of Exchange Act (45 & 46 Vict. c. 61)   66
        s. 72   10
        Married Women's Property Act (45 & 46 Vict. c. 75)
        s. 17   285, 318
1892   Foreign Marriage Act (55 & 56 Vict. c. 52)   299, 301
        s. 22   299
1906   Marine Insurance Act (6 Edw. 7 c. 68)   194
1907   Evidence (Colonial Statutes) Act (7 Edw. 7 c. 16)   34
1920   Administration of Justice Act (10 & 11 Geo. 5 c. 81)
        109, 126, 127, 179
        s. 9(2)(b)   111
        s. 9(2)(d)   120
1924   Carriage of Goods by Sea Act (14 & 15 Geo. 5 c. 22)
        215, 394
1925   Administration of Estates Act (15 & 16 Geo. 5 c. 23)
        s. 33   287
        Law of Property Act (15 & 16 Geo. 6 c. 20)
        s. 35   287
        s. 36   287
        s. 53(1)(b)   61, 208
        s. 75(5)   244
        s. 136   253
        s. 137   257
        s. 177   273
        s. 184   61

1926 Adoption of Children Act (16 & 17 Geo. 5 c. 29)   353
Legitimacy Act (16 & 17 Geo. 5 c. 60)   25, 298
  s. 1   353
  s. 8   30, 353
1932 Administration of Justice Act (22 & 23 Geo. 5 c. 55) s. 2(1) 269
1933 Foreign Judgments (Reciprocal Enforcement) Act (23 & 24 Geo. 5 c. 13)   109, 126, 127, 128, 179
  s. 1(2)(a)   127
    (b)   125
  s. 2(2)   128
  s. 4(1)
    (a)(iii)   121
    (iv)   119
    (v)   121
    (b)   128
    (2)(a)
      (i)   113, 114
      (ii)   113
      (iii)   115
      (iv)   111, 113
      (v)   115
    (3)(a)   117
    (b)   117
  s. 8   129
1934 Law Reform (Miscellaneous Provisions) Act (24 & 25 Geo. 5 c. 41)   223
1945 Bretton Woods Agreement Act (8 & 9 Geo. 6 c. 19)   372
1947 Exchange Control Act (10 & 11 Geo. 6 c. 14)   213, 371
Foreign Marriage Act (10 & 11 Geo. 6 c. 33)   299, 301
1948 Law Reform (Personal Injuries) Act (11 & 12 Geo. 6 c. 41) 213, 236, 238
1949 Finance Act (12, 13 & 14 Geo. 6 c. 47) s. 28(2)   252
Marriage Act (12, 13 & 14 Geo. 6 c. 76)   314
1950 Arbitration Act (14 Geo. 6 c. 27) Part II   179, 181, 182
  s. 27   180
  s. 35(1)(a)   182
    (b)   182
  s. 36(1)   182
    (2)   182
  s. 37(1)   182
    (2)   182

s. 39   182
s. 40(b)   182
1954   Law Reform (Enforcement of Contracts) Act (2 & 3 Eliz. 2 c. 34)   62
1958   Variation of Trusts Act (6 & 7 Eliz. 2 c. 53)   291
s. 1(1)   291
s. 2(2)   291
1959   Legitimacy Act (7 & 8 Eliz. 2 c. 73)   26, 298
1960   Marriage (Enabling) Act (8 & 9 Eliz. 2 c. 29)   303
s. 1(1)   304
(3)   304
1963   Wills Act (c. 44)   10, 31 53, 55, 272, 393
s. 1   26, 272
s. 2(1)(a)   272
(b)   272, 275
(c)   275
s. 3   18, 26, 272
s. 4   273
s. 6(1)   272
(2)   272
(3)   272
1964   Diplomatic Privileges Act (c. 81)   389
1966   Arbitration (International Investment Disputes) Act (c. 41)   185, 393
1967   Uniform Laws on International Sales Act (c. 45)   214
1968   Consular Relations Act (c. 18)   389
International Organisations Act (c. 48)   389
1969   Family Law Reform Act (c. 46) s. 1(1)   48, 209
Administration of Justice Act (c. 58) Part II   173
1970   Equal Pay Act (c. 41)
s. 1(a)(11)   214
1971   Carriage of Goods by Sea Act (c. 19)   10, 215
Recognition of Divorces and Legal Separations Act (c. 53)   10, 27, 29, 53, 117, 323, 324, 325, 328, 394
1972   Maintenance Orders (Reciprocal Enforcement) Act (c. 18)   171
Civil Evidence Act (c. 30)
s. 4(1)   34
(2)   33
(4)   33
(5)   34
1973   Matrimonial Causes Act (c. 18)
s. 1(1)   320
ss. 11–13   321

s. 11   316, 317
    (d)   314, 316
s. 12   310, 311, 321
    (c)   310
s. 13   321
s. 14(1)   321
s. 16   321
s. 24   292
    (1)(c)   281
s. 46
    (2)   320
s. 47(1)   317, 319
    (2)   319
Domicile and Matrimonial Proceedings Act (c. 45)   10,
51, 55, 320, 323
s. 1(1)   47
    (2)   48
s. 3(1)   48, 50
s. 4(1)   49
    (2)   50
    (4)   50
    (5)   50
s. 5(2)   55, 320
    (3)   321
    (4)   320
    (5)   320
    (6)   90
s. 6(5)   321
Sched. 1 para. 8   90
              para. 9   90
1974   Trade Union and Labour Relations Act (c. 52)
s. 18   62
1975   Evidence (Proceedings in other Jurisdictions) Act (c. 34)
12, 393
Inheritance (Provision for Family and Dependants) Act
(c. 63)   318
Sex Discrimination Act (c. 65)
s. 6   214
s. 10(1)   214
1976   Legitimacy Act (c. 51)   26
s. 1
    (1)   298, 351
    (2)   351

s. 2   352
s. 3   352
s. 5   353
s. 10(1)   353
Fatal Accidents Act (c. 30)   66, 239
Adoption Act (c. 36)   10, 353
    s. 6   354
    s. 13(3)   354
    s. 14(2)(a)   354
    s. 15(2)(a)   354
    s. 17   355
    s. 22(1)   354
    s. 38   356
        (1)(c)   355
        (1)(d)   355
    s. 39   39, 49
        (5)   356
    s. 44   356
    s. 46(5)   356
    s. 62(2)   354
        (3)   354
    s. 72(2)   355
Race Relations Act (c. 74)
    s. 4   214
    s. 8   214
1977   Administration of Justice Act (c. 38) s. 4   66
Unfair Contract Terms Act (c. 30)   202, 236, 238
    s. 26   214
    s. 27
        (1)   214
        (2)   214
1978   State Immunity Act (c. 33)   389
1979   International Monetary Fund Act (c. 29)   372
Arbitration Act (c. 42)   181
Sale of Goods Act (c. 54)
    ss. 12–15   245
    ss. 17–19   245
    s. 18   245
    ss. 21–5   245
    s. 25(1)   248, 249
    s. 48   250

1980   Protection of Trading Interests Act (c. 11)
         s. 2   104
         s. 3   104
         s. 5   104, 126
             (2)(a)   126
                (b)   126
         s. 6   126
         Limitation Act (c. 58)   63
         s. 3   63
         s. 17   63
1981   International Organisations Act (c. 9)   389
         Supreme Court Act (c. 54)
         ss. 20–4   161
         s. 25(1)   269
         s. 37(1)   84
         s. 49(3)   84
         s. 51   82
         s. 69(5)   33
         s. 114(2)   269
         s. 152(4)   269
1982   Civil Jurisdiction and Judgments Act (c. 27)   71, 86, 109,
         128, 131, 287, 394
         s. 2   132
         s. 3   73, 132, 190
         s. 4(1)   173
         s. 6   173
         s. 7   174
         s. 10   175
         s. 16   175
         s. 17   175
             (1)   175
         s. 18(2)(e)   179
         s. 19   175
         s. 25   167
             (1)   77
             (3)   77
         s. 30   262
         s. 32   107, 117
         s. 33(1)(a)   114, 158
                (b)   114
                (c)   114
         s. 34   124

ss. 41–6   37, 53
s. 41(2)   139
     (3)   139
     (4)   139
     (6)   139
     (7)   139
s. 42(3)   139
     (4)   139
     (5)   139
     (6)   139
     (7)   139, 178
s. 43   139, 178
s. 44   139
s. 45(2)   139
     (3)   139
s. 46   139
s. 49   166
Sched. 1 (Brussels Convention, 1968)   91, 123
     Art. 1   134, 153, 171
          (1)   171
          (4)   140
     Art. 2   136, 146, 151, 191
     Arts. 2–23   137
     Art. 3   137, 173
     Art. 4   137, 167
     Art. 5   140
          (1)   140–4, 145, 147, 149, 157, 160, 192, 203
          (3)   80, 144–7, 175
          (5)   147–9
          (6)   287
          (8)   175
     Arts. 5–6   137
     Art. 6   140
          (1)   149–50
          (2)   150–1, 154
          (3)   151–2
     Art. 6A   140–75
     Arts. 7–12A   152
     Art. 8(2)   139
     Arts. 13–15   152, 154

Art. 13   139
Art. 16   137, 153, 154, 159, 164, 175
      (1)   140, 153, 261, 264, 265, 266
Art. 17   137, 144, 151, 153, 154–7, 158, 159, 164,
             165, 175
Art. 18   114, 137, 158–9, 164
Art. 19   159, 164
Art. 20   159
Art. 21   136, 159, 164, 165, 166
Art. 22   136, 160, 164, 166
Art. 23   165, 166
Art. 24   126, 167, 168
Art. 25   168
Art. 26   168
Art. 27   160, 168–72, 173
Art. 28   168, 169, 172
Art. 29   173
Art. 30   173
Art. 31   173
Art. 32   173
Art. 34   168, 173
Art. 36   173
Art. 37   173
Art. 38   174
Art. 40   173
Art. 41   173
Art. 42   174
Art. 44   174
Art. 45   174
Art. 52(1)   138
      (2)   138
Art. 53   138
Art. 55   174
Art. 56   174
Art. 57   160
Art. 59   137, 174
Art. 63   131
Sched. 1   132
Sched. 2   132
Sched. 3   132
Sched. 4   175

Art. 5(3)   175
Art. 5(8)   175
Art. 6A   175
Sched. 5   175
Sched. 6   179
Sched. 7   179
Administration of Justice Act (c. 53)   65
    s. 18   273
1983   Matrimonial Homes Act (c. 19)   318
       Mental Health Act (c. 20) s. 96   287
1984   Foreign Limitation Periods Act (c. 16)   10, 18, 60, 63,
       212, 238, 385
       s. 1(1)   64
          (5)   64
       s. 2(1)   64
          (2)   64
          (3)   64
       s. 3   64, 129
       s. 4   64
       s. 5   65
       s. 6   66
       Matrimonial and Family Proceedings Act (c. 42) Part III
       328
1985   Companies Act (c. 6)   82, 139
       s. 360   289
       s. 691   83
       s. 694A(2)   82
            (3)   82
       s. 695   83
       s. 725(1)   82
          (2)   82
          (5)   82
       Sched. 21A para. 3(e)   82
       Child Abduction and Custody Act (c. 60)   10, 55, 56,
       339, 347, 393
       s. 15   343
       s. 18   343
       Sched. 1 (Hague Convention, 1980)   339
          Art. 3   340
          Art. 4   340
          Art. 5(a)   340
              (b)   340

Arts. 8–19   342
Art. 11   340
Art. 12   340, 342
Art. 13   340
Art. 17   342
Art. 18   342
Art. 19   342
Art. 21   340
Sched. 2 (European Convention, 1980)   339, 342
Art. 1
        (a)   342
        (b)   342
        (c)   342
        (d)   343
Art. 5
        (1)   342
        (2)   342
Art. 7   343
Arts. 8–19   342
Art. 8   343
Art. 9   343
        (3)   343
Art. 10   342, 343
Art. 11   342
Art. 12   342
Art. 15   343
Art. 17   343
1986   Family Law Act (c. 55)
Part I   335, 336, 337
s. 1   337
s. 1(1)(d)   337
s. 2(1)   337
    (2)   337
    (3)   337
s. 2(A)   337
s. 3   337
    (2)   337
s. 5   337
s. 6   338
s. 25   338
s. 27   338
s. 28   338

s. 29(1)   338
    (2)   338
s. 30   338
s. 31   338
ss. 33–5   337
s. 41   337
Part II   10, 53, 117, 323, 393
s. 44(1)   326
    (2)   323
s. 45   324, 326
ss. 46–9   324
s. 46(1)   325, 327
    (2)   325
    (3)(a)   324
        (b)   325
    (4)   326
    (5)   13, 37, 324
s. 47(1)   327
    (2)   326, 328
s. 48   327
s. 49   326
s. 50   27, 29, 307, 308
s. 51   328
s. 51(1)   328
    (3)(a)   121, 328
        (b)   330
        (c)   122, 328
    (4)   330
s. 52(5)   324
s. 54(1)   324
Part III
s. 55   333
s. 56   357
s. 57   357
s. 58(1)   333, 357
    (5)(a)   333
    (6)   333
s. 65(3)   333
Insolvency Act (c. 45) s. 213   135
1987   Family Law Reform Act (c. 42)   348
s. 22   357
Finance Act (c. 16)   371

Recognition of Trusts Act (c. 14)   9, 10, 286, 394
  s. 1(1)   286
  s. 1(2)   287
  s. 1(3)   296
  s. 1(4)   287
  s. 1(5)   286
  Sched. 1 (Hague Convention, 1986)
    Art. 2(1)   287
    Art. 3   286–7
    Art. 4   287
    Art. 6   287, 288
    Art. 7   287
    Art. 8(2)(h)   292
    Art. 9   289
    Art. 10   289, 291
    Art. 11(1)   289
        (2)   289
        (3)   289
    Art. 12   289
    Art. 13   290
    Art. 15   290, 292
    Art. 16
        (1)   290
        (2)   290
        (3)   290
    Art. 17   288
    Art. 18   291
    Art. 22   286
1988 Income and Corporation Taxes Act (c. 1)   318
      Foreign Marriage (Amendment) Act (c. 14)   299,
      312
      Road Traffic Act (c. 52)   144
1989 Children Act 1989 (c. 41)   336, 393
  s. 1(1)   338
  s. 4   336
  s. 5   335
    (3)   335
  s. 8   334, 336, 347
  s. 92(7)   335
  s. 100   334
      Law of Property (Miscellaneous Provisions) Act (c. 34)
  s. 2   208

1990   Contracts (Applicable Law) Act (c. 36)   10, 96, 180, 189, 394
    s. 2(1)   190
        (2)   190, 210
        (3)   191
    s. 3   190
    Sched. 1 (Rome Convention, 1980)   190
        Art. 1
            (1)   191
            (2)   191
                (a)   208
                (b)   278
            (3)   192, 254
            (4)   192
        Art. 2   191
        Art. 3   267
            (1)   192, 193, 194, 195, 197, 203, 206, 210
            (2)   205
            (3)   193, 197, 213
            (4)   196, 206
        Arts. 3–6   206, 210
        Art. 4   142, 195, 196, 198, 201, 202, 203, 204
            (1)   192, 194, 198
            (2)   190, 198, 200
            (3)   198, 201, 267
            (4)   198, 201
            (5)   198, 199
        Art. 5   202
            (1)   202
            (2)   202, 208, 213
            (3)   202, 203
            (4)   203
            (5)   203
        Art. 6   203
            (1)   203, 213
            (2)   202, 203
                (a)   203
                (b)   203
        Art. 7
            (1)   213, 217, 218
            (2)   197, 213, 290

Art. 8   196, 206
    (1)   206, 212
    (2)   206
Art. 9   196, 205, 209
    (4)   208
    (5)   208
    (6)   208, 213
Art. 10
    (1)   210
        (a)   210
        (b)   211
        (c)   64, 65, 211
        (d)   63, 212, 219
        (e)   210
    (2)   211
Art. 11   191, 196
Art. 12   257, 258
    (1)   254, 256, 257
    (2)   254, 256, 257
Art. 14   61, 192
    (2)   62
Art. 15   27, 204
Art. 16   213, 217, 374
Art. 17   192
Art. 18(2)   190
Art. 19(2)   191
Art. 20   219
Art. 21   219
Art. 23   219
Art. 24   219
Sched. 2   190
Sched. 3 (Brussels Protocol, 1988)   190
    Art. 2   191
    Art. 3   191
1991   Civil Jurisdiction and Judgments Act 1991 (c. 12)   71,
109, 128, 131, 132, 287, 394
    Sched. 1 (Lugano Convention, 1989)
    Art. 5(1)   143
    Art. 6(1)   150
    Art. 16(1)   266
    Art. 54(B)(3)   172
    Art. 57(4)   172

1992 Social Security and Benefits Act (c. 4)
       s. 121(B)   318
       s. 147(5)   318
1994 Sale and Supply of Goods Act (c. 35)   246
1995 Private International Law (Miscellaneous Provisions) Act
       (c. 42)   10
       Part II   317
       s. 5(1)   317
          (2)   317
       s. 6(1)   317
          6(2)–(5)   317
          6(6)   317
       s. 8(2)   318
       Part III   221, 228
       s. 9(4)   229
          (5)   27, 229, 234
          (6)   233
       s. 10   225, 228, 233
       s. 11   228, 230, 231, 233, 239
       s. 11(1)   229
          (2)   229
          (3)   229
       s. 12   231, 233
          (1)   231, 232, 239
          (2)   231, 232
       s. 13   225, 227
       s. 14   235, 237
       s. 14(2)   233
          (3)(a)   235
          (3)(b)   231
          (4)   238
       Sched. para. 2   317
       para. 4   318
1996 Employment Rights Act (c. 18)
       s. 204(1)   214
       Arbitration Act (c. 23)
       Part I   184
       s. 1(c)   184
       s. 9   96, 184
          (4)   184
       s. 33(2)   183
       s. 66   179, 182, 183

ss. 85–7, 184
s. 99   182
Part III   179–83
s. 100(1)   183
       (2)   183
s. 101(1)   183, 185
            (a)   183
            (b)   183
s. 102(1)(a)   183
            (b)   183
            (c)   183
s. 103(1)   183
       (2)   183
       (3)   184
       (4)   183
1999   Adoption (Inter-Country Aspects) Act (c. 18)   355

Table of cases

A, *re* [1970] Ch. 665   346

A (A Minor) (Abduction), *re* [1988] 1 FLR 365   341

A (Foreign Access Order: Enforcement), *re* [1996] 1 FLR 561   342, 343

A (Minors) (Abduction: Custody Rights), *re* [1992] Fam. 106   341

A (Minors) (Abduction: Custody Rights), *re* (No. 2) [1993] Fam. 1   341

A (Minors) (Abduction: Habitual Residence), *re* [1996] 1 WLR 25   56

A (A Minor) (Wrongful Removal of Child), *re* [1988] Fam. Law. 383   341

Abidin Daver, The [1984] AC 398   86, 88, 95, 99

Abouloff *v.* Oppenheimer (1882) 10 QBD 295   119, 120, 184

Abu Dhabi Arbitration (1952) 18 ILR no. 37   392

ACE Insurance SA-NV *v.* Zurich Insurance Co., [2000] 2 All ER (Comm.) 449, (2001) *The Times*, 27 February   166

Achillopoulos, *re* [1928] Ch. 433   270

Adams *v.* Cape Industries plc [1990] Ch. 433   111, 113, 115, 121, 361

Adams *v.* Clutterbuck (1883) 10 QBD 403   266

Adams *v.* National Bank of Greece and Athens SA [1958] 2 QB 59   32, 244, 271, 362; [1961] AC 255   19, 58, 212, 246

Addison *v.* Addison [1955] NI 1   312

Adriatic, The [1931] P 241   194

Aganoor's Trusts, *re* (1895) 64 LJ Ch. 521   31, 32, 270

Agnew *v.* Lansforsakringsbolagens A/B [2000] 2 WLR 497   141, 152

AIG Group (UK) Ltd *v.* The Ethniki [1998] 4 All ER 301   200; [2000] 1 All ER 556   141

Aiglon *v.* Gau Shan Co. Ltd [1993] 1 Ll.R 164   150

Airbus Industrie GIE *v.* Patel [1996] ILPr. 230, [1997] 2 Ll.R 8, [1999] AC 19   101, 103, 104, 104, 125

Akai Pty Ltd *v.* People's Insurance Co. [1998] 1 Ll.R 90   107
Akande *v.* Balfour Beatty Construction Ltd [1998] ILPr. 110   114
Alabama Claims Arbitration (1872) Moore, International Arbitrations,
   653   359
Albaforth, The. *See* Cordoba Shipping Co. *v.* National State Bank NJ
Al Battani, The [1993] 2 Ll.R 219   87
Albeko Schuhmaschinen *v.* Kamborian Shoe Machine Co. Ltd (1961)
   111 LJ 519   206
Alberti, *re* [1955] 1 WLR 1240   275
Alcock *v.* Smith [1892] 1 Ch. 238   245, 247
Ali *v.* Ali [1968] P 564   315
Alves *v.* Hodgson (1797) 7 TR 241   63, 207
Ambrose *v.* Ambrose [1961] 25 DLR (2d) 1   30
Amin Rasheed Shipping Corporation *v.* Kuwait Insurance Co. [1982]
   1 WLR 961; [1983] 1 WLR 228; [1984] AC 50   27, 75, 76, 79,
   117, 193, 195, 199, 204, 205, 377
Andros, *re* (1883) 24 Ch. D 637   352
Angelic Grace, The [1995] 1 Ll.R 87   107, 185
Anglo-Iranian Oil Co. *v.* Jaffrate [1953] 1 WLR 246   250, 365, 389
Annesley, *re* [1926] Ch. 692   13, 20, 22, 24, 25, 26, 37, 273
Antérist *v.* Crédit Lyonnais [1986] ECR 1951   157
Anton *v.* Bartolo (1891) Clunet 1171   277
Anziani, *re* [1930] 1 Ch. 407   246, 255
Apt *v.* Apt [1948] P 83   18, 296, 310
Arab Monetary Fund *v.* Hashim [1993] 1 Ll.R 543   224
Arab Monetary Fund *v.* Hashim [1996] 1 Ll.R 589   230
Arcado sprl *v.* Haviland SA [1988] ECR 1539   141, 192
Arkwright Mutual Insurance Co. *v.* Bryanston Insurance Co. Ltd [1990]
   2 QB 649   152, 166
Armadora Occidental SA *v.* Horace Mann Insurance Co. [1977] 1
   WLR 1098   199
Armagas Ltd *v.* Mundogas SA [1985] 3 WLR 640, [1986] AC 71
   224, 231
Armar Shipping Co. *v.* Caisse Algérienne d'Assurance (1981) 1 WLR
   207   204, 205
Armitage *v.* Attorney-General [1906] P 135   322, 356
Armitage *v.* Nanchen (1983) 4 FLR 293   122
Armour *v.* Thyssen Edelstahlwerke A/G [1991] 2 AC 339   248
Ashurst *v.* Pollard [2001] 2 WLR 722   135, 265
Askew, *re* [1930] 2 Ch. 259   21, 22, 25, 26, 352
Askin *v.* Absa Bank Ltd [1999] ILPr. 471   92, 99
Atlantic Emperor, The. *See* Marc Rich & Co.

Atlantic Song, The [1983] 2 Ll.R 394   97
Atlantic Star, The [1973] QB 283; [1974] AC 436   85, 86, 88
Attock Cement Co. Ltd *v.* Romanian Bank for Foreign Trade [1989] 1 WLR 1147   200
Attorney-General *v.* Rowe (1862) 1 H & C 31   46
Attorney-General for Alberta *v.* Cook [1926] AC 444   47
Attorney-General for New Zealand *v.* Ortiz [1982] QB 349 1; [1984] AC 1   6, 364, 366, 367, 368, 370
Attorney-General for the United Kingdom (HM) *v.* Heinemann Publishers Australia Pty Ltd (No. 2) (1988) 165 CLR 30   370, 371
Attorney-General (HM) *v.* Wellington Newspapers Ltd [1988] 1 NZLR 129   371
Augustus *v.* Permanent Trustee Co. (Canberra) Ltd (1971) 124 CLR 245   289
Australian Commercial Research & Development Ltd *v.* ANZ McCaughan Merchant Bank Ltd [1989] 3 All ER 65   95

B (A Minor) (Abduction), *re* [1994] 2 FLR 249   341
B (A Minor) (Child Abduction: Father's Rights), *re* [1999] Fam. 1   57
B (Minors) (Abduction) (No. 2), *re* [1993] 1 FLR 993   56
B's Settlement, *re* [1940] Ch. 54   335, 346
B *v.* B (Abduction: Custody Rights), *re* [1993] Fam. 32   340, 341
B-M (Wardship Jurisdiction), *re* [1993] 1 FLR 979   51
Babcock *v.* Jackson (1963) 12 NY 2d 473; [1963] 2 Ll.R   234, 280
Baindail *v.* Baindail [1946] P 122   209, 317
Bamgbose *v.* Daniel [1955] AC 107   318, 349, 351
Banco, The [1971] P 137   83
Banco Atlantico *v.* The British Bank of the Middle East [1990] 2 Ll.R 504   93, 95
Banco de Bilbao *v.* Sancha [1938] 2 KB 176   57
Banco de Vizcaya *v.* don Alfonso de Borbon y Austria [1935] 1 KB 140   364, 365
Bank of Africa Ltd *v.* Cohen [1902] 2 Ch. 129   210, 267, 275
Bank of Baroda *v.* Vysya Bank Ltd [1994] 2 Ll.R 87   200
Bank of Credit and Commerce Hong Kong Ltd *v.* Sonali Bank [1995] 1 Ll.R 227   99
Bank of Ethiopia *v.* National Bank of Egypt and Liguori [1939] Ch. 513   57
Bank of Tokyo *v.* Karoon [1987] AC 45n   101
Bank Saderat Iran *v.* Farsneshani (1982) Comm. LR 111   365
Bank voor Handel en Scheepvaart NV *v.* Slatford [1953] 1 QB 248   246, 364, 367

Bankes, *re* [1902] 2 Ch. 333   207, 278
Bankers Trust Co. *v.* PT Jakarta International Hotels and Development [1999] 1 Ll.R 910   107, 185
Bankers Trust International plc *v.* PT Dharmalas Sakti Sejahtera [1996] CLC 252   106
Banque Cantonale Vaudoise *v.* Waterlily Maritime Inc. [1997] 2 Ll.R 347   164
Barcelona Traction, Power & Light Co. Case ICJ 1970, 3   59
Barclays Bank International *v.* Levin Bros. (Bradford) Ltd [1977] QB 270   66
Barnett's Trusts, *re* [1902] 1 Ch. 847   271
Bata *v.* Bata [1948] WN 366   81, 228
Bavaria and Germanair *v.* Eurocontrol [1977] ECR 1517   134, 174
Beamish *v.* Beamish (1861) 9 HL Cas. 274   300
Beatty *v.* Beatty [1924] 1 KB 807   125
Beaumont, *re* [1893] 3 Ch. 490   48, 49, 50
Bell *v.* Kennedy (1868) LR 1 Sc. & Div. 307   38, 42
Benarty, The [1985] QB 325   97, 215
Benincasa *v.* Dentalkit srl [1998] 1 All ER (EC) 135   153, 158
Berchtold, *re* [1923] 1 Ch. 192   244
Berezovsky and Glanchkow *v.* Michaels [2000] 1 WLR 1004   81, 95, 228
Berghoefer GmbH *v.* ASA, SA [1985] 1 CMLR 13   155
Berisford (SW) plc *v.* New Hampshire Insurance [1990] 2 QB 631   166
Berkovits *v.* Grinberg [1995] Fam. 142   325
Berliner Industriebank *v.* Jost [1971] 2 QB 463   127
Bernkrant *v.* Fowler 55 Cal. 2d 588 (1961)   62
Berny, The [1979] QB 80   83
Berthiaume *v.* Dastous [1930] AC 79   296, 322
Bertrand *v.* Ott [1978] ECR 1431   152
Bethell, *re* (1887) 38 Ch. D 220   313, 314
Bettinson's Question, *re* [1956] Ch. 67   285
Bier *v.* Mines de Potasse d'Alsace [1976] ECR 1735, [1978] QB 708   80, 145
Birtwhistle *v.* Vardill (1839) Cl. & F 895   275
Bischoffsheim, *re* [1948] Ch. 79   348, 349–51
Black *v.* Yates [1992] 2 QB 526   123, 128
Black-Clawson International Ltd *v.* Papierwerke-Waldhof Aschaffenburg A/G [1975] AC 591   63, 64, 129
Blanckaert & Willems *v.* Trost [1981] ECR 819   148
Bliersbach *v.* McEwen 1959 SC 43   297

Blohn *v.* Desser [1962] 2 QB 116   115, 116, 127
Blue Nile Shipping *v.* Iguana S & F [1998] ILPr. 446   163
BMG Trading Ltd *v.* AS McKay [1998] ILPr. 691   87
Bodley Head *v.* Flegon [1972] 1 WLR 680   209
Boettcher *v.* Boettcher [1949] WN 83   329
Boissevain *v.* Weil [1949] 1 KB 482; [1950] AC 327   371
Boldrini *v.* Boldrini [1932] P 9   45
Bonacina, *re* [1912] 2 Ch. 394   18, 192, 206, 382
Bondholders Securities *v.* Manville [1933] 4 DLR 699   209
Bonython *v.* Commonwealth of Australia [1951] AC 201   195, 197,
    204, 210
Boocock *v.* Hilton International Co. [1993] 1 WLR 1065   83
Boss Group Ltd *v.* Boss France SA [1997] 1 WLR 351   140, 143
Bouygues Offshore SA *v.* Caspian Shipping Co. (Nos. 1, 3, 4 and 5)
    [1998] 2 Ll.R 461   107
Bozzelli's Settlement, *re* [1902] 1 Ch. 751   304, 348
BP Exploration Co. (Libya) Ltd *v.* Hunt [1976] 1 WLR 788   79,
    204
BP Exploration Co. (Libya) Ltd *v.* Hunt (No. 2) [1979] 1 WLR 783;
    [1981] 1 WLR 232   66
Brabo, The [1949] AC 326   77
Bradford *v.* Young (1885) 29 Ch. D 617   273
Brailey *v.* Rhodesia Consolidated Ltd [1910] 2 Ch. 95   34
Brandsma qq *v.* Hanse Chemie A/G (1997) 16 May. *See* [1998] LMCLQ
    35   256
Brazendale & Co. Ltd *v.* Saint Frères [1970] 2 Ll.R 34   182
Breen *v.* Breen [1964] P 144   35, 307
Bremer *v.* Freeman (1857) 10 Moo. PC 306   272
Brenner *v.* Dean Witter Reynolds Inc. [1995] All ER (EC) 278   153
Brereton *v.* Canadian Pacific Railway (1897) 29 OR 57   262
Briesemann, *in b.* [1894] P 260   269
Brinkibon Ltd *v.* Stahag Stahl GmbH [1980] 2 Ll.R 556; [1983] 2 AC
    34   13, 78, 79, 206
Bristow *v.* Sequeville (1850) 5 Exch. 275   34, 63
Britannia SS Insurance Association *v.* Ausonia Assicurazione SpA [1984]
    2 Ll.R 98   206
British Aerospace plc *v.* Dee Howard Co. [1993] 1 Ll.R 368   79,
    97, 98
British Airways Board *v.* Laker Airways [1985] AC 58   104, 105,
    106
British South Africa Co. *v.* Companhia de Moçambique [1893] AC
    602   261

British South Africa Co. *v.* de Beers Consolidated Mines Ltd [1910] 2 Ch. 502   267

Brodin *v.* A/R Seljan 1973 SC 213   213, 237

Brokaw *v.* Seatrain UK Ltd [1971] 2 QB 476   368

Brook *v.* Brook (1861) 9 HL Cas. 193   302, 348

Brown *v.* Brown (1982) 3 FLR 212   43, 46

Brown *v.* Collins (1883) 25 Ch. D 56   336

Brown *v.* Thornton (1827) Ad. & E 185   63

Buchanan *v.* Rucker (1808) 9 East. 192   110

Buckland *v.* Buckland [1968] P 296   310

Bumper Development Corp. Ltd *v.* Commissioner of Police of the Metropolis [1991] 1 WLR 1362   35

Buswell *v.* Inland Revenue Commissioners [1974] 1 WLR 1631   42, 44

C (Abduction: Consent), *re* [1996] 1 FLR 414   341

C *v.* C (Abduction) (Rights of Custody) [1989] 1 WLR 654   341

Cable (Lord), *re* [1977] 1 WLR 7   368, 371

Callwood *v.* Callwood [1960] AC 659   284

Caltex Trading Pty Ltd *v.* Metro Trading International Inc. [2000] All ER (Comm.) 108   74

Camdex International Ltd *v.* Bank of Zambia (No. 2) [1997] CLC 714   370

Cammell *v.* Sewell (1858) 3 H & N 617 affd (1860) 5 H & N 728   247, 248

Campbell, Connelly & Co. *v.* Noble [1963] 1 WLR 252   253, 254, 255

Canada Trust Co. *v.* Stolzenberg (No. 2) [2000] 3 WLR 376   136

CAPAC *v.* International Good Music Inc. [1963] 37 DLR (2d) 1   228

Carl Zeiss Stiftung *v.* Rayner & Keeler Ltd (No. 2) [1965] Ch. 525; reversed [1967] 1 AC 853   57, 129, 365

Carr *v.* Fracis Times & Co. [1902] AC 176   230

Carrick *v.* Hancock (1895) 12 TLR 59   111

Casdagli *v.* Casdagli [1919] AC 145   51

Castanho *v.* Brown & Root Ltd [1981] AC 557   87, 101

Castrique *v.* Imrie (1870) LR 4 HL 414   35, 118

Catterall *v.* Catterall (1847) 1 Rob. Ecc. 580   300

Celia (SS) *v.* Volturno (SS) [1921] 2 AC 544   65

Century Credit Corporation *v.* Richard (1962) 34 DLR (2d) 291   248, 249

Cesena Sulphur Co. *v.* Nicholson (1876) 1 Ex. D 428   58
Chadha *v.* Dow Jones & Co. Inc. [1999] 23 LS Gaz. R 34   81
Chailease Finance Corp. *v.* Crédit Agricole Indosuez [2000] 1 All ER (Comm.) 399   143
Chaney *v.* Murphy [1948] WN 130   77
Channel Tunnel Group *v.* Balfour Beatty Construction Ltd [1993] AC 334   106, 184
Chaplin *v.* Boys [1968] 2 QB 1 189; [1971] AC 356   29, 60, 65, 221, 223, 225, 226, 230, 233, 385
Charm Martime Inc. *v.* Kyriakou [1987] 1 Ll.R 433   129
Charron *v.* Montreal Trust Co. (1958) 15 DLR (2d) 240   209
Chartered Mercantile Bank of India *v.* Netherlands India Steam Navigation Co. (1883) 10 QBD 521   238
Chaudhary *v.* Chaudhary [1985] Fam. 19   324, 329
Chaudry *v.* Chaudry [1976] Fam. 148   318
Chellaram *v.* Chellaram [1985] Ch. 409   9, 288
Cheney *v.* Conn [1968] 1 WLR 242   389
Cheni *v.* Cheni [1965] P 85   304, 315
Chetti *v.* Chetti [1909] P 67   306
Chiwell *v.* Carlyon (1897) 14 SC 61   283, 284
Choice Investments *v.* Jeromnimon [1981] QB 149   66
Church of Scientology of California *v.* Commissioner of Metropolitan Police (1976) 120 Sol. Jo. 690   224, 225, 231
Cia. Colombiana de Seguros *v.* Pacific Steam Navigation Co. [1965] 1 QB 101   253, 254
Citadel Insurance *v.* Atlantic Union Insurance [1982] 1 Ll.R 543   201
Citi-March Ltd *v.* Neptune Orient Lines Ltd [1996] 1 WLR 1367   75, 98
Cleveland Museum of Art *v.* Capricorn International SA [1990] 2 Ll.R 166   83, 90, 95
Clore, *re* (No. 2) [1984] Simon's Tax Cases 609   40
Coast Lines Ltd *v.* Hudig and Veder Chartering NV [1972] 2 QB 34   79, 195
Cohen *v.* Rothfield [1919] 1 KB 410   101
Cohn, *re* [1945] Ch. 5   18, 60, 61
Coleman *v.* Shang [1961] AC 481   318
Collens, *re* [1985] Ch. 505   275
Collier *v.* Rivaz (1841) 2 Curt. 855   20, 21, 24, 25, 26, 272
Colorado, The [1923] P 102   67
Colt Industries *v.* Sarlie (No. 1) [1966] 1 WLR 440   72, 111
Colt Industries *v.* Sarlie (No. 2) [1966] 1 WLR 1287   127
Communications Ltd *v.* Communication Telesystem International [1999] 2 All ER (Comm.) 33   98

Compagnie Tunisienne de Navigation SA *v.* Compagnie d'Armement Maritime SA [1971] AC 572   180, 195, 196

Compton *v.* Bearcroft (1769) 2 Hagg. Con. 444n.   297

Connelly *v.* RTZ plc [1998] AC 554   87, 92, 93, 166, 167

Connor *v.* Connor [1974] 1 NZLR 632   125, 368

Continental Bank NA *v.* Aeakos Companhia Naviera SA [1994] 1 WLR 588   97, 107, 163

Cook Industries *v.* Galliher [1979] Ch. 439   263, 264

Cooke's Trusts, *re* (1887) 56 LJ Ch. 637   47, 279

Cooper *v.* Cooper (1888) LR 13 App. Cas. 88   279

Copin *v.* Adamson (1875) LR 1 Ex. D 17   115

Corcoran *v.* Corcoran [1974] VR 164   225, 226

Cordoba Shipping Co. *v.* National State Bank, NJ, The Albaforth [1984] 2 Ll.R 91   75

Coreck Maritime GmbH *v.* Handelsveem BV (2000) *The Times*, 1 December   155

Coupland *v.* Arabian Gulf Oil Co. [1983] 1 WLR 1136   220, 222, 224, 236

Courtney, *re, ex parte* Pollard (1840) Mont. & Ch. 239   263, 267

Cramer *v.* Cramer [1987] 1 FLR 116   42

Cranstown *v.* Johnston (Lord) (1796) 3 Ves. 170   263

Crédit Lyonnais *v.* New Hampshire Insurance Co. [1997] 2 Ll.R 1   199

Crédit Suisse Financial Products *v.* Société Générale d'Entreprises [1997] ILPr. 165   155

Crédit Suisse First Boston (Europe) Ltd *v.* MLC (Bermuda) Ltd [1999] 1 All ER (Comm.) 237   107

Crédit Suisse First Boston (Europe) Ltd *v.* Seagate Trading Co. Ltd [1999] 1 All ER (Comm.) 261   107

Crick *v.* Hennessy [1973] WAR 74   117

Crowe *v.* Kader [1968] WAR 122   316

Cruh *v.* Cruh [1945] 2 All ER 545   45

Cruickshanks *v.* Cruickshanks [1957] 1 WLR 564   46

Crumpton's Judicial Factor *v.* Finch-Noyes 1918 SC 378   50

Cruse *v.* Chittum [1974] 2 All ER 940   55

Culling *v.* Culling [1896] P 116   301

Cunnington, *re* [1924] 1 Ch. 68   273

Custom Made Commercial Ltd *v.* Stawa Metallbau GmbH [1994] ECR I-2913   143

Cutcliffe, *re* [1940] Ch. 565   244

D (an infant), *re* [1943] Ch. 305   335

D *v.* D [1994] 1 FLR 38   323, 329

DVA v. Voest Alpine [1997] 2 Ll.R 279 CA   107
Daarnhouwer & Co. NV v. Boulos [1968] 2 Ll.R 259   114
Dallal v. Bank Mellat [1986] QB 441   179, 183, 185
D'Almeida Araujo v. Sir Frederick Becker & Co. Ltd [1953] 2 QB 329
    65
Dalmia Cement Ltd v. National Bank of Pakistan [1975] QB 9   179,
    182
Dalmia Dairy Industries Ltd v. National Bank of Pakistan [1978] 2
    Ll.R 223   182
Dalrymple v. Dalrymple (1811) 2 Hagg. Con. 54   295
Dansommer A/S v. Andreas Götz [2000] ILPr. 127   265
Danvaern Productions A/S v. Schuhfabriken Otterbeck GmbH & Co.
    [1995] ECR I-2053   152
Davenport v. Corinthian Motor Policies at Lloyd's 1991 SLT 774
    144
Davidsson v. Hill [1901] 2 KB 606   239
Dearle v. Hall (1823) 2 Russ. 1   251
Debaecker and Plouvier v. Bouwman [1985] ECR 1779   169, 170
De Béeche v. South American Stores Ltd [1935] AC 148   34, 371
De Beers Consolidated Mines v. Howe [1906] AC 455   58
De Bloos v. Bouyer [1976] ECR 1497   141, 148
De Bonneval v. De Bonneval (1838) 2 Curt. 856   145
De Cavel v. De Cavel (No. 1) [1979] ECR 1055   135, 168
De Cavel v. De Cavel (No. 2) [1980] ECR 731   135
De Cosse Brissac v. Rathbone (1861) 6 H & N 301   118
De Dampierre v. De Dampierre [1988] AC 92   90, 95, 320
Deichland, The [1990] 1 QB 361   139, 174
De Jager v. Attorney-General of Natal [1907] AC 36   335
De la Vega v. Vianna (1830) 1 B & Ad. 284   66
De Nicols, re (No. 2) [1900] 2 Ch. 410   281, 283
De Nicols v. Curlier [1900] AC 21   18, 280, 283
Denby v. Hellenic Mediterranean Lines Co. Ltd [1994] 1 Ll.R 320
    169
Denilauler v. Couchet Frères [1980] ECR 1553   168
De Reneville v. De Reneville [1948] P 100   312
Deschamps v. Miller [1908] 1 Ch. 856   263
Desert Sun Loan Corp. v. Hill [1996] 2 All ER 847   114, 130
Deutsche Schachtbau- und Tiefbohrgesellschaft mbH v. Ra's Al
    Khaimah National Oil Co. [1987] 3 WLR 1023 (*on appeal*) v. Shell
    International Petroleum Co. [1990] 1 AC 295   184, 260
De Wilton, re [1900] 2 Ch. 481   302, 348
De Wolf v. Cox [1976] ECR 1759   173

De Wutz v. Hendricks (1824) 2 Bing. 314   216, 374
Di Savini v. Lousada (1870) 18 WR 425   341
Distillers Co. Ltd (Biochemicals) v. Thompson [1971] AC 458   230
Doetsch, re [1896] 2 Ch. 836   68
Domicrest Ltd v. Swiss Bank Corp. [1999] QB 548   143, 147
Donaldson v. Donaldson [1949] P 363   46
Donohoe v. Armco Inc. [2000] 1 All ER (Comm.) 425   107
Dougherty & Co. v. Krimke 105 NJL 470 (1929)   249, 250
Dresser UK Ltd v. Falcongate Freight Management Ltd, The Duke of
    Yare [1992] 2 QB 502   163, 166
Drouot Assurances v. Consolidated Metallurgical Industries (CMI
    Industrial Sites) [1999] QB 497   162
Duchess of Orleans, HRH, in re (1859) 1 Sw. & Tr. 253   269
Duijnstee v. Goderbauer [1983] ECR 3663   154
Duke v. Andler [1932] SCR 734   263
Duke of Marlborough v. Attorney-General [1945] Ch. 78   278
Duke of Wellington, re [1947] Ch. 506; affd [1948] Ch. 118   23,
    25, 262, 275, 377
Dulles' Settlement, re (No. 2) [1951] Ch. 842   74, 114, 116
Dumez France SA and Tacoba v. Hessische Landesbank [1990] ECR
    I-49   133, 146
Duncan v. Lawson (1889) 41 Ch. D 394   275, 276
Duncan v. Motherwell Bridge & Engineering Co. 1952 SC 131   213
Dunlop Pneumatic Tyre Co. Ltd v. A/G Cudell & Co. [1902] 1 KB
    342   82
Dynamics Corporation of America, re [1976] 1 WLR 757   66
Dynamit A/G v. Rio Tinto Co. [1918] AC 292   216, 374

E (Children) (Abduction: Non-Convention Country), re (1999) The
    Times, 7 July   347
E (D), re [1967] Ch. 761   347
E v. E (Child Abduction: Intolerable Situation) [1998] 2 FLR 980
    341
East India Trading Co. Inc. v. Carmel Exporters & Importers Ltd
    [1952] 2 QB 439   181
Easterbrook v. Easterbrook [1944] P 10   311
ED & F Man (Sugar) Ltd v. Haryanto [1991] 1 Ll.R 429   123
Edwards v. Carter [1893] AC 360   279
Effer v. Kantner [1982] ECR 825   140
Egbert v. Short [1907] 2 Ch. 205   111
Egerton's Will Trusts, re [1956] Ch. 593   281
Egon Oldendorff v. Libera Corporation [1995] 2 Ll.R 64   194, 206

Egon Oldendorff *v.* Libera Corporation (No. 2) [1996] 1 Ll.R 380
  194
Egyptian Delta Land & Investment Co. *v.* Todd [1929] AC 1   58
EI Pont de Nemours *v.* Agnew [1987] 2 Ll.R 585   91, 95
EI Pont de Nemours *v.* Agnew (No. 2) [1988] 2 Ll.R 240   91
El Ajou *v.* Dollar Land Holdings plc [1994] 2 All ER 685   33
El Amria, The [1982] 2 Ll.R 119   97
Eli Lilley & Co. *v.* Novo Nordisk A/S [2000] ILPr. 73   167
Elefanten Schuh *v.* Jacqmain [1981] ECR 1671   156, 158, 159
Eleftheria, The [1970] P 94   97
Ellis *v.* McHenry (1871) LR 6 CP 228   118, 122
Emanuel *v.* Symon [1908] 1 KB 302   110, 112, 113, 115, 116
Embiricos *v.* Anglo-Austrian Bank [1905] 1 KB 677   245, 247
Emery *v.* Emery 45 Cal. 2d 421 (1955)   234
Emery's Investment Trusts, *re* [1959] Ch. 410   369, 374
EMI Records Ltd *v.* Modern Music Karl-Ulrich Walterbach GmbH
  [1992] QB 115   168
Empresa Exportadora de Azucar *v.* Industria Azucerera Nacional SA,
  The Playa Larga [1983] 2 Ll.R 171   367, 370
Enforcement of an English Anti-Suit Injunction, *re* the [1997] ILPr.
  320   107
English *v.* Donnelly 1958 SC 494   213
Enohin *v.* Wylie (1862) 10 HLC 1   269
Entores *v.* Miles Far East Corporation [1955] 2 QB 327   13, 78,
  206
Eroglu *v.* Eroglu [1994] 2 FLR 287   328, 329
Esso Malaysia, The [1978] QB 198   239
Estate Frankel *v.* The Master [1950] (1) SA 220   282
European-Asian Bank *v.* Punjab & Sindh Bank [1981] 2 Ll.R 651;
  [1982] 2 Ll.R 356   88, 92
Eurosteel Ltd *v.* Stinnes A/G [2000] All ER (Comm.) 964   19
Evans Marshall & Co. Ltd *v.* Bertola SA [1973] 1 WLR 349   15, 96
Ewing *v.* Orr-Ewing (1885) 10 App. Cas. 453   269

F (A Minor) (Abduction) (Custody Rights), *re* [1991] Fam. 23   347
F (A Minor) (Child Abduction), *re* [1992] 1 FLR 548   56, 57
F *v.* F (A Minor) (Custody: Foreign Order), *re* [1989] Fam. 1   344
Farrell *v.* Long [1997] QB 842   140
Fehmarn, The [1958] 1 WLR 159   96
Feist *v.* Société Intercommunale Belge d'Electricité [1934] AC 161
  386
Felthouse *v.* Bindley (1862) 11 CB (NS) 869   207

Feyerick v. Hubbard (1902) 71 LJKB 509   115
Finnish Marine Insurance Co. Ltd v. Protective National Insurance
    Co. [1990] 1 QB 1078   80
Fitzgerald, re [1904] 1 Ch. 573   275
Flynn, re (No. 1) [1968] 1 WLR 103   47
Folliott v. Ogden (1790) 3 Term. Rep. 726   362
Forbes v. Simmons (1914) 20 DLR 100   111
Forgo, l'Affaire (1883) 10 Clunet 64   20, 21, 22
Forsikringsaktieselkapet Vesta v. Butcher [1968] 2 All ER 488; [1989]
    AC 862   195
Forsyth v. Forsyth [1891] P 363   292
Foster v. Driscoll [1929] 1 KB 470   217, 218, 362, 374, 379
Frankfurther v. WL Exner Ltd [1947] Ch. 629   364
Frecchia del Nord, The [1989] 1 Ll.R 388   166
Freke v. Carbery (1873) LR 16 Eq. 461   244
Fuld, re (No. 3) [1968] P 675   22, 25, 26, 40, 42, 45, 60, 271
Furse, re [1980] 3 All ER 839   41, 43

G (A Minor) (Abduction), re [1989] 2 FLR 473   341
G (A Minor) (Child Abduction) (Enforcement), re [1990] 2 FLR 325
    343, 344
G (A Minor) (Enforcement of Access Abroad), re [1993] Fam. 216   66
GAF Corporation v. Anchem Products Inc. [1975] 1 Ll.R 601   75
Gaetano and Maria, The (1882) 7 PD 137   238
Gamlestaden plc v. Caisse de Suecia SA [1994] 1 Ll.R 433   157
Gascoine v. Pyrah [1994] ILPr. 82   149
Gasque v. Inland Revenue Commissioners [1940] 2 KB 80   157
Gatty v. Attorney-General [1951] P 444   38
General Steam Navigation v. Gouillou (1843) 11 M & W 877   68
Gerling Konzern v. Amministrazione del Tesoro [1983] ECR 2503
    155, 158
GIE Groupe Concorde v. Master of the Vessel Suhadiwarno Panjan
    [1999] 2 All ER (Comm.) 700   143
Gill and Duffus Landauer Ltd v. London Export Corpn GmbH [1982]
    2 Ll.R 627   78
Glencore International v. Metro-Trading [2001] All ER (Comm.) 103
    246
Godard v. Gray (1870) LR 6 QB 139   109, 118
Goenaga, in the Estate of [1949] P 367   269
Goetschius v. Brightman 245 NY 186 (1927)   249
Goff v. Goff [1934] P 107   292
Goodman's Trusts, re (1881) 17 Ch. D 266   352

Gourdain v. Nadler [1979] ECR 733   135
Government of India v. Taylor [1955] AC 491   125, 366, 368, 369
Government of Kuwait v. Sir Frederick Snow & Partners [1984] AC
    426   183
Grant v. Easton (1883) 13 QBD 302   123
Grant v. McAuliffe 41 Cal. 2d 859 (1953)   234
Gray v. Formosa [1963] P 259   122, 361
Grell v. Levy (1864) 16 CB (NS) 73   216, 370
Grey's Trusts, re [1892] 3 Ch. 88   352
Group Josi Reinsurance Co. SA v. Universal General Insurance Co.
    [2000] 3 WLR 467   136, 152
Grove, re (1887) 40 Ch. D 216   352
Grupo Torras SA and Others v. Sheikh Fahad Mohammed Al-Sabah
    [1996] 1 Ll.R 7   35, 153
Gsponer's Marriage, re (1988) FLR 164   341
Guaranty Trust Corporation of New York v. Hannay [1918] 2 KB 623
    35
Guardianship of an Infant Case ICJ 1958, 55   390
Gubisch Maschinenfabrik A/G v. Palumbo [1987] ECR 49   160,
    161, 163
Guépratte v. Young (1851) 4 De G & Sm. 217   278
Guinness v. Miller 291 Fed. 768 (1923)   382

H, re [1966] 1 WLR 381   347
H (A Child) (Abduction: Rights of Custody), re [2000] 2 WLR 337
    340
H (Minors) (Abduction: Acquiescence), re [1998] AC 72   341
H (Minors) (Abduction) (Custody Rights) [1991] 2 AC 476   340
H v. H [1954] P 258   310
HB (Abduction: Children's Objections), re [1998] 1 FLR 422   342
Hack v. Hack (1976) 6 Fam. Law. 177   55
Hacker v. Euro Relais [1992] 3 ILPr. 515   265
Hagen, The [1908] P 189   75
Hagerbaum, re [1933] IR 198   352, 353
Haji Ioannou v. Frangos [1999] 1 WLR 337   162
Halcyon Isle, The [1981] AC 221   67, 70
Halcyon the Great, The [1975] 1 Ll.R 515   66
Hall (R & H) & WH Pim Jr, re (1928) 139 LT 50   65
Halley, The (1868) LR 2 PC 193   222, 239
Hamlyn v. Talisker Distillery [1894] AC 202   180, 195
\Haque v. Haque (1962) 108 CLR 230   27
Harben v. Harben [1957] 1 WLR 261   336

Hardwick Game Farm *v.* Suffolk Agricultural Poultry Producers Association [1966] 1 WLR 287   246
Harris *v.* Quine (1869) LR 4 QB 653   14, 63, 64, 129
Harris *v.* Taylor [1915] 2 KB 580   144
Harrods (Buenos Aires) Ltd, *re* [1992] Ch. 72   91, 166, 167
Harrop *v.* Harrop [1920] 3 KB 386   125
Hashmi *v.* Hashmi [1972] Fam. 36   349, 351
Haumschild *v.* Continental Casualty Co. 7 Wis. (2d) 130 (1959)   234
Hawthorne, *re* (1883) 23 Ch. D 743   263
Hayward, decd, *re* [1997] Ch. 45   135
Heidberg, The [1994] 2 Ll.R 287   168
Helbert Wagg & Co. Ltd's Claim, *re* [1956] Ch. 323   30, 212, 250, 365, 371, 374
Hellman's Will, *re* (1866) LR 2 Eq. 363   272
Helstan Securities Ltd *v.* Hertfordshire CC [1978] 3 All ER 262   253
Henderson *v.* Henderson [1967] P 77   39, 42
Hendrickman *v.* Magenta Druck & Verlag GmbH [1997] QB 421   170
Henry *v.* Geoprosco International Ltd [1976] QB 726   74, 111, 117
Herceg Novi *v.* The Ming Galaxy [1998] 4 All ER 238   99
Herman *v.* Meallin (1891) 8 WN (NSW) 38   111
Hesperides Hotels *v.* Aegean Turkish Holidays [1979] AC 508   262
HIB Ltd *v.* Guardian Insurance Co. [1997] 1 Ll.R 412   199
Hilton *v.* Guyot 159 US 113 (1895)   110
Hiscox *v.* Outhwaite [1992] 1 AC 562   183
Hodge *v.* Club Motor Insurance Agency (1974) 2 ALR 421   234
Hoffman *v.* Krieg [1988] ECR 645   170
Hollandia, The [1982] 2 WLR 556; [1983] 1 AC 565   10, 97, 215
Holman *v.* Johnson (1775) 1 Cowp. 341   8, 369
Hooper *v.* Gumm (1867) LR 2 Ch. App. 282   248
Hooper *v.* Hooper [1959] 1 WLR 1021   26
Hope *v.* Hope (1854) 4 De GM & G 328   335, 336
Hopkins *v.* Hopkins [1951] P 116   55
Hoskins *v.* Matthews (1855) 8 De GM & G 13   46
Hough *v.* P & O Containers Ltd [1999] QB 834   151, 154
House of Spring Gardens Ltd *v.* Waite [1991] 1 QB 241   120, 130
Hoyles, *re* [1911] 1 Ch. 179   244
Huber *v.* Steiner (1835) 2 Bing. NC 202   14, 63
Huntington *v.* Attrill [1893] AC 150   14, 125
Hurll, *re* [1952] Ch. 722   30
Hussain *v.* Hussain [1983] Fam. 26   314, 316
Hutter *v.* Hutter [1944] P 95   111

Hyde *v.* Hyde & Woodmansee (1866) LR 1 P & D 130   313, 314, 315

Igra *v.* Igra [1951] P 404   329
Indian Endurance, The. *See* Republic of India
Industrial Diamond Supplies *v.* Riva [1977] ECR 2175   173
Indyka *v.* Indyka [1969] 1 AC 33   117, 323
Inglis *v.* Robertson [1898] AC 616   247
Inglis *v.* Usherwood (1801) 1 East. 515   247
Inland Revenue Commissioners *v.* Bullock [1976] 1 WLR 1178   41
Inland Revenue Commissioners *v.* Duchess of Portland [1982] Ch. 314   48
Inland Revenue Commissioners *v.* Lysaght [1928] AC 234   54
Interdesco SA *v.* Nullifire Ltd [1992] 1 Ll.R 180   168, 173
International Credit and Investment Co. (Overseas) Ltd *v.* Shaikh Kamal Adham [1999] ILPr. 302   89
International Tank & Pipe SAK *v.* Kuwait Aviation Fuelling Co. KSC [1975] 2 QB 224   180, 181
Ioannis Daskalelis, The [1974] 1 Ll.R 174   67
IP Metal *v.* Ruote OZ spa [1993] 2 Ll.R 60   154, 155
Iran Vojdan, The [1984] 2 Ll.R 380   205
Irvani *v.* GKH Montage GmbH [1990] 1 WLR 667   62
Isaac Penhas *v.* Tan Soo Eng [1953] AC 304   299, 300
Isabelle Lancray SA *v.* Peters und Sickert K/G [1990] ECR I-2725   170
Ispahani *v.* Bank Melli Iran [1998] Ll.R (Bank.) 133   218
Israel Discount Bank of New York *v.* Hadjipateras [1984] 1 WLR 137   118, 120, 122
Iveagh *v.* Inland Revenue Commissioners [1954] Ch 364   288
Iveco Fiat SpA *v.* Van Hool SA [1986] ECR 3337   155
Ivenel *v.* Schwab [1982] ECR 1891   142

J (A Minor) (Abduction), *re* [1990] 2 AC 562   55, 57, 340
JA (A Minor) (Child Abduction: Non-Convention Country), *re* [1998] 1 FLR 231   347
J *v.* C [1970] AC 668   347
Jabbour *v.* Custodian of Israeli Absentee Property [1954] 1 WLR 139   113, 252, 365, 370
Jacobs *v.* Crédit Lyonnais (1884) 12 QBD 589   212
Jacobson *v.* Frachon (1927) 138 LT 386   121
Jakob Handte & Co. GmbH *v.* Société Traitements Mecano-Chimiques [1992] ECR I-3967   141
Jalakrishna, The [1983] 2 Ll.R 628   87

James, *re* (1908) 98 LT 438   46
Jarrett *v.* Barclays Bank plc [1999] QB 1   266
Jeannot *v.* Fuerst (1909) 25 TLR 424   121
Jenner *v.* Sun Oil Co. [1952] 2 DLR 526   228
Jet Holdings Ltd *v.* Patel [1990] 1 QB 335   119, 121
Johnson, *re* [1903] 1 Ch. 821   21
Johnson *v.* Coventry Churchill International Ltd [1992] 3 All ER 14
    224, 226, 230, 232
Johnstone *v.* Beattie (1843) 10 Cl. & Fin. 42   335, 346
Johnstone *v.* Pedlar [1921] 2 AC 262   335
Jones's Estate, *re* 192 Iowa 78 (1921)   47, 52, 53
Jones *v.* Trollope and Colls Cementation Overseas Ltd (1990) *The
    Times*, 26 January   64
Jordan Grand Prix *v.* Baltic Insurance Group [1999] 2 AC 127   152
Joyce *v.* Director of Public Prosecutions [1946] AC 347   336
Joyce *v.* Joyce [1979] Fam. 93   329
Jugoslavenska Oceanska Plovidba *v.* Castle Investment Co. (The Kezara)
    [1974] QB 292   66
Jurisdiction of the Courts of Danzig Case PCIJ Ser. B no. 15 (1928)
    389

K (A Minor) (Abduction), *re* [1990] 1 FLR 387   344
K (Abduction: Consent: *Forum Conveniens*), *re* [1995] 2 FLR 211   56
Kahler *v.* Midland Bank Ltd [1950] AC 24   212, 371
Kalfelis *v.* Schröder, Munchmayer, Hengst & Co. [1988] ECR 5565
    144, 149
Kapur *v.* Kapur [1984] 5 FLR 920   56, 320
Kaufman, *in b.* [1952] P 325   269
Kaufman *v.* Gerson [1904] 1 KB 591   216, 374
Kehr, *re* [1952] Ch. 26   268
Ker's Settlement Trusts, *re* [1963] Ch. 533   291
Kelly *v.* Selwyn [1905] 2 Ch. 117   258
Kendall *v.* Kendall [1977] Fam. 208   119, 329
Kenward *v.* Kenward [1952] P 124   310
King of Italy *v.* de Medici (1918) 34 TLR 623   370
King of the Hellenes *v.* Brostrom (1923) 16 Ll.R 167   370
Kinnear *v.* Falconfilms NV [1996] 1 WLR 920   151
Kleinwort Benson Ltd *v.* Glasgow City Council [1996] QB 57   175
Kleinwort Benson Ltd *v.* Glasgow City Council [1999] AC 153   141,
    144
Kleinwort Sons & Co. *v.* Ungarische Baumwolle A/G [1939] 2 KB 678
    372
Kloebe, *re* (1884) 28 Ch. D 175   67, 268

Kloeckner & Co. A/G *v.* Gatoil Overseas Inc. [1990] 1 Ll.R 177   164
Klomps *v.* Michel [1981] ECR 1593   169, 170
Kochanski *v.* Kochanska [1958] P 147   300
Kohnke *v.* Karger [1951] 2 KB 670   65, 129
Kolsky *v.* Mayne Nickless Ltd [1970] 3 NSWR 511   226, 231
Komninos S, The [1990] 1 Ll.R 541 [1991] 1 Ll.R 370   64, 195
Kongress Agentur Hagen GmbH *v.* Zeehage BV [1990] ECR I-1845
    133, 150
Koop *v.* Bebb (1951) 84 CLR 629   230
Korner *v.* Witkowitzer [1950] 2 KB 128   63
Kotia *v.* Nahas [1941] AC 403   22
Kraut (Jean) A/G *v.* Albany Fabrics Ltd [1977] QB 182   16
Kroch *v.* Rossell [1937] 1 All ER 725   18, 228
Krombach *v.* Bamberski (2000) *The Times*, 30 March   169, 173
Kursell *v.* Timber Operators & Contractors Ltd [1927] 1 KB 298
    219
Kurz *v.* Stella Musical Veranstaltungs GmbH [1992] Ch. 196   156,
    157, 158
Kuwait Oil Tanker Co. SAK *v.* Al Bader [1997] 1 WLR 1410   223
Kwok Chi Leung Karl *v.* Commissioner of Estate Duty [1988] 1 WLR
    1035   252

L, *re* [1974] 1 WLR 250   246
L (Abduction: Pending Criminal Proceedings), *re* [1999] 1 FLR 433
    341
LTU *v.* Eurocontrol [1976] ECR 1541   134, 168
Langley's Settlement Trusts, *re* [1962] Ch. 541   309, 363, 381
Lashley *v.* Hog (1804) 4 Paton 581   282, 283
Laurie *v.* Carroll (1958) 98 CLR 310   72
La Van *v.* Danyluk (1970) 75 WWR 500   226
Lawrence *v.* Lawrence [1985] Fam. 106   27, 29, 302, 304, 305,
    307
Lazard Brothers *v.* Midland Bank [1933] AC 289   33, 35, 57
Lazarewicz *v.* Lazarewicz [1962] P 171   300
Leathertex Divisione Sintetici spa *v.* Bodetex BVBA [1999] 2 All ER
    (Comm.) 769   141
Lecouturier *v.* Rey [1910] AC 262   364
Lee *v.* Abdy (1886) 17 QBD 309   255
Lee *v.* Lau [1967] P 14   314
Le Feuvre *v.* Sullivan (1855) 10 Moo. PC 1   257, 258
Lemenda Trading Co. Ltd *v.* African Middle East Petroleum Co. Ltd
    [1988] QB 448   217

Le Mesurier *v.* Le Mesurier [1895] AC 517   322
Lepre *v.* Lepre [1965] P 52   122
Leroux *v.* Brown (1852) 12 CB 801   14, 62
Levene *v.* Inland Revenue Commissioners [1928] AC 217   54
Lewis *v.* Lewis [1956] 1 WLR 200   55
Lexmar Corp. *v.* Nordisk Skibsrederforening [1997] 1 Ll.R 289   164
Libyan Arab Bank *v.* Bankers Trust Co. [1989] QB 728   200
Libyan Arab Foreign Bank *v.* Manufacturers Hanover Trust Co. [1988] 2 Ll.R 494   200
Liddell's Settlement Trusts, *re* [1936] Ch. 365   262
Lieber *v.* Göbel [1994] ECR I-2535   264
Limerick *v.* Limerick (1863) 4 Sw. & Tr. 252   300
Lindsay *v.* Miller [1949] VLR 13   289
Littauer Glove Corporation *v.* FW Millington Ltd (1928) 44 TLR 746   112, 172
Liverpool Marine Credit Co. *v.* Hunter (1868) LR 3 Ch. App. 479   248
Lloyd *v.* Guibert (1865) LR 1 QB 185   238
Lloyd-Evans, *re* [1947] Ch. 695   45
Lloyd's Register of Shipping *v.* Société Campenon Bernard [1995] All ER (EC) 531   149
Lodge *v.* Lodge (1963) 107 Sol. Jo. 437   297
Logan *v.* Bank of Scotland (No. 2) [1906] 1 KB 141   111
Lord Advocate *v.* Jaffrey [1921] 1 AC 146   47
Lorentzen *v.* Lydden & Co. Ltd [1942] 2 KB 202   364
Lorillard, *re* [1922] 2 Ch. 638   270
Loucks *v.* Standard Oil Co. of New York 224 NY 99 (1918)   380
Lubbe *v.* Cape plc [2000] 1 WLR 1545   88, 92, 93, 100, 166
Luck's Settlement Trusts, *re* [1940] Ch. 864   352
Lundgren *v.* O'Brien (No. 2) [1921] VLR 361   309
Luther *v.* Sagor [1921] 3 KB 532   246, 365
Lynch *v.* Provisional Government of Paraguay (1871) LR 2 P & D 268   31, 32, 270, 276, 298, 364

M (Abduction: Habitual Residence), *re* [1996] 1 FLR 887   56
M (Minors) (Residence Order: Jurisdiction), *re* [1993] 1 FLR 495   56, 57
M *v.* M (Abduction: England and Scotland), *re* [1997] 2 FLR 263   56
McCabe *v.* McCabe [1994] 1 FCR 257   296
Macalpine *v.* Macalpine [1958] P 35   119, 121, 329
Macartney, *re* [1921] 1 Ch. 522   122
Macaulay *v.* Macaulay [1991] 1 All ER 866   171

McElroy *v.* McAllister 1949 SC 110   63, 221, 223, 224, 225, 230

McFeetridge *v.* Stewarts & Lloyds Ltd 1913 SC 773   209

Machado *v.* Fontes [1897] 2 QB 231   223, 230

Maciej Rataj, The. *See* The Tatry

McKain *v.* RW Miller & Co. (SA) Pty Ltd (1991) 17 CLR 1   225

McKee *v.* McKee [1951] AC 352   346

Mackender *v.* Feldia [1967] 2 QB 590   75, 78, 91

McKenzie, *re* (1951) 51 SR (NSW) 293   39

MacKinnon *v.* Iberia Shipping Co. 1955 SC 20; [1954] 2 Ll.R 372   239

McLean *v.* Pettigrew [1945] 2 DLR 65   230

Macmillan Inc. *v.* Bishopsgate Investment Trust plc (No. 3) [1996] 1 WLR 387   19, 26, 252, 256

Macmillan Inc. *v.* Bishopgate Investment Trust plc (No. 4) [1999] CLC 417, 478   35

McMillan *v.* Canadian Northern Railway [1923] AC 120   230

MacShannon *v.* Rockware Glass Ltd [1977] 1 WLR 376; [1978] AC 795   88

Mahadervan *v.* Mahadervan [1964] P 233   62

Maharanee of Baroda *v.* Wildenstein [1972] 2 QB 283   72, 73, 85, 111

Mainschiffahrts-Genossenschaft eG (MSG) *v.* Les Gravières Rhénanes SRL [1997] QB 731   144, 155

Maldonado, *re* [1954] P 223   16, 271

Male *v.* Roberts (1800) 3 Esp. 163   9, 209

Mamdani *v.* Mamdani [1984] 5 FLR 699   329

Manifold, *re* [1962] Ch. 1   270, 275

Manners *v.* Pearson [1898] 1 Ch. 581   65

Mansouri *v.* Singh [1986] 2 All ER 619   373

Manta Lines Inc. *v.* Sofianites [1984] 1 Ll.R 14   74

Maraver, *re* (1828) 1 Hagg. Ecc. 498   271

Marc Rich & Co. *v.* Societa Italiana Impianti SA, The Atlantic Emperor [1991] ECR I-3855   133, 136

Mariannina, The [1983] 1 Ll.R 12   195, 205, 206

Marinari *v.* Lloyds Bank plc [1996] QB 217   146

Marshall, *re* [1957] Ch. 263   356

Martin, *re* [1900] P 211   13, 37, 46, 274

Martin *v.* Nadel [1906] 2 KB 26   240

Martin Peters *v.* Zuid Nederlandse AV [1983] ECR 987   141, 192

Marvin Safe Co. *v.* Norton 48 NJL 410 (1886)   249

Mary Moxham, The (1876) 1 PD 107   231

Masters *v.* Leaver [2000] ILPr. 387   121

Matthews *v.* Kuwait Bechtel Corporation [1959] 2 QB 57   76, 236

Maudslay, *re* [1900] 1 Ch. 602   261

Mauroux *v.* Pereira [1972] 1 WLR 962   75, 79

May *v.* May [1943] 2 All ER 146   46

Mecklermedia Corp. *v.* DC Congress GmbH [1998] Ch. 40   146, 162

Meeth *v.* Glacetal [1978] ECR 2133   156

Mehta *v.* Mehta [1945] 2 All ER 690   315

Meisenhelder *v.* Chicago & NW Railway 170 Minn. 317 (1927)   27

Mercantile Investment & General Trust Co. *v.* River Plate etc. Co. [1892] 2 Ch. 303   264

Mercedes-Benz A/G *v.* Leiduck [1996] 1 AC 285   77

Mercury Communications Ltd *v.* Communication Telesystem International [1999] 2 All ER (Comm.) 33   157, 167

Mercury Publicity Ltd *v.* Wolfgang Loerke GmbH (1991) *The Times*, 21 October   142

Messianiki Tolmi, The [1984] 1 Ll.R 266   74

Messier Dowty *v.* Sabena SA (No. 2) [2001] 1 All ER 275   150, 162

Metall und Rohstoff A/G *v.* Donaldson Lufkin and Jenrette Inc. [1990] 1 QB 391   80, 224, 230

Metropolitan Water Board *v.* Dick, Kerr & Co. [1918] AC 119   219

Mette *v.* Mette (1859) 1 Sw. & Tr. 416   302

Middleton *v.* Janverin (1802) 2 Hagg. Conn. 437   297

Midland Bank plc *v.* Laker Airways Ltd [1986] QB 689   105

Midleton's Settlement, *re* [1947] Ch. 583   244

Milford, The (1858) Swa. 362   67

Miliangos *v.* George Frank (Textiles) Ltd [1976] AC 443   66

Miliangos *v.* George Frank (Textiles) Ltd (No. 2) [1977] QB 489   66

Miller *v.* Teale (1954) 92 CLR 406   309

Milliken *v.* Pratt 125 Mass. 374 (1878)   209

Minalmet GmbH *v.* Brandeis Ltd [1992] ECR I-5661   169, 170

Mohamed *v.* Knott [1969] 1 QB 1   304

Mohamed *v.* Bank of Kuwait and Middle East KSC [1996] 1 WLR 1483   92, 100

Mölnlycke AB *v.* Procter & Gamble Ltd [1992] 1 WLR 1112   144, 150

Monaco *v.* Monaco (1937) 157 LT 231   346

Monterosso Shipping Co. *v.* ITWF [1982] 3 All ER 841   62, 201

Moran *v.* Moran 1997 SLT 541   56

Morguard Investments Ltd *v.* de Savoye (1990) 76 DLR (4th) 256   117

Morris *v.* Baron & Co. [1918] AC 1   62
Mostyn *v.* Fabrigas (1774) 1 Cowp. 161   8
Motala *v.* Attorney-General (1992) 2 FLR 261, [1992] 1 AC 281
    349, 351
Mount Albert Borough Council *v.* Australasian Temperance etc.
    Assurance Society Ltd [1938] AC 224   211
Moynihan *v.* Moynihan [1997] 1 FLR 59   41
Muduroglu *v.* TC Ziraat Bankasi [1986] QB 1225   88
Mulox IB Ltd *v.* Geels [1993] ECR I-4075   142
Multinational Gas Co. *v.* Multinational Gas Services Ltd [1983] Ch.
    258   77
Municipal Council of Sydney *v.* Bull [1909] 1 KB 7   368
Murphy *v.* Sivajothi [1999] 1 WLR 467   115
Musurus, *re* [1936] 2 All ER 1666   271
Myerson *v.* Martin [1979] 1 WLR 1390   72

N (Minors) (Abduction), *re* [1991] FLR 413   341, 342
Nabi *v.* Heaton [1981] 1 WLR 1052   318
Nachimson *v.* Nachimson [1930] P 217   313
National Bank of Greece and Athens SA *v.* Metliss [1958] AC 509
    57
National Mortgage and Agency Co. of New Zealand *v.* Gosselin (1922)
    38 TLR 832   78
Naviera Amazonica Peruana SA *v.* Cia Internacional de Seguros del
    Peru [1988] 1 Ll.R 116   181
Nelson *v.* Bridport (1845) 8 Beav. 527   30, 31, 35, 262, 266
Nessa *v.* Adjudication Officer [1999] 1 WLR 737   55
Netherlands State *v.* Rüffer [1980] ECR 3807   134
New Hampshire Insurance Co. *v.* Strabag Bau A/G [1990] 2 Ll.R 61
    148
Newmarch *v.* Newmarch [1978] Fam. 79   329
Newtherapeutics Ltd *v.* Katz [1991] Ch. 226   153
New York Breweries Co. Ltd *v.* Attorney-General [1899] AC 62   269
New York Life Insurance Co. *v.* Public Trustee [1942] 2 Ch. 101
    252
Nile Rhapsody, The [1994] 1 Ll.R 374   158, 166, 167
Norris *v.* Chambres (1861) 3 De GF & J 583   263, 264
Norton *v.* Florence Land and Public Works Co. (1877) Ch. D 332
    67
Norton's Settlement, *re* [1908] Ch. 471   111
Nouvion *v.* Freeman (1889) 15 App. Cas. 1   127
Nova (Jersey) Knit *v.* Kammgarn Spinnerei GmbH [1977] 1 WLR 713
    185

Novello & Co. Ltd *v.* Hinrichsen Edition [1951] Ch. 595   364
Nugent *v.* Vetzera (1866) LR 2 Eq. 704   346
Nunneley *v.* Nunneley (1890) 15 PD 186   292

Obikoya *v.* Silvernorth (1983) *The Times*, 6 July   74
O'Callaghan *v.* Thomond (1810) 3 Taunt. 82   68
Oceanic Sun-Line Special Shipping Co. Inc. *v.* Fay (1988) 15 CLR
  197   99
Ochsenbein *v.* Papelier (1873) 8 Ch. App. 695   119
Offshore International SA *v.* Banco Central SA [1977] 1 WLR 399
  200
Ogden *v.* Ogden [1909] P 46   14, 297, 301, 306
Ohochuku *v.* Ohochuku [1960] 1 WLR 183   314
O'Keefe, *re* [1940] Ch. 124   23, 24, 26
Onobrauche *v.* Onobrauche (1978) 8 Fam. Law 107   315
Oppenheim *v.* Mahomed Haneef [1922] 1 AC 482   182
Oppenheimer *v.* Cattermole [1976] AC 249   250, 365
Oppenheimer *v.* Louis Rosenthal & Co. A/G [1937] 1 All ER 23   80,
  100
Overseas Union Insurance Ltd *v.* New Hampshire Insurance Ltd [1992]
  QB 434   152, 160, 164
Owens Bank Ltd *v.* Bracco [1992] 2 AC 443   120
Owens Bank Ltd *v.* Bracco (No. 2) [1994] QB 509   154
Owens Bank Ltd *v.* Etoile Commerciale SA [1995] 1 WLR 44   120

P (Abduction: Non-Convention Country), *re* [1997] 1 FLR 780   347
P (GE) (An Infant), *re* [1965] Ch. 568   55, 335, 336
Padolecchia *v.* Padolecchia [1968] P 314   303, 304, 306
Paget's Settlement, *re* [1965] 1 WLR 1046   291
Paine, *re* [1940] Ch. 46   303, 349
Papadopoulos *v.* Papadopoulos [1930] P 55   118
Parkasho *v.* Singh [1968] P 233   315
Parlement Belge, The (1879) 4 PD 179, affd (1880) 5 PD 197   389
Parojcic *v.* Parojcic [1958] 1 WLR 1280   310, 311
Parouth, The [1982] 2 Ll.R 351   206
Pemberton *v.* Hughes [1899] 1 Ch. 781   118
Pendy Plastic Products BV *v.* Pluspunkt [1982] ECR 2723   169, 170
Peninular and Oriental Steam Navigation Co. *v.* Shand (1865) 3 Moo.
  PC (NS) 272   195
Penn *v.* Baltimore (Lord) (1756) 1 Ves. Sen. 444   263
Pepin *v.* Bruyère [1902] 1 Ch. 24   275
Perrini *v.* Perrini [1979] Fam. 84   27, 116, 301, 304, 305, 306,
  307, 316

Perutz *v.* Boehmische Discount Bank 304 NY 533 (1953)   374
Peter Buchanan Ltd *v.* McVey [1955] AC 516n.   366, 368
Petereit *v.* Babcock International Holdings Ltd [1990] 1 WLR 550
    174
Petrotrade Inc. *v.* Smith [1999] 1 WLR 457   136
Philip Alexander Futures and Securities Ltd *v.* Bamberger [1997] ILPr.
    73, 104   107
Philipson-Stow *v.* Inland Revenue Commissioners [1961] AC 727
    273, 276, 289
Phillips *v.* Eyre (1870) LR 6 QB 1   30, 31, 221, 222, 225, 226, 228,
    230
Phoenix Marine Inc. *v.* China Ocean Shipping Co. [1999] 1 All ER 139
    34
Phrantzes *v.* Argenti [1960] 2 QB 19   122, 235
Pioneer Container, The [1994] 2 AC 324   89, 98
Plozza *v.* South Australian Insurance Co. [1963] SASR 122   234
Plummer *v.* Inland Revenue Commissioners [1988] 1 WLR 292
    42
Po, The [1991] 2 Ll.R 206   166, 174
Ponticelli *v.* Ponticelli [1958] P 204   296, 312
Porter *v.* Freudenberg [1916] 1 KB 857   72
Potinger *v.* Wightman (1817) 3 Mer. 67   48
Potter *v.* Broken Hill Pty Co. Ltd (1906) 3 CLR 479   261
Powell Duffryn plc *v.* Petereit [1992] 3 ILPr. 300   141, 155
Power Curber International Ltd *v.* National Bank of Kuwait [1981] 1
    WLR 1233   200, 252, 260
Preston *v.* Preston [1965] P 411   300
Price *v.* Dewhurst (1837) 8 Sim. 279   120
Price Mobile Home Centres Inc. *v.* National Trailer Convoy of Canada
    (1974) 44 DLR (3d) 433   248
Priest, *re* [1944] Ch. 58   273
Princess Paley Olga *v.* Weisz [1929] 1 KB 718   246, 365, 366
Prins Bernhard, The [1964] P 117   83
Provincial Treasurer of Alberta *v.* Kerr [1933] AC 710   245
Pugh *v.* Pugh [1951] P 482   303
Puttick *v.* Attorney-General [1980] Fam. 1   45

Qatar Petroleum Producing Authority *v.* Shell International Petroleum
    [1983] 2 Ll.R 35   75, 76
Quazi *v.* Quazi [1980] AC 744   325, 328
Queensland Mercantile Agency Co. Ltd, *re* [1891] 1 Ch. 536 affd
    [1892] 1 Ch. 219   260, 261

QRS I Aps *v.* Frandsen [1999] 1 WLR 2169   134, 368

Qureshi *v.* Qureshi [1972] Fam. 173   314, 324

R, *re* (1981) 2 FLR 416   347

R (A Minor) (Abduction), *re* [1992] 1 FLR 105   341

R *v.* Barnet London Borough Council, *ex parte* Nilish Shah [1983] 2 AC 309   54, 56

R *v.* Bham [1966] 2 QB 159   314

R *v.* Brentwood Superintendent Registrar of Marriages, *ex parte* Arias [1968] 2 QB 956   26, 28, 29, 303, 305, 307

R *v.* Crown Court at Harrow, *ex parte* UNIC Centre Srl [2000] 1 WLR 2112   134

R *v.* International Trustee for the Protection of Bondholders A/G [1937] AC 500   5, 30, 31, 195, 205

R *v.* Millis (1843–4) 10 Cl. & F 534   299

R *v.* Registrar-General of Births, Deaths and Marriages, *ex parte* Minhas [1977] QB 1   325

R *v.* Sagoo [1975] QB 885   317

R *v.* Sarwan Singh [1962] 3 All ER 612   317

R *v.* Secretary of State for the Home Department, *ex parte* Ghulam Fatima [1985] QB 190; [1986] AC 527   325

Radhakrishna Hospitality Service Private Ltd *v.* EIH Ltd [1999] 2 Ll.R 249   100

Radwan *v.* Radwan (No. 2) [1973] Fam. 35   301, 304, 316

Raffenel, *in b.* (1863) 3 Sw. & Tr. 49   46

Raiffeisen Zentralbank Osterreich A/G *v.* Five Star Trading LLC [2000] All ER (Comm.) 897, (2001) *The Times*, 21 February   256

Rainford *v.* Newell-Roberts [1962] IR 95   116

Ralli Brothers *v.* Compania Naviera Sota y Aznar [1920] 2 KB 287   212, 218, 371

Ramsay *v.* Liverpool Royal Infirmary [1930] AC 588   41, 42

Rank Film Distributors Ltd *v.* Lanterna Editrice SrL [1992] 3 ILPr. 58   140, 163

Raulin *v.* Fischer [1911] 2 KB 93   125

Razelos *v.* Razelos (No. 2) [1970] 1 WLR 392   285

Red Sea Insurance Co. Ltd *v.* Bouyges SA [1995] 1 AC 190   226, 227, 237

Reed *v.* Reed (1969) 6 DLR (3d) 617   297, 306, 307

Regazzoni *v.* KC Sethia (1944) Ltd [1958] AC 301   217, 362, 374, 379

Régie Nationale des Usines *v.* Maxicar spa (2000) *The Times*, 23 May   169

Reichert *v.* Dresdner Bank A/G [1990] ECR I-27   264
Reichert *v.* Dresdner Bank A/G (No. 2) [1992] ECR I-2149   145
Rena, K, The [1979] QB 377   185
Rennie Car Sales *v.* Union Acceptance Corporation (1955) 4 DLR 822
    249
Republica de Guatemala *v.* Nunez [1927] 1 KB 669   255, 258
Republic of Haiti *v.* Duvalier [1990] 1 QB 202   167
Republic of India *v.* Indian Steamship Co. Ltd (The Indian Endur-
    ance) [1993] AC 410   124, 128
    (No. 2) [1998] AC 878   83, 124, 128, 162
Réunion Européenne SA *v.* Spliethoff's Bevrachtingskantoor BV [2000]
    QB 90   141, 147, 149
Richards *v.* McLean [1973] 1 NZLR 521   228
Risdon Iron and Locomotive Works *v.* Furness [1906] 1 KB 49   57
Risk *v.* Risk [1951] P 50   314
Robert *v.* Robert [1947] P 164   312
Robinson *v.* Bland (1760) 2 Burr. 1077   88
Rohr *v.* Ossberger [1981] ECR 2431   158
Rome *v.* Punjab National Bank (No. 2) [1989] 1 WLR 1211   83
Rose Mary, The. *See* Anglo-Iranian Oil Co. *v.* Jaffrate   250, 365,
    389
Rosler *v.* Hilbery [1925] Ch. 250   75, 76, 77
Rösler *v.* Rottwinkel [1985] ECR 95, [1986] QB 33   265, 266
Ross, *re* [1930] 1 Ch. 377   22, 24, 25, 26, 262, 273, 391
Ross *v.* Ross [1930] AC 1   20, 44
Rothnie, The [1996] 2 Ll.R 206   98
Rossano *v.* Manufacturers Life Insurance Co. [1963] 2 QB 352   125,
    199, 260, 368
Rosseel NV *v.* Oriental Commercial and Shipping (UK) Ltd [1990] 1
    WLR 1387   183
Rousillon *v.* Rousillon (1880) 14 Ch. D 351   110, 116, 122, 216,
    374
Royal Bank of Scotland *v.* Cassa di Rispiarmo Delle Provincie Lombardo
    [1992] ILPr. 411   141
Royal Boskalis Westminster NV *v.* Mountain [1999] QB 674   216,
    218
Ruding *v.* Smith (1821) 2 Hagg. Con. 371   299
Rutten *v.* Cross Medical [1997] All ER (EC) 121   142

Saab *v.* Saudi American Bank [1999] 1 WLR 1861   82, 92
S (Abduction: Return into Care), *re* [1999] 1 FLR 843   341
S (A Minor) (Abduction), *re* [1991] 2 FLR 1   341, 342

S (A Minor) (Abduction: Custody Rights) [1993] Fam. 242   341
S (A Minor) (Custody: Habitual Residence), re [1998] AC 750   56
SA Consortium General Textiles v. Sun and Sand Agencies [1978] QB 279 126, 362
Sadler v. Robins (1808) 1 Camp. 253   125
SB (An Infant), re [1968] Ch. 204   354
St Pierre v. South American Stores Ltd [1936] 1 KB 382   85, 261
St Pierre v. South American Stores Ltd [1937] 1 All ER 206; 3 All ER 349   63
Salotti v. Rüwa [1976] ECR 1831   155
Sanders v. Van der Putte [1977] WCR 2383   265
Sanicentral v. Collin [1979] ECR 3423   134, 154
Santos v. Illidge (1860) 8 CB (NS) 861   363
Sargasso, The, [1994] 3 All ER 180   166
Sarrio SA v. Kuwait Investment Authority [1997] 1 Ll.R 113, [1999] AC 32   162, 163, 167
Sar Schotte v. Parfums Rothschild [1987] ECR 4905   148
Saxby v. Fulton [1909] 2 KB 208   33
Sayers v. International Drilling Co. [1971] 1 WLR 1176   195, 234, 236
Scarpetta v. Lowenfeld (1911) 27 TLR 509   121
SCF Finance Co. v. Masri (No. 3) [1987] QB 1028   259
Schemmer v. Property Resources Ltd [1975] Ch. 273   125
Scherrens v. Maenhout [1988] ECR 3791   265
Schibsby v. Westenholz (1870) LR 6 QB 155   109, 110, 113, 380
Schnapper, re [1936] 1 All ER 322   272
Schneider's Estate, re 96 NY Supp. 2d 652 (1950)   20
Schorsch Meier GmbH v. Hennin [1975] QB 416   66
Schuler (L) A/G v. Wickman Machine Tools Sales Ltd [1974] AC 235 205
Schwebel v. Ungar (1963) 42 DLR (2d) 622; affd (1964) 48 DLR (2d) 644   28, 29, 308
Scott v. Attorney-General (1886) 11 PD 128   309, 381
Scott v. Pilkington (1862) 2 B & S 11   127
Scott v. Seymour (1862) 1 H & C 219   227
Scrimshire v. Scrimshire (1752) 2 Hagg. Con. 395   8, 295
Scullard, re [1957] Ch. 107   47
Seaconsar Far East Ltd v. Bank Markazi Jomhouri Islami Iran [1994] 1 AC 438   75
Seale's Marriage Settlement, re [1961] Ch. 574   291
Sebba, re [1959] Ch. 166   33
Segoura v. Bonakdarian [1976] ECR 1851   154, 155

Sehota, *re* [1978] 1 WLR 1506   318
Sellars *v.* Sellars 1942 SC 206   46
Selot's Trusts, *re* [1902] 1 Ch. 488   363, 381
Sennar, The (No. 2) [1985] 1 WLR 490   97, 130
Serbian and Brazilian Loans Cases PCIJ Ser. A, nos. 20, 21 (1929)
   386, 390, 391
Services Europe Atlantique Sud *v.* Stockholm Rederiaktiebolaget Svea,
   The Folias, The Despina R [1979] AC 685   66
Sfeir *v.* National Insurance Co. of New Zealand Ltd [1964] Ll.R 330
   112
Sharif *v.* Azad [1967] 1 QB 605   372, 373, 374
Sharif *v.* Sharif (1980) 10 Fam. Law 216   329
Sharpe *v.* Crispin (1869) LR 1 P & D 611   50
Sharps Commercials Ltd *v.* Gas Turbines Ltd [1956] NZLR 819
   117
Shaw *v.* Gould (1868) LR 3 HL 55   27, 302, 348, 349, 350, 351
Shearson Lehmann & Hutton *v.* TVB GmbH [1993] ECR I-139   152
Shenavai *v.* Kreischer [1987] ECR 239   141, 142
Shevill *v.* Presse Alliance SA [1995] 2 AC 18; [1996] 3 All ER 929
   81, 146, 228
Showlag *v.* Mansour [1995] 1 AC 431   123
Sierra Leone Telecommunications Ltd *v.* Barclays Bank plc [1998] 2
   All ER 821   200
Sill *v.* Worswick (1791) 1 H Bl. 665   245
Sim *v.* Robinow (1892) 19 Rettie 665   87
Simonin *v.* Mallac (1860) 2 Sw. & Tr. 67   297
Sindh, The [1975] 1 Ll.R 372   97
Singh Batra *v.* Ebrahim [1982] 2 Ll.R 11   371
Sinha Peerage Claim, The [1946] 1 All ER 348n.   315, 318
Sirdar Gurdyal Singh *v.* Rajah of Faridkote [1894] AC 670   110,
   111, 116
Siskina, The [1979] AC 210   77
Six Constructions Ltd *v.* Humbert [1989] ECR 341   142
Slater *v.* Mexican National Railway 194 US 120 (1904)   379
Smith, *re* [1916] 2 Ch. 206   263, 267
Smith, Kline & French Laboratories Ltd *v.* Bloch [1983] 1 WLR 730
   87
Smith, Kline & French Laboratories Ltd *v.* Bloch [1985] ECC 230
   105
Société Commerciale de Réassurance *v.* ERAS International Ltd [1995]
   2 All ER 278   150
Société Coopérative Sidmetal *v.* Titan International Ltd [1966] 1 QB 828
   117

Société d'Informatique Service Realisation Organisation v. Ampersand
    Software BV [1994] ILPr.55; [1996] QB 127   133, 169
Société du Gaz de Paris v. Société Anonyme de Navigation 'Les
    Armateurs Français' 1926 SC 13   89
Société Française Bunge SA v. Belcan NV [1985] 3 All ER 378   66
Société Nationale Industrielle Aerospatiale v. Lee Kui Jak [1987] AC
    871   101
Society of Lloyd's v. White (2000) The Times, 14 April   107
Sohio Supply Co. Ltd v. Gatoil (USA) Inc. [1989] 1 Ll.R 588   97
Soleimany v. Soleimany [1999] QB 785   184, 218, 219
Solo Kleinmotoren GmbH v. Boch [1994] ECR I-2237   168
Somafer v. Saar-Ferngas A/G [1978] ECR 2183   147, 149
Somersett's case (1771) 20 St. Tr. 1   363
Sonntag v. Waidmann [1993] ECR I-1963   134, 170
Sottomayor v. Barros (No. 1) (1877) 3 PD 1   209, 302, 306
Sottomayer v. de Barros (No. 2) (1879) 5 PD 94   306
Soulié, l'Affaire (1910) Clunet 888   20
Source Ltd v. TUV Rheinland Holding A/G [1998] QB 54   142,
    145
South Carolina Insurance Co. v. Ass. Maatschappij 'de Zeven
    Provincien' NV [1987] AC 24   106
South India Shipping Co. v. Export-Import Bank of Korea [1985] 1
    WLR 585   82, 83
Sperling v. Sperling (1975) (3) SA 707   30, 32, 282
Spiliada Maritime Corporation v. Cansulex Ltd [1987] AC 460   75,
    84, 87, 90, 91
Spitzley v. Sommer Exploitation [1985] ECR 787   159
Spurrier v. La Cloche [1902] AC 446   195
Srini Vasan v. Srini Vasan [1946] P 67   317
Standard Chartered Bank Ltd v. Inland Revenue Commissioners [1978]
    1 WLR 1160   252
Standard Steamship Owners' Protection and Indemnity Association
    (Bermuda), The v. Gann [1992] 2 Ll.R 528   79, 98
Starkowski v. Attorney-General [1954] AC 155   30, 31, 32, 270,
    297, 300
Star Texas, The [1993] 2 Ll.R 445   195, 205
State of Norway's Application, re (Nos. 1 and 2) [1990] 1 AC 723
    369
Stone v. Stone [1958] 1 WLR 1287   46
Stransky v. Stransky [1954] P 428   55
Stuart v. Marquess of Bute (1869) 9 HL Cas. 440   335, 346
Submarine Telegraph Co. v. Dickson (1864) 15 CB (NS) 759   239
Sussex Peerage Case (1844) Cl. & F 85   309

Swan, Will of (1871) 2 VR (IE & M) 47   306
Swedish Central Railway Co. Ltd *v.* Thompson [1925] AC 495   58, 59
Swiss Bank Corporation *v.* Boehmische Industrial Bank [1923] 1 KB 673   259
Syal *v.* Heyward [1948] 2 KB 443   119
Sydney Express, The [1988] 2 Ll.R 257   158
Szalatnay-Stacho *v.* Fink [1947] KB 1   221
Szechter *v.* Szechter [1971] P 286   45, 310, 311

T, *re* [1968] Ch. 704   346
T (Children) (Abduction: Custody Rights), *re* (2000) *The Times*, 24 April   342
Taczanowska *v.* Taczanowski [1957] P 301   26, 296, 299, 300
Tagus, The [1903] P 44   67
Tallack *v.* Tallack [1921] P 211   292
Tallmadge, *re* 181 NY Supp. 336 (1919)   20
Tamari and Tamari *v.* Bernhard Rofhfos [1980] 2 Ll.R 553   201, 204
Tatry, The [1999] QB 515n.   124, 160–2, 163
Taylor *v.* Caldwell (1863) 3 B & S 826   219
Taylor *v.* Hollard [1902] 1 KB 676   128
Tee *v.* Tee [1974] 1 WLR 213   40, 45, 46, 47
Tesam Distribution Ltd *v.* Shuh Mode Team GmbH (1989) *The Times*, 22 October   140
Tessili *v.* Dunlop A/G [1976] ECR 1473   133, 143
Tezcan *v.* Tezcan [1992] 87 DLR (4th) 503   280
'Tilly Russ' Ms *v.* Haven [1984] ECR 2417, 2 QB 931   154, 155
Toepfer International GmbH *v.* Molino Boschi srl [1996] 1 Ll.R 510   107, 162, 164
Toepfer International GmbH Société Cargill France [1998] 1 Ll.R 379   107
Tojo Maru, The [1972] AC 242   238
Tomkinson *v.* First Pennsylvania Banking & Trust Co. [1961] AC 1007   34, 372 (see also United Railways of Havana and Regla Warehouses Ltd)
Topolski *v.* The Queen (1978) 90 DLR (3d) 66   30
Toprak Mahuselleri Ofisi *v.* Finagrain [1979] 2 Ll.R 98   372
Torok *v.* Torok [1973] 1 WLR 1066   327
Tracomin SA *v.* Sudan Oil Seeds Ltd (No. 1) [1981] 1 WLR 1026   107, 114, 117, 118
Tracomin SA *v.* Sudan Oil Seeds Ltd (No. 2) *ibid.* at 1031   107, 185

Trasporti Castelleti Spedizioni Internazionale Spa *v.* Hugo Trumpy
   Spa [1999] ILPr. 492   154
Travers *v.* Holley [1953] P 246   116, 322
Trendtex Trading Corporation *v.* Central Bank of Nigeria [1977]
   QB 529   33, 389
Trendtex Trading Corporation *v.* Crédit Suisse [1980] 3 All ER 734;
   [1980] QB 629; [1982] AC 679   88, 253, 254
Trepca Mines Ltd, *re* [1960] 1 WLR 1273   117
Tropaioforos, The [1967] 1 Ll.R 410   100
Trufort, *re* (1887) 36 Ch. D 600   21
Tubantia, The [1924] P 78   239
Tucker, *in b.* (1864) 3 Sw. & Tr. 585   268
Turnbull *v.* Walker (1892) 67 LT 767   116
Turner *v.* Grovit [2000] 1 WLR 1034   107, 165
Tyburn Productions Ltd *v.* Conan Doyle [1991] Ch. 75   261

UBS A/G *v.* Omni-Holding A/G [2000] 1 WLR 916 42   135
Udny *v.* Udny (1869) 1 LR Sc. & Div. 441   38, 39, 40, 45, 47
Union International Insurance Co. Ltd *v.* Jubilee Insurance Co. Ltd
   [1991] 1 WLR 45   78
Union National des Coopératives Agricoles de Cereales *v.* Catterall
   [1959] 2 QB 44   181
Union of India *v.* McDonnell Douglas Corp. [1993] 2 Ll.R 48   181
Union Transport plc *v.* Continental Lines [1992] 1 WLR 15   141
Union Trust Co. *v.* Grosman 245 US 412 (1918)   209
Unit Construction Co. Ltd *v.* Bullock [1960] AC 351   58, 59
United Bank of the Middle East *v.* Clapham (1981) *The Times*, 20 July
   74
United City Merchants *v.* Royal Bank of Canada [1983] 1 AC 168
   372, 373, 374
United Railways of Havana and Regla Warehouses Ltd, *re* [1960] Ch.
   62 affd sub nom. Tomkinson *v.* Pennsylvania Banking and Trust Co.
   [1961] AC 1007   27, 204, 212
United States of America *v.* Harden (1963) 41 DLR (2d) 721   368
United States of America *v.* Inkley [1989] QB 255   125
United States of America *v.* Ivey (1995) 130 DLR (4th) 674   370
Unterweser Reederei GmbH *v.* Zapata Offshore Co., The Chaparral
   [1968] 2 Ll.R 158   79
Urquhart *v.* Butterfield (1887) 37 Ch. D 357   50

V (Abduction: Habitual Residence), *re* [1995] 2 FLR 992   56
V *v.* B (A Minor) (Abduction) [1991] 2 FLR 292   56
Vadala *v.* Lawes (1890) 25 QBD 310   119

Valentine's Settlement, *re* [1965] Ch. 831   355, 356
Van Bogaard *v.* Laumen [1997] QB 759   135
Van Dalfsen *v.* Van Loon [1991] ECR I-4743   174
Van Grutten *v.* Digby (1862) 31 Beav. 561   207, 278
Vanquelin *v.* Bouard (1863) 15 CB (NS) 341   118, 269
Van Uden Maritime BV *v.* Kommanditgesellschaft in Firma Deco-Line
     [1999] 2 WLR 1181   136, 167
Varna (No. 2), The [1994] 2 Ll.R 41   100
Velasco *v.* Coney [1934] P 143   273
Vervaeke *v.* Smith [1983] 1 AC 145   123, 170, 328, 361
Viditz *v.* O'Hagan [1900] 2 Ch. 87   280
Vishva Ajay, The [1989] 2 Ll.R 558   87
Viskase Ltd *v.* Paul Kiefel GmbH [1999] 1 WLR 1305   143
Visser, *re* [1928] Ch. 877   368
Vita Food Products Inc. *v.* Unus Shipping Co. [1939] AC 277   193,
     215
Vogel *v.* RA Kohnstamm Ltd [1973] QB 133   115, 115, 116
Volvox Hollandia, The [1988] 2 Ll.R 361   161
Von Linden, *in b.* [1896] P 148   269
Voth *v.* Manildra Flour Mills Pty Ltd (1990) 171 CLR 538   99

W *v.* H [1982] ECR 1189   135, 167
Wahl *v.* Attorney-General (1932) 147 LT 382   45
Wallach, *re* [1950] 1 All ER 199   47
Walpole *v.* Canadian Northern Railway [1923] AC 113   230
Warren *v.* Warren [1972] Qd.R 386   225, 234
Warter *v.* Warter (1890) 15 PD 152   309, 381
Waterford Wedgwood plc *v.* David Nagli Ltd [1999] ILPr. 9   147,
     151
Watkins *v.* North American Land and Timber Co. Ltd (1904) 20 TLR
     534   73
Way *v.* Way [1950] P 71   310
Wayland, *re* [1951] 2 All ER 1041   275
Webb *v.* Webb [1994] QB 696   265
Welch *v.* Tennent [1891] AC 639   284
West (Richard) & Partners (Inverness) Ltd *v.* Dick [1969] Ch. 424
     263
Westacre Investments Inc. *v.* Jugoimport SPDR Holding Co. Ltd [1999]
     QB 740, [2000] QB 238   184
Weston's Settlements, *re* [1969] 1 Ch. 223   291
Whicker *v.* Hume (1858) 7 HLC 124   37
White & Tennant 31 W Va. 790 (1888)   40

Whitworth Street Estates (Manchester) Ltd v. James Miller & Partners
    Ltd [1970] AC 583   181, 204, 205
Wier's Case (1607) 1 Rolle Ab. 530 K 12   8
Wilby, re [1956] P 174   356
Wilks, re [1935] Ch. 645   268
Williams Bros. v. ET Agius Ltd [1914] AC 510   65
Williams & Glyn's Bank v. Astro Dinamico [1984] 1 WLR 438   74
Williams & Humbert Ltd v. WH Trademarks (Jersey) Ltd [1986] AC
    368   364, 365
Willoughby, re (1885) 30 Ch. D 324   336
Wilson, re [1954] Ch. 733   356
Wilson, Smithett & Cope Ltd v. Terruzzi [1976] QB 683   372, 373
Winans v. Attorney-General [1904] AC 287   41, 43, 46
Windeatt's Will Trusts, re [1969] 1 WLR 692   291
Winkworth v. Christie, Manson & Woods [1980] Ch. 496   26, 246,
    247, 250
Witted v. Galbraith [1893] 1 QB 577   77
Wolfenden v. Wolfenden [1946] P 61   299, 300
Wolff v. Oxholm (1817) 6 M & S 92   68, 365
Wood v. Wood [1957] P 254   327
World Harmony, The [1967] P 341   82
Worms v. de Valdor (1880) 49 LJ Ch. 261   363, 381
Wright's Trusts, re (1856) 2 K & J 595   352

X v. Y [1990] 1 QB 220   167
X A/G v. A Bank [1983] 2 All ER 464   13, 258
Xin Yang, The [1996] 2 Ll.R 217   167

Zaal v. Zaal [1983] 4 FLR 284   329
Zanelli v. Zanelli [1948] 64 TLR 556   45, 320
Zeevi (J) & Sons Ltd v. Grindlay's Bank (Uganda) Ltd 37 NY 2d 320
    (1978)   373
Zelger v. Salinitri [1980] ECR 89   144
Zelger v. Salinitri (No. 2) [1984] ECR 2397   166
Zigurds, The [1932] P 113   67
Zivnostenka Banka National Corp. v. Frankman [1950] AC 57   371
Zollverein, The (1856) Swab. 96   238
Zoneheath Associates Ltd v. China Tianjin International Economic
    and Technical Cooperative Corp. [1994] CLC 348   260

Part I

General principles

1 Introduction

The subject-matter

The English conflict of laws is a body of rules whose purpose is to assist an English court in deciding a case which contains a foreign element. It consists of three main topics, which concern respectively: (i) the jurisdiction of an English court, in the sense of its competence to hear and determine a case; (ii) the selection of the appropriate rules of a system of law, English or foreign, which it should apply in deciding a case over which it has jurisdiction (the rules governing this selection are known as 'choice of law' rules); and (iii) the recognition and enforcement of judgments rendered by foreign courts or awards of foreign arbitrations.

If the case contains no foreign element, the conflict of laws is irrelevant. If an Englishman and woman who are both British citizens, domiciled and resident in England, go through a ceremony of marriage in England and later, when they are both still domiciled and resident here, the wife petitions an English court for a divorce, no foreign element is involved. No problem of jurisdiction arises and any questions about the validity of the marriage or the grounds upon which a divorce can be granted, as well as any procedural or evidential matters, are all governed by English law alone. The same is true if two Englishmen in England contract here for the sale and purchase of goods to be delivered from Oxford to Cambridge with payment in sterling in London, and the seller later sues the buyer and serves him with a writ in England.

But if we vary the facts and suppose that in the first example at the time the wife petitions for divorce the husband is domiciled and resident in France, and that the ceremony had taken place in France and the husband argues that it did not comply with the requirements of French law so that there is no marriage to dissolve, the conflict of laws becomes relevant. The husband's absence raises the question of the court's jurisdiction, and his argument raises that of whether French or English law is to determine the validity of the marriage.

Or suppose that in the second situation the seller is an Englishman in England who agrees to sell goods in England to a French buyer in France, to be delivered in France and paid for in sterling into an English bank in Paris. The question arises as to whether the seller can invoke the jurisdiction of the English court against the buyer, who is still in France, if he wishes to sue him for breach of contract or failure to pay the price. The further question may also arise as to which law, English or French, is to be applied to determine the parties' rights and obligations should the English court possess jurisdiction.

It will be seen from these examples that a question of jurisdiction and one of choice of law may both be involved in a particular case. But they can arise independently. The court may clearly have jurisdiction, as it has in the divorce case, but it has to answer the choice of law question. Or there may be no question as to what law to apply, as would be the case in the contract example if the parties had stipulated that English law should govern their agreement, but there would be a question whether the court has jurisdiction. Recognition and enforcement of foreign judgments is a wholly independent matter. Choice of law does not arise in combination with it.

These are only examples. A jurisdictional question can arise in any kind of case; it usually does so because the proposed defendant is not in England when the claimant tries to serve him with the process of the English court.[1] A choice of law problem can arise in any civil action. The conflict of laws is concerned with all of the civil and commercial law. (It is not concerned with criminal, constitutional or administrative cases.)[2] It covers the law of obligations, contract and tort, and the law of property both immovable and movable, whether a question of title arises *inter vivos* or by way of succession. It is concerned also with family law, including marriage and divorce, and guardianship and the relations of parent and child. Recognition or enforcement of a judgment in some civil or commercial matter may be called for whether it was for breach of contract or a tort (delict) or dealt with the ownership of property or concerned status, such as a decree of divorce or nullity of marriage or a custody or adoption order.

---

[1] This is not true in matrimonial cases, where statutory rules of jurisdiction exist; see pp. 319–20, 321 below. In some cases the English court may not have jurisdiction even though the defendant is in England, as where, for example, he is a foreign ambassador or consul. The jurisdictional immunities of foreign diplomatic and consular agents, as well as foreign states or governments, now rest on statute. They will not be dealt with in this book; reference should be made to works on public international law.

[2] But questions of, for example, validity of marriage or recognition of divorces may be involved in matters of British citizenship, immigration and social security.

The name

Two names for the subject are in common use; however, they are interchangeable. Neither is wholly accurate or properly descriptive. The name 'conflict of laws' is somewhat misleading, since the object of this branch of the law is to eliminate any conflict between two or more systems of law (including English law) which have competing claims to govern the issue which is before the court, rather than to provoke such a conflict, as the words may appear to suggest. However, it was the name given to the subject by A. V. Dicey, when he published his treatise, the first coherent account by an English lawyer of its rules and principles, in 1896[3] and it has been hallowed by use ever since.

Another name is 'private international law', which is in common use in Europe. This is even more misleading than 'conflict of laws', and each of its three words requires comment. 'Private' distinguishes the subject from 'public' international law, or international law *simpliciter*. The latter is the name for the body of rules and principles which governs states and international organisations in their mutual relations. It is administered through the International Court of Justice, other international courts and arbitral tribunals, international organisations and foreign offices, although, as part of a state's municipal or domestic law, it is also applied by that state's courts.[4] Its sources are primarily to be found in international treaties, the practice of states in their relations (or custom) and the general principles of municipal legal systems.[5] Private international law is concerned with the legal relations between private individuals and corporations, though also with the relations between states and governments so far as their relationships with other entities are governed by municipal law, an example being a government which contracts with individuals and corporations by raising a loan from them.[6] Its sources are the same as those of any other branch of municipal law, which is to say that English private international law is derived from legislation and decisions of English courts.

---

[3] The latest, 13th edition, *The Conflict of Laws*, called Dicey and Morris (Morris being one of its most distinguished editors) was published by Stevens (London) in 2000. It is still the most authoritative textbook.

[4] The question whether international law is part of English law will not be pursued here.

[5] Statute of the International Court of Justice, Article 38. This also states that textbooks on the subject and judicial decisions are subsidiary means for the determination of the rules to be applied by the International Court.

[6] See *R* v. *International Trustee for the Protection of Bondholders A/G* [1937] AC 500 HL, where it was held that certain bonds issued in New York by the British Government were governed by New York law.

'International' is used to indicate that the subject is concerned not only with the application by English courts of English law but of rules of foreign law also. The word is inapt, however, in so far as it might suggest that it is in some way concerned with the relations between states (it is even more inapt if it suggests 'nations' rather than states).[7] The relationship between public and private international law will be discussed more fully later.[8]

The word 'law' must be understood in a special sense. The application of the rules of English private international law does not by itself decide a case, as does that of the rules of the law of contract or tort. Private international law is not substantive law in this sense, for, as we have seen, it merely provides a body of rules which determine whether the English court has jurisdiction to hear and decide a case, and if it has, what system of law, English or foreign, will be employed to decide it, or whether a judgment of a foreign court will be recognised and enforced by an English court.

Geographical considerations

For the purpose of the English conflict of laws, every country in the world which is not part of England and Wales is a foreign country and its foreign law. This means that not only totally foreign independent countries such as France or Russia, or independent Commonwealth countries, such as India or New Zealand, are foreign countries but also British Colonies such as the Falkland Islands. Moreover, the other parts of the United Kingdom – Scotland and Northern Ireland – are foreign countries for present purposes, as are the other British Islands, the Isle of Man, Jersey and Guernsey. It may be that the rules of another system are identical with those of English law, or that they are found in legislation such as the Companies Act 1985 which extends to both England and Scotland. But if say, New Zealand or Scots law falls to be applied by an English court, it is nonetheless New Zealand or Scots law which is being applied, and not English law, even though these are identical.[9]

---

[7] The rules of private international law apply between, for example, England and Scotland, which are not separate states. The English and Scots may be regarded as separate nations but that is not why the rules so apply; it is because they have separate legal systems.

[8] Ch. 23 below.

[9] Though see *Attorney-General for New Zealand* v. *Ortiz* [1984] AC 1 HL where certain statutes of New Zealand which were in the same terms as English statutes were interpreted by resort to English case law. This case is discussed at pp. 366–7 below.

In the case of foreign countries with a federal constitutional organisation, reference to the foreign country or law is not generally to the state in an international sense, but to one of the component parts thereof, if these are regarded in the constitutional law of that country as being separate entities having separate legal systems. Thus, the reference is not usually to the United States of America, but to a state therein, such as New York or California, or to Canada, but to a province, for example Ontario or Quebec, or to Australia, but to one of its states, such as Victoria or New South Wales.[10]

Glossary of terms employed

Conflicts lawyers commonly employ some Latin terms, which are a convenient and short way of saying certain things which are in common use. Some of these are:

Lex causae – the law which governs an issue. The following are examples:

Lex actus – the law governing a transaction, such as the applicable law of a contract.

Lex domicilii – the law of a person's domicile.

Lex fori – the law administered by the court hearing the case. English law is the *lex fori* for an English court.

Lex loci actus – the law of the place where a transaction is concluded; in relation to the conclusion of a contract called *lex loci contractus* and to the celebration of a marriage, *lex loci celebrationis*.

Lex loci delicti commissi – the law of the place where a tort is committed.

Lex loci solutionis – the law of the place of performance (of a contract).

Lex situs – the law of the place where property is situated.

---

[10] However, it is obvious that for the purpose of determining a person's nationality, which is rarely necessary in the conflict of laws, it is the United States, Canada or Australia which must be referred to. In the case of Canada and Australia a person would probably be regarded as domiciled there rather than in a province or state for the purpose of recognition of divorces granted there, since the divorce laws of those countries refer to divorces of persons domiciled in Canada or Australia. See p. 38 note 4 below.

2   Characteristics of the English conflict of laws

Late development

Compared with other branches of English law, a systematic body of rules on the conflict of laws only came into being at a comparatively late stage. The earliest cases appear to have concerned the enforcement of foreign judgments.[1] An eighteenth-century case, which is still of binding authority, concerned the validity of a foreign marriage.[2] Lord Mansfield, who, more than any judge, was connected with the development of a body of commercial law in the latter half of the eighteenth century, gave judgments concerning foreign contracts,[3] torts[4] and the duty to give effect to, and sometimes to deny effect to, foreign laws.[5]

It can be said with some confidence that the subject began to burgeon in the latter part of the nineteenth century, which at the same time saw the development (after 1857) of family law and the coming into existence of a coherent body of commercial law, since that period witnessed a rapid expansion of international trade and financial transactions. In those years, the courts evolved more sophisticated rules as regards domicile, the validity of marriages and recognition of foreign legitimations, formulated the modern doctrine of the proper law of the contract, laid down the rule governing liability for torts committed abroad and adopted clear rules and principles for the recognition and enforcement of foreign judgments. In order to formulate these principles the English courts had to rely more on the writings of jurists than was usual with them; Huber and the American Story J are notable examples. These were also foreign jurists, for it was not until A. V. Dicey published his *Conflict of Laws* in 1896, that any English writer attempted to set down the existing rules in a systematic fashion and to formulate a theoretical basis for them and to extract coherent principles from them.

[1] *Wier's* case (1607) 1 Rolle Ab. 530 K 12.
[2] *Scrimshire* v. *Scrimshire* (1752) 2 Hagg. Con. 395.
[3] *Robinson* v. *Bland* (1760) 2 Burr. 1077.   [4] *Mostyn* v. *Fabrigas* (1774) 1 Cowp. 161.
[5] *Holman* v. *Johnson* (1775) 1 Cowp. 341.

Because of this feature, it is sometimes dangerous nowadays to rely on older authorities.[6] Moreover, even decisions of those years or of the early years of the twentieth century are unreliable or, to our eyes, confused. Some questions remain unanswered: for example, what law governs capacity to conclude a commercial contract?[7] or, does capacity to make a will of movable property depend on the law of the testator's domicile at the time he makes a will or at the time of his death? The conflict rules regarding trusts *inter vivos*, other than those arising from marriage settlements, were the subject of almost no clear English decisions.[8] Other topics remain, surprisingly, the subject of considerable doubt, and the indeterminacy of the rules which do exist is due, perhaps, to unclear principle and analysis.

One other matter should be mentioned. Until quite recently, questions concerning choice of law could fairly be said to have predominated over jurisdictional problems. During the last thirty or so years this has been completely reversed and for reasons which may become apparent, it is fair to say that the English courts have come to be almost entirely preoccupied with jurisdiction and enforcement of foreign judgments (the law relating to which is concerned with questions of jurisdiction) rather than with choice of law rules.

Legislation

Until fairly recently, the English conflict of laws was characterised by lack of legislative interference; practically all its rules were judge-made. A few statutes did exist, in particular Acts of 1868, 1920 and 1933 concerning recognition and enforcement of foreign judgments, but these did not contain any choice of law rules; this was true also of statutory provisions which extended divorce jurisdiction from 1937 onwards. A few isolated examples of statutory provisions could be found, which contained choice of law rules dealing with particular topics, such as the Bills of Exchange Act 1882, section 72. A rarity was the Legitimacy Act 1926 which not only introduced legitimation by subsequent marriage into English law, but provided for recognition of foreign legitimations by furnishing rules which are simpler than the common law rules.

---

[6] See, for example, *Male* v. *Roberts* (1800) 3 Esp. 163.

[7] The Rome Convention, 1980, on contractual obligations does not apply to the capacity of natural persons (Art. 1(2) (a)). See pp. 208–9 below.

[8] One case, *Chellaram* v. *Chellaram* [1985] Ch. 409, was concerned with a trust *inter vivos* other than one created by a marriage settlement. It was held there that the English court had the power to remove a trustee of an Indian trust. For trusts, see the Recognition of Trusts Act 1987, ch. 17 below.

n has increasingly affected the conflict of laws during ears, partly because of the need to implement inter- tions dealing with the subject. Indeed, a considerable iglish conflict of laws is now statutory. Statutes include)63,[9] the Adoption Act 1976,[10] the Family Law Act 1900, Part II,[11] the Evidence (Proceedings in other Jurisdictions) Act 1975[12] and the Child Abduction and Custody Act 1985.[13] They also include the Recognition of Trusts Act 1987[14] and the Contracts (Applicable Law) Act 1990.[15] Statutes which owe their origins to the Law Commission are the Foreign Limitation Periods Act 1984[16] and the Private International Law (Miscellaneous Provisions) Act 1995, which deals with capacity to contract a polygamous marriage[17] and choice of law in tort.[18] The Domicile and Matrimonial Proceedings Act 1973, the Unfair Contract Terms Act 1977[19] and the Carriage of Goods by Sea Act 1971 also contain provisions relevant to the conflict of laws.[20]

---

[9] This dealt with the formal validity of wills and is in compliance with the Hague Convention on the Forms of Testamentary Dispositions, 1961. See p. 272 below.

[10] This enacted the Convention on Adoption of Children, 1965; it has been amended by the Children Act 1975. See p. 355 below.

[11] This replaces the Recognition of Divorces and Legal Separations Act 1971, which enacted the Convention of the same name, 1970. See pp. 323–30 below.

[12] This enacts the Convention on the Taking of Evidence Abroad, 1968.

[13] This enacts the Hague Convention on Child Abduction, 1980, and the complementary Council of Europe Convention on Recognition and Enforcement of Custody Orders, 1980; see pp. 339–45 below.

[14] This implements the Hague Convention on the Law Applicable to Trusts and their Recognition, 1986. See ch. 17.

[15] This implements the Rome Convention on the Law applicable to Contractual Obligations, 1980. See ch. 12.315–17 below.

[16] Pp. 63–4 below.   [17] Pp. 315–17 below

[18] Ch. 13 below.   [19] Especially s. 27, p. 24 below.

[20] As to the effect of the last of these, see *The Hollandia* [1983] 1 AC 565 HL, p. 215 below.

3　Choice of law rules

Analysis

The conflict of laws, in so far as it is concerned with the choice of the applicable law, consists of only a small number of rules; the problems tend to arise, as in most areas of the law, with the exceptions. But, for the moment, we will stay with the general rules. These can all be stated in the same simple form, for example:

(a) The formal validity of a marriage is governed by the law of the place of celebration.
(b) Capacity to marry is governed by the law of the parties' domiciles.
(c) Succession to movable property is governed by the law of the last domicile of the deceased.
(d) Succession to immovable property is governed by the *lex situs*.
(e) Procedure is governed by the *lex fori*.
(f) Contracts are governed (in general) by the law intended by the parties.

Some issues are governed by more than one system of law, either (i) cumulatively, as: at common law liability for alleged torts committed abroad is governed by both the *lex fori* (English law) and the law of the place where the event took place; or (ii) alternatively, as: formal validity of contracts is governed by either the law of the place of contracting or by the applicable law.

These rules can all be analysed in the same manner. Thus: 'succession to immovables is governed by the *lex situs*' falls into two parts: (i) 'succession to immovables' and (ii) '*situs*'. '[F]ormal validity of a marriage is governed by the law of the place of celebration' falls into (i) 'formal validity of marriage' and (ii) 'place of celebration'.

The parts as in (i) are sometimes called 'operative facts', but a more accurate name for them is, perhaps, 'legal categories'. They are like pigeon-holes into which the legal issue disclosed by the facts of cases may be placed. The parts as in (ii) are called 'connecting factors', since they connect the legal categories to the applicable law.

There are not many legal categories; they may be ascertained by looking at the headings and sub-headings of most of the chapters of this book; similarly there are not many connecting factors.

This may seem fairly straightforward, but there are difficulties about it. Problems may occur because of conflicts between different legal systems and they may arise in three ways.

(1) The case may fall into one legal category in the view of the *lex fori* (English law) but into another by the foreign law which is alleged to be the *lex causae*, or applicable law. Thus, English law may regard the case as being concerned with formalities of marriage, but French law may regard it as raising the question of capacity to marry.

(2) English law and the foreign (say, French) law may agree on the legal category, and on the connecting factor. But this conceals a latent conflict, because the two laws mean different things by the connecting factor. Thus, under both laws succession to movables is governed by the law of the last domicile of the deceased. However, by the English law of domicile, he died domiciled in France; under French law he died domiciled in England.

(3) There is a patent conflict between the respective choice of law rules, since they employ different connecting factors, as where English law regards succession to movables as governed by the law of the domicile, but by the foreign law it is governed by the law of the nationality.

(1) involves the question of 'characterisation'; (2) involves the question of the interpretation of the connecting factor; (2) and (3) both involve the doctrine of *renvoi*.

These three will be dealt with in the following order: (i) the connecting factor, since it is the easiest, (ii) characterisation and (iii) *renvoi*.

Connecting factors

The connecting factors employed by the conflict of laws are not very numerous. They include the personal law (domicile, habitual residence and, very rarely, nationality), the place where the transaction takes place (as place of celebration of a marriage or the place of contracting), the place of performance (as in contracts), the intention of the parties, the *situs* (the place where property is situated) and the place where the court (forum) is sitting.

Since the conflict of laws forms part of English law, English law alone can determine when a foreign law is to be applied. It follows from this that English law must not only select the connecting factor, it must also say what it means. This is clear, though it is only in respect of two connecting factors, domicile and, for jurisdictional purposes, the place of contracting, that authority exists.

Thus, if both English and French law use domicile as a connecting factor, but by English law a person is domiciled in France and by French law in England, he will be regarded by an English court as domiciled in France. In Re *Annesley*[1]

> Mrs A died domiciled in France according to English law. By French law she had never acquired a domicile there. Russell J held that Mrs A died domiciled in France.

In two cases[2] the English courts have determined, by applying rules of the English law of contract, whether a contract was concluded in England or abroad. In fact, in neither case did either party think it worth arguing that the matter should be determined by a foreign law.

There can be no doubt that if it should be necessary to determine the *situs* of property, for example, a bank account at a New York bank's English branch, English law would apply, and the *situs* would be England, even if by New York law it would be New York.[3]

There are two exceptions to this general rule. These are: (i) nationality – this can only be determined by French law if a person is alleged to be a French national; (ii) for jurisdictional purposes, two statutes provide that in certain cases, domicile shall be as determined by the foreign law in question.[4]

There is also a quasi-exception. If, as in Re *Annesley*,[5] the English court decides that a person died domiciled in France, but continues by applying *renvoi* (which will shortly be discussed),[6] and pretends that it is a French court, it is then applying the French conflict rules and not those of English law and this will entail a determination that the deceased died domiciled in England.

Characterisation

We have seen that the process known as 'characterisation' is sometimes necessary because English law may regard a case as falling into one

---

[1] [1926] Ch. 692. The case was complicated by *renvoi*. See pp. 20–7 below. See also Re *Martin* [1900] P 211.
[2] *Entores* v. *Miles Far East Corporation* [1955] 2 QB 327; *Brinkibon* v. *Stahag Stahl GmbH* [1982] 2 AC 34 HL See pp. 78, 206 below.
[3] See *X A/G* v. *A Bank* [1983] 2 All ER 464.
[4] See Family Law Act 1986, s. 46(5) p. 324 below; Civil Jurisdiction and Judgments Act 1982, Sched. 1 (this is the EC Convention on Jurisdiction and Enforcement of Judgments in Civil and Commercial Matters, 1968) Art. 52(2) (see p. 138 below).
[5] [1926] Ch. 692.   [6] See pp. 20–7 below.

legal category but the relevant foreign law believes it to belong in a different one. This process is undertaken also in cases which do not contain a foreign element; a court may be called upon to determine whether the issue sounds in contract or in tort, or whether property is realty or personalty, but it is obviously more difficult where a foreign element is present.

Examples of characterisation are to be found throughout this book, where they are discussed in some detail. They include questions such as whether two different requirements of French law, that a French domiciliary required his parents' consent to his marriage, which was celebrated in England, concerned formal validity, which was a matter for English law, or capacity to marry and so was governed by French law. In two cases it was held that these French requirements concerned formal validity and so were irrelevant in the case.[7] In another case the question was whether a rule of English law which required that in order for an action to be brought on a contract there must be written evidence thereof, was a rule of evidence and thus procedural, so that it applied by virtue of the *lex fori* to a contract governed by French law. It was held that it was procedural, and applied.[8] In several cases the question was whether a rule of a foreign law requiring an action to be brought within a certain period of time was substantive and applicable, or whether it was procedural and irrelevant. The courts held that it was procedural.[9] The question has arisen whether a sum awarded as part of a judgment by a foreign court and described by the foreign law as a penalty, though it was not so regarded by English law, should be characterised as a penalty or not. It was held that English law governed the matter, and it was not a penalty.[10]

It will be observed from these examples that the English courts have generally characterised the issue before them according to their own notions; this will be illustrated further.[11]

The problem of characterisation is one of the most difficult in the conflict of laws, and it has generated an enormous amount of writing in many languages. It might well be thought that its difficulties and obscurities increase in direct proportion to the increase in the quantity

---

[7] *Simonin* v. *Mallac* (1860) 2 Sw. & Tr. 67; *Ogden* v. *Ogden* [1908] P 46 CA; p. 297 below.

[8] *Leroux* v. *Brown* (1852) 12 CB 801. See p. 62 below.

[9] See, for example, *Huber* v. *Steiner* (1835) Bing. NC 202; *Harris* v. *Quine* (1869) LR 4 QB 653.

[10] *Huntington* v. *Attrill* [1893] AC 150 PC (on appeal from Ontario). The English courts will not enforce a judgment for a sum they regard as a penalty.

[11] See pp. 17–19 below.

of juristic discussion of it.[12] There is considerable difference of opinion as to how the problem should be solved. The courts are usually criticised for solving it the wrong way and nearly all the cases referred to above have been the subject of severe criticism. It is true that the solutions arrived at have caused, or are capable of causing, considerable difficulties. This is so much so that in one area, limitation of actions, Parliament has had to step in and turn the law round.[13] It is not sought to add to the confusion here, it is merely desired to state the problem, illustrate it, discuss briefly the chief methods which writers have suggested as solutions for it, and to illustrate the whole matter by giving some English cases by way of example.

Before proceeding further it has to be said that there has been very great debate and confusion right at the start of the inquiry as to what it is that is characterised. Is it a 'legal relation', 'a legal claim', 'a legal question', 'a factual situation', the 'facts of the case', or 'the rule of English (or foreign) laws'? The real question is whether it is the facts or factual situation, or a legal question. Since some aspects of characterisation clearly do not involve the facts this leads to the conclusion that it is a legal question.

It is proposed to adopt this view. One reason is that although any case, of course, involves the facts, what the choice of law rule points to is the legal rules of some system. The facts are those data which enable the judge to formulate, as he must always do, a legal issue which leads to the application of a legal rule. A judge or a lawyer is not interested in facts *in vacuo*, and they cannot be characterised in the abstract, but only by formulating the legal categories; these are categories of legal questions.

Various solutions to the problem of characterisation have been put forward; four will be mentioned.

The lex fori *theory*

This was proposed by the German and French writers, Kahn[14] and Bartin,[15] who 'discovered' the problem in the 1890s. It has been the

---

[12] Not all the literature is itself confusing. For a short, clear account see A. V. Dicey and J. H. C. Morris, *The Conflict of Laws*, 13th edn, by L. Collins and others (London, Stevens, 2000) ch. 2. Two more advanced and also comprehensible discussions are by K. Lipstein, 'Conflict of Laws 1921–71, the Way Ahead' [1972B] 67 *CLJ* 77–83 and O. Kahn-Freund, 'General Principles of Private International Law' (1974–III), *Recueil des Cours*, vol. 143, 369–82.

[13] Foreign Limitation Periods Act 1984. See pp. 63–4 below.

[14] F. Kahn, 'Gesetzkelten', in *Jehrings Jahrbucher* vol. 30 (1891) 1–143.

[15] F. Bartin, *De L'impossibilité d'arriver à la suppression définitive des Conflits des Lois* (Paris, Clunet, 1897), 225–55, 466–95, 720–38. The most comprehensive discussion of this

prevailing theory on the Continent, and by and large has been adopted in practice by the English courts. According to this theory the court should characterise the issue in accordance with the categories of its own domestic law, and foreign rules of law in accordance with their nearest analogy in the same law. Thus, a French rule requiring parental consent to marriage should be characterised as pertaining to formalities, since English law so regards its own rules regarding parental consent.

Objections raised to the *lex fori* theory are that its application may result in a distortion of the foreign rule and render it inapplicable in cases in which the foreign law would apply it, and vice versa. Moreover if there is no close analogy in the domestic law (as there is no analogy in English law to the matrimonial property regime known to foreign laws), the theory does not work. Lastly, its proponents sometimes seem to suggest that it is facts alone which have to be classified, but this is not so; it is facts which are presented in the light of a foreign law.

The lex causae *theory*

According to this theory, classification should be effected by adopting the categories of the governing law. It is sometimes suggested that at least one English decision is based on this method, though this is, perhaps, doubtful.[16] There are two serious objections to this theory. First, the whole purpose of characterisation is to discover what law governs the issue. To say that the governing law dictates the process of characterisation is to argue in a circle, for how can we know what the governing law is until the process of characterisation is completed?[17] Secondly, if there are two possible foreign laws to govern the matter, and they characterise the issue differently, which is to be adopted by the English court? It may be added that the adoption of this theory could compel the adoption of idiosyncratic foreign characterisation, such as the well-known rule of Maltese law that a Maltese person can only be validly married, wherever the ceremony takes place, if he or she goes through a ceremony before a Roman Catholic priest. The court would have to resort to public policy to avoid this consequence.

topic in English is that by A. H. Robertson, *Characterisation in the Conflict of Laws* (Cambridge, Mass., Harvard University Press, 1940). It was introduced to English-speaking lawyers by E. G. Lorenzen in 1920. His article, published in that year, is reproduced in his *Selected Articles on the Conflict of Laws* (New Haven, Yale University Press, 1947).

[16] Re *Maldonado* [1954] P 233; see p. 271 below.

[17] M. Wolff denied that circularity need be involved: *Private International Law*, 2nd edn (Oxford University Press, 1950) 156, but his arguments are not entirely convincing.

Analytical jurisprudence and comparative law

This theory was espoused by the author of the encyclopaedia of comparative conflict of laws, Ernst Rabel,[18] and views similar to his were advanced in England by W. E. Beckett,[19] who said that conflicts rules should use 'conceptions of an absolutely general character', and that

> These conceptions are borrowed from analytical jurisprudence, that general science of law, based on the results of the study of comparative law, which extracts from this study essential general principles of professedly universal application – not principles based on, or applicable to, the legal system of one country only.

This is at first sight attractive, but it has its drawbacks. First, few universal principles are disclosed by analytical jurisprudence and comparative law which would be of assistance in this area. Secondly, though comparative law may disclose similarities between legal systems, it may also disclose differences, which it is hardly capable of resolving; thus it may show that requirements of parental consent to marriage pertain to formalities in some systems or to capacity in others or do not exist in others, but this does not tell us how in the case before us these differences are to be settled. Thirdly, it is rather impractical; it would be asking too much of legal advisers and judges to undertake the exercise involved, and one cannot imagine them doing so. This method would certainly add to the length and cost of litigation.

Falconbridge's views

The Canadian lawyer, Falconbridge, proposed a two-stage process.[20] The first stage, a task for the *lex fori*, is to define the scope of the legal category, the categories not being those of the domestic legal system but of its private international law, and the second is to examine the relevant foreign rule in its own context to see whether it can be fitted into the legal category in question.

English courts and characterisation

The English courts have not consciously adopted any one doctrine or theory. Indeed, the question of characterisation has only been referred

---

[18] E. Rabel, *The Conflict of Laws, a Comparative Study*, 2nd edn, vol. I (Ann Arbor, University of Michigan, 1968).

[19] (1934) 15 *BYIL* 46. Beckett was then Assistant Legal Adviser and later Legal Adviser to the Foreign Office.

[20] J. D. Falconbridge, *Selected Essays in the Conflict of Laws*, 2nd edn (Toronto, Canada Law Book Co., 1954), 50. Similar views were expressed earlier by L. Raape (1934–IV), *Recueil des Cours*, vol. 50, 477.

to *expressis verbis* in few cases. But the *lex fori* theory, modified in some cases so as to approximate to Falconbridge's view, seems to represent the actual method employed by the courts. With one exception,[21] they do not apply foreign classifications as such; indeed in two cases, they are directed to ignore the foreign characterisation. By the Wills Act 1963,[22] they are instructed to ignore certain foreign classifications of rules concerning the validity of wills as relating to capacity and treat those rules as laying down formal requirements only. By the Foreign Limitation Periods Act 1984 they must, in a conflict case, generally treat rules of both English and foreign law governing the period within which an action must be brought as pertaining to substance and not procedure, irrespective of their classification by the domestic law to which they belong.[23]

In practice, the English courts formulate the issue and define the ambit of the legal category for themselves, and then they determine whether a question posed by a foreign rule comes into that category. An example of this is Re *Cohn*.[24]

> A mother and her daughter, domiciled in Germany, were killed by the same bomb in a German air-raid in London and it could not be shown which died first and which survived the other.

Succession was governed by German law under which the daughter's estate could only succeed under her mother's will if she had survived the mother. By section 184 of the English Law of Property Act 1925 she, being the younger, was presumed to have survived her mother. Uthwatt J held that this rule was not one of evidence and did not apply. The corresponding provision of German law, under which the two were deemed to have died simultaneously, he held to be part of the law of inheritance and so applicable. Thus he categorised the issue before him as one of succession and then held that the question presented by the German law came within that category.

The limits of the legal categories adopted in a conflicts case do not necessarily coincide with the domestic classifications of English law. Thus, 'contract' has been extended to include an Italian agreement unsupported by consideration[25] and the implied contract imposed upon matrimonial property by French law;[26] these concepts are unknown to

---

[21] That is, as to whether property is movable or immovable.   [22] S. 3. See p. 272 below.
[23] See p. 63 below.   [24] [1945] Ch. 5.   [25] Re *Bonacina* [1912] 2 Ch. 394 CA.
[26] *De Nicols* v. *Curlier* [1900] AC 21 HL. The concept of formality of marriage was extended to cover the question of the validity of a proxy marriage in *Apt* v. *Apt* [1948] P 83 CA.

English domestic law. Two cases which demonstrate the technique described here when a foreign concept is unknown to English law, and two which coincided with an English legal concept, are the 'Greek bank' cases, where a question of universal succession by a corporation and two regarding contractual liability were in issue.

In the first of these cases, *National Bank of Greece and Athens SA* v. *Metliss*,[27] the House of Lords held that a Greek law which merged two banking corporations into a single new one and transferred by way of universal succession, a concept not known to English law, the rights and liabilities of the old banks to the new one, was a law affecting status, and applied since Greek law as the law of the place of incorporation governed the issue, so that the new bank was liable on a guarantee of certain bonds. But it held that a moratorium law affecting liability thereon was a matter of contract law and, since the contract was governed by English law as the proper law of the bonds and guarantee, the new bank's liability was unaffected by it. In subsequent proceedings, the House held in *Adams* v. *National Bank of Greece and Athens SA*[28] that a further Greek law enacted after the earlier decision and which purported to absolve the new bank retrospectively from liability on the guarantee was no defence to an action thereon for the same reason.

In *Macmillan Inc.* v. *Bishopsgate Investment Trust plc* (No. 3),[29] where the claimant company sought the return of shares it owned in another company which its own controller, Robert Maxwell, had fraudulently pledged to a third party, the Court of Appeal rejected the claimant company's argument that the question should be classified as restitutionary. It emphasised that it was not the *claim* but the *issue* which fell to be characterised; in the instant case this issue concerned title to intangible movable property and was thus governed by the *lex situs* of the shares, whose application the claimant company was trying to avoid.

In one situation, however, the English courts abandon their own domestic classification, and adopt one which is generally adopted in systems of law which are not derived from the common law. For the purpose of the conflict of laws, they classify property into movables and immovables, rather than personalty and realty. Moreover, they determine into which category given property falls in accordance with its *lex situs* and not with English law.[30]

---

[27] [1958] AC 509, applied in *Eurosteel* v. *Stinnes A/G* [2000] All ER (Comm.) 964.
[28] [1961] AC 255.   [29] [1996] 1 WLR 387, CA.   [30] See pp. 243–4 below.

Renvoi

Meaning

Renvoi is a technique for solving problems which arise out of differences between the connecting factor used by English law and that of the law to which the English connecting factor leads. Such differences may be either (i) that English law and the *lex causae*, say, French law, use the same connecting factor for the legal category, for example, domicile, but mean different things by it,[31] or (ii) English law and the *lex causae*, say, Italian law, use different connecting factors for the legal category, domicile and nationality respectively.[32]

The English court might in such cases apply English law on the ground that a French court would decide the case in accordance with English law (this is called remission) or might apply German law on the ground that an Italian court would apply German law (this is called transmission). This process is known as *renvoi*.

The topic is bedevilled by rather intemperate academic discussion; most writers are, in general, hostile to *renvoi*, but courts in many states have adopted it.[33] It is perhaps fair to say that it got a bad reputation internationally from the case which was its *fons et origo*, the decision of the Court of Cassation of France in *Forgo*'s case in 1883.[34]

> Forgo, an illegitimate Bavarian national, was born with a domicile in Bavaria, but lived most of his life in France without ever acquiring a 'domicil' under French law. He left movable property in France but no relatives except for some remote collateral relatives of his mother. These could not succeed him under French law, and under French law the property, being ownerless, would go to the French state. Under Bavarian law they could succeed. The French courts would determine the question by applying Bavarian law but the state argued that the Bavarian courts would apply French law, and the French courts should do likewise.

The court held in favour of the French state's arguments. The result was that the French Treasury got its hands on the property to the exclusion of the collateral relatives.

---

[31] See, for example, Re *Annesley* [1926] Ch. 692.   [32] See Re *Ross* [1930] 1 Ch. 377.

[33] United States courts did so in Re *Tallmadge* 181 NY Supp. 336 (1919); Re *Schneiders' Estate* 96 NU Supp. (2d) 652 (1950).

[34] 10 Clunet 64; see also *L'Affaire Soulié* (1910) Clunet 888. In fact, the real and earlier originator was an English judge, Sir Herbert Jenner, in *Collier* v. *Rivaz* (1841) 2 Curt. 855, though he never used the French term *renvoi*.

The real question is: what does the English court mean by the 'foreign law' it is proposing to apply? As Maugham J put it in Re *Askew*,[35] 'When the English courts refer the matter to the law of Utopia as the *lex domicilii*,[36] do they mean the whole of that law or do they mean the local or municipal law which in Utopia would apply to Utopian subjects?' This poses the problem neatly, though, as far as the English courts are concerned, the words 'the whole of that law' need a little more refinement.

There are three possibilities. The first is that by the law of Utopia is meant Utopian law *minus its conflict rules*, so that we apply, for example, the Utopian domestic law of succession. This has been done in many cases without question, and it is what is done in contract cases.[37]

The second is that by the law of Utopia is meant its law *including its conflict rules but minus its conflict rules applying* renvoi, *if it has any*. This is sometimes called the 'single' or 'partial' *renvoi*, or *renvoi simpliciter*. Thus, if the Utopian courts would apply English or Swiss law to decide the case, so will the English courts. This is what happened in *Forgo's* case, and what, in part, Sir Herbert Jenner did in *Collier* v. *Rivaz*,[38] when he applied English law to uphold the validity of four codicils to a will made in Belgium by an Englishman domiciled there. The codicils were formally valid under English, but not under Belgian, law. But the Belgian courts would, if they had had to decide the case, have applied English law as the law of the nationality of the testator.[39]

The third meaning of the 'law of Utopia' is all the relevant law of Utopia *including its conflict rules and* renvoi *if they include it*. This is sometimes called the 'double' or 'total' or 'English' (since it appears to be peculiar to English law) *renvoi*. Another name for it is the 'foreign court' doctrine since the English court first decides by its own conflict rule to apply Utopian law and then pretends to be the Utopian court or, more plausibly, asks how that court would decide the case. If it would apply English law and by English law mean English law *including its conflict rules minus* renvoi, then the Utopian court would apply Utopian law. So, then, will the English court do the same.

---

[35] [1930] 2 Ch. 259.
[36] This is only an example; the same issue can arise if the courts refer the matter to the law of Utopia as the *lex situs*.
[37] See p. 204 below.
[38] (1841) 2 Curt. 855. This meaning of 'the foreign law' was applied in Re *Johnson* [1903] 1 Ch. 821, a case of transmission. See also Re *Trufort* (1887) 36 Ch. D 600.
[39] The will and two other codicils were admitted to probate on the ground that they were valid by Belgian law, that is, by the first possibility. The judge was being pragmatic rather than doctrinaire, and was evidently trying to fulfil the testator's intentions.

This third meaning was first adopted by Russell J in Re *Annesley*,[40] a case which concerned the material or essential validity of the terms of a will.

> An English testatrix had lived in France for fifty-six years. She died leaving a will of movable property. The English court held that she died domiciled in France, so that French law governed the validity of her will. By French law it was partly invalid because she was not free to dispose of all her property in the way she had done, since she had not provided for certain persons who were entitled by law to a share.

By French law also the validity of the will was governed by the law of Mrs Annesley's last domicile, but by French law she died domiciled in England. So English law would be applied by a French court. However, by means of *renvoi* it would apply the English conflict rule, so that it would (as in *Forgo*'s case) apply the French law of succession.

The court applied the French law of succession and held the will partly invalid.

On the other hand, in Re *Ross*[41]

> An English testatrix died domiciled in Italy leaving movable property in England and Italy and immovable property in Italy. Succession to all her property was, therefore, governed by Italian law as the *lex domicilii* and the *lex situs*. The will was partly invalid by Italian law. But the Italian court would apply English law as her national law, but not apply *renvoi*.

Therefore, Luxmoore J applied English domestic law and held the will valid.

In two cases which involved German law, which in this respect was like French law but unlike Italian law, the English court applied German law. These were Re *Askew*[42] which concerned legitimation by subsequent marriage, and Re *Fuld* (No. 3)[43] which concerned the formal validity of a will of movable property.

This perhaps eccentric technique appears to be the doctrine at present adhered to by the English courts. It is fair to say, however, that no appeal court has so far had the opportunity to rule on the matter.[44] An American writer once said that:

Notwithstanding the great authority of Westlake and Dicey it may reasonably be hoped that, when the doctrine with all its consequences is squarely presented to

---

[40] [1926] Ch. 692.   [41] [1930] 1 Ch. 377.   [42] [1930] 2 Ch. 259.   [43] [1968] P 675.
[44] However, *renvoi* (in its 'single' form) was stated by the Privy Council in *Kotia* v. *Nahas* [1941] AC 403. But its application in that case was prescribed by a local Palestine law.

the higher English courts, they will not hesitate to reject the decisions of those courts that have lent colour to *renvoi* in the English law.[45]

Arguments against renvoi

Several arguments have been advanced against *renvoi* by writers.

(a) It is said to be difficult to ascertain whether the foreign system of law does or does not apply *renvoi*. This reflects the almost lachrymose remarks of Wynn Parry J in Re *Duke of Wellington*[46] when faced with deciding whether Spanish law did or did not adopt it.[47]

This difficulty is no greater than that of ascertaining any other rule of foreign law, such as its rules about communication of the acceptance of an offer. It is ascertained in the usual ways.[48] Because of the great controversy the doctrine has engendered amongst writers of various nationalities since 1883, the attitude of many legal systems to *renvoi* is quite well known. This objection to it seems either misguided or exaggerated.[49]

(b) It is claimed that by applying *renvoi* an English court is surrendering to a foreign court, in that instead of applying the English choice of law rule it is effectively applying the French or Italian choice of law.

This is, of course, true, but only occurs because our choice of law rule leads to the application of French or Italian law. This process is undertaken only because our courts wish to undertake it. Moreover, as we have seen, the question (to quote Maugham J) is: what do the English courts mean by the law of Utopia? This surely cannot be described as an abdication in favour of Utopian conflict of laws.

(c) A difficulty arises if the foreign court, should it be seised of the case, would apply the law of a person's nationality. If a person is a national of a federal state or one which, like the United Kingdom, contains several territories each possessing its own system of law, reference to his national law is meaningless, since it could be one of several laws. Re *O'Keefe*[50] is usually held up to ridicule in this context.

---

[45] Lorenzen, *Selected Articles*, 53.
[46] [1947] Ch. 506, affd without reference to this point [1948] Ch. 118 CA.
[47] There were conflicting decisions of Spanish courts and conflicting opinions of writers. It is not clear from the report how the point arose. The Court of Appeal disposed of the case without mention of *renvoi*.
[48] For proof of foreign law, see ch. 4 below.
[49] Countries with codes often provide for the matter. When Parliament wishes to exclude *renvoi* it can do so and often does. For examples see pp. 26–7 below.
[50] [1940] Ch. 124.

A woman of British nationality died intestate in Italy, leaving movable property. By English conflict of laws succession was governed by Italian law, since she died domiciled there. By Italian law it was governed by her national law and Italian courts reject *renvoi*. Though she was born in India, her domicile of origin was Ireland, since her father was domiciled there when she was born. She had only paid one short visit to Ireland, she had stayed rather longer in England, but the only country in which she had settled was Italy.

Crossman J held that, in these circumstances, the law of her nationality should be taken to mean that part of the British Empire to which she 'belonged' and that this was the southern part of Ireland, then (1940) Eire, now the Irish Republic.[51]

This does seem odd in a way since she had hardly ever been to Ireland and Eire did not exist when she was born or went to Ireland. But what else was the court to do? Eire was a more realistic choice than any other part of the British Isles or Commonwealth (her name suggests it, for one thing).[52] In any case the objection misses the target; it was not *renvoi* but the use by Italian law of nationality as a connecting factor added to there being no one system of law throughout the British Isles which caused the trouble. If further inquiries had been made as to how the Italian courts would have decided the actual case, a different and maybe more realistic answer might have been forthcoming. Italian jurists have suggested that Italian domestic law would have been applied.

(d) There is no logical reason why the process should ever stop. Moreover, the English 'double *renvoi*' only operates at all because the courts of other countries reject it. Thus, if French courts adopted our method, in Re *Annesley*[53] the English court would apply French law, the French court English law and so on *ad infinitum*. This is, of course, true. But if some foreign law (as, for example, New South Wales) also used the double *renvoi* method, and these horrendous consequences were to ensue, one cannot help thinking that our courts would put a stop to it somehow.[54]

(e) Re *Annesley*[55] would have been decided the same way if Russell J had simply applied French domestic law. This is true, but is not true of, for example, Re *Ross*,[56] Re *O'Keefe*[57] or *Collier* v. *Rivaz*.[58]

---

[51] It should be noted carefully that this was not, as many students seem to think, a case of the revival of the domicile of origin (as to which see pp. 47, 51–2 below). Mrs O'Keefe died domiciled in Italy.

[52] It is curious that Re *Ross* [1930] 1 Ch. 377 comes in for no similar criticism.

[53] [1926] Ch. 692.   [54] It would be better not to plead *renvoi* at all.

[55] [1926] Ch. 692.   [56] [1930] 1 Ch. 377.

[57] [1940] Ch. 124.   [58] (1841) 2 Curt. 855.

Arguments in favour of renvoi

There are some arguments in favour of the application of *renvoi*.

(a) Though it does not necessarily achieve uniformity of decision, which its opponents say that its proponents claim it does,[59] it tends towards it, as in Re *Ross*. If it is not employed, determination of rights is more than likely to depend on where the action is brought. If one action is brought in England and another in, say, Italy, conflicting decisions of the English and the Italian court might well result.

(b) The use of *renvoi* might achieve the legitimate expectation of a person as it did in *Collier* v. *Rivaz*, Re *Ross* or Re *O'Keefe*. This, of course, does not always ensue; in one or two cases, such as Re *Annesley* or Re *Fuld* (No. 3),[60] a will has been to some extent upset. But in Re *Askew*[61] a person was held to have been legitimated who would, without *renvoi* being employed, have been held to have been a bastard by reason of what was then a gap in English domestic law.[62]

(c) It appears to be agreed on all sides, or at any rate conceded, that if the choice of law rule requires the application of the *lex situs* to questions concerning immovable property, *renvoi* should be applied. For if Italian law says that the person entitled to Italian land is the one who is entitled to succeed by English law, it would be pointless for the English court to insist that it should be whoever is so entitled under the Italian law of succession. It could do nothing to enforce its view.

Summary

So there are respectable arguments both for and against the application of *renvoi*. But it is suggested that the matter is not as important in practice as the writing about it might suggest. It has not been applied uniformly in respect of all the English choice of law rules, nor in respect of any one of them. In some decided cases, no resort has been made to *renvoi*, presumably because neither party, in proving the relevant foreign law, proved its rules of the conflict of laws. Moreover, as we shall see, the English courts do not apply *renvoi* in connection with some of their choice of law rules, where 'Utopian law' is taken to mean only Utopian domestic law without its conflict rules, and, because of certain

---

[59] Not even the complete elimination of differences between choice of law rules of various conflicts systems would do this; it could only be done by all legal systems having identical rules for each legal question.

[60] [1968] P 675.   [61] [1930] 2 Ch. 259.

[62] The Legitimacy Act 1926 did not allow an *adulterinus* to be legitimated.

legislation, it is not nowadays nearly as important as it was in areas in which it has in the past been applied.

Areas of application

English courts have employed *renvoi* in one form or another in respect of:

(a) Formal validity of wills of movables (and immovables[63]): *Collier* v. *Rivaz*,[64] Re *Fuld*.[65] But now the Wills Act 1963, section 1 provides seven systems of law (and eight in the case of immovables) to test the validity of a will. The rules are the domestic rules thereof.[66]

(b) Essential or material validity of wills of movables: Re *Trufort*,[67] Re *Annesley*,[68] Re *Ross*.[69]

(c) Succession to movables on intestacy: Re *O'Keefe*.[70]

(d) Essential validity of wills of movables: Re *Ross*.

(e) Almost certainly, succession to immovables on intestacy.

(f) Title to movables by transfers *inter vivos*. This was suggested by Slade J in *Winkworth* v. *Christie, Manson & Woods*.[71] In *Macmillan Inc.* v. *Bishopsgate Investment Trust plc*,[72] Staughton LJ in the Court of Appeal said that *renvoi* did not apply to the determination of title to shares in a company. It is hard to see why it should not. The other two Lords Justice did not mention the point.

(g) Almost certainly, title to immovables *inter vivos*.

(h) Legitimation by subsequent marriage: Re *Askew*.[73] This has been of little importance since the removal of the former bar on legitimation of *adulterini* in 1959.[74]

(j) Formal validity of marriage. In *Taczanowska* v. *Taczanowski*[75] the Court of Appeal was willing to apply Polish law by way of reference from Italian law (*lex loci celebrationis*) if this would have meant the marriage was valid. But it did not and the marriage was instead held valid as being a good common law marriage.[76]

(k) Capacity to marry. In *R* v. *Brentwood Superintendent Registrar of Marriages*, ex parte *Arias*,[77] a person's capacity to remarry after a

---

[63] There is no actual decision regarding a will of immovables.
[64] (1841) 2 Curt. 855.   [65] [1968] P 675.   [66] S. 3.   [67] (1887) 36 Ch. D 600.
[68] [1926] Ch. 692.   [69] [1930] 1 Ch. 377.   [70] [1940] Ch. 124.
[71] [1980] Ch. 496. The learned judge was, however, asked only whether English or Italian domestic law governed the effect of a sale of goods in Italy.
[72] [1996] 1 WLR 387, CA.   [73] [1930] 2 Ch. 259.
[74] Legitimacy Act 1959. See now Legitimacy Act 1976.
[75] [1957] P 301 CA. See also *Hooper* v. *Hooper* [1959] 1 WLR 1021, which is not, perhaps, a true example of *renvoi*.
[76] See p. 300 below.   [77] [1968] 2 QB 956.

recognised foreign divorce was tested by reference from the law of his domicile to that of his nationality, by which he had no capacity. This is of less significance now, since this decision was reversed as regards capacity to remarry in England after a recognised foreign divorce by the Recognition of Divorces and Legal Separations Act 1971.[78]

By statute, *renvoi* plays no part in the law of contract[79] or tort.[80]

The incidental question

The problem of the so-called incidental question arises when, in the course of deciding a case, an issue which is subsidiary to the actual issue to be decided arises. Thus, entitlement to share in the estate of a deceased person may depend on whether the person in question is legitimate or illegitimate, and this in turn may depend on the validity of his parents' marriage as in *Shaw* v. *Gould*.[81]

For the problem to arise there must be (1) a principal or main question governed by English conflict rules by the law of country A, and (2) a subsidiary or incidental question in the same case, which could arise on its own and is governed by the law of country B. Also (3) the application of the law of A must produce a result different from that which would follow from the application of the law of B.

In only very few cases has this situation arisen. It did not arise in *Shaw* v. *Gould*, since all the issues involved were governed by the same law.[82]

Writers express different views on whether the answer to the subsidiary issue should, when the problem arises, decide the case in which event the law governing the principal issue would not be given its usual effect, or whether the latter law should be applied so that international harmony as to the result might more easily be achieved.

---

[78] S. 7. It seemed that the decision would continue to apply if the remarriage was celebrated abroad, but see *Lawrence* v. *Lawrence* [1985] Fam. 106, and see now Family Law Act 1986, s. 50; p. 307 below.

[79] Contracts (Applicable Law) Act 1990, Sched. 1 (Rome Convention, 1980), Art. 15. The same was true at common law. See *Amin Rasheed Shipping Corporation* v. *Kuwait Insurance Co.* [1984] AC 50. Also Re *United Railways of Havana Ltd* [1960] Ch. 52 CA.

[80] Private International Law (Miscellaneous Provisions) Act 1995, s. 9(5).

[81] (1868) LR 3 HL 55, p. 349 below.

[82] I.e. English law. Nor did it arise in *Perrini* v. *Perrini* [1979] Fam. 84, since the main question (capacity to marry) and the subsidiary question (recognition of a foreign nullity decree) were both governed by English law. It did arise in an American case: *Meisenhelder* v. *Chicago & NW Railway* 170 Minn. 317 (1927), and in an Australian case: *Haque* v. *Haque* (1962) 108 CLR 230. See Dicey and Morris, *Conflict of Laws*, 13th edn, 45–64.

The problem arose in one Canadian and two English cases. In all three the principal question concerned capacity to marry (or remarry) and in all three the subsidiary issue was the recognition of a foreign divorce decree. In the Canadian case and the first of the English cases, the court applied the law governing the principal issue and effectively excluded the law which would have governed the subsidiary issue had it arisen on its own. In the second English case, the court allowed the main question to be determined by the answer to the subsidiary question. These cases are discussed later on,[83] but will be dealt with reasonably fully at this point.

In the Canadian case, *Schwebel* v. *Ungar*[84]

> H[1] and W were Jews domiciled in Hungary. They left Hungary for Israel but *en route* obtained a divorce in Italy. They both arrived in Israel where W acquired a domicile. She then went to Ontario and there married H[2] who was domiciled in Ontario.

Under Ontario conflict rules W had capacity to marry H[2] since her capacity to marry was governed by Israeli law at the time of the marriage. Since Israeli law recognised the Italian divorce, it regarded her as a single woman. But by Ontario conflict rules that divorce was not recognised since at the time it was obtained the parties were still domiciled in Hungary, whose courts had not granted it and did not recognise it. Therefore, in the eyes of the Ontario court W was still married to H[1], and H[2], who was domiciled in Ontario, had no capacity to marry her. The court, applying Israeli law and ignoring Ontario law, which governed the subsidiary issue, held the marriage valid.

The converse situation arose in England in the *Brentwood Marriage* case.[85]

> H and W were domiciled in Switzerland, where a divorce was obtained. This was recognised in England. H was an Italian national and by Swiss law his capacity to marry was governed by Italian law as his national law. By Italian law the Swiss divorce was not recognised so that under Italian and Swiss law he could not remarry.

The English court, like the Canadian court, concentrated on the issue of H's capacity to marry to the exclusion of the recognition of his divorce, applied the law of his domicile[86] and held that he could not remarry in England, though in the eyes of English law he was an unmarried man.

---

[83] See pp. 307–8 below.
[84] (1962) 42 DLR (2d) 622 affd (1964) 48 DLR (2d) (Supreme Court of Canada).
[85] [1968] 2 QB 956.   [86] This is an example of *renvoi* by transmission.

In one sense *Schwebel* v. *Ungar* might be regarded as satisfactory, but the *Brentwood Marriage* case as unsatisfactory, since the former promoted freedom to marry and the latter denied it. Indeed, the *Brentwood Marriage* case has since been reversed by statute, in that H's incapacity would now be disregarded.[87]

From another point of view *Schwebel* v. *Ungar* is equally unsatisfactory. If it represented English law it would mean that a person who is domiciled here could marry someone who, in the eyes of English law, is a married person, that is to say, contract a bigamous union and in so doing commit a crime here. It is not clear that *Schwebel* v. *Ungar* would be followed in England, but it is thought that it would not.

In the second English case, *Lawrence* v. *Lawrence*,[88] the facts were basically the same as the *Brentwood Marriage* case[89] except that the remarriage had taken place abroad. This being so, and the legislative provision which reversed the latter case not being applicable where the remarriage takes place outside the United Kingdom, one would have expected the decision to have been the same and the remarriage to have been held invalid.

But the Court of Appeal, without saying the *Brentwood Marriage* case was wrong, held that because the court must recognise the foreign divorce the wife was free to remarry, though she had no capacity to do so under the law of her domicile.[90] It thus made the incidental question effectively determine the main question. Indeed, the majority specifically said that the question of capacity to marry in the usual sense did not arise. It is submitted that this was highly dubious at common law.[91] However, it was enacted into law by the Family Law Act 1986, section 50.

The time factor

Problems may sometimes arise in the conflict of laws because over a period of time changes take place in the law. A change may take place in a conflict rule of the *forum*. This occurred for example with the Wills Act 1963,[92] and in *Chaplin* v. *Boys*.[93] Here, the questions which may arise are whether the new rule affects transactions or relationships already

---

[87] Family Law Act 1986, s. 50.   [88] [1985] Fam. 106.   [89] [1968] 2 QB 956.

[90] The Court thus extended s. 7 of the Recognition of Divorces etc. Act 1971 to remarriages outside the United Kingdom in spite of the limiting words therein, and achieved a reform proposed by the Law Commission in Report no. 137 (1984) and enacted by the Family Law Act 1986, s. 50.

[91] Purchas LJ expressly dissented from this view; he held that the remarriage was valid on another ground which is even more dubious. Anthony Lincoln J had decided that the remarriage was valid on another ground which is perhaps slightly less dubious, since he regarded the question in the same light as did the court in the *Brentwood Marriage* case.

[92] See p. 272 below.   [93] [1971] AC 356 HL. See pp. 223–4 below.

entered into or a status already acquired, and whether the new rule entirely supersedes the old one.[94] Or a change may take place in the connecting factor, for example, a change in a person's domicile or in the *situs* of movable property. Some connecting factors, such as the *situs* of immovables or the place of commission of a tort, cannot change. These two kinds of change will not be pursued further.

The most difficult problems arise in respect of changes in the *lex causae*; for example, New York law, the law governing a subsisting contract, is altered by legislation, or a marriage which was formally invalid by the law of the place of celebration when celebrated is subsequently validated by or under that law. The problem has always existed, but did not attract much learned or judicial attention until recent times.[95]

Examples which will be found in this book concern the following: (i) *tort*: in *Phillips* v. *Eyre*[96] an act which was a tort in Jamaica was later justified by Jamaican legislation, thus making the act not actionable in tort in England; (ii) *contract*: in *R* v. *International Trustee for the Protection of Bondholders A/G*[97] a provision of New York law, the applicable law, which rendered a gold clause in a contract void, and in Re *Helbert Wagg & Co. Ltd*'s Claim[98] a moratorium imposed by a German law which had the effect of discharging a debtor from liability under a contract which was governed by German law, were given effect; (iii) *formal validity of marriage*: in *Starkowski* v. *Attorney-General*[99] a marriage which was formally invalid by Austrian law when it was celebrated in that country was held to have been validated by its registration under the provisions of a later Austrian law; (iv) *succession to immovables*: in *Nelson* v. *Bridport*,[100] the *lex situs* (law of Sicily) was changed after the death of a testator so as to invalidate interests created by his will in land in Sicily.

It will be observed that in all these cases effect was, apparently, given to the change in the *lex causae*,[101] but in two cases[102] it was not. They

---

[94] It has been held that the statutory rules for recognition of foreign legitimations by subsequent marriage contained in the Legitimacy Act 1926, s. 8, did not displace the common law rules: Re *Hurll* [1952] Ch. 722.

[95] Two important articles by F. A. Mann, 'The Time Element in the Conflict of Laws' (1954) 31 *BYIL* 217, and J. K. Grodecki, 'Conflicts of Laws in Time' (1959) 35 *BYIL* 58, were published after the decision in *Starkowski* v. *Attorney-General* [1954] AC 155 HL below.

[96] (1870) LR 6 QB 1.   [97] [1937] AC 500 HL.   [98] [1956] Ch. 323.

[99] [1954] AC 155. It was distinguished in a Canadian case on capacity to marry: *Ambrose* v. *Ambrose* (1961) 25 DLR (2d) 1 (British Columbia).

[100] (1845) 8 Beav. 527.

[101] This was done in a South African case concerning laws governing matrimonial property: *Sperling* v. *Sperling* (1975) (3) SA 707, and in a Canadian case on the same matter: *Topolski* v. *The Queen* (1978) 90 DLR (3d) 66.

[102] Three, if one includes *Ambrose* v. *Ambrose*, note 99 above.

concerned *succession to movables*. In *Lynch* v. *Provisional Government of Paraguay*[103] a law of Paraguay which purported to invalidate the will of a testator who had died domiciled there was denied effect, and the will was held valid as regards property in England. This was followed in Re *Aganoor's Trusts*[104] where interests in movable property in England bequeathed by the will of a person who died domiciled in Padua were held not to have been invalidated when, later, the Austrian law was supplanted by Italian law upon Italy succeeding to the territory of Padua, Italian law regarding the interests as invalid.

It should be added that, as regards the *formal validity of wills*, provision is made in the Wills Act 1963[105] whereby a change in one of the applicable laws after the will is made or after the testator's death is to be given effect if it validates the will, but not if it invalidates it.

The general view of the cases mentioned appears to be that a reference to the *lex causae* should be a reference to that law in its entirety, including any changes in it between the relevant event and the date of its application. On this view the cases in (i) to (iv) are correct and *Lynch*'s case and Re *Aganoor's Trusts* wrong.[106]

But a more subtle analysis suggests that they are all correct. Lipstein[107] has drawn attention to the need to distinguish between 'once and for all' acts or events which are over and done with and those which form part of a continuing relationship. Thus, the death of a testator is a 'once and for all' event, but the entry into a contract is not, for the contractual relationship may continue for many years. *Lynch*'s case[108] is an example of the former, *R* v. *International Trustee for the Protection of Bondholders A/G*[109] of the latter. A law enacted subsequent to the death of a testator cannot affect the succession to the testator, which has already taken place, but it can affect the contractual relationship, which is still subsisting. Further, one must characterise the rule of the *lex causae* to determine what it is concerned with and whether it is in fact applicable at all.

Examined thus, *Nelson* v. *Bridport*[110] and Re *Aganoor's Trusts*[111] which, prima facie, appear quite incompatible, are reconcilable (and Re *Aganoor's Trusts* carries *Lynch*'s case with it). The Sicilian law in the former case did not invalidate the will, but was concerned with the

---

[103] (1871) LR 2 P & D 268.   [104] (1895) 64 LJ Ch. 521.
[105] S. 6(3). The Act applies to wills of immovables as well as wills of movables.
[106] In *Starkowski* v. *Attorney-General* [1954] AC 155 the House of Lords rather feebly tried to distinguish *Lynch*'s case.
[107] K. Lipstein, 'Conflict of Laws 1921–71, the Way Ahead' [1972B] 67 *CLJ*, 96–100. Lipstein's arguments appear entirely correct.
[108] (1871) LR 2 P & D 268.   [109] [1937] AC 550.
[110] (1845) 8 Beav. 527.   [111] (1895) 64 LJ Ch. 521.

invalidity of subsisting interests in immovable property in Sicily and thus was correctly applied as its *lex situs*. The Italian law in Re *Aganoor's Trusts* likewise purported to invalidate subsisting interests in property, but since the property was in England, it was not part of the *lex situs*, which was English law. By English law those interests were valid. It may be added that, as Diplock J observed in *Adams* v. *National Bank of Greece and Athens SA*,[112] the Paraguayan law in *Lynch's* case was not really concerned to invalidate the will, but to expropriate to that state the property bequeathed to it. But again, the *lex situs* of the property was English law and Paraguayan law did not govern title to it.

At first sight, the two cases, *Phillips* v. *Eyre*[113] and *Starkowski* v. *Attorney-General*,[114] do not fit this explanation, since the act had taken place and was 'over and done with' when the tort was committed and the ceremony of marriage was performed. But this is not really so; in *Phillips* v. *Eyre*, the *lex causae* governing tort liability was English law, and the result reflected a rule of that law which gave justificatory effect to the conduct in question if it was justified where it was done. In *Starkowski's* case it is arguable that the parties remained subject to Austrian law after they were 'married', by reason of their domicile there. The Austrian validating law was passed in June 1945, the month after the wedding, and they only left Austria for England in July 1945.

---

[112] [1958] 2 QB 59 at 76, 77.   [113] (1870) LR 6 QB 1.
[114] [1954] AC 155. For a discussion of variations on the facts of this case and suggestions that have been made for dealing with them, should they arise, see pp. 297–8 below. On the analysis reproduced here, the Austrian law should have had no effect, had it been enacted after the parties had acquired a domicile in England. (However, this was not the view adopted in *Sperling* v. *Sperling* (1975) 3 SA 707.)

4   Proof of foreign law

Status of rules of foreign law

In an action before an English court, a party who relies on the rules of a foreign system of law must plead and prove them. Normally, the courts will not take judicial notice of the rules of foreign law,[1] except that the House of Lords, which is a court of appeal in civil cases from England, Scotland and Northern Ireland, will take judicial notice of the laws of all three countries in hearing appeals from the courts of any one of them.

In this respect rules of foreign law differ from those of public international law; moreover, the rules of public international law have the status of rules of law in an English court, because it is part of the law of England.[2] Rules of foreign law have the status of facts. But they are unusual facts, because, unlike other facts, they need only be proved to the satisfaction of the judge, not that of the jury.[3]

At common law, a particular rule of foreign law must be proved afresh each time it is pleaded, because the foreign law may have changed since the previous occasion on which it was proved to and accepted by an English court.[4]

However, the Civil Evidence Act 1972[5] now provides that where any question of foreign law has been determined in any civil or criminal proceedings[6] by a court other than one which can take judicial notice of foreign law, then any finding made or decision on that question in the earlier proceedings shall, if reported or recorded in citable form, be

---

[1] *El Ajou* v. *Dollar Land Holdings plc* [1994] 2 All ER 685. But in *Saxby* v. *Fulton* [1909] 2 KB 208 CA at 211 notice was taken of the 'notorious' fact that gaming was lawful at Monte Carlo. This was heretical. As to proof of foreign law, see generally R. G. Fentiman, *Foreign Law in English Courts* (Oxford University Press, 1999).

[2] See, for example, *Trendtex Trading Corporation* v. *Central Bank of Nigeria* [1977] QB 529 CA.

[3] Supreme Court Act 1981, s. 69(5).

[4] *Lazard Brothers* v. *Midland Bank* [1933] AC 289 HL. But cf. Re *Sebba* [1959] Ch. 166.

[5] S. 4(2).   [6] These are defined in s. 4(4).

admissible in evidence in proving the foreign law, and this will be taken as established unless the contrary is proved.[7]

A finding or decision is taken to be reported or recorded in citable form only if it is in writing in a report or transcript which could be cited as authority if the question had been a question as to English law.[8]

A foreign statute or law cannot be put before the court without an expert to explain it, nor can books of authority or decisions of courts, since they might require interpretation to enable the court to understand them correctly.[9] The required method of proof is by expert witnesses.

Method of proof

An expert testifying to foreign law may give his evidence orally or by affidavit.[10] Who is an expert is not easy to state. Ideally, it should be a judge or lawyer qualified to practise in the relevant foreign country but this was never an exclusive requirement.

For example, an English banker with years of banking experience in London who had gained great knowledge of South American banking practices was preferred to a Chilean lawyer who had practised there for four years, to inform the court of the meaning of 'first class bills on London' appearing as a phrase in leases of premises in Chile.[11] Academic qualifications by themselves are not enough,[12] but the Reader at the Inns of Court School of Law in Roman-Dutch law who had no experience of practice in Southern Rhodesia but had practised for a time in the Transvaal, was allowed to give evidence of the law of Southern Rhodesia.[13]

That there never was an absolute requirement that an expert witness must be a practitioner is made clear by the Civil Evidence Act 1972, which professes to be declaratory. This provides that:[14]

---

[7] Unless, that is, the finding or decision conflicts with another one on the same question adduced in the same proceedings as that other. For a discussion of the weight to be given to the previous English decision see *Phoenix Marine Inc.* v. *China Ocean Shipping Co.* [1999] 1 All ER (Comm.) 139.

[8] Civil Evidence Act 1972, s. 4(5).

[9] For a statutory exception to this see the admissibility of copies of statutes of the legislature of a British possession (which term includes independent Commonwealth countries including republics) in the Evidence (Colonial Statutes) Act 1907.

[10] There is a statutory power for a court to state a case for the courts of a British possession as to a question of its law: British Law Ascertainment Act 1859. This is rarely used.

[11] *De Béeche* v. *South American Stores* [1935] AC 148 HL.

[12] *Bristow* v. *Sequeville* (1850) 5 Exch. 275.

[13] *Brailey* v. *Rhodesia Consolidated Ltd* [1910] 2 Ch. 95.   [14] S. 4(1).

It is hereby declared that in civil proceedings a person who is suitably qualified to do so on account of his knowledge or experience is competent to give expert advice as to [foreign law] . . . irrespective of whether he has acted or is entitled to act as a legal practitioner there.

Duty of the English court

If an expert's evidence is uncontradicted or if the experts are agreed, the judge cannot reject the evidence and form his own opinion from his own researches.[15] But the evidence does not have to be accepted if the witness is obviously unreliable or the evidence is preposterous.[16] If the witness puts a foreign code, decision or textbook in evidence, the court is entitled to look at the parts he puts in evidence,[17] and where the evidence of experts upon its interpretation conflicts, the court can arrive at its own conclusions.[18] The court must not, however, examine the parts not put in evidence.

If the experts disagree, the court must make up its own mind on the evidence. If the courts of the country have not decided a point, or there are conflicting decisions therein, the court must still decide it.[19] If the point has been decided by a foreign court, the English court must accept the decision unless it is clearly absurd or inconsistent with the rest of the evidence.[20] The expert should, in the case of a question concerning the interpretation of a foreign statute, state and explain the relevant foreign rules of statutory interpretation.[21]

In two recent cases, *Grupo Torras* v. *Sheikh Fahad Mohammed Al-Sabah*[22] and *Macmillan Inc.* v. *Bishopsgate Investment Trust* (No. 4),[23] the duties of the Court of Appeal have been considered. That court said that it should not be so reluctant to disturb the trial judge's findings of fact as is usually the case, where the fact is a rule of foreign law; it has interfered with the judge's finding where that was contrary to the agreement of the experts.[24] It has also said that where the judge's view of he construction of a foreign statute was in accordance with the English

---

[15] *Bumper Development Corp. Ltd* v. *Commissioner of Police of the Metropolis* [1991] 1 WLR 1362 CA.

[16] *Grupo Torras SA* v. *Sheikh Fahad Mohammed Al-Sabah* [1996] 1 Ll.R 7 CA.

[17] See *Nelson* v. *Bridport* (1845) 8 Beav. 527; *Lazard Brothers* v. *Midland Bank* [1933] AC 289 HL.

[18] See *Nelson* v. *Bridport* (1845) 8 Beav. 527.

[19] See *Breen* v. *Breen* [1964] P 144; Re *Duke of Wellington* [1947] Ch. 506.

[20] *Guaranty Trust Corporation of New York* v. *Hannay* [1918] 2 KB 623 CA.

[21] See, for example, *Castrique* v. *Imrie* (1870) LR 4 HL 414 at 430.

[22] [1996] 1 Ll.R 7 CA.   [23] [1999] CLC 417, CA.

[24] As in the *Bumper* case, [1991] 1 WLR 1362 CA.

rules of interpretation in the absence of any evidence that the foreign court would apply different rules, the Court of Appeal is entitled, and indeed bound, to form its own view of the meaning of the statute. If foreign law is not proved, the court will apply English law.

5   Domicile and residence

Meaning of domicile

Domicile is a connecting factor which links a person with a particular legal system, and the law of his domicile is his personal law. That law determines, in principle, whether a man or woman has legal capacity to marry, and how the estate of a deceased person is to be distributed. If a married person is domiciled in England, the English courts have jurisdiction to dissolve or annul his or her marriage. If a married person is domiciled in, say, France, then a divorce decree granted by the French courts to or against that person will be recognised in England. Apart from the conflict of laws itself, domicile is of significance in other areas of the law, especially tax law.

Since it is a connecting factor, a person's domicile must be ascertained by applying English law, and not in accordance with the rules of a foreign legal system.[1]

The general meaning of domicile is 'permanent home'. This seems clear enough, but the view expressed by Lord Cranworth V-C in *Whicker* v. *Hume* (1858)[2] that a person's domicile is what he regards as his permanent home is far too simplistic and, indeed, somewhat misleading. It is true that for most people their domicile coincides with their permanent home. However, domicile is a legal concept and a person's 'basic' domicile is his domicile of origin, which is ascribed to him by law at his birth, and is not necessarily the country of his family's permanent home at that time. His domicile of dependence, whilst he is a minor, is the same as that of both or one of his parents, even though he may have no home with either. The ascertainment of a person's domicile of choice does depend upon showing that he intended to establish

---

[1] Re *Martin* [1900] P 211; Re *Annesley* [1926] Ch. 692. By way of exception, but for jurisdictional and not for choice-of-law purposes, statutes have provided for reference to the foreign definition of domicile (Family Law Act 1986, s. 46(5)) and a definition different from that which is considered in this chapter (Civil Jurisdiction and Judgments Act 1982, ss. 41–6). As to the latter see pp. 138–9 below.
[2] HLC 124 at 160.

a permanent home in a particular country, but even so, what the law regards as permanent may not strike a layman as such.

A person must be domiciled in a 'law district'. This coincides with a state such as France, Italy or Germany if that state possesses only one system of law. But this is not so if the state is a federal state or one which, like the United Kingdom, contains several different districts, each having its own legal system. Thus, a person must be domiciled in, say, Iowa or California and not the United States of America, or England or Scotland, not the United Kingdom. If an Englishman goes to the United States intending to stay there permanently but does not settle in any one of the fifty states of the Union, he continues to be domiciled in England.[3]

No person can be without a domicile. A domicile is ascribed to a person by law as his domicile of origin or of dependence. As will be seen, he will keep such a domicile unless and until he acquires another by choice, and if he abandons a domicile of choice his domicile of origin will revive and be his domicile unless and until he acquires another domicile of choice. This inability of anyone to be without a domicile is a feature of the English law which makes domicile preferable as a connecting factor for determining the personal law to any other, since a person can be without a residence, a home or a nationality. Another advantage is that no one can have more than one domicile for any one purpose at the same time;[4] he can, however, have more than one residence, home or nationality.

These general principles were first clearly enunciated by Lord Westbury in *Udny* v. *Udny* in 1869.[5]

There are three kinds of domicile: domicile of origin, domicile of choice and domicile of dependence.

Domicile of origin

A person's domicile of origin depends on the domicile of one of his parents at the time of his birth, not on where he was born, nor on his

---

[3] *Gatty* v. *Attorney-General* [1951] P 444. A person whose domicile of origin was in Jamaica but who came to Great Britain intending to stay here permanently did not acquire a domicile of choice and lose his Jamaican domicile until he decided to settle in Scotland rather than England: *Bell* v. *Kennedy* (1868) LR 1 Sc. & Div. 307 HL. Australia and Canada are similar to the United States and the United Kingdom in this respect, but see note 4 below.

[4] Or, probably, for any purpose. But it may be that if, as in Australia, there is a federal divorce law, a person could, for the purpose of recognition of his divorce, be regarded as domiciled in Australia and not, say, Victoria. Canada also has a federal divorce law.

[5] (1869) 1 LR Sc. & Div. 441 HL.

parents' residence at that time. In *Udny* v. *Udny*,[6] for example, Colonel Udny was born and then lived in Tuscany, where his father resided as British consul. But his father was domiciled in Scotland, so the Colonel's own domicile of origin was Scotland.

The rules for the ascertainment of the domicile of origin are: (i) a legitimate child takes his father's domicile, (ii) an illegitimate child and (iii) (possibly) a posthumous child, that is a legitimate child born after his father's death, both take his mother's domicile, and (iv) a foundling[7] or one whose parents' domicile is unknown is domiciled in the place where he is found or born. In one situation only, (v) the domicile of an adopted child, the domicile of origin can be changed after the child's birth. By statute,[8] an adopted child becomes thenceforth for all legal purposes the child of his adoptive parents, so he takes their domicile[9] as his domicile of origin.

A minor's domicile may change after his birth, but any new domicile he acquires is a domicile of dependence and not of origin (except where he is adopted); that remains the domicile he acquired at birth.[10]

Domicile of choice

Differences between domicile of origin and domicile of choice

Domicile of origin and domicile of choice can be distinguished in three ways:

First, the domicile of origin is ascribed to a person by law and does not depend on his own acts or intentions; a domicile of choice is acquired if a person goes to live in a country with the intention to remain there permanently. Secondly, it is more tenacious than a domicile of choice. A domicile of origin can only be lost by intentional acquisition of another one, but a domicile of choice can be lost simply by leaving the relevant country intending not to return. If that should

---

[6] *Ibid.*

[7] There is no English authority. In the Australian case Re *McKenzie* (1951) 51 SR (NSW) 293, an illegitimate child whose mother's domicile was unknown was held to have his domicile of origin where he was born.

[8] Adoption Act 1976, s. 39. This does *not* apply to legitimated children. A legitimated child, whatever domicile of dependence he may acquire on legitimation, retains his domicile of origin derived from that of his mother at his birth.

[9] Or that of his parent if adopted by only one person. Since 1973 a married woman can have a domicile separate from her husband's. If a child is adopted by parents who have different domiciles, presumably he takes his new father's domicile.

[10] This may be important if a person acquires a domicile of choice after his majority. If he then abandons it without acquiring another, it is his domicile of origin, not that of dependence, which will revive: *Henderson* v. *Henderson* [1967] P 77.

happen, then, unless another domicile of choice is acquired, the domicile of origin revives. This, the 'revival' of the domicile of origin, is a third distinguishing feature. It was established by *Udny* v. *Udny* in 1869.[11]

> Colonel Udny was born in Tuscany where his father, then domiciled in Scotland, was British consul. Thus Scotland was his domicile of origin. He later acquired a domicile of choice in England, but then fled to France to evade his creditors. He thereby abandoned his English domicile, but did not acquire one in France.

The House of Lords held that when the Colonel left England, his Scottish domicile of origin automatically revived; he did not need to go and live in Scotland in order to reacquire it.[12]

Requirements for acquisition

A domicile of choice is acquired by a combination of two things, the *factum* of actual presence or residence in a country, and the *animus*, that is, the requisite intention. The two must coincide. If a person goes to a country and then leaves it, but later wishes to return there for good without actually returning, he will not acquire a domicile in that country. However, provided the necessary intention exists, even a stay of a few hours will suffice.[13]

The chief problems in this area concern the definition of the requisite intention and the proof of its existence in the particular case.

The requisite intention may be defined as that of permanent or indefinite residence; the person must intend, at the relevant time, to stay in a country for good, or at least for an unlimited period.[14] If he does so, it does not matter that he later changes his mind, so long as he does not actually leave the country.

If, however, he intends to reside in a country for a fixed time, say five years, or for an indefinite time, but thinks that he will leave some day, then he does not acquire a domicile of choice there. If the possibility of departing is in his mind, however, that possibility must depend upon a real contingency and not a fanciful one (such as if he won the football

---

[11] (1869) 1 LR Sc. & Div. 441 HL. See also *Tee* v. *Tee* [1974] 1 WLR 213 CA.
[12] The revival of the domicile of origin is one of the most severely criticised rules of the English law of domicile. The criticism is discussed at p. 51 below.
[13] As in the celebrated American case of *White* v. *Tennant* (1888) 31 W Va. 790.
[14] See Re *Fuld* (No. 3) [1968] P 675. For a case where the requisite intention was not proved see Re *Clore* (No. 2) [1984] STC 609.

pools), nor one which is too vague. For example, compare *IRC* v. *Bullock*[15] with Re *Furse*.[16] In the former case, Group Captain Bullock, a Canadian, lived in England for forty-four years. He had married an Englishwoman and in deference to her wishes set up home in England. He often expressed an intention to return to Nova Scotia should she predecease him.

The Court of Appeal held that he had not acquired a domicile in England. Group Captain Bullock's intention indeed depended upon a contingency which might not occur, but it was quite possible that it would, for it was nearly as likely that his wife would predecease him as that he would predecease her.

But in Re *Furse* an American, who owned a farm in England where he lived and worked and had his family after 1923, had considered returning to New York from time to time but after the 1940s had abandoned searches for a house in the United States. Thereafter he stayed on his farm and said nothing except that he might go back to the United States if he ceased to be capable of leading an active life on the farm.

It was held[17] that he had acquired a domicile of choice in England, since his intention to leave was vague and indefinite. There was no pressure on him to stay here, and he was wholly integrated into the community in which he lived.[18]

Re *Furse*[19] also demonstrates that residence in a country for a particular limited purpose does not in itself create a domicile of choice there. It was argued that Mr Furse had acquired a domicile of dependence in England because, when he was a minor, his father had himself acquired a domicile of choice in England. But his father had only come to England with the children after his wife had died in order to get them away from what he regarded as the undesirable influences of his wife's family, and he had returned to New York, where he died. So the father did not have any intention to remain in England and make his permanent home here, and thus did not acquire an English domicile of choice.

Physical residence and the requisite intention must coincide at the relevant time. If they do not, it is immaterial that the intention can be shown to have been formulated at some subsequent time.

---

[15] [1976] 1 WLR 1178 CA.   [16] [1980] 3 All ER 838.
[17] By Fox J, distinguishing *IRC* v. *Bullock* and *Ramsay* v. *Liverpool Royal Infirmary* [1930] AC 588. See p. 42 below.
[18] Unlike Mr Winans in *Winans* v. *Attorney-General* [1904] AC 287; see p. 43 below.
[19] [1980] 3 All ER 838.

In the well-known case of *Bell* v. *Kennedy*[20]

> Mr Bell left Jamaica, his domicile of origin, as he said, 'for good', and went to Scotland intending to reside there. But when he arrived he could not make his mind up as between Scotland and England, though he remained in Scotland. His wife died.

It was held that at that time his, and his wife's, domicile was still in Jamaica. Shortly afterwards he bought an estate in Scotland and settled there, but it was only then that he acquired a domicile of choice in Scotland.

In the more recent case, *Plummer* v. *IRC*,[21]

> Miss Plummer had an English domicile of origin. During the tax years 1983–5, she spent 492 days in England and 189 in Guernsey with her grandmother, mother and sister who resided there. She said she regarded Guernsey as her home and would like to live there permanently, after getting experience by working in television elsewhere.

It was held that she had not, in 1983–5, acquired a domicile of choice in Guernsey.

Burden and standard of proof

The burden of proving the acquisition of a domicile of choice rests on the person who alleges it. It seems that the standard of proof is that required in ordinary civil cases, that is, proof upon a balance of probabilities, though there is some doubt about this.[22]

Some cases concerning rather unusual people are often cited in order to show that the burden of proof is extraordinarily difficult to discharge. Thus, in *Ramsay* v. *Liverpool Royal Infirmary*[23]

> George Bowie, a Scotsman born in Glasgow with a Scottish domicile of origin, stopped working when he was thirty-seven and when he was forty-six went to Liverpool to live with (or sponge off) members of his family. He died there aged eighty-seven. He had only left Liverpool

---

[20] (1868) LR 1 Sc. & Div. 307. For some obscure reason this case is often thought, especially by students, to be concerned with the revival of the domicile of origin. But it is not; the domicile of origin had not been replaced by a domicile of choice. See also *Cramer* v. *Cramer* [1988] 1 FLR 116.

[21] [1988] 1 WLR 292. The judgment is complicated by Hoffman J's belief that he had to invent a new rule for people who have more than one residence at the same time. It is submitted that this was both unnecessary and confusing.

[22] In *Henderson* v. *Henderson* [1967] P 77 it was said that a higher standard was required. But see Scarman J in *Re Fuld* (No. 3) [1968] P 675 with whom the Court of Appeal in *Buswell* v. *IRC* [1974] 1 WLR 1631 agreed, rejecting the standard required in criminal cases.

[23] [1930] AC 588 HL.

on two short trips, and refused to return to Glasgow, even for his mother's funeral. He always took a Glasgow newspaper, and called himself a 'Glasgow man', stating this in his will. He made a will which was formally invalid under English law, but valid by Scots law.

The House of Lords held that he died domiciled in Scotland. Though his residence in England was lengthy, it was 'colourless' and motivated only by his attachment to a member of his family who would keep him despite his disinclination to work. The burden of proving his acquisition of a domicile in England had not been discharged. His will was thereby held to be valid.

In *Winans* v. *Attorney-General*[24]

> An American, whose domicile of origin was in New Jersey, came to England and took tenancies of furnished houses in Brighton, one of which he kept until his death there thirty-seven years later. He spent parts of each year in England, Germany, Scotland and Russia, but during the last four years of his life, he confined himself to Brighton on medical advice. His two abiding preoccupations were looking after his health and a project which never came to fruition of building 'cigar' or 'spindle' shaped vessels for sale to the United States in order to wrest the carrying trade from the British. He acquired part of a waterfront in Baltimore to build the ships and talked of returning there to develop the scheme. He disliked the English and never mixed with them socially.

The House of Lords held that he did not die domiciled in England; the Crown had not adduced sufficient evidence of any fixed and determined purpose positively to acquire a domicile of choice in England, and had not discharged the burden of proof incumbent upon it.

But these cases are on the edge of the law, and possess somewhat extraordinary features. In other cases, the burden of proof has not been so difficult to discharge.[25] Two, more recent, cases concerned with the domicile of Americans may be contrasted with *Winans* v. *Attorney-General*: *Re Furse*,[26] also a tax case, and *Brown* v. *Brown*,[27] a divorce case.

> In the latter, the husband, an American citizen, joined an American company and came to England in its employ in 1966. He married here in 1969, and in the same year was posted to Rome for three years, but kept his membership of London clubs.[28] A child was born

---

[24] [1904] AC 287 HL.

[25] In *Winans* v. *Attorney-General* [1904] AC 287 the decision of the House of Lords was by a two-to-one majority; the majority of all the judges who heard the case held that he died domiciled in England.

[26] [1980] 3 All ER 838. See p. 41 above.   [27] (1982) 3 FLR 212 CA.

[28] Including the MCC, membership of which may be regarded as a rather un-American activity.

in 1971. In 1972 Mr Brown returned to London with his family and bought a flat, and the child was entered for an English prep. school and Eton. In 1977 he was once again posted to Rome for three years, and rented the flat to a friend so he could get it back when he wanted it. His wife refused to return with him in 1980 and he petitioned for divorce. She challenged the statement in his petition that he was domiciled in England.

It was held by the Court of Appeal that, though he was still a United States citizen, he had spent only forty-eight days out of fifteen years in the United States and that by his uncontroverted evidence he had succeeded in proving that he had a settled intention to make a permanent home in England.

Evidence of intention

Any evidence may be relevant to prove the intention. No piece of evidence is necessarily decisive, and evidence which is decisive in one case may be entirely discounted in another. Declarations of the person concerned are viewed warily. For one thing, they may be selfserving. Further, though they are admissible in evidence, they must be scrutinised carefully to ascertain the person to whom, the purpose for which and the circumstances in which they are made. A person who is not a private international lawyer who is asked by, for example, the Inland Revenue where he is domiciled, may not appreciate what the question means and his answer may not be held against him.[29]

The declaration must be consistent with the person's other behaviour, and must, in any case, be put into effect by conduct. In *Ross* v. *Ross*[30]

> The question was whether a Scotsman who had no fixed home was domiciled in New York. He told his business associates that he intended to remain there. But he always referred to Scotland as 'home', and in an affidavit he swore he was a domiciled Scotsman.

The House of Lords held that the statements to his associates were admissible in evidence, but since they were not consistent with the rest of it, a New York domicile was not established.

Domicile as a social bond

Domicile denotes a social, not a political, attachment to a particular country. This is shown by cases which concerned persons who became

---

[29] *Buswell* v. *IRC* [1974] 1 WLR 1631 CA.   [30] [1930] AC 1 HL.

naturalised in a state or persons who were deported or were subject to possible deportation. If a person becomes naturalised in a country this may be evidence of his intention to acquire a domicile there,[31] but it may not necessarily be so. He may want to become a national of one state without wishing altogether to sever his social ties with the country of his domicile.[32]

An alien who is liable to be deported from England, and whose stay here may, therefore, be cut short, may nevertheless intend to stay in England and make it his permanent home so far as he is able to do so. In *Boldrini* v. *Boldrini*,[33] for example, an Italian who was working as a waiter in England was registered as an alien under the then aliens legislation and was liable to deportation. He was nevertheless held to have acquired a domicile here. The same was true of an alien in respect of whom a deportation order had been made.[34]

However, an illegal entrant to England[35] cannot acquire a domicile here. This is a rule based on English public policy; an English court might well hold that an illegal entrant to another country had obtained a domicile there.

Motive and freedom of choice

Motive must be distinguished from intention. The fact that a person has what might be regarded as an unworthy motive in going to a country, for example, to escape payment of taxes, does not prevent the court from holding that he has formed the necessary intention to reside permanently there.

Generally speaking a person's intention must be the result of a free choice; but all that this means is that the fact that, for instance, his residence is a result of his fleeing from justice or from oppression or enemy invasion, may make it perhaps less likely that he has the requisite intention, but if there is adequate evidence of such an intention, there is nothing to stop the court holding that he has acquired a domicile of choice.

Thus, on the one hand, in Re *Lloyd-Evans*[36] a person had a domicile of choice in Belgium. He came to England in 1940 after the German

---

[31] *Tee* v. *Tee* [1974] 1 WLR 213 CA.
[32] *Wahl* v. *Attorney-General* (1932) 147 LT 382 HL; Re *Fuld* (No. 3) [1968] P 675.
[33] [1932] P 9 CA; *May* v. *May* [1943] 2 All ER 146; *Zanelli* v. *Zanelli* [1948] 64 TLR 556; *Szechter* v. *Szechter* [1971] P 286.
[34] *Cruh* v. *Cruh* [1945] 2 All ER 545. [35] *Puttick* v. *Attorney-General* [1980] Fam. 1.
[36] [1947] Ch. 695; see also *De Bonneval* v. *De Bonneval* (1838) 1 Curt. 856. In *Udny* v. *Udny* (1869) 1 LR Sc. & Div. 441 HL, Colonel Udny fled to France to evade his English creditors. It was held that he had not acquired a domicile there.

invasion of that country, but he intended to return if and when the Germans were expelled. It was held that he died domiciled in Belgium. On the other hand, in Re *Martin*[37] a French professor who had committed a crime in France fled to England in 1870 and stayed for twenty years. Two years after he could no longer be prosecuted in France he returned there. It was held that in 1874 he was domiciled in England.

The point is also illustrated by cases concerning invalids. If a person goes to a country for the temporary purpose of treatment he will obviously not acquire a domicile there; nor, it was held in Re *James*,[38] which concerned a sick Welshman who went to South Africa, if he is told he is mortally ill and decides to go there to alleviate his sufferings, since he acts under a kind of compulsion. But if he is not mortally ill, and only believes he has more chance of being well or getting better in another country, as in *Hoskins* v. *Matthews*,[39] he will be held to have been 'exercising a preference and not acting upon a necessity' and to have acquired a domicile there.

A person who is sent to a country for employment there usually does not acquire a domicile there,[40] but he may do so.[41] A serviceman posted to another country for service will not usually acquire a domicile there, but again he may do so. In *Donaldson* v. *Donaldson*[42] an RAF officer stationed in Florida decided to stay there after demobilisation, and brought his wife and child there; it was held that he had acquired a domicile in Florida. In the converse case of *Stone* v. *Stone*,[43] a United States serviceman was held to have acquired a domicile in England, where he had been posted.

Abandonment of domicile of choice (or dependence)

In order to abandon a domicile of choice, the requisite intention to do so must be carried into effect and the person must actually leave the country of his domicile of choice. If he does not, that domicile continues to adhere whatever his wishes. In in b. *Raffenel*,[44] a widow who had

---

[37] [1900] P 211. See *Moynihan* v. *Moynihan* [1997] 1 FLR 59 (refugee from British justice got a domicile in the Philippines).

[38] (1908) 98 LT 438; see also *Winans* v. *Attorney-General* [1904] AC 287 HL.

[39] (1855) 8 De GM & G 13.

[40] *Attorney-General* v. *Rowe* (1862) 1 H & C 31. In *Tee* v. *Tee* [1974] 1 WLR 213 CA an Englishman who had acquired a domicile in the United States did not get one in Germany on being sent there.

[41] *Brown* v. *Brown* (1982) 3 FLR 212 CA.

[42] [1949] P 363. See also the Scots case of *Sellars* v. *Sellars* 1942 SC 206 and see *Cruickshanks* v. *Cruickshanks* [1957] 1 WLR 564.

[43] [1958] 1 WLR 1287.   [44] (1863) 3 Sw. & Tr. 49.

a domicile of dependence with her husband in France went on board a cross-channel ferry at Calais intending to sail to England, her domicile of origin, and stay here. Before the ship left France, she fell ill and had to return to land where she died. She died domiciled in France.

Provided, however, he has actually physically left, the person need not have formed a positive determination never to return; he has lost the domicile of choice merely by having no intention to go back to the country.[45]

If no other domicile of choice is acquired, the domicile of origin revives.[46] Thus, had Mrs Raffenel's boat crossed the boundary of French territorial waters, she would have died domiciled in England. This rule is often very severely criticised; it does not represent the law in the United States,[47] where the domicile of choice continues until a new domicile of choice is acquired.[48]

Domicile of dependence

Married women

Until 1 January 1974, as a matter of law, a married woman automatically possessed the domicile of her husband even if he and she lived apart and even though they were judicially separated.[49] Only if their marriage was void or after it had been annulled or dissolved or after her husband's death could she have her own domicile, separate from his.[50]

However, by the Domicile and Matrimonial Proceedings Act 1973,[51] from and after 1 January 1974, the domicile of a married woman is ascertained in the same way as is that of an adult male. This rule applies to women who were married either before or after that date. If, immediately before then, a woman was married and had her husband's domicile by dependence, she is to be regarded as retaining that domicile

---

[45] Re *Flynn* (No. 1) [1968] 1 WLR 103 which concerned the estate of the late Errol Flynn, the film actor. The judgment of Megarry J should be read for its entertainment value. It was approved in *Tee* v. *Tee* [1974] 1 WLR 213 CA.

[46] *Udny* v. *Udny* (1869) LR 1 Sc. Div. 441; *Tee* v. *Tee.*

[47] Re *Jones's Estate* 192 Iowa 78 (1921). It has been abolished in the Antipodes.

[48] This criticism is discussed at p. 51 below.

[49] *Attorney-General for Alberta* v. *Cook* [1926] AC 444 PC; *Lord Advocate* v. *Jaffrey* [1921] 1 AC 146 HL.

[50] A wife could live in another country from her husband's and if she intended to live there permanently then on his death she would immediately acquire a domicile there, even though she was unaware that she was a widow: Re *Cooke's Trusts* (1887) 56 LJ Ch. 637; Re *Scullard* [1957] Ch. 107. Cf. Re *Wallach* [1950] 1 All ER 199.

[51] S. 1(1). The Act is not retrospective and the common law rules still have to be applied to determine the domicile of a married woman before 1 January 1974.

as her domicile of choice, unless and until she acquires another domicile of choice or her domicile of origin revives on or after 1 January 1974. It has been held that her previous domicile of dependence must continue as a 'deemed' domicile of choice until she actually departs from, say, England for another country.[52]

Minors

A minor is a person who is aged under eighteen.[53] But a person can, since 1 January 1974, acquire his own domicile when he attains his sixteenth birthday or, if he is below that age, upon marriage.[54]

The domicile of dependence of a legitimate minor is, with the exception discussed below,[55] that of his father, and changes automatically if his father changes his own domicile. That will also remain his domicile after his father's death until the minor becomes sixteen. It may, however, after his father's death follow that of his mother. But if his *mother* changes her domicile, the minor's domicile does not necessarily alter. The mother has a power to change the minor's domicile along with her own, but she must positively change it and must not abstain from doing so. If she does exercise this power she must not, it seems, do so fraudulently, that is, for a purpose other than for the benefit or welfare of the minor.[56] Thus in Re *Beaumont*[57]

> Mr and Mrs B were domiciled in Scotland. They had several children all of whom had a Scottish domicile of origin and of dependence. The father died and Mrs B then married N. They went to live in England where they acquired a domicile. They took all the children to live with them with the exception of Catherine, who was left in Scotland with her aunt, with whom she had lived since her father's death. Catherine attained her majority and shortly thereafter died in Scotland.

The Court of Appeal held that Catherine died domiciled in Scotland, since her mother had not exercised her power to alter her domicile.

---

[52] S. 1(2) *IRC* v. *Duchess of Portland* [1982] Ch. 314. This decision is not, however, free from difficulty: see J. A. Wade, 'Domicile: a Re-examination of Certain Rules' (1983) 32 *ICLQ* 1.

[53] Family Law Reform Act 1969, s. 1(1). Before 1 January 1970 it was twenty-one.

[54] Domicile and Matrimonial Proceedings Act 1973, s. 3(1). This does not operate retrospectively. A person can only obtain a new domicile on or after marriage when he is below sixteen if he is domiciled abroad, since a person domiciled here cannot marry until he is that age.

[55] See pp. 49–50 below.

[56] Not, for example, to acquire better rights of succession to the child's property: see *Potinger* v. *Wightman* (1817) 3 Mer. 67.

[57] [1893] 3 Ch. 490 CA.

It should be observed that Catherine remained with her aunt for all purposes; the case would probably have been different if she had been left in Scotland for a limited and temporary purpose, for example, to remain at school there in order to finish her education.

The domicile of origin of an illegitimate child is, as we have seen, that of his mother when he is born. Most writers say that Re *Beaumount* applies to an illegitimate child's domicile during his minority.[58] It is not at all clear that this is so. The domicile which Catherine retained was that acquired from her father, that is, her domicile of origin. That which an illegitimate child would retain would be the one derived from his mother. Moreover, Catherine remained in the country of her domicile of origin. Suppose X is born in France and illegitimate, when his mother is domiciled in New Zealand. If his mother acquires a domicile in England leaving X in France, then, if his domicile does not automatically change, X will remain domiciled in New Zealand, a country in which he has never set foot, until he is sixteen at least. This does not look very sensible.

Re *Beaumont* does not seem a very satisfactory decision nowadays, when men and women are equal in law (although it had good reasons behind it when it was decided).[59] The situation should have been properly dealt with in 1973, when reforms, about to be discussed, were made by statute, in respect of a minor's domicile.

If, as is thought, a legitimated child acquires a domicile of dependence upon his father when he is legitimated, his domicile will thereafter be ascertained as if he were legitimate. The same must be true of a child who is adopted by a man and wife, since he takes the adoptive parents' (presumably the father's) domicile as his domicile of origin.[60]

One problem was dealt with in a not very lucid manner in the Domicile and Matrimonial Proceedings Act 1973. It concerned the domicile of a minor whose parents had been divorced before 1 January 1974 or after that date were separated, and lived in different countries and acquired separate domiciles, and who lived exclusively with the mother. The Act provides[61] that where the parents of a child, including an adopted child under sixteen, are alive but live apart, the child's domicile of dependence

---

[58] See, for example, A. V. Dicey and J. H. C. Morris, *The Conflict of Laws*, 13th edn (London, Stevens, 2000), 140.

[59] Until 31 December 1973, a married woman's domicile automatically changed with that of her husband. So if N had left his wife and acquired a domicile in Peru, her domicile and that of her children, including Catherine, would have become Peruvian. But the unity of domicile of husband and wife was, as has been said (p. 47 above), abolished as from 1 January 1974.

[60] See Adoption Act 1976, s. 39. The same problem arises in the case of a child who is adopted by a woman alone as in the case of the illegitimate child just discussed.

[61] S. 4(1).

is that of his father. But if he has a home with his mother and none with his father, his domicile is that of his mother. Once he acquires his mother's domicile under this provision he retains it until he is sixteen even if he ceases to have a home with her, unless he has at any time a home with his father.[62]

Two questions arise out of this. First, the statutory rules appear to apply only to the domicile of dependence since they envisage the child's domicile of origin being that of his father. Suppose he is legitimate but his parents separate before he is born. Presumably his domicile of dependence is that of his mother, but his domicile of origin that of his father, in which case his domicile changes immediately after his birth. This seems very artificial.

Second, suppose the child acquires a domicile with his mother under the Act, then goes to live with his father on 1 February, and his father dies on 2 February. He reacquires the domicile of his father. Thereafter, the statutory rule ceases to govern, and the common law rules, including Re *Beaumont*,[63] apply. Moreover, since the Act is concerned with a situation where the parents are alive, it may be that Re *Beaumount* will apply after the father dies, even though the child had not reacquired a home with him. None of this seems satisfactory; it would have been better had Parliament made it clear that the Act continued to apply, or better still, abolished the common law rule in Re *Beaumont* altogether.

Mental patients

It appears that the domicile of a mentally disordered person cannot be changed by his own act since he is unable to form the requisite intention,[64] and thus he retains the domicile he had when he became insane.[65]

There is authority for the proposition that if a person becomes insane during his minority[66] his domicile of dependence can be changed by an alteration of the domicile of the parent upon whom he is dependent, even if this takes place after he attains majority, but that if he becomes insane after he attains majority, his domicile cannot be changed for him.[67]

---

[62] S. 4(2). The common law continues to apply in order to ascertain the minor's domicile at any time *before* 1 January 1974. By s. 4(4) and (5) the statutory rule does not apply to illegitimate children. But if the child is illegitimate he has his mother's domicile anyway.

[63] [1893] 3 Ch. 490 CA.   [64] *Urquhart* v. *Butterfield* (1887) 37 Ch. D 357 CA.

[65] *Crumpton's Judicial Factor* v. *Finch-Noyes* 1918 SC 378.

[66] I.e. when under the age of sixteen: Domicile and Matrimonial Proceedings Act 1973, s. 3(1).

[67] *Sharpe* v. *Crispin* (1869) LR 1 P & C 611 at 628. This is aptly stigmatised as 'irrational' by G. C. Cheshire and P. M. North, *Private International Law*, 13th edn by P. M. North and J. J. Fawcett (London, Butterworths, 1999) 157.

Criticism and reform of the law of domicile

General

Some features of the law of domicile have long been criticised. The rules were, for the most part, laid down by judges in Victorian times, and it is argued that, though they may have been quite satisfactory as reflecting social factors then in existence, they are nowadays artificial or inadequate.

However, the only reform in the law has been the Domicile and Matrimonial Proceedings Act 1973. As we have seen, this discarded the common law unity of domicile between married persons and made some limited reforms in relation to the domicile of minors.[68]

Two frequently voiced complaints remain. The first concerns the alleged difficulty, which arises from the presumption of the continuance of the domicile of origin, in establishing the acquisition of a domicile of choice.[69] The other concerns the revival of the domicile of origin.[70]

These are sometimes unfavourably compared with the corresponding rules in United States law. They demonstrate the tenaciousness of the domicile of origin; the American rules do not. But the contrast can be explained. When the rules were being formulated England was not a country of immigration as was the United States, and it was more a country of emigration. But many Englishmen went abroad for particular, temporary purposes, such as governing the Empire, especially India, or to make their fortune, intending to return home. The courts would be slow to hold that such people had acquired a domicile in the country to which they had gone.[71] But United States courts could not possibly have presumed that immigrants from, say, Poland, Italy or Ireland were still domiciled there; they had come to America to escape from persecution or hardship in Europe and did, in fact, intend to make a new life in the New World.

The same considerations underlie the doctrine of revival of the domicile origin and explain its absence from American law. If an Englishman did acquire a domicile abroad, in New Zealand, for example, and then decided to leave that country, it was probable that he intended to return home. The law reflected what usually happened. Such a doctrine could not have been contemplated by United States courts. If an Italian

---

[68] Whether this exercise in law reform has been entirely successful is perhaps open to doubt: see pp. 49–50 above.

[69] See pp. 42–4 above. There is also doubt as to the standard of proof required.

[70] See p. 47 above.

[71] The concept of an 'Anglo-Indian' domicile which found favour at one time was rejected in *Casdagli* v. *Casdagli* [1919] AC 145 HL. No such place as 'Anglo-India' ever existed.

had settled in Illinois and then decided to go west to California to seek his fortune, but having set off met his death at the hands of American Indians somewhere between the two states, it would have been preposterous to hold that he died domiciled in Italy.

Attempts were made in the 1950s to abolish the presumption of the continuance of the domicile of origin and replace it by a presumption that a person is domiciled in his country of residence, but Bills[72] introduced into the House of Lords for this purpose were lost or withdrawn in consequence, it appears, of representations from American businessmen resident and working in England, who saw that if the burden of proving that they were not domiciled here was placed on them, it would be much more likely that the Revenue would successfully claim that they had acquired such a domicile and that they would, therefore, be liable to pay more by way of United Kingdom taxes.

It is submitted, however, that the difficulty of proving the acquisition of a domicile of choice is not, in practice, as great as is often suggested.[73]

As to the revival of the domicile of origin,[74] neither the English nor the opposed American principle that a domicile of choice continues until another is acquired is entirely unobjectionable. In the American case, Re *Jones's Estate*,[75]

> Jones was born in Wales with an English domicile of origin. He sired an illegitimate daughter. To escape paying for his sin, he went in 1883 to the United States, married there, amassed a fortune, and became an American citizen. By Iowa law he acquired a domicile in Iowa. In May 1914 his wife died. He decided to leave Iowa and return to live out his days with his sister in Wales. On 1 May 1915 he sailed in the *Lusitania* from New York but it was sunk on the high seas off the Irish coast by a German submarine. By Iowa law his illegitimate daughter succeeded to his estate, but by English law it went to his brothers and sisters.

The Supreme Court of Iowa held that, since his domicile of choice continued until he acquired another and because he never got to England, he died domiciled in Iowa.

This is hardly satisfactory in that it frustrated Jones's intentions, which were to reacquire his connection with English law and to avoid having any responsibility for his illegitimate daughter. It is also just as artificial as the revival of the domicile of origin, since it makes the devolution of a person's estate depend on the law of a country which he has left, wishing never to return to it.

---

[72] Domicile Bills 1958 and 1959.   [73] See pp. 42–4 above.
[74] See p. 47 above.   [75] 192 Iowa 78 (1921).

The best solution in such a case might be to deem a person to be domiciled in the country to which he intended to go. This would be reasonable in a case with the facts of Re *Jones's Estate* but it is not always safe to rely on unfulfilled intentions. If the submarine had not sunk the *Lusitania*, Jones would have reached England. But suppose it had been scheduled to call at Cherbourg? We do not know that if it had done so and Jones had been still alive he would have remained on board; he might have disembarked and stayed in France.

Possible solutions to these problems in the law of domicile, if they really are serious problems, are either to regard the law as beyond redemption and abandon it as a connecting factor or make another connecting factor an alternative to domicile. Nationality is, in general, too artificial and has little to recommend it. Successive Hague Conventions on Private International Law have resulted in a compromise between those systems which adopt domicile in our sense and those which adopt nationality and have produced 'habitual residence' which is like domicile, shorn of its technicalities, as a connecting factor side by side with domicile and nationality.[76]

The Law Commission's proposals (1987)

The Law Commission considered the law of domicile and, in 1987,[77] made proposals for far-reaching reforms. It had earlier, in 1984,[78] rejected the possibility of abandoning domicile as a connecting factor in favour of habitual residence. It included in its Report a draft Bill.

It proposed that the domicile of origin should be discarded. Instead it put forward rules for determining the domicile of children at birth and until their sixteenth birthday. The domicile of such a person should be determined as follows:

(i) he should be domiciled in the country with which he is, for the time being, most closely connected.

(ii) where the child's parents are domiciled in the same country and he has his home with either or both of them, it would be presumed,

---

[76] See Wills Act 1963, enacting the Convention on the Forms of Testamentary Dispositions, 1961; Family Law Act 1986, Part II, replacing the Recognition of Divorces and Legal Separations Act 1971, enacting the Convention of the same name, 1970. The Brussels Convention, 1968, and the Lugano Convention, 1989, on Jurisdiction and Enforcement of Judgments in Civil and Commercial Matters use domicile as the basic test for jurisdiction. For the enactment of this into English law see the Civil Jurisdiction and Judgments Act 1982, ss. 41–6, pp. 138–9 below.

[77] Report 168 (1987). For comment see P. B. Carter, 'Domicile: the Case for Radical Reform' (1987) 36 *ICLQ* 713.

[78] Working Paper no. 88 (1984).

unless the contrary be shown, that he is most closely connected with that country.

(iii) where the parents are not domiciled in the same country and he has a home with one and not with the other, it would be presumed, unless the contrary be shown, that he is most closely connected with the country in which the parent with whom he has his home is domiciled.

No person or court could override or abrogate these rules.

No special rule is required for a person who marries or becomes a parent when under the age of sixteen.

The normal civil standard of proof on a balance of probabilities would apply in all disputes about domicile.

As to the acquisition of a domicile of choice, a person of sixteen or over would be able to acquire one if he is present in a country with the requisite intention and no higher or different quality of intention should be required if the alleged change of domicile is from one acquired at birth than from any other domicile. The requisite intention would be merely to settle in a country for an indefinite period and should be determined without reference to any presumption. The revival of the domicile at birth would be replaced by the continuance of the existing domicile until another is acquired.

If enacted, these recommendations would have brought about great simplification and improvement in the law of domicile. However, they have not been proceeded with.[79]

Ordinary residence

A person's residence is where he lives. It is a question of fact. For the purpose of statutory provisions in which it is found 'ordinary residence' appears to differ from 'residence *simpliciter*'.[80] For the purpose of taxing statutes it has been held to mean 'residence' in a place with some degree of continuity and apart from accidental or temporary absence.[81] In *IRC* v. *Lysaght*[82] it was held, in a case concerning a person who lived in Ireland but spent about a week in each month in England living in hotels when on business there, that a person can have his ordinary residence in each of two places and so, surprisingly perhaps, that he was ordinarily resident in England as well as in Ireland.

---

[79] Law Commission no. 239 (1995) (Annual Report) p. 10, n. 24.
[80] *R* v. *Barnet LBC*, ex parte *Nilish Shah* [1983] 2 AC 309 HL (ordinary residence for eligibility for a grant for further education).
[81] *Levene* v. *IRC* [1928] AC 217 HL.   [82] [1928] AC 234 HL.

A person can continue to be ordinarily resident in one country though he is actually resident on business elsewhere, especially if he continues to maintain a home in that country.[83] It has been held that a minor who usually lived in England with one parent continued to be ordinarily resident there, though he had been removed abroad by the other parent and had resided with that parent in the other country for some time.[84]

Habitual residence *(obviously in place of domicile)*

This connecting factor has been employed in several statutes, some of which are based upon international conventions which employ the term either in addition to, or in place of, domicile. Thus, it is used as an alternative to domicile in respect of the jurisdiction of the English courts to grant decrees of divorce, judicial separation and nullity of marriage,[85] and in respect of the law governing the formal validity of wills.[86] It is used as an alternative to domicile and nationality as a basis for the jurisdiction of a foreign court when recognition of an overseas divorce is in issue.[87] It has relevance in the choice of law rules for contract[88] and plays a part in the laws of taxation, immigration and social security.

In *Cruse* v. *Chittum*,[89] an early case which concerned the recognition of an overseas divorce, habitual residence was said to denote 'regular physical presence which must endure for some time'. In several cases, the courts have said that it is a question of fact; this has turned out to be over-optimistic and, unavoidably, perhaps, legal rules have developed.

Some principles were stated by Lord Brandon in the leading case, Re *J (A Minor: Abduction)*.[90] Habitual residence must be understood in the natural and ordinary meaning of those words and is a question of fact to be decided in the light of the circumstances of the case.[91] Unlike

---

[83] This is illustrated by cases concerning the ordinary residence of a wife under statutory provisions which gave the English court jurisdiction to grant her a divorce if her husband was domiciled abroad: *Hopkins* v. *Hopkins* [1951] p 116; *Stransky* v. *Stransky* [1954] P 428; *Lewis* v. *Lewis* [1956] 1 WLR 200. These provisions were repealed by the Domicile and Matrimonial Proceedings Act 1973.

[84] Re *P (GE) (An Infant)* [1965] Ch. 568 CA. Thus the English court had jurisdiction to make a custody order in respect of him. See p. 136 below.

[85] Domicile and Matrimonial Proceedings Act 1973, s. 5(2).   [86] Wills Act 1963, s. 1.

[87] Family Law Act 1986, s. 46(1).   [88] See pp. 198–204 below.

[89] [1974] 2 All ER 940. Cf. *Hack* v. *Hack* (1976) 6 Fam. Law. 177.

[90] [1990] 2 AC 562 HL, a case on the Child Abduction and Custody Act 1985 (see for this Act pp. 339–43 below). For a learned general discussion see P. Rogerson, 'Habitual Residence: the New Domicile' (2000) 49 *ICLQ* 87.

[91] *Nessa* v. *Chief Adjudication Officer* [1991] 1 WLR 737 HL.

domicile, it cannot be acquired in a single day, since 'an appreciable period of time and a settled intention to reside on a long-term basis'[92] are necessary. The 'settled intention' need not be an intention to stay in the country permanently or indefinitely.[93] Like domicile, it is immediately lost by leaving a country with a settled intention not to return.

Although in several cases,[94] habitual residence has been said to differ not at all from *ordinary residence*, there are at least two differences between them. A person can have only one habitual residence but may have more than one ordinary residence at any one time. Whereas ordinary residence can be acquired in a single day, habitual residence needs an appreciable period of time.[95]

Habitual residence differs from domicile in several respects. It is not ascribed to a person at birth; the intention required for its acquisition is different and a previous habitual residence does not revive on the abandonment of one which has been subsequently acquired. It is, however, abandoned in the same way as domicile is abandoned. Therefore, a person can be without an habitual residence.[96]

As regards the habitual residence of children, the fact that a child may be without one may deprive him or her of the protection of the Child Abduction and Custody Act 1985 if he or she is abducted. Most of the reported cases about habitual residence have been decided under this Act. The courts have held that a child's habitual residence may change with that of a parent with whom the child lives and who is exercising rights of custody.[97] If the parents live together and the child lives with them, he or she has their habitual residence.[98] If they have joint responsibility, neither can change the child's habitual residence by wrongfully removing or retaining the child in breach of the other party's rights.[99] Both parents must consent.[100] A court order may change the

---

[92] Habitual residence can change quite quickly: Re *S (A Minor) (Custody: Habitual Residence)* [1998] AC 750 HL; *V* v. *B (A Minor) (Abduction)* [1991] 2 FLR 992.

[93] Re *B (Minors) (Abduction)* (No. 2) [1993] 1 FLR 993; *M* v. *M (Abduction) (England and Scotland)* [1997] 2 FLR 263 CA.

[94] See, for example, *Kapur* v. *Kapur* [1984] 5 FLR 920, quoting Lord Scarman in *R* v. *Barnet LBC*, ex parte *Nilish Shah* [1983] 2 AC 309 at 344. See also *M* v. *M (Abduction: England and Scotland)* [1997] 2 FLR 263 CA.

[95] Re *V (Abduction: Habitual Residence)* [1995] 2 FLR 992.

[96] Re *M (Abduction: Habitual Residence)* [1996] 1 FLR 887 CA; *Moran* v. *Moran* 1997 SLT 541.

[97] Re *M (Minors) (Residence Order: Jurisdiction)* [1993] 1 FLR 495 CA; Re *G (A Minor) (Enforcement of Access Abroad)* [1993] Fam. 216 CA.

[98] Re *A (Minors) (Abduction: Habitual Residence)* [1996] 1 WLR 25.

[99] Re *M (Abduction: Habitual Residence)* [1996] 1 FLR 887 CA.

[100] Re *K (Abduction: Consent: Forum Conveniens)* [1995] 2 FLR 211 CA; one parent may acquiesce (see Re *F (A Minor) (Child Abduction)* [1992] 1 FLR 548 CA).

child's habitual residence.[101] If one parent has lawful custody his or her habitual residence is also that of the child.[102] If the child is made a ward of court, the court's consent is needed to change the child's habitual residence.[103] This habitual residence 'of dependence', like that of domicile, probably ceases at the age of sixteen.

Companies

Status and domicile

The personal law of a company is that of its domicile, which means the law of the place of its incorporation.[104] To this it owes its existence, and that law governs also its dissolution[105] and its capacity to contract. The law of the place of incorporation dictates who can sue (or cause it to sue) and be sued on its behalf,[106] and governs the extent to which a member can be personally liable for its debts.[107] It also governs its status after an amalgamation.

In *National Bank of Greece and Athens SA* v. *Metliss*[108]

> Sterling mortgage bonds governed by English law were issued by a Greek bank in 1927 and guaranteed by the National Bank of Greece, a Greek bank. In 1941 payment of interest on the bonds ceased. In 1949 the Greek Government passed a moratorium extinguishing liability on the bonds. In 1953 another Greek decree amalgamated the National Bank with the Bank of Athens into a new bank, the National Bank of Greece and Athens, which the decree declared to be the 'universal successor' of the two banks. In 1955 a bondholder claimed arrears of interest from the new bank.

The House of Lords held that he could do so, since the status of the new bank and the effects thereof were governed by Greek law. The

---

[101] Re *F (A Minor) (Child Abduction)* [1992] 1 FLR 548 CA.

[102] Re *J (A Minor) (Abduction: Custody Rights)* [1990] 2 AC 562 HL; Re *M (Minors) (Residence Order: Jurisdiction)* [1993] 1 FLR 495 CA in which case it was said that lawful custody means the child being in physical care of the parent.

[103] Re *B-M (Wardship Jurisdiction)* [1993] 1 FLR 979; Re *B (A Minor) (Abduction: Father's Rights)* [1999] Fam. 1.

[104] *Gasque* v. *IRC* [1940] 2 KB 80. A company registered in England, Wales or Scotland cannot change its domicile since it cannot alter its place of registration. For domicile under the Civil Jurisdiction and Judgments Act 1982, see pp. 138–9 below.

[105] *Lazard Brothers* v. *Midland Bank* [1933] AC 289 HL. Winding up of foreign companies in England will not be dealt with here.

[106] *Bank of Ethiopia* v. *National Bank of Egypt and Liguori* [1937] Ch. 413; *Banco de Bilbao* v. *Sancha* [1938] 2 KB 176 CA; *Carl Zeiss Stiftung* v. *Rayner & Keeler Ltd* (No. 2) [1967] 1 AC 853 HL.

[107] *Risdon Iron and Locomotive Works* v. *Furness* [1906] 1 KB 49 CA.

[108] [1958] AC 509 HL.

moratorium law was said not to have affected the old bank's liability since that was a matter for the proper law of the contract, English law. Subsequently, a decree provided that this status should not carry with it liability under the bonds. But the House of Lords held that this affected the obligations thereunder, and since these were governed by English law the new Greek decree was irrelevant. (It was also said that if it had affected status, it would be disregarded in so far as it was meant to have retrospective effect.)[109]

Residence

The residence of a company, which is chiefly important for tax purposes, is determined not by the place of its incorporation, but by where its 'central management and control' is exercised.[110]

Thus in *De Beers Consolidated Mines* v. *Howe*[111]

> A diamond company was incorporated in South Africa and had a head office there. A board of directors there handled day-to-day adminis-trative matters. Another board in London, which joined with that in South Africa in making major policy decisions, in fact controlled them because most of the directors lived in London. Meetings of members and mining operations and sales of diamonds took place in South Africa.

The House of Lords held that the company should be assessed for tax as resident in the United Kingdom, since the central management and control was actually exercised there, where it 'kept house and did busi-ness'. In *Egyptian Delta Land & Investment Co.* v. *Todd*,[112] where the company simply maintained in England an office, a register of members and a local secretary to comply with minimum legal requirements, but its active secretary, directors, seals, books and bank account were all in Cairo, it was held to be resident in Egypt. It is, for this purpose, irrelevant where the central management and control should be exercised under the company's constitution, if it is, in fact, exercised elsewhere, as in the case of foreign subsidiaries who were held to be resident in England since they were wholly controlled by their English holding company.[113]

If the test is 'central management and control' it is difficult to see how this can be in more than one country. But such was held to be the case in *Swedish Central Railway Co. Ltd* v. *Thompson*,[114] and Lord

---

[109] *Adams* v. *National Bank of Greece and Athens SA* [1961] AC 255 HL.
[110] *Cesena Sulphur Co.* v. *Nicholson* (1876) 1 Ex. D 428.
[111] [1906] AC 455 HL.   [112] [1929] AC 1 HL.
[113] *Unit Construction Co. Ltd* v. *Bullock* [1960] AC 351 HL.   [114] [1925] AC 295 HL.

Radcliffe said in *Unit Construction Co. Ltd* v. *Bullock*[115] that this might be true where it is impossible to identify one country or the control is 'peripatetic'.

It should be noted that the test of residence may be different for a different purpose, for example enemy character, and the test stated above is not the test of residence for jurisdictional purposes.[116]

Nationality of a company is determined by the law of the place of incorporation.[117]

[115] [1960] AC 351 HL. He was not very happy with the *Swedish Central Railway* case.
[116] See pp. 82–3 and 112–13 below.
[117] Nationality is unimportant in the conflict of laws. The law of the place of incorporation is the national law of a company for the purposes of public international law. See *Barcelona Traction Power & Light Co. Case*, ICJ (1970), 3.

6   Substance and procedure

Matters of procedure are governed by the *lex fori*, English law, whatever be the *lex causae*, for example, the French governing law of a contract. Whether a question is procedural or substantive has presented difficulties of classification, as has the question of whether a foreign rule of law affects procedure or substance. It is easy enough to state that substantive issues are those which concern the existence of a right whereas procedural issues are those which concern the method and means of enforcement of a right. But acute difficulties may be encountered in deciding whether even an English rule is procedural or substantive. Thus, in *Chaplin* v. *Boys*[1] the majority of the House of Lords regarded the question whether a victim of the tort of negligence could recover damages for pain and suffering as concerned with remoteness of damage, whereas the minority appeared to think that it was a question of quantification of damages. Remoteness is a question of substance, quantification one of procedure.

Matters have been made worse by the almost inveterate habit of English judges of classifying questions and rules of law as procedural,[2] so leading them to apply English law. In one context the result led to such difficulties that Parliament intervened.[3]

In what follows, three topics will be discussed in some detail: (a) evidence, (b) limitation of actions and (c) remedies. Two others, (d) priorities and (e) parties to an action, will be mentioned briefly.

Evidence

Questions of evidence, such as what has to be proved, how it may be proved, and the sufficiency of proof, are clearly procedural. The same is true of the burden of proof. In Re *Fuld* (No. 3),[4] three codicils to a will

---

[1] [1971] AC 356.

[2] But see *Chaplin* v. *Boys* and Re *Cohn* [1945] Ch. 5, where a different approach was adopted.

[3] Foreign Limitation Periods Act 1984.   [4] [1968] P 675.

executed by a testator who died domiciled in Germany were challenged
on the ground that he lacked testamentary capacity because of illness, and
that he did not 'know and approve' of their contents. Scarman J held
that whether illness affected capacity was a matter for German law, the
lex causae, but that, the burden of proof being a procedural matter, the
English rule to the effect that in cases of doubt 'knowledge and approval'
must be affirmatively demonstrated to have existed must be applied.

But this question is complicated by the existence of presumptions in
English and foreign laws. These may be presumptions of law, which are
either irrebuttable, as until 1993 that a boy under the age of fourteen is
incapable of sexual intercourse,[5] or rebuttable, as is that of legitimacy.
Or they may be presumptions of fact, such as the presumption of sanity.
It is obvious that some presumptions, such as the one concerning a boy
under fourteen, are substantive in effect since their application determines
the outcome of the case. In one case this view led to conflicting English
and German presumptions both being classified as substantive and the
latter, which formed part of the *lex causae*, was applied. In Re *Cohn*[6]

> A mother and daughter, both domiciled in Germany, were killed to-
> gether in an air raid on London and it was impossible to determine for
> the purpose of deciding a question of entitlement to the mother's
> estate, which died first. By English law,[7] the mother, being older, was
> presumed to have died first, by German they were presumed to have
> died simultaneously.

It was held that, though the method of proof was a matter of procedure, this was of no use when it was impossible to decide who died first.
The issue was really substantive, and German law as the *lex causae*
applied.

The Rome Convention on the Law Applicable to Contractual Obligations (1980) does not apply to evidence (Art. 1(2)(b)). But Article 14
provides that the contract's applicable law, not the *lex fori*, governs, to
the extent that it contains, *in the law of contract*, rules which raise
presumptions of fact or determine the burden of proof. Though some
foreign laws of contract may contain such rules, there appear to be
none in the English law of contract.

As respects the manner of proof, such as whether written evidence is
required,[8] this was held in the old and much criticised decision in

---

[5] This was only true of the criminal law; it did not apply in civil cases.
[6] [1945] Ch. 5.   [7] Law of Property Act 1925, s. 184.
[8] This is of much less importance than it used to be since English law now only requires
written evidence of declarations of trusts of land (*ibid.* s. 53(1)(b)) and contracts of
guarantee (Statute of Frauds 1677, s. 4).

Leroux v. *Brown*[9] to be a question of procedure and so governed by English law.

> By an oral agreement made in France an English resident agreed to employ the plaintiff, a French resident, in France for more than a year. The contract was valid and enforceable by its French proper law, but though valid was not enforceable by English law since it was not evidenced by writing as required by the Statute of Frauds 1677.[10]

The court, influenced by the fact that the relevant English statutory provision began with the words 'no action shall be brought', held that the issue and the English rule were procedural, that the latter applied and that the contract could not be enforced. This decision has been attacked[11] on the grounds that the issue was effectively one of substance since it made no difference whether the contract was invalid or only unenforceable – the claimant lost either way – and that the English rule could have been outflanked if the claimant had either done some act in part performance of the contract or recovered judgment in France and then enforced that judgment in England. The case was not followed in California.[12]

It seems that *Leroux* v. *Brown* would now be decided differently. The Rome Convention, 1980, Article 14(2) provides that a contract may be decided by the methods of English law or by those of the applicable law or by those of the law of the place of contracting. It needs only to apply the last two types of rule if it can administer them. Suppose that a guarantee is governed by French law or was given in France, and French law treats a verbal guarantee as valid and allows it to be proved by oral evidence. Since English courts can obviously hear oral evidence, they must admit such testimony of the guarantee.

---

[9] (1852) 12 CB 801.
[10] Since the Law Reform (Enforcement of Contracts) Act 1954, such a contract is no longer required to be evidenced in writing.
[11] It was criticised by Willes J in two cases, but apparently approved by the House of Lords in *Morris* v. *Baron & Co.* [1918] AC 1. It was recently approved by the Court of Appeal in *Irvani* v. *G. and H. Montage GmbH* [1990] 1 WLR 667 CA. In *Mahadervan* v. *Mahadervan* [1964] P 233, the conclusiveness of a foreign certificate of marriage was treated as a question of substance. In *Monterosso Co. Ltd* v. *International Transport Workers' Federation* [1982] 3 All ER 841 CA, it was held that a requirement of the Trade Union and Labour Relations Act 1974, s. 18 that a collective agreement should be conclusively presumed not to have been intended to be a legally enforceable contract unless it stated that the parties intended it to be so was a matter of substance and, since the agreement in question was not governed by English law, the requirement did not apply.
[12] *Bernkrant* v. *Fowler* 55 Cal. 2d 588 (1961).

Whether particular evidence is admissible, as for example, an unstamped document,[13] or a copy of a foreign document,[14] or whether oral evidence may be introduced to vary, add to or contradict a written document,[15] is a question of procedure. But whether oral evidence is admissible in order to interpret a written document is a matter of substance and so governed by the *lex causae*.[16]

Limitation of actions

Rules governing the period of time during which an action must be brought are, in legal systems generally, of two kinds: first, those which merely bar the action, which are procedural; second, those which extinguish the plaintiff's rights, which are substantive. Most English rules are of the first type.[17] Moreover the English courts have almost always regarded a rule of foreign law in the same light, usually in reliance upon its literal wording.[18] The result has been that the English rule has almost always been applied. Many foreign systems regard their own limitation rules as substantive, and the conflict of characterisation can lead to undesirable results, especially where an action abroad has been dismissed on the ground that a limitation period has expired, but an English action is allowed to continue.[19]

The Law Commission criticised the existing law in 1982[20] and its recommendations were enacted in the Foreign Limitation Periods Act 1984.[21] The matter is also dealt with as regards actions on contracts by Article 10(1)(d) of the Rome Convention, 1980 which states that prescription and limitation of actions are governed by the contract's

---

[13] *Bristow* v. *Sequeville* (1850) 5 Exch. 275. It is otherwise if the foreign law renders an unstamped document a nullity: *Alves* v. *Hodgson* (1797) 7 TR 241.

[14] *Brown* v. *Thornton* (1827) 6 Ad. & E 185.

[15] *Korner* v. *Witkowitzer* [1950] 2 KB 128 CA (this type of evidence is usually inadmissible in an English court by virtue of the so-called parol evidence rule).

[16] *St Pierre* v. *South American Stores Ltd* [1937] 1 All ER 206; 3 All ER 349 CA.

[17] See Limitation Act 1980. Exceptions are s. 3 (conversion of goods) and s. 17 (land) where title is extinguished. Where a statute such as the Fatal Accidents Act 1976 creates a right of action and prescribes a period for bringing it, the rule is one of substance: see *McElroy* v. *McAllister* 1949 SC 110.

[18] See, for example, *Huber* v. *Steiner* (1835) 2 Bing. NC 202.

[19] See *Harris* v. *Quine* (1869) LR 4 QB 653, and *Black-Clawson International Ltd* v. *Papierwerke-Waldhof Aschaffenburg A/G* [1975] AC 591 HL (where the German court regarded the German rule as one of substance). See p. 129 below.

[20] Report no. 114 (1982).

[21] For a commentary, see P. B. Carter, 'The Foreign Limitation Periods Act 1984' (1985) 101 *LQR* 68–78.

applicable law. The Act provides that all limitation periods,[22] both English and foreign, and whether the latter are classified as substantive or procedural by the foreign courts, should be classified as substantive so that the foreign rule would be applied.[23] But this would not prevent the court refusing in its discretion to apply the foreign rule on the ground of public policy,[24] or where its application would cause undue hardship.[25] Any extension of the limitation period allowed under the foreign law is to be given effect except where it is extended because of either party's absence from the jurisdiction;[26] otherwise, if a party were to stay out of that jurisdiction permanently, the case would never be decided. A foreign judgment on a limitation point is now regarded as a judgment on the merits and so provides a good defence to a further action here on the same cause of action.[27]

Remedies

A claimant can only obtain English remedies and so cannot obtain a remedy which exists by the *lex causae* but not in English law. He can, however, obtain a remedy available under English law but not by the *lex causae*. Thus, a decree of specific performance might be awarded, though this is not obtainable in the courts of the country whose law governs the contract. But the claimant will not be granted an English remedy if this would effectively alter the right he has acquired by the foreign law.[28]

Article 10(1)(c) of the Rome Convention, 1980 states that the applicable law governs the consequences of breach of a contract, but within the limits of the powers conferred on the court by English procedural law. This may ensure that the applicable law decides, for example, whether the innocent party can rescind the contract on account of its

---

[22] As defined in s. 4.
[23] S. 1(1). *Renvoi* is excluded: s. 1(5). The Law Commission also recommended that the effect given by our courts to the foreign rule should be that given to it by the foreign courts, i.e. whether it bars the remedy or extinguishes the right. This is not mentioned in the Act.
[24] S. 2(1) and (2).
[25] S. 2(2), which was applied in *Jones* v. *Trollope and Colls Cementation Overseas Ltd* (1990) *The Times*, 26 January and at first instance in *The Komninos S* [1990] 1 Ll.R 541 (*revd* on other grounds: [1991] 1 Ll.R 370 CA) but not in *Arab Monetary Fund* v. *Hashim* [1993] 1 Ll.R 543.
[26] S. 2(3).
[27] S. 3. Thus *Harris* v. *Quine* (1869) LR 4 QB 653 and *Black-Clawson International Ltd* v. *Papierwerke-Waldhof Aschaffenburg A/G* [1975] AC 591 HL are no longer law. The Act applies to arbitrations (s. 5) and to the Crown (s. 6).
[28] *Phrantzes* v. *Argenti* [1960] 2 QB 19.

breach. It may also encourage the court to refer the availability of a remedy such as specific performance to that law. But it need not grant specific performance if, in the circumstances, English law does not permit it to do so.

In respect of damages, two questions must be distinguished. These are (i) remoteness of damage, or for what types of damage can the claimant recover? which is a question of substance, and (ii) measurement or quantification of damages, which is a procedural matter. The former is governed by the *lex causae*, the latter by the *lex fori*. In contract, the position can be illustrated by sub-contract losses; in general these are not recoverable under English law.[29] This is a matter of remoteness of damage, and if, as in *D'Almeida Araujo* v. *Sir Frederick Becker & Co. Ltd*,[30] damages are recoverable under the (Portuguese) proper law, they will be awarded by the English court. How much money the claimant will receive in respect of such losses depends on English law exclusively. The same is true of damages in tort. So, whether damages for pain and suffering[31] or damages for loss of expectation of life[32] are recoverable is for the *lex causae* to determine. How much can be awarded for these is a matter for the *lex fori*.[33] However, Article 10(1)(c) of the Rome Convention, 1980 provides that the applicable law determines *the assessment of damages for breach of contract* so far as it is governed by rules of law which, of course, it is.

Until 1975, the English courts could only award damages in sterling,[34] and even if the proper law of the contract was foreign and the money of account and the money of payment were in foreign currency, the damages had to be converted into sterling. The rate of conversion was the exchange rate at the date of breach of contract or when the debt was payable or when a loss was suffered by means of a tort being committed.[35] This 'breach date' rule, as opposed to the 'judgment date' rule, resulted during the early and mid-1970s, when the pound suffered a catastrophic fall in value, in injustice to foreign creditors, who saw the real value of the debt they were owed or the damages they were entitled to decline considerably between the date of breach and the date of

---

[29] *Williams Bros.* v. *ET Agius Ltd* [1914] AC 510 HL. But if the sub-sale was in the contemplation of the parties it may be taken into account: Re *Hall (R & H)* v. *WH Pim Jr* (1928) 139 LT 50.

[30] [1953] 2 QB 329.   [31] See *Chaplin* v. *Boys* [1971] AC 356 HL.

[32] These were abolished in English law by the Administration of Justice Act 1982.

[33] See *Kohnke* v. *Karger* [1951] 2 KB 670.

[34] *Manners* v. *Pearson* [1898] 1 Ch. 581, 593 CA; *Tomkinson* v. *First Pennsylvania Banking & Trust Co.* [1961] AC 1007 HL.

[35] See, for example, *SS Celia* v. *SS Volturno* [1921] 2 AC 544 HL (tort).

judgment, which might be years later. By a revolution engineered mainly by Lord Denning MR[36] in a case in which the Court of Appeal disregarded the precedents, for which it was castigated by the House of Lords, the House of Lords itself reversed the old law and held that in certain cases the English courts could give judgment in foreign currency.[37] This would only have to be converted into sterling if the judgment required enforcement, in which case the conversion would take place at the date at which enforcement is sought.

This case, *Miliangos* v. *George Frank*,[38] concerned an action for a debt arising out of a contract whose foreign proper law was that of the country in whose currency judgment was requested. But the new rule was extended to cover a claim on a bill of exchange[39] and to damages for breach of contract.[40] It was further extended to cases of contract where the governing law was English law, and to tort, in cases[41] in which it was held that the claimant may recover in the currency in which his loss was effectively felt, having regard to the currency in which he normally operates or with which he has the closest connection; failing any evidence of which, it would be the currency in which the loss was incurred. The rule has also been applied to, for example, garnishee orders,[42] claims against a company in liquidation[43] and claims for restitution.[44]

The method of execution, for example, whether attachment of a debt or execution on land or goods is available, is determined by the *lex fori*.[45]

---

[36] The first shots were fired when the Court of Appeal held in 1973 that an arbitrator could make an award in foreign currency: *Jugoslavenska Oceanska Plovidba* v. *Castle Investment Co.* (The Kezara) [1974] QB 292 CA.

[37] *Schorsch Meier GmbH* v. *Hennin* [1975] QB 416. In *The Halcyon the Great* [1975] 1 Ll.R 515 it was held that the Admiralty Marshal could sell a ship for dollars.

[38] [1976] AC 443. The whole episode concerns the doctrine of precedent rather than the conflict of laws.

[39] *Barclays Bank International* v. *Levin Bros. (Bradford) Ltd* [1977] QB 270. Certain provisions of the Bills of Exchange Act 1882, which were in issue in that case, were repealed by the Administration of Justice Act 1977, s. 4.

[40] *Kraut (Jean) A/G* v. *Albany Fabrics Ltd* [1977] QB 182.

[41] *Services Europe Atlantique Sud* v. *Stockholms Rederiaktiebolaget Svea*; *The Folias* and *The Despina R* [1979] AC 685; see also *Société Française Bunge SA* v. *Belcan NV* [1985] 3 All ER 378.

[42] *Choice Investments* v. *Jeromnimon* [1981] QB 149.

[43] Converted as at the date of the winding-up order: Re *Dynamics Corporation of America* [1976] 1 WLR 757.

[44] *BP Exploration Co. (Libya) Ltd* v. *Hunt* (No. 2) [1979] 1 WLR 783 at 840–1; [1981] 1 WLR 232 CA. With respect to interest see *Miliangos* v. *George Frank (Textiles) Ltd* (No. 2) [1977] QB 489.

[45] See *de la Vega* v. *Vianna* (1830) 1 B & Ad. 284.

Priorities

The question of what law governs the priority of assignments of single debts or other interests will be discussed later.[46] In the case of priorities of claims against funds administered by an English court, such as winding up, bankruptcy and administration of insolvent estates, it is clear that English law as the *lex fori* orders priorities.[47] The same is true of claims against a ship when the court is exercising its Admiralty jurisdiction.[48] Thus, in *The Tagus*:[49]

> Claims were brought against an Argentine ship. The master claimed a lien for wages and disbursements on several voyages. Under Argentine law he only had priority for the lien for the last voyage; under English law this extended to all voyages.

It was held that the English rule applied.

In this case and *The Zigurds*[50] the interest which arose under the foreign law was one with which English law was familiar. If it is not, the foreign law governing the transaction under which one of the competing interests arose will have to be consulted to ascertain what the interest amounts to, but English law will determine whether it amounts to a maritime lien and what its priority will be. Thus, in *The Halcyon Isle*:[51]

> An English bank was the mortgagee of a ship. She was repaired in New York. By New York law the repairers had a maritime lien for the price of the repairs. The ship left New York and arrived in Singapore where the mortgagees arrested her. She was sold by court order.

The Privy Council held that the mortgagees had priority over the New York repairers or 'necessaries men'. These may have had a maritime lien under New York law, but had none by the *lex fori* (Singapore) which determined what classes of events gave rise to a maritime lien and priority between such liens.[52]

Priority of claims against foreign land is presumably governed by the *lex situs*.[53]

---

[46] See pp. 257–9, 261 below.   [47] Re *Kloebe* (1884) 28 Ch. D 175.
[48] *The Milford* (1858) Swa. 362.
[49] [1903] P 44. This decision is criticised in G. C. Cheshire and P. M. North, *Private International Law*, 13th edn (London, Butterworths, 1999), 83.
[50] [1932] P 113.   [51] [1981] AC 221 PC.
[52] The majority (Lords Diplock, Elwyn-Jones and Lane) said that the decision of the Supreme Court of Canada to the contrary in *The Ioannis Daskalelis* [1974] 1 Ll.R 174 was based on a misunderstanding of *The Colorado* [1923] P 102 CA. Lords Salmon and Scarman supported the Supreme Court's understanding of *The Colorado* and effectively described the judgment of the majority as a breach of the comity of nations and natural justice and a denial of private international law.
[53] *Norton* v. *Florence Land and Public Works Co.* (1877) 7 Ch. D 332.

Parties

A question may arise as to whether a party is a proper plaintiff in, or a proper defendant to, an action. Is this procedural or substantive?

An example of this is to be found in the law of assignments of intangibles (choses in action). In English law an equitable assignor or assignee must join the other as a party but a statutory assignor or assignee need not do so. In the case of an equitable assignee is this a procedural requirement? If so, it applies even though it is not required by the *lex causae*. If it is substantive, it does. In one early case,[54] it seems to have been governed by the *lex fori*, but this was also the *lex causae*. In another, which concerned an assignment of an Irish judgment debt, it was held to be substantive and the claimant could sue in his own name since Irish law allowed this.[55]

Another example is a requirement of some systems that if X is a member of a firm, the firm's creditors cannot sue him without having sued the firm first, and that a surety or guarantor cannot be sued before the principal debtor. (This is the converse of English law.) If (a) the *lex causae* regards him as under no liability until the firm or principal is sued, this is substantive and its rule applies; if (b) he is liable thereunder but can only be sued after all other remedies have been exhausted, this is procedural and is ignored. This distinction was drawn in *General Steam Navigation* v. *Goulliou*,[56] but the court was equally divided as to whether the French law was of type (a) or (b).

---

[54] *Wolff* v. *Oxholm* (1817) 6 M & S 92.
[55] *O'Callaghan* v. *Thomond* (1810) 3 Taunt. 82.
[56] (1843) 11 M & W 877. A Spanish rule was held to be of type (b) and inapplicable in Re *Doetsch* [1896] 2 Ch. 836.

Part II

Jurisdiction and foreign judgments

7 Jurisdiction of the English courts

'Jurisdiction' means the competence of the courts to hear and decide a case. For the purpose of determining the jurisdiction of the English courts, actions are of two kinds.

(i) Actions *in personam*: these are actions brought to compel a defendant to do or to refrain from doing something or to pay damages. Jurisdiction over such actions depends primarily, though not exclusively, on the defendant's presence in England. This chapter is mainly concerned with actions *in personam*.

(ii) Actions *in rem*: these are actions against ships and aircraft when jurisdiction depends upon the presence of the ship or aircraft in England.

It should be added that, in some cases, such as divorce or nullity of marriage, sometimes called 'actions *quasi in rem*' since they involve determination of personal status, jurisdiction is entirely statutory. These are dealt with separately.

Jurisdiction in actions *in personam*

In such actions, including actions in contract and tort and those respecting property other than ships and aircraft, jurisdiction may, in cases where the defendant is not present in England when the action is started, be acquired if the defendant submits to the jurisdiction and, in some situations, where the court allows him to be served with a claim form.

The Civil Jurisdiction and Judgments Act 1982, which incorporates into United Kingdom law the EC Convention on Jurisdiction and Enforcement of Judgments in Civil and Commercial Matters, 1968 (known as the Brussels Convention), enacted distinct rules governing jurisdiction in cases concerning such matters where the defendant is domiciled in a member state of the EU, as well as rules governing jurisdiction over defendants domiciled in other parts of the United Kingdom. The Civil Jurisdiction and Judgments Act 1991 enacts into United Kingdom law the parallel Convention of 1989 with countries which are members of the European Free Trade Area (the Lugano Convention). There are thus four sets of rules, respecting (i) EU domiciliaries, (ii) EFTA domiciliaries, (iii) domiciliaries of the United Kingdom, and (iv) the rest of the world's population.[1]

The first three of these will be dealt with later;[2] here we are only concerned with the fourth and last.

Presence

If the defendant is in England when he is served with a claim form or equivalent document the courts have jurisdiction;[3] if he is not, then (generally) they have none.[4]

It matters not that the defendant is only here as a casual traveller or for a few hours or minutes, provided that he has not been tricked or kidnapped into coming here.

Thus in *Colt Industries* v. *Sarlie* (No. 1)[5]

> A New York company got a judgment in New York against a Frenchman and sought to enforce it in England. Process was served on him at a London hotel where he was staying for one night.

It was held that the court had jurisdiction over him.

The same was true in the rather exotic case of *Maharanee of Baroda* v. *Wildenstein*[6]

> The Maharanee lived in Paris as did M. Wildenstein. They were both members of the 'international set' and shared interests in fine art and racehorses. The Maharanee had bought from M. Wildenstein at Sotheby's a painting described in the sale catalogue as 'La Poésie' by Boucher, 'a girl in pale blue and white drapery reclining, holding a book and a lyre'. She learned that it was probably a copy and worth much less than she had paid for it. She took out a writ in England, claiming rescission of the contract and repayment of the price, and within a year had it served on the defendant when he had come over from France on a short visit, at Ascot races.

---

[1] There rules will continue to apply to EU, EFTA and UK domiciliaries in so far as the case falls outside the statutory provisions.

[2] See ch. 10 below.   [3] For the position with respect to companies see pp. 82–3 below.

[4] The courts may permit service by an alternative method (formerly substituted service) if the defendant was here but went abroad to evade service. CPR Rule 6.8. See *Porter* v. *Freudenberg* [1916] 1 KB 857 CA; *Laurie* v. *Carroll* (1958) 98 CLR 310; *Myerson* v. *Martin* [1979] 1 WLR 1390 CA.

[5] [1966] 1 WLR 440.   [6] [1972] 2 QB 283 CA.

The court clearly had jurisdiction; the contrary was not argued (it was being asked to stay the action). Both in taking out the writ and in serving it the Maharanee was doing no more than our law permits, even though it may have ruined M. Wildenstein's day at the races. 'Some might regard her action as bad form; none can legitimately condemn it as an abuse of the legal process', said Edmund Davies LJ.

The principle is often criticised as 'exorbitant' and it is sometimes suggested that residence rather than mere presence should be required. It is expressly suppressed as regards EU and UK domiciliaries by the Civil Jurisdiction Act 1982 and the Brussels Convention.[7] But three points may be made: (i) it has the virtue of simplicity – it is obvious if a person is here, but it is not so obvious where he is resident or domiciled; (ii) its harshness, if it has that quality, can be tempered by the court exercising its discretion to stay the action if it thinks it should more properly have been brought elsewhere;[8] (iii) the two cases which have been discussed were both out of the ordinary. Mr Sarlie was served in consequence of a nice piece of detective work. M. Wildenstein's racing habits were perfectly well known to the Maharanee, and she and her advisers knew that he could often be found at an English racecourse. How many claimants know when a potential defendant has arrived for a short visit here?

Service of a claim form on a defendant who has been tricked into coming within the jurisdiction or who has been brought here after being kidnapped will, however, be set aside.[9]

Submission

An absent defendant may confer jurisdiction on the court by submission. This may arise from express agreement or from conduct.[10] There are four possibilities:

(a) *The defendant accepts service of process.* This occurs where he instructs an English solicitor to accept service on his behalf and has notified in writing the party serving the claim form,[11] or where he acknowledges service without applying to the court to decide that it has no jurisdiction.[12]

---

[7] Art. 3.
[8] For staying of actions see ch. 8 below. In the *Baroda* case, the Court of Appeal removed a stay imposed by Bridge J.
[9] *Watkins* v. *North American Lands etc. Co.* (1904) 20 TLR 530 HL.
[10] Submission cannot confer jurisdiction on a court to entertain proceedings which are beyond its competence under English law: for example, in divorce cases or those concerning nullity of marriage and actions which raise the question of title to foreign land.
[11] CPR Rule 6.4(2); in principle, service must be on the solicitor.   [12] CPR Rule 11.5.

(b) *The defendant pleads to the merits.* If the defendant pleads to the merits of the case, such as by disputing liability for breach of contract, he thereby submits, but not if he merely argues that the court has no jurisdiction over him.[13] But a defendant who requests the court to stay the action is taken to have submitted, since he impliedly admits that jurisdiction exists.[14] But if, at the same time as he asks for a stay pending the outcome of proceedings abroad, he also argues that the court lacks jurisdiction, he does not submit.[15] Moreover, a defendant who challenges the issue of an interim injunction to restrain him from removing his assets out of England (a freezing injunction) is not taken to have submitted to the jurisdiction any further.[16]

(c) *The defendant contracts to submit.* Where a contract contains a term providing that, in the event of a claim being issued in relation to the contract, the claim form may be served by a method specified in the contract and a claim form containing only a claim in respect of that contract is issued, the claim form is deemed to be served on the defendant if it is served by such a method.[17] If no such provision for service is included, and the defendant is abroad, the court may permit service on him in its discretion.[18]

(d) *A claimant who is abroad sues a defendant here.* This gives the court jurisdiction over a counterclaim by the defendant if it arises out of a matter which is related to the claim, but not if it is unrelated to it.[19]

Extended jurisdiction by service abroad

The Civil Procedure Rules, Rule 6.20 gives authority to the court to assume jurisdiction over absent defendants in certain specified situations by permitting the service of claim forms on them.[20] In applying for

---

[13] CPR Rule 11. Re *Dulles' Settlement* (No. 2) [1951] Ch. 842 CA, though in *Henry* v. *Geoprosco International Ltd* [1976] QB 726 CA, which concerned a foreign judgment, it was thought the defendant in Re *Dulles' Settlement* (No. 2) had submitted in another way.

[14] *The Messianiki Tolmi* [1984] 1 Ll.R 266 CA. An application for discovery of documents is inconsistent with an appearance solely to contest the jurisdiction and so amounts to a submission: *Caltex Trading Pty Ltd* v. *Metro Trading International Inc.* [2000] 1 All ER (Comm.) 108.

[15] *Williams & Glyn's Bank* v. *Astro Dinamico* [1984] 1 WLR 438 HL.

[16] *Obikoya* v. *Silvernorth* (1983) *The Times*, 6 July.

[17] CPR Rule 6.15(1). See *Manta Lines Inc.* v. *Sofianites* [1984] 1 Ll.R 14 CA.

[18] Under CPR Rule 6.20(5)(d), p. 79 below. If the claim falls within the Brussels or Lugano Conventions (see ch. 10 below) the claim form may be served out of the jurisdiction without need for permission: *ibid.* Rule 6.19. See p. 133 below.

[19] See *United Bank of the Middle East* v. *Clapham* (1981) *The Times*, 20 July CA.

[20] The present rules came into force in 2000 and replace the former RSC Order 11 rule 1(i).

permission to serve a claim form out of the jurisdiction the claimant must produce written evidence to the effect, *inter alia*, that he believes the claim has a reasonable prospect of success.[21] In *Seaconsar Far East Ltd* v. *Bank Markazi Jomhouri Islami Iran*[22] the House of Lords held that, as to the merits of the claim, the claimant needs to show only that there is a serious issue which he wishes to be tried.

The court has full discretion to permit or refuse to permit service out of the jurisdiction. The factors which it should take into account have been enunciated in a number of cases.[23] These are: (1) the court should be 'exceedingly careful' before it allows the writ to be served abroad; (2) any doubt as to the construction of the rule should be resolved in the defendant's favour; (3) the claimant should make 'full and fair' disclosure in the written evidence given in support of his application for permission, since this is made without notice; (4) permission should be refused if the case is within the letter, but not within the spirit, of the rules; (5) the court should consider whether it is or is not the appropriate forum. *Forum conveniens* in this context was the subject of the important decision of the House of Lords in *Spiliada Maritime Corporation* v. *Cansulex Ltd (The Spiliada)*,[24] which will be discussed more fully in the next chapter.[25] It has always been relevant to applications for leave to serve out of the jurisdiction under the former RSC Order 11. The claimant always had to show that the English court is the suitable one for trial of the action; it is now made clear by CPR Rule 6.21 (2A) that '[t]he court will not give permission unless satisfied that England and Wales is the proper place in which to bring the claim'. Also, the court should lean against assuming jurisdiction where the claimant has agreed to submit to the jurisdiction of a foreign tribunal. For example, leave was refused in *Mackender* v. *Feldia*.[26] In that case Diplock LJ emphasised that this extended jurisdiction conflicts with the basic principle of comity.[27]

---

[21] CPR Rule 6.21(1)(b).   [22] [1994] 1 AC 438 HL.

[23] *The Hagen* [1908] P 109; *Rosler* v. *Hilbery* [1925] Ch. 250; *GAF Corporation* v. *Anchem Products Inc.* [1975] 1 Ll.R 601; *Qatar Petroleum* v. *Shell International Petroleum* [1983] 2 Ll.R 35 CA; with respect to (5) compare *Mauroux* v. *Pereira* [1972] 1 WLR 962 (permission refused), and *Cordoba Shipping Co.* v. *National State Bank NJ* [1984] 1 Ll.R 91 CA (permission granted).

[24] [1987] AC 460 HL.   [25] Pp. 87–90.

[26] [1967] 2 QB 590 CA. However, permission may be granted, particularly if the claimant wishes to sue defendants some of whom are here and some abroad, to avoid multiplicity of actions and inconsistent decisions. *Evans Marshall & Co. Ltd* v. *Bertola SA* [1973] 1 WLR 349; *Citi-March Ltd* v. *Neptune Orient Lines* [1996] 1 WLR 1367.

[27] In spite of a suggestion to the contrary by Denning LJ in Re *Dulles' Settlement* (No. 2) [1951] Ch. 842 CA, it is clear that the English courts would not recognise jurisdiction assumed by a foreign court. See *Amin Rasheed Shipping Corporation* v. *Kuwait Insurance Co.* [1984] AC 50 HL.

These factors were effectively restated in general terms by the House of Lords in *Amin Rasheed Shipping Corporation* v. *Kuwait Insurance Co.*,[28] where their Lordships held unanimously that English law governed a contract so that permission could be granted. Nevertheless, also unanimously, they refused permission to serve the defendant in Kuwait, since justice could equally well be done there.

The several grounds of the rule will now be examined, but it should be emphasised that the case may fall within more than one ground, so, although there may be some reason why permission cannot be granted under one ground, it may be granted under another.[29] The grounds are as follows:

(1) *Domicile*: if 'a claim is made for a remedy against a person domiciled within the jurisdiction' though he is abroad. Domicile here means not domicile in the normal sense, but in the sense in which it is defined and employed in the Civil Jurisdiction and Judgments Act 1982, sections 41–6.[30]

(2) *Injunction*: if an injunction is sought ordering the defendant to do or refrain from doing an act within the jurisdiction. The injunction must be the remedy which is really sought and must not be asked for solely to induce the court to assume jurisdiction as was the case in *Rosler* v. *Hilbery*.[31]

(3) *Necessary or proper party*: if a claim is made against someone on whom the claim form has been or will be served and (a) there is between the claimant and that person a real issue which it is reasonable for the court to try, and (b) the claimant wishes to serve the claim form on another person who is a necessary or proper party to that claim.[32]

    If D^1 has been or will be served,[33] either in England or under another head of CPR Rule 6.20, D^2 who is a 'necessary' or, though not necessary, is a 'proper' party[34] to the action may then be served. This is useful where the claimant wishes to sue alleged joint tortfeasors, or where he has one claim against one party and

---

[28] [1984] AC 50.

[29] For example, *Matthews* v. *Kuwait Bechtel Corporation* [1959] 2 QB 57 CA (leave not possible under the tort ground but possible under a contract ground).

[30] CPR Rule 6.18(g): see pp. 138–9 below.   [31] [1925] Ch. 250.

[32] This ground is also available where the claim is a CPR Part 20 claim, i.e. a counterclaim or claim for indemnity or contribution: *ibid.* Rule 6.20(3A).

[33] The words 'or will be' reverse the decision in *Kuwait Oil Tanker Co. SAK* v. *Al Bader* [1997] 1 WLR 1410 CA, which required that another defendant must already have been served.

[34] See *Qatar Petroleum* v. *Shell International Petroleum* [1983] 2 Ll.R 35 CA.

a different claim against another arising from the same transaction and D^2 cannot be served under another head.

If it is clear that the claim against D^1 is bound to fail, as where he could not possibly be liable and is a mere 'dummy', sued in order to get D^2 before the court, permission will not be given. Thus, in *Witted* v. *Galbraith*.[35]

> A ship belonging to D^2, a domiciled Scotsman, arrived in the Thames, where D^1, a London broker, had her unloaded. C's husband was killed during the unloading. C sued D^1 and tried to serve D^2 in Scotland.

C was refused permission, since D^1 could not possibly have been liable to C. On the other hand it seems that if D^1 *could* be liable to C, though he could not satisfy any judgment, being bankrupt or, if a company, in liquidation, D^2 may be served, even though the action against D^1 was brought for the predominant purpose of suing D^2.[36]

If there is no purpose in suing D^2 since full recovery is possible from D^1, the court may refuse permission to serve D^2.[37] D^2 is neither a necessary nor a proper party if he clearly has a defence to the claim.[38]

(4) *Interim remedies*: if a claim is made under the Civil Jurisdiction and Judgments Act 1982, s. 25(1).[39]

(5) *Contract*: if a claim is made in respect of a contract. This has four different subheads which are alternatives. Service may be permitted if a claim is made in respect of a contract in the following situations.

The contract may be one which

---

[35] [1893] 1 QB 577; *The Brabo* [1947] AC HL (D'immune).

[36] *Multinational Gas Co.* v. *Multinational Gas Services Ltd* [1983] Ch. 258 CA. Lawton LJ dissented. Presumably if C's *only* purpose is to serve D^2 leave will be refused.

[37] *Chaney* v. *Murphy* [1948] WN 130 CA. See also *Rosler* v. *Hilbery* [1925] Ch. 250.

[38] *Multinational Gas Co.* v. *Multinational Gas Services Ltd* [1983] Ch. 258 CA. (Lawton and Dillon LJJ. May LJ dissented on this point.)

[39] It was held in *The Siskina* [1979] AC 210 HL that where the claimant had no other cause of action in England and all that he sought was a 'Mareva' (now 'freezing') injunction to restrain the defendant from removing assets hence, permission could not be granted. This was reversed as regards cases in which proceedings have been started in a country which is a party to the Brussels or Lugano Conventions: Civil Jurisdiction and Judgments Act 1982, s. 25. However, *The Siskina* was followed in *Mercedes-Benz A/G* v. *Leiduck* [1996] AC 284 PC but these decisions were reversed by SI 1997 no. 302, made under the 1982 Act, s. 25(3), and the court now has power to grant interim relief under s. 25(1) in relation to proceedings commenced or to be commenced in countries which are not party to the Brussels or Lugano Conventions, though no proceedings are taking place in England.

(a) 'was made within the jurisdiction'.[40] Whether the contract was made here or abroad is decided by the English law of contract. If the offeror is here and the acceptance is received by him, the contract is made here. If communication of acceptance is by post and the English 'posting rule' applies, then if the letter of acceptance is posted in, say, New York, the contract is not made here. The 'posting rule' was not applied to acceptance by telex in two well-known cases. In *Entores* v. *Miles Far East Corporation*,[41] the claimant made an offer from England to the Netherlands by telex. The defendants in the Netherlands replied by a telex message which was received in England. The contract was made in England. In the converse situation in *Brinkibon* v. *Stahag Stahl GmbH*,[42] it was held to have been made outside England.

> The buyers were in England, the sellers in Austria. B made an offer to S by telex, S 'accepted' subject to modifications. S asked B to open a letter of credit under which S could receive payment through an Austrian bank. B opened the credit in London and sent a confirming telex to S. S then purported to withdraw.

It was held that S's telex was not an acceptance of B's offer but a counter-offer, so that his telex did not conclude a contract here. B's opening of the credit in London was not an acceptance of S's counter-offer. This was accepted by B's confirming telex which was received in Austria, so the contract was made there and B was refused permission to serve S.

(b) 'was made by or through an agent trading or residing within the jurisdiction'. The contract need not be concluded by the agent here (if it was it would fall under (a)). It is sufficient that the agent here was a means of communication to his principal abroad, who himself concluded the contract abroad.[43] The agent must have acted on behalf of the defendant. Permission cannot be granted to the claimant if the agent acted for him.[44]

---

[40] If the contract was made here but it contains a foreign jurisdiction clause leave will not usually be granted: *Mackender* v. *Feldia* [1967] 2 QB 590 CA.

[41] [1955] 2 QB 327 CA.   [42] [1983] 2 AC 34 HL.

[43] *National Mortgage and Agency Co. of New Zealand* v. *Gosselin* (1922) 38 TLR 832.

[44] *Union International Insurance Co. Ltd* v. *Jubilee Insurance Co. Ltd* [1991] 1 WLR 415. See also *Gill and Duffus Landauer Ltd* v. *London Export Corporation GmbH* [1982] 2 Ll.R 627 CA.

(c) 'is governed by English law'. That is to say that the contract, wherever made, has English law as its applicable law. There are many cases on the matter, which is fully discussed later in the chapter on contract.[45]

(d) 'contains a term to the effect that the court shall have jurisdiction to hear and determine any action in respect of the contract'. This is an example of submission, as previously explained.[46] It differs in one respect from the rest of CPR Rule 6.20. It appears that if permission is sought under this head the court does not have to be as cautious about permitting service as it does when requested under the other heads. In *Unterweser Reederei GmbH* v. *Zapata Offshore Co., The Chaparral*:[47]

> C, a German company, agreed to tow an oil rig of D, an American company, from Louisiana to Italy. The towage agreement quaintly referred all disputes to 'the London Court of Justice', which the English High Court took to refer to itself. The tug had to take refuge in a port in Florida. Each party alleged the other to have breached the agreement. D started an action *in rem* in Florida. C countered by suing D for damages in England and asked leave to serve D in the United States. Permission was granted, the court saying that it was its policy to hold parties to their agreements.

In *British Aerospace plc* v. *Dee Howard Co.*,[48] the court said that the proper approach in such a case is to regard the proceedings as being brought as of right.

(6) *Breach of contract*: 'if a claim is made in respect of a breach of contract committed within the jurisdiction'.

English law determines where the breach was committed.[49] An example is where X who is abroad sends his agent to England or

---

[45] See ch. 12 below; *Amin Rasheed Shipping Corporation* v. *Kuwait Insurance Co.* [1984] AC 50 HL (permission not granted). For other examples see *Coast Lines Ltd* v. *Hudig & Veder NV* [1972] 2 QB 34 CA; *Mauroux* v. *Pereira* [1972] 1 WLR 962; *BP Exploration Co. (Libya) Ltd* v. *Hunt* [1976] 1 WLR 788.

[46] See p. 74 above, CPR Rule 6.15.

[47] [1968] 2 Ll.R 158 CA. Proceedings in the United States were stayed by the Supreme Court.

[48] [1993] 1 Ll.R 368; see also *Standard SS Owners Protection Indemnity Association (Bermuda)* v. *Gann* [1992] 2 Ll.R 328.

[49] *Brinkibon Ltd* v. *Stahag Stahl GmbH* [1980] 2 Ll.R 556 CA: the court held that the repudiatory acts took place in Austria, so the breach of contract was not committed in England where the telex informing B of this was received. The House of Lords did not deal with the point.

writes to his agent here, telling him to repudiate a contract and he does so. Another is where X who is abroad employs C in England and terminates his employment here, even though the contract of employment is governed by a foreign law.[50]

(7) *Contract, negative declaration*: 'if a claim is made for a declaration that no contract exists where, if the contract was found to exist, it would comply with the conditions set out in (5)'.[51]

(8) *Tort*: 'if a claim is made in tort where *either* (a) the damage was sustained within the jurisdiction *or* (b) the damage sustained abroad resulted from an act committed within the jurisdiction'.

This replaces the provision in the Rules of the Supreme Court until 1983, which required that the tort should have been committed here. This caused many problems in determining whether the tort was committed in England,[52] but they have ceased to exist. This ground was first redrafted in 1983 in the light of the interpretation of the Brussels Convention, 1968, Article 5(3) (which gives jurisdiction to the courts of the state where the harmful event took place) in *Bier* v. *Mines de Potasse d'Alsace*.[53] The European Court of Justice said the harmful event took place either where the defendant misconducted himself or where the claimant suffered damage, at the claimant's option. In *Metall und Rohstoff A/G* v. *Donaldson, Lufkin and Jenrette Inc.*[54] service was allowed on the defendants in New York. They had, when there, sent inducements to persons in England to persuade the latter to break their contracts with third parties here. The claim was for the tort of inducing breach of contract and the damage was sustained in England.

In several libel cases it has been held that, where the defamatory statement has been composed abroad but sent to England where it was published, the tort was committed here or (since 1983) that the damage was sustained here. Most of these cases concern statements in foreign newspapers whose circulation in this country is nowhere near as great as the circulation in the foreign country and the courts have granted permission for the defendant to be served

---

[50] *Oppenheimer* v. *Louis Rosenthal & Co. A/G* [1937] 1 All ER 23 CA.
[51] This reverses the decision in *Finnish Marine Insurance Co. Ltd* v. *Protective National Insurance Co.* [1990] 1 QB 1078.
[52] For some cases decided under this provision see pp. 228–30 below.
[53] [1978] QB 708. For further discussion see p. 145 below.   [54] [1990] 1 QB 391 CA.

if the claimant can show that the libel has some connection with England in the sense that he has a reputation here.[55]

(9) *Enforcement*: if 'a claim is made to enforce any judgment or arbitral award'. The judgment or award may be an English judgment or award or a foreign judgment or award.

(10) *Property*: if 'the whole subject matter of a claim relates to property located within the jurisdiction'. The property may be immovable or movable (including intangible) property; however, it is more important in the case of immovable property, since the English courts do not recognise the jurisdiction of foreign courts over English land.

(11) *Trust*: if 'a claim is made for any remedy which might be obtained in proceedings to execute the trusts of a written instrument where (a) the trusts ought to be executed according to English law; *and* (b) the person on whom the claim form is to be served is a trustee of the trust'. The trust property need not be, or have been, in England.

(12), (13) *Administration of estates, probate*: if 'a claim is made for any remedy which might be obtained in proceedings for the administration of the estate of a person who died domiciled' in England or a 'claim is made in probate proceedings, which includes a claim for the rectification of a will'.

(14) *Constructive trustee*: if 'a claim is made for a remedy against the defendant as constructive trustee where the defendant's alleged liability arises out of acts committed' in England. The acts need not have been committed by the trustee personally but by some third party.

(15) *Restitution*: if 'a claim is for restitution where the defendant's liability arises out of acts committed' in England. This ground was introduced in 1990.

(16) *Claims for duties and taxes*: if 'a claim is made by the Commissioners of Inland Revenue against a defendant who is not domiciled in Scotland or Northern Ireland'.

---

[55] Service was allowed in *Kroch* v. *Rossell et Cie* [1937] 1 All ER 725 and *Berezovsky and Glanchkov* v. *Michaels* [2000] 1 WLR 1004 HL. See also *Shevill* v. *Presse Alliance SA* [1995] 2 AC 18 HL (a case within the Brussels Convention, 1968, Art. 5(3)) (see p. 146 below). It was refused in *Chadha* v. *Dow-Jones & Co. Inc.* [1999] 23 LS Gaz. R 34 CA and in *Bata* v. *Bata* [1948] WN 366 in which the statement was contained in a letter sent from Switzerland to England.

(17) *Costs orders*: if 'a claim is made by a party to proceedings for an order that the court exercise its power[56] to make a costs order in favour of or against a person who is not a party to those proceedings'.

(18) *Claims under statutes*.[57]

Companies

Since a company, being a corporate person, has no real existence, it can have no actual presence or residence in England. However, at common law, a company will be deemed to be within the jurisdiction if it carries on business here.[58] There are numerous cases on this, but they are not often of importance in practice nowadays, because of the statutory provisions about to be considered.[59] They may help, however, to determine whether for the purpose of those provisions, a company has a place of business here.[60] As regards the service of process of the court upon a company, the provisions of the Companies Act 1985 are of greater significance than the common law rules.

If a company is registered in England service should be served by leaving the document (claim form, etc.) at or sending it by post to the company's registered office here.[61] If a company is incorporated abroad,[62] by amendments to the Companies Act 1985[63] it may fall into one of two categories. First, *if it has a branch* in Great Britain it must register the names and addresses of persons authorised to accept service of process *in respect of the business of the branch*; the document is sufficiently served if it is addressed to any such person and is left at or sent by post to that address.[64] Secondly, if it has *an established place of business* in Great Britain, which *is not a branch*, the company must register the

---

[56] Under the Supreme Court Act 1981, s. 51.

[57] The enactments (or statutes) are specified in practice directions.

[58] The same test determines whether it is present or resident in a foreign country, for the purpose of recognition and enforcement of a foreign judgment against it. See pp. 112–13 below.

[59] See, for example, *Dunlop Pneumatic Tyre Co. Ltd* v. *A/G Cudell & Co.* [1902] 1 KB 342 CA and *The World Harmony* [1967] P 341.

[60] For a modern example see *South India Shipping Co.* v. *Export-Import Bank of Korea* [1985] 1 WLR 585.

[61] Companies Act 1985, s. 725(1).

[62] That is, outside Great Britain and Gibraltar. As to service on a company registered in Scotland see Companies Act 1985, s. 725(2)(5).

[63] SI 1992 no. 3719.

[64] Companies Act 1985, s. 694A, Sched. 21A, para. 3(e), s. 694A(2). As to service where there is default see *ibid.*, s. 694A(3). As to the meaning of 'branch' and carrying on of the business of the branch, see *Saab* v. *Saudi American Bank* [1999] 1 WLR 1861 CA.

names and addresses of one or more persons resident in Great Britain who are authorised to accept service on its behalf; service may be effected on a person so named.[65] There is *no limitation* to the business of the branch. It seems that the latter provision will seldom operate, since the entity in Great Britain will either be a branch or will usually conduct its own business rather than that of the foreign company, as normally is the case of a subsidiary or an agent.[66]

In all these cases service may be effected under the Civil Procedure Rules, Part 6,[67] that is, by leaving it with a person holding a senior position in the company, by post, by leaving the document at the principal office of the company or at any place of business it may have within the jurisdiction which has a real connection with the claim through a document exchange, fax or other means of electronic communication.

These provisions seem unnecessarily complex and should be simplified.

Jurisdiction in actions *in rem*

An Admiralty action *in rem* is one against a ship.[68] It is begun by affixing the claim form to the formal defendant, the ship.[69] So it cannot be served out of jurisdiction. Either the wrongdoing ship or one under the same ownership (but only one of them) may be sued.[70] The law is contained in the Supreme Court Act 1981, section 21–4. In *Republic of India* v. *Indian Steamship Company Ltd.*[71] in 1998, the House of Lords held that the action was in substance against the ship's owner. It is a device to persuade the owner to submit to the jurisdiction.

---

[65] Companies Act 1985, s. 691: *Boocock* v. *Hilton International Co.* [1993] 1 WLR 1063 CA; *Rome* v. *Punjab National Bank* (No. 2) [1989] 1 WLR 1211 CA. As to service in default, see Companies Act 1985, s. 695.

[66] *South India Shipping Co.* v. *Export-Import Bank of Korea* [1985] 1 WLR 585 seems to have involved a branch of the defendant company. For a rare case in which a commercial agent had power to bind a Panamanian company by contracts and the agent's place of business in London was held to be also that of the company, see *Cleveland Museum of Fine Art* v. *Capricorn Art International SA* [1990] 2 Ll.R 166, discussed at p. 90–1 below.

[67] Rule 6.2(2).

[68] It lies also against cargo, freight, aircraft and hovercraft, but this rarely occurs.

[69] This constitutes notice to persons interested in the ship. Leaving the form with the captain or master is ineffective: *The Prins Bernhard* [1964] P 117.

[70] *The Banco* [1971] P 137; *The Berny* [1979] QB 80

[71] [1998] AC 878 HL p. 124 below, and see *The Tatry* [1999] QB 515n. p. 162 below.

8   Staying of English actions and restraint of foreign proceedings

The English court has an inherent power, which is contained also in the Supreme Court Act 1981, section 49(3), to stay any action which is frivolous or vexatious or otherwise an abuse of the process of the court.

It also has the power to restrain, by injunction, persons subject to its jurisdiction from instituting or continuing proceedings in foreign courts. The power of the court to grant injunctions generally is to be found in section 37(1) of the same Act.

Staying of English actions

General principles

Until relatively recent times, the courts denied that English law contained any general doctrine of *forum non conveniens*, by virtue of which a court will decline to exercise the jurisdiction it possesses because it is not the most suitable court to hear the case but some foreign court is.[1] But the law on this matter underwent considerable development after 1972 when a process of 'liberalisation' set in. For some time, the principles upon which a court should exercise its discretion to stay or not to stay an action in favour of a foreign court were a matter of considerable doubt and it was not until 1986 that the courts adopted coherent guidelines. Then, in *Spiliada Maritime Corporation* v. *Cansulex Ltd (The Spiliada)*,[2] the House of Lords introduced some order into the confusion which it had itself generated in the first place.

The Spiliada laid down the basic principle that English proceedings may be stayed where there is another *clearly* more appropriate forum for

---

[1] It was explained in the previous chapter (p. 75) that *forum non conveniens* has always governed cases in which the court is asked to exercise its discretion to allow service out of the jurisdiction under CPR Rules 6.20 *et seq.*, esp. 6.21 (2A), but there it is being asked to assume jurisdiction over an absent defendant.
[2] [1987] AC 40 HL.

trial of the action in which justice can be done. The onus is on the defendant to prove that this is the case as the claimant should not be deprived of the advantage of proceedings here merely on the balance of convenience. At one time the English court would stay its own proceedings only where it was vexatious and oppressive to the defendant not to do so.[3] The test of vexation and oppression was difficult to satisfy except where the claimant had commenced proceedings against the defendant in more than one forum.[4] When coupled with jurisdiction based upon mere presence of the defendant within the territory, a claimant could 'forum shop', that is, look around and sue in England if that was where he was more likely to succeed, even when its courts had no real connection with the claim or either party.[5] On the one hand, as Lord Denning MR once noted, England is a good place to shop for justice, both for the quality of the goods and the speed of the service.[6] On the other hand, in an increasingly international world, the combination of the rules come to be regarded as xenophobic.

Although forum shopping is a term of abuse, used by both the courts and private international lawyers, having rules which allow a claimant to choose a forum which suite the claimant best is not necessarily prejudicial to justice.[7] If all other things are equal, it is to both parties' advantage to have a speedy and inexpensive final judgment from a single forum. This may be best effected in a forum which has many factual connections to the case and the parties.[8] However, the court has to be aware of the tactics of international litigation. A claimant may be bringing proceedings in an expensive, claimant-friendly forum in order to drive the defendant into settling the dispute. Equally, a defendant may be wanting to defend the claim only in a slow and expensive forum, hoping that the claimant will die or run out of money before trial. The different disclosure of evidence requirements in different countries can be used either by claimants to prove their case more easily or by

---

[3] *St Pierre* v. *South American Stores Ltd* [1936] 1 KB 382 CA. This was known as the *St Pierre* test.

[4] In three cases decided between 1906 and 1908 (*Logan* v. *Bank of Scotland* (No. 2) [1906] 1 KB 141 CA, *Egbert* v. *Short* [1907] 2 Ch. 205 and *Re Norton's Settlement* [1908] 1 Ch. 471 CA) a stay was ordered, but in all of them the claimant was suing in England and not in the natural forum in order to vex and harass the defendant into agreeing to compromise his legal rights.

[5] *Maharanee of Baroda* v. *Wildenstein* [1972] 2 QB 283 CA.

[6] *The Atlantic Star* [1973] QB 364 at 382 CA.

[7] After all, it is accepted wisdom in a liberal economy that freedom of choice is advantageous.

[8] See the earlier discussion in ch. 7 above in the related area of service out of the jurisdiction in which these factors are also important.

defendants to make the evidence more difficult to find. In some courts there may be more security against the defendant's failure to meet an award of costs or better protection of the claimant from a defendant hiding assets from enforcement of a judgment. A foreign court may be unwilling to respect the choice of law clause and so the result on the merits may be different, to the claimant's or the defendant's advantage. The English court has to weigh all these factors against each other so as to achieve justice to both parties.

An early example of the English court's realisation that these factors should be important in determining whether or not to stay its proceedings was *The Atlantic Star*.[9] An action *in rem* was brought by a Dutch shipowner against a Belgian shipowner. The only connection with England was that the Belgian ship's sister ship had been arrested when it had arrived in English waters. The English court had jurisdiction under a statute which incorporated an international convention. These facts led the House of Lords, by a bare majority, to hold that a stay should be granted of the action. They followed the long practice of the Scottish courts which had adopted a doctrine of *forum non conveniens* to limit the effect of exorbitant jurisdictional rules based upon mere presence of the defendant's property in Scotland.[10] In 1984 in *The Abidin Daver*[11] the House of Lords expressly admitted the doctrine into English law.

> A Cuban vessel was in collision with a Turkish vessel in the Bosphorus within Turkish waters.[12] An action was started by the Turkish owners in the Turkish court in Istanbul. The Cuban owners began an action *in rem* in the English Admiralty Court. The Turkish owners asked for a stay of this action.

The Court of Appeal, reversing the judge at first instance, refused the stay. The House of Lords restored the judge's order. The Turkish court[13] was the natural and more appropriate forum. It was the forum with the most real and substantial connection with the case. Therefore, unless the claimant could show by cogent evidence that justice could not be achieved in Turkey, the English proceedings should be stayed. The English court should not continue with its proceedings in a spirit

---

[9] [1974] AC 436 HL.

[10] This was abolished by the Civil Jurisdiction and Judgments Act 1982, which, *inter alia*, created a new statutory scheme for the jurisdiction of the Scots courts.

[11] [1984] AC 398 HL.

[12] In the words of Sir John Donaldson MR in the Court of Appeal, 'If the evidence on each side was correct we have reached the classic case of a collision between two anchored ships at least one mile apart.'

[13] From whose windows the place of the accident could be seen.

of chauvinism but should be mindful of comity. Justice could be done elsewhere than in England.[14] In determining where justice was to be done the case placed emphasis on personal or juridical advantages to the claimant and this led to a number of difficulties. Different courts expressed very different views about certain factors, in particular whether the prospect of recovering higher damages in one country's courts rather than another's is such a legitimate advantage.[15] As with many other of these 'legitimate advantages', what is the claimant's advantage is the defendant's disadvantage.

However, the doctrine of *forum non conveniens* was really only established properly by Lord Goff of Chievely in *The Spiliada* in 1986.[16] He laid down authoritative guidelines for establishing the *forum conveniens* both with regard to staying of English actions and for service out of the jurisdiction. This case did not in fact concern a stay of proceedings, but an application for permission to serve the defendant out of the jurisdiction in British Columbia under what are now CPR Rules 6.20 *et seq*. The principle behind *forum non conveniens* has always applied in such cases and Lord Goff said that the doctrine applies in the same way to applications to serve out of the jurisdiction and to those which request a stay of English proceedings which are brought as of right. The distinction between them is that the claimant has to ask the court to exercise its discretion to allow service out of the jurisdiction so that the burden of persuading the court lies on him, whereas the defendant has that burden if he wants a stay. The guidelines laid down in Lord Goff's speech for judges to follow in deciding how to exercise their discretion are based largely on Scots cases.[17] Lord Goff pointed out that the word *conveniens* is not really apt, since the question is not whether or not a court is convenient but whether it is suitable or appropriate for the trial of the action. The guidelines are as follows:

[14] The House of Lords was not particularly polite about the Master of the Rolls extolling the virtues of the English Admiralty court.

[15] In *Castanho* v. *Brown & Root Ltd* [1981] AC 557 HL and *Smith, Kline & French Laboratories Ltd* v. *Bloch* [1983] 1 WLR 730 CA, both of which were applications to restrain American proceedings. In the former, the prospect of higher damages in Texas was, but in the latter that of higher damages in New York was not, regarded as passing the test. Lord Goff has reiterated that lower damages in the *forum conveniens* was not of itself a ground for refusing a stay (*Connelly* v. *RTZ* [1998] AC 854 at 872). However, where the claimant would recover little or nothing at all abroad that may be sufficient to allow English proceedings to continue: see *The Jalakrishna* [1983] 2 Ll.R 628, *The Vishva Ajay* [1989] 2 Ll.R 558, *The Al Battani* [1993] 2 Ll.R 219 and *BMG Trading Ltd* v. *AS McKay* [1998] ILPr. 691 CA.

[16] [1987] AC 460 HL. Lord Goff may be regarded as the architect of the modern law concerning both staying of English actions and restraining foreign proceedings.

[17] Especially *Sim* v. *Robinow* (1892) 19 R 665 at 668 per Lord Kinnear.

(1) A stay will only be granted if the court is satisfied that there is another available court having competent jurisdiction which, because the case could be tried there suitably for the interest of the parties and the ends of justice, is appropriate for the trial.[18]

(2) In general the burden of persuading the court to exercise its discretion to grant a stay rests on the defendant, although in respect of any matter raised by either party to persuade it one way or the other, the burden lies on the party who raises it.

(3) The defendant must show not only that England is not the natural or appropriate forum but that there is one other forum which is clearly or distinctly more appropriate.[19] A distinctly more appropriate forum did exist in the leading cases in which a stay had been granted, such as *The Atlantic Star*,[20] *MacShannon* v. *Rockware Glass Ltd*,[21] *Trendtex Trading Corporation* v. *Credit Suisse*[22] and *The Abidin Daver*.[23]

(4) The court must first look for factors which point to another forum, defined by Lord Keith in *The Abidin Daver* as 'that with which the action had the most real and substantial connection'. These include factors affecting convenience or expense (including availability of witnesses) and others, such as which law governs the relevant transaction, or the respective places of residence or business of the parties.

(5) If the court concludes that no such forum exists, a stay will almost certainly be refused.

(6) If it concludes that there is a *prima facie* more appropriate forum a stay will normally be granted. But if the claimant (on whom the evidential burden now lies) can show that circumstances beyond those under (4) exist why a stay should not be granted, such as that he will clearly not be able to obtain justice in the foreign court,[24] a stay will be refused.

A 'legitimate personal or juridical advantage' for the claimant, such as higher damages, a more complete procedure for disclosure of evidence, the award of interest and a longer limitation period, is no longer

---

[18] More recently, the House of Lords has emphasised that only the parties' private interests have a bearing on the court's decision. Public interest, questions of judicial *amour propre* and political considerations have no part to play: *Lubbe* v. *Cape plc* [2000] 1 WLR 1545 at 1561, 1566 HL.

[19] There was no such forum in *European-Asian Bank* v. *Punjab & Sindh Bank* [1982] 2 Ll.R 356 CA, where the case could have been heard in either India or Singapore, but neither provided a more appropriate forum than did England.

[20] [1974] AC 43 HL (Belgium).   [21] [1978] AC 795 HL (Scotland).

[22] [1982] AC 679 HL (Switzerland).

[23] [1984] AC 398 HL (Turkey). See also *Muduroglu* v. *TC Ziraat Bankasi* [1986] QB 1225 CA (Turkey).

[24] See further p. 92 below.

decisive; it is a factor to be taken into account,[25] but no more. It cannot be decisive since the claimant's advantage is gained at the defendant's expense. As Lord Sumner put it in a leading Scottish case:[26]

I do not see how one can guide oneself profitably by endeavouring to conciliate and promote the interests of both these antagonists, except in that ironical sense, in which one says that it is in the interests of both that the case should be tried in the best way and in the best tribunal and that the best man should win.

If *The Spiliada* had been a case in which an action had been begun against a defendant present here it would not have been stayed. Two factors present in the case were emphasised. The first was what was called the *Cambridgeshire* factor, after the name of a ship which had been involved in previous litigation concerned with the same matters as was *The Spiliada*, and in which a considerable amount of expert scientific evidence had been amassed in England and much work had been done by lawyers in England. This made it much more sensible to try the action here rather than in British Columbia, the alternative forum, for if an action had to be brought there, all this work might have to be started over again. Thus a trial in England would be much cheaper. Secondly, any action in British Columbia (the alternative forum) appeared to be time-barred whereas an English action was not. The claimants would not be penalised for not starting an action in British Columbia by staying their action, if England was otherwise the natural forum. However, care must be taken not to overemphasise either of these factors as being decisive in all cases. For example, a claimant must act reasonably in allowing a time limit in a foreign court to expire. Thus, the Privy Council in *The Pioneer Container*[27] stayed an action commenced in Hong Kong. The action had in fact been brought in violation of an exclusive jurisdiction clause in favour of the courts of Taiwan since the action was time-barred there. The claimants tried to argue that commencing proceedings in Taiwan was so very expensive and that the time-bar (of one year) was so short that they had acted reasonably in not pursuing an action there. Unsurprisingly, the court disagreed and stayed the Hong Kong proceedings notwithstanding that that left the claimants without any remedy.

---

[25] An advantage may relate to the aftermath of the trial – for example, the relative ease of enforcement of an English judgment as compared with a foreign judgment – in third countries: *International Credit and Investment Co. (Overseas) Ltd* v. *Sheikh Kamal Adham* [1999] ILPr. 302 CA.

[26] *Société du Gaz de Paris* v. *SA de Navigation 'Les Armateurs Français'* 1926 SC (HL) 13 at 22.

[27] [1994] 2 AC 324 PC.

It is clear that in *The Spiliada* the House of Lords was trying, in laying down these guidelines, to discourage appeals in this type of case. If the trial judge were to exercise his discretion according to Lord Goff's principles, then, according to Lord Templeman, 'an appeal should be rare and the appellate court should be slow to interfere'.

These remarks have not prevented the publication of many reports of (mainly) commercial cases in which the *Spiliada* principles have been applied, but only a few of these will be discussed here, in order to illustrate their application.

First, there are some cases in which a stay was granted. In *De Dampierre* v. *De Dampierre*,[28] Lord Goff's guidelines were held to apply in a divorce case, where the power to stay English proceedings was contained in a statute.

> A husband and wife, both French nationals, had married in France and moved to London where the wife had a child. The husband bought them a home in London, but soon the wife established a business in New York. She took the child there and severed her tenuous connection with England. The marriage foundered. The husband sought a divorce in France, the wife petitioned in England.

The Domicile and Matrimonial Proceedings Act 1973[29] provides that the court can stay the English proceedings when proceedings are also brought abroad, if it appears that 'the balance of fairness (including convenience) between the parties to the marriage is such that it is appropriate for the [foreign] proceedings . . . to be disposed of before further steps are taken in the [English] proceedings'.

The wife's proceedings were stayed. France was the natural forum and she could get all the redress she was entitled to by French law in the French courts.

In *Cleveland Museum of Art* v. *Capricorn Art International SA*[30]

> Capricorn (D¹), a company registered in Panama and having (it was held) a place of business in England, owned an ancient Pakistani Ghandara reliquary. It agreed to lend it to the Cleveland Museum (C) for exhibition in the United States. An English company (D²) collected it in London and sent it to C in Cleveland, Ohio. A plaque on it was missing on arrival. D¹ sued C and D² in Ohio for breach of the loan agreement, breach of bailment and negligence. C obtained a stay of D¹'s action in Ohio pending the outcome of its own attempt to sue D¹ in England. D¹ asked for a stay, arguing that Ohio was the more appropriate forum.

---

[28] [1988] AC 92 HL.   [29] S. 5(6), Sched. 1, para. 9(1)(b).   [30] [1990] 2 Ll.R 166.

Hirst J applied the basic *Spiliada* principle and held that, taking all the facts into consideration, the continuance of the English action would result in additional expense, inconvenience and delay. It was merely likely, not certain, that the Ohio court would make its stay permanent. So, if the English action continued, there might be concurrent proceedings here and in Ohio. A stay was granted.

In Re *Harrods (Buenos Aires) Ltd*,[31] where there was no *lis alibi pendens*,

> A company was registered in England but its business and administration were carried on in Argentina. Its two shareholders were Swiss companies. The one which held the minority of the shares petitioned for the compulsory winding up of the company under the Insolvency Act 1986 and for relief from prejudicial conduct under ss. 459–61 thereof; it requested the court to order the majority shareholder to buy it out. No such remedy existed in Argentina but by Argentine law the minority could sue the majority for damages.

The Court of Appeal, reversing Harman J,[32] held that the *Spiliada* principles applied to such petitions and, by a majority, that a stay should be granted; Argentina was clearly the natural forum and the petitioner could get justice there even though the relief it might obtain was not exactly the same as that which existed in England.[33]

Secondly, there are some cases in which a stay was refused. In *El Pont de Nemours* v. *Agnew*[34] the claimants (C) were held liable in a products liability action in Illinois. The damages included an award of punitive damages, which could not have been awarded against them under English law. C sued thirteen defendants (Ds) on an insurance policy to recover the amount of the damages. Ds 1 to 3 were in England and Ds 4 to 13 were served out of the jurisdiction.

Ds then brought an action in Illinois for a declaration that they were not liable to pay out on the policy because it was contrary to Illinois (though not English) public policy for insurers to indemnify the insured for a punitive damages award. Ds 1 to 3 asked for a stay of the English action.

The Court of Appeal refused a stay. Applying the *Spiliada* principles, it held that England was the more suitable forum. The insurance policy

---

[31] [1992] Ch. 72 CA.

[32] He had decided that proceedings on such petitions are not adversarial, so the *Spiliada* principles could not apply.

[33] Since the English court had jurisdiction in this case under the Brussels Convention on Jurisdiction in Civil and Commercial Cases, 1968, the question arose whether it could stay the action in favour of the courts of a non-contracting state. The Court of Appeal held that it could, but the House of Lords referred the matter to the European Court of Justice for an interpretive decision. See further ch. 10 p. 166 below.

[34] [1987] 2 Ll.R 585 CA. The claimant failed to restrain concurrent proceedings started by the defendants in Illinois.

contained no express choice of law but, it was held, English law did govern the contract. Defendants 1 to 3 (who were, of course, English companies carrying on the relevant business in England) had not shown that Illinois was the more appropriate forum. The claimants, on the other hand, had demonstrated a strong arguable case for relief in England, where no reason existed why they should not be able to claim on the policy in respect of the punitive damages.

In *Saab* v. *Saudi American Bank*[35] the Court of Appeal refused to stay proceedings, notwithstanding that there were two alternative more appropriate fora. The claim concerned an agreement by a Saudi Arabian bank to market around the world some securities in a Lebanese company for the claimants. The agreement was to be partly performed in London. However, this case raised many questions about the defendant bank and the Lebanese company. The court carefully balanced all the factors and decided that although both Saudi Arabia and the Lebanon were appropriate neither was more appropriate than the other. A stay was refused as the defendant had not discharged the onus of showing a clearly more appropriate forum.

Where the claimant can show that the foreign court will not give him justice, the English court has refused to stay its proceedings even where it is not at all a *forum conveniens*. For example, in *Mohammed* v. *Bank of Kuwait and Middle East KSC*[36] the claimant was an Iraqi employee of the defendant bank, who had been working in Kuwait before the Gulf War. He was suing for wages and an account of money he had deposited with his employer. As the claimant could show that he would not at the time the action was commenced be likely to have a fair trial in Kuwait the action was continued in England. In contrast, in *Askin* v. *Absa Bank*[37] the English proceedings were stayed in favour of South Africa as the claimant had failed to make out his allegations that he would not have a fair trial of the action and that his life would be in danger there.

Two recent decisions in which the House of Lords refused a stay of English proceedings repay closer attention. They are *Connelly* v. *RTZ*[38] and the more recent *Lubbe* v. *Cape plc.*[39] The facts of the cases were substantially similar. The claimants had been employed in Namibia and South Africa respectively by the local subsidiaries of the defendants who were 'parent' companies incorporated and doing business in England.

---

[35] [1999] 1 WLR 1861 CA. See also *European Asian Bank* v. *Punjab & Sindh Bank* [1981] 2 Ll.R 651; [1982] 2 Ll.R 350 CA (neither India nor Singapore was more appropriate than the other and a stay was refused).

[36] [1996] 1 WLR 1483 CA.   [37] [1999] ILPr. 471 CA.

[38] [1998] AC 854 HL.   [39] [2000] 1 WLR 1545 HL.

Such companies are obviously subject to the English courts' jurisdiction.[40] The employment was dangerous and the claimants had all suffered injury.[41] Their claims were primarily against their employer, a subsidiary company. The parent companies were joined to the actions in England as the claimants were more likely to be able to enforce a judgment against them than against their subsidiaries.[42] To strengthen their cases they claimed that the parent company owed them a duty to ensure a safe system of work throughout the group of companies owned by the parent. In *Connelly* v. *RTZ* the claimant was a Scotsman who after working abroad came back to live in England and was diagnosed with cancer of the throat. Although he conceded that Namibia was the forum with the most real and substantial connection, Mr Connelly could not achieve justice there in a practical way as he was unable to afford to take action there where legal aid was unavailable. In England he could obtain legal aid and take advantage of conditional fee arrangements with his solicitors and experts to fund his action. Also, much of the evidence depended upon medical expert witnesses who were easily available in England but not in Namibia. The complexity of the case meant that the claimant could not achieve justice abroad without the medical evidence and the expense was considerable. The action was allowed to proceed here although ultimately Mr Connelly lost on the merits.[43]

In *Lubbe* v. *Cape plc*[44] an action was brought in England by a few claimants in a similar position to Mr Connelly, except that almost all of them were South African and did not live here. Following *Connelly*, the Court of Appeal allowed the action to proceed. More than 3,000 other claimants from South Africa then joined the action. The defendants, another English company, sought a stay and were unsuccessful in the House of Lords. Lord Bingham reiterated that in stay cases the onus was on the defendant to show that there was another forum in which justice could be done in the interests of all the parties. The issues which were important in this case involved the responsibility of the parent company and were most likely to be connected to England where the documents and evidence were to be found. Secondly, there were the individual personal injury matters, such as the medical examination of the claimants, the diagnosis of their injuries and evidence of possible

---

[40] The Court of Appeal in *Banco Atlantico* v. *British Bank of the Middle East* [1990] 2 Ll.R 504 CA had unsurprisingly demanded clear and strong grounds before the English court would stay such an action against companies incorporated and doing business here.

[41] Usually cancer from working with asbestos or uranium.

[42] Some claimants were unable to recover in their 'home' jurisdiction due to limitations on an employer's liability.

[43] [1999] CLC 533.   [44] [2000] 1 WLR 1545 HL.

causation. These were most likely to be connected to South Africa. Given the number of claimants, South Africa was found to be the natural forum. However, this was a case where litigation in the natural forum was outweighed by the interests of justice. The claimants were unlikely to be able to obtain financial help in South Africa but had the advantage of contingency fee arrangements in England. This of itself was probably insufficient to prevent a stay. However, this action was now a complex group action involving many claimants and possible other defendants might be joined to the action. This type of action was new to South African courts and could be more efficiently dealt with in England.

Special factors

Three factors need special attention. These are the weight to be attached to (a) proceedings existing abroad between the parties (*lis alibi pendens*), (b) the applicable law, and (c) jurisdiction and arbitration agreements. As to (c) such agreements are often placed in a separate category in any discussion of the *forum conveniens*. They are usually held to be decisive of the *forum conveniens* even if the dispute has no connection with the chosen forum. However, occasionally both the courts and commentators regard the presence of jurisdiction or arbitration clauses as merely a factor to be considered.

Lis alibi pendens

There are particular problems when proceedings between the parties are taking place in another country. These may have been started by the defendant or the claimant, or even a third party in a complex multi-party action. Duplication of proceedings can often be unfair to both parties. Each party may be subject to two sets of costs, and the time and trouble necessary to conduct two proceedings is unnecessary. The risk of conflicting judgments is not conducive to overall justice and may lead to an unseemly rush to judgment. However, deciding which court's proceedings should continue and which should not be allowed to continue raises difficult issues. Either the English court can stay its own proceedings in favour of the other court, or the English court may decide that it should try to prevent the proceedings continuing in the other court. The latter option, often known as an anti-suit injunction, is discussed below.[45] The mere fact of proceedings having been commenced

---

[45] As to anti-suit injunctions see pp. 100–8 below.

elsewhere is not of itself enough to make that court the *forum conveniens*.[46] However, where the claimant has commenced both sets of proceedings he may be required to elect in which court to proceed.[47] The foreign proceedings may have been commenced for purely tactical reasons, in a distinctly inappropriate forum, or they may not be very far advanced. In such cases the *lis alibi pendens* is not very significant. However, where the foreign proceedings are in an appropriate forum and are well under way, the English court will stay its proceedings in the interests of justice.[48]

Applicable law

The applicable law can be seen as an important factor in locating the *forum conveniens*. Where the parties have chosen a law to govern their relationship, most usually in a contract, it is often more efficient and more conducive to the correct result if their dispute is decided in the courts of the country of that system of law. This is especially so if the law is likely to be difficult for another court to apply or if that court might apply its country's public policy.[49] In defamation cases the applicable law is English law (at least in part).[50] These cases are best decided in the English courts.[51] However, when the applicable law can be easily applied by another court then the factor is not very weighty. In England, foreign law is treated as a matter of fact and is usually proved by expert testimony. This may or may not be the case in the other forum. But where there is certainty about the rules or where there are similarities between the systems concerned the applicable law has little weight. For example, English law of contract can be easily applied in New York. The English court will stay proceedings in favour of New York where that would be the *forum conveniens* notwithstanding an English choice of law clause. Where, on the other hand, the foreign court will not apply the applicable law (particularly where that has been expressly chosen by the parties) then the English court is likely to decide that justice cannot be done in the foreign court and refuse a stay.[52]

---

[46] *De Dampierre* v. *De Dampierre* [1988] AC 92 HL.
[47] *Australian Commercial Research and Development* v. *ANZ McCaughan Merchant Bank Ltd* [1989] 2 All ER 65, 70.
[48] This was the case in *The Abidin Daver* [1984] AC 398 HL and in *Cleveland Museum of Art* v. *Capricorn* [1990] 2 Ll.R 166.
[49] This factor weighed heavily in favour of the English court in *EI Pont de Nemours* v. *Agnew* [1987] 2 Ll.R 585.
[50] The choice of law rules in defamation remain those of double actionability (see ch. 13 below). A role for English law is therefore inevitable in these case.
[51] *Berezovsky* v. *Michaels* [2000] 1 WLR 1104 HL.
[52] *Banco Atlantico SA* v. *British Bank of the Middle East* [1990] 2 Ll.R 504 CA.

Jurisdiction and arbitration agreements

Jurisdiction clauses are a relatively common way in which parties to contracts seek to establish a court in which any disputes between them will be settled. Arbitration clauses seek to remove any dispute from the courts and instead to have the issue decided by arbitration. By statute, the English courts must stay any action and remit the parties to arbitration, either in England or abroad, where a valid arbitration agreement exists.[53] Arbitration will be dealt with later.[54]

If an action is brought in England in contravention of an agreement to confer exclusive jurisdiction on a foreign court, the English court is faced with two conflicting policies. One dictates that persons should not be allowed by agreement to oust the jurisdiction of the English courts,[55] the other that persons must be held to their agreements. The courts usually resolve this conflict by favouring the latter policy. This has the important consequence that the burden of convincing the court *not* to exercise its discretion so as to stay the action is borne by the claimant, who is acting in breach of contract in suing in England.

It must be emphasised that it is *exclusive* jurisdiction clauses which are under consideration here. If the clause is non-exclusive, it merely adds to the number of courts (the English court being one) which have jurisdiction and does not purport to oust the jurisdiction of any of them. An exclusive jurisdiction clause is meant to oust the jurisdiction of any court except the chosen one.

The law which governs the clause[56] determines (a) whether the clause is valid.[57] It also determines (b) whether the clause provides for exclusive or only non-exclusive jurisdiction.[58] An exclusive jurisdiction clause operates so as to exclude the jurisdiction of all courts except the chosen courts, which alone are intended to have jurisdiction. A non-exclusive jurisdiction clause is designed to confer jurisdiction upon courts which might not otherwise possess it. Should the governing law be English law, then whether the parties intend the jurisdiction clause to be exclusive or non-exclusive is a matter of construction of the contract, as was

---

[53] Arbitration Act 1996, s. 9.   [54] See ch. 11 below.

[55] See *The Fehmarn* [1958] 1 WLR 159 CA, where the court held that the English elements in the case outweighed the Russian elements and refused to stay the action because of the Russian jurisdiction clause.

[56] This will usually be the applicable law of the whole contract, but it might not be. As will be seen, the choice of law rules contained in the Rome Convention on Contractual Obligations, 1980 (enacted into English law by the Contracts (Applicable Law) Act 1990) do not apply to jurisdiction and arbitration clauses, which are specifically excluded from the Convention. See further ch. 12 below.

[57] *Mackender* v. *Feldia* [1967] 2 QB 590, 598 CA.

[58] *Evans Marshall & Co. Ltd* v. *Bertola SA* [1973] 1 WLR 349.

held in, for example *Sohio Supply Co.* v. *Gatoil (USA) Inc.*[59] by the Court of Appeal. It also decides (c) whether the clause covers the matter in dispute.[60] Furthermore, (d) as the House of Lords held in *The Hollandia*,[61] the clause must not contravene an English statute.

The principles to be applied and the factors to be considered when the court is asked to stay proceedings were stated by Brandon J in *The Eleftheria*,[62] which concerned a contract for carriage of goods by sea from Romania to Hull, in which a clause referred disputes to the courts of the state where the carrier conducted his business. The carrier was Greek and carried on business in Greece. The vessel was arrested at Hull and the defendant asked for a stay of proceedings and their reference to the court at Piraeus. Brandon J stated that all the circumstances of the case should be taken into account but said that particular matters for consideration are: (i) in what country the evidence of fact is or is more easily available, and the effect of this on the convenience and expense of trial; (ii) whether the law of the foreign court applies and if so whether it differs materially from English law; (iii) the closeness of the connection of either party with the countries concerned; (iv) whether the defendants genuinely desire trial abroad or are only seeking procedural advantages in being sued there; and (v) whether the claimants would be prejudiced by the case being tried abroad because they would (a) be deprived of security for claims, (b) be unable to enforce a judgment obtained there, (c) be faced with a time-bar not applicable in England, or (d) be unable to get a fair trial for political, racial, religious or other reasons.

Applying these tests to the case in hand, the court stayed the action; most of the evidence was in England, but Greek law differed from English law in material respects.

The Eleftheria was approved by the Court of Appeal in *The El Amria*,[63] in which the claim was for damages for breach of contract and negligence in respect of the storage and custody of potatoes which had been conveyed from Alexandria to Liverpool. The contract contained an exclusive Egyptian jurisdiction clause. The dispute really concerned the

---

[59] [1989] 1 Ll.R 588; see also *British Aerospace plc* v. *Dee Howard Co.* [1993] 1 Ll.R 368; *Continental Bank NA* v. *Aeakos* [1994] 1 WLR 888 CA. For a discussion of this matter in the context of Article 17 of the Brussels and Lugano Conventions see p. 163 below.

[60] *The Sindh* [1975] 1 Ll.R 372 CA.

[61] [1983] 1 AC 565 HL; compare *The Benarty* [1985] QB 325 CA. See further p. 215 below.

[62] [1970] P 94.

[63] [1982] 2 Ll.R 119 CA. Brandon LJ, as he had become, approved it. It was further approved by the House of Lords in *The Sennar* [1985] 1 WLR 490 at 500, per Lord Brandon of Oakbrook, as he had by then become. *The El Amria* was applied in *The Atlantic Song* [1983] 2 Ll.R 394.

speed of discharge at Liverpool, so the evidence was in England. Further and vitally, the claimants were suing not only the cargo carriers but the Liverpool port authorities, so that if both actions were tried here, the possibility of there being conflicting English and Egyptian decisions would be avoided. A stay was refused. The test is known, therefore, as the *Eleftheria* test or the *El Amria* test.

In *The Pioneer Container*[64] bills of lading contained an exclusive jurisdiction clause in favour of Taiwan. Notwithstanding that proceedings could not now go ahead in Taiwan as they were time-barred, the Privy Council stayed the proceedings before them. Lord Goff held that the parties should be held to their bargain. The undoubted disadvantages to the claimants of having to provide a large sum of money as security in Taiwan and a short time-bar were insufficient to justify the stay requested. Having chosen a forum, a party could not then argue that the procedures of that forum were disadvantageous, nor that the forum was inappropriate or lacked connection with the dispute. Something more is necessary. An example of this is *Citi-March Ltd* v. *Neptune Orient Lines Ltd*[65] where there were several parties to the action which were not bound by the exclusive jurisdiction clause in favour of Singapore. Colman J considered that the risk of conflicting judgments was sufficient to justify refusing to stay the English proceedings in breach of the clause.

The *Eleftheria* test bears a very close resemblance to the *Spiliada* test. In fact, they must necessarily be more or less identical, since they concern the same thing, the staying of English actions. The only real difference is that, as has been pointed out, where the defendant is asking for a stay in a case where there is no jurisdiction clause, the burden of proof, as it were, rests on him. Where there is such a clause, the burden of proof is on the claimant.

In *The Rothnie*,[66] it was held that the same principle effectively applied where the clause conferred merely *non-exclusive* jurisdiction on the foreign court. This was a strong indication that the chosen court (Gibraltar) was the appropriate court and the action was stayed in its favour.

Submission to the English courts or arbitration

It is unlikely that a stay of English proceedings will be granted when the parties have agreed to English jurisdiction or arbitration.[67]

---

[64] [1994] 2 AC 324 PC.   [65] [1995] 1 WLR 1367.   [66] [1996] 2 Ll.R 206.
[67] See *The Standard Steamship and Indemnity Association Ltd* v. *Gann* [1992] 2 Ll.R 528; *British Aerospace plc* v. *Dee Howard Co.* [1993] 1 Ll.R 368; *Communications Ltd* v. *Communication Telesystem International* [1999] 2 All ER (Comm.) 33.

Criticisms of the *forum non conveniens* doctrine

Some states of the United States have a similar doctrine of *forum non conveniens* but the European countries have not apparently needed it. Indeed many are very sceptical of the doctrine as it is based on a judge's discretion. Under the Brussels Convention *lis alibi pendens* is recognised as the basis for staying proceedings of any court seised after the one which is first seised if the claim concerns the same parties and the same subject matter. This is a non-discretionary, automatic stay.[68] *Forum non conveniens* has its critics and has not been followed in Australia.[69] It can be said to be too uncertain and wasteful of resources. Parties are put to considerable expense in order for the English court even to be able to decide whether it should hear the merits of the case. However, the jurisdictional question may be the only real dispute in the case. Once the court which is to hear the merits is decided the actual result may be entirely clear. Therefore the parties may themselves want this jurisdictional dispute decided as carefully as possible.

The balance between a necessarily rough-and-ready decision 'to be decided in hours not days' and a careful weighing up of all the factors is not easy to strike. In particular, it can be difficult to determine the truth of the facts relied upon by both parties at this early, interlocutory stage before disclosure. Finding the most appropriate forum, taking into account all the factors and finely balancing all the interests, may therefore not be possible. Nevertheless, a decision has to be taken and the appellate courts should be slow to intervene. The stronger party may be dragging out the jurisdictional issue to induce the weaker party to settle the case.

The court has said that it must not investigate the quality of justice, including procedural rules, that can be achieved abroad.[70] Thus in *Herceg Novi* v. *The Ming Galaxy*[71] a lower foreign limitation of financial

---

[68] See ch. 9 below. The only possible scope for a discretionary doctrine of *forum non conveniens* as is now accepted in England is in Article 22, where a court second seised *may* stay its own proceedings if the subject matter is merely related to that in proceedings in another contracting state's court.

[69] The High Court of Australia kept the test of vexation and oppression in *Oceanic Sun-Line Special Shipping Co. Inc.* v. *Fay* (1988) 165 CLR 197. However, this was clarified in *Voth* v. *Manildra Flour Mills Pty Ltd* (1990) 171 CLR 538 when the High Court held that if Australia was a clearly inappropriate forum then the test of vexation and oppression was satisfied, and the proceedings would be stayed.

[70] *The Abidin Daver* [1984] AC 398 HL. In *Askin* v. *Absa Bank* [1999] ILPr. 471 the Court of Appeal was very critical of the claimant's arguments that he would not achieve justice in South Africa because the defendant bank was in conspiracy with fraudsters. See also *BCCHK* v. *Sonali Bank* [1995] ILI.R 227.

[71] [1998] 4 All ER 238 CA.

liability under a different international convention from the one applied by English courts did not militate against a stay in favour of the foreign court. To do so would confirm the alleged chauvinism of the English courts and affront comity. However, the test requires the court to make a decision about substantial justice between the parties. At some point the quality of justice in foreign courts must become important. The claimant may argue that justice is impossible abroad due to the foreign court's bias on racial or political grounds,[72] to its lack of commercial[73] or procedural expertise[74] or to excessively lengthy delays there.[75] Although a claimant is required to provide cogent and convincing evidence of such factors before they can carry any weight, a decision involving them is necessarily one on the quality of justice.

Restraining foreign proceedings

The English court cannot prohibit a foreign court from hearing an action. However, it may restrain *a party*, subject to its jurisdiction, from starting or continuing proceedings in that foreign court. These orders are colloquially known as 'anti-suit injunctions' and are enforced by using the procedure of contempt of court. This is draconian. Someone in contempt may be prevented from taking further part in English proceedings which could result in summary judgment and costs orders against them; or, their assets may be seized or, in sufficiently heinous cases, the party may be imprisoned. The party to be restrained must be subject to the English court's jurisdiction by being present here to be served with the order, or by being a party to proceedings here by submission or even if the English court has assumed jurisdiction by allowing service on an absent defendant under CPR Rule 6.20.[76]

There has been an enormous growth in the use of these orders in recent years. Proceedings in more than one jurisdiction on the same claim and between the same parties are unnecessarily expensive and risk conflicting judgments. The English court maintains that anti-suit injunctions are not a direct interference with the foreign court as they operate *in personam*. However, the court does recognise the breach of comity inherent in these injunctions and therefore requires a 'sufficient interest' of the English court to justify the use of the discretionary

---

[72] *Oppenheimer* v. *Louis Rosenthal* [1937] 1 All ER 23 (a CPR Rule 6.20 case); *Mohammed* v. *Bank of Kuwait and Middle East KSC* [1996] 1 WLR 1483 CA.
[73] *The Varna* (No. 2) [1994] 2 Ll.R 41 (stay granted).
[74] *Lubbe* v. *Cape plc* [2000] 1 WLR 1545 HL.
[75] *Radhakrishna Hospitality Service Private Ltd* v. *EIH Ltd* [1999] 2 Ll.R 249.
[76] *The Tropaioforos* [1962] 1 Ll.R 410.

power.[77] Otherwise there is a risk that the English court might wrongly arrogate to itself the power to decide which is the most appropriate court for determining the dispute.

In *Airbus Industrie GIE* v. *Patel*[78] Lord Goff laid down the following categories of cases in which the power is exercised, but it must be stressed that these categories are not closed. The underlying principle is that the English court exercises its power to restrain a party from proceeding abroad because the ends of justice require it.[79]

Vexatious or oppressive foreign proceedings

The original ground for the grant of the injunction required the proceedings abroad to be vexatious and oppressive to the party asking for the order.[80] There was a time when the courts thought that the principles of *forum conveniens* might be appropriate to decide whether to grant an anti-suit injunction.[81] However, a decision merely that England is the appropriate forum should not be sufficient to justify the interference with the foreign court. Bringing an action in an inconvenient or inappropriate court is not of itself enough to be vexatious and oppressive. The Privy Council in *SNIA* v. *Lee Kui Jak*[82] accepted that the *Spiliada* criteria were insufficient and required something more. The foreign proceedings must also be causing injustice, not mere inconvenience. The facts of *SNIA* v. *Lee Kui Jak* were complex.

> The respondents were the widow and administrators of a man who was killed when a helicopter crashed in Brunei. This had been manufactured in France by the appellant French company (SNIA), which had a Texas subsidiary. The helicopter was owned by a British company and serviced by its Malaysian subsidiary (M) under contract to a Brunei company. The respondents brought proceedings against SNIA in Brunei, in France and in Texas alleging faulty design and manufacture. They sued in Texas because they were advised that product liability law was more favourable to them under Texas law than under Brunei law and that higher damages were probably obtainable there. Their Texas attorneys carried out pre-trial discovery and examination of witnesses in Texas and France and the Texas trial was fixed for 1 July 1987. In December 1986 SNIA applied to the Brunei court for an injunction to restrain the Texas action. (The French proceedings had

---

[77] *Airbus Industrie GIE* v. *Patel* [1999] AC 119 HL.   [78] *Ibid.*   [79] *Ibid.* at p. 133.
[80] See, for example, *Cohen* v. *Rothfield* [1919] 1 KB 410 CA.
[81] *Castanho* v. *Brown and Root (UK) Ltd* [1981] AC 557 at 574 HL. Application of *forum non conveniens* in such a situation was strongly queried in *Bank of Tokyo Ltd* v. *Karoon* [1989] AC 45n. CA.
[82] *Société Nationale Industrielle Aerospatiale* v. *Lee Kui Jak* [1987] AC 871 PC.

been dropped). This was refused. SNIA undertook to the Brunei Court of Appeal that they would expedite a hearing in Brunei. SNIA also served a contribution notice on M, who would accept Brunei jurisdiction but not that of Texas.

The Brunei Court of Appeal applied *The Spiliada* and refused the injunction. The Privy Council allowed the appeal and held that the Texas proceedings should be enjoined. This was a case, as it happened, in which a stricter and, as the Privy Council held, more correct test than that of *forum non conveniens* was satisfied.

Lord Goff, delivering the advice of the Board, said that the court cannot restrain foreign proceedings on the sole ground that England is the natural forum. Rather, the English court will usually, where a remedy for a particular wrong is available in both an English and a foreign court, only restrain a person from pursuing proceedings in the foreign court if his doing so would also be vexatious or oppressive to the other party. (This sounds like the original test, which was, as we have seen, used in earlier times for applications for stays of actions in the English courts.) The English court must not only conclude that it is the natural forum but must also take account of and balance the respective justice and injustice caused to the parties if an injunction was granted or if it was not. So, as a general rule, the court will not grant an injunction if, by doing so, it would deprive the claimant in the foreign action of advantages he might have in the foreign forum, of which it would be unjust to deprive him.

In *SNIA* v. *Lee Kui Jak* itself, clearly the Brunei court was the natural forum since every factor in the case pointed to it. The accident occurred there and Brunei law, which differed from Texas law in several respects, governed the claim. The deceased had had his residence and principal place of business in Brunei, where the respondents resided, as did any witnesses of fact. Nothing at all connected the action with Texas. The activities of the Texas lawyers could not make the Texas court the natural forum; they were in no way comparable with the *Cambridgeshire* activities which had played a significant role in the *Spiliada* case.[83]

Moreover, any injustice caused to the respondents by depriving them of possible higher damages in Texas was cancelled out by injustice to SNIA which would arise from depriving them of trial in Brunei. M, the Malaysian company, had been the respondent's prime target and had settled with them. M, it will be recalled, had agreed to submit to Brunei jurisdiction but not that of Texas. So if the latter action were to continue and SNIA were to be held liable, they would have to start a separate action against M in Brunei for contribution and SNIA's liability

---

[83] See p. 89 above.

might have to be established afresh. The continuance of the Texas action would clearly be oppressive to SNIA.

In *Airbus Industrie GIE* v. *Patel*,[84] the courts were faced for the first time with a request for an anti-suit injunction to restrain the defendants from proceeding in a foreign court, when the alternative forum was not the English court and there were no substantive proceedings here.

> D and others (Ds) suffered death and injury in a plane crash at Bangalore, India. They or their relatives wished to sue Airbus in Texas, but Airbus obtained an order in the nature of an anti-suit injunction from the Indian court prohibiting Ds from suing Airbus anywhere except India. Since Ds resided in England the Indian order was ineffective so Airbus asked the English court to enforce the Indian order, or alternatively to issue its own anti-suit injunction. The English court had jurisdiction since Ds were resident here.

Colman J held, correctly, that in cases not within the Brussels or Lugano Conventions, only foreign money judgments can be enforced.[85] He further held that, although he had power to issue an English anti-suit injunction, the facts of this case did not warrant his doing so. The Court of Appeal[86] held that the learned judge had misdirected himself and that the injunction should be granted. However, the House of Lords reversed this extraordinary judgment and rescinded the injunction.

In his speech Lord Goff of Chievely emphasised the need to observe comity towards foreign courts and held that as a general principle England and its courts must have some interest in the litigation (which in this case it did not) to justify interfering indirectly with the exercise by a foreign court of its jurisdiction. Such interference is only justifiable if the foreign court has, for example, claimed jurisdiction on some extremely internationally exorbitant basis.

It may be observed that the Court of Appeal's main objection to the Texas court's hearing the case was that, at the time, they had no doctrine of *forum non conveniens* and quite a lot of Lord Goff's speech was devoted to this topic (by the time he delivered the speech, Texas had adopted the doctrine). It is not altogether clear what this really had to do with it. It seems quite unwarranted for the English courts to reprobate foreign courts[87] for not applying *forum non conveniens* when the former only avowedly adopted it thirteen years earlier.[88]

---

[84] [1999] AC 119 HL.   [85] [1996] ILPr. 465.   [86] [1997] 2 Ll.R 8 CA.

[87] As Lord Goff himself observes, this could only be with regard to common law courts anyway; civil law systems do not operate the doctrine. It has no place in the Brussels and Lugano Conventions: see p. 133 below.

[88] See p. 187 above.

Unconscionable foreign proceedings

Airbus Industrie GIE v. *Patel* was a case similar to the so-called 'single fora' cases in which proceedings between the parties are impossible in England, because, for example, English law provides no cause of action. In these cases the English court should be even more reluctant to enjoin the foreign proceedings. This is because if the claimant cannot sue in the foreign court, the claimant's rights may not be capable of being vindicated anywhere. However, the English court has granted an injunction where the bringing of the foreign proceedings is unconscionable so long as the English court had a sufficient interest in or connection with the action. The situation is exemplified by actions for damages under the United States' Anti-Trust Laws and the decision in *British Airways Board* v. *Laker Airways Ltd.*[89]

The case arose out of the collapse and liquidation of Laker Airways in early 1982. The British liquidator commenced proceedings in the United States under, *inter alia*, the US Anti-Trust Laws,[90] alleging that two British airlines had conspired with other airlines and aircraft manufacturers to bring about the collapse of Laker. If he won, he would be entitled to treble damages.[91] The two airlines asked the court to restrain the liquidator from his action in the United States, arguing that it would be unjust to them and contrary to public policy for it to continue.

Parker J refused. The defendant could show that to grant an injunction would be unjust since the anti-trust action could only be pursued in America. If he could not sue there he could not sue anywhere.

The Secretary of State then made an Order[92] and general directions under the Protection of Trading Interests Act 1980 which had the effect of prohibiting the United Kingdom airlines from complying with any requirement or prohibition under the Anti-Trust Acts and with any requirement for production of certain evidence in the US actions.[93] The Court of Appeal thought this made all the difference by rendering a proper trial in the United States impossible.

But the House of Lords, speaking through Lord Diplock, reversed this decision on the narrow ground that since the airlines were seeking an injunction they must show that they had a pre-existing cause of

---

[89] [1985] AC 58 HL. British Caledonian Airways were co-claimants.
[90] Sherman Act 1890, Clayton Act 1914.
[91] I.e. the actual compensation trebled. This would not be enforceable here by reason of the Protection of Trading Interests Act 1980, s. 5, but could be enforced against assets in the United States.
[92] Protection of Trading Interests (US Anti-trust Measures) Order 1983.
[93] The Order and directions were made under ss. 2 and 3 of the 1980 Act. An attempt to have these declared *ultra vires* failed.

action for which an injunction would be a remedy, or some legal or equitable right arising from a contract (as where there is an English jurisdiction clause) or from the other party's unconscionable conduct (as where there would be a good defence under English law)[94] not to be sued in the foreign court on the foreign cause of action, since the court's power to grant an injunction is limited to these circumstances. The airlines had no such cause of action or right.[95]

It can be said that though the House's decision put an end to a conflict between the English and the United States courts, it hardly answers the objection to allowing one British company to sue two other British companies in a foreign court when it could not do so here. Nor does it give much weight to the argument, based on public policy, against making the executive and the courts appear to be speaking with different voices on a matter which affects relations with another state.[96]

In a subsequent decision of the Court of Appeal, *Midland Bank v. Laker Airways*,[97] which arose out of the same dispute, *British Airways Board v. Laker Airways* was distinguished and an injunction restraining Laker's liquidator from continuing anti-trust litigation in the USA against two English banks was restored. It was held that it would be unjust and unconscionable for them to be subjected to such litigation in respect of acts done in England and intended to be governed by English law when they had no relevant presence or activities in the United States.

But the House of Lords' decision was applied in *Smith, Kline & French Laboratories Ltd v. Bloch*,[98] in which Dr Bloch began an action in the United States based, not on breach of contract as was an earlier action he had brought there and which had been enjoined, but on the anti-trust laws. Moreover, his action was not against the English subsidiary of an American company, as in reality it had been in the earlier proceedings he had brought in the United States, but against the American parent company alone. The court refused to grant an injunction against him.

---

[94] Such as estoppel, election, waiver or laches (lapse of time caused by delay).

[95] This is all developed from Lord Diplock's own judgment in *The Siskina* [1979] AC 210, 256 HL.

[96] The argument which had prevailed in the Court of Appeal was disclaimed by the airlines before the House of Lords. Lord Diplock showed that it was based on a misconstruction of the Protection of Trading Interests Act 1980 and a misapprehension of the effect of the directions made under it. Public policy was not infringed since there was no invasion of United Kingdom sovereignty in US courts applying their law to activities which took place in part in the United States. But the British Government was arguing that the United States was in breach of treaty.

[97] [1986] QB 689 CA.   [98] [1985] ECC 230 CA.

Another case which seems to fall for discussion here is *South Carolina Insurance Co* v. *Assurantie Maatschappij 'de Zeven Provincien' NV*,[99] although there were proceedings in existence in England. But what it sought to restrain the defendants from doing abroad they could not do under English law. The House of Lords lifted an injunction against the defendants, who were parties to an action in England, from continuing proceedings in the United States which they had started so as to obtain pre-trial discovery of evidence from the claimants for use in the English action. Such pre-trial discovery is not normally permitted in England. The House of Lords held that the case did not fall into one of those categories insisted on by Lord Diplock in *British Airways Board* v. *Laker Airways* as being those in which an injunction can be granted. The defendants' conduct was not unconscionable; they were entitled to get their evidence wherever they could and by any lawful means.[100]

One difficulty to which this case gave rise is that, although Lord Brandon, for the majority, said that Lord Diplock's categories of case in which an injunction can be granted were exclusive, Lords Mackay and Goff clearly thought that they were not, saying that the court's power to grant injunctions, being quite unfettered by statute,[101] is not restricted to such types of case. In *Channel Tunnel Group Ltd* v. *Balfour Beatty Construction Ltd*,[102] Lord Mustill was of the opinion, perhaps, that Lord Diplock's views represent the law, but Lord Browne-Wilkinson, with whom two other Law Lords agreed, had serious reservations and sympathised with the views of Lords Mackay and Goff. The matter is not, therefore, altogether beyond doubt.[103]

Submission to English jurisdiction: proceedings started abroad

Where a claimant starts proceedings abroad in disregard of a clause in a contract submitting to the jurisdiction of the English courts or to arbitration here, the court will be more likely to restrain the foreign proceedings than it will be if no such clause exists. The Court of Appeal granted an injunction to restrain further Swiss proceedings between

---

[99] [1987] AC 24 HL. Compare *Bankers Trust International plc* v. *PT Dharmalas Sakti Sejahtera* [1996] CLC 252, where an injunction was granted restraining proceedings in New York for the same purpose. However, the English proceedings were already completed and the New York action was highly speculative.

[100] Any prejudice the claimants might suffer, such as increased costs, was self-inflicted, since they had refused to cooperate in the English proceedings.

[101] Supreme Court Act 1981, s. 37(1).   [102] [1993] AC 334 HL.

[103] The matter was not mentioned in *Airbus Industrie GIE* v. *Patel* [1999] 1 AC 119 HL.

Swiss buyers and Sudanese sellers in *Tracomin SA* v. *Sudan Oil Seeds Ltd* (No. 2)[104] when the buyers had sued the sellers to judgment in the Swiss courts in violation of an English arbitration clause. (Such a foreign judgment could not be enforced in England.)[105]

Millett LJ observed in *The Angelic Grace*[106] that there is no difference in this respect between an arbitration clause and an exclusive jurisdiction clause; both confer on the claimant a legal right not to be sued abroad. Good reason must be shown by the party who is acting in breach of agreement why an injunction should not be granted.[107] In *Bouygues Offshore SA* v. *Caspian Shipping Co.* (Nos. 1, 3, 4 and 5),[108] where there were several parties some of whom were not subject to the jurisdiction clause, an injunction was refused. One might also be refused so as to avoid multiplicity of proceedings in litigation where a foreign court is the *forum conveniens*. Otherwise, as was held in *Toepfer International GmbH* v. *Société Cargill France*,[109] little or no weight should be given to *forum non conveniens* or to the risk of inconsistent judgments.

Delay in applying for an injunction or the claimant's submission to the jurisdiction of the foreign court or the making of an application to it for a stay of its proceedings which then fails may cause an injunction to be refused[110] as will the existence of genuine reasons for supposing the clause is invalid[111] or where the dispute does not clearly fall within the clause.[112]

It was held in *Philip Alexander Securities and Futures Ltd* v. *Bamberger*[113] that where the foreign court did not regard itself as obliged to stay its

---

[104] [1981] 1 WLR 1026 at 1031.

[105] Civil Jurisdiction and Judgments Act 1982, s. 32. In *Tracomin SA* v. *Sudan Oil Seeds Ltd* (No. 1) [1983] 1 WLR 1026, the entry into force of this provision during proceedings to enforce the Swiss judgment already obtained was held to preclude its recognition or enforcement: see p. 117 below.

[106] [1995] 1 Ll.R 87 at 96 CA (arbitration clause); *Continental Bank NA* v. *Aeakos Companhia Naviera* [1994] 1 WLR 588 CA, *Turner* v. *Grovit* [2000] 1 WLR 1034 CA (both discussed more fully at pp. 163–5 below); *Society of Lloyd's* v. *White* (2000) *The Times*, 14 April.

[107] *Akai Pty Ltd* v. *People's Insurance Co. Ltd* [1998] 1 Ll.R 90. Damages will not usually be an adequate remedy for breach of such an agreement.

[108] [1998] 2 Ll.R CA.   [109] [1997] 2 Ll.R 98, [1997] 2 Ll.R 279 CA.

[110] For discussion of such factors see *Toepfer International GmbH* v. *Molina Boschi Srl* [1996] 1 Ll.R 510; *Akai Pty Ltd* v. *People's Insurance Co. Ltd* [1998] 1 Ll.R 90 at 107–8; *DVA* v. *Voest Alpine* [1997] 2 Ll.R 279, CA.

[111] *Crédit Suisse First Boston (Europe) Ltd* v. *Seagate Trading Co. Ltd* [1999] 1 All ER (Comm.) 261; cf. *Bankers' Trust Co.* v. *PT Jakarta International Hotels and Development* [1999] 1 All ER (Comm.) 785.

[112] *Crédit Suisse First Boston (Europe) Ltd* v. *MLC (Bermuda) Ltd* [1999] 1 All ER (Comm.) 237; *Donohoe* v. *Armco Inc.* [2000] 1 All ER (Comm.) 425.

[113] [1997] 1 ILPr. 73, 104 CA. See Re *the Enforcement of an English Anti-Suit Injunction* [1997] ILPr. 320.

proceedings in the face of the English injunction which it regarded as an infringement of its sovereignty, an injunction should not be granted. It has been suggested that the courts may be becoming more careful in asserting their jurisdiction under an exclusive jurisdiction clause;[114] indeed, in the case just mentioned the Court of Appeal suggested that the courts' existing approach might need reconsideration.

---

[114] See G. C. Cheshire and P. M. North, *Private International Law*, 13th edn (London, Butterworths, 1999) 372.

9   Foreign judgments

An English court may find itself called upon to recognise or enforce a judgment rendered by a foreign court. Certain types of judgment, by their nature, only require recognition. These include foreign divorce and nullity decrees. Others, including all judgments *in personam*, may on occasions only need to be recognised, as when a defendant pleads that he had satisfied a judgment given in the claimant's favour. But the court may be asked to enforce a foreign judgment, such as a maintenance order, or any judgment for damages.

The law governing the matter has become somewhat complex. Six different sets of rules exist. These deal with, respectively, judgments of courts (i) of other EU countries, (ii) of other parts of the United Kingdom, (iii) of EFTA countries,[1] (iv) of Commonwealth countries to which the Administration of Justice Act 1920 applies, (v) of countries to which the Foreign Judgments (Reciprocal Enforcement) Act 1933 applies and (vi) of other countries to which rules of common law apply.[2] It is the last of these with which this chapter is chiefly concerned.[3]

Basis of recognition and enforcement

Since the mid-nineteenth century the theory adopted by the English courts to explain their recognition and enforcement of foreign judgments has been the doctrine of 'obligation'. This means that a judgment rendered by a foreign court of competent jurisdiction imposes upon the defendant a duty or obligation to obey it and discharge it and confers a correlative right on the claimant to enforce that obligation through the English courts. This was clearly enunciated in *Schibsby* v. *Westenholz*[4] by Blackburn J.

---

[1] (i), (ii) and (iii) are discussed in ch. 10 below.
[2] (v) applies to judgments of courts of some EU and EFTA countries to which the rules of the Civil Jurisdiction and Judgment Acts 1982 and 1991 do not apply.
[3] Reference to the rules of the 1933 Act will be made where these are apposite.
[4] (1870) LR 6 QB 155, quoting *Godard* v. *Gray* (1870) LR 6 QB 139.

The adherence of the English courts to this theory explains the ease with which a foreign judgment may be recognised or enforced in England compared with the position under the laws of some other countries. These may only be willing to enforce a foreign judgment if the courts of the state in which the judgment was rendered would enforce a judgment of the court which is requested to enforce it.[5]

Jurisdiction of the foreign court

It is essential to the recognition and enforcement of a foreign judgment that the court which rendered it had jurisdiction in the eyes of the English court. It is not enough that it had jurisdiction under its own rules. In the celebrated case of *Buchanan* v. *Rucker*[6] in which a judgment was obtained in Tobago where the defendant had never been, by means of substituted service upon him effected by nailing a copy of the summons to the court-house door as permitted by Tobago law, Lord Ellenborough enquired, 'Can the island of Tobago pass a law to bind the whole world? Would the world submit to such an assumed jurisdiction?' He then answered his own questions in the negative.

If the foreign court did not have jurisdiction in our view the judgment cannot be recognised or enforced in England. If it did, the judgment will, in most cases, be recognised or enforced, since any defences other than lack of jurisdiction are few and strictly circumscribed.[7]

The usual starting point for an exposition of this topic is a passage from the judgment of Buckley LJ in *Emanuel* v. *Symon*:[8]

In an action in personam there are five cases in which the courts of this country will enforce a foreign judgment: (1) where the defendant is a subject of the foreign country in which the judgment has been obtained; (2) where he was resident in the foreign country when the action began; (3) where the defendant in the character of plaintiff has selected the forum in which he is afterwards sued; (4) where he has voluntarily appeared; and (5) where he has contracted to submit himself to the forum in which the judgment was obtained.

Of these five categories, the first is open to very serious doubt.[9] (3), (4) and (5) are three different examples of ways in which the defendant confers jurisdiction by submission.

---

[5] Compare the decision of the United States Supreme Court in *Hilton* v. *Guyot* 159 US 113 (1895). For the meaning of 'reciprocity' in enforcing judgments when the foreign court has assumed jurisdiction in a situation in which the English courts might have done the same, see *Schibsby* v. *Westenholz* and see pp. 116–17 below.

[6] (1808) 9 East. 192. See also *Sirdar Gurdyal Singh* v. *Rajah of Faridkote* [1894] AC 670 PC.

[7] For the defences which may be raised see pp. 119–23 below.

[8] [1908] 1 KB 302 CA. He was, in fact, repeating observations by Fry J in *Rousillon* v. *Rousillon* (1880) 14 Ch. D 351.

[9] See p. 116 below.

Presence or residence

Buckley LJ's second category, 'where [the defendant] was resident in the foreign country when the action began' calls for examination of two matters.

First, by using the words 'when the action began' it seems that he was referring to when process of the foreign court was served on the defendant and not when it was issued from that court. In *Adams* v. *Cape Industries plc*[10] the Court of Appeal thought it meant the former. The defendant's residence or presence at the former and not the latter time is what gives an English court jurisdiction.[11] It is clearly not enough that, as in *Sirdar Gurdyal Singh* v. *Rajah of Faridkote*,[12] the defendant was present in the foreign country when the claimant's cause of action arose, for example, when he allegedly committed a breach of contract or a tort, but had left it before any proceedings started at all.

Secondly, it is not entirely clear whether 'residence', the word used by Buckley LJ, is required or whether the defendant's physical presence, however transitory, is enough. Three considerations point to 'residence'. It is favoured by most writers, is the word used by Buckley LJ and is employed in statutes concerning the enforcement of foreign judgments.[13] By this, presumably, residence coupled with physical presence is what is meant and not residence alone. One can be present in Utopia without being resident there, but one can also be resident without actually being present there.

Three arguments favour 'presence' being the link. First, it is the basis of the jurisdiction of the English court.[14] Secondly, it was clearly held in *Carrick* v. *Hancock*[15] that the defendant's mere presence in Sweden caused him to owe allegiance to the Swedish laws and courts and the latter, therefore, had jurisdiction over him. (Admittedly, the case is not a very strong one, for there was evidence that the defendant had submitted to their jurisdiction.) Thirdly, it has the virtue of simplicity, for it is easier to tell whether someone is present in a country than to ascertain whether he is resident there. In *Adams* v. *Cape Industries plc*[16] the court was of the view, without deciding the point, that presence was the test.

---

[10] [1990] Ch. 433 CA.   [11] See pp. 72–3 above.   [12] [1894] AC 670 PC.

[13] Foreign Judgments (Reciprocal Enforcement) Act 1933, s. 4(2)(a)(iv); Administration of Justice Act 1920, s. 9(2)(b) ('ordinary residence').

[14] See, for example, *Colt Industries* v. *Sarlie* (No. 1) [1966] 1 WLR 440; *Maharanee of Baroda* v. *Wildenstein* [1972] 2 QB 283 CA; and see pp. 72–3 above.

[15] (1895) 12 TLR 59. Lord Russell of Killowen was quite specific on this point. The decision was foreshadowed in Australia in *Herman* v. *Meallin* (1891) 8 WN (NSW) 38 and followed in Canada in *Forbes* v. *Simmons* (1914) 20 DLR 100.

[16] [1990] Ch. 433 CA.

Presence or residence of companies

In the case of a company, its presence or residence has to be determined in a way which takes account of its being a legal and, therefore, imaginary person and not a natural one. It would be wrong to regard it as present or resident where it is incorporated or has its registered office, since these may be dictated solely by convenience and not be in the place or country where the company carries on its business activities.

The courts have therefore held that a corporation is present or resident in a foreign country when it indulges in 'some carrying on of business at a definite, and, to some reasonable extent, permanent place'[17] there.

It must be stressed that this test is not additional to the grounds enumerated by Buckley LJ in *Emanuel* v. *Symon*[18] and does not apply to natural persons, but is the equivalent for a company of physical presence or residence in the case of a natural person.

The test has only been discussed in four reported cases and in none of them did the court decide that the company in question was present or resident in the relevant country. Thus, in *Littauer Glove Corporation* v. *FW Millington*[19] the service of process on an English company's managing director at a customer's office when he was visiting New York on his company's business as its salesman, staying in hotels there, did not give the New York courts jurisdiction.

In *Sfeir* v. *National Insurance Co. of New Zealand Ltd*[20] the presence in Ghana of an agent for a New Zealand insurance company did not satisfy the test, since it only did minor business on the latter's behalf and for other companies. The New Zealand company was not resident in Ghana. In *Vogel* v. *RA Kohnstamm Ltd*[21] the presence of a 'contact man' in Israel, who merely sought out customers there for an English company and acted as the latter's means of communication with those customers but had no power to conclude contracts on the company's behalf, did not amount to presence in Israel of the company itself.

If a company has no fixed place of business of its own in a foreign country, but has an agent there who has full authority to conclude contracts on its behalf without first submitting them to the company for

---

[17] *Littauer Glove Corp.* v. *FW Millington (1920) Ltd* (1928) 44 TLR 746, per Salter J. The test, which has been applied by courts in other Commonwealth countries, is said to be the same as that adopted at common law to determine whether a company is resident in England. There are many cases on this, though their importance is nowadays relatively small. See p. 82 above.

[18] [1908] 1 KB 302 CA.   [19] (1928) 44 TLR 746.

[20] [1964] 1 Ll.R 330, a case under the Administration of Justice Act 1920.

[21] [1973] QB 133. The English company had no office of its own in Israel.

approval, it will, it seems, be regarded as residing at the agent's place of business in that foreign country.[22]

In the case of a group of companies, the presence of a subsidiary may amount to the presence of the parent company in the foreign country. But this will only be so if the subsidiary is doing the parent's business so that its business is that of the parent. The subsidiary must be the agent of the company. However, the relationship of principal and agent must be made out and does not exist solely because of the parent–subsidiary nexus. In *Adams* v. *Cape Industries plc*[23] the court held that it had not been made out and refused to disregard the separate legal personalities of an English parent and its subsidiaries in the United States. The former was held not to be present in the United States.

The requirement laid down in the Foreign Judgments (Reciprocal Enforcement) Act 1933 is more stringent than the common law test for it entails that the company should have its *principal* place of business, not merely 'any' place of business, in the foreign country.[24]

Submission

The third, fourth and fifth of Buckley LJ's categories in *Emanuel* v. *Symon*[25] are cases of submission to the jurisdiction by a defendant who is not otherwise subject to it.

(a) If the defendant was the claimant (or counterclaimant) in the foreign court and judgment was given against him on a counterclaim, he is taken to have submitted in respect of the counterclaim.[26]

(b) If the defendant makes a voluntary appearance in the proceedings and if he pleads to the merits of the case, he thereby submits to the jurisdiction even though he also contests the court's jurisdiction.[27] Formerly it was unclear whether, at common law, a defendant who appeared solely to argue that the court had no jurisdiction over him had thereby submitted, so that if the argument was decided against him and judgment was given against him on the merits, the

---

[22] See *Jabbour* v. *Custodian of Israeli Absentee Property* [1954] 1 WLR 139. The cases on whether a foreign company has a place of business in England bear this out.

[23] [1990] Ch. 433 CA, see J. G. Collier, note [1990] 49 *CLJ* 416. The Court of Appeal applied English company law. For a detailed discussion in the context of 'lifting the veil of incorporation', see L. C. B. Gower, *Modern Company Law*, 6th edn (London, Sweet and Maxwell, 1997) 168–74.

[24] S. 4(2)(a)(iv).   [25] [1908] 1 KB 302.

[26] See also *Schibsby* v. *Westenholz* (1870) LR 6 QB 155 at 161; 1933 Act, s. 4(2)(a)(ii).

[27] 1933 Act, s. 4(2)(a)(i).

judgment was enforceable in England.[28] But the Civil Jurisdiction and Judgments Act 1982, s. 33(1)(a) provides that an appearance to contest the jurisdiction of the foreign court is not for that reason alone to be regarded as a submission thereto.[29]

In *Henry* v. *Geoprosco International*[30] it was held that where a defendant had appeared before the foreign court to ask it (i) to stay the action and remit it to arbitration in accordance with an agreement between the parties and (ii) otherwise to decline in its discretion to exercise such jurisdiction as it could assume under its own rules, he had thereby submitted to its jurisdiction.[31] Section 33(1)(b) of the 1982 Act now provides that (i) is no longer to amount to a submission.[32] But (ii) is not changed so that if, for example, the defendant were to appear to ask the court not to allow service on him out of the jurisdiction, it appears that this would amount to submission. It is thought that if, as some foreign laws require him to do, a defendant who wishes to contest the jurisdiction at the same time also formally files his possible defences on the merits, he does not thereby submit provided he does not argue the case on its merits.[33] A defendant does not submit if he enters a conditional appearance and seeks to set aside permission to serve process of the court outside the jurisdiction.[34]

At common law, an appearance to protect property about to be seized in the foreign country was a voluntary submission, whereas an appearance to protect property already seized was not. By section 33(1)(c) of the 1982 Act an appearance solely for either of these purposes is not now to be treated as submission.[35]

---

[28] In Re *Dulles' Settlement* (No. 2) [1951] Ch. 842, Denning LJ thought not, but the case did not concern a foreign judgment and it was explained away in *Henry* v. *Geoprosco International Ltd* [1976] QB 726 CA where *Daarnhouwer & Co. NV* v. *Boulos* [1968] 2 Ll.R 259, which decided that this was not a submission, was overruled. *Harris* v. *Taylor* [1915] 2 KB 580 CA and *Henry* v. *Geoprosco* did not decide that such a defendant was deemed to have submitted, but tended to suggest that he had.

[29] This was already provided by the 1933 Act, s. 4(2)(a)(i). In *Desert Sun Loan Corp.* v. *Hill* [1996] 2 All ER 847 CA it was held that a finding of a foreign court that a defendant had authorised a lawyer to act on his behalf and so had submitted could create an issue estoppel (as to which see pp. 129–30 below) and prevent the issue of authority being relitigated. However, in that case the US court did not find that the defendant had submitted.

[30] [1976] QB 726 CA.

[31] The reason was that he had admitted that the court *could* exercise jurisdiction over him.

[32] Applied in *Tracomin SA* v. *Sudan Oil Seeds Ltd* (No. 1) [1983] 1 WLR 662, affd *ibid.* 1026 CA. The arbitration was to be held in England.

[33] This is the position under the Brussels Convention, Art. 18: see p. 158 below.

[34] *Akande* v. *Balfour Beatty Construction Ltd* [1998] ILPr. 110 at 114–16 (registration of a Nigerian judgment under the 1920 Act set aside).

[35] This brought the common law into line with the 1933 Act, s. 4(2)(a)(i).

Submission to the jurisdiction of the foreign court in one action is not submission in another action, though both actions arise out of the same allegations.[36] On the other hand, a party's submission to the jurisdiction in an action against him is also a submission in respect of a claim against him by a co-defendant where that claim is connected with the subject matter of the original action.[37]

(c) A defendant who had previously agreed, either directly, by a contract with the claimant,[38] or indirectly, as for example, by taking shares in a foreign company whose constitution provides for submission of disputes arising out of membership therein to the jurisdiction of a foreign court and a method of service of proceedings upon him, is taken to have submitted to that court's jurisdiction in respect of such disputes.[39]

It seems that such an agreement must be express; in any event it cannot be implied merely from entry into a contract which is governed by the law of the foreign country concerned, if the contract contains no jurisdiction or arbitration clause referring to that country.[40] Nor can it be implied from membership in a foreign company whose constitution contains no provision with respect to jurisdiction over disputes arising out of membership.[41] In *Emanuel* v. *Symon*[42] it was held that mere entry into a partnership is not an agreement to submit to the courts of the country where the partnership owns property or carries on business. Indeed, the argument that there can be an 'implied submission' has been judicially rejected.[43]

Office or place of business

Statute provides for one case of 'special' jurisdiction. Where an individual or corporation has an office or place of business in the foreign country, its courts have jurisdiction over proceedings in respect of a transaction effected through that office or place of business.[44] No decision supports this as a rule of common law.

---

[36] *Adams* v. *Cape Industries plc* [1990] Ch. 433, per Scott J.
[37] *Murphy* v. *Sivajothi* [1999] 1 All ER 72.
[38] *Feyerick* v. *Hubbard* (1902) 71 LJKB 509.
[39] *Copin* v. *Adamson* (1875) LR 1 Ex. D 17 CA; 1933 Act, s. 4(2)(a)(iii).
[40] *Vogel* v. *RA Kohnstamm Ltd* [1973] QB 133. A jurisdiction clause in a contract may lead to an inference as to the governing law (see p. 194 below), but the converse is not true.
[41] See *Copin* v. *Adamson* (1875) LR 1 Ex. D 17 CA.
[42] [1908] 1 KB 302 CA. This was not followed in *Blohn* v. *Desser* [1962] 2 QB 116 which can be distinguished in that the case concerned the relations of partners *vis-à-vis* third parties, whereas *Emanuel* v. *Symon* concerned an internal dispute, but *Blohn* v. *Desser* is widely regarded as wrong on this point.
[43] *Vogel* v. *RA Kohnstamm Ltd* [1973] QB 133.
[44] 1933 Act, s. 4(2)(a)(v). This is known as 'special' jurisdiction, because it does not include any disputes other than those mentioned.

Where the foreign court has no jurisdiction

In addition to the cases already mentioned where the Civil Jurisdiction and Judgments Act 1982 denies jurisdiction, it is clear, or tolerably clear, that in several other situations a foreign court will not be regarded as having jurisdiction. These are all cases which are not mentioned as bases of jurisdiction in the 1933 Act.

Mere possession of property in the foreign country[45] and mere presence of the defendant there at the time the cause of action arose[46] are not enough to give its courts jurisdiction. Moreover, although Buckley LJ mentioned nationality in *Emanuel* v. *Symon*, it has been doubted whether this is a basis of jurisdiction,[47] and so has domicile, for nationality or domicile by themselves alone provide too tenuous a connection with a foreign country or its courts.

It has been suggested[48] that reciprocity would allow an English court to recognise and enforce a foreign judgment when the foreign court has assumed jurisdiction in a case in which the English court could itself assume jurisdiction by allowing service on an absent defendant under CPR Rule 6.20.[49] But this suggestion is open to several objections, the chief of which is that it is the very one which was rejected in *Schibsby* v. *Westenholz*,[50] a case in which the English court refused to enforce a judgment given by a French court in favour of a Dane against other Danes, resident and carrying on business in London, who had not been to France. Another is that since service out of the jurisdiction under CPR Rule 6.20 is discretionary, then if the same is true of the equivalent foreign rules, the English court could not be certain that the foreign court, in assuming jurisdiction, had exercised its discretion in precisely the same way as the English court itself would have done. Thus precise reciprocity is difficult to achieve.

Although this principle of reciprocity was applied at common law to recognition of foreign divorces[51] and nullity decrees,[52] it has been

---

[45]   *Emanuel* v. *Symon* [1908] 1 KB 302 CA.

[46]   *Ibid.*; *Sirdar Gurdyal Singh* v. *Rajah of Faridkote* [1894] AC 670 PC; *Rousillon* v. *Rousillon* (1880) 14 Ch. D 351.

[47]   See *Blohn* v. *Desser* [1962] 2 QB 116; *Rossano* v. *Manufacturers Life Insurance Co.* [1963] 2 QB 352; *Vogel* v. *RA Kohnstamm Ltd* [1973] QB 133. It is supported by dicta in several cases. It was rejected by the Irish Supreme Court in *Rainford* v. *Newell-Roberts* [1962] IR 95.

[48]   By Denning LJ in Re *Dulles' Settlement* (No. 2) [1951] Ch. 842 CA at 851. This was *obiter* since the question in that case was whether the English court had jurisdiction.

[49]   As to this see pp. 74–82 above.

[50]   (1870) LR 6 QB 155, and see *Turnbull* v. *Walker* (1892) 67 LT 767.

[51]   *Travers* v. *Holley* [1953] P 246 CA.

[52]   *Perrini* v. *Perrini* [1979] Fam. 84. But only after abolition with respect to divorces.

abolished by statute with regard to these,[53] and courts both in England[54] and in the Commonwealth[55] have rejected reciprocity as a ground for recognition and enforcement of judgments *in personam*. Moreover, the rule laid down in *Indyka* v. *Indyka*[56] that a foreign divorce decree should be recognised if there was a 'real and substantial connection' between the petitioner and the court which granted it, is inapt for judgments *in personam*. This rule was also abolished as regards foreign divorces and annulments.[57] It does not appear to have been relied on in respect of a judgment *in personam*.[58]

Under the 1933 Act, a foreign court is denied jurisdiction solely because the subject matter of the judgment is immovable property outside the foreign country.[59]

The Civil Jurisdiction and Judgments Act 1982, by section 32(1), applies to all judgments the rule already contained in section 4(3)(b) of the 1933 Act that, unless the defendant agreed to submit or brought the original proceedings himself or counter-claimed or otherwise submitted to the jurisdiction of the foreign court, the judgment cannot be recognised or enforced if the proceedings were brought in violation of an agreement between the parties to settle the dispute otherwise than by proceedings in that country's courts.[60]

What are not defences to enforcement

Once it is established that the foreign court had jurisdiction, the claimant will be able to enforce the judgment in England unless the defendant can raise a defence. In general he is not permitted to reopen the case and cause it to be re-argued on the merits, so as to show that the

---

[53] Recognition of Divorces and Legal Separations Act 1971, s. 6 (repealed and replaced by the Family Law Act 1986, Part II).

[54] Re *Trepca Mines Ltd* [1960] 1 WLR 1273 CA; *Société Coopérative Sidmetal* v. *Titan International Ltd* [1966] 1 QB 828 (a case under the 1933 Act, which does not mention reciprocity); *Amin Rasheed Shipping Corporation* v. *Kuwait Insurance Co.* [1984] AC 50 HL.

[55] *Sharps Commercials* v. *Gas Turbines Ltd* [1956] NZLR 819; *Crick* v. *Hennessy* [1973] WAR 74.

[56] [1969] 1 AC 33 HL.   [57] See Family Law Act 1986, Part II.

[58] The Canadian Supreme Court has recently adopted this test, but in the context of intra-provincial judgments: *Morguard Investments Ltd* v. *de Savoye* (1990) 76 DLR (4th) 256.

[59] S. 4(3)(a). The same is doubtless true at common law.

[60] This provision deals with a point at issue in *Henry* v. *Geoprosco International Ltd* [1976] QB 726 CA. It was applied in *Tracomin* v. *Sudan Oil Seeds Ltd* (No. 1) [1983] 1 WLR 1026 CA.

decision of the foreign court was wrong. Thus, very few defences are available and all, to a greater or lesser extent, reflect public policy. Before discussing these, it is convenient to say what is not a defence.

An error of fact or law on the part of the foreign court is not a defence, even though that court applied the wrong law or, though it applied the correct law, it got it wrong. This is exemplified by *Godard* v. *Gray*,[61] where a French court made an obvious error as to the rules of English law it had purported to apply. The defendant cannot adduce evidence which could have been produced to the foreign court.[62] On the other hand, it seems that he can adduce fresh evidence which was not available at the time of the trial if it can be shown that had this evidence been before it, that court would have arrived at a different result.[63] Nor can he raise and defence which could have been pleaded before the foreign court.[64]

Moreover, it was held in *Vanquelin* v. *Bouard*[65] that it was no defence that, although the courts of France had jurisdiction over the defendant, the particular French court which gave the judgment lacked the competence to do so under French law. The reason is that the foreign court (or a court of appeal from it), not an English court, is the proper tribunal to decide whether it has exceeded its jurisdiction. This is a question of foreign, not English law. This is certainly true if the judgment is by the foreign law valid until set aside for excess of jurisdiction. But there is some authority for the further proposition that where, under the foreign law, the judgment is void and totally destitute of effect, it will not be recognised or enforced here.[66]

So, 'if a judgment is pronounced by a foreign court over persons within its jurisdiction and in a matter with which it is competent to deal, English courts never investigate the propriety of the proceedings . . . unless they offend against English views of substantial justice'.[67]

---

[61] (1870) LR 6 QB 139. See also *Castrique* v. *Imrie* (1870) LR 4 HL 414; *Tracomin* v. *Sudan Oil Seeds Ltd* (No. 1) [1983] 1 WLR 1026 CA.

[62] *De Cosse Brissac* v. *Rathbone* (1861) 6 H & N 301.

[63] In the case mentioned in note 62 it was not alleged that the French court would have arrived at a different result. A foreign judgment is in the same position as an English judgment in this respect.

[64] *Ellis* v. *McHenry* (1871) LR 6 CP 228; *Israel Discount Bank of New York* v. *Hadjipateras* [1984] 1 WLR 137 CA.

[65] (1863) 15 CB (NS) 341; *Pemberton* v. *Hughes* [1899] 1 Ch. 781 CA (foreign divorce decree).

[66] *Papadopoulos* v. *Papadopoulos* [1930] P 55 (Cyprus nullity decree not recognised since the court had been expressly deprived of power to grant divorce or nullity decrees). See also *Castrique* v. *Imrie* (1870) LR 4 HL 414 (a French judgment *in rem*) where it was suggested that the foreign court must act within the jurisdiction conferred upon it by the foreign state. This was entirely *obiter*.

[67] *Pemberton* v. *Hughes* [1899] 1 Ch. 781 at 790 per Lindley MR.

Defences to enforcement

Although all the available defences are, perhaps, based on public policy, it is convenient to deal with them separately.

Fraud

The first is fraud on the part of the foreign court or of the claimant.[68] If the court itself acted fraudulently, as where it acted on a bribe, the judgment obviously will not be enforced.[69] Fraud on the part of the claimant may take one of two forms. Either it is 'collateral fraud' which vitiates the jurisdiction of the foreign court by inducing it to assume jurisdiction which otherwise it would not have done. There is no doubt that this will cause the foreign judgment to be refused recognition[70] or enforcement[71] here. In *Jet Holdings Ltd* v. *Patel*,[72] it was made clear that a decision of the foreign court that there was no collateral fraud is not binding on the English court.

Or, it may be that the fraud vitiates the foreign judgment on the merits of the case, where, for example, the court is misled into giving judgment in the claimant's favour, which it otherwise would not have done. But the English courts go further than this, for they allow the case to be reopened on the merits, so it was held in *Abouloff* v. *Oppenheimer*,[73] contrary to normal principle. Thus they may enter into an investigation of the facts which were in issue before and investigated earlier by the foreign court. The faint jurisdiction for this is that, since the foreign court could not have known of the facts which were fraudulently concealed from it, it could not have ruled on them. Writers regard this as no real justification, though it seems not unfair of the English court to refuse to allow the fraudulent person to reap the fruit of his fraud.

Less justifiable is *Syal* v. *Heyward*[74] where it was held that the judgment debtor could raise the defence of fraud even though he knew the

---

[68] See the 1933 Act, s. 4(1)(a)(iv).

[69] If the judge accepted the bribe, he would hardly be regarded thereafter as acting in accordance with natural justice, unless, of course, he accepted a bribe from both sides.

[70] A case at common law in which a foreign divorce was refused recognition on this ground is *Macalpine* v. *Macalpine* [1958] P 35. A Bolivian divorce was denied recognition on the ground that recognition would be 'manifestly contrary to public policy' under Recognition of Divorces and Legal Separations Act 1971, s. 8, which had no separate heading of 'fraud'. *Kendall* v. *Kendall* [1977] Fam. 208. See p. 329 below.

[71] *Ochsenbein* v. *Papelier* (1873) 8 Ch. App. 695.   [72] [1990] 1 QB 335 CA.

[73] (1882) 10 QBD 295 CA; *Vadala* v. *Lawes* (1890) 25 QBD 310 CA.

[74] [1948] 2 KB 443, a case under the 1933 Act concerning an Indian judgment. The defendant had entered no defence at all in the Indian action.

facts on which it was based at the time of the proceedings abroad, but had not pleaded them in those proceedings.[75]

In the most recent decision on the matter, *Owens Bank Ltd* v. *Bracco*,[76] the House of Lords declined to overrule *Abouloff* v. *Oppenheimer*. A court in St Vincent had given judgment for the claimant after refusing to allow the defendants to raise a plea of fraud after the claimant's case had closed. The House of Lords held that the defendants could raise the plea in enforcement proceedings in England. The case concerned registration under the Administration of Justice Act 1920. Section 9(2)(d) allows this to be set aside if the judgment 'was obtained by fraud'. The House held that the phrase must be given the meaning it had at common law in 1920 and that it still has that meaning at common law.

One unfortunate effect of this decision is that it creates a distinction between judgments of courts in countries which are not parties to the Brussels and Lugano Conventions and of those which are. As will be seen,[77] the English courts have applied a very narrow view of fraud in the context of convention judgments and thereby almost entirely eliminated it as a defence to recognition and enforcement of such judgments.

In a more recent decision, *Owens Bank Ltd* v. *Etoile Commerciale Ltd*,[78] the Privy Council showed little enthusiasm for *Owens Bank Ltd* v. *Bracco*. It evaded that decision by holding that the defendant's attempt to raise the defence of fraud, of which there was no prima facie evidence, should be struck out in the interests of justice as an abuse of the process of the court, thus providing a possible means of escape.

Natural justice

If the foreign court acted in breach of natural justice, the judgment may not be enforced. Thus, if it acts in effect as judge in its own cause,[79] it offends against the maxim *nemo judex in causa sua*, and if it refuses to

---

[75] This seems to distinguish fraud from, for example, duress. But see the odd case of *Israel Discount Bank of New York* v. *Hadjipateras* [1984] 1 WLR 137 CA. The general principle, as we have seen, is that any defence on the merits should have been pleaded in the foreign court.

[76] [1992] 2 AC 443 HL. See J. G. Collier, note [1992] 51 *CLJ* 44 for criticism.

[77] Pp. 168–9 below.

[78] [1995] 1 WLR 44 PC. Issue estoppel may also, but rarely, be used to defeat the defence of fraud: see *House of Spring Gardens* v. *Waite* [1990] 1 QB 241 CA (p. 130 below). Abuse of the process of the court really explains the type of estoppel in issue in the latter case, so the two categories may be the same, or at least they may be alternatives.

[79] As in *Price* v. *Dewhurst* (1837) 8 Sim. 279.

allow the defendant to plead his case, it offends against the maxim *audi alteram partem*.[80]

However, there is no reported case in which a defendant has successfully pleaded the latter in resisting enforcement.

Thus, the court's reliance on its own rules in refusing to allow a party to give evidence on his own behalf[81] or the acceptance by the foreign court of biased evidence[82] do not vitiate the proceedings, provided the defendant's case has actually been heard. In *Jeannot v. Fuerst*[83] lack of notice of the proceedings was not a denial of natural justice. But in that case the judgment debtor had agreed to submit to the jurisdiction and was taken to know of the French court's rules as to service. Moreover he had had the right, of which he had not availed himself, to come in and defend the proceedings before or after execution of the judgment. Lack of notice due to the claimant's having deceived the foreign court into hearing the case when it otherwise would not have done so may amount to a fraud on the court.[84]

In *Adams v. Cape Industries plc*[85] the Court of Appeal said that a judgment could not be enforced if the trial was conducted in a manner which was not contrary to natural justice in the sense just explained but amounted to a denial of substantive justice. The foreign court had adopted a method of assessing damages which was irregular by its own rules and of which the defendants had not been told. This is a little dubious. The irregularity in question was a misapplication of the court's own laws; an error of law by the foreign court is not a defence to enforcement. However, the Court of Appeal applied the decision in the later case, *Masters v. Leaver*.[86]

Public policy

With respect to other situations involving English public policy,[87] there appears to be only one case, other than two which concerned recognition

---

[80] It appears that a finding by the foreign court that it had observed the rules of natural judgment is, like a finding that there had been no fraud, not binding on the English court: *Jet Holdings Ltd v. Patel* [1990] 1 QB 335 CA.

[81] *Scarpetta v. Lowenfeld* (1911) 27 TLR 509.

[82] *Jacobson v. Frachon* (1927) 138 LT 386. But in that case, which was concerned with recognition of a foreign judgment, the evidence was of an expert nominated by one party which the French court was not bound to accept. The decision might have been different if (i) it had been bound to accept it and (ii) the expert had been nominated by the party, knowing he would be biased and mislead the court.

[83] (1909) 25 TLR 424.

[84] See *Macalpine v. Macalpine* [1958] P 35, note 70 above. See also Family Law Act 1986, s. 51(3)(a)(i), p. 329 below, and 1933 Act, s. 4(1)(a)(iii).

[85] [1990] Ch. 433 CA.   [86] [2000] ILPr. 387 CA.

[87] Public policy is a ground for non-registration under the 1933 Act, s. 4(1)(a)(v).

of nullity decrees,[88] where a foreign judgment has not been recognised or enforced. In *Armitage* v. *Nanchen*,[89] a man against whom a Swiss court had made a maintenance order sought to have its registration set aside, arguing that to enforce it would be contrary to public policy, because the Swiss court had followed procedures different from those of English courts, and because it had relied more heavily on certain evidence than an English court would have done. But in rejecting these arguments the court said that if the foreign court had followed its own procedure and the judgment was untainted by fraud or other delinquency, an English court would only reject the judgment on the ground of public policy if it was so offensive in their eyes as to be a denial of natural justice.

This view of the matter seems both sensible and correct and puts in doubt Re *Macartney*.[90]

> A man domiciled in England left his fiancée in Malta, where she gave birth to his daughter. The Maltese court ordered him to pay maintenance for his daughter, and that after his death it should be paid from his estate, during her entire life.

Astbury J refused to enforce this order against the estate. One ground for his decision was that the cause of action was unknown to English law, a reason which cannot now be supported.[91] The other was that it was contrary to public policy to enforce an award of perpetual maintenance in favour of an illegitimate child against his or her father and his estate. This seems to be stretching public policy rather far. The decision appears to rest upon a misreading by Astbury J of the judgment of Fry J in *Rousillon* v. *Rousillon*,[92] but it has been, possibly, followed in a rather unsatisfactory judgment of the Court of Appeal in *Israel Discount Bank of New York* v. *Hadjipateras*.[93]

---

[88] *Gray* v. *Formosa* [1963] P 259 CA, followed unwillingly in *Lepre* v. *Lepre* [1965] P 52, recognition being refused on the ground of lack of substantial justice. See also Family Law Act 1986, s. 51(3)(c), p. 329 below.

[89] (1983) 4 FLR 293.

[90] [1921] 1 Ch. 522.

[91] In *Phrantzes* v. *Argenti* [1960] 2 QB 19 CA, it was held that an action brought in England would not fail, provided the English court can give a suitable and adequate remedy, merely because the cause of action was unknown to English law.

[92] (1880) 14 Ch. D 351. Astbury J appears to have thought that Fry J was speaking of public policy in the context of the action to enforce the French judgment; but he spoke of it in the context of the alternative action to enforce the contract on which the French judgment had been based.

[93] [1984] 1 WLR 137 CA. The case is criticised in J. G. Collier, note [1984] 43 *CLJ* 47, where it is pointed out that it could have been decided on the simple ground that the defence sought to have been raised here should have been pleaded in the New York proceedings, and could not be raised now: cf. *Ellis* v. *McHenry* (1871) LR 6 CP 228.

In *Vervaeke* v. *Smith*,[94] the House of Lords held that if a foreign judgment reflects the foreign notion of public policy and a previous English judgment with which the foreign judgment conflicts reflects English ideas of public policy, English public policy will prevail.

Conflicting judgment: *res judicata*

In *Vervaeke*, the House of Lords held that where, as in that case, a foreign judgment is irreconcilable with a previous English judgment, the English judgment is *res judicata* and the foreign judgment will not be recognised or enforced. The Privy Council in *Showlag* v. *Mansour*[95] applied this to the situation where two irreconcilable foreign judgments were in issue.

> In 1990 an English court held that M had stolen some of S's money. In 1991 an Egyptian court held that S had given M the money, so he had not stolen it. S's legal representatives brought an action in Jersey to recover some of the money, which had found its way there. M relied by way of defence on the second Egyptian judgment, as giving rise to *res judicata*.

It was held that the English judgment itself constituted *res judicata* and being first in time must be recognised and given effect by the Jersey court.[96]

Methods of enforcement

At common law

A foreign judgment is enforced at common law by an action begun by a claim form in which the claim is for payment of the sums due under the judgment.[97] The former rule that the claimant had the option of suing again in England on the original cause of action was abolished by the Civil Jurisdiction and Judgments Act 1982, s. 34, which prevents a further action in England on the same cause of action. This apparently sensible measure could lead to unhappy consequences and did so in *Black* v.

---

[94] [1983] 1 AC 145 HL (foreign nullity decree). This principle was applied in respect of an Indonesian judgment in the remarkably complex case, *ED & F Man (Sugar) Ltd* v. *Yani Haryanto* [1991] 1 Ll.R 429 CA. The reasoning is wide enough to apply also where the foreign judgment precedes the English judgment.

[95] [1995] 1 AC 431 PC, on appeal from a court in Jersey.

[96] The Privy Council derived this, in part, from the Brussels Convention, 1968, Art. 27(5) which prevents a court of one contracting state from recognising a judgment of another contracting state which is irreconcilable with an earlier judgment of a non-contracting state. See pp. 171–2 below. Jersey is not a party to the Brussels Convention.

[97] The basis of the action is *indebitatus assumpsit*: *Grant* v. *Easton* (1883) 13 QBD 302.

Yates[98] where the claimant had recovered on account of the death of her husband in Spain damages to an amount which was only a fraction of what she could have recovered in England. She could not, partly because of section 34, sue for the rest in England the English defendant (and effectively) his English insurer. However, in *Republic of India* v. *Indian Steamship Co. Ltd*,[99] the House of Lords held that section 34 did not deprive the English courts of jurisdiction over such an action. It merely created a statutory estoppel in favour of the defendant, so preventing him from being sued again on the same cause of action. But he could waive this, for example by agreement, so allowing the claimant to sue again in England.

This case returned to the House of Lords five years later;[100] it held that the defendants had not waived their defence under section 34, nor were they estopped by convention or by acquiescence from relying on it. The facts which gave rise to this litigation were:

> In a fire on D's ship a small number of its cargo of artillery shells were jettisoned and the rest were damaged. In 1988 the claimant cargo owners sued D in India in an action *in personam* for short delivery (i.e. for not delivering the jettisoned shells) and obtained a judgment for the equivalent of £7,200 in December 1989. In August 1989 C started English proceedings *in rem* against D's ships in respect of damage to the whole cargo for £2.6 million.

In No. 2 the House of Lords held that the claimant's action was barred by section 34. The words in that section, 'no proceedings may be brought' on a cause of action in respect of which judgment has been given in his favour, included proceedings which were started before the foreign judgment was obtained and covered proceedings continued after that time. The House held that the English and Indian proceedings arose from the same cause of action, since they arose out of the same contract and the same breach thereof and out of the same incident. If the breaches were different, they arose out of the same facts.

The House also held that, as section 34 requires, the two proceedings were between the same parties, although the English action was *in rem* and the Indian action against the shipowners *in personam* against the shipowners, since both are usually in substance against the latter.[101]

A judgment must satisfy three conditions if it is to be enforced. These are as follows.

---

[98] [1992] 2 QB 246.　　[99] [1993] AC 410 HL.

[100] *Republic of India* v. *Indian Steamship Co. Ltd* (No. 2) [1998] AC 878 HL.

[101] This point, which is nothing in particular to do with the conflict of laws, settles a controversy which has gone on for a long time. In arriving at its conclusion the House of Lords relied to some extent on the decision of the European Court of Justice in *The Tatry* [1999] QB 513n. which is discussed at ch. 10 pp. 161–2 below.

The judgment must be for a debt or fixed sum of money

A sum is not fixed (nor is the judgment final and conclusive, a further requirement discussed below) if it is for an amount which is variable at some time in the future,[102] nor if it is for damages and costs which are subject to assessment, since the entire sum is not then ascertained nor ascertainable.[103] An injunction ordered by a foreign court is not enforceable at common law.[104]

The judgment must not be for tax nor a penalty

The judgment must not be for a tax.[105] Nor may it be for a penalty.[106] A fine, for a criminal offence, is clearly a penalty. A judgment of a foreign court by way of damages awarded to the claimant may be coupled with a fine; if so, the damages may be severed from the fine and judgment for the former enforced.[107]

An award of damages may be assimilated to a fine and be regarded as a penalty though it is not imposed in criminal proceedings, but is recoverable in a civil action, if it is payable to the foreign state or other public authority by way of punishment rather than as compensation.[108] In *USA* v. *Inkley*,[109] a sum of money due under a bail bond given by the defendant in criminal proceedings against him in the United States was held to be a penalty and unenforceable in England, though it was recoverable in civil proceedings in the United States. The correctness of this decision cannot be doubted, though its justice can.

It is not a penalty in the eyes of English law, even though the foreign law under which it is imposed regards or even describes it as such, if it is payable to a private individual.

Thus, in the leading case, *Huntington* v. *Attrill*,[110] enforcement was sought in the Canadian courts of a New York judgment for a sum

---

[102] Compare two cases concerning enforcement of foreign maintenance orders at common law: *Harrop* v. *Harrop* [1920] 3 KB 386 and *Beatty* v. *Beatty* [1924] 1 KB 807.

[103] *Sadler* v. *Robins* (1808) 1 Camp. 253. A sum is ascertainable if it can be ascertained by a 'simple arithmetical calculation', *Beatty* v. *Beatty* [1924] 1 KB 807.

[104] *Airbus Industrie GIE* v. *Patel* [1996] ILPr. 465 per Colman J from whose judgment on this point there was no appeal.

[105] The English courts will not enforce directly or indirectly a claim by way of action by a foreign revenue authority: see pp. 368–9 below. Nor will an action on a foreign judgment for tax be enforced. *Government of India* v. *Taylor* [1955] AC 491 HL; *Rossano* v. *Manufacturers Life Insurance Co.* [1963] 2 QB 352. See also 1933 Act, s. 1(2)(b).

[106] *Ibid.*   [107] *Raulin* v. *Fischer* [1911] 2 KB 93.

[108] A sum is not a tax or penalty if it is awarded for services rendered such as payment to a legal aid fund: *Connor* v. *Connor* [1974] 1 NZLR 632.

[109] [1989] QB 255 CA.

[110] [1893] AC 150 PC. See also a case which concerned the appointment of a receiver of a company by a foreign court: *Schemmer* v. *Property Resources Ltd* [1975] Ch. 273.

awarded to private individuals against the officers of a company under a New York statute which described it as a penalty. The Privy Council, reversing the Ontario court, held that the judgment was not for a penalty and so could be enforced. Lord Denning MR made the point clearly in *SA Consortium General Textiles* v. *Sun and Sand Agencies*,[111] a case in which objection was raised to the enforcement of part of a French judgment for 10,000 francs awarded on account of the defendant's 'résistance abusive', or unjustifiable opposition to the claimant's claim, on the ground that the sum was for punitive or exemplary damages and so a penalty. His Lordship said,[112] 'The word "penalty" in the statute means,[113] I think, a sum payable to the state by way of punishment and not a sum payable to a private individual, even though it is payable by way of exemplary damages.'

The view has been put forward that a judgment in favour of a private individual or corporation for 'treble damages', that is, for the actual damage suffered multiplied by three, under the United States Anti-Trust Laws[114] may be unenforceable as being a penalty, on the grounds that it is imposed *in terrorem*. It is thought that on principle this is not so, and that the whole judgment could be enforced here. But the question is now academic, since section 5 of the Protection of Trading Interests Act 1980 prevents the enforcement[115] of a judgment for 'multiple damages'[116] in its entirety, and not only for the non-compensatory part.[117] An even more draconian provision which is a means of retaliation against the application of the Anti-Trust Laws is contained in section 6 of the Act, which enables a person who has paid a sum in compliance with a judgment for 'multiple damages' to recover the amount paid, but only to the extent by which the total exceeds the compensatory element.[118]

---

[111] [1978] QB 279 CA, a case under the 1933 Act.
[112] Lord Denning MR actually regarded the claim as one for compensatory damages anyway.
[113] The case concerned an application for the registration of a judgment of a French court under the 1933 Act.
[114] Sherman Act 1890, Clayton Act 1914.
[115] By action at common law or by registration under the 1920 or 1933 Acts (see pp. 127–8 below).
[116] Defined as a 'judgment for an amount arrived at by doubling, trebling or otherwise multiplying a sum assessed as compensation for the loss or damage sustained' by the person in whose favour the judgment was rendered.
[117] S. 5(2)(a). Under s. 5(2)(b) any judgment based on a *foreign rule of law* which the Secretary of State has designated by Order-in-Council whether for multiple damages or not is made unenforceable or non-registrable. No such Order has been made.
[118] Cf. s. 5.

The judgment must be final and conclusive

The foreign judgment must be final and conclusive in the court which rendered it.[119] If it can be reopened in the same court by further proceedings in which defences can be raised, which could not have been pleaded in the earlier proceedings, a judgment in respect of the latter cannot be enforced.[120]

On the other hand, a judgment is final even though it may be the subject of an appeal, and even though an appeal has been lodged. If the foreign court has granted a stay of execution of the judgment pending the outcome of the appeal, the English court may stay enforcement proceedings.[121] A judgment is also final even though under the foreign law execution cannot yet be levied in respect of it, for reasons other than a grant of a stay.[122]

By statute

Two statutes provide for enforcement of judgments given by courts in certain foreign countries by the method of registration with the relevant English court, rather than by way of action.[123] The Administration of Justice Act 1920 applies to judgments rendered in some countries in the Commonwealth.[124] The most important at present is the Foreign Judgments (Reciprocal Enforcement) Act 1933, which applies to some Commonwealth judgments, and allows the enforcement by registration on a reciprocal basis of their judgments. It has also been extended by Order-in-Council to judgments of some non-Commonwealth countries with which the United Kingdom has concluded a convention.[125]

The chief distinctions between the Acts of 1920 and 1933 are that under the former, registration of the foreign judgment is in the discretion

---

[119] See also 1933 Act, s. 1(2)(a).

[120] *Nouvion* v. *Freeman* (1889) 15 App. Cas. 1 HL (Spanish 'remate' proceedings). See also *Blohn* v. *Desser* [1962] 1 QB 116.

[121] See generally *Colt Industries* v. *Sarlie* (No. 2) [1986] 1 WLR 1287 CA; *Scott* v. *Pilkington* (1862) 2 B & S 11.

[122] See *Berliner Industriebank* v. *Jost* [1971] 2 QB 463 CA. Note that in this case the German judgment could not be enforced by registration under the 1933 Act since the German Tribunal was not a 'court' within the meaning of the Act.

[123] The technical details of these statutes will not be dealt with here.

[124] See Reciprocal Enforcement of Judgments (Administration of Justice Act 1920, Part II) (Consolidation) Order 1984, SI 1984 no. 129.

[125] The countries to which the Act at present applies are: France*, Belgium*, Norway*, Germany*, Austria*, The Netherlands*, Israel, Italy*, India, Pakistan, Bangladesh, Jersey, Guernsey, Isle of Man, Suriname, Tonga, Canada and the Canadian provinces (except Quebec), Australia, the Australian States and the Australian Capital Territory. Those marked * are, in so far as the judgment is one to which the 1982 Act applies, outside the scheme.

of the English court and the judgment creditor does not have to register the judgment; he may enforce it by action at common law,[126] whereas under the latter, the court must register a judgment which fulfils the Act's requirements and the creditor cannot enforce it at common law. But registration of a judgment must, under the 1933 Act, be set aside if it is incapable of registration, if the foreign court lacked jurisdiction, if the judgment debtor did not receive sufficient notice of the proceedings and did not appear in them, if the judgment was obtained by fraud or if its registration and enforcement would be contrary to public policy, or if the rights under the judgment were not vested in the person who registered it. The court may also set registration aside if it is satisfied that the matter in dispute before the foreign court had already been finally decided by another judgment.[127]

When a judgment has been registered under the 1933 Act it has the same force as an English judgment.[128]

The other statutes which provide for registration of foreign judgments are the Civil Jurisdiction and Judgments Acts 1982 and 1991, which will be dealt with separately.[129]

Foreign judgment as a defence

Action estoppel

A foreign judgment, like an English judgment, operates by way of estoppel and prevents the parties or their privies (that is, persons claiming through the parties) from reopening it, since it is *res judicata*.[130] Thus, not only is it generally incontrovertible evidence, if the defendant was unsuccessful, that the obligation sought to be enforced was imposed on him,[131] but also, if he satisfied the judgment, that he has been discharged from that obligation.[132] He therefore has a good defence if, as in *Taylor* v. *Hollard*,[133] the claimant sues him here in order to enforce the judgment, and this is so, even though the defendant's satisfaction of

---

[126] The same was true of the Judgments Extension Act 1868.   [127] 1933 Act, s. 4(1)(b).
[128] *Ibid.*, s. 2(2).   [129] See ch. 10 below.
[130] Since the Civil Jurisdiction and Judgments Act 1982, s. 34, the claimant who has obtained a foreign judgment must enforce it and cannot sue on the cause of action: see *Republic of India* v. *Indian Steamship Co.* (No. 1) [1993] AC 410 HL; (No. 2) [1998] AC 878 HL.
[131] See pp. 109–10 above.   [132] See *Black* v. *Yates* [1992] 2 QB 246.
[133] [1902] 1 KB 676. The defendant had discharged a South African judgment which the claimant had obtained in order to enforce an English one; the South African court had only given judgment for part of the sum due under the English one. See also *Black* v. *Yates* [1992] 2 QB 246.

the judgment was not enough to satisfy the claim. But it was held in *Kohnke* v. *Karger*[134] that satisfaction by one defendant of a judgment against him does not discharge a co-defendant from his liability, and the claimant can sue him for any loss in excess of that compensated for by the first defendant.

Moreover, a defendant can always plead a judgment of a foreign court in his favour as a defence if he is sued again in England by the same claimant on the same cause of action. The judgment must, of course, be final and conclusive. If it is not, it is no defence if the claimant sues again in England.[135]

Issue estoppel

Cause of action estoppel prevents a party from asserting or denying a cause of action. Issue estoppel arises where the determination of an action has involved the court in determining an issue or a number of issues essential in reaching its decision. This applies to both English and foreign proceedings and even if the second action in which the issue is said to occur arises out of a different cause of action.[136] The leading case concerned foreign proceedings. In *Carl Zeiss Stiftung* v. *Rayner & Keeler Ltd* (No. 2),[137] in the course of proceedings in West Germany an issue was decided which, it was argued, was the same as one before the English court in subsequent proceedings. The House of Lords held that issue estoppel applies to foreign proceedings, but that three conditions must be satisfied for the parties to be estopped: (i) the issue before the English court must be identical with that determined by the foreign court; (ii) the foreign decision must be final and on the merits; and (iii) the parties or their privies must be identical. For differing reasons the five members of the House held that these conditions were not satisfied.[138]

---

[134] [1951] 2 KB 670. But if the defendant's payment has compensated the claimant fully, he obviously cannot recover anything from the co-defendant.

[135] At common law (*Harris* v. *Quine* (1869) LR 4 QB 653) and under the 1933 Act, s. 8 (*Black-Clawson International Ltd* v. *Papierwerke-Waldhof Aschaffenburg A/G* [1975] AC 591 HL) this was so only if the foreign judgment was on the merits and not on a procedural ground such as the running of time under a limitation statute. This is reversed by the Foreign Limitation Periods Act 1984, s. 3. See p. 64 above. In *Charm Maritime Inc.* v. *Kyriakou* [1987] 1 Ll.R 433 CA the evidence did not establish that a claimant whose action in Greece had been dismissed on procedural grounds could no longer litigate in Greece.

[136] If the judgment is *in rem* it binds the whole world, if *in personam*, the parties and their privies.

[137] [1967] 1 AC 853 HL.

[138] Lord Reid thought that (i) was not satisfied, Lords Guest, Upjohn and Wilberforce thought that (ii) was not satisfied, Lords Reid, Hodson, Guest and Upjohn that (iii) was not satisfied.

In *The Sennar* (No. 2)[139] the House of Lords held that they were satisfied. The question had arisen in Dutch proceedings whether the action between sellers and buyers fell within a clause in the bill of lading which provided that 'all actions under this contract of carriage' should be decided exclusively by the courts of the Sudan. The Dutch court held that it did. In subsequent proceedings in England it was contended that it did not, and that the Dutch decision was not binding, since it was not on the merits.

It was held that the issue was *res judicata* and the action was stayed.[140]

In an unusual case, *House of Spring Gardens* v. *Waite*,[141] issue estoppel was used to prevent a foreign judgment being reopened in England on the ground of fraud.

> In a first Irish action (before the Brussels Convention (1968) entered into force for Ireland) judgment was given for the claimants. In a second Irish action the defendants sought to have the earlier judgment set aside as having been fraudulently obtained. This action was dismissed. When Cs sought to enforce the first judgment D sought to raise the defence of fraud in the English proceedings. But for the second Irish judgment (which was not itself tainted by fraud) he could have done so.[142]

It was held by the Court of Appeal that he was estopped by the second Irish judgment from doing this.

---

[139] [1985] 1 WLR 490 HL.

[140] The decision of the Dutch court seems at first sight to have been on a procedural point only, since it was concerned with which country's courts were to decide a dispute. But it can be said to have decided the substance of the dispute which was before both the Dutch and English courts, that is, did the Sudanese courts have exclusive jurisdiction over a claim framed in tort? In *Desert Sun Loan Corp.* v. *Hill* [1996] 2 All ER 847 CA the Court of Appeal clearly regarded estoppel as applicable to a foreign court's decision on a purely procedural point: see p. 114 note 20 above.

[141] [1990] 1 QB 241 CA.   [142] See pp. 118–19 above.

10   Jurisdiction and judgments in the European Union and EFTA

General: Civil Jurisdiction and Judgments Acts 1982 and 1991; Brussels Convention, 1968; Lugano Convention, 1989

The Civil Jurisdiction and Judgments Act 1982 signified a radical departure from the common law and statutory rules as regards the jurisdiction of the English courts over persons who are domiciled in other member states of the European Community and with respect to the recognition and enforcement of judgments of the courts of other member states. It incorporates into English law the provisions of the EC Convention on Jurisdiction and Judgments in Civil and Commercial Matters, 1968 (the Brussels Convention).[1]

Article 220 of the EC Treaty obliged the original members of the EC to enter into negotiations to secure for their nationals simplification of formalities governing the recognition and enforcement of judgements, but the framers of the 1968 Convention went further and laid down rules of jurisdiction as well. Article 63 of the Convention itself required any new member states to accept the Convention as a basis for negotiations for their accession to the treaties contemplated by Article 220 of the EC Treaty, including the 1968 Convention itself. Ultimately, after some adjustments were made to the 1968 Convention, an Accession Convention by which the three new member states[2] agreed to accede to the 1968 Convention and to the subsequent Protocol on Interpretation of 1971 was signed in 1978. Greece acceded in 1982 and by the San Sebastian Convention, 1989, Spain and Portugal did likewise.

The 1982 Act has the main purpose of implementing the 1968 Convention (as amended by the Accession Conventions of 1978, 1982 and 1989) and the Protocol of 1971. It also contains rules of jurisdiction and rules for the enforcement of judgments as between the constituent parts of the United Kingdom.[3] The Act gives the Conventions the force

---

[1] This entered into force in 1973. For the EU Regulation see pp. 175–8 below.
[2] The United Kingdom, Republic of Ireland and Denmark.   [3] See p. 174–5 below.

of law in the United Kingdom and requires judicial notice to be taken of them. They are set out 'for convenience of reference' with the Act.[4]

The Lugano Convention, concluded in 1989 by the EC member states and those of the European Free Trade Area (Austria, Finland, Iceland, Norway, Sweden and Switzerland) operates parallel to the Brussels Convention. A handful of rather irritating exceptions apart, its text is identical to that of the Brussels Convention. It will only be referred to in this chapter in order to point out the differences between the two Conventions.[5]

Interpretation of the Brussels Convention

The Act (section 3) provides that any question as to the meaning of the Conventions must, if not referred to the Court of Justice of the European Communities for a preliminary ruling, be determined in accordance with the principles laid down by decisions of that Court. The reports of Mr Jenard on the 1968 Convention and the 1971 Protocol, of Professor Schlosser on the 1978 Accession Convention and of Messrs Almeida Cruz, De Santos Real and Jenard on the 1989 Accession Convention may be considered in this connection and appropriate weight given to them.[6]

If the House of Lords considers that a decision on a question of interpretation is necessary to enable it to give judgment, it must refer a question to the European Court of Justice for its opinion.[7] Any other appellate court may make such a reference.[8]

The European Court of Justice has already been called upon to interpret the 1968 Convention in over a hundred cases. The Court has had to decide whether the provision in question should be interpreted in accordance with its meaning under the law of a contracting state, because it is either the *lex fori* or the *lex causae*, or in accordance with the basic principles of the Convention itself, which are sometimes called

---

[4] S. 2. The English texts are contained in Sched. 1 (1968 Convention), Sched. 2 (1971 Protocol) and Sched. 3 (the relevant provisions of the Accession Convention). But reference may be made to other language versions. The consolidated English version of the text of the Convention, as amended, is to be found in the Civil Jurisdiction and Judgments (Amendment) Order 1990 (SI 1990 No. 2591). The text is set out only 'for convenience of reference' because all the different language versions are equally authentic.

[5] It was enacted into United Kingdom law by the Civil Jurisdiction and Judgments Act 1991.

[6] These were the rapporteurs of the bodies which drafted the respective instrument.

[7] In some cases, the Court of Appeal or High Court *must* do so.

[8] This may be contrasted with the position under the EC Treaty, Art. 177, where *any* court may do so.

'community' or 'Convention' principles. It has, except in one case,[9] opted for the latter method.

Objectives and characteristics of the Convention

The objective of the Convention, like that of Article 220 of the EC Treaty, is to secure the free movement of judgments throughout the member states of the Community and to ensure that judgments of the courts of each contracting state are accorded 'full faith and credit' (to use the words of the US Constitution) by the courts of all the others. The European Court of Justice has emphasised this several times.[10] It has also frequently said that other objectives are the attainment of legal certainty and the protection of persons domiciled in the European Union. Moreover, in *SISRO* v. *Ampersand Software BV*[11] the Court made it clear that the Convention, in particular the procedures for enforcement of judgments that it contains, constitutes 'an autonomous and complete system independent of the legal systems of the contracting states'. The procedural rules of domestic law continue to apply where the Convention does not;[12] but where it does apply, those rules are superseded. The Convention lays down uniform rules governing jurisdiction of the domestic courts of member states and then provides that recognition and enforcement of judgments of such courts are, with very limited exceptions, to be automatic.

The Convention departs in five main ways from the existing principles of English law governing jurisdiction and recognition and enforcement of judgments. First, jurisdiction exercised on the basis of the defendant's presence in England alone is prohibited. Secondly, if the defendant is outside England but the action falls within the jurisdiction of the English courts, service upon him is a matter of right and not merely within the courts' discretion.[13] Thirdly, if the English court has jurisdiction it has no discretion to stay the action on the ground that a court of another contracting state is a more convenient form. It can only stay an action or decline jurisdiction if such a court has already been seised of the case.[14] Fourthly, the grounds of refusal of recognition or enforcement

---

[9] *Tessili* v. *Dunlop A/G* [1976] ECR 1473, and see p. 143 below. For examples, see many of the decisions discussed in this chapter.

[10] See, for example, *Dumez France and Tracoba* v. *Hessische Landesbank* [1990] ECR 49; *Marc Rich & Co. A/G* v. *Societa Italiana Impianti SA (The Atlantic Emperor)* [1991] ECR I-3855.

[11] [1996] QB 127 ECJ. See J. G. Collier, note [1996] 55 *CLJ* 9.

[12] See *Kongress Agentur Hagen GmbH* v. *Zeehage NV* [1990] ECR I-1845.

[13] See CPR Rule 6.19. See ch. 7 above.

[14] Whether, if the English court has jurisdiction under the Convention, it can stay the action in favour of a court in a non-contracting state is a controversial question. See p. 166 below.

of judgments are very limited indeed, especially as regards investigation of the jurisdiction of the court which pronounced the judgment. Fifthly, judgments other than money judgments can be enforced, as can judgments which are not final and conclusive.

Scope of the Convention

The Convention applies to all 'civil and commercial matters', whatever the nature of the court or tribunal which hears the case.[15] On the other hand, as the European Court of Justice decided in *LTU* v. *Eurocontrol*,[16] it does not extend to cases involving the exercise of its powers by a public authority. The Court also determined that a concept of 'civil and commercial matters' should be given a community meaning.

> LTU, a German air carrier, disputed the validity of charges imposed by Eurocontrol, an international organisation which provided air safety services. Eurocontrol obtained a judgment in Belgium, the Belgian court expressly finding that the matter was commercial in nature. When the German court was asked to enforce this judgment it referred the question of interpretation to the European Court.

It was held that this was not a 'civil or commercial matter' and that enforcement of the judgment therefore fell outside the scope of the Convention.[17] In *Netherlands* v. *Rüffer*[18] a claim by the Dutch public waterways authority for reimbursement of the costs of removing the wreck of a German vessel after a collision was likewise held to fall outside the term 'civil and commercial matters'. The English courts have held that an action by a local authority acting under its statutory powers to bring forfeiture proceedings in respect of goods which are suspected of infringing trade marks is one to enforce private rights (a victim of infringement could bring such proceedings) and is not an exercise of public authority. It is a civil matter and therefore within the Convention.[19]

The Convention does not extend, in particular, to revenue,[20] customs or administrative matters. Four classes of case are expressly excluded.

---

[15] Title I, Art. 1. This includes employment law: *Sanicentral* v. *Collin* [1979] ECR 3423.
[16] [1976] ECR 1541; cf. *Sonntag* v. *Waidmann* [1993] ECR I-1963.
[17] This was followed by a further reference by the German court in *Bavaria and Germanair* v. *Eurocontrol* [1977] ECR 1517 where it was said that this did not preclude enforcement under the provisions of a bilateral convention which is also limited to civil and commercial matters; the term need not mean the same thing in both conventions. The Court declined any power to interpret such bilateral conventions.
[18] [1980] ECR 3807.
[19] *R* v. *Crown Court at Harrow*, exparte *UNIC Centre Srl* [2000] 1 WLR 2112.
[20] In *QRS 1 Aps* v. *Frandsen* [1999] 1 WLR 2169 CA it was held that the term 'revenue matters' includes an 'indirect' claim by a foreign state for tax. See further ch. 21, pp. 368–9 below.

(1) Status or legal capacity of natural persons, rights in property arising out of a matrimonial relationship, wills and succession. The Court has four times had to interpret this provision. In the first case it gave a judgment not noted for its clarity,[21] but in the second, *De Cavel* v. *De Cavel* (No. 2),[22] it emphasised that the exclusion of these matters does not necessarily exclude questions ancillary to the principal claim and which are not infected by it. Maintenance payments arising out of divorce proceedings are within the Convention, but the Court made clear that protective measures granted during divorce proceedings to prevent a spouse removing matrimonial property fall outside it.[23] So do measures designed to secure delivery up of a document to prevent it being used as evidence in an action respecting a husband's management of his wife's property if such management was closely connected with the marriage relationship.[24] In *Van Bogaard* v. *Laumen*[25] the Court held that the order of an English court for the payment by one ex-spouse to the other on divorce of a lump sum and to transfer property to her did not relate to 'rights in property arising out of a matrimonial relationship' if its purpose was to ensure the former spouse's maintenance and so fell within the scope of the Convention. (The problem the Dutch court had faced arose from the fact that English law permits the making of orders for lump sum payments and not only periodical payments and that it does not contain the institution of matrimonial property regimes, as do continental systems. English courts, unlike continental courts, can vary existing property rights.)

(2) Bankruptcy, proceedings relating to winding up of insolvent companies, judicial arrangements, compositions and analogous proceedings.[26] In Re *Hayward*[27] an English court held that a claim by a trustee in bankruptcy to recover the bankrupt's share in immovable property for the benefit of the bankrupt's estate was not a matter of bankruptcy and therefore fell within the Convention.[28] The decision is not above criticism since a trustee in bankruptcy can only pursue the bankrupt's property by virtue of his own title, which he derives

---

[21] *De Cavel* v. *De Cavel* (No. 1) [1979] ECR 1055.

[22] [1980] ECR 731.   [23] This was the subject of the first case: *ibid*.

[24] *W* v. *H* [1982] ECR 1189.   [25] [1997] QB 759 ECJ.

[26] This was interpreted in *Gourdain* v. *Nadler* [1979] ECR 733 so that a claim against company directors for fraudulent or wrongful trading (Insolvency Act 1986, s. 213) may be excluded. But a claim by the liquidator to recover debts due to the company is not excluded. This claim does not arise in bankruptcy.

[27] [1997] Ch. 45. *Gourdain* v. *Nadler* was applied by an English court in *UBS A/G* v. *Omni Holding A/G* [2000] 1 All ER (Comm.) 42 and *Ashurst* v. *Pollard* [2000] 2 WLR 722 CA.

[28] See further p. 265 below.

only from the bankruptcy. Winding up of solvent companies is not excluded.[29]

(3) Social security.

(4) Arbitration. The exact scope of this exception is not clear. It includes the power to set aside an award or to appoint or dismiss an arbitrator. In *The Atlantic Emperor*,[30] the European Court held that the appointment of an arbitrator and any preliminary question, such as the validity of the arbitration clause, are excluded from the Convention, which is concerned with the free movement of judgments, not of arbitration awards. That Court has also held that interim measures sought from a court (under Article 24) in respect of a dispute which is decided by arbitration are ancillary measures which do not concern the arbitration but are parallel to it and so can be within the Convention.[31] Whether the exception excludes all matters agreed to be referred to arbitration, as the United Kingdom contends, has been left open.[32]

Jurisdiction

General rule

The basic principle and the general rule governing jurisdiction is that persons domiciled in a contracting state, whatever their nationality, must be sued in the courts of that state alone.[33] In *Canada Trust Co.* v. *Stolzenberg* (No. 2)[34] the House of Lords held that the relevant domicile is a person's domicile at the time the claim form is issued, not when it is served on him, should he have changed his domicile in the interim (the point arose in the context of Article 6(1)).[35] The domicile or nationality of the claimant is generally irrelevant, as the European Court held in *Group Josi Reinsurance Co. SA* v. *Universal General Insurance Co.*[36] It must be emphasised that, as will be seen, some provisions of the

---

[29] But creditors' voluntary winding-up is excluded.

[30] *Marc Rich & Co. A/G* v. *Societa Italiana Impianti SA* [1989] 1 Ll.R 548 CA [1991] ECR I-3855.

[31] *Van Uden Maritime BV* v. *Kommanditgesellschaft in Firma Deco-Line* [1999] 1 All ER (Comm.) 385 ECJ.

[32] Schlosser Report, Official Journal of the European Communities, OJC 59, 5 March 1979, para. 62.

[33] Art. 2. Persons who are not nationals of a state in which they are domiciled are to be governed by the rules of jurisdiction applicable to nationals of that state: *ibid.*

[34] [2000] 3 WLR 376; see also *Petrotrade Inc.* v. *Smith* [999] 1 WLR 457 CA. Compare the decisions on when a court is 'seised' for the purposes of Arts. 21 and 22, p. 166 below.

[35] See p. 149 below.   [36] [2000] 3 WLR 1625 ECJ.

Convention apply and in some situations confer jurisdiction on the courts of a particular country, irrespective of the defendant's domicile.

The jurisdiction of the courts of the defendant's domicile is comprehensive and covers all matters within the scope of the Convention.[37] This rule is subject to two exceptions. A defendant cannot be sued in the courts of his domicile if some other court has exclusive jurisdiction[38] or if the defendant is a party to a contractual agreement to submit to another jurisdiction.[39]

It is also exclusive of the jurisdiction of the courts of all other contracting states, except where the Convention gives special (or concurrent) jurisdiction to other courts as well over certain matters, so that a defendant can be sued also in the courts of a country other than that in which he is domiciled,[40] or where the defendant voluntarily submits to the jurisdiction of another court.[41]

Certain bases of jurisdiction which are used by courts of certain contracting states are suppressed as against persons domiciled in other contracting states. These include arrest of assets, as was the case in Scotland; nationality, as in France; presence of assets, as was the case in Germany; and casual presence, as in England.[42]

But it should be stressed that these are only suppressed as against persons domiciled in other contracting states. With respect to persons domiciled elsewhere, they are expressly preserved and are given a greater force than they previously possessed, since (subject to the provisions as to exclusive jurisdiction) as against such persons jurisdiction is determined by the *lex fori*.[43] Thus the English courts retain jurisdiction over a casual visitor domiciled somewhere in the United States, and can assume jurisdiction over him under CPR Rule 6(20). This point is important since a judgment given on such a basis *must* be enforced in other member states. Thus, if a domiciled New Yorker has assets in Germany and under German law a German court has jurisdiction over him for that reason alone, a German judgment must be enforced against him here.[44] This, of course, is not true at common law or under

---

[37] Art. 3.   [38] Art. 16. See pp. 264–6 below.   [39] Art. 17. See pp. 154–8 below.
[40] Arts. 5–6; 7–12A (Insurance); 13–15 (consumer contracts).
[41] Art. 18. See p. 156 below.   [42] Art. 3.   [43] Art. 4.
[44] This consequence could be avoided if the United Kingdom were to enter into a convention with the United States obliging it not to enforce such judgments: Art. 59. But although such a draft convention was initialled, further implementation has not been proceeded with. It is this possibility of enforcement which led the United States to object to the Convention. A Convention with Canada was signed in 1984: Cmnd 9337, and the United Kingdom gave an undertaking under Art. 59. It entered into force in 1987. A Convention with Australia was concluded in 1991: Cmnd 1394.

existing statutes, so, for example, a Polish or Israeli judgment cannot be enforced in such a case.

Domicile: definition

Domicile is a key concept in the Conventions. However, the framers of the 1968 Convention left it undefined, since the word means much the same thing in the laws of each of the original six member states, being equivalent to habitual residence. Although domicile is not the same as habitual residence in English and Irish law, no definition was included in the Accession Convention of 1978, and the definition of domicile is that which it bears under the domestic laws of the several contracting states. So, in order to assimilate English law to continental systems, the 1982 Act contains a new definition of domicile in English law for the purpose of the Convention.

Article 52(1) of the Convention provides that, in order to decide whether a party is domiciled in England, an English court must apply English law. If he is not, to find if he is domiciled in another contracting state the court must apply that state's law, so that if he is or is not domiciled in France according to French law, he is or is not domiciled there in English eyes accordingly (Article 52(2)).[45] If he is not domiciled in that state, or is alleged to be domiciled in a non-contracting state, the court must apply English law to determine his domicile.

Article 53 provides that the domicile of a company or other legal person or association is where it has its seat. English private international law determines whether a company is domiciled here.

The rules laid down in the 1982 Act for the determination of domicile cannot be said to lack complexity, and it is unfortunate perhaps that the term 'habitual residence' could not be substituted for 'domicile' in the Act because the Convention also employs the term 'habitual residence'.

It must be emphasised that these rules only apply if it is sought to bring an action in the English courts. They do not and obviously cannot apply to determine the defendant's domicile if it is sought to sue him in the Italian courts. In such a case, as the Convention says, Italian law or Italian private international law determines whether a person or a company is domiciled in Italy.

Individuals

An individual is domiciled in the United Kingdom or a particular part of it if he is both resident in and has a substantial connection with it. If

---

[45] Thus, here the connecting factor is not interpreted by the *lex fori*.

he is resident in the United Kingdom but has no substantial connection with any particular part of it, he is domiciled in the part in which he is resident. In the absence of proof to the contrary, residence for three months is presumed to be a substantial connection.[46] An individual is domiciled in a non-contracting state, for example Poland, only if he is resident there and has a substantial connection with it. In this case, no presumption arises from length of residence.[47]

Corporations and associations

A corporation or association's domicile is at its seat. The Act provides that its seat is in the United Kingdom if either (a) it was incorporated or formed under the law of a part thereof and has its registered office or some other official address therein or (b) its central management or control is exercised in the United Kingdom.[48] It has its seat in a particular part of the United Kingdom by the application of either of those tests or if it has a place of business in that part.[49] Thus, a company registered under the Companies Act 1985 which has its registered office in England, its central management and control in Scotland and a place of business in Northern Ireland, has its seat and, therefore, its domicile in England, Scotland and Northern Ireland and can be sued in any of these countries.

If the corporation or association does not have its seat in the United Kingdom, to decide where its seat is, the same test is applied as for the United Kingdom.[50] But it does not have its seat in a contracting state if that state's courts do not regard it as having its seat there.[51]

Separate provision is made for the domicile of insurers and suppliers of goods, services or credit to customers.[52] A trust is domiciled in that part of the United Kingdom with whose law it has the closest and most real connection.[53] The Crown in right of the United Kingdom has its seat in every part thereof.[54]

---

[46] 1982 Act, s. 41(2), (3), (6). A person is domiciled in a place (for example, Birmingham) if he is domiciled in the part of the United Kingdom which contains that place and he is resident in that place: *ibid.*, s. 41(4).

[47] *Ibid.*, s. 41(7).   [48] *Ibid.*, s. 42(3).

[49] *Ibid.*, s. 42(4). As to its domicile in a place, which is only relevant for liability of co-defendants and insurance, see *ibid.*, s. 42(5).

[50] *Ibid.*, s. 44. See 1968 Convention, Arts. 8(2), 13.

[51] 1982 Act, s. 42(7). See *The Deichland* [1990] 1 QB 361 CA.

[52] 1982 Act, s. 44. See 1968 Convention, Arts. 8(2), 13.

[53] 1982 Act, s. 45(3). A trust is only domiciled in the United Kingdom if it is by s. 45(3) domiciled in a part thereof: s. 45(2).

[54] *Ibid.*, s. 46.

Special jurisdiction

In addition to being liable to be sued in the country in which he is domiciled a person domiciled in a member state may also be sued in another state in certain cases. If the claimant sues the defendant in that other state, the jurisdiction of the courts of the defendant's domicile is ousted. Such special (or concurrent) jurisdiction exists in twelve cases. These are (Article 5): (1) contract, the place of performance of the obligation; (2) maintenance, the place of the claimant's domicile or habitual residence;[55] (3) tort, the place where the harmful event occurred; (4) damages or restitution for a criminal offence, the place where the prosecution takes place; (5) a claim arising out of the running of a branch or agency or other establishment, the place where that is situated; (6) trust, where the trust is domiciled;[56] (7) salvage claims, where the cargo or freight is arrested; also (Article 6): (8) over co-defendants, the court of the domicile of one of the defendants; (9) where a third party is sued in an action on a warranty or guarantee or other third party proceedings, the court which is seised of the original proceedings; (10) counterclaims, the court where the original claim was brought; (11) contract claims, if the action can be combined with an action *in rem* in immovable property, the courts of the *situs* thereof[57] (this would cover a claim on a contract of mortgage of land); and (Article 6(A)): (12) limitation of liability actions (in the case of ships), the court having jurisdiction in an action relating to liability arising from the use or operation of the ship.

The cases which will be discussed in detail here are (1), (3), (5), (8), (9) and (10).

Contract (Article 5(1))

The typical situation in which this jurisdiction is invoked is when the claimant is domiciled in country A and the defendant in country B and the claimant argues that the place of performance of the defendant's obligation is in A.[58] This jurisdiction exists even though the defendant denies the existence of the contract,[59] or even if the claimant does so,[60]

---

[55] For the meaning of 'claimant' see *Farrell* v. *Long* [1997] QB 842 ECJ.

[56] The trust must arise out of an *inter vivos* settlement; if it arises out of a will or intestacy it is not within the Convention at all: Art. 1(4).

[57] For exclusive jurisdiction over immovable property see Art. 16(1), pp. 264–7 below.

[58] For a learned and highly critical discussion see J. Hill, 'Jurisdiction in Matters relating to a Contract under the Brussels Convention' (1995) 44 *ICLQ* 591.

[59] *Effer* v. *Kantner* [1982] ECR 825. See also *Tesam* v. *Schuh Mode* (1989) *The Times*, 24 October, and *Rank Film Distributors* v. *Lanterna Editrice SrL* [1991] 3 ILPr. 58.

[60] *Boss Group Ltd* v. *Boss France SA* [1997] 1 WLR 351 CA.

though not, the House of Lords held in *Kleinwort Benson Ltd* v. *Glasgow City Council*,[61] if the contract has already been held to be void.

'Contract' is an autonomous community concept; it includes, for example, membership of an association, according to the European Court in *Martin Peters* v. *Zuid Nederlandse AV*.[62] In *Jakob Handte GbmH* v. *Traitements Mecano-Cliniques Des Surfaces*[63] the Court held that it did not include a case where a sub-purchaser sues the manufacturer of goods since in such a case there is no 'undertaking freely entered into' between the two.

The obligation in question need not, it appears, be part of the contract itself provided that it is closely associated with it. In *Agnew* v. *Lansforsakringsbolaget AB*,[64] the House of Lords held, by a bare majority, that an obligation to make disclosure in pre-contract negotiations could constitute the obligation in question, which gave those words their ordinary meaning. The 'obligation' referred to is the obligation which is the basis of the claim, not any other obligation under the contract. In *De Bloos* v. *Bouyer*,[65] where the claimant alleged a breach of a distributorship agreement, the European Court insisted on this meaning (and held the obligation to be that of the grantor), so as to limit the number of contractual obligations which could confer jurisdiction, since the number of courts having jurisdiction should be strictly limited. Where more than one obligation is sued on then, that Court said in *Shenavai* v. *Kreischer*,[66] the national court must determine what is the principal obligation, but it did not say how the national court was to do this. In *Union Transport plc* v. *Continental Lines SA*,[67] where the defendants were domiciled in Belgium and the claimants in England, the latter sued the former for failure to nominate a vessel in London and to provide one in Florida. The House of Lords held that the nomination was the principal obligation, because until the vessel was nominated, it

---

[61] [1997] AC 153 HL.

[62] [1983] ECR 987, which was applied in *Arcado Sprl* v. *Haviland* [1988] ECR 1539 to claims for payment of commission under an agency agreement and for repudiation of the agreement. See also *Powell Dyffryn* v. *Petereit* [1992] ILPr. 300 (company's articles).

[63] [1993] 4 ILPr. 404. See also *Réunion Européenne* v. *Spliethoff's Bevrachtingskantoor BV* [2000] QB 690 ECJ where it was held that no such undertaking existed between the consignee of goods and the actual maritime carrier of them who was not named in the bills of lading.

[64] [2000] 2 WLR 497 (Lugano). This settled a difference of opinion between the lower courts. The majority were Lords Nicholls, Woolf MR and Cooke; Lords Hope and Millett strongly dissented.

[65] [1976] ECR 1497, followed in England in, for example, *Royal Bank of Scotland* v. *Rispiarmo delle Provincie Lombard* [1992] 3 ILPr. 411 CA.

[66] [1987] ECR 239.

[67] [1992] 1 WLR 15. See *AIG Group (UK) Ltd* v. *The Ethniki* [2000] 2 All ER 566 CA. This does not apply absent such obligation: *Leathertex Sinetici* v. *Boditex* [1992] 2 All ER (Comm.) 769 ECJ.

was not known which vessel had to be provided. So the English court had jurisdiction over the claimant's claim in respect of that and any accessory obligations. In *Source Ltd* v. *TUV Rheinland Holding A/G*,[68] on the other hand, S, a UK company, required a certificate of quality of goods which were to be imported from China and Taiwan. It asked TUV to examine the goods and prepare a report on them to be presented in England. S sued TUV in England contending that the inspection had been conducted negligently and the report was inaccurate. The Court of Appeal declined jurisdiction, holding that the main obligation was the inspection of the goods, which took place in China and Taiwan, not the presentation of the report.

However, in *Ivenel* v. *Schwab*,[69] the European Court, by a piece of judicial legislation,[70] made an exception for employment contracts, based on the Rome Convention, 1980, Article 4 of which introduced into the law relating to contractual obligations the doctrine of characteristic performance.[71] It held that in such contracts the place where characteristic performance is due is where the employment takes place, whatever the obligation sued on and whether it is the employee or the employer who sues, at least where the action is based on several obligations to be performed in different states. This is to protect the employee by ensuring the application of employment legislation in force at his place of work.

But this interpretation does not extend beyond employment contracts in the strict sense, which the Court said is one which 'creates a continuing relationship which places the employee in the context of a certain business organisation'.

In *Shenavai* v. *Kreischer*,[72] the Court refused to apply the exception to a case where an architect sued for his fees, holding that the place of performance of the obligation was where the fees were payable. Moreover, in *Six Construction* v. *Humbert*[73] it held that Article 5(1) did not apply at all if the employee works in various places, mostly outside the contracting states.

Article 5(1) was amended in the San Sebastian Convention to deal expressly with employment contracts and reads

> . . . (i) in matters relating to individual contracts of employment, this place [of performance of the obligation] is that where the employee habitually carries out his work.

---

[68] [1998] QB 54 CA.   [69] [1982] ECR 1891.

[70] The Brussels Convention nowhere specifically mentioned employment contracts, though it made special provisions for consumer and insurance contracts: see pp. 152–3 below.

[71] This is discussed at pp. 198–200 below.

[72] See *Mercury Publicity Ltd* v. *Wolfgang Loerke GmbH* (1991) *The Times*, 21 October.

[73] [1989] ECR 341. See *Mulox IB Ltd* v. *Geels* [1993] 4 ILPr. 608; *Rutten* v. *Gross Medical Ltd* [1997] All ER (EC) 121 ECJ.

or (ii) if the employee does not habitually carry out his work in any one country, the employer may also be sued in the courts for the place where the business which engaged the employee was or is now situated.

Three points should be noted. (a) In (i) either party can sue the other in England, if that is where the employee works, but in (ii) only the employer can be sued here. Thus, if an English employee works all over the place, even outside all the contracting states, then he can sue his employer (but the employer cannot sue him) in France if the employer is domiciled there, or in England if the employer engaged the worker through a place of business here, or in Germany if that place of business has been moved to Germany.[74] (b) In (ii) account is taken of a change of the place of business after the employee has been engaged. (c) These provisions are not limited to actions in which there are claims relating to different obligations to be performed in different states.

The Lugano Convention is identical as to (i) but differs as to (ii) by which both employer and employee may be sued in England and which says only that 'this place shall be the place of business through which he was engaged'. That is to say, the Lugano Convention does not expressly take account of a change of the place of business. Apparently, the reason for the differences between the current Brussels Convention and the Lugano Convention is that the EU member states desire to protect employees more than do EFTA states.

It might have been more sensible if in both Conventions employment contracts had been taken out of Article 5(1) and dealt with in a separate provision, as were consumer and insurance contracts.

The European Court held in *Tessili* v. *Dunlop*[75] that, to decide where the obligation is to be performed, the domestic court should employ its own conflict of laws rules, and later, in *Custom Made Commercial Ltd* v. *Stawa Metallbau GmbH*,[76] that this is so when these rules are contained in an international convention. The European Court has more recently affirmed and applied these two decisions in *GIE Groupe Concorde* v. *Master of the Vessel Suhadiwarno Panjan*.[77]

---

[74] If an exclusive jurisdiction clause confers jurisdiction on an Italian court then, generally speaking, the parties can sue each other only in Italy.

[75] [1976] ECR 1473.

[76] [1994] ECR I-219.

[77] [1999] 2 All ER (Comm.) 700 ECJ. As to English decisions see *Boss Group Ltd* v. *Boss France SA* [1997] 1 WLR 351 CA, *Domicrest Ltd* v. *Swiss Bank Corp.* [1999] QB 548 and *Chailease Finance Corp.* v. *Crédit Agricole Indosuez* [2000] 1 All ER (Comm.) 399 (place of payment under letter of credit), in all of which England was held to be the place of performance, and *Viskase Ltd* v. *Paul Kiefel GmbH* [1999] 1 WLR 1305 CA where it was held that Germany, not England, was such place.

If the parties agree on, say, England as the place of performance of the obligation, whether they do so orally or in writing, the agreement (provided it is effective under the conflict rules of the law which governs the contract and is not a sham) effectively confers jurisdiction on the English courts.[78] This is important if the agreement on the place of performance is oral or in a form which does not satisfy the requirements of Article 17, which deals with jurisdiction clauses.[79] By such agreement the parties can orally oust the jurisdiction of the courts of the defendant's domicile, which they cannot do by virtue of Article 17. However the agreement must not be a sham and concluded solely for avoiding the formal requirements of Article 17. In *MSG* v. *Les Gravières Rhénanes SARL*[80]

> The parties, who were German and French, agreed orally that the former should charter to the latter an inland-waterway vessel. After the negotiations had been completed the former sent the latter a commercial letter of confirmation containing a pre-printed statement: 'The place of performance is Würzburg [Germany] and the courts for the place have exclusive jurisdiction.' Its invoices also mentioned that forum. The French company did not challenge the letter of confirmation and paid the invoices. The vessel loaded gravel, mainly in France, and carried it on the Rhine and unloaded it in France. Würzburg is not in France and is nowhere near the Rhine.

The European Court held that the oral agreement was not governed by Article 5(1) but by Article 17, since it was not designed to determine the place where the person liable was actually to perform his obligations but solely to attempt to confer jurisdiction on the courts of the designated place.

Tort (Article 5(3))

In *Kalfelis* v. *Schröder, Munchmayer*,[81] the European Court held that the words 'tort, delict or quasi-delict' must be given a community meaning and include any action which calls a defendant's liability in question and which does not involve matter relating to a contract. In England it was held in *Mölnlycke AB* v. *Procter & Gamble Ltd*[82] that a claim for infringement of a patent is within Article 5(3). But in *Kleinwort Benson Ltd* v. *Glasgow City Council*[83] it was held that a claim to restitution of

---

[78] *Zelger* v. *Salinitri* [1980] ECR 89.   [79] See pp. 154–8 below.
[80] [1997] QB 731 ECJ.   [81] [1988] ECR 5565.   [82] [1992] 1 WLR 1112 CA.
[83] [1999] AC 153 HL. See also the decision of the Scots court in *Davenport* v. *Corinthian Motor Policies at Lloyd's* 1991 SLT 774, where it was held that a statutory right under the road Traffic Act 1988, s. 151, of the victim of a driver's negligence to enforce a judgment against the latter's insurer did not fall within Art. 5(3) since the dispute was not over what had happened in Scotland.

moneys paid under a contract which had earlier been held to be void did not fall within Article 5(3).

This decision is understandable, because if B has given A money and A still has it then it seems curious to talk of 'the harmful event occurring' anywhere. It is submitted that it is also correct, since the judgment in *Kalfelis* v. *Schröder, Munchmayer* has been misunderstood through mistranslation of the German language; what the Court said was not 'the defendant's liability' but his 'liability *for damages*' and A is scarcely liable for damage to B.

But the Court does not seem itself to have been altogether consistent. In *Reichert* v. *Dresdner Bank* (No. 2)[84] an action permitted by French law (*action paulienne*) whereby a creditor seeks to revoke a transfer of property rights by his debtor which the creditor regards as a fraud on his rights (this is similar to a 'fraudulent preference', or as it is now called, a 'preference' in English insolvency law) was held not to be within Article 5(3). It appears, however, that the real question, which does not seem to have been argued, was not whether the French action was within Article 5(3) but whether the claimant's action was in respect of a delict committed in France. If his allegations were true, it clearly was.

In *Kalfelis* v. *Schröder, Munchmayer*[85] it was also held that Article 5(3) must be interpreted strictly in the sense that a court which is competent to deal with part of a claim founded upon a tort is not necessarily competent to deal with another part founded upon non-tortious (for example, contractual) grounds. If the claimant finds that this puts him to the inconvenience of suing in several courts, his remedy is, of course, to sue in those of the defendant's domicile. In *Source Ltd* v. *TUV Rheinland Holding A/G*,[86] the English court held that this decision operated to exclude a claim which could be brought on the same facts under a contract or independently of a contract. Both related to the contract and, since the court had held that S could not bring a contractual claim in the United Kingdom under Article 5(1), it was similarly excluded from bringing a claim here in tort.

The 'place where the harmful event occurred' means both the place where the defendant acted and the place where the claimant suffered the harm or damage. In *Bier* v. *Mines de Potasse d'Alsace*[87]

> A French defendant was alleged to have poured effluents into the Rhine from the French bank and damaged the Dutch claimant's property in Holland. The European Court of Justice held that both the French and Dutch courts had jurisdiction.

[84] [1992] ECR I-2149.   [85] [1988] ECR 5565.
[86] [1998] QB 54 CA.   [87] [1976] ECR 1735, [1978] QB 708.

This was a sensible ruling because the French courts had jurisdiction on the basis of the defendant's domicile anyway, so any other interpretation would have rendered Article 5(3) to a large extent otiose.[88]

The decision in the *Bier* case was applied by the English courts and followed by the European Court with respect to actions for defamation in *Shevill* v. *Presse Alliance SA*.[89]

> S and others sued a French newspaper for libel. S was domiciled in England. The defendants accepted that the articles were false. S sought damages in respect of publication in England, where the paper's daily circulation was about 230. In France it was over 200,000.

The European Court held that since publication occurred in England, the harm to the claimants' reputations was suffered here and the English courts had jurisdiction, though only in respect of that harm. The courts of other contracting states would also have jurisdiction in respect of similar harm. The Court held that the criteria for assessing whether the event is harmful and the evidence and extent of the harm suffered by the claimant are those of the substantive law determined by the domestic rules of private international law. The House of Lords[90] gave effect to this judgment, holding that when English law presumes that publication of a defamatory statement is harmful without specific proof of actual damage, Article 5(3) is applicable.

The European Court has held that Article 5(3) is not applicable if the damage complained of is merely an indirect consequence of the harm suffered by the immediate victim of the wrongful act. In *Dumez France and Tracoba* v. *Hessische Landesbank*[91] it was held that a French company could not sue in France for loss it claimed to have suffered as the result of losses to its German subsidiaries caused by alleged wrongful acts in Germany by the defendant German banks. Subsequently the Court applied this reasoning where the claimant himself alleged that he had suffered only consequential damage, in the very curious case, *Marinari* v. *Lloyds Bank*.[92]

> M, domiciled in Italy, lodged with a Manchester branch of Lloyds Bank promissory notes of an exchange value of US $752,500,000

---

[88] But not entirely. The defendant might be domiciled elsewhere. Thus, if in the *Bier* case, it had been domiciled in Germany, the German (by Art. 2), the French and the Dutch (both by Art. 5(3)) courts would all have had jurisdiction. In *Mecklermedia Corp.* v. *DC Congress GmbH* [1998] Ch. 40, it was held that, in the tort of passing off allegedly committed by a German-domiciled defendant, the harmful event was the harm done to the claimant's goodwill in England and their reputation, since that was a direct effect on their property.

[89] [1995] 2 AC 18 ECJ. See C. F. Forsyth, note [1995] 54 *CLJ* 515.

[90] [1996] 3 All ER 929 HL.   [91] [1990] ECR I-49.

[92] [1996] QB 217 ECJ. See J. G. Collier, note [1996] 55 *CLJ* 216.

issued by a province of the Philippines in favour of a Lebanese company. After the naturally surprised bank staff opened the envelope they called the police, who arrested M but later released him. He returned to Italy and brought an action there against the bank, claiming the value of the notes, compensation for damage he claimed to have suffered by his arrest, breach of several contracts (it is quite unclear what these could have been) and injury to his reputation.

The court held that, in so far as these events had occurred in Italy, they were merely adverse financial consequences of any direct harm suffered in England and the Italian courts had no jurisdiction.

In *Réunion Européenne SA* v. *Spliethoff's Bevrachtingskantoor BV*[93] the court held, in effect, that the French courts had no jurisdiction under Article 5(3) over Dutch domiciled defendants, when the physical damage had already occurred to goods when they were on the high seas, merely because the damage was discovered when they were inspected in France.

This principle was applied by an English court in *Domicrest Ltd* v. *Swiss Bank Corp.*[94] in the context of negligent misstatement or misrepresentation. The Swiss domiciled defendants were alleged to have made representations to the claimants in England which had caused them to release goods in Switzerland and Italy, whereby the claimants suffered financial losses in England. It was held that the court had no jurisdiction under Article 5(3).[95]

Branches, agencies and other establishments (Article 5(5))
The situation envisaged by this provision is one in which the claimant is in England and a German company, acting through its branch in England, has concluded a contract with the claimant. The claimant now wishes to sue the German company in England.

In *Somafer* v. *Saar-Ferngas*,[96] the European Court of Justice gave the words 'branch, agencies or other establishment' a 'community' meaning which, it said, was 'dictated by the interests of legal certainty'.

C brought an action in Germany which arose out of D's having blown up a bunker for the Ministry of the Interior of Saarland. D was a French company with its registered office and principal place of business in France. D's notepaper bore a business address in Germany. In fact, D's business there was carried on by one of its employees and D was not entered in a commercial register as a branch.

[93] [2000] QB 90.
[94] [1999] QB 548 (Lugano Convention) and in *Waterford Wedgwood plc* v. *David Nagli Ltd* [1999] ILPr. 9.
[95] It was, however, held that it had jurisdiction under Art. 5(1): see p. 149 above.
[96] [1978] ECR 2183.

The Court said that strict criteria had to be met and that the defendant must have a local place of business or management and be materially equipped to negotiate for it. The Advocate-General (M. Mayras) rejected the application of any doctrine of 'holding-out'; the reality, not appearance of control by the defendant, must be demonstrated. This seems rather unfair to a claimant who may justly complain that the defendant led him to believe that its representative was a branch or agency.[97]

The applicable test, that is, whether the branch or agency is subject to the defendant's direction or control, was reaffirmed by the Court in *De Bloos* v. *Bouyer*.[98] It held that a Belgian holder of an exclusive sales concession from a French supplier did not pass the test. In *Blanckaert and Willems* v. *Trost*[99] the Court held that an independent commercial agent who merely negotiated the defendant's business, who was free to arrange his own business and to decide how much time to devote to the defendant and who represented others and merely transmitted orders to the defendant was not a 'branch agency or other establishment' of the latter.[100]

It is not clear, however, why the 'direction and control' test should be applied to an 'establishment' other than a branch or agency.

In a more recent case, *Sar Schotte GmbH* v. *Parfums Rothschild SARL*,[101] a subsidiary company in a group carried on business through its parent.

> C, a German company, wished to sue D, a French company (Rothschild) in Germany. D was a wholly owned subsidiary of a German parent company (also called Rothschild). C claimed the price of goods delivered and argued that the German parent was an 'establishment' of D.

The Court held that Article 5(5) would apply if a company established in one contracting state, while it did not operate a dependent branch, agency or other establishment in another state, carried out its activities there through an independent company with a separate legal personality which had the same name and management, which transacted business in its name and which it used as an extension of itself.

The Court also said that the connection between a dispute and the domestic court which was asked to hear it was to be assessed not only on the basis of the legal relationship between the two companies but also by observing the behaviour of the two companies and the way in which they presented themselves to third parties.

---

[97] But see *Sar Schotte GmbH* v. *Parfums Rothschild SARL* [1987] ECR 4905.
[98] [1976] ECR 1497.   [99] [1981] ECR 819.
[100] See also *New Hampshire Insurance Co.* v. *Strabag Bau A/G* [1990] 2 Ll.R 61.
[101] [1987] ECR 4905.

The result is somewhat surprising in view of *Somafer* v. *Saar Ferngas* and clearly represents an acceptance of 'holding-out' and 'appearance' rather than 'reality' in the case of companies in a group. However, it is not often that the decision will help a claimant, for usually members of a group of companies act for themselves and not, as in the *Sar Schotte* case, as an extension of the business of one or all of the others.

It is essential that the dispute must arise out of the operations of the branch etc., such as out of a contract entered into by it, which it did not do in the *Somafer* case.

In the *Somafer* case the Court suggested that if the dispute arose out of a contract, the contract must be one which the defendant has to perform in the country in which the branch is situated. In most cases, of course, such a contract would fall within Article 5(1) and make Article 5(5) almost redundant. For this reason, among others, the Court overruled this dictum in *Lloyd's Register of Shipping* v. *Campenon Bernard*,[102] where the defendant was English and had concluded in France, through its French branch, a contract which was to be performed in Spain by its Spanish branch. Other reasons given were that Article 5(5) contained no such limitation and that it was based on the requirement that when concluding the contract the other party should know with whom he is dealing. The French court had jurisdiction under Article 5(5).

Co-defendants (Article 6(1))

If D is one of a number of co-defendants one of whom is domiciled in England, he can be sued here, though he is not domiciled in England. Thus, if D^1 and D^2 have committed a tort entirely in France, D^1 being domiciled in England and D^2 in Italy, C can sue D^1 in England and join D^2 as co-defendant to the action. It is important to note that D^1 *must* be domiciled here; D^2 *cannot* be joined if the English court has only special jurisdiction over D^1.[103]

In *Kalfelis* v. *Schröder, Munchmayer*,[104] the European Court held that, for Article 6(1) to apply, there must be a connection between the actions against the various defendants of such a kind that it is expedient to determine the actions together to avoid the risk of irreconcilable judgments resulting from separate proceedings in different states. In *Gascoine* v. *Pyrah*[105] where D^1, who was domiciled in England, had agreed to arrange for D^2, who was domiciled in Germany, to give a veterinary report on a show-jumping horse which was in France, and it

---

[102] [1995] All ER (EC) 531.
[103] This was emphasised by the European Court in *Réunion Européenne SA* v. *Spliethoff's Bevrachtingskantoor BV* [2000] QB 690 ECJ.
[104] [1988] ECR 5565.   [105] [1994] ILPr. 82 CA.

was alleged that D^2 did so negligently in Germany, the Court of Appeal held that this requirement was satisfied.[106] In *SCOR* v. *Eras International Ltd* (No. 2),[107] Potter J summarised the situations in which there could be a risk of irreconcilable judgments which would justify the application of Article 6(1), as those in which there might be (i) irreconcilable findings of fact, (ii) irreconcilable decisions based on those facts (though the outcome might depend on the application of different rules of law) and (iii) no irreconcilability of facts or decisions but different remedies.

In *Aiglon Ltd* v. *Gau Shan Co. Ltd*,[108] an English court correctly held that if it has jurisdiction under Article 6(1), this is mandatory, not permissive, and the court cannot stay the action on the ground of *forum non conveniens*.

Third parties (Article 6(2))

A defendant can be sued 'as a third party in an action on a warranty or guarantee or in any other third party proceedings [if the English court] is seised of the original proceedings unless these were instituted solely with the object of removing him from the jurisdiction of the court which would be competent in his case'.

Thus, if A sues B, domiciled in England, B may join T, domiciled in France, as a third party to the action, provided A did not sue B only for the purpose of getting B to remove T from the jurisdiction of the French courts.

It must be emphasised that (unlike Article 6(1)), this does not require that B is domiciled in England; it suffices that B is domiciled in Italy and the English court has jurisdiction over him under, for example, Article 5(1).[109]

The European Court held, in *Kongress Agentur Hagen GmbH* v. *Zeehage NV*,[110] that Article 6(2) does not *require* the court actually to exercise jurisdiction over the third party and it may apply its own procedural rules (such as that proceedings may be struck out as being an abuse of

---

[106] The court said that the test for 'necessary or proper party' under CPR Rule 6.20(3) (see pp. 76–7 above), being a liberal one, could not be adopted by analogy in view of the European Court's stricter interpretation of Art. 6(1). See also *Möhnlycke AB* v. *Procter & Gamble Ltd* [1992] 1 WLR 1112 CA. The claimant cannot rely on Art. 6(1) if he wishes to join the foreign defendant only in order to obtain discovery of documents from him.

[107] [1995] 2 All ER 278. The actions against the various defendants must be related when the proceedings are instituted and there must be a risk at that time of irreconcilable judgments: *Messier Dowty Ltd* v. *Sabena SA* [2001] 1 All ER 275 CA.

[108] [1993] 1 Ll.R 164, a case under the Lugano Convention, Art. 6(1).

[109] A French court has held that Art. 6(2) does not apply if the original defendant is domiciled in a non-contracting state and jurisdiction is based on him on exorbitant grounds, e.g. casual presence.

[110] [1990] ECR 1845.

the process of the court) in order to determine whether the action is admissible, provided that the effectiveness of the Convention is not prejudiced, as by causing delay.[111]

In the same case, the European Court said that Article 6(2) is based on the existence of a particularly close connecting factor between a dispute and the court which may be called upon to hear it. This was held to be the case in *Kinnear* v. *Falconfilms NV*.[112]

> The actor, Roy Kinnear, was injured during the shooting of a film and died in hospital in Madrid. His administrators commenced proceedings in England against the film company, the producer and the director of the film. These defendants contended that Mr Kinnear had died not from his injuries but from the medical malpractice of the Spanish hospital and the surgeon who had treated him.

The court held that English law allowed the joinder of third parties, so they were 'any other third party proceedings', and that there existed a sufficiently close connecting factor between itself and the dispute; here, some alleged tortfeasors wished to reduce their liability to reflect the liability of others for the claimant's damage and this might be impossible unless all parties were before the same court. This could be effected in England but not, apparently, in Spain. Moreover, the issues involved in the two claims largely overlapped.

Like general jurisdiction under Article 2 and the other special jurisdictions, jurisdiction cannot be exercised under Article 6(2) if the third party is also a party to an exclusive jurisdiction clause as in *Hough* v. *P&O Containers Ltd*,[113] where H sued P&O, domiciled in England, and P&O sought to bring in B+V, domiciled in Germany, as third parties. However a contract between P&O and B+V contained a clause which was valid under Article 17 of the Convention and conferred jurisdiction on German courts. It was held that this agreement overrode Article 6(2) and the court had no jurisdiction over B+V. Though this result was unavoidable, it is, as Rix J observed, unsatisfactory, since it gives rise to a multiplicity of jurisdictions and of actions.

Counterclaims (Article 6(3))

A person may be sued 'on a counterclaim arising from the same contract or facts on which [his] original claim was based, in the court in

---

[111] The Court said, in particular, that the action on the guarantee should not be dismissed on the ground that the guarantor resides, or is domiciled, in another contracting state. In *Waterford Wedgwood plc* v. *David Nagli Ltd* [1999] ILPr. 9, the English court emphasised its discretion and declined to allow Art. 6(2) to be relied on when there existed no active original action.
[112] [1996] 1 WLR 920.   [113] [1997] QB 842.

which the original claim is pending'. So if A, domiciled in France, sues B, domiciled in England, in an English court, B may sue A in the same court on a counterclaim. This is restricted to claims by which defendants seek pronouncement of a separate judgment or decree and does not cover defences, in particular a set-off against the original claim.[114]

Insurance and consumer contracts

Special rules exist for these types of contract. Those regarding insurance (Section 3, Articles 7–12A) are as follows.[115] The insured may sue the insurer where either of them is domiciled. Where the defendant is a co-insurer he may also be sued where the leading insurer is sued. Where an insurer is not domiciled in a member state but has a branch, agency or other establishment in such a state and the dispute arises out of the operation of such a branch, agency or other establishment, he is deemed to be domiciled in that state and may be sued there.[116]

The insurer may bring a counterclaim against the insured in the courts of the latter's domicile. The insurer need not be domiciled in a contracting state; but the counterclaim must be against the original insured claimant and not against other defendants.[117]

A jurisdiction agreement is only effective if (a) it was entered into after the dispute has arisen, or (b) it allows the policy-holder, insured or beneficiary to bring proceedings in courts other than those mentioned above, or (c) it is concluded between a policy-holder and an insurer both of whom are domiciled in the same contracting state and it confers jurisdiction on the courts of that state even if the harmful event were to occur abroad, or (d) (with exceptions) it is concluded with a policy-holder who is not domiciled in a contracting state, or (e) it relates to a contract of insurance which covers certain risks.[118]

The rules for consumer contracts (Section 4, Articles 13–15), which are designed to afford extra protection to consumers,[119] are as follows.

---

[114] *Danvaern Production A/S* v. *Schufabriken Ofterbeck Gmbh & Co.* [1995] ECR I-2053.

[115] These do not apply to reinsurance: *Group Josi Reinsurance Co. SA* v. *Universal General Insurance Co.* [2000] 3 WLR 1625, ECJ, *Agnew* v. *Lansförsäkringsbølagens HB* [2000] 2 WLR 497 HL.

[116] See *Berisford (S & W) plc* v. *New Hampshire Insurance Co.* [1990] 2 QB 631; *Arkwright Mutual Insurance Co.* v. *Bryanston Insurance Co. Ltd* [1990] 2 QB 649; *Overseas Union Insurance Ltd* v. *New Hampshire Insurance Co.* [1992] QB 434.

[117] *Jordan Grand Prix Ltd* v. *Baltic Insurance Group* [1999] 2 AC 127 HL.

[118] These risks are listed in Art. 12A.

[119] *Bertrand* v. *Ott* [1978] ECR 1431. A person who is not the original 'consumer', but is his assignee, cannot rely on these provisions: *Shearson Lehmann & Hutton* v. *TVB GmbH* [1993] ECR I-139.

A consumer[120] may sue the supplier where either is domiciled.[121] Where the supplier is not domiciled in a contracting state but has a branch, agency or other establishment in a contracting state, he is deemed to be domiciled there. However, a consumer may generally only be sued where he is domiciled. He may also be sued elsewhere by agreement. But the normal rules respecting conferring jurisdiction by agreement[122] do not apply. An agreement only confers jurisdiction over a consumer if (a) it was concluded after the dispute arose or (b) it allows the consumer to bring proceedings in a place other than those already indicated or in a member state in which both he and the supplier were domiciled or habitually resident when the contract was concluded.[123]

Exclusive jurisdiction

In certain categories of cases, listed in Section 5, Article 16, courts other than those of the defendant's domicile have exclusive jurisdiction and that of the courts of the domicile is ousted.[124] The jurisdiction of the courts having jurisdiction in such cases cannot be excluded by agreement or by submission by the defendant to the courts of another state. There are five types of dispute; these, and the courts having exclusive jurisdiction, are:

(i)   proceedings having as their object rights *in rem* or tenancies of immovable property: the courts of the *situs* of the property (as will be shown, an exception to this, concerning tenancies, was introduced in 1989);

(ii) proceedings concerning the validity of a company's[125] constitution, its nullity or dissolution[126] or decisions of its organs (such as its board of directors):[127] the courts of the state where it has its seat;

---

[120] A contract concluded by a person who is not at the time engaged in business, with a view to setting up a business, is not a consumer contract: *Benincasa* v. *Dentalkit Srl* [1998] All ER (EC) 1 ECJ.

[121] The courts of the state in which the consumer is domiciled have jurisdiction if the supplier is domiciled in a contracting state or is deemed to be domiciled there: *Brenner* v. *Dean Witter Reynolds Inc.* [1995] All ER (EC) 278 ECJ.

[122] Under Art. 17: see pp. 154–8 below.

[123] The first of these will be discussed later. Thus if the consumer is domiciled in France and the supplier in Germany, but both are habitually resident in Belgium, and the contract confers jurisdiction on the Belgian courts, if they then get a domicile in Ireland and Italy respectively, the Belgian courts have jurisdiction.

[124] Another type of exclusive jurisdiction is conferred by agreement. Art. 17: see pp. 154–8 below.

[125] Also other legal persons or associations.

[126] This does not include the winding-up of an insolvent company, which is not within the Convention at all (Art. 1: see p. 135 above). But it does include the winding-up and reorganisation of a solvent company.

[127] *Newtherapeutics Ltd* v. *Katz* [1991] Ch. 226; see also *Grupo Torras SA* v. *Sheikh Fahad Mohammed Al-Sabah* [1996] 1 Ll.R 7 CA.

(iii) proceedings in respect of entries in a register: the courts of the place where the register is kept;

(iv) industrial property, the registration or validity of patents, trade marks or designs, or other such interests: the courts of the place where their deposit or registration has been applied for or has taken place;

(v) enforcement of judgments: the courts of the state where the judgment is to be or has been enforced.[128]

The first of these will be discussed later.[129]

Submission

Submission by agreement (prorogated jurisdiction)

An agreement to submit a dispute to the jurisdiction of the courts of a particular contracting state ousts the jurisdiction of the courts of all the others,[130] except those which possess exclusive jurisdiction under Article 16.[131] Article 17, as amended by the Accession Convention, 1978 and the San Sebastian Convention, provides, in effect, that: If the parties, one or more of whom is domiciled in a contracting state, have agreed that a court or the courts of a contracting state are to have jurisdiction to settle any disputes which have arisen or may arise in connection with a particular legal relationship, that court or those courts shall have exclusive jurisdiction.

Such an agreement must be either (a) in writing or evidenced in writing, or (b) in a form which accords with practices which the parties have established between themselves[132] or (c) in international trade or commerce, in a form which accords with a usage of which the parties are or ought to have been aware[133] and which in such trade or commerce is widely known to, and regularly observed by, parties to contracts of

---

[128] *Duijnstee* v. *Goderbauer* [1983] ECR 3363; *Owens Bank* v. *Bracco* (No. 2) [1994] QB 509 ECJ. See R. G. Fentiman, note [1994] 53 *CLJ* 239; E. Peel, note (1994) 110 *LQR* 386.

[129] Ch. 14, pp. 264–6 below.

[130] In *Hough* v. *P&O Containers Ltd* [1998] 2 All ER 978 the jurisdiction of the English court over a German third party under Art. 6(2) was held to be ousted by a German exclusive jurisdiction clause in a contract between the English defendant and the third party: see p. 151 above.

[131] Exclusive jurisdiction derived from Art. 17 is not, therefore, as exclusive as that derived from Art. 16. An agreement in a consumer contract is also ineffective if it does not comply with Arts. 13–15. Art. 17 contains a provision about trust instruments.

[132] This incorporates the decisions in *Segoura* v. *Bonakdarian* [1976] ECR 1851 and *Ms 'Tilly Russ'* v. *Haven and Vervaebedriff Nova NV (The Tilly Russ)* [1984] ECR 2417, [1985] QB 931; *IP Metal* v. *Ruote* [1993] 2 Ll.R 60.

[133] Discussed by the European Court in *Trasporti Casteltetti Spedizione Internazionale SpA* v. *Hugo Trumpy* [1999] 10 ILPr. 492.

the type in the particular trade or commerce concerned.[134] For example, in *IP Metal Ltd* v. *Ruote OZ SpA*,[135] the Court of Appeal held that an oral agreement for the sale of aluminium, which was confirmed by a telex which contained an English jurisdiction clause, was within Article 17, since the telex evidenced the jurisdiction agreement in writing and it was in a form which accorded with a usage of the trade in aluminium.

The original version required that the agreement must be in writing or evidenced in writing, and the European Court at first interpreted this very strictly,[136] but the subsequent amendments (made largely at the behest of the United Kingdom) and later decisions of the Court itself have done much to relax the formal requirement. Thus the Court has held that an agreement which is confirmed in writing by one party and not objected to by the other in reasonable time is valid.[137] If a contract between A and B contains a stipulation for the benefit of C, who may be, for example, a beneficiary under an insurance contract or the transferee of a bill of lading,[138] and the contract contains a jurisdiction clause, C can rely on the clause though he has not signed the contract, provided Article 17 is satisfied between A and B and their conduct was obvious.[139] Further, an agreement is valid if it is in writing and renewed orally, provided the applicable national law allows it to be renewed without the requirement of writing, even though the contract itself requires renewal to be in writing.[140]

An English court has held[141] that where the written contract expressly refers, by way of incorporation, to other written terms which include a jurisdiction clause, the profferee of the contract, by signing it without reservation, must be taken to have agreed in writing to those terms, even though he has no available copy of them.

The European Court held, in *Powell Duffryn plc* v. *Petereit*,[142] that a jurisdiction clause in a company's articles, covering disputes between the company and its shareholders, was within Article 17.

---

[134] In *MSG* v. *Les Gravières Rhénanes* [1997] QB 731 ECJ, the European Court gave a detailed explanation of this requirement and said it is for the domestic court to determine whether it had been fulfilled.

[135] [1993] 2 Ll.R 60 CA.

[136] *Salotti* v. *Ruwa* [1976] ECR 1831; *Segoura* v. *Bonakdarian*. These cases seem to have been overruled: *Iveco/Fiat SpA* v. *Van Hool SA* [1986] ECR 3337.

[137] *Berghoefer GmbH* v. *ASA SA* [1985] ECR 2699; *The Tilly Russ*, [1984] ECR 2417, [1985] QB 931.

[138] See *Coreck Maritime* v. *Handelsveem* (2000) *The Times*, 1 December, ECJ.

[139] *Gerling Konzern* v. *Amministrazione del Tesoro* [1983] ECR 2503.

[140] *Iveco/Fiat SpA* v. *Van Hool SA* [1986] ECR 3337; *The Tilly Russ* [1984] ECR 2417, [1985] QB 931.

[141] *Crédit Suisse Financial Products* v. *Société General d'Entreprises* [1997] 8 ILPr. 65.

[142] [1992] ILPr. 300; the Court said such a clause did not, like one in a contract, need to be specifically brought to the shareholder's attention. It sufficed that the articles were available to him.

National law cannot be relied upon to invalidate an agreement which is formally valid under Article 17.[143]

The parties may select one or more courts in different countries, for example as in *Meeth* v. *Glacetal*,[144] where exclusive jurisdiction was conferred on the German courts over actions against the German party (D) and on the French courts over those against the French party (C). But it is not clear that an agreement which conferred jurisdiction on the French and German courts over all disputes between the parties, at the claimant's option, would be valid. It would not seem to chime with the words 'a court or the courts of *a* contracting state'.[145]

A problem may arise where the defendant either claims a set-off or counterclaims. In *Meeth* v. *Glacetal* C sued D in the German courts where D claimed a set-off against C. The European Court held that since this arose out of the transaction in respect of which C was suing D, it could be determined by the German court in spite of the agreement that C was only to be sued in France.[146]

It should be observed that Article 17 operates independently of the defendant's domicile; it is enough that the claimant is domiciled in a contracting state. Moreover, if an agreement of the type in question is concluded by parties none of whom is domiciled in a contracting state, say, between a Canadian company and an Australian company, which confers jurisdiction on the English courts, the courts of other contracting states have no jurisdiction unless the English courts decline jurisdiction or unless the defendant waives the clause.

Article 17 also provides that if the jurisdiction clause was included for the benefit of only one of the parties, he retains the right to bring proceedings in any other court which has jurisdiction under the Convention. Suppose the agreement confers jurisdiction on the French courts, which are those of C's domicile. If this was for C's benefit, D can only sue C in France, but C can sue D in France or Germany (if D is domiciled there) or any other court which has special jurisdiction over D.

---

[143] *Sanicentral* v. *Collin* [1979] ECR 3423 (the clause was invalid in French law by being incorporated into an employment contract); *Elefanten Schuh* v. *Jacqmain* [1981] ECR 1671 (Belgian law invalidated the clause since the language used in it was not that prescribed by that law).

[144] [1978] ECR 2133.

[145] But see Hoffman J in *Kurz* v. *Stella Musical Veranstaltungs GmbH* [1992] Ch. 196, who appears to believe this would be valid.

[146] It is unclear whether the German court could have considered a counterclaim arising out of a different transaction. Advocate-General Mayras thought not, for this would be independent of the claimant's claim whereas a set-off operates by way of defence to such a claim.

In *Antérist* v. *Crédit Lyonnais*[147] the European Court held that the common intention to confer an advantage on one of the parties must be clear from the terms of the clause (i.e. it must say so) or from evidence therein or the surrounding circumstances. There is no presumption that the choice was for the benefit of one party simply because the chosen court is that of the country where he was domiciled.

As we have seen,[148] Article 17 was amended by the San Sebastian Convention to include a provision about employment contracts.

In matters relating to individual contracts of employment an agreement conferring jurisdiction shall have legal force only if it is entered into after the dispute has arisen [or if the employee invokes it to seise courts other than those for the defendant's domicile or those specified in Article 5(1)].

The words in square brackets do not appear in the Lugano Convention, Article 17 of which is otherwise the same as that of the Brussels Convention. So, if the agreement is entered into before the dispute arises, that is to say, where it is in the original contract of employment, the Lugano Convention invalidates it altogether. However, the Brussels Convention only invalidates it if the employer invokes it; but if the employee wishes to rely on it he may do so. In other words it can give the employee another choice of court in addition to those of the employer's domicile or of his own place of habitual employment.

A jurisdiction agreement is typically used either to restrict jurisdiction by, for example, confining this to the courts of the defendant's domicile and excluding all those which might have special jurisdiction (an exclusive jurisdiction clause), or to bestow jurisdiction upon courts which would otherwise not possess it (a non-exclusive jurisdiction clause).

Is a non-exclusive jurisdiction clause capable of conferring exclusive jurisdiction by Article 17? The wording does not preclude this; it does not say the clause must confer *exclusive* jurisdiction, only confer jurisdiction, in order to give a court exclusive jurisdiction. In *Kurz* v. *Stella Musical Veranstaltungs GmbH*,[149] Hoffman J appears to have held (though this is not entirely clear) that a non-exclusive jurisdiction clause could have this effect as far as exclusion of the jurisdiction of other courts under the Convention goes.

---

[147] [1986] ECR 1951.   [148] P. 143 above.
[149] [1992] Ch. 196, followed in *Gamlestaden plc* v. *Caisse de Suecia SA & Hans Thulin* [1994] 1 Ll.R 433 and *Mercury Communication Ltd* v. *Communication Telesystem International* [1999] 2 All ER (Comm.) 33.

Naturally, the Convention does not deal with a case where parties are domiciled in contracting states, but confer jurisdiction on the courts of a non-contracting state, say New York. It is not clear what criteria a court in a contracting state should apply to decide whether to give effect to such a provision.

The Convention, equally naturally, does not mention the situation where all or some of the parties to a contract are domiciled in contracting states, but agree to confer exclusive jurisdiction on the courts of a non-contracting state, New York, for example. If an English court is asked to exercise jurisdiction which it otherwise possesses under the Convention, it may stay the action in favour of the chosen court, or so the Court of Appeal held in *The Nile Rhapsody*.[150]

Finally, in *Benincasa* v. *Dentalkit Sr 1*[151] the European Court held that a jurisdiction clause is effective, even if it is sought to have the entire contract, including the jurisdiction clause, declared void.

Jurisdiction conferred by agreement can be circumvented by the defendant's voluntary submission to another court under Article 18.

Submission by appearance

By Article 18, a defendant who enters a voluntary appearance before a court of a member state which is not otherwise entitled to exercise jurisdiction thereby confers jurisdiction upon it, unless another state's courts have exclusive jurisdiction under Article 16. An appearance for the sole purpose of contesting the jurisdiction is not a submission[152] nor does the defendant voluntarily submit if, at the same time as he objects to the court's jurisdiction, he also formally files defences to the merits if so required by the domestic law, provided that he continues to maintain his objection.[153] It has been held in England that where the defendant objects to the jurisdiction and asks for time to prepare his defence, he has not submitted.[154] It has also been held that an application for a stay of proceedings is not a submission.[155]

---

[150] [1994] 1 Ll.R 374 CA (where the chosen courts were those of Egypt), p. 166 below.

[151] [1998] 1 All ER (EC) 135.

[152] Compare the position regarding submission to a foreign court in connection with the recognition and enforcement of foreign judgments under English Law: Civil Jurisdiction and Judgments Act 1982, s. 33(1)(a), pp. 113–14 above.

[153] *Rohr* v. *Ossberger* [1981] ECR 2431; *W* v. *H* [1982] ECR 1189; *Gerling Konzern* v. *Amministrazione del Tesoro* [1983] ECR 250. See also *Elefanten Schuh* v. *Jacqmain* [1981] ECR 1671.

[154] *Kurz* v. *Stella Musical Veranstaltungs GmbH* [1992] Ch. 196.

[155] *The Sydney Express* [1988] 2 Ll.R 257. *Sed quaere.* This would seem to be an admission that the court has jurisdiction. For the position at common law, see p. 114 above.

A court can acquire jurisdiction by this method, though another state's court has been given jurisdiction under Article 17. To this extent, therefore, contractually agreed jurisdiction is not entirely exclusive.[156]

It is not clear whether Article 18 applies if the defendant is domiciled in a non-contracting state.[157]

Refusal of jurisdiction and staying proceedings

By Article 19, if the courts of one member state have exclusive jurisdiction under Article 16, those of other states must decline it of their own motion. By Article 20, courts of states other than that of the defendant's domicile must do likewise if the defendant does not enter an appearance, unless they have exclusive or special jurisdiction. A court must stay proceedings if it is not shown that the defendant has received the document instituting them in time to arrange his defence, or that sufficient steps have been taken to this end.

Lis pendens and staying of actions

The doctrine of *forum non conveniens*, which has been evolved by the English courts in recent times,[158] has no application in cases to which the Convention applies. The only cases in which the English courts may decline jurisdiction or stay proceedings in favour of the courts of another contracting state is where the latter also have jurisdiction under the Convention and proceedings were begun therein before they were started in England, that is, cases of *lis alibi pendens*.

The same cause of action (Article 21)

Where the proceedings in, say, Germany and those in England involve *the same cause of action* and are *between the same parties*, then if the German court was *first seised*, the English court must of its own motion stay its proceedings until the German court decides whether it has jurisdiction. If and when it so decides, the English (or any other) court must decline jurisdiction in favour of the German court.[159]

---

[156] *Elefanten Schuh* v. *Jacqmain* [1981] ECR 1671. A claimant can confer jurisdiction on a court if he submits to a counterclaim by the defendant under a transaction which is separate from that which is the subject of the claimant's claim, provided it is covered by the terms of the contractual agreement: *Spitzley* v. *Sommer Exploitation* [1985] CMLR 507.

[157] It does not say so, but Art. 17 does say so and a submission under Art. 18 overrides an agreement within Art. 17.

[158] See ch. 8 above.

[159] Art. 21 was amended by the San Sebastian Convention, but only to put the requirements of declining and of staying the other way round from the original version.

In *Overseas Union Insurance Co.* v. *New Hampshire Insurance Co.*[160] the European Court, on a reference from the English courts, held that Article 21 was not restricted to cases where the defendant was domiciled in a contracting state (it was a United States company) and, not surprisingly, that the second (English) court could not at this stage examine the first (French) court's jurisdiction.

The question has arisen several times: what is meant by the same cause of action? This presents no difficulty if A sues B for breach of contract in Germany, where B is domiciled, and then A sues B in England, whose courts have jurisdiction under Article 5(1). However, in *Gubisch Maschinenfabrik A/G* v. *Palumbo*,[161] the European Court held that the concept of *lis pendens* has a community meaning.

> G, a German company, sued P, an Italian, in Germany for the price due under a contract between them. Then P sued G in Italy, claiming annulment of the contract. G argued that Article 21 applied so that the Italian court must decline jurisdiction.

The European Court agreed. It pointed out that if the Italian court annulled the contract, a German judgment would not, by virtue of Article 27(3),[162] be recognised or enforced against P in Italy. P's action was in effect a defence to G's action; therefore the two proceedings involved the same cause of action. This result is mildly surprising. The two causes of action were clearly *related* and so fell within Article 22 but they do not seem to be the same. The decision may be, and has been, criticised as encouraging forum shopping.

But the European Court applied the same reasoning where the actions were the other way round and the action for a declaration of non-, or limitation of, liability preceded the 'substantive' action for damages based on the defendant's liability.

In the important case of *The Tatry* (1994)[163]

> A cargo of soya bean oil, belonging to a number of owners, on board the *Tatry* (T) was discharged in October 1988 partly in Rotterdam and partly in Hamburg and it was complained that the cargo had been contaminated during the voyage. In November 1988, T's owners (who also owned the *Maciej Rataj* (MR)) brought an action in the Netherlands against the cargo owners, except one of them (Phibro (P)), for a declaration that they were not liable, or fully liable, for the alleged contamination. In September 1989 actions *in rem* were started in England against the T and the MR, which had been arrested in Liverpool

[160] [1992] 1 QB 434 ECJ.   [161] [1982] ECR 461 ECJ.   [162] See p. 170 below.
[163] [1999] QB 515 note ECJ, [1995] All ER (EC) 229. The full title is *Owners of Cargo lately laden on board Tatry* v. *Owners of Maciej Rataj* and it is usually called either *The Tatry* or *The Maciej Rataj*. The former is adopted here.

by the cargo owners, including P. The jurisdiction of the English courts derived from an international convention of 1952,[164] which was expressly preserved by the Brussels Convention, Article 57.[165]

Among the five questions put by the Court of Appeal to the European Court was, did the Dutch and English proceedings involve the same cause of action? The latter court repeated observations it had made in *Gubisch* v. *Palumbo* that, unlike the English version of Article 21, other language versions spoke not just of the 'same cause of action', but of the 'same object' and the English text should be given the same meaning: the 'object of the action' meant the end the action had in view. In the present case, the issue of liability was the object of both the Dutch and English actions. The negative terms of the former action and the positive terms of the latter action did not make any difference. The fact that damages were sought in the English action was only the consequence of a finding of liability; the seeking of a declaration of non-liability implies that the party who seeks it disputes any obligation to pay damages. The result is that the English court must decline jurisdiction.

This decision was met by considerable criticism from English practitioners and writers,[166] mainly because, even more than *Gubisch* v. *Palumbo*, it encourages 'forum shopping' in allowing a prospective defendant in the courts of one state to make a 'pre-emptive strike' in the courts of another, by asking for a negative declaration there. It is argued that there is a 'natural forum' for the trial of an action, that forum being where it is sought to establish the defendant's liability. Moreover, the English courts have, on the whole, been rather hostile to actions for negative declarations because they are often requested for tactical reasons, in order to pre-empt claims which have not been fully formulated.[167] There is some force in these criticisms, but they must be understood in the light of the fact that the Conventions do not reflect any notion of the 'natural forum' and do not make any value judgment between jurisdiction based on domicile and alternative bases of jurisdiction, should any of these be established. Further, as the Advocate-General pointed out, in *The Tatry* itself, the English court only had jurisdiction because the ship turned up in an English port and the English court had no closer connection with the dispute than had the Dutch court. Also, the English court's relative hostility towards

---

[164] The International Convention for the Unification of Certain Rules relating to the arrest of seagoing ships, 1952, implemented by the Supreme Court Act 1981, ss. 20–4.

[165] See p. 172 below.

[166] See B. Davenport, note (1995) 111 *LQR* 336; A. Briggs, note (1995) *LMCLQ* 161; R. G. Fentiman, note [1995] 54 *CLJ* 261.

[167] See *The Volvox Hollandia* [1988] 2 Ll.R 361.

negative declarations is not altogether shared by those in European countries, and in the United States and in England itself they are frequently resorted to, for good reasons, by insurers and reinsurers.[168]

Examples of subsequent cases in which English courts have held that two actions did not involve the same cause of action are *Toepfer International* v. *Molin Boschi*,[169] where the defendant's Italian action was for damages and the claimant's action in England was to prevent further proceedings in Italy; *Sarrio* v. *Kuwait Investment Authority*,[170] where the claimant's action in Spain against the defendants was for sums which the latter's subsidiary had failed to pay under a contract and their actions in England were for damages against the defendant for damages for negligent misstatement which had induced the claimants to enter into separate contracts; *Mecklermedia Corp.* v. *DC Congress*,[171] where a German action by the defendants against the claimant licensees was for breach of patent and the claimants' own action in England against them was for passing off the defendants' products as the claimants'. (In all these cases, it was held that the actions might well be, or were, *related*,[172] in which case all the English court need do was, by virtue of Article 22, stay its own proceedings.)

Another question put to the European Court in *The Tatry* was whether the two actions were between the same parties. At first instance[173] Sheen J had held that, since the Dutch action was *in personam* against the shipowners and the English action was *in rem* against the ship itself, the parties were not the same. The Court held that the term had a Convention meaning, that the formal technical distinction drawn in English law was irrelevant and, since both actions were in substance against the shipowners, the parties were in effect identical.[174]

In another case, *Drouot Assurances SA* v. *Consolidated Metallurgical Industries (CMI Industrial Sites)*,[175] the European Court held that for an insurer and the insured to be regarded as the same party, there must be a sufficient degree of identity between their interests. It appeared to the

---

[168] See A. S. Bell, 'The Negative Declaration in Transnational Litigation' (1995) 111 *LQR* 674. See now *Messier-Dowty Ltd* v. *Sabena* (No. 2) [2001] 1 All ER 275 CA.

[169] [1996] 1 Ll.R 510.   [170] [1996] 1 Ll.R 650.

[171] [1998] Ch. 40, where it was also held that the actions were not between the same parties.

[172] See *Sarrio* v. *Kuwait Investment Authority* [1999] AC 32 HL, p. 163 below, on this point, and *Haji Ioannou* v. *Frangos* [1999] WLR 337 CA.

[173] [1991] 2 Ll.R 458.

[174] Since *The Tatry*, the House of Lords has held, partly in reliance on it, that most English actions *in rem* are merely a procedural device to get the owners of the ship before the court and the action is, in substance, against them: *The Indian Endurance* (No. 2) [1998] AC 878: see pp. 83, 124, 128 above.

[175] [1998] QB 497 ECJ.

Court that an action by the insurer of a ship against the owner and insurer of its cargo was not between the same parties as one between the latter and the owner and charterer of the ship (not its insurer) concerning general average contributions. (The Dutch domestic court was also told that Dutch domestic procedural rules were irrelevant in this context.)

Related actions (Article 22)

When proceedings in, say, Germany and England are not concerned with the same cause of action, but are only related to each other, in other words, 'when they are so closely related that it is expedient to hear and determine them together to avoid the risk of irreconcilable judgments', the English (and other) courts need only stay their proceedings while the German action is pending at first instance.[176]

It will be recalled that, in *The Tatry*, one claimant in the English action was not a party to the Dutch proceedings. The European Court said that, although Article 21 did not apply to Phibro's action, Article 22 could do. The concept of 'related actions' had to be interpreted broadly and so as to cover all cases where there was a risk of conflicting decisions, even if the different judgments could be separately enforced and their legal consequences were not mutually exclusive. Article 22 is designed to improve the co-ordination of the exercise of judicial functions within the European Union and to avoid conflicting and contradictory decisions. Subsequently, in *Sarrio* v. *Kuwait Investment Authority*,[177] the House of Lords also held that the concept must be given a broad and common-sense meaning, avoiding an over-sophisticated approach.

Whether Articles 21 and 22 apply to a case in which the English court is not the one first seised, but its jurisdiction is derived from a jurisdiction agreement which is valid under Article 17, was one question before the Court of Appeal in *Continental Bank NA* v. *Aeakos Cia Naviera SP*,[178] and the answer it gave, rather controversially, was 'no'.

CB, an American bank with branches in many countries, gave a loan facility to A, a Greek group of companies. The agreement was governed by English law and A, it said, 'irrevocably submits to the jurisdiction of the English courts', which the Court of Appeal held was an exclusive English jurisdiction clause. A defaulted on its repayments. A

---

[176] This has less scope since *Gubisch* v. *Palumbo* [1987] ECR 49. But see the English case of *Dresser UK Ltd* v. *Falcongate Freight Management Ltd (The Duke of Yare)* [1992] QB 502. Art. 22 also provides for consolidated actions. (See also *Rank Film Distributors* v. *Lanterna Editrice SrL* [1992] 3 ILPr. 58.)

[177] [1999] AC 32 HL: see p. 162 above and see *Blue Nile Shipping* v. *Iguana S&F* [1998] ILPr. 440 CA.

[178] [1994] 2 All ER 540 CA.

brought an action in a Greek court claiming damages against CB. Then, CB issued a claim form in England against A to restrain it from continuing its action in breach of the jurisdiction clause.

Both the Greek (under Article 3) and the English (under Article 17) courts had jurisdiction. Clearly the Greek courts were first seised. Assuming that the two proceedings concerned the same cause of action, or were related actions, the first question was, should the English court decline jurisdiction under Article 21 or stay the proceedings under Article 22? In arriving at its answer, the Court of Appeal relied on the fact that under Article 17 the English courts had 'exclusive' jurisdiction and therefore the Greek courts had none, and it also relied on previous first instance decisions.[179]

This decision, which has been followed several times by courts which have been bound by the Court of Appeal,[180] has been regarded as wrong by almost every commentator who has written about it.[181] It overlooks the statement by the European Court in *Overseas Union Insurance Ltd* v. *New Hampshire Insurance Co.*[182] that 'in no case is the court second seised in a better position than the first court seised to determine whether the latter has jurisdiction'. Although that case did not involve an exclusive jurisdiction clause, it is wide enough to cover such a situation. Also, the Court of Appeal seems to have thought that when Article 17 confers exclusive jurisdiction, it means 'altogether exclusive'. But this is not so; Article 17 is in Section 6 of the Convention, headed 'prorogated [or conferred] jurisdiction' together with Article 18. Section 5 is headed 'exclusive jurisdiction'; it contains only Article 16. Article 16 jurisdiction really is exclusive; it displaces all other bases of jurisdiction and cannot itself be displaced by agreement or voluntary submission. Article 17 jurisdiction is not so exclusive; it can be waived by the partner for whose benefit it was inserted and can be displaced by voluntary submission (Article 18).[183] Moreover, when Article 19 requires a court to decline jurisdiction of its own motion, it must do so only in favour of a court which has exclusive jurisdiction by virtue of Article 16, not Article 17 as well.

Further, Article 17 is only concerned with formal validity; if the jurisdiction agreement complies with its requirements, the Greek court

---

[179] *Kloeckner & Co. A/G* v. *Gatoil Overseas Inc* [1990] 1 Ll.R 177; *Denby* v. *Hellenic Mediterranean Lines* [1994] 1 Ll.R 320.

[180] See *Toepfer International GmbH* v. *Molin Boschi Srl* [1996] 1 Ll.R 43; *Lexmar Corp.* v. *Nordiskskibsrederforening* [1997] 1 Ll.R 289; *Banque Cantonale Vaudoise* v. *Waterlily Maritime* [1997] 2 Ll.R 347.

[181] P. Rogerson, note [1994] 53 *CLJ* 241; A. Briggs, note (1994) *LMCLQ* 158; J. Hill, *The Law Relating to International Commercial Disputes*, 2nd edn (1998) 250, 336.

[182] [1992] 1 QB 434 ECJ, p. 160 above.   [183] See pp. 156–8 above.

should decline jurisdiction. But that court could perfectly well decide that it does not so comply, or that it is intrinsically invalid or that it does not cover the dispute in question. The last two matters are governed by the agreement's applicable law. In the present case that law was English law; but there is no reason to suppose that the Greek courts would or could not apply English law. If the Greek courts decided that the clause was invalid or irrelevant for any of these reasons, they could proceed to judgment. The English court would apparently do the same. In such a case there is a risk of irreconcilable judgments, which it is an objective of the Convention to avoid. For these reasons, among others,[184] it is submitted that the decision in *Continental Bank NA* v. *Aeakos* is wrong.

To make matters even more wrong, the Court of Appeal, without considering whether it is permissible under the Convention to do so, issued an injunction to restrain A from continuing its Greek proceedings. There is nothing whatever in the Convention to countenance this.

It must, however, be added that in a later decision, *Turner* v. *Grovit*,[185] the Court of Appeal went even further and held that the English courts have a discretion, which that court exercised, to restrain continuance of proceedings in another Convention country, in cases other than those in which the English courts have jurisdiction under Article 17. These include cases in which they are, in their view, first seised under Article 21 (though the foreign court would not regard Article 21 as applicable) and cases wherein neither Article 17 nor Article 21 is applicable but the English court believes that the foreign proceedings were only commenced in order to harass and oppress a party to existing English litigation; conduct which amounts to abuse of the process of the court. The court said that nothing in the Convention prevented it from restraining the foreign proceedings. On the other hand, there is nothing in the Convention which warrants it and the decision does not seem to be correct.

Exclusive jurisdiction (Article 23)

In the rare case where an action falls within the exclusive jurisdiction of the English court and of those courts in other contracting states, the English court must decline jurisdiction in favour of another court, if the latter was first seised of the action.

In *Owens Bank Ltd* v. *Bracco* (No. 2)[186] the European Court held that Article 23 did not apply where the courts of two contracting states

---

[184] See literature cited at note 181 above, for other reasons.
[185] [2000] 1 WLR 1034.   [186] [1994] QB 509 ECJ. See also p. 120 above.

(Italy and England) were asked to enforce a judgment of a court in a non-contracting state, in that case St Vincent and the Grenadines.

When a court is seised

A question which has arisen is, when, for the purposes of Articles 21, 22 and 23, is the English court 'seised' of proceedings? The European Court said in *Zelger* v. *Salinitri* (No. 2)[187] that it is when they are 'definitively pending'. However, it held that this must be determined by domestic law. It was held in *The Freccia del Nord*[188] that for action *in rem* and by the Court of Appeal in *The Duke of Yare*[189] that, with possible exceptions for actions *in personam*, an English court is seised not when the claim form is issued but when it is served on the defendant. Subsequently, in *The Sargasso*[190] the same court held that there are no exceptions to this rule and that where service out of the jurisdiction has been permitted the court is seised only when the absent defendant is served.

It is not entirely clear whether, if an English court has jurisdiction under the Convention, it can stay the action on the ground that a court in a *non-contracting* state is the *forum conveniens*. In two cases at first instance, *Berisford (S&W) plc* v. *New Hampshire Insurance Co.*[191] and *Arkwright Mutual Insurance Co.* v. *Bryanston Insurance Co. Ltd,*[192] it was held that it cannot, but these decisions were overruled by the Court of Appeal in Re *Harrods (Buenos Aires) Ltd.*[193] The Court of Appeal relied on section 49 of the Civil Jurisdiction and Judgments Act 1982, which preserves the power of the Court to stay proceedings where this 'is not inconsistent with' the Brussels Convention, and said that since the Convention was concerned only with relations between courts of contracting states, to stay proceedings in favour of the courts of Argentina was not inconsistent with it. The House of Lords referred the matter to the European Court of Justice, but the case was settled. Re *Harrods (Buenos Aires) Ltd* has been applied in other cases,[194] including *The Nile Rhapsody,*[195] where the courts of the non-contracting state (Egypt) were the courts mentioned in an exclusive jurisdiction clause. More often, the courts have avoided the issue by refusing to stay the English action[196] or

---

[187] [1984] ECR 2397 ECJ.   [188] [1989] 1 Ll.R 388.
[189] *Dresser UK Ltd* v. *Falcongate Freight* [1992] QB 502 CA.
[190] *Nesté Chemicals SA* v. *DK Line SA* [1994] 3 All ER 180 CA.
[191] [1990] 2 QB 631.   [192] [1990] 2 QB 649.   [193] [1992] Ch. 72 CA.
[194] *The Po* [1992] 1 Ll.R 206, where the court had jurisdiction under a specialised convention.
[195] [1994] 1 Ll.R 382 CA. See also *ACE Insurance SA-NV* v. *Zurich Insurance Co.* [2000] 2 All ER 449, (2001) *The Times*, 27 February, CA, where the defendant was domiciled in a contracting state to the Lugano Convention.
[196] *Connelly* v. *RTZ Corp. plc* [1998] AC 854 HL; *Lubbe* v. *Cape plc* [2000] 1 WLR 1545 HL; Lord Bingham cast doubt on Re *Harrods (Buenos Aires) Ltd.*

for some other reason.[197] It has been held that it is not inconsistent with the Convention to stay proceedings where the English court has jurisdiction under a non-exclusive jurisdiction clause.[198]

In *Sarrio SA* v. *Kuwait Investment Authority*[199] the Court of Appeal held that where the subject matter of the proceedings is within the scope of the Convention but the defendant is not domiciled in a contracting state, the English court may stay proceedings in favour of the courts of another contracting state (Spain). It said that this is because by Article 4 of the Convention jurisdiction is determined in such a case by domestic law and the English rules regarding jurisdiction include the power to stay on the ground of *forum non conveniens*.

Provisional or protective measures

An example of such measures is an interim injunction. The courts of any contracting state may be asked to grant such a measure even if the courts of another have jurisdiction over the case itself.[200]

Recognition and enforcement of judgments

Title III of the Convention deals with recognition and enforcement of judgments rendered by the courts of other contracting states on the basis of the jurisdictional rules just expounded.

Types of judgment

The Convention covers all types of judgment and not, as at common law or under existing statutes, only those for sums of money. Thus, any decree, order, writ of execution, determination of costs and so forth is

---

[197] In *Connelly* v. *RTZ Corp. plc*, the Court of Appeal had stayed the action and said that the question raised by *Re Harrods (Buenos Aires) Ltd* was advanced too late in the proceedings [1996] QB 361 CA. In *The Nile Rhapsody* [1994] 1 Ll.R 382 CA, a reference to the European Court was refused because of the delay and expense it would involve. See also *Eli Lilley & Co.* v. *Novo Nordisk A/S* [2000] ILPr. 73 CA.

[198] *Mercury Communications Ltd* v. *Communication Telesystems International Ltd* [1999] 2 All ER (Comm.) 33.

[199] [1997] 1 Ll.R 113 CA (reversed by the House of Lords on another point); see also *The Xin Yang* [1996] 2 Ll.R 217.

[200] Art. 24. This applies only to such provisional measures as are within the scope of the Convention, unlike those in *W* v. *H* [1982] ECR 1189. See *Van Uden Maritime BV* v. *Kommanditgesellschaft in Firma Deco-Line* [1999] 2 WLR 1181 ECJ. The English courts can grant such measures by the Civil Jurisdiction and Judgments Act 1982, s. 25; *Republic of Haiti* v. *Duvalier* [1990] 1 QB 202. The defendant need not be domiciled in England: *X* v. *Y* [1990] 1 QB 220.

included.[201] The judgment need not be final or conclusive. The judgment must be rendered in a case within the scope of the Convention, that is, in a civil or commercial matter, and not within those matters specifically excluded from its jurisdictional provisions.[202] Although provisional measures, such as an interim injunction, are within the Convention and are enforceable, provided the defendant was amenable to the jurisdiction,[203] the rights of defence must have been observed and they cannot be enforced if they were ordered in the absence of the defendant and intended to be enforced without advance notice to him.[204] Thus, an English freezing (formerly *Mareva*) injunction will usually not, and a search (formerly *Anton Piller*)[205] order could not, be enforced in another contracting state. A similar German order was refused enforcement in England.[206] If protective measures are sought to prevent the removal of assets from the jurisdiction pending trial of an action, they should be requested in the country where the assets are (as Article 24 provides) and not where the trial is to take place, should that be elsewhere.

A settlement, even if it is supervised or approved by a court, is not a judgment but an authentic instrument.[207]

Recognition

Recognition is to be automatic. The judgment need not be final or conclusive or *res judicata*. If the outcome of proceedings in a court depends on the determination of an incidental question of recognition, that court has jurisdiction over the question.[208]

There are six possible defences to recognition.[209] These also apply to enforcement of a judgment:[210]

(1) Where recognition is contrary to the requirements of English public policy; but this does not apply with respect to the jurisdiction of the foreign court. This defence seems to include a judgment obtained by fraud, since fraud is not treated as a separate defence. But here the scope of fraud is considerably narrower, it appears, than it is at common law. In *Interdesco SA* v. *Nullifire Ltd*,[211] which was approved

---

[201] Art. 25: see *The Heidberg* [1994] 2 Ll.R 287.
[202] *LTU* v. *Eurocontrol* [1976] ECR 1541.
[203] *De Cavel* v. *De Cavel* (No. 1) [1979] ECR 1055.
[204] *Denilauler* v. *Couchet frères* [1980] ECR 1553, 1570.
[205] Which permits the plaintiff to search the defendant's premises for offending goods, mainly in copyright cases.
[206] *EMI Records Ltd* v. *Modern Music Karl-Ulrich Walterbach GmbH* [1992] QB 115.
[207] See Art. 51 and *Solo Kleinmotoren GmbH* v. *Boch* [1994] ECR I-2237 ECJ.
[208] Art. 26.   [209] Arts. 27, 28.   [210] Art. 34.
[211] [1992] 1 Ll.R 180. As to fraud in relation to other foreign judgments, see pp. 119–20 above.

by the Court of Appeal in *SISRO* v. *Ampersand Software BV*,[212] it was held that even where the defendant could produce fresh evidence of fraud, if redress lay in the foreign jurisdiction (and it appears that it does lie in all the courts of all the contracting states) the defendant should pursue his remedy there and the English court cannot determine the question of fraud.

In the only case in which the European Court has held that Article 27(1) could be relied on, *Krombach* v. *Bamberski*,[213] it stated that public policy could only be resorted to if recognition or enforcement of a judgment of another contracting state would be at variance to an unacceptable degree with the legal order of the requested state, comprising a manifest breach of a rule of law regarded as essential or a right recognised as fundamental in the legal order of the state. It held that a French judgment for civil compensation against a German domiciliary in criminal proceedings in which French law forbade counsel to appear on his behalf need not be recognised or enforced by the German courts, since entitlement to fair legal process is a fundamental human right.[214]

The narrow scope of public policy described in that case was reiterated in *Régie Nationale des Usines Renault SA* v. *Maxicar SpA*,[215] where the European Court held that it did not permit refusal of recognition or enforcement of a judgment which was alleged to be vitiated by error of domestic law, even of EU law. The court said that Article 27(1) must be interpreted narrowly since it constitutes an obstacle to one of the fundamental objectives of the Convention, that is, the free movement of judgments.

(2) If the judgment was a default judgment (that is, one given against a defendant who did not appear) and the defendant was not duly served with notice of the proceedings in time for him to prepare his defence. The European Court has insisted repeatedly that the right of defence must be observed.[216] The question whether the defendant was duly served is one to be answered by the court which is asked to recognise or enforce the judgment, even though the court which gave it believed that the right of defence had been observed.[217] There is, therefore, a double check.

---

[212] [1994] ILPr. 55.   [213] (2000) *The Times*, 30 March.

[214] The Court emphasised that, as Art. 28 provides, public policy cannot be used to question the jurisdiction of the foreign court, see p. 173 below.

[215] (2000) *The Times*, 23 May.   [216] *Klomps* v. *Michel* [1981] ECR 1593.

[217] *Pendy Plastic Products BV* v. *Pluspunkt* [1982] ECR 2723; *Debaecker and Plouvier* v. *Bouwman* [1985] ECR 1779; *Minalmet GmbH* v. *Brandeis* [1993] 4 ILPr. 132.

It has also been very strict about this. For example, in *Hendrikman* v. *Magenta Bruck*,[218] it treated a judgment as having been given in default of appearance where a lawyer had, in fact, appeared on the defendants' behalf; however, they were unaware that he had done so.

The conditions for the application of Article 27(2) are: (a) the judgment must have been given in default of the defendant's appearance; (b) the defendant was not served with the document commencing the proceedings or (c) though he was so served, this was not in time for him to arrange his defence; (d) the claimant must show the defendant was duly served, etc. With respect to (a), it should be observed that a judgment remains one given in default and cannot be recognised, even if the defendant subsequently became aware of it but did not appeal against it[219] and even if he tried unsuccessfully to have the judgment set aside.[220] On the other hand, Article 27(2) does not apply where the defendant has appeared, provided he has been informed as to the substance of the case against him and has been enabled to arrange his defence.[221] With respect to (b) and (c), if there is a defect in service under the law of the foreign court, the English court cannot waive it.[222] Whether service was effected in sufficient time is a question of fact, not of the law, of either the court of origin or the requested court.[223]

(3) If the judgment is not reconcilable with an English judgment given in a dispute between the same parties.[224] The English judgment may have been rendered before or after the foreign judgment. Moreover, the English judgment need not itself be within the Convention. In *Hoffman* v. *Krieg*,[225]

> A Dutch court granted a divorce. A German court, which did not recognise this divorce, granted W maintenance against H, a German living in the Netherlands, on the footing that they were still married to each other.

The European Court held that the German order was clearly not reconcilable with the Dutch divorce, so was not enforceable in the Netherlands, even though divorce decrees, being a matter of status,

---

[218] [1997] QB 426 ECJ.   [219] *Minalmet GmbH* v. *Brandeis* [1993] 4 ILPr. 132.

[220] *Klomps* v. *Michel* [1981] ECR 1593; *Pendy Plastic Products BV* v. *Pluspunkt* [1982] ECR 2723; *Hendrikman* v. *Magenta Bruck & Verlag GmbH* [1997] QB 426 ECJ.

[221] *Sonntag* v. *Waidmann* [1993] ECR I-1963 (D appeared in criminal proceedings in which damages were also claimed against him).

[222] *Isabelle Lancray* v. *Peters und Sickert A/G* [1990] ECR I-2725.

[223] *Debaecker and Plouvier* v. *Bouwman* [1985] ECR 1779.

[224] For the common law see *Vervaeke* v. *Smith* [1983] 1 AC 145 HL: p. 123 above.

[225] [1988] ECR 645.

are excluded from the Convention.[226] This decision was applied by an English court, in refusing to enforce an Irish maintenance order, in *Macaulay* v. *Macaulay*.[227]

(4) If, in order to arrive at its judgment, the foreign court had decided a preliminary question as to status, legal capacity, matrimonial property, wills or succession (which are not matters within the Convention)[228] in a way which conflicts with a rule of English private international law, unless the same result would follow from the application of that rule. This is not very likely to occur, and in England would be mainly relevant in maintenance proceedings. For example, suppose a Dutch court had held H and W to be married and had granted W a maintenance order against H. By English conflicts rules they are not married. The order cannot be recognised. But if by those rules, even if they differ from the corresponding Dutch rules, H and W are married, the order must be recognised and enforced.

(5) If the judgment is irreconcilable with an earlier judgment in a *non-contracting* state (a) on the same cause of action and (b) between the same parties, provided (c) that the earlier judgment is entitled to recognition or enforcement in England by English law.

> C sues D in New York. D is resident in New York but domiciled in France. The New York court dismisses the action. C sues D again on the same cause of action in France. The French court gives a judgment in favour of C.

Since the judgments are based on the same cause of action and are between the same parties and since the New York court had jurisdiction by English law because of D's residence there and its judgment is entitled to recognition in England, the French judgment is not recognised here. On the other hand:

> C, an English company, sues D, a French company, in New York, for non-payment for goods delivered to France. The New York court assumes jurisdiction on the basis of D's managing director's presence in New York on holiday, and gives judgment for C. D then gets a French judgment against C for damages when the goods explode and damage D's French factory.

---

[226] Art. 1(1). The Court held that Art. 27(1) did not apply to this situation.

[227] [1991] 1 All ER 866. The facts were similar, though not identical, to *Hoffman* v. *Krieg* (an Irish court had recognised the English divorce, but continued the maintenance order made before the divorce). Moreover, it was sought to enforce the order under the Maintenance Orders Act 1972, rather than the Convention. But that Act contains a defence in similar terms to Art. 27(2); the court held that the 1972 Act must be given the same construction.

[228] Art. 1: see p. 135 above.

The French judgment must be recognised here, since (a) the two judgments do not arise from the same cause of action, and (b) the New York judgment is not entitled to recognition at common law.[229] (Nor are the two judgments irreconcilable.)

It is not entirely clear whether the Convention requires recognition in a case such as the following:

> C obtains a judgment in New York against D who was not present or resident there and did not submit to the court's jurisdiction. It is not enforceable at common law in England. C enforces it against D in France where D is domiciled under the Convention. (C is said to thereby 'launder' it.)

The better opinion is that the English court need not recognise or enforce the French judgment,[230] though nothing in the wording of Article 27(5) says this.

The Convention is silent as to what the English court should do if it is presented with irreconcilable judgments of the courts of two contracting states. This problem, by reason of the provisions concerning the declining of jurisdiction and staying of actions,[231] should not arise, but it might, if a foreign court has not applied them correctly. It has been suggested that the first to be registered in England should be recognised and the other not, since when registered, a judgment is entitled to be ranked as an English judgment, in which event Article 27(3) would apply.[232] If neither has been registered, and only recognition is required, possibly the judgment first rendered will be recognised.

(6) The sixth defence is provided in Article 28. This is that the jurisdiction on which the foreign court acted conflicted with the Convention's provisions on insurance or consumer contracts or with Article 16 (exclusive jurisdiction). An example is a German judgment concerning French land, though even here the English court would be bound by the German court's finding of fact, including presumably a finding that the land was in Germany![233]

If none of these defences exists, Article 28 states that the basis on which the foreign court took jurisdiction may not be reviewed even on the ground of public policy. The draconian nature of this prohibition is

---

[229] See *Littauer Glove Corp.* v. *FW Millington Ltd* (1928) 48 TLR 746 (p. 112 above).
[230] See P. Droz, *Compétence judiciaire et effets de jugements dans le marché commun* (Paris, Dalloz, 1972) 270–1.
[231] Arts. 21–3, pp. 159–66 above.
[232] Jenard-Moller Report on the Lugano Convention, p. 79.
[233] The Lugano Convention contains two more defences in Arts. 54B(3) and 57(4).

illustrated by *Krombach* v. *Bamberski*[234] where a French court had convicted a German domiciled defendant of manslaughter in Germany of a French national, having assumed jurisdiction over the defendant on the basis of the victim's nationality, and then in a later judgment in parallel civil proceedings ordered him to pay compensation. As regards the civil action, the French jurisdiction is not one which can be exercised over a person domiciled in a contracting state and is, indeed, expressly suppressed by Article 3 of the Convention. Nevertheless, the European Court held that Article 28 precluded Article 27(1) being relied upon to resist enforcement for this reason. Article 29 states that in no circumstances may a judgment be reviewed as to its substance (or merits). Article 34 repeats this as respects enforcement.

Moreover, the English courts may only stay proceedings for recognition (or enforcement) if an ordinary appeal has been lodged in the foreign court.[235]

Enforcement

Method of enforcement
A judgment which is entitled to recognition can be enforced. A judgment is enforced in England by registration with the High Court.[236] This applies to all types of judgment, and is not restricted to money judgments. The common law methods of enforcement are not available for judgments within the Convention.[237] Application for registration is made without notice;[238] the defendant may apply to the High Court for registration to be set aside and if he fails in this he may appeal once only on a point of law.[239] If the application is refused, the applicant may, on giving notice to the defendant, reapply to the High Court.[240] Either party may appeal once only on a point of law.[241] In England, appeal lies to the Court of Appeal or to the House of Lords under the 'leap-frog' procedure.[242]

Stay of enforcement
If an ordinary appeal[243] is pending in the courts of the state where the judgment was given, or the time for such appeal has not expired, the

---

[234] (2000) *The Times*, 30 March. See, however, p. 169 above for the other point involved in the case which *did* allow art. 27(1) to operate.
[235] Arts. 30, 40. As to the meaning of 'ordinary appeal' see note 243 below.
[236] Arts. 31, 32; 1982 Act, s. 4(1).   [237] *De Wolf* v. *Cox* [1976] ECR 1759.
[238] Art. 34.   [239] Arts. 36 and 37.   [240] Art. 40.   [241] Art. 41.
[242] 1982 Act, s. 6; Administration of Justice Act 1969, Part II.
[243] That is, one forming part of the ordinary course of the action, not being a request for reopening the case or for a new trial: see *Industrial Diamond Supplies* v. *Riva* [1997] ECR 2175, where it was held that the concept should be given a community meaning; see also *Interdesco SA* v. *Nullifire Ltd* [1992] 1 Ll.R 180.

English court may stay enforcement proceedings until the determination of the appeal or expiry of that time. Or enforcement may be made conditional on the provision of security.[244]

Miscellaneous

Parts of a judgment which are enforceable under the Convention may be severed from those which are not, and enforced.[245] Provision is made for legal aid.[246] No security, bond or deposit may be required of an alien or person domiciled abroad.[247] Under the 1982 Act, section 7, interest is payable on a registered judgment in accordance with and at the rate provided for by the law of the state where the judgment was given.

Relationship of the 1968 Convention to other conventions

Except in relation to matters to which the Convention does not apply it supersedes the United Kingdom's Conventions for Reciprocal Enforcement of Judgments with Belgium, the Federal Republic of Germany, France, Italy and the Netherlands, and the 1933 Act no longer applies to them.[248] The Convention does not affect international conventions to which the United Kingdom is a party and which, in relation to particular matters, govern jurisdiction and enforcement of judgments.[249] The United Kingdom may enter into conventions with third states obliging itself not to recognise or enforce judgments of other member states against persons domiciled or habitually resident in the third states on the jurisdictional grounds which are suppressed as against persons domiciled in member states.[250]

Intra-UK jurisdiction and judgments

Although the Convention does not deal with the division of jurisdiction and enforcement of judgments between the courts of the constituent parts of the United Kingdom, this had to be legislated for and the 1982 Act contains provisions to this end.[251]

---

[244] Art. 38: see *Van Dalfsen* v. *Van Loon* [1992] ILPr. 5 ECJ; *Petereit* v. *Babcock International Holdings Ltd* [1990] 1 WLR 350.
[245] Art. 42.   [246] Art. 44.   [247] Art. 45.   [248] Arts. 55–6.
[249] Art. 57; *Bavaria and Germanair* v. *Eurocontrol* [1997] ECR 1517. An example is maintenance orders under the Hague Convention of 1973. For maritime conventions, see *The Deichland* [1990] 1 QB 361 CA. Compare *The Po* [1990] 2 Ll.R 206 CA. For a lucid discussion see T. C. Hartley, note (1989) 105 *LQR* 640.
[250] Art. 59: see pp. 137–8 above.
[251] It also contains a new code of jurisdictional rules for the Scottish courts.

The Act sets out a modified version of the jurisdictional rules of the Convention.[252] It omits, for example, the insurance provisions.[253] There is no provision regarding exclusive jurisdiction in the case of industrial property,[254] and no requirement that a contractual submission should be in writing.[255] The Act makes clear that special jurisdiction exists in the courts of the place where the harmful event occurs in tort cases, not only when it has occurred, but where its occurrence is threatened.[256] The Act does not apply to certain specified proceedings, for example proceedings under the Companies Acts, proceedings respecting registration or validity of patents, trademarks or designs, or appeals from or review of decisions of tribunals.[257]

With respect to enforcement of judgments of United Kingdom courts, money judgments can be enforced by registering in the English court a certificate of the court which gave the judgment.[258] Provision is made for the enforcement of non-money judgments, including injunctions and decrees of specific performance, provided they are not interlocutory.[259] Provision is also made for recognition of judgments by way of defence.[260]

In *Kleinwort Benson Ltd* v. *City of Glasgow*[261] the European Court held that it had no power to give interpretative rulings on provisions of the 1982 Act, other than those which are provisions of the Brussels Convention itself.

EU Council Regulation (2000)

In 1998, the contracting states to the Brussels Convention, 1968 concluded a new convention which was to replace the earlier one. However, after the amendment of the EC Treaty by the Treaty of Amsterdam of 1997, the Council of the EU, relying upon Article 65 of the EC Treaty which gives it authority over the field of judicial cooperation in civil matters, took over the new convention and, on 22 December 2000, promulgated it as a Regulation ((EC) No. 44/2001),[262] which enters into force and becomes directly applicable in the law of member states (except Denmark, which opted out of it) on 1 March 2002.[263] It

---

[252] Ss. 16–17; Sched. 4.   [253] Sched. 1, Arts. 7–12A.
[254] Cf. Sched. 1, Art. 16.   [255] Cf. Sched. 1, Art. 17.
[256] Cf. Sched. 4, Art. 5(3). Also new Arts. 5(8) and 6A.
[257] 1982 Act, s. 17(1); Sched. 5. The Act allocates jurisdiction over trusts and consumer contracts: s. 10.
[258] S. 18; Sched. 6.
[259] S. 18; Sched. 7. This is not applicable to bankruptcy, winding-up or administration of estates, maintenance orders, status or legal capacity.
[260] S. 19.   [261] [1996] QB 57 ECJ.
[262] Official Journal of the European Communities L12, 16 January 2000, p. 1.
[263] Art. 76. The Regulation replaces the term 'contracting state' with 'member state'.

replaces the Brussels Convention as between the member states, except Denmark.

The Regulation's principles are the same as those of the Brussels Convention and its actual terms are not much different. The principal alterations to the Brussels Convention are as follows:

In the *jurisdiction* provisions, Article 5(1) is amended by removal of the words which refer to employment contracts, which are governed by a new chapter 3, section 5. The deleted words are replaced in Article 5(1) by the following:

> For the purpose of Article 1 and unless otherwise agreed, the place of performance of the obligation in question shall be:
> In the case of the sale of goods, the place in a Member State where, under the contract, the goods were delivered or should have been delivered, in the case of the provision of services, the place in a Member State where, under the contract, the services were provided or should have been provided.

Article 5(3) is amended so as to confer special jurisdiction in matters relating to tort, delict or quasi-delict not only on 'the courts for the place where the harm occurred' but also upon the place 'where it may occur'. Article 6(1), which confers special jurisdiction over co-defendants, is amended, so as to reflect the case law, to require that the claims against the defendants 'are so closely connected that it is expedient to hear and determine them together to avoid the risk of irreconcilable judgments resulting from separate proceedings'.

The new chapter 2, section 5, concerning jurisdiction over actions about individual contracts of employment, substantially gathers in one place the provisions which were inserted into Articles 5(1) and 17 of the Brussels Convention when it was amended by the San Sebastian Convention.[264] These provisions are motivated by a desire to give protection to employees.

An employer who is not domiciled in a member state but has a branch, agency or other establishment in one is deemed to be domiciled in that state in respect of disputes arising out of its operations (Article 18(2)). Article 19 provides that an employer domiciled in a member state may be sued either in the courts of that state or in another member state. In another state it may be sued in the courts of the place where the employee habitually carries out his work or where he did so, or, if the employee does not or did not habitually carry out this work in any one country, in the courts of the place where the business which engaged the employee is or was situated. Article 20 states that the employer may bring proceedings only in the courts of the

---

[264] See pp. 142–3 above.

state where the employee is domiciled (though the employer may bring a counterclaim in the court where the employee's claim is pending). A jurisdiction agreement is only effective if it was entered into after the dispute had arisen, or, if it was entered into before a dispute had arisen, it allows the employee to sue the employer in courts other than those mentioned in Article 19 (Article 21).

Article 17 of the Brussels Convention[265] is re-enacted in Article 25 of the Regulation, amended to provide that 'any communication by electronic means which provides a durable record of the [jurisdiction] agreement shall be equivalent to "writing"'. Point (4) of Article 17 is deleted and point (5) is transferred to Article 21 of the Regulation.

The provisions concerning *lis pendens* and related actions (Articles 21 to 23 of the Convention),[266] renumbered as Articles 27 to 29 of the Regulation, are amplified by the inclusion of a new Article 30. This provides a definition of when a court is 'seised' of proceedings; the matter is no longer left to be decided by domestic law.[267] A court will be deemed to be seised:

1. at the time when the document instituting the proceedings or an equivalent document is lodged with the court, provided that the plaintiff has not subsequently failed to take the steps he was required to take to have service effected on the defendant, or
2. if the document has to be served before being lodged with the court, at the time when it is received by the authority responsible for service, provided that the plaintiff has not subsequently failed to take the steps he was required to take to have the document lodged with the court.

In the provisions about *recognition of judgments*, Article 34 of the Regulation (Article 27 of the Convention),[268] which lays down the grounds of non-recognition, now requires as to (1) that recognition must be 'manifestly' contrary to the public policy of the requested state. (It is unclear what difference the inclusion of this word adds.) (2), which concerns default judgments, is restricted by the addition of the words 'unless the defendant failed to commence proceedings to challenge the judgment when it was possible for him to do so'. (4) (conflicts of rules of private international law) is deleted and (5) is extended to apply also to a judgment which is irreconcilable with an earlier judgment given in *another member state*. There are some amendments to the procedural requirements for *enforcement* (Regulation, Articles 38 to 56).

One other alteration concerns 'domicile'. In the text of the new 1998 Convention the term 'domicile' was to have been replaced by 'habitual

---

[265] See pp. 154–8 above.   [266] See pp. 159–66 above.
[267] See pp. 166–7 above.   [268] See pp. 168–73 above.

residence' but the Regulation retains 'domicile'. The Regulation (Article 59) continues to refer the definition of 'domicile' to the internal law of the forum state, as in Article 52 of the Brussels Convention. However, the Regulation (Article 60) replaces Article 53[269] of that Convention and supplies a common definition of the domicile of a company or other legal person or a company or association of natural and legal persons. This is where it has its 'statutory seat' (which for the purposes of the United Kingdom and Ireland means the registered office or, where there is no such place anywhere, the place under the law of which the formation took place), or its central administration or principal place of business.

---

[269] See pp. 138–9 above. This means that the Civil Jurisdiction and Judgments Act, ss. 42 and 43 are superseded.

11 Arbitration

An arbitration award usually arises out of a contract to submit a dispute to settlement by arbitration. Such an award has not the same effect in English law as a judgment, and if it requires enforcement the assistance of a court is needed. An English arbitration award (i.e. one made in England, whoever is the arbitrator) may be enforced by an action in the courts, or by summary procedure under the Arbitration Act 1996, section 66, by an originating summons made *ex parte* asking for leave of the court.

A foreign arbitration award (i.e. any award made in a foreign country)[1] can be enforced in England in several different ways: (a) at common law, by securing an English judgment; (b) if the award is within the Geneva Convention (1927) and the Protocol on Arbitration Clauses (1923) – for which provision is made by Part II of the Arbitration Act 1950[2] – or is within the New York Convention (1958), enacted into law by the Arbitration Act 1996, Part III (ss. 100–4),[3] either by action at common law or under the 1996 Act, section 66; (c) even if it is not within these statutory provisions, under section 66;[4] (d) if it has been made enforceable by a foreign judgment, by an action on the judgment; (e) if it was made in a country to which the Administration of Justice Act 1920, Part II, or the Foreign Judgments (Reciprocal Enforcement) Act 1933 extends, as if it were a judgment rendered by a court in that country;[5] (f) if it was made in another part of the United Kingdom and enforceable there as a judgment, it is enforceable by registration in England.[6]

---

[1] Even though not rendered under the law of such country: *Dallal* v. *Bank Mellat* [1986] QB 441.

[2] See p. 182 below.

[3] See pp. 182–5 below, where the relationship between the Conventions and the Acts is mentioned.

[4] *Dalmia Cement Ltd* v. *National Bank of Pakistan* [1975] QB 9.

[5] For these Acts see pp. 127–8 above. If the award falls within the 1933 Act the claimant can only enforce the award by registration under the Act, and cannot bring any other proceedings for enforcement. In other cases, he has the option of proceeding in the ways mentioned in (a) to (d).

[6] Civil Jurisdiction and Judgments Act 1982, s. 18(2)(e), Schedules 6 and 7: see pp. 174–5 above.

An arbitration award, as such, cannot be enforced in England under the Brussels and Lugano Conventions, which are concerned only with the free movement of judgments. They specifically exclude arbitration from their scope.[7] An award has to be converted into a judgment to be enforceable under the Conventions.

Common law

There are three conditions for enforcement at common law: (i) the parties must have submitted to arbitration by an agreement which is valid by its governing law, (ii) the award must be valid by the law which governs the arbitration proceedings and (iii) it must be final.

The agreement to arbitrate

The arbitrator's jurisdiction is derived from the agreement. Thus the validity, interpretation and effect of the agreement is governed, as with any other contract, by its applicable law.[8] Whether the particular dispute is within the agreement is determined by this law,[9] as is, for example, the question whether an English court can extend the time for submission to arbitration. Thus, in *International Tank & Pipe SAK* v. *Kuwait Aviation Fuelling Co. KSC*,[10] although the arbitration was to be held in Kuwait, the contract was expressed to be governed by English law, so it was held the court could grant an extension of time.[11]

The applicable law is also determined in the same way as is that of any contract. Suffice it to say that if the parties to the agreement state what law is to govern it, that will generally be conclusive: if they do not, it will be inferred by the court from the contract's terms and surrounding circumstances, failing which it will be governed by the system of law with which it has its closest and most real connection.[12] A selection of a particular country as the place of arbitration will, in the absence of an express choice of law to the contrary, almost certainly give rise to the inference that the country's law governs it, though this is not necessarily so.[13]

---

[7] See ch. 10 above, especially p. 136.
[8] See ch. 12 below. This law is usually the same as that which governs the contract as a whole. An example is *Hamlyn* v. *Talisker Distillery* [1894] AC 202 HL.
[9] *The Sindh* [1975] 1 Ll.R 372.
[10] [1975] 2 QB 224 CA.
[11] Under the Arbitration Act 1950, s. 27. But, of course, in that case the arbitration, to be held in Kuwait, had not begun.
[12] See pp. 194–5 below. The Contracts (Applicable Law) Act 1990 does not apply to arbitration. Its principles are, however, the same as those of the common law.
[13] The leading case at common law is *Compagnie Tunisienne de Navigation SA* v. *Compagnie d'Armement Maritime SA* [1971] AC 572 HL.

The law of the arbitration proceedings

This, usually called the *lex arbitri*, governs such matters as the procedure of the arbitration, and whether the arbitrator can be compelled to state a case for the opinion of the court, as well as whether the award is final. That it could be a different law from the proper law of the contract was made clear in *Whitworth Street Estates (Manchester) Ltd* v. *James Miller & Partners Ltd*[14] where arbitration proceedings were held in Scotland. The House of Lords held by a majority that English law governed the contract, but it held unanimously that Scots law governed the arbitration itself, so that the arbitrator could not be compelled to state a case, though under the then English law he could.[15] Thus, in the absence of an expressly chosen law to govern the proceedings, they will be governed by the law of the country where they are to take place.[16]

The finality of the award

This requirement means that the award must be final under the foreign law, but this is directed to determining whether it is final in the English sense. If, under the law governing the proceedings, they cannot be reopened before the same arbitrator, it is final for this purpose. The question is, whether the award disposes of all the points in dispute. If it is final in this sense, it can be enforced here, even though it could not be enforced in the foreign country. This was established by the Court of Appeal in *Union National des Coopératives Agricoles Cereales* v. *Catterall*[17] (a case under the Arbitration Act 1950, Part II, but it is beyond doubt that the principle is the same at common law), where, by Danish law, a Danish award required a judgment in order to enforce it. The reason was made plain, and is indeed obvious: if the English court insisted on a foreign judgment it would be enforcing the judgment and not the award which would, as such, be deprived of real effect in England.[18]

An award which is otherwise enforceable may, nevertheless, not be enforced if one of several defences can be raised. The available defences are not as clear as are those available in respect of foreign judgments,

---

[14] [1970] AC 583; *International Tank & Pipe SAK* v. *Kuwait Aviation Fuelling Co. KSC* [1975] 2 QB 224 CA.

[15] English law on this was changed by the Arbitration Act 1979 which had for its prime objective the reduction of judicial interference in arbitrations.

[16] See generally *Naviera Amazonica Peruana SA* v. *Compania Internacional de Seguros de Peru* [1988] 1 Ll.R 116 CA and *Union of India* v. *McDonnell Douglas Corp.* [1993] 2 Ll.R 48.

[17] [1959] 2 QB 44.

[18] If the party did obtain a foreign judgment on the award, he could, of course, enforce the judgment: *East India Trading Co. Inc.* v. *Carmel Exporters & Importers* [1952] 2 QB 439.

but they cannot be very different. Thus (i) the arbitrators' lack of jurisdiction,[19] (ii) fraud,[20] (iii) public policy, (iv) breach of natural justice, are all, presumably, defences.

Statutes

Arbitration Act 1950, Part II

This deals with awards made in pursuance of an arbitration agreement[21] other than one governed by English law[22] between persons who are subject to the jurisdiction of different countries which are declared by Order-in-Council to be parties to the Geneva Convention, 1927. 'Subject to the jurisdiction' means that the parties must reside in, or carry on business in, two states that are parties to that Convention and that the contract containing the submission to arbitration must have resulted from business conducted therein.[23] Further, the award must have been made in a territory specified by Order-in-Council as a state party to the Convention.[24] In *Catterall*'s case,[25] for example, the arbitration was between French buyers and English sellers and was held in Denmark. The conditions for enforcement are similar to common law,[26] and enforcement is, again, either by action or under section 66.[27] The defences are similar to those at common law.[28]

Arbitration Act 1996, Part III

This legislation, which is designed to replace the Arbitration Act 1950, Part II,[29] was originally enacted in the Arbitration Act 1975 which it replaces in identical terms. It enabled the United Kingdom to become

---

[19] Discussed in *Dalmia Dairy Industries Ltd* v. *National Bank of Pakistan* [1978] 2 Ll.R 223 CA.

[20] *Oppenheim* v. *Mahomed Haneef* [1922] 1 AC 482 PC.

[21] The Protocol on Arbitration Clauses, 1923, must apply to the agreement: s. 35(1)(a).

[22] *Ibid.*, s. 40(b).

[23] *Brazendale & Co. Ltd* v. *Saint Frères* [1970] 2 Ll.R 34. The countries must have been declared to be parties by an Order-in-Council; if they have not, it is not enough to show that they are actually parties: *Dalmia Cement Ltd* v. *National Bank of Pakistan* [1975] QB 9. For a list of states declared to be parties see SI 1984 no. 1168.

[24] Arbitration Act 1950, s. 35(1)(b).   [25] [1959] 2 QB 44.

[26] Arbitration Act 1950, s. 37(1). As to 'finality' see *ibid.*, s. 39. For grounds for non-enforcement see *ibid.*, s. 37(2).

[27] *Ibid.*, s. 36(1). An award may be relied on by way of defence: *ibid.*, s. 36(2).

[28] Fraud and natural justice are not mentioned but would be covered by public policy: *ibid.*, s. 37(1)(e).

[29] Part II of the 1950 Act is expressly preserved as regards foreign awards which are not New York Convention awards: Arbitration Act 1996, s. 99.

a party to the New York Convention on the Recognition of Foreign Arbitral Awards of 1958 which was intended to replace the Geneva Convention. The New York Convention and the 1996 Act, Part III (sections 100 to 104) create a simpler scheme.

A 'Convention' award is one made in pursuance of an arbitration agreement in the territory of a state, other than the United Kingdom, which is a party to the Convention.[30] An award is to be treated as 'made' at the seat of the arbitration, regardless of where it was signed, despatched or delivered to any of the parties.[31] An award may be enforced by way of an action at common law or, under section 66 of the 1996 Act, by summary procedure.[32] An award is binding between the parties for all purposes.[33] The arbitration agreement must be in writing[34] and it is an implicit requirement that the award is in writing.[35]

By section 103 of the Act the court has a discretion to refuse enforcement in eight cases only:[36] (a) if a party to the arbitration agreement was under an incapacity by his personal law; (b) if the arbitration agreement was invalid under the law to which the parties submitted it (or, if none, the law of the place where the award was made);[37] (c) if the defendant was not given proper notice of the appointment of the arbitrator or of the proceedings or was otherwise unable to present his case; (d) if the award was outside the scope of the agreement; (e) if the composition of the tribunal or the procedure was not in accordance with the agreement, or if there was no agreement as to these matters by the law of the country where the arbitration took place; (f) if the award is not yet binding or has been set aside or suspended by a competent authority of the country in which, or under the law of which, it was made.[38]

---

[30] S. 100(1). An Order-in-Council stating that a state is a party is conclusive evidence of the fact: s. 100(3). But presumably it can be proved otherwise that a state is a party. For states parties to the Convention see: SI 1984 no. 1168, 1989 no. 1348. An award made in a contracting state before it became a party is within the Act: *Government of Kuwait* v. *Sir Frederick Snow & Partners* [1984] AC 426 HL.

[31] Arbitration Act 1996, s. 100(2)(b), reversing the unfortunate decision of the House of Lords in *Hiscox* v. *Outhwaite* [1991] 1 AC 562 HL that the award in an arbitration held in England was 'made' in France, where the arbitrator happened to sign it.

[32] Arbitration Act 1996, s. 101(2).   [33] *Ibid.*, s. 101(1).

[34] *Ibid.*, ss. 100(2), 102(1)(b).

[35] Since a claimant must produce an authenticated award or certified copy (*ibid.*, s. 102(1)(a)).

[36] A part of the award outside the scope of the agreement may be severed from that which is within it and the latter part enforced (*ibid.*, s. 103(4)).

[37] See *Dallal* v. *Bank Mellat* [1986] QB 441.

[38] Arbitration Act 1996, s. 103(1), (2). An award becomes binding on its publication. This is not affected by an agreement made before publication that any proceedings to confirm or vacate it will be brought in the courts of a particular country: *Rosseel NV* v. *Oriental Commercial and Shipping (UK) Ltd* [1990] 1 WLR 1387.

These objections must be made by the party who is resisting enforcement, but in two cases either a party may object or the court of its own motion may refuse enforcement: if (g) the award is in respect of a matter which is not capable of settlement by arbitration; or if (h) enforcement would be contrary to public policy.[39] An award will be refused recognition on this ground if it is based on a contract which is illegal by the law of England.[40] Fraud is not a separate objection but there is no doubt that an award which has been procured by fraud will be refused enforcement for reasons of public policy.[41] In *DST* v. *Raknoc*[42] it was held by the Court of Appeal that it was not contrary to public policy to enforce an award when the arbitrators had been allowed by the agreement to select the law to govern the arbitration and had selected not the domestic law of any country, but the internationally accepted principles of law governing contractual relations.

An English court has an inherent discretionary power to stay any action brought in breach of an arbitration agreement. If submission to arbitration is contained in a written agreement the Arbitration Act 1996, s. 9[43] provides that the court *must* stay an action brought in violation of it; there is no discretion in the matter.[44]

---

[39] Arbitration Act 1996, s. 103(3).

[40] *Westacre Investments Inc.* v. *Jugo-Import SDPR Holiday Co. Ltd* [1999] QB 740, affirming Colman J [1999] QB 740; *Soleimany* v. *Soleimany* [1999] QB 789 CA.

[41] In the *Westacre* case it was held that this was only so if new evidence which might have affected the arbitrator's conclusion was not available at the time of the hearing or of an application to a foreign court to set aside the award. The court declined to apply the rules regarding fraud as a defence to enforcement of a foreign judgment as exemplified by *Abouloff* v. *Oppenheimer & Co.* (1882) 10 QBD 295: see ch. 9 p. 119 above.

[42] *Deutsche Schachtbau- und Tiefbohrgesellschaft mbH* v. *Ra's al Khaimah National Oil Co. Ltd* [1987] 3 WLR 1023 CA. The point was not argued in the House of Lords: see [1990] 1 AC 295 HL.

[43] Section 1(c) provides that 'in matters governed by Part I [of the Act which includes s. 9] the court *should not* intervene except as provided by this Part' (emphasis added). But, with regard to the statutory predecessor of section 1(1) in *Channel Tunnel Group* v. *Balfour Beatty Construction Ltd* [1993] AC 334 HL, the House held that whether or not the dispute resolution procedure in issue in that case was an agreement falling within the Arbitration Act, the court had a discretionary power, which the House relied on, to order a stay, rather than on the statutory power. Note that section 1(c) says only 'should not' not 'must not'. Matters not governed by Part I would include oral arbitration agreements and alternative dispute resolution.

[44] Heretofore domestic arbitration agreements only attracted statutory discretionary stays (see Arbitration Act 1950, s. 4(1)). It was intended to continue to distinguish these agreements from 'non-domestic' ones in the 1996 Act, since ss. 85–7 modify s. 9. But these provisions have not been brought into operation and it is likely they will be repealed or amended. At present, domestic agreements are not excepted from s. 9.

But the court has a power to refuse a stay if satisfied that the arbitration agreement is null and void, or inoperative or incapable of being performed.[45]

The court may restrain by injunction the bringing of proceedings in a foreign court in disregard of an arbitration clause.[46]

International investment disputes

It should also be mentioned that an award made by the International Centre for the Settlement of Investment Disputes, created under the World Bank Convention of 1965, in an investment dispute between a contracting state and a national of another state may be enforced under the Arbitration (International Investment Disputes) Act 1966, by registration in the High Court.

Foreign award as a defence

A foreign award is binding between the parties for all purposes and can be relied on by them by way of defence, set off or otherwise in legal proceedings in the United Kingdom.[47] In *Dallal* v. *Bank Mellat*[48] it was held that this was so even though the award was rendered by a tribunal which did not operate under Dutch law; indeed it might not have been valid by that law. The tribunal, which sat at The Hague, was created by agreements between the United States and Iran in order to settle claims of nationals of each of those states against the other state.

---

[45] Arbitration Act 1996, s. 9(4). The fact that the defendant would be financially incapable of fulfilling part of the award does not mean that the agreement is incapable of fulfilment: *The Rena K* [1979] QB 377. In *Nova (Jersey) Knit* v. *Kammgarm Spinnerei GmbH* [1977] 1 WLR 713 HL the dispute was not in respect of a matter agreed to be submitted to arbitration.

[46] *Tracomin SA* v. *Sudan Oil Seeds Co. Ltd* (No. 2) [1983] 1 WLR 1026; *The Angelic Grace* [1995] 1 Ll.R 87; *Bankers Trust Co.* v. *PT Jakarta International Hotels and Development* [1999] 1 Ll.R 910, where Cresswell J said there is no difference in this respect between an arbitration clause and a jurisdiction clause, as to which see ch. 8 pp. 106–8 above.

[47] Arbitration Act 1996, s. 101(1).   [48] [1986] QB 441.

Part III

Law of obligations

12   Contract

The law on this topic has fairly recently been the subject of major legislation. Over the years the English courts built up a considerable amount of case law concerning contracts in the conflict of laws. This was especially so as regards the basic concept of the proper law of the contract, the law which governed most contractual issues. However, as regards some contractual issues, such as the effect of mistake, misrepresentation and illegality, and capacity to contract, there was either no, or only rather obscure, case law. The common law rules continue to govern contracts concluded before 1 April 1991 and to apply to certain issues which might arise out of contracts concluded after that date.

The Contracts (Applicable Law) Act 1990; Rome Convention, 1980

On 1 April 1991 there entered into force the Contracts (Applicable Law) Act 1990, which enacted into United Kingdom law the Convention on the Law Applicable to Contractual Obligations, 1980 (the Rome Convention), concluded between the then member states of the European Community.[1] This Convention was designed to achieve harmonisation of the relevant conflicts rules of the member states and was said to be a logical and necessary consequence of the Brussels Convention of 1968 on Jurisdiction and Judgments in Civil and Commercial Matters.[2] It has also been argued that it introduces certainty into the rules of the conflict of laws. Whether one should accept these arguments and whether harmonisation or certainty will be achieved is a matter on which there is room for differences of opinion, especially as regards certainty.

---

[1] For commentaries on the Act and the Convention, see A. V. Dicey and J. H. C. Morris, *The Conflict of Laws*, 13th edn (London, Stevens, 2000) 1195–1283; G. C. Cheshire and P. M. North, *Private International Law*, 13th edn (London, Butterworths, 1999), ch. 18.

[2] See ch. 10 above. However, the Rome Convention is based on the voluntary agreement of the EC member states and is not derived from the obligation under Art. 220 of the Treaty of Rome, as is the case with the Brussels Convention.

The idea of a Convention was first put forward by the Benelux countries to the EEC Commission in 1967. The Commission appointed a Committee of Experts to consider the law applicable to both contractual and non-contractual obligations. This Committee produced a draft convention in 1972, but in 1978 non-contractual obligations were omitted as being topics on which the divergence of national laws was much wider than it was on contractual obligations.

There has been some difference of opinion as to the extent to which the Convention's principles and rules resemble those of the English common law. It is submitted that the two sets of principles and rules do not differ in any fundamental way. This is particularly true of the rules for the ascertainment of the applicable law (as the proper law is now called) and of its scope. Elaboration of the relevant rules is to be found in the provision concerning formal validity, for example. Among new elements, hitherto unknown to English law (by their names anyway), are the concept of 'mandatory rules' which appears in several Articles and that of the presumption of 'characteristic performance' contained in Article 4(2) as an aid in determining the applicable law when none has been selected by the parties.

The Contracts (Applicable Law) Act 1990, referred to in this chapter as 'the Act', enacts by section 2(1) not only the Rome Convention ('the Convention')[3] but also the Greek Accession Convention concluded in 1984 and the Protocol of 1988 (the Brussels Protocol) on interpretation of the Rome Convention by the European Court of Justice.[4]

Interpretation of the Rome Convention

The Act provides (section 3)[5] that any question as to the meaning or effect of any of the provisions of the Convention shall, if not referred to the European Court of Justice, be determined in accordance with the principles laid down by, and any relevant decision of, that Court. Judicial notice is to be taken of any decisions of or expression of opinion by the European Court. The Official Report of Professors Giuliano and Lagarde (the Official Report)[6] may also be considered in this connection. It should be added that Article 18 of the Convention states that regard should be had to the international character of its rules and of the desirability of achieving uniformity in its interpretation and application.

---

[3] Except for the provisions referred to in s. 2(2) (Arts. 7(1) and 10(1)(e)).
[4] The three instruments are set out in Scheds. 1, 2 and 3 respectively for ease of reference.
[5] Compare Civil Jurisdiction and Judgments Act 1982, s. 3, pp. 132–3 above.
[6] Official Journal of the European Communities 1980 No. C. 282(1).

The Brussels Protocol (Article 2) lays down which courts may request the European Court to give an opinion on interpretation, if they consider that a decision on the question is necessary to enable them to give a judgment.[7] In the United Kingdom these courts are (a) the House of Lords and other courts from which no further appeal is possible and (b) any court when acting as an appeal court. Moreover, by Article 3 the 'competent authority' in the United Kingdom may, if a United Kingdom judgment has become *res judicata*, ask for a ruling of the European Court if that judgment conflicts with the interpretation given to a provision by the European Court or in a judgment given in another contracting state. Any such ruling does not affect the decision of the United Kingdom court in any way.

Sphere of application of the Rome Convention

Article 1(1) of the Convention provides that its rules apply to contractual obligations in any situation which involves a choice between the laws of different countries and Article 2 that the law specified by the Convention applies though it is not the law of a contracting state. Thus it applies not only if the choice is between the laws of contracting countries, English and French law, for example, but also if it is between the laws of a contracting and a non-contracting country, such as English and New York law, or between those of non-contracting states, such as New York law and Swiss law. It also applies between the different laws of the United Kingdom, since this state has not availed itself of the freedom accorded to it by Article 19(2) to 'contract out' in this respect.[8]

The matters to which the Convention does not apply are (Article 1(2)) questions involving the status or capacity of natural persons,[9] contractual obligations relating to wills and succession, rights in property arising out of a matrimonial relationship, rights and duties arising from a family relationship, parentage, marriage or affinity (including maintenance in respect of illegitimate children). Nor does it apply to negotiable instruments, arbitration[10] and choice of court agreements, company law and the law of other bodies corporate or unincorporate (such as partnerships), to questions of the authority of an agent to bind his principal (or a

---

[7] Compare the position under the Brussels Convention, 1968, Art. 2 whereby certain courts *must* refer a question of interpretation to the Court.
[8] The Act, s. 2(3).   [9] Subject to Art. 11, p. 208 below.
[10] Thus the Convention rules apply to all the terms of a contract except to an arbitration clause contained therein, to which the common law rules apply. This seems unsatisfactory, and it is hoped that a court would apply the same choice of law rules to all of the contract.

company's organs or those of other bodies corporate or unincorporate) to a third party, to trusts or evidence and procedure.[11] Also excepted are contracts of insurance which cover risks situated in the territories of EC member states, but not contracts of reinsurance.[12]

The Convention is not retrospective and only applies to contracts made after its entry into force for the United Kingdom (Article 17). This was 1 April 1991.

Characterisation

The Convention does not define 'contract' or 'contractual obligation'. The English courts have given a wider meaning to the notion of a contract in private international law than it possesses under domestic English law. In one case a court regarded an Italian agreement unsupported by consideration as a contract.[13] Presumably, the European Court will interpret 'contract' in the way it has interpreted 'matters relating to a contract' in the context of the Brussels Convention, 1968, Article 5(1), and give the phrase an autonomous community or convention meaning, though so far the Court's guidance on this has not been particularly illuminating.[14]

The applicable law

The concept of the applicable law of a contract, which has been known to the English courts as the 'proper law', is fundamental to this topic. That law governs, as will be seen, almost, if not quite all, contractual issues. Indeed, that is why it exists. In the guise of the 'putative' applicable law it governs the formation and the existence of a contract. In respect of some issues, other laws than the applicable law may have to be taken into account. All this is as true of the Convention as it was of the traditional English choice of law rules.

The basic rules for the ascertainment of the applicable law are contained in Articles 3(1) and 4(1) of the Convention, which provide that a contract 'shall be governed by the law chosen by the parties. Their choice must be *express* or demonstrated with reasonable certainty by the terms of the contract or the circumstances of the case', failing which,

---

[11] Subject to Art. 14: p. 62 above.   [12] Art. 1(3) and (4).
[13] Re *Bonacina* [1912] 2 Ch. 394.
[14] See, for example, *Martin Peters* v. *ZNAV* [1983] ECR 987; *Sprl Arcado* v. *Haviland SA* [1988] ECR 1351, discussed at p. 141 above.

'the contract shall be governed by the law of the country with which it is most closely connected'. All this bears a remarkable resemblance to the English courts' approach, as set out in the speeches of Lords Diplock and Wilberforce in the leading modern case, *Amin Rasheed Shipping Corporation* v. *Kuwait Insurance Co.*,[15] which concerned a contract contained in an insurance policy. The former judge said:

[T]he first step is to examine the policy to see whether the parties have, by its express terms, or by necessary implication . . . evinced a common intention as to the system of law by reference to which their mutual rights and obligations under it are to be ascertained.

Lord Wilberforce added that if no intention is expressed and none can be inferred, then, 'it is necessary to seek the system of law with which the contract has its closest and most real connection'. We will call this an 'imputed' applicable law.

Express choice of law

Article 3(1) clearly treats an express choice of law as conclusive. This reflects the English traditional view as expressed by Lord Wright in *Vita Food Products Inc.* v. *Unus Shipping Co.*[16] It rejects claims which have been advanced by writers that the principle of the parties' autonomy is limited by a doctrine whereby parties are not allowed to evade the application of the rules of a system of law which they do not like by resorting to another system. No such general doctrine of evasion of law exists in English private international law.[17] Article 3(3) allows for the possible application of rules of some other system and goes some way to prevent evasion of what are called 'mandatory rules', but this does not, as will be seen, altogether nullify the parties' selection of a law to govern their contract; indeed it confirms their freedom of choice. It also confirms that the chosen law need have no connection with the contract.

After a perusal of the following pages, it may well be concluded that it is highly desirable, to say the least, that the parties should always clearly state what law is to govern their contract, unless agreement upon this is impossible.

---

[15] [1984] AC 50 HL.   [16] [1939] AC 277 PC.
[17] Lord Wright said that it was difficult to think of any qualification of the parties' freedom 'provided the intention expressed is *bona fide* and *legal* and there is no reason for avoiding the choice on the grounds of public policy'.

Inferred choice of law

Article 3(1) provides that if the parties have not expressed a choice of law ('this contract shall be governed by French law'), such a choice must be 'demonstrated with reasonable certainty,[18] by the terms of the contract or the circumstances of the case'.

This is conceptually distinct from what we may call the 'imputed' choice of law which operates in the absence of an express or inferred choice and is envisaged by Article 4(1). However, applying the distinction in a given case may not be an easy task. Indeed, in the *Amin Rasheed* case Lord Diplock, with whom three other Law Lords agreed, was able to conclude that English law was the proper law by inference from the terms of the contract and the surrounding circumstances, whereas the majority of the Court of Appeal and Lord Wilberforce were unwilling to draw such an inference and held that English law governed by reason of the 'closest and most real connection' test. This may have been, on the facts, the more realistic view. The provisions of the Rome Convention do not do anything to resolve this matter. With this warning in mind, examples will briefly be given of the factors which have sometimes (though sometimes not) led the English courts to make such an inference as to the applicable law.

The Official Report gives examples of factors which may enable an inference to be made. These include: the use of a standard form, for example a Lloyd's policy of marine insurance;[19] a previous course of dealing under contracts containing a choice of law clause, whose omission from the instant contract is not the consequence of a decision to change the parties' policy; a choice of court or arbitration clause (this has nearly always led the English courts to draw the inference that if there is such a clause providing for settlement of disputes in England, the parties intended English law to govern, as they did in *Egon Oldendorff* v. *Libera Corp.*,[20] a

---

[18] In the *Amin Rasheed* case [1984] AC 50 HL Lord Diplock said it must be a *necessary* inference. But the Official Report, p. 17 says the choice must be *real*. There is, therefore, probably no great difference between the formulations.

[19] *The Adriatic* [1931] P 241 CA, but see *Amin Rasheed Shipping Corporation* v. *Kuwait Insurance Co.* [1984] AC 50 HL, where the policy was a standard Lloyd's policy, as set out in the Marine Insurance Act 1906, Sched. 1. The House of Lords inferred that English law was the governing law not from the fact that the policy was in English form, since such policies are in use throughout the world, but because the parties' rights and obligations could only be determined by reference to that Act and its judicial interpretation.

[20] [1995] 2 Ll.R 64 (Mance J) (No. 2) [1996] 1 Ll.R 380 (Clarke J). The contract was an English insurance contract containing standard clauses with well-known meanings in English law.

case decided under Article 3(1));[21] a reference to rules of a particular system of law, as for example, the inclusion of provisions of the French Civil Code; an expressly chosen law to govern related transactions.

In the past, the English courts have sometimes, but not always, drawn an inference from such factors as the currency and place of payment,[22] the status of the parties (as, for example, that one is a government)[23] and from the supposed intention of the parties to create or include a valid contract or term thereof, such as an exemption clause (inference *in favorem negotii*).[24] The status of such factors under the Convention is not entirely clear.

If no inference can be drawn, the Court will have to resort to the rules in Article 4 of the Convention.

Scission of the contract

Article 3(1) says that 'by their choice the parties can select the law applicable to the whole or a part only of the contract'. Thus, the Convention introduces the possibility of what is known as 'depecage' or 'scission' of the contract, whereby they can split it up and make different parts subject to different laws. Presumably, if they expressly choose the law to govern one part and do not deal with other parts, the law applicable to those others will be selected by resort to Article 4 and the law of the country or countries with which those parts are most closely connected will be the applicable law.

This possibility is recognised by English common law[25] but is highly unusual and most inconvenient. The advisability of including it in the

---

[21] See, for example, *Hamlyn* v. *Talisker Distillery* [1894] AC 202 HL; *Spurrier* v. *La Cloche* [1902] AC 446 PC; *The Mariannina* [1983] 1 Ll.R 12 CA; *The Komninos S.* [1991] 1 Ll.R 370 CA. In *Compagnie Tunisienne de Navigation SA* v. *Compagnie d'Armement Maritime SA* [1971] AC 572 HL, the House of Lords held that the inference could be rebutted, and that in spite of there being an English arbitration clause in the contract, the latter was governed by French law. No such inference can be drawn when the contract provides for arbitration in alternative places: *The Star Texas* [1993] 2 Ll.R 445 CA (London or Beijing).

[22] *R* v. *International Trustee for the Protection of Bondholders A/G* [1937] AC 500 HL (payment in US dollars; New York law governed), but this can be rebutted. US dollars, for example, are often used in international trade: *Amin Rasheed Shipping Corporation* v. *Kuwait Insurance Co.* [1984] AC 50 HL.

[23] *Bonython* v. *Commonwealth of Australia* [1951] AC 201 PC, but see *R* v. *International Trustee* case (previous note).

[24] *Peninsular and Oriental Steam Navigation Co.* v. *Shand* (1865) 3 Moo. PC (NS) 272. In *Sayers* v. *International Drilling Co.* [1971] 1 WLR 1176 CA, the exemption clause was valid by Dutch but not by English law; Dutch law governed. The converse was the case in *Coast Lines Ltd* v. *Hudig and Veder Chartering NV* [1972] 2 QB 34 CA.

[25] See *Forsikringsaktieselskapet Vesta* v. *Butcher* [1986] 2 All ER 488; affirmed on different grounds by the Court of Appeal and the House of Lords: [1989] AC 852.

Convention was questioned. The Official Report[26] says that the choice must be logically consistent and that repudiation for non-performance could hardly be subject to two laws, one for the seller and one for the buyer. In case of such an inconsistency resort must be had to Article 4 instead to find the applicable law.

Consent of the parties to the choice

Article 3(4) of the Convention provides that the existence and validity of the consent of the parties to the choice of the applicable law shall be determined in accordance with the provisions of Articles 8 (existence and material validity), 9 (formal validity) and 11 (a case of incapacity). These will be discussed later.

Failure of an express choice of law to take effect

If the express choice of law does not, for some reason, take effect it does not necessarily follow that it is totally useless. An express choice may fail to take effect in a case where a system of law is not nominated directly (as by saying 'French law'). The problem was discussed by members of the House of Lords in *Compagnie Tunisienne de Navigation SA* v. *Compagnie d'Armement Maritime SA*.[27]

A contract contained in a charter-party which had no connection with England other than an English arbitration clause (clause 18), provided (clause 13) that it should be 'governed by the law of the flag of the vessel carrying the goods'. It further provided (clause 28) that shipments were to be made in 'tonnage owned or controlled or chartered by French ship-owners'. It seems, therefore, that it was envisaged that vessels flying the French flag should primarily be employed. In fact the shipments were made in French, Norwegian, Swiss, Bulgarian and two Liberian ships.

The majority of the House held that clauses 13 and 28 together sufficiently pointed to an express choice of French law.

But consideration was given to what the position would be if it did not. As to this, the views of their Lordships were equally divided. Lords Morris and Diplock thought that if clause 13 did not have the positive effect of making French law the governing law, it could nevertheless be relied upon to show the intention of the parties by inference and thus that French law was the governing law and in so doing to rebut any inference from clause 18 that English law was the proper law. Lords

---

[26] P. 17.   [27] [1971] AC 572 HL.

Dilhorne and Wilberforce thought that if the clause had not achieved its purpose it must be struck out and ignored.[28] The former view is surely to be preferred; clause 13 was, after all, agreed by the parties as a term of the contract and was not void.

Mandatory rules

Article 3(3) limits the application of the chosen law by providing that this 'shall not, where all the other elements relevant to the situation at the time of the choice are connected with one country only, prejudice the application of rules of the law of that country which cannot be derogated from by contract'.

The concept of 'mandatory rules', which also appears elsewhere in the Convention, will be more fully discussed later.[29] However, the purpose of this provision is to prevent evasion of mandatory rules of law where what is fundamentally a domestic contract is turned into a conflicts case solely by virtue of the parties' choice of a foreign law to govern their contract. Thus, if what is entirely a Dutch contract containing a clause which offends a mandatory rule of Dutch law is expressed to be governed by French law, an English court must apply the Dutch rule to that clause. There is no reason why the same should not be done if the contract is really English; the provisions of the Unfair Contract Terms Act 1977 could be applied so as to control an exemption clause therein which is valid by French law, by the courts of England or of any contracting state.[30]

The law of the country with which all the relevant connections exist must be examined to see whether the rule is one which cannot be derogated from by contract.

Imputed applicable law

Article 4(1) provides that, in the absence of choice, the applicable law is to be 'the law of the country with which the contract is most closely connected'.[31] It then adds that 'a severable part of the contract which has a closer connection with another country may by way of exception be governed by the law of that other country'.[32] It is hoped that courts will be reluctant to split a contract in this way.

---

[28] They selected French law as the system with which the contract had its closest and most real connection.

[29] Pp. 213–15 below.

[30] An English court might rely on Art. 7(2) but this deals with a slightly different kind of mandatory rule. See p. 213 below.

[31] Compare *Bonython* v. *Commonwealth of Australia* [1951] AC 201 PC.

[32] Compare Art. 3(1). See p. 195 above.

Article 4 goes on to give three presumptions for determining with which country the contract is most closely connected and then by paragraph (5) restates the principle set out in (1). It seems that one first applies the presumptions and then looks to see whether, in the words of Article 4(5), the presumption in Article 4(2) cannot operate or those in Article 4(3) and (4) are to be disregarded in the circumstances of the case, and only then one looks for the closest connection.

Article 4(2): characteristic performance

This is the most novel, controversial and seemingly peculiar of the presumptions. It provides that the contract is presumed to be most closely connected with the country 'in which the party who is to effect the *performance which is characteristic of the contract* has, at the time of the conclusion of the contract, his habitual residence'. (Not, it should be noted, where he is to effect performance.) Thus, where A's performance is characteristic of the contract, suppose

> A is habitually resident in England and contracts with B in France. Wherever A is bound to perform his contractual obligations (England, France, Italy or Brazil) English law is presumed to be the applicable law. This is so even if, by the time he has to perform them, A is habitually resident in Japan.

It is then provided that if A is a corporate or unincorporated 'body', for example, a company or partnership, for its 'habitual residence' read 'central administration'. Thus

> If A is a company registered in New York but its central administration is in England, then, in the above circumstances, English law is presumed to be the applicable law.
> But if A is registered in England but its central administration is in Germany, German law is presumed to be that law.

However, there is a caveat to these provisions. If A, whether an individual or a 'body', entered into the contract *in the course of A's trade or profession*, for example, where A is a manufacturer selling his or its own manufactured goods, then

(i)   If A's *principal place of business* is in England, *English* law is presumed to be the applicable law.
(ii) If it is in England but A has *a place of business in France* and has to perform his or its obligation through such place of business (for example, a warehouse there), *French* law is presumed to be the applicable law.
(iii) If A (an individual) has his habitual residence in England and has his principal place of business in France, but has to perform his

obligation through a place of business in Germany, German law is presumed to be the applicable law.

But, as was said earlier, if the characteristic performance cannot be determined, this presumption does not apply (Article 4(5)).

If this remarkably convoluted provision has been understood, note should be taken of the following comments.

It is strange that the Convention should contain any presumptions when in recent times courts, especially the English courts, have deprecated their employment. In earlier cases, the English courts did use presumptions, for example, that the law of the place of contracting should govern the contract, or that if performance was to take place elsewhere, the law of the place of performance should do so. The law of the flag carried by a ship was presumed to govern contracts of affreightment or charter-parties. But in some of these situations and in others, the presumption was sometimes not applied or was easily rebutted.

Moreover, the notion of 'characteristic performance' is, it seems, probably derived from Swiss law (it is now in a Swiss statute), which is slightly odd since Switzerland is not an EU member state and so cannot be a party to the Convention.

What is 'characteristic' performance? There is no problem in the case of unilateral contracts, but how is it to be determined in the case of bilateral contracts? In the Official Report[33] it is suggested that, in the case of a contract for the supply of goods or services, it is the provision of the goods or services, not the payment for them, which is the characteristic performance. While it is true that payment of money characterises any type of contract (except barter) and so does not distinguish between the different types, the reasons the rapporteurs give for their suggestion are not wholly convincing.[34]

It is, however, possible to surmise that the English courts had already adopted something akin to a doctrine of characteristic performance (without using or, indeed, having heard of the concept) in that the courts have looked to see what type of contract the case is about and then said that that type of contract is normally governed by a certain law.

Thus, an insurance contract has been held to be governed by the law of the insurer's place of business.[35] A contract contained in a bank

---

[33] P. 20.   [34] Dicey and Morris, *Conflict of Laws*, 13th edn, 1237.

[35] *Rossano* v. *Manufacturers Life Insurance Co.* [1963] 2 QB 352; *Crédit Lyonnais* v. *New Hampshire Insurance Co.* [1997] 1 Ll.R at 6 CA, a case under Art. 6(2) of the Convention, as was *HIB Ltd* v. *Guardian Insurance Co.* [1997] 1 Ll.R 412, which concerned an insurance broking contract: the broker was in England; English law was held to apply. This law was not applied in *Amin Rasheed Shipping Corporation* v. *Kuwait Insurance Co.* [1984] AC 50 HL or in *Armadora Occidental SA* v. *Horace Mann Insurance Co.* [1977] 1 WLR 1098 CA.

account has been held to be governed by the law of the country in which the account is held and not of that where the bank's head office is situated.[36] The same conclusion was reached by applying the presumption of characteristic performance in *Sierra Leone Telecommunications Co. Ltd* v. *Barclays Bank plc*.[37] The case concerned the applicable law of a bank account of a Sierra Leone company at an English branch of an English bank which also had a branch in Sierra Leone. Cresswell J held that it was the bank whose performance was characteristic of the contract and the contract was entered into in the course of its trade. Its performance was to be effected through a place of business in England so English law was the applicable law of Sierratel's bank account. (The same would have been true if the bank had its principal place of business in France.) A banker's credit has been held to be governed by the law of the country in which the beneficiary can draw on it, as has a performance bond given by a bank to secure payment on a contract.[38]

This is also the result by the application of Article 4(2) to banker's credits. In *Bank of Baroda* v. *Vysya Bank*:[39]

> Indian buyers instructed V bank, an Indian bank, to issue a letter of credit in favour of Irish sellers with an office in London. The credit provided it should be advised to the seller through B bank, also an Indian bank, at its London branch. B bank confirmed the credit and paid the sellers under it. V bank withdrew its authorisation to B bank to claim reimbursement from V bank before the due date, whereon B bank sought permission to serve V bank out of the jurisdiction on the ground, *inter alia*, that the contract between the two banks was governed by English law. Whether it was so governed depended on the application of Article 4.

Mance J. held that this contract, between the issuing and confirming bank, was governed by English law. The contract was one of agency; the characteristic performance was that of the confirming bank (B bank). Since that was to be effected through its London branch (a 'place of business other than its principal place' of business), by article 4(2) English law was the applicable law.

[36] *X A/G* v. *A Bank* [1983] 2 All ER 464; *Libyan Arab Bank* v. *Bankers Trust Co.* [1989] QB 728; *Libyan Arab Foreign Bank* v. *Manufacturers Hanover Trust Co.* [1988] 2 Ll.R 494.

[37] [1998] 2 All ER 821. A similar example was given by Colman J in the context of reinsurance contracts in *AIG Group (UK) Ltd* v. *The Ethniki* [1998] 4 All ER 301 at 310.

[38] *Offshore International SA* v. *Banco Central SA* [1977] 1 WLR 399, approved in *Power Curber International Ltd* v. *National Bank of Kuwait* [1981] 1 WLR 1233 CA; *Attock Cement Co. Ltd* v. *Romanian Bank for Foreign Trade* [1989] 1 WLR 1147 CA.

[39] [1994] 2 Ll.R 187. Mance J also considered what law would have governed some of the contracts which might also have existed between the parties. See for a discussion, Dicey and Morris, *Conflict of Laws*, 13th edn, 1425–7.

Closest connection

The determination of the system of law or country with which the contract is most closely connected gives the court freedom to select almost whatever law it pleases, a freedom which is not limited by the Convention, as it was not limited at common law.

English courts have held that commodity agreements, for the sale of coffee,[40] for example, and similar contracts, such as those of reinsurance, are governed by the law of the country in which the relevant market, like the London Coffee Exchange or Lloyd's, is situated.[41] In a case concerning a labour agreement, written in the English language and to which an international workers' union having its headquarters in London was a party but which was negotiated in Spain on its behalf by a Spanish union and concerned crews recruited in Spain by a Maltese shipowning company, the contract was held to have its closest and most real connection with Spanish law.[42]

Presumptions regarding immovable property and carriage

Article 4 contains two presumptions for dealing with particular types of contract. By Article 4(3), a contract, in so far as it concerns *immovable property* or a right to use such property, is presumed to be most closely connected with the country of its *situs*. This presumption, it seems, does not extend to contracts for construction or repair of immovable property.[43]

By Article 4(4) *contracts for the carriage of goods* by all methods of transport (but not contracts for the carriage of passengers) are subject to another presumption. Where the country in which, when the contract is concluded, the carrier (i.e. the person who agrees to carry the goods, whether he does the carrying himself or arranges for someone else to do so) has his principal place of business *is also* the country where the place of loading or of discharge or the principal place of business of the consignor is situated, then the contract is presumed to be most closely connected with that country. Where these factors are not present, no resort can be had, in ascertaining the law governing a contract for the sale of goods, to the presumption based on characteristic performance. Thus, the country with which the contract is most closely connected will have to be discovered without its aid.[44]

---

[40] *Tamari and Tamari* v. *Bernhard Rofhfos* [1980] 1 Ll.R 55 CA.
[41] *Citadel Insurance* v. *Atlantic Union Insurance* [1982] 2 Ll.R 543.
[42] *Monterosso Shipping Ltd* v. *International Transport Workers' Federation* [1982] 3 All ER 841 CA.
[43] Official Report, p. 21.
[44] Art. 21 of the Convention ensures that any rules in the Hague Convention on the Law Applicable to the Sales of Movables will prevail over those of the Convention.

Special rules: consumer and employment contracts

The Convention contains special rules for determining the law applicable to some consumer contracts and to individual employment contracts, to protect the weaker party.

Consumer contracts (Article 5)

These rules apply (Article 5(1)) to a contract whose object 'is the supply of goods or services to a person ("the consumer") for a purpose which can be regarded as being outside his trade or profession, or a contract for the provision of credit for that object'.[45]

They do not apply to all such contracts but only to a rather limited number. Indeed, since most English consumers buy from English suppliers (even of foreign manufactured goods) under contracts governed by English law, only a very limited number of transactions of the kind envisaged in Article 5(2) are likely to come before the English courts.

These transactions are those in which, say, in England,

(i)   the conclusion of the contract was preceded by a specific invitation addressed to the consumer (C) or by advertising by a French supplier (S) and C had taken in England all the steps necessary on his part for the conclusion of the contract (that is, sent his order from England), or

(ii) S or his agent received C's order in England, or

(iii) in cases of *sale of goods only*, C travelled from England to France and ordered the goods there, S having arranged C's journey to France in order to induce C to buy them (cross-border shopping, of a kind) then.

If French law governs the contract as a result of an express or inferred choice, C retains the protection of any mandatory rules of English law[46] if he is habitually resident here. If he is habitually resident in Germany, he retains the protection of such rules of German law, though not of English law.

If there is no such choice of law, Article 4 does not operate so as to determine the applicable law. Instead, Article 5(3) provides that the contract is governed by English or German law in the above situations. This is not a *presumption* but a *rule of law*.[47]

These provisions apply to contracts for the supply of package holidays, which are a combination of travel and accommodation at an inclusive

---

[45] The Official Report, p. 23, says the purpose of Art. 5(1) is protection of the consumer.
[46] For example, of the Unfair Contract Terms Act 1977.
[47] Compare Art. 6(2) concerning individual employment contracts, p. 203 below.

price (Article 5(5)).[48] They do not otherwise apply to a contract of carriage or to a contract for the provision of services which are to be rendered exclusively elsewhere than where C has his habitual residence, for example where C, habitually resident in England, is provided with a hotel room in Majorca. Articles 3 and 4 apply to such contracts (Article 5(4)).

Individual employment contracts (Article 6)

Article 6(1) provides that a choice of law made by the parties shall not deprive the employee of the mandatory rules of the law which would govern the contract under Article 6(2) in the absence of such choice. Thus, if a French employer (F) employs an English employee (E) to work in England and French law is expressed to govern the contract and, but for that, English law would (by Article 4) be the applicable law, the United Kingdom employment protection legislation will apply in favour of E.

Where there is no chosen law, two rules are put forward in Article 6(2) (these are really presumptions)[49] and Article 4 does not apply. (a) The applicable law is that of the country where the employee habitually carries out his employment, even if he is temporarily employed in another country. Thus, in the previous example, English law governs the contract even if E is temporarily working in Holland. (b) If the employee habitually works in more than one country, then the law of the country in which is situated the employer's place of business through which the employee was engaged governs the contract. So, if E was employed through F's place of business (i) in England, English law governs, (ii) in France, French law governs, (iii) in New York, New York law governs.[50] These rules do not apply if the contract appears from the circumstances as a whole to be more closely connected with another country, say, Italy, in which case Italian law is the applicable law. This is why the rules are merely *presumptions*.

It is unclear how it is to be decided whether a contract is one of employment or is a contract for services. Presumably, the European Court would give the term 'contract of employment' an autonomous community meaning, that being the one it has adopted in connection with Article 5(1) of the Brussels Convention.[51]

---

[48] Even if C is habitually resident in England and the holiday starts from the Netherlands to go to Spain (Official Report, p. 25).

[49] Compare Art. 5(3) concerning consumer contracts, p. 202 above.

[50] Employment legislation, such as the Employment Rights Act 1996, may only apply if the employment in question is in the enacting country. It does not seem that Art. 6(2)(b) should require the application of the above Act if the employee works outside Great Britain, so as to confer on him greater protection than our legislation provides.

[51] See pp. 142–3 above.

System of law or country?

Where there is no express or inferred choice of law, is it that system of law, or that country, with which the contract has its closest and most real connection, which is the applicable law, if they are different?[52] In *Amin Rasheed Shipping Corporation* v. *Kuwait Insurance Co.*[53] the contract had little connection with England, but was redolent of English law. The majority of the Court of Appeal and Lord Wilberforce selected English law as the system with which the contract was most closely and really connected. This terminology was used by Lord Simonds in *Bonython* v. *Commonwealth of Australia*,[54] and this seems to be the correct formulation,[55] though in *Whitworth Street Estates (Manchester) Ltd* v. *James Miller & Partners Ltd*,[56] members of the House of Lords wished to combine the two formulations.

However, Article 4 of the Rome Convention speaks of the 'law of the country with which it is most closely connected'. Whether the English courts will distinguish between 'system of law' and 'country' in applying the Convention is a matter for speculation. If they do, then the finding in *Whitworth* v. *Miller* that English law governed, though the contract was more closely connected with Scotland, would be reversed.

Renvoi

Renvoi plays no part in the ascertainment of the applicable law. Indeed, Article 15 excludes its application throughout the Convention. This accords with English common law.[57]

The time at which the applicable law is determined

Two matters are involved here. First, the parties' intention must be established at the time the contract is concluded. So must the country with which it is most closely connected. The English courts have held that there could not be a 'floating' proper law which is determined retrospectively by acts which at the time of contracting were in the future

---

[52] If they choose a governing law, the parties invariably state, for example, 'this contract should be governed by the law of England'. Unless their knowledge of English were minimal they would hardly say it should be 'governed by England'.

[53] [1984] AC 50, and see [1982] 1 WLR 961 CA.   [54] [1951] AC 201.

[55] Several decisions bear this out: *Rossano* v. *Manufacturers Life Insurance Co.* [1968] 2 QB 352; *BP Exploration Co. (Libya) Ltd* v. *Hunt* [1976] 1 WLR 788; *Armar Shipping Co.* v. *Caisse Algérienne d'Assurance* [1981] 1 WLR 207 CA; *Tamari and Tamari* v. *Bernhard Roflhfos* [1980] 2 Ll.R 553 CA.

[56] [1970] AC 583.

[57] Re *United Railways of Havana and Regla Warehouses Ltd* [1960] Ch. 52 CA; *Amin Rasheed Shipping Corporation* v. *Kuwait Insurance Co.* [1984] AC 50 HL.

and uncertain,[58] though it is possible, if unusual, to select a system of law to govern the contract unless a court holds that it is not to be applied and another system is the applicable law should this occur.[59]

Article 3(2) of the Convention allows the parties to agree to change the applicable law to another system than that which previously governed it, whether as a result of an earlier choice under Article 3 or of other provisions of the Convention. This power is subject to two provisos. So as to avoid doubts as to the validity of the contract in the period before it is exercised, such a change does not prejudice the formal validity of the contract established under Article 9.[60] Moreover, acquired rights of third parties are not to be adversely affected.

Secondly, in *Whitworth Street Estates (Manchester) Ltd* v. *James Miller & Partners Ltd*[61] and in the *Amin Rasheed*[62] case the House of Lords held that the intention of the parties must be determined by their conduct at the time the contract was concluded. Subsequent acts are only relevant if they show the parties intend to vary the contract (or, now, the applicable law) by a new one, or lead to a party being estopped from denying his intention at the time of contracting. This is an aspect of the general rule that a contract cannot be interpreted in the light of the parties' subsequent conduct.[63] Whether this is the case under the Convention is unclear.

If the rules of the applicable law change after the contract was concluded this may vary or discharge the parties' contractual obligations.[64] But this simply follows from the principle that the applicable law, whatever its rules are, governs such matters and has nothing to do with deciding what system is the applicable law. It is only mentioned for the sake of completeness.

Putative applicable law

Though this term is not used in the Convention, the concept itself is employed therein. In some cases, such as where it is argued that no contract ever existed, because, for example, the offer was not accepted, then,

---

[58] *Armar Shipping Co.* v. *Caisse Algérienne d'Assurance* [1981] 1 WLR 207 CA; *The Iran Vojdan* [1984] 1 WLR 380; *The Star Texas* [1993] 2 Ll.R 445 CA. A contract cannot exist in a 'legal vacuum' (*Amin Rasheed* case at p. 65 per Lord Diplock).
[59] *The Mariannina* [1983] 1 Ll.R 12 CA. (Provision for arbitration in England and English law is to apply, but if the arbitration clause is held to be unenforceable, the dispute is to be decided by the Greek courts who are to apply Greek law.)
[60] See p. 207 below.   [61] [1970] AC 583 HL.   [62] [1984] AC 500 HL.
[63] *L Schuler A/G* v. *Wickman Machine Tool Sales Ltd* [1974] AC 235 HL.
[64] See for example *R* v. *International Trustee for the Protection of Bondholders A/G* [1937] AC 500 HL.

if there never was a contract, there can logically be no applicable law. To answer this type of problem the English courts adopted the not particularly logical device of asking what law would govern the contract, assuming that there is a valid contract, and then applying that law, since there is no other satisfactory way of answering the question. There was, however, some disagreement among the writers whether an expressly chosen law could be the putative governing law, though in one case, *The Mariannina*,[65] Ackner LJ seems to have had no difficulty in thinking that it could be.

The Convention effectively adopts the device of the putative applicable law and envisages that an expressly chosen law can rank as such. Article 8 provides, *inter alia*, that 'the existence and validity of a contract or of any term of a contract, shall be determined by the law which would govern it under this Convention [by Articles 3 to 6] if the contract or term were valid'.[66]

Formation of the contract and reality of agreement

The place at which a contract was concluded is determined, for the purpose of jurisdiction, by English law.[67] Since the place of contracting is a connecting factor, presumably it is determined by English law for the purpose of choice of law.

Whether a contract has been concluded at all is determined by the putative applicable law (Article 8(1)). This provision was applied in *Egon Oldendorff* v. *Libera Corp.*[68] so that English law as determined by Article 3(1) decided whether a contract existed. It also decided whether the English arbitration clause had been incorporated into the contract. This covers all matters affecting the existence of a contract, such as requirements of offer and acceptance, consideration, misrepresentation and mistake, and their effects. It also governs the validity of a contract term, such as a choice of law clause. This seems to reflect the English common law rules.[69]

As regards the giving of consent, such as the reality of an 'acceptance', Article 8(2) provides that:

Nevertheless, a party may rely upon the law of the country in which he has his habitual residence to establish that he did not consent if it appears from the

---

[65] [1983] 1 Ll.R 12 CA.   [66] See also Art. 3(4).
[67] *Entores* v. *Miles Far East Corporation* [1955] 2 QB 327 CA; *Brinkibon* v. *Stahag Stahl GmbH* [1982] 2 AC 34 HL (formerly RSC Order 11 rule 1).
[68] [1995] 2 Ll.R 64.
[69] *The Parouth* [1982] 2 Ll.R 351 CA; *Britannia SS Insurance Association* v. *Ausonia Assicurazioni* [1984] 2 Ll.R 98 CA; *Albeko Schuhmaschinen* v. *Kamborian Shoe Co. Ltd* (1961) 111 LJ 519 (communication of acceptance); *Re Bonacina* [1912] 2 Ch. 394 CA (consideration).

circumstances that it would not be reasonable to determine the effect of his conduct [by the putative proper law].

This would deal with a situation such as the following:

> A in country X writes to B in England offering to sell him goods and saying that if he does not hear from B within a week he will regard B as having agreed. By English law B's silence does not amount to an acceptance of A's offer.[70] By X law, the applicable law, it does.

The jurist, Wolff,[71] suggested that if B wishes to enforce the 'agreement' against A, he should be allowed to do so, but if he does not wish to, A cannot enforce the contract against B.

Formal validity

Whether a contract is void for non-compliance with a rule of law that it must be concluded in a certain form, for example, in writing or by deed or notarial act, was at common law determined, it seems, by the proper law or by the law of the place of contracting, so that if it was valid by either of these laws its validity would be upheld.[72]

The Rome Convention (Article 9), which does not define formal validity,[73] adopts this and elaborates on it.

(1) A contract concluded between persons who are in the same country is valid if it satisfies the formal requirements of the applicable law or of the law of the country where it was concluded.

> So, if A and B when in France conclude there a contract governed by English law, the contract is valid if it conforms with the formalities of either French or English law.

(2) Where persons are in different countries, the contract is formally valid if it is so by the applicable law or by the law of either of those countries.

> So, if A in Germany and B in France conclude a contract governed by English law, the contract is valid if it conforms with the formalities of German, French or English law.

---

[70] *Felthouse* v. *Bindley* (1862) 11 CB (NS) 869.

[71] *Private International Law*, 2nd edn (Oxford University Press, 1950) 439.

[72] See cases on marriage settlements for the applicable law's relevance: *Van Grutten* v. *Digby* (1862) 3 Beav. 561; Re *Bankes* [1903] 2 Ch. 333; and, as to the law of the place of contracting, see *Alves* v. *Hodgson* (1797) 7 TR 241.

[73] The Official Report (p. 92) says that 'form' might be considered 'as including every external manifestation required on the part of a person expressing the will to be legally bound, and in the absence of which such expression of will would not be regarded as fully effective'.

(3) Where a contract is concluded by an agent, the country where the
agent acts is the relevant country for the purposes of (1) and (2).

These rules do not apply to a consumer contract concluded in the
circumstances described in Article 5(2).[74] Such a contract's formal
validity is governed by the law of the consumer's country of habitual
residence (Article 9(5)).

A contract regarding a right in immovable property or a right to use
it (e.g. a tenancy) is subject to the mandatory requirements of the *lex
situs* if it imposes them irrespective of where the contract is concluded
and of the applicable law.[75]

By Article 9(4) an act relating to an existing or contemplated contract
is valid if it complies with the applicable or putative applicable law or
that of the place where the act was done. This includes notice of
termination, remission of a debt, rescission or repudiation.[76] It seems
that it would also cover acts involving offers and acceptances since
these relate to a contemplated contract.

Capacity to contract

Capacity of a natural person to contract is excluded from the Convention.[77] This is because under the laws of most European countries
capacity is a matter of status rather than of contract. The common law
conflicts rules continue to apply. (However, a relevant provision is Article
11, which says that where a contract is concluded between persons who
are in the same country a person can only invoke his incapacity under
the law of another country if, at the time of contracting, the other party
was aware or would have been aware of it had he not been negligent.)

What law governs the capacity of a natural person to conclude a
commercial contract is a matter for some speculation, for there is a
dearth of English authority on the point. The question is of comparatively
little practical importance, perhaps, since large commercial concerns
are companies whose capacity is governed by their 'personal' law, that
is the law of their place of incorporation. With respect to individuals, in
the English context few problems can occur, since the only categories
of person whose contractual capacity is limited are mental patients,[78]

---

[74] See p. 202 above.
[75] Art. 9(6). Such mandatory requirements of English law are that a conveyance must be
by deed (Law of Property Act 1925, s. 53(1)(b)) and a contract for the sale of land
must be in writing (Law of Property (Miscellaneous Provisions) Act 1989, s. 2).
[76] Official Report, p. 29.   [77] Art. 1(2)(a).
[78] Whose property is usually under the control of the Court of Protection.

intoxicated persons and minors. The significance of contractual incapacities of minors was reduced by the lowering of the age of majority.[79]

There are several possibilities. The governing law may be (1) that of the domicile of the person alleged to be under the incapacity; (2) that of the place of contracting; (3) the law applicable to the contract. Application of the first could work unjustly towards the other party[80] and the second is unsatisfactory if the place of contracting is 'fortuitous'.[81]

Only two English cases touch on the point. In the early case, *Male v. Roberts*,[82] the decision appears to be equally consistent with the law of the place of contracting and with what would now be called the proper law.[83] The issue was probably quasi-contractual rather than contractual and it was not shown that the law of Scotland, where the defendant, an infant circus performer, had incurred a debt for 'liquors of various sorts', differed from English law. In the much more modern case, *Bodley Head v. Flegon*,[84] which concerned the copyright in Alexander Solzhenitsyn's novel, *August 1914*, the author had signed in Moscow a power of attorney authorising a Swiss lawyer to deal in the author's works outside the Soviet Union. It was argued that the author had no capacity under Soviet law, the law of the place of contracting and of his domicile, to contract with the lawyer. The argument was rejected on the ground that Russian law had not been shown to have the effect contended for, though the court suggested that Swiss law as the applicable law possibly governed the question.

In this state of the authorities, the writers favour the applicable law.[85] Although they do not seem to say so in terms, this appears to mean the putative applicable law,[86] which here should mean the proper law

---

[79] Family Law Reform Act 1969, s. 1, reduced this from twenty-one to eighteen.

[80] It finds support in dicta in cases concerning marriage and matrimonial property settlements: e.g. *Sottomayor* v. *de Barros* (No. 1) (1877) 3 PD 1 CA; *Baindail* v. *Baindail* [1946] P 122. These seem to have little relevance to commercial contracts. But the US Supreme Court has favoured the law of the domicile: *Union Trust Co.* v. *Grosman* 245 US 412 (1918).

[81] It is supported, however, by *McFeetridge* v. *Stewarts & Lloyds Ltd* 1913 SC 773 (Scotland); *Bondholders Securities* v. *Manville* [1933] 4 DLR 699 (Canada); *Milliken* v. *Pratt* 125 Mass. 374 (1878).

[82] (1800) 3 Esp. 163.

[83] Lord Eldon LC used the words 'the law of the country where the contract arose must govern the contract'. At that time the *lex loci contractus* governed all contract issues.

[84] [1972] 1 WLR 680. The case receives much attention in Cheshire and North, *Private International Law*, 13th edn, 593, but very little in Dicey and Morris, *Conflict of Laws*, 13th edn, 1274.

[85] *Charron* v. *Montreal Trust Co.* (1958) 15 DLR (2d) 240 (Ontario) favours this. Cases previously referred to are consistent with this, for the law of the place of contracting and the proper law were the same.

[86] Since if a contract is void for incapacity (or any other reason) it cannot have a proper law.

ascertained by looking for the system of law with which the transaction has its closest and most real connection, ignoring any express choice of law, at any rate if that law was chosen in order to confer capacity which otherwise would not exist.[87] In the present context this seems correct.

It has been suggested that if a party lacks capacity by the applicable law but has it under his personal law, the contract should be valid.[88]

The *lex situs*, it appears, governs not only capacity to convey or to create an interest in land, but also capacity to contract to do so.[89]

Scope of the applicable law: interpretation, performance, breach, termination

Article 10(1) of the Convention sets out five matters which *in particular* are governed by the applicable law determined in accordance with Articles 3 to 6 and 12. The fifth, 'the consequences of nullity of the contract', being regarded in English and Scots law as a quasi-contractual and not a contractual matter, was made the subject of a permitted reservation by the United Kingdom and does not have the force of law in the United Kingdom (1990 Act, s. 2(2)). The words 'in particular' have been emphasised because their presence demonstrates that other issues, indeed all issues other than formal validity, the existence of capacity and material validity are governed by the applicable law alone.

The particular matters mentioned in Article 10(1) are:

(a) Interpretation

This represents the English rule.[90] If the parties have selected one law to govern the contract and another to interpret its terms, the latter will be employed to construe the contract, since this method of 'splitting' the contract is permitted by Article 3(1). However, if the question is as to the meaning of a currency, for example, what are Dutch guilders, this surely must be determined by the law of the country whose currency is referred to.

---

[87] Dicey and Morris, *Conflict of Laws*, 1271–5; Cheshire and North, *Private International Law*, 592–5.

[88] Dicey and Morris, *Conflict of Laws*, 1275.

[89] *Bank of Africa* v. *Cohen* [1902] 2 Ch. 129 CA. This is one of the most severely criticised decisions in the English conflict of laws: see p. 287 below.

[90] *Bonython* v. *Commonwealth of Australia* [1951] AC 201 PC.

(b) Performance

Since to perform a contractual obligation is merely one way of obtaining one's discharge from and extinguishing such an obligation, performance could well have been included in another category. The Official Report[91] includes these issues as involving performance:

> The diligence with which the obligation must be performed, conditions as to the time and place of performance; the extent to which the obligations can be performed by a person other than the party liable . . . joint and several obligations, alternative obligations, divisible and indivisible obligations, pecuniary obligations; where performance consists of the payment of a sum of money, the conditions relating to the discharge of the debtor who has made the payment, the appropriation of the payment, the receipt etc.

This provision coincides with the position under English common law. (See, for example, *Mount Albert Borough Council* v. *Australasian Temperance & Assurance Society.*)[92]

Article 10(2) is based upon the distinction that the above matters are substantive issues but that the manner of performance is not, since it provides that 'In relation to the manner of performance and the steps to be taken in the event of defective performance regard shall be had to the law of the country in which performance takes place.'

As to what is meant by the manner of performance, the Official Report says[93] this is a matter for the *lex fori* to decide, but gives as examples rules governing public holidays, the manner in which goods are to be examined and the steps to be taken if they are refused. An example from the common law is the *Mount Albert* case in which the Privy Council held that the obligation to pay X pounds was a matter of interpretation, governed, as between Australian and New Zealand law, by the applicable law. When it was decided which of these was meant, the currency in which the amount must be discharged was referred to the law of the place of performance.

A question raised by Article 10(2) is, what effect is to be given to that law? It does not say that it *must* be applied, only that regard may be had to it.[94] This seems to introduce a discretion and its concomitant uncertainty.

(c) Consequences of breach

The Convention's words are 'within the limits of the powers conferred on the court by its procedural law, the consequences of breach, including the assessment of damages insofar as it is governed by rules of law'.

---

[91] Pp. 32–3.   [92] [1938] AC 224 PC.   [93] P. 33.
[94] The Official Report (p. 33) offers little useful guidance.

This, we are told,[95] includes such matters as 'the liability of the party in breach, claims to terminate the contract for breach and any requirement of service of notice on the party to assume his liability'.

It has been the rule of English common law that remoteness of damage (for what consequences of breach the defendant is liable) and heads of damage are matters of substance, governed by the applicable law. This is confirmed by Article 10(1)(c). However, the assessment or computation of the damages is procedural and governed by the *lex fori*. This seems to be modified by the Convention and the applicable law will apply in so far as that law regards the matter as governed by rules of law.

The remedies available under the applicable law, such as damages or specific performance, will have to be granted by the English courts. But if English procedural law does not allow a certain remedy, for example, periodical payments or, in the particular situation, specific performance, such remedies need not be awarded.[96]

(d) The various ways of extinguishing obligations, and prescription and limitation of actions

At English common law the applicable law decides whether a contractual obligation has been discharged by frustration[97] or breach[98] or by novation (by which one party is discharged from his obligations and succeeded by another person)[99] or whether a moratorium, allowing of delay, can postpone performance.[100] This is clearly the situation under the Convention.

That the applicable law governs prescription and limitation of actions has been the case since the English Foreign Limitation Periods Act 1984, one reason for whose enactment was the possible entry into force of the Convention.[101]

Illegality

At common law, it was clear that a contract which was illegal by the law which governed it would not be enforced in England.[102] This rule is enshrined in the Convention (Article 8(1)). However, even if the

---

[95] *Ibid.*
[96] G. C. J. Morse, *Halsbury's Current Statutes Annotated* (London, Butterworths, 1990) 30.
[97] *Ralli Brothers* v. *Compania Naviera Sota y Aznar* [1920] 2 KB 287 CA. Or by *force majeure: Jacobs* v. *Crédit Lyonnaise* (1884) 12 QBD 589 CA.
[98] *Ibid.*
[99] Re *United Railways of Havana and Regla Warehouses Ltd* [1960] Ch. 52 CA.
[100] Re *Helbert Wagg & Co. Ltd's Claim* [1956] Ch. 323; *Adams* v. *National Bank of Greece and Athens SA* [1961] AC 255 HL.
[101] See further pp. 63–4 above.   [102] *Kahler* v. *Midland Bank Ltd* [1950] AC 24 HL.

contract was legal by the proper law, it was sometimes argued that the contract might be refused enforcement if it was illegal by some other law, such as that of the place of performance. But the Convention makes no reference to this law or to the law of the place of contracting or to that of the residence or place of business of the debtor, so it can be assumed that these are not relevant.

However, closely connected with the question of illegality are two other matters which are dealt with in the Convention. The first is the application of mandatory rules (Articles 3(3), 5(2), 6(1), 7(2) and 9(6)). (Article 7(1), which also deals with such rules, has not been enacted into United Kingdom law, since this country made a permissible reservation to the Convention with respect to it.) Secondly, the courts can continue to apply the rules of English public policy (Article 16).

Mandatory rules

Article 3(3) defines such rules as rules of law 'which cannot be derogated from by contract, hereinafter called "mandatory rules"'. The use of the word 'hereinafter' seems to signify that the term 'mandatory rules' means the same thing in all the subsequent provisions in which it appears. But, in the unenacted Article 7(1) and in Article 7(2) it means something different and has a narrower effect, being 'rules of law . . . [which are mandatory] irrespective of the law otherwise applicable to the contract'.

One thing is clear: the rules must be mandatory by the system of law of which they are a part.

Article 7(2) provides that nothing in the Convention 'shall restrict the application of the rules of the forum in a situation where they are mandatory irrespective of the law otherwise applicable to the contract'. Whether a rule of English law has this overriding effect is determined by English law and if it is contained in a statute it is a matter of its interpretation. Most mandatory rules, it is thought, are contained in statutes. Thus, in *Boissevain* v. *Weil*,[103] the forerunner of the now repealed Exchange Control Act 1947 was applied to a contract entered into in Monaco under Monégasque law. The Scots courts applied Scottish statutes in a number of cases, though the contracts were arguably not governed by foreign laws.[104]

---

[103] [1950] AC 327 HL.
[104] *English* v. *Donnelly* 1958 SC 494 (Hire Purchase (Scotland) Act); *Brodin A/R* v. *Seljan* 1973 SC 213 (Law Reform (Personal Injuries) Act 1948); *Duncan* v. *Motherwell Bridge & Engineering Co.* 1952 SC 131 (Truck Acts) (though the contract may have been governed by Scots law anyway).

Provisions of some modern statutes concerning employment are made to apply whatever the chosen law of the contract if work is to be done under it in this country. An example is the Employment Rights Act 1996, section 204(1).[105] A notable statute in this connection is the Unfair Contract Terms Act 1977 under which parties to a contract of sale or hire-purchase cannot exclude or restrict certain of the seller's or owner's implied contractual undertakings by a term of the contract and can only as against a party not dealing as a consumer exclude or restrict others in so far as the contract term satisfies the condition of reasonableness. Section 27(2) provides that these provisions have effect notwithstanding any contract term which applies or purports to apply the law of some country outside the United Kingdom where either or both of the following apply: (i) in making the contract one of the parties dealt as a consumer when he was habitually resident in the United Kingdom and the essential steps in the making of the contract were taken in this country, in which case the provisions of the Act prevail; (ii) if the court or arbitrator concludes that the term was imposed wholly or mainly for the purpose of enabling the party who imposed it to evade the operation of the Act. Thus where a party is not a consumer the expressly chosen law will apply unless it was incorporated as an evasion device.[106]

It may be added that section 27(1) of the Act contains the unusual provision that if the parties have chosen the law of some part of the United Kingdom and that without such choice the contract would be governed by some other (for example, Japanese) law the provisions of the Act do not apply as part of the law of England. So an exemption or limiting clause in the contract would be effective. This was enacted so as not to discourage foreign businessmen from coming to England to settle their disputes here.[107]

It must be emphasised that the legislation mentioned here does not preclude the application of the chosen law to other aspects of the contract, and that it clearly reinforces, rather than negates, the view that in principle the parties have freedom to choose either a foreign or an English system of law to govern their contract, though the chosen system has little or no connection with the contract.

The statutes dealt with so far purport to limit *directly* the effect of the chosen law. The limitation may, however, operate *indirectly*.

---

[105] See also Equal Pay Act 1970, s. 1(a)(11); Sex Discrimination Act 1975, ss. 6, 10(1); Race Relations Act 1976, ss. 4, 8.

[106] This provision does not apply to an international supply contract within the definition in the Uniform Laws on International Sales Act 1967: s. 26.

[107] Law Commission: Second Report on Exemption Clauses, no. 69 (1975), para. 232.

An example is the Carriage of Goods by Sea Act 1971, as applied by the House of Lords in *The Hollandia*.[108] This decision came after the Hague Rules, which were at issue in the *Vita Foods*[109] case, had been revised. The object of the new Rules, known as the Hague-Visby Rules of 1968, which were enacted into English law by the 1971 Act, was to close the gap revealed by that case and to secure uniformity in the application of the Rules by courts in contracting states. By the revised Rules, which apply to shipments both out from and into contracting states, a shipowner can only rely on a clause limiting his liability in respect of the cargo ('package limitation') to a certain sum, and any provision in the contract of carriage 'lessening his liability' below what sum is null and void.

The Hollandia concerned a contract for the carriage of a machine from Scotland[110] to the Dutch West Indies, which was transshipped at Amsterdam. The bill of lading specified that the Dutch court should have exclusive jurisdiction over disputes arising from it and that Dutch law should govern the contract. The Netherlands had not enacted the revised Rules but adhered to the old Hague Rules under which the shipowner could 'lessen his liability' to an amount below the sum permitted by the revised Rules. The machine was damaged and the claimants sued in England.

The defendants asked for a stay of proceedings in England, relying on the Dutch jurisdiction clause.

The Court of Appeal and the House of Lords both held that the trial judge had erred in granting a stay. The reason was that since to grant a stay on the basis of the jurisdiction clause would result in the case being tried in the Netherlands, whose court would apply Dutch law, the shipowners' liability would be lessened below the sum allowed by the Hague-Visby Rules. These, as enacted by the 1971 Act (unlike the original Hague Rules as enacted by the 1924 Act), have 'the force of law' in the United Kingdom, and so rendered the Dutch jurisdiction and choice of law clauses null and void by United Kingdom law. There was nothing, therefore, upon which the defendants could rely in requesting a stay of the English proceedings.

Public policy

The difference between mandatory rules and rules of public policy lies mainly in their effect on a contract. In principle, the former have an

---

[108] [1983] 1 AC 565, distinguished in *The Benarty* [1985] QB 325 CA.
[109] [1939] AC 277 PC. See p. 193 above.
[110] Scotland being part of the United Kingdom, the English court was sitting in the country of shipment, which was not the case in the decision referred to in the preceding note.

inclusionary effect, in that the mandatory rules are written into the contract, whereas rules of public policy are exclusionary in that, generally, they exclude the operation of a rule of law which would otherwise apply.

Article 16 of the Convention provides that: 'The application of a rule of law of any Country specified by this Convention may be refused only if such application is manifestly contrary to public policy.' The use of the word 'manifestly' signifies that the exception must be restrictively applied and that the court must 'find special grounds for upholding an objection' based on public policy.[111]

The English courts have in the past refused to enforce contracts governed by a foreign law because to apply a rule of that law which regards the contract as valid would lead to a result which would infringe English public policy. Examples are: a champertous contract,[112] an agreement to stifle a prosecution,[113] an agreement in restraint of English trade,[114] and a contract which involved trading with the enemy.[115] In *Royal Boskalis NV* v. *Mountain*,[116] it was held that making contractual payments in violation of United Nations sanctions enacted into Dutch law was akin to trading with the enemy for the purposes of public policy. In the same case it was said that a contract obtained by a class of duress so unconscionable might, as a matter of public policy, override the law which governs it.

One kind of contract which has been refused enforcement is one whose enforcement might be regarded as contrary to international comity and, perhaps exaggeratedly, is said to be likely to imperil the relations of the Crown with a foreign friendly power (that is, one with which this country is not actually at war). So the English courts will not enforce a contract whose performance requires the doing of an act in a foreign friendly country which is an offence by its law. Nor will they enforce a contract the parties to which intend either to do themselves or to procure a third party to do such an act which is unlawful in such a country. In *De Wutz* v. *Hendricks*[117] a contract to raise money to assist a rebellion in

---

[111] Official Report, p. 38. See also other statutes based on international conventions, such as the Family Law Reform Act 1986, Part II, s. 51(3)(c), based on the Hague Convention on Recognition of Divorces and Legal Separations, 1970, p. 329 below. The Report states that public policy includes also European Community public policy, an integral part of the public policy of member states.

[112] *Grell* v. *Levy* (1804) 16 CB (NS) 73.

[113] See *Kaufman* v. *Gerson* [1904] 1 KB 591 CA.

[114] *Rousillon* v. *Rousillon* [1880] 40 Ch. D 351.

[115] *Dynamit A/G* v. *Rio Tinto Co.* [1918] AC 292 HL.

[116] [1999] QB 674 CA, in which one party to a contract governed by the law of Iraq intended that it should be performed in the Netherlands in contravention of Dutch sanctions against Iraq.

[117] (1824) 2 Bing. 314.

Crete, and in *Foster* v. *Driscoll*[118] a contract for the supply and sale of whisky which it was intended should be smuggled into the United States and ultimately sold and consumed there in violation of the Prohibition laws,[119] was not enforced.

In a third case, *Regazzoni* v. *KC Sethia (1944) Ltd*,[120] a seller in India agreed to sell jute bags to a Swiss buyer for delivery to Genoa. The seller knew that the buyer intended to resell and deliver them to South Africa, and they both knew that under Indian law it was a criminal offence to export jute to South Africa from India, where the jute was to be obtained. The House of Lords refused to enforce the contract.

In all three cases, the contract was governed by English law, but even more importantly in the present context, if its governing law had been that of another country by which it was perfectly unobjectionable, the result would have been the same, since the decisions rested on English public policy.

Suppose that the contracts in these cases had been governed by French law, then it is arguable that they show that the English court is actually giving effect to a mandatory rule of a foreign law, and that the cases exemplify the situation envisaged in Article 7(1) which allows the court to give effect 'to the mandatory rules of another country with which the situation has a close connection, if and insofar as, under the law of the latter country, these rules must be applied whatever the law applicable to the contract'. Since this provision has not been enacted into United Kingdom law, the continued existence of this principle of English law cannot be based upon it and can only be accommodated under Article 16(1). It might be said, however, that in this situation the effect of the application of public policy is to include rules of foreign law, those of the Ottoman Empire, the United States and India respectively, rather than to exclude them, so that the appropriate provision of the Rome Convention is Article 7(1). However, this article was the subject of a reservation by the United Kingdom so, as we have seen, has not the force of law in this country and non-enforcement of such contracts is no longer authorised. Moreover, it is submitted that public policy is being used to exclude a rule of French law which makes the contract valid; the law of the third country is treated by the English

---

[118] [1929] 1 KB 470 CA.

[119] Prohibition of the purveying of alcohol was then part of the US Constitution by the Eighteenth Amendment of 1918. This unfortunate experiment was terminated by the Twenty-first Amendment in 1933.

[120] [1958] AC 301 HL. The act envisaged must be unlawful. If it merely contravenes the foreign public policy it will only be refused enforcement if it is also contrary to English public policy: *Lemenda Trading Co. Ltd* v. *African Middle East Petroleum Co. Ltd* [1988] QB 448.

court as a fact which produces a situation in which it would be contrary to public policy to apply the French rule.

In any event, the *Regazzoni* principle has been applied more recently by the Court of Appeal in *Royal Boskalis Westminster NV* v. *Mountain*,[121] where it was accepted that it applied where *one* party (the Government of Iraq) intended that the contract should be performed in a manner which breached Dutch law. That Court refused, in *Ispahani* v. *Bank Melli Iran*,[122] to enforce banking arrangements whose object was to transfer funds out of Bangladesh in contravention of that country's exchange control laws. Moreover, in *Soleimany* v. *Soleimany*,[123] it declined to enforce an Israeli arbitration award, which was based on a contract governed by Jewish law, to export carpets from Iran in violation of Iranian revenue and exchange control laws, basing its decision on the *Regazzoni* principle.

Supervening illegality

For the sake of completeness, it should be added that in the past it has been often supposed by writers and courts that refusal to enforce a contract by reason of its illegality by the law of the place of performance is exemplified by the decision in *Ralli Brothers* v. *Compania Naviera Sota y Aznar*,[124] in which Spanish shippers contracted with English charterers in London to carry goods from Calcutta to Barcelona. They were to be paid £50 per ton freight in Barcelona on delivery there. After the voyage had begun, but before the goods arrived at Barcelona, a Spanish law enacted that freight must not exceed £10 per ton. The charterers agreed to pay the £10 but no more. An action for the balance in the English courts failed.

It has been argued that this decision exemplifies Article 7(1) of the Convention, and, like cases such as *Foster* v. *Driscoll*,[125] now falls to be considered as an application of public policy.

The case, clearly, has nothing to do with the application of mandatory rules or of public policy, being wholly distinct from such situations. In the *Ralli Brothers* case, there was no attempt to evade Spanish mandatory rules; the parties, at the time of contracting, were wholly innocent of any nefarious intent and no such rules then existed. In spite of some remarks in the judgments, the Court of Appeal clearly treated the Spanish law as a frustrating event, relying on cases of supervening illegality by

---

[121] [1999] QB 674 CA. The contract was governed by the law of Iraq.
[122] [1998] Ll.R (Bank.) 133 CA, where it was stated that this rule is not a conflicts rule but one of domestic English law.
[123] [1999] QB 789 CA.   [124] [1920] 2 KB 287 CA.   [125] [1929] 1 KB 470 CA.

British legislation.[126] Since English law was the applicable law, it followed that the contract was frustrated, Spanish legislation having the effect of preventing full performance.[127]

It follows that if the applicable law had been the law of Utopia, and that law did not regard the Spanish legislation as a frustrating event, or if the law of Utopia had no doctrine of frustration, then an English court should have awarded the claimants the unpaid freight.[128]

If the case illustrates any provision of the Convention, it is submitted that the most appropriate one is Article 10(1)(d), since enactment of the Spanish law extinguished (in part) the defendant's obligation, and this is a matter which is governed by the applicable law.

Community law: other conventions

Article 20 provides for the precedence over the rules of the Convention of provisions concerning choice of law contained in acts of the Institutions of the European Communities or in national laws harmonised in consequence of such acts.

Article 21 provides that the Convention does not prejudice the application of international conventions, such as several concerning carriage, to which the United Kingdom is a party, or any to which it may become a party, such as Hague Private International Law Conventions. That on the Law Applicable to International Sales of Movables (1955) numbers among its parties several EC member states but not, as yet, the Untied Kingdom.[129] That on Trusts (1986) is now part of the law of the United Kingdom.

---

[126] For example, *Metropolitan Water Board* v. *Dick, Kerr & Co.* [1918] AC 119 HL.

[127] This was pointed out long ago by Dr F. A. Mann, 'Proper Law and Illegality in Private International Law' (1937) 18 *BYIL* 97. The continued confusion is incomprehensible. In *Soleimany* v. *Soleimany* [1999] QB 789 CA, the Court of Appeal had no difficulty in distinguishing initial from supervening illegality. The *Ralli Brothers* case is just like *Kursell* v. *Timber Operators & Contractors Ltd* [1927] 1 KB 298 CA which concerned the effect of Latvian legislation on an (apparently English) contract. Like the latter it merely shows that whether an English contract is frustrated by events abroad is matter of English law. See p. 212 above. See also F. M. B. Reynolds, note (1992) 108 *LQR* 553.

[128] This is scarcely shocking. English law knew no such doctrine until *Taylor* v. *Caldwell* (1863) 3 B & S 826.

[129] See Articles 24 and 23 for the procedure to be followed if a contracting state wishes to become a party to such a Convention. Article 23 also applies if such a state wishes to introduce a new choice of law rule for a category of contract which is within the Convention.

13   Tort

Selection of the governing law

The selection of the law which is to govern tort liability is conceptually one of the most difficult problems in the conflict of laws, at any rate if the vast amount of learned discussion given to it by the writers is anything to go by. Much of the modern academic discussion and most of the case law emanates from the United States, and it is on this topic that American methodologies and methodologists chiefly concentrate. There has been little English case law on the question (though much more in Australia and Canada). This may suggest either that there is little litigation about torts committed abroad, or that litigants here do not trouble to prove any relevant rules of foreign law, perhaps because these rules are little different in effect from English rules of tort law in many cases.[1]

Also, the relative profuseness of the case law from the United States and the Commonwealth as compared with our own meagre collection is easily explained. In those countries there are several different jurisdictions; in North America about sixty. Of course, there are several in the British Isles. But a very great number of modern cases in all countries have arisen out of road traffic accidents; it is easier to drive a car across a land frontier than to cross the sea with it, and England's only land boundary is with Scotland.

Several different choice of law rules have been proposed from time to time as being the most appropriate, but some which have been adopted abroad have ceased to be applied there. One is the law of the place where the tort was committed (*lex loci delicti commissi*). This has found favour on the Continent of Europe and was the prevailing rule in the United States until its disadvantages, which had already led to its being outflanked, caused it to be abandoned in most states after 1962 in favour of a more flexible but more amorphous rule.

The *lex fori* has also been suggested as the governing law. This is easy to apply and is superficially attractive. Its earliest advocates had in mind

[1] For an example of this, see *Coupland* v. *Arabian Gulf Oil Co.* [1983] 1 WLR 1136 CA.

that tort is akin to crime, and that domestic courts apply only their own law to determine criminal liability. The idea that the *lex fori* should be applied reflects a feeling that domestic courts cannot be expected to give a remedy when this is not available in wholly domestic cases. This is not thought to be the case, however, in other areas of the law such as contract,[2] and it is not in itself an insuperable obstacle to the application of the *lex loci*. Moreover, except for some family law matters, the *lex fori* does not govern substantive issues in the conflict of laws.

In revulsion from the unfortunate decision of the Scottish Court of Session in *McElroy* v. *McAllister*,[3] J. H. C. Morris put forward a third choice of law rule as the most appropriate.[4] This is the 'proper law' of the tort, adopted by way of analogy with the proper law of the contract. The proper law is that with which the event has its closest and most real connection.[5] Something like this or variants of it have been taken up in the United States by courts and writers since 1962.[6] However, this doctrine need not detain us further at this point, since one of the few things which are clear from the leading English case, *Chaplin* v. *Boys*,[7] is that it is not the common law choice of law rule.[8]

As will be seen, discussion of theory is now somewhat redundant. The English common law rule still applies, but only to defamation actions. Otherwise, legislation in the form of the Private International Law (Miscellaneous Provisions) Act 1995, Part III governs all other actions in tort.

Common law choice of law rule

The common law choice of law rules may be stated as follows:

When the tort is committed in England, English law alone applies: *Szalatnay-Stacho* v. *Fink*.[9]

When the conduct takes place abroad, liability is determined by English law, subject to the condition that, if liability exists by English law, it must also be civilly actionable in damages by the law of the place where it took place. This is known as the rule in *Phillips* v. *Eyre*,[10] as

---

[2] See ch. 12 above.   [3] 1949 SC 110, discussed at p. 223 below.
[4] 'The Proper Law of a Tort' (1951) 64 *Harvard Law Review* 888.
[5] In *McElroy* v. *McAllister* this would almost certainly have been Scots law.
[6] *Babcock* v. *Jackson* (1963) 12 NY 2d 473; [1963] 2 Ll.R 286 (New York Court of Appeals).
[7] [1971] AC 356 HL.
[8] It was, however, one of the two possibilities put forward for consideration by the Law Commission in its Working Paper no. 8 of 1985 but was not recommended in its Report no. 193 of 1990.
[9] [1947] KB 1 CA (a defamation case).   [10] (1870) LR 6 QB 1.

interpreted in *Chaplin* v. *Boys*,[11] as the latter was explained by the Court of Appeal.[12] In *Phillips* v. *Eyre* an action for assault was brought in England against the Governor of Jamaica, the alleged tort having been committed in Jamaica. This was a tort by English law and would have been so by Jamaican law, but after the deed was done, the Jamaican legislature passed an Act of Indemnity, relieving the governor of liability. It was held that the claimant could not recover here. In a celebrated judgment Willes J said, in words which have sometimes since been treated as if they were contained in a statute, that conduct abroad is actionable as a tort in England if:

(1) it is of such a character as to make it actionable as a tort had it been committed here [i.e. English law applies], and (2) it is *not justifiable* by the law of the place where it was committed.

In *Phillips* v. *Eyre* itself, (1) was satisfied, but (2) was not, so the claimant's action failed.

The first requirement was derived from the decision of the Privy Council in *The Halley* (1868).[13]

> An action was brought by the owners of a Norwegian ship against those of a British ship arising out of a collision in Belgian waters, caused by the negligence of a Belgian pilot on board the latter ship. His presence was required by Belgian law. By Belgian law the British owners were liable for his negligence; by the then English law they were not.

The defendants were held not liable. None of the justifications can withstand examination, yet all five members of the House of Lords in *Chaplin* v. *Boys* approved *The Halley*. This was the only point on which they all said the same thing, though it was the one point not in issue in the case.

This requirement has always been more harshly criticised than the second requirement, though it has given rise to fewer problems in its application. As will be seen,[14] it has been removed by statute in respect of all torts except defamation.

The second requirement, that the conduct must be 'not justifiable' by the local law, has proved more troublesome and has been given different meanings at different times. In *Phillips* v. *Eyre*[15] itself, the word 'justifiable' meant precisely that, for the governor's conduct was 'justified' by the subsequent legislation. In other contexts, it could mean one of several things: (i) the conduct must be a tort by the local law, or (ii)

---

[11] [1971] AC 356 HL.
[12] See, in particular, *Coupland* v. *Arabian Gulf Oil Co.* [1983] 1 WLR 1136 CA.
[13] (1868) LR 2 PC 193.   [14] See p. 225 below.   [15] (1870) LR 6 QB 1.

the claim must be in some way civilly actionable thereby, or (iii) though the claim is not civilly actionable, the conduct is 'wrong' by that law. This would include conduct which attracts criminal liability only.

At first, 'justifiable' was taken to mean (i). In *The Mary Moxham*,[16] action in respect of damage caused by an employee to a pier in Spain, it was held that the defendant employers, not being vicariously liable by Spanish law, themselves bore no tortious liability and so were not liable in England.

But in *Machado v. Fontes*,[17] meaning (iii) was adopted.

> An action was brought in respect of an alleged libel published in Brazil. According to the evidence, by Brazilian law the defendant was under no civil liability at all, but could be prosecuted for a criminal offence.

It was held that the existence of criminal liability under Brazilian law meant that the libel was 'not justifiable' by the *lex loci*, so the claimant could obtain such damages as were available under English law. His ability to get such damages though he could not do so by the *lex loci* hardly seems what Willes J had in mind by the words 'not justifiable'.

Unsatisfactory though this consequence was, the repudiation of *Machado v. Fontes* and the adoption of meaning (ii) by the Scottish Court of Session in *McElroy v. McAllister*[18] led to an even more unfortunate, and indeed preposterous, result.

> The pursuer's late husband was injured in an accident in Shap in England, forty miles south of the border, when in a lorry being driven by another employee while they were on the business of their Scottish employer. All parties were Scots. She sued as her husband's executrix-dative in Scotland claiming (1) under Scots law (*lex fori*), *solatium*; (2) and (3) by English law under the Law Reform Act 1934 on behalf of his estate and under the Fatal Accidents Act; (4) by both laws the funeral expenses.

(1) was not actionable in English law (*lex loci*) and (2) and (3) were not actionable under Scots law (*lex fori*) so (4) being the only head of damage recoverable under both laws, all the widow obtained were the funeral expenses. Apart from other considerations, this result is absurd.

The choice of the law rule was examined afresh by the English courts, including the House of Lords, in *Chaplin v. Boys*[19] but in a most confused manner.

---

[16] (1876) 1 PD 107.   [17] [1897] 2 QB 231 CA.
[18] 1949 SC 110. It was this case which caused Morris to advocate the 'proper law of the tort' as the governing law.
[19] [1971] AC 356 HL applied to a pre-Act tort in *Kuwait Oil Tanker Co. SAK v. al Bader* (2000) *The Times*, 30 May.

The claimant and defendant were both English servicemen who had been posted on duty to Malta. They met for the first time when the defendant, in his motor car, collided with the claimant, on his motorcycle, and injured him. The car was insured in England. The claimant was released from the services and soon got a job. He sued the defendant, who admitted negligence. The only issue was about the amount of damages the claimant could recover. Under English and Maltese law he could recover his actual pecuniary losses, but these were small. But under English law, though not Maltese law, he could recover damages for pain and suffering. Could he obtain such damages here?

All three courts which heard the case (Milmo J, the Court of Appeal by a majority (Lord Upjohn and Lord Denning MR, Diplock LJ dissenting) and the House of Lords unanimously) held that the claimant could recover but the members of the House gave different reasons for this. The *ratio decidendi* of their decision is not easy to discern, but it is unnecessary to subject the speeches of their Lordships to close analysis to discover it, since in several subsequent cases the Court of Appeal has said what it is. In *Church of Scientology of California* v. *Commissioner of the Metropolitan Police*,[20] which concerned an alleged libel written in England and published in Germany, and in *Coupland* v. *Arabian Gulf Oil Co.*,[21] where the tort was committed in Libya, the *ratio* of *Chaplin* v. *Boys*[22] was stated to be contained in the speech of Lord Wilberforce, that is to say, that as a general rule the defendant's conduct must be

actionable as a tort according to English law, subject to the condition that civil liability in respect of the relevant claim exists as between the actual parties under the law of the foreign country where the act was done.

This is, of course, the rule as it was applied in *McElroy* v. *McAllister*.[23]

The general rule can be stated in different words as follows. If the claimant cannot prove liability in tort under English law as the *lex fori*, he will fail. If he can do so then he will win unless the defendant shows he has a defence by the *lex loci*. Should the defendant do this, then the

---

[20] This was reported only in (1976) 120 Sol. Jo. 690, but is examined fully by Hodgson J in the *Coupland* case.

[21] [1983] 1 WLR 1136 Hodgson J and CA; see also *Armagas Ltd* v. *Mundogas SA* [1986] AC 717 CA and *Metall und Rohstoff A/G* v. *Donaldson, Lufkin and Jenrette Inc.* [1990] 1 QB 391 CA. It has also been adopted in a number of judgments given at first instance, for example, *Johnson* v. *Coventry Churchill International Ltd* [1993] 3 All ER 14; *Arab Monetary Fund* v. *Hashim* [1993] 1 Ll.R 543.

[22] [1971] AC 356 HL.   [23] 1949 SC 110.

claimant must show he can, nevertheless, recover under that law. If he does so he wins, if he does not do so, he loses.

The rule in *Phillips* v. *Eyre* has been abolished in respect of all torts committed after 1 May 1996[24] but is preserved as respects defamation,[25] and it continues to apply to all torts committed before 1 May 1996.

Displacement of the general rule

If the general rule had been applied in *Chaplin* v. *Boys*, the claimant would have lost. In fact, he won. The explanation for this has been derived from the speech of Lord Wilberforce, who said that there are exceptional cases in which with respect to the particular issue the general rule can be departed from on clear and satisfactory grounds and the system of law having the most significant relationship with the issue and the parties can be applied instead.

If such an exception had been applied in *McElroy* v. *McAllister*,[26] the pursuer would have recovered *solatium* at least, though not those sums which were available only under English law.

There are but few examples of later cases in which the exception was applied, so it is not quite clear when this will be done. Indeed, Lord Wilberforce's exception has been strongly criticised for its vagueness and for the unpredictability of its application. However, it is sometimes suggested that it might be easier to exclude the general rule where the parties had some relationship before the tort was committed, as where they were spouses or common employees. Thus in the Queensland case, *Warren* v. *Warren*[27]

> A husband and wife, domiciled and resident in Queensland, where their car was registered and insured, were driving in New South Wales when the wife was injured by her husband's negligent driving. She could sue him in Queensland, where the action was brought, but not under New South Wales law.

It was held that New South Wales law could be disregarded and Queensland law, as the most suitable law, applied instead. But a pre-tort

---

[24] Private International Law (Miscellaneous Provisions) Act 1995, s. 10.
[25] *Ibid.*, s. 13.   [26] 1949 SC 110.
[27] [1972] QdR 386, see also *Corcoran* v. *Corcoran* [1974] VR 164. These cases are only mentioned to illustrate the point. The High Court of Australia has since held that the exception is inapplicable, in intra-Australian cases at any rate: *McKain* v. *RW Miller & Co. (SA) Pty Ltd* (1991) 174 CLR1.

relationship is not essential, as *Chaplin* v. *Boys*[28] shows. It might be easier to displace the general rule where it is not basic liability which is at issue, but some consequential question, such as heads of liability or whether the parties can sue each other, or where contributory negligence is raised by way of defence.

In *Johnson* v. *Coventry Churchill International Ltd*[29] the exception was applied by an English court:

> The claimant, it was decided, was employed by the defendant English company to work in Germany. He was injured while working there. He could not recover damages under German law, nor was he eligible for compensation under a German state scheme. He could recover damages under English law.

It was held that German law could be ignored and that the claimant could recover under English law alone. There was a pre-tort nexus between the parties; the defendants were insured in England and, the court held, German law was not, in its own terms, interested in the matter.

Three questions remained after *Chaplin* v. *Boys*. Two have been answered.

The first was, would the first requirement of the rule in *Phillips* v. *Eyre* be displaced in a suitable case so that English law would not be applied, the foreign law alone governing the matter? This was answered by the Privy Council in *Red Sea Insurance Co.* v. *Bouyges*[30] where the *lex loci* (Saudi Arabian law) was alone applied.

The second question was whether the second requirement of the general rule would only be displaced if English law was then applied. If in *Chaplin* v. *Boys*[31] the parties had been French servicemen serving in Chad, would the court have applied French law? This situation has not arisen, but there seems no reason why this should not be done and Lord Wilberforce's remarks are wide enough to encompass it. The third question was, would the *lex loci* be displaced in the converse case, assuming the parties to be American servicemen posted to this country? Since the rule in *Phillips* v. *Eyre* is concerned with torts committed abroad, this seems less likely, and English law alone would continue to be applied.

---

[28] This was one ground for the decision in *La Van* v. *Danyluk* (1970) 75 WWR 500 (British Columbia), where Washington State was the *locus delicti*. *Kolsky* v. *Mayne Nickless Ltd* (1970) 3 NSWR 511 was not approved on this point in *Corcoran* v. *Corcoran* [1974] VR 164.
[29] [1992] 3 All ER 14.   [30] [1995] AC 190 PC.   [31] [1971] AC 356 HL.

Defamation: the general rule applied

Therefore, since these rules still apply to defamation:[32]

If the defendant's words are not defamatory, or do not refer to the claimant, or have not been published to a third party, or the defendant can rely on a defence, such as justification, absolute privilege, qualified privilege or fair comment and in the case of the last two defences cannot be shown to have been motivated by malice, they are not actionable in tort by English law. The claimant will therefore lose. He will do so if the defendant is not vicariously liable for the defamation committed by someone else.

If the statement is actionable by the claimant against the defendant under English law, the former will nevertheless lose if the defendant can show he is not liable to the claimant under the foreign law. So if, for example, there exists only criminal liability under that law, or he is not vicariously liable by that law, or the claimant is his wife and by the foreign law spouses cannot sue each other, or there exist thereunder defences, such as those mentioned in the previous paragraph, the action will fail.

Defamation: displacement of the general rule

No decided cases concern defamation but a possible example is where one domiciled Englishman (D) defames another domiciled Englishman (C) to a third domiciled Englishman (T) in Italy. Italian law would be disregarded and English law alone applied. If all three were Italian then, following *Red Sea Insurance* v. *Bouyges*, English law would be displaced and Italian law alone applied.[33]

The place where the tort is committed

It is easy to decide where a tort is committed if all the elements necessary to constitute liability occur in one country. Where they take place in different countries, it is not so easy to decide. As will be seen,[34] the common law on this matter was not entirely consistent but in recent times the English courts adhered to a test of deciding where the substance of the tort occurred. Almost all the relevant cases did not concern choice of law but service out of the jurisdiction and whether the tort had been

---

[32] Defamation includes for this purpose libel, slander, slander of title, slander of goods or other malicious falsehood or any claim under the law of another country corresponding thereto: Private International Law (Miscellaneous Provisions) Act 1995, s. 13.

[33] See *Scott* v. *Seymour* (1862) 1 HLC 219, 235 (assault by one Englishman on another one in Naples).

[34] See p. 230 below.

committed in England (or in the country whose courts were asked to allow service out of the jurisdiction).[35] The decisions in the defamation cases all held that where a defamatory statement was written or spoken in one country but published in another country then, since publication is the gist of the action, the country where publication took place was where the tort was committed. The only 'choice of law' case concerned defamation. In *Church of Scientology of California* v. *Commissioner of Metropolitan Police*,[36] the alleged libel was contained in a report composed in England and sent to West Berlin (Germany). The Court of Appeal held that the tort was committed in Germany, that is, where the substance of the tort occurred.

The Private International Law (Miscellaneous Provisions) Act 1995

Part III (sections 9–15) of the Act entered into force on 1 May 1996. Section 10 abolishes the rules of common law as set forth above in respect of all torts except, as section 13 provides, defamation. The exclusion of defamation came about during the passage of the Bill through the House of Lords in consequence of a sustained campaign by the media which was fearful of being exposed to liability under some oppressive foreign law and in respect of publications they might make abroad and being deprived of protection afforded by English law.

Moreover, the Act is not retrospective and the common law rules apply to torts committed before 1 May 1996 (section 14(1)).

The applicable law: the general rule

The effect of sections 10 and 11 is to remove the first requirement of the rule in *Phillips* v. *Eyre* and make the second requirement alone the general rule.

---

[35] *Bata* v. *Bata* [1948] WN 366 (letter written in Switzerland and posted to England where the claimant lived and the letter was read; the tort was committed in England). See also the decision of the European Court of Justice in *Shevill* v. *Presse Alliance* [1995] 2 AC 18, a case on the Brussels Convention, 1968, Art. 5(3) (see also p. 146 above). See also the Canadian cases, *Jenner* v. *Sun Oil Co.* [1952] 2 DLR 526 and *CAPAC* v. *International Good Music Inc.* [1963] 37 DLR (2d) 1. Compare with *Bata* v. *Bata*, *Kroch* v. *Rossell* [1937] 1 All ER 325 where a foreign newspaper was distributed here, but the vast majority of copies were distributed in France or Belgium. The claimant had no real reputation in England to be injured. Service was, in the court's discretion, refused. In the converse situation, where an article defamatory of a person outside New Zealand was published outside that country though written therein, the New Zealand court refused to allow service on one of the absent defendants: *Richards* v. *McLean* [1973] 1 NZLR 521. For a recent decision on this point see *Berezovsky* v. *Michaels* [2000] 1 WLR 1004 HL.

[36] (1976) 120 Sol. Jo. 690.

By section 11(1), 'The general rule is that the applicable law is the law of the country in which the events constituting the tort or delict in question occur.' Section 9(5) expressly excludes *renvoi*.

Two matters need discussion:

(1) Since section 9(4) provides that 'the applicable law shall be used for determining the issues arising in a claim, including in particular *the question whether an actionable tort or delict has occurred*', it follows that the English court, provided that it classified the action as one in tort, may have to enforce liability for conduct which is a tort by the law of the country where the conduct occurred, though the actor does not incur any liability at all under English law. Such is the case with liability for invasion of privacy, as has been observed by many commentators.[37]

(2) If all the elements of the tort occur in say, France, as where A negligently drives his car on a French road and hits and injures B, French law is the applicable law. If he does the same on an English road, English law determines A's liability to B.

With respect to cross-border torts, where some elements occur in one country and some in another, section 11(2) provides solutions to some of the problems.

Personal injury

Where the cause of action is in respect of personal injury or death resulting from personal injury, the applicable law is that of the country where the individual was when he sustained the injury.

If A in Germany shoots an arrow across the border with France and hits and injures B in France with it, French law applies. If B is brought to England and dies here, French law is still the applicable law.

Section 11(3) says that 'personal injury' includes disease or any impairment of physical or mental condition. So, if B comes to England and here, as a result of being struck by the arrow, contracts dermatitis or blood poisoning, loses temporarily or permanently the use of his right arm, or becomes insane, French law is the applicable law.

Property damage

Where the cause of action is in respect of damage to property, the law of the country where the property was when it was damaged applies.

So, if in the above example, B's car was damaged, French law applies. It applies also if, in consequence of the crash, no damage was observed at the time but the car falls apart after it is brought to England.

---

[37] Some control might be exercised by reference to section 14, discussed at p. 235 below.

Other torts

With respect to other torts, such as misrepresentation, inducing breach of contract and other economic torts, the applicable law is that of the country in which the most significant element or elements of the events occurred. No further elaboration of 'significance' is given and the courts will have to work this out and apply it for themselves. Presumably, they will derive guidance from cases decided under the common law and adopt something like the 'substance of the tort' test, which was adumbrated in *Distillers Co. (Biochemicals) Ltd* v. *Thompson*[38] (a personal injury case) and applied also in non-personal injury cases like *Metall und Rohstoff AG* v. *Donaldson, Lufkin and Jenrette Inc.*[39] in which the Court of Appeal held that where a conspiracy took place in New York to induce a breach of contract in England, the tort was committed in England.

Application of the lex loci

It follows from section 11 that if by the foreign law the defendant is not liable to the claimant, the claimant will lose.[40]

It will be a good defence that only criminal liability exists under the foreign law[41] or that the conduct was authorised[42] or justified[43] by that law. It appears that it will also be a good defence to an action in tort that the claimant is not entitled under the *lex loci* to an award of damages based on the defendant's causal responsibility, but under a statutory insurance scheme for workmen's compensation[44] or, as in New Zealand, for any personal injuries, since the defendant is under no civil liability and the injured party can recover whether or not the defendant's conduct was actionable. Although the defendant's conduct makes him liable in principle, the claimant will fail if his particular interest is not recognised by the *lex loci* (for example a claim for *solatium*)[45] or the head of damage is not recoverable[46] or the damages claimed are

---

[38] [1971] AC 458 PC.

[39] [1990] 1 WLR 391 CA. See also *Arab Monetary Fund* v. *Hashim* [1996] 1 Ll.R 589 CA (bribery).

[40] This is implicit in *Chaplin* v. *Boys* [1971] AC 356 HL. In this and the text accompanying notes 41 to 48 the illustrations are taken from common law discussions.

[41] *Ibid.*, overruling *Machado* v. *Fontes* [1897] 2 QB 231 and, it seems, *McLean* v. *Pettigrew* [1945] 2 DLR 65.

[42] *Carr* v. *Fracis Times & Co.* [1902] AC 176 HL.

[43] *Phillips* v. *Eyre* (1870) LR 6 QB 128.

[44] *Walpole* v. *Canadian Northern Railway* [1923] AC 113 PC; *McMillan* v. *Canadian Northern Railway, ibid.*, at 120. See also *Johnson* v. *Coventry Churchill International Ltd* [1993] 3 All ER 14.

[45] *McElroy* v. *McAllister* 1949 SC 110; cf. *Koop* v. *Bebb* (1951) 84 CLR 629 (Australia).

[46] *Chaplin* v. *Boys* [1971] AC 356 HL (had the general rule applied).

too remote. If the claimant cannot sue the defendant, as for example, a husband his wife or vice versa, or a gratuitous passenger his driver, he will fail. If someone may be liable, but not the defendant, since he is not, for example, vicariously liable, the defendant cannot be made liable here.[47]

If contributory negligence is a complete defence by the *lex loci* the claimant will fail, but if it gives rise to apportionment of damages by the *lex loci* and by the English law, he can, in the circumstances, recover in full; it was held in Australia that in such a case the *lex loci* affects the measure of damages only, and since that issue, being procedural, is governed by the *lex fori*, the claimant can recover in full.[48]

The applicable law: displacement of the general rule

Section 12 allows the court to displace the law applicable by section 11 and apply the law of another country, either England or a third country, to decide whether a tort has been committed or to decide a particular issue.

Section 12(1) provides that:

(1) If it appears, in all the circumstances, from a comparison of –
  (a) the significance of the factors which connect a tort or delict with the country whose law would be the applicable law under the general rule; and
  (b) the significance of any factors connecting the tort or delict with another country,
that it is substantially more appropriate for the applicable law for determining the issues arising in the case, or any of those issues, to be the law of the other country, the general rule is displaced and the applicable law for determining those issues or that issue (as the case may be) is the law of that other country.

This is somewhat similar to Lord Wilberforce's exception in *Chaplin* v. *Boys*.[49] As we have said, that exception has been criticised for its vagueness and unpredictability. Section 12(1) makes one thing clear, that displacement of the general rule may result in the application of the law of a third state, not just of either the *lex fori* or the *lex loci*.

Further than that, however, it makes matters no clearer than they were before. The statutory provision is less vague, but it is in a statute and so is naturally more carefully expressed than Lord Wilberforce's

---

[47] *The Mary Moxham* (1876) 1 P & D 107; *Armagas Ltd* v. *Mundogas SA* [1985] 3 WLR 640 CA. See also the *Church of Scientology* case (1976) 120 Sol. Jo. 690 CA.

[48] *Kolsky* v. *Mayne Nickless Ltd* [1970] 3 NSWR 511. If this is so, the result would be the same in this country: 1995 Act, s. 14(3)(b).

[49] [1971] AC 356 HL.

statement, which was all his own work. But its application seems no more predictable; this object is not attained simply by using more words which are more carefully chosen in which to express oneself.

Section 12(1) requires that one must look for the factors which connect the tort or the issue with the country where the tort was committed, for example, Malta, and those which connect it with another country, for example England or France, compare the *significance* of the respective factors and then decide whether it would be *substantially more appropriate* to apply English or French law instead of Maltese law.

Section 12(2) provides that the factors which may be taken into account include, in particular: (i) those relating to the parties (such as their residence and domicile); (ii) those relating to any of the events which constituted the tort in question (such as where the defendant's conduct took place and where its consequences were felt); (iii) those relating to any of the circumstances of the events which constitute the tort in question; and (iv) those relating to any of the consequences of those events (such as loss which is consequential upon the commission of the tort in another country).

These factors are not exclusive; others not expressly mentioned in section 12(2) may be considered. One can only speculate as to what these might be.

Thus the factors which may be taken into account constitute an open class. They are far more numerous than those mentioned by Lord Wilberforce, which are merely the connection with the occurrence and with the parties.

Section 12(1) states that it must then be decided whether it is *substantially* more appropriate to apply a law other than the *lex loci*. Apart from the obvious meanings, that it must not be only *marginally* or *slightly* more appropriate but need not be *overwhelmingly* so, no guidance is given as to when it is substantially more appropriate.

In the light of all this and the fact that it is not entirely clear how the relative significance of the various factors is to be assessed, it is difficult to forecast how the courts will apply section 12. Perhaps the few common law cases such as *Chaplin* v. *Boys*, *Johnson* v. *Coventry Churchill*[50] and *Red Sea Insurance Co.* v. *Bouyges*[51] may be relied on by way of illustration but even this is not entirely clear.[52]

Last, in the case of 'cross-border' torts, section 12(1) will usually only be resorted to where the claim arises from personal injury or property damage. For other torts, the determination of the place where

---

[50] [1991] 3 All ER 14.   [51] [1995] 1 AC 190 PC.
[52] See G. C. Cheshire and P. M. North, *Private International Law*, 13th edn (London, Butterworths, 1999) 643–5.

the tort occurred and thus of the applicable law under section 11 will already have involved consideration of the significance of the elements connected with the tort.

Tort committed in England

It is clear that Parliament intended that Part III of the 1995 Act should apply to torts committed in England as well as to those which take place abroad. In such cases English law would apply by virtue of section 11 but it could be displaced under section 12 and French law, for instance, applied instead. Indeed section 9(6), which provides that 'this Part applies in relation to events occurring [in England] as it applies in relation to events occurring in another country' clearly has this effect. However, it equally clearly conflicts with section 14(2), which provides that 'Nothing in this Part affects any rules of law (including rules of private international law) abolished by section 10.'

However, section 10 only abolished the application of 'both the law of the forum and the law of another country for the purpose of determining whether a tort of delict is actionable' and Lord Wilberforce's exception. But this did not apply to torts committed in England. The contradiction of section 9(6) by section 14(2) should have been avoided by redrafting the latter provision when the former was inserted by the House of Lords.

It is possible, though not very plausible,[53] to reconcile these provisions. One hopes that a court would prefer section 9(6) to section 14(2) and give effect to what is known to have been Parliament's intention.

Ways of avoiding the application of the lex loci

There are four ways in which the application of the foreign law indicated by section 11 of the Act can be avoided should it be thought inappropriate, unsatisfactory or obnoxious.

Displacement
This is by resorting to section 12. It needs no further elaboration.

Characterisation
Whereas displacement involves classifying the cause of action or the issue as tort, characterisation involves characterising the claim or issue as something else and applying the appropriate and different choice of

---

[53] See *ibid.*, 625.

law rule. The 1995 Act contains a provision which is probably meant to say this but it is remarkable only for the ineptitude of its drafting. Section 9(5) says that '[t]he characterisation for the purposes of private international law of issues arising in a claim as relating to tort or delict is a matter for the courts of the forum'. Quite apart from the pleonasm (the English word 'court' means the same as the Latin word 'forum') involved, this is a statement of the obvious; if an action is before an English court, how could a Scottish or French court characterise any-thing? Presumably what is meant is that the court before which an action is brought should classify the issues involved in accordance with its own laws (the *lex fori*) and not with another law, for example, the foreign *lex causae*.

The characterisation technique has been adopted occasionally by the courts of several countries. The United States courts did so, before they abandoned the *lex loci* as the governing law in *Babcock* v. *Jackson* in 1962;[54] this method thereafter was no longer needed. Australian courts have occasionally adopted this method, as in *Sayers* v. *International Drilling Co.*,[55] did the majority of the Court of Appeal in England, though perhaps accidentally rather than on purpose.

Thus, whether spouses can sue each other in tort has been treated as a matter of family law and so governed by the parties' personal law.[56] This was an alternative ground for the application of Queensland law in *Warren* v. *Warren*,[57] to avoid the rule of New South Wales law which prevented a wife suing her husband in tort. Whether a cause of action survived against the estate of a deceased tortfeasor was treated by the California Supreme Court in *Grant* v. *McAuliffe*[58] as a matter of adminis-tration of estates and governed by the law of the court administering the estate, the *lex fori*. This could be done also in respect of survival of a cause of action to the victim's estate. Whether a victim can sue directly the tortfeasor's insurers has been regarded as a question of contract[59] or quasi-contract.[60] But in only one case has this kind of characterisation been applied in England.[61] When it has been applied in the United States and Australia it has led to the application of the *lex fori*, though under a different guise.

---

[54] [1963] 2 Ll.R 286.   [55] [1971] 1 WLR 1176 CA.
[56] *Haumschild* v. *Continental Casualty Co.* 7 Wis. (2d) 130 (1959). See also *Emery* v. *Emery* 45 Cal. 2d 421 (1955) (whether a child could sue his parent).
[57] [1972] QdR 386.   [58] Cal. 2d 859 (1953).
[59] *Plozza* v. *South Australian Insurance Co.* [1963] SASR 122.
[60] *Hodge* v. *Club Motor Insurance Agency* (1974) 2 ALR 421.
[61] *Sayers* v. *International Drilling Co.* [1971] 1 WLB 1176.

Public policy

At common law, the rule in *Phillips* v. *Eyre* required that the tort should
be actionable as such by English law, so there was no need to resort to
public policy to exclude the application of foreign law. Now that the *lex
loci* alone has become the applicable law an exception to its application
on the ground of English public policy is needed. So section 14(3)(a)
provides that nothing in the Act 'authorises the application of the law of
a country outside [England] . . . in so far as to do so – (i) would conflict
with principles of public policy'.

Public policy will be discussed more fully later.[62] It must be emphasised here that the scope of public policy in the conflict of laws is
narrow and the rule of foreign law would have to be very objectionable
to be excluded for this reason: for example, rules which prohibit certain
persons suing or recovering damages on racial, political, religious or
other discriminatory grounds.

But a rule of foreign law cannot be rejected simply because no such rule
exists in English law[63] or because it is different from the corresponding
rule of English law. Apart from the fact that it cannot be said that the
English rules of tort law are adequate or perfect, if we were to adopt
this position we might as well abandon choice of law altogether. Moreover since the main purpose of the 1995 Act was to eliminate English
law from the matter and to make the *lex loci* the applicable law it would
be to turn the legislation on its head if the courts at the slightest opportunity decided to exclude the foreign law and apply English law instead.
Nor is a foreign law contrary to public policy because its application
leads to the claimant losing his case or recovering lower damages than
he would obtain if English law applied. The claimant often loses even if
English law applies.

Failure to plead to prove foreign law

Since the parties must plead and prove such rules of foreign law as they
wish to rely on and need not do so if they do not so wish, they can
compel the court to apply English law rather than the foreign law by
not pleading or proving the latter. This matter has been discussed
already.[64]

Exemption clauses in contracts of service

The inclusion of an exemption clause in a contract can cause peculiar
difficulties if one party thereto sustains injury by the tortious conduct of

[62] See ch. 21 below.   [63] See *Phrantzes* v. *Argenti* [1960] 2 QB 19.   [64] Ch. 4 above.

another or of persons employed by that other. One type of exemption clause, namely a term in a contract of service which exempts an employer from liability for an injury suffered by an employee by the negligence of a fellow employee during their common employment, may or may not be effective,[65] depending upon whether the issue is treated as tort or as a contract. Indeed, one way in which to avoid the application of the choice of law rule for tort is to sue in contract instead of, or alternatively to, suing in tort. The latter option was envisaged in *Matthews* v. *Kuwait Bechtel Corporation*[66] and in *Coupland* v. *Arabian Gulf Oil Co.*,[67] but in neither case did the contract contain an exemption clause.

The validity of such a clause was treated as a purely contractual issue by the majority of the Court of Appeal in *Sayers* v. *International Drilling Co.*[68]

> An action was brought by an English employee of a Dutch company who was engaged to work on an oil rig in Nigerian waters. His contract was what Dutch law termed an 'international contract' and under Dutch law the exemption clause was valid. It was invalid by English law.

The majority (Salmon and Stamp LJJ) held that Dutch law was the proper law so that the exemption clause provided a good defence.

The case is, therefore, an example of avoiding the application of the tort rule, but its impressiveness is reduced by the fact that it was not suggested that Nigerian law as *lex loci delicti commissi* was of any relevance. Lord Denning MR regarded the case as being concerned with tort liability, correctly it is thought, but he then got into difficulties of his own devising, first by his statement of the tort choice of law rule:

> In considering that claim we must apply the proper law of the tort, that is, the law of the country with which the parties and the acts done have the most significant connection. That is how I put it in *Boys* v. *Chaplin*. I think it is confirmed by what Lord Wilberforce said in the House of Lords, though he put it with more scholarship and precision than I could hope to do.

Lord Wilberforce would have been astonished by this economium, since this is exactly what he did not say; he used the proper law only by way of exception to the 'double actionability' rule.[69] Secondly, however, Lord Denning MR continued, almost perversely, to hold that the proper law of the tort was Dutch law, but that the proper law of the contract was English law. (Had he held them both to be Dutch law or both English law, there would have been no trouble.) Which then, was to

---

[65] Such exemption clauses were outlawed in English law by the Law Reform (Personal Injuries) Act 1948 and the Unfair Contract Terms Act 1977.
[66] [1959] 2 QB 57.   [67] [1983] 1 WLR 1136 CA.
[68] [1971] 1 WLR 1176 CA.   [69] See p. 225 above.

decide the case, Dutch or English law? Lord Denning MR got himself out of his quandary of his own making by holding that the 'proper law of that issue' should govern, and that this was for some obscure reason Dutch law, so that the exemption clause was valid and a good defence.

If the issue is treated as one of tort as, it is submitted, correctly, a Scots court did in *Brodin* v. *A/R Seljan*,[70] three situations must be considered:

(i) The clause is *invalid* by the *lex loci* but *valid* by the contract's applicable law. The clause affords *no defence* under the *lex loci*, so the claimant's action *succeeds*.

(ii) The clause is *valid* both by the *lex loci* and by the contract's applicable law. The clause affords *a defence* under the *lex loci* so the claimant's action *fails*.

(iii) The clause is *valid* by the *lex loci* but *invalid* by the contract's proper law (i.e. the converse of (i)). At first sight the clause is a defence by the *lex loci* so the action should *fail*. This cannot be correct; if the clause is invalid by the law governing the contract in which it is contained, there is no exemption clause upon which the *lex loci* can operate. The claimant's action should, therefore, *succeed*.

One may further suggest that the issue is really one in tort. From the above, it will be seen that only in (i) does it make any difference to the claimant, who will win if he sues in tort but *lose* if he sues in contract. It makes no difference in (iii) since he will win whether he sues in tort or in contract, or in (ii) since he will lose whichever option he takes.

The Law Commission declined to recommend any statutory provision, which is why there is none in the 1995 Act, seemingly because the matter is too difficult. This, it may be thought, rather overestimates the problems involved.

Savings, especially procedure and mandatory rules

Section 14 of the 1995 Act lists several 'savings' which in fact preserve exceptions to the common law rules. Section 14(2) and public policy (section 14(3)(a)) have already been discussed. A third is concerned with foreign penal, revenue or other public laws which will be discussed later.[71]

The fourth saving is for rules of evidence pleading or practice or questions of procedure. These continue to be governed by the *lex fori*, English law alone.[72] It should be recalled that, in consequence of the

---

[70] 1973 SC 213.   [71] Ch. 21 below.   [72] See ch. 6 above.

Foreign Limitation Periods Act 1984, limitation of actions has in effect ceased to be a matter of procedure and has become one of substance[73] so that, in a tort action, it is the foreign period of limitation which will apply and not the English period.

The fifth saving is for 'mandatory rules', which have been discussed in the previous chapter,[74] though section 14(4) does not use the term. Although this is not made clear, it is thought that, as the Law Commission in its draft Bill did make clear,[75] this refers to mandatory rules of English law and not of some foreign law. It is to be hoped that the provision will be interpreted in this sense.

Maritime torts

Torts committed on the high seas

Torts not committed on one ship

When an alleged tort has not been committed entirely on one ship, as where the act of omission results in a collision, the English court will determine liability in accordance with 'the general maritime law as administered in England'.[76] This is 'in truth nothing more than English law'.[77] Internationally agreed rules governing collisions at sea have been given statutory effect in English law.[78]

In *Chartered Mercantile Bank of India* v. *Netherlands India Steam Navigation Co.*[79]

> P shipped cargo in D's vessel, whose nationality was Dutch. Owing to the negligence of D's servants it collided on the high seas with another Dutch ship. P's rights against D were governed by English, not Dutch, law.

---

[73] See pp. 63–4 above.   [74] See pp. 213–15 above.

[75] Law Commission Report No. 193 (1990) Appendix A. It is not entirely clear what rules of English law are mandatory rules for this purpose; among those suggested are some contained in statutes, if Parliament intended them to have overriding effect, such as the Law Reform (Personal Injuries) Act 1948 (see p. 236 above) and provisions of the Unfair Contract Terms Act 1977. Whether any common law rules can be regarded as mandatory is somewhat doubtful, although the draftsman of the 1995 Act, unlike the Law Commission, seems to have thought so.

[76] See *The Zollverein* (1856) Swab. 96, i.e. English rules for maritime questions; *The Gaetano and Maria* (1882) 7 PD 137, 143 per Brett LJ; *The Tojo Maru* [1972] AC 242 HL at 290–1.

[77] *Lloyd* v. *Guibert* (1865) LR 1 QB 115 at 133 per Willes J.

[78] Convention on Revision of International Regulations Preventing Collisions at Sea, 1972 (Cmnd 3471) and Collision Regulations and Order 1977 (SI 1977 no. 982) as amended. This is also extended to hovercraft.

[79] (1883) 10 QBD 521.

The English courts, it seems, apply English law to all torts, such as trespass, committed on the high seas.[80] This includes such statutes as, upon their construction, extend to such cases.[81]

Thus in *The Esso Malaysia*,[82]

> A Panamanian and a Russian vessel collided on the high seas. This was caused by the negligence of the master and crew of the former. A member of the crew of the Russian vessel was drowned.

His personal representatives were entitled to recover damages in England from the owners of the Panamanian ship under the Fatal Accidents Act 1976.

Torts committed on one ship

Here the rule in *Phillips* v. *Eyre*[83] will apply. For this purpose the *lex loci* will be that of the country of the ship's flag, and, if the country of that flag has more than one law, the law of the place of registry.

Torts committed in foreign national or territorial waters

Torts not committed on one ship

Liability in such cases is governed by the 1995 Act, s. 11 so, generally, the law of the coastal state will be applicable.

Torts committed on one ship

The same was held by the Scots courts at common law to be the case.[84] It would be more sensible to displace the general rule by relying on section 12(1) where this is appropriate.

Torts committed on aircraft

Authority on the question of the law governing liability is lacking. It may be that if the aircraft is over the high seas English law will apply, but if it is over a foreign country section 11 of the 1995 Act will generally apply, the subjacent country being the *locus delicti*.

---

[80] See *Submarine Telegraph Co.* v. *Dickson* (1864) 15 CB (NS) 759; *The Tubantia* [1924] P 78.
[81] *Davidsson* v. *Hill* [1901] 2 KB 606.   [82] [1978] QB 198.   [83] (1870) LR 6 QB 1.
[84] *MacKinnon* v. *Iberia Shipping Co.* [1954] 2 Ll.R 372 and see *The Halley* (1868) LR 2 PC 193.

Part IV

Property and succession

14 Property *inter vivos*

Characterisation

The first question concerning title to property is how rights therein are to be characterised. In English domestic law they are for historical reasons categorised into real and personal property. This pays no regard to the physical characteristics of the property and the division does not coincide with a distinction between land, which is by its nature immovable, and movable objects such as a car or a diamond, which are tangible, and debts or copyrights which are intangible but nevertheless are capable of being owned. Thus in English domestic law certain interests in land such as leases are personal property, though called 'chattels real'.

This classification, being unknown to most systems of law, since these usually categorise property as either immovable (which term includes all interests in land and the buildings thereon) or movable, is obviously wholly inapt for the purpose of the conflict of laws. Therefore, the English courts abandon their domestic classification and for that purpose adopt the distinction between immovables and movables.

Moreover, to determine whether an item of property is one or the other, classification is affected not by English notions, but according to the *lex situs* of the property. This is obviously sensible, since for our courts to classify it in a manner opposed to that of the *lex situs* would often be a waste of time, as there may be little our courts could do to enforce their ideas and solutions.

For example, if A dies intestate, domiciled in England and owning a farm in Ruritania with animals on it, then if the animals are classified as movable, they will be inherited by whoever is entitled to them under English law, since intestate succession to movables is governed by the law of the last domicile of the deceased. But if they are regarded as immovables (for foreign laws also have their idiosyncrasies) because they are 'attached' to the farm, they will descend to whoever is entitled to them by Ruritanian law, since the *lex situs* governs intestate succession to immovables. The English court will regard cows as immovables if Ruritanian law so classifies them.

Leasehold land in England, though regarded as personal property by English law, the *lex situs* and by Irish law, the law of the testator's domicile, has been held to be an interest in an immovable and a bequest of it governed by English law.[1] An interest of a mortgagee of land in Ontario who died domiciled in England was likewise held to be an interest in an immovable and his bequest of it was governed by Ontario law.[2] In Re *Berchtold*[3] English land held on trust for sale which by English law was, in consequence of the equitable doctrine of conversion, regarded as already sold and therefore as money, which is movable property, was held to be an immovable.

> Berchtold died domiciled in Hungary possessed of freehold land in England, which was settled on trust for sale with power to postpone sale. The question arose, whether one set of persons entitled under Hungarian law, or another entitled under English law, should take the land. The former would succeed if the interest was movable property, the latter if it was immovable. The former argued that since English law regarded land held on trust for sale as personalty it was movable property and Hungarian law applied. The latter replied that the first question was whether it was immovable or movable. Since land is immovable by English law, the interest was an interest in an immovable, so English law governed. Only then might the question whether it was realty or personalty arise, in order to determine who, under English law, was entitled to it.

The court decided in favour of the claimants under English law.

Title to property

Title to property is, in general, governed by its *lex situs*, whether it is immovable or movable, except that succession to movable property is governed by the law of the last domicile of the deceased.[4] In this chapter only title to property derived from *inter vivos* transactions will be dealt with.[5] The discussion will be concerned first with tangible movables, concerning which the *lex situs* rule can be stated with some confidence, and then with intangible movables, of which the same cannot be said.

---

[1] *Freke* v. *Carberry* (1873) LR 16 Eq. 461.   [2] Re *Hoyles* [1911] 1 Ch. 179 CA.
[3] [1923] 1 Ch. 192. As to settled land, where the Law of Property Act 1925, s. 75(5), provides that capital monies representing its sale are 'land', and land is an immovable, see Re *Cutcliffe* [1940] Ch. 565, and compare Re *Midleton's Settlement* [1947] Ch. 583 CA.
[4] See Diplock J in *Adams* v. *National Bank of Greece and Athens SA* [1958] 2 QB 59.
[5] For succession see ch. 15 below.

Movable property: tangible movables

Things such as cars, jewels and books are tangible movables. Here it is vital to distinguish between contractual issues (if there is a contract) and proprietary questions. The English Sale of Goods Act 1979, for example, contains some rules, such as those respecting implied terms in a contract for the sale of goods,[6] which are concerned with contractual issues and others which are concerned with proprietary issues, such as those governing passing of property in goods and the acquisition of title from a non-owner.[7] The former issues are governed, in principle, by the applicable law of the contract, but the proprietary issues by the *lex situs* of the property. For example:

> By section 18 rule 1 of the Sale of Goods Act 1979 there is a presumption that, in the absence of any contrary intention, where there is an unconditional contract for the sale of specific goods in a deliverable state, property (i.e. ownership) passes at the time the contract is made and not at the time of delivery or payment or both, if these take place later. Suppose that X sells a car to Y by a contract made in England and governed by English law, and the car is then in Utopia. Suppose, further, that by Utopian law property passes only on delivery of the goods to the buyer.

English law governs the contractual issues, such as whether X was in breach of contract or of a term of the contract. But Utopian law determines whether title has passed to Y. If the car has not been delivered to him title has not passed and X is still the owner.

In the past, three other choice of law rules have been suggested. One is the law of the domicile of the parties, in accordance with the maxim *mobilia sequuntur personam*.[8] But, as the Privy Council observed in *Provincial Treasurer of Alberta* v. *Kerr*,[9] this now only explains the rule that succession to movables is governed by the law of the domicile.[10] The law of the domicile is difficult to apply if the parties have different domiciles: which law is to dictate who owns the goods?

Another suggested rule is that the *lex loci actus*,[11] that is, the law of the place where the transaction took place, governs title. In our hypothetical example it would be English law. This finds some support in *Alcock* v. *Smith*[12] and *Embiricos* v. *Anglo-Austrian Bank*,[13] but these

---

[6] See ss. 12–15.   [7] See especially ss. 17–19, 21–5.
[8] *Sill* v. *Worswick* (1791) 1 H Bl. 665.   [9] [1933] AC 710 PC at 721.
[10] This obviates the complications inherent in applying the *lex situs* if the deceased left property in different countries.
[11] Which under the name of *lex loci celebrationis* governs forms of marriage.
[12] [1892] 1 Ch. 238 CA.   [13] [1905] 1 KB 677 CA.

concerned bills of exchange and the *lex loci actus* and the *lex situs* must, of necessity, coincide in their case, since in order to put a signature on a cheque or to deliver it one must possess it.[14] Nowadays the *lex loci contractus* does not even govern contractual issues except formalities and then only optionally,[15] and has fallen out of favour in the present context.

A third suggested rule is that the *lex actus*, that is, the proper law of the transaction, governs. In the example given this also would be English law. It was once much favoured by Cheshire. But those who suggest it should apply overlook the conceptual distinction between contractual and proprietary questions. The *lex actus* is useless where there is one transaction in country A followed by another in B, or where there is no transaction between X and Y, as where Y steals X's ring in Scotland, then brings it to England and (before 1994) sold it here in market overt[16] to Z, thus giving him title to it.

Application of the *lex situs* is supported by dicta in several cases,[17] and seems the most satisfactory rule, mainly because of its simplicity and certainty, except where the goods are in transit (though this is of little importance since transfer in such cases is usually effected by delivery of documents of title).

Devlin J said in *Bank voor Handel en Scheepvaart NV* v. *Slatford*,[18] 'there is little doubt that it is the *lex situs* which, as a general rule, governs the transfer of movables when effected contractually'.

It is also supported by decided cases, such as those concerning laws expropriating property enacted by foreign states or governments.[19] In *Winkworth* v. *Christie, Manson & Woods*[20] Slade J held that the effect of a transaction in Italy in respect of a painting previously stolen in England but in Italy at the relevant time should be determined by Italian law and not English law. In that case, the judge was asked to determine as between English and Italian domestic law, but he thought that if the Italian court would have applied English law by way of *renvoi*, it would be open to the claimant to argue that the English court should apply English law. This seems unobjectionable.

---

[14] Title ot a bill of exchange is transferred by delivery (in the case of a bearer bill) or endorsement by signing it and delivery (in the case of an order bill).
[15] See pp. 207–8 above.   [16] Abolished by Sale and Supply of Goods Act 1994.
[17] Re *Anziani* [1930] 1 Ch. 407, 420 per Maugham J; *Adams* v. *National Bank of Greece and Athens SA* [1958] 2 QB 59 per Diplock J; *Hardwick Game Farm* v. *Suffolk Agricultural Poultry Producers Association* [1966] 1 WLR 287, 330 per Diplock J.
[18] [1953] 1 QB 248 at 257.
[19] See, for example, *Luther* v. *Sagor* [1921] 3 KB 532 CA; *Princess Paley Olga* v. *Weisz* [1929] 1 KB 718 CA discussed at p. 365 below.
[20] [1980] Ch. 496. Also *Glencore International A/G* v. *Metro Trading* [2001] All ER (Comm.) 103.

For the purpose of further discussion, two situations will be distinguished:

(a) Where the *situs* remains constant in one country. That country's law will determine title to the goods;[21]

(b) Where the *situs* is changed by the goods being moved from one country to another the problem is slightly, but not much, more complicated.

(i) If X acquired title by the law of country A when the goods were there, his title will be recognised in England unless when they are subsequently in B[22] a transaction takes place there which by the law of B gives title to Y, in which event Y's title will prevail over X's.

(ii) If the facts are the same but no transaction takes place in B, or if one does take place there, but does not by the law of B give title to Y, X's title will continue to be recognised.

Thus, in the early case of *Cammell* v. *Sewell*[23]

> X, a domiciled Englishman, owned a cargo of timber, title to which he had acquired by Russian law when it was in Russia. It was shipped from Russia to England on a Prussian vessel, which was wrecked on the coast of Norway. The ship's master sold the timber to Y in Norway; this gave Y title under Norwegian law, but not by English law. Y brought the timber to England and X sued him here.

The court held that Y's title acquired by Norwegian law when the timber was in Norway prevailed over that of X.

The case illustrates proposition (i) where A was Russia and B Norway and proposition (ii) where A was Norway and B England.

The same result follows where the goods were in B, then were taken to A and brought back to B, where B is England. In *Winkworth* v. *Christie, Manson & Woods*[24] works of art were stolen from England where they were owned by Mr William Wilberforce Winkworth and taken to Italy where they were bought by Dr Paolo del Pozzo d'Annone, who later sent them back to England to be auctioned. Slade J held that Italian law should determine whether Dr d'Annone had acquired title. Nothing had occurred with respect to the paintings after they had

---

[21] *Inglis* v. *Usherwood* (1801) 1 East. 515 (Russian law determined the effect of a stoppage in transit when the goods were there); *Inglis* v. *Robertson* [1898] AC 616 HL (validity of a pledge in England of goods in Scotland determined by Scots law).

[22] Whether B is England or a third country.

[23] (1858) 3 H & N 617, 638, affd (1860) 5 H & N 728. See also *Alcock* v. *Smith* [1892] 1 Ch. 238 CA and *Embiricos* v. *Anglo-Austrian Bank* [1905] 1 KB 677 CA.

[24] [1980] 1 Ch. 496.

arrived in England which, under English law, would deprive him of any title he might have acquired by Italian law.

These simple propositions also explain what seem more complex cases concerning retention or reservation[25] of title on a sale of goods or on letting them on hire purchase, or third party encumbrances such as liens, pledges or mortgages. Apart from the fact that what X has retained or acquired is often (but not always) a right less than full ownership, these cases are not particularly difficult to follow if the principles already stated are borne in mind. The real point at issue is often only what the law of B (and sometimes A) means and what its effect on X's rights really is.

The same two possibilities exist:

(i) A transaction takes place in B which, by its law, has the effect of overriding X's title or right. This is proposition (i) above. It is exemplified (as, indeed, is proposition (ii)) by the Canadian case, *Century Credit Corporation* v. *Richard.*[26]

> When a car was in A (Quebec) X sold it to Y by a conditional sale agreement under which property in it was to remain in X until the price was fully paid. This was effective under Quebec law. Y took the car to B (Ontario) and resold it to Z who had no notice of X's rights. Under Ontario law (a) a conditional sale must be registered for X's reservation of his title to be effective and (b) since Y had agreed to buy the car and was in possession of it, a sale by him to Z would give Z good title, as it would in England by the Sale of Goods Act 1979, section 25(1).

The Ontario Court held, as to (a), that this rule did not affect X's rights reserved in Quebec since it did not prevent their being recognised, just as in *Cammell* v. *Sewell*[27] the fact that English law would not have given to the sale in Norway the effect it had under Norwegian law did not prevent that effect being recognised in England. But as to (b) since the sale to Z took place when the car was in Ontario and by the law of Ontario had the effect of overriding X's title, Z's title prevailed over X's rights.

---

[25] So, the effect of what are known as *Romalpa* clauses, whereby sellers of materials to manufacturers reserve the legal ownership of the materials or the goods into which they are made or the monetary proceeds of the sale thereof, is to some extent governed by these principles. The decided cases, mainly Scottish ones, in which the conflict of laws aspect might have been determined did not, for various reasons, deal with it. See, for example, *Armour* v. *Thyssen Edelstahlwerke A/G* [1991] 2 AC 339 HL.

[26] (1962) 34 DLR (2d) 291; *Price Mobile Home Centres Inc.* v. *National Trailer Convoy of Canada* (1974) 44 DLR (3d) 443. It is also illustrated by the old English cases, *Hooper* v. *Gumm* (1867) LR 2 Ch. App. 282 and *Liverpool Marine Credit Co.* v. *Hunter* (1868) LR 3 Ch. App. 479.

[27] (1853) 3 H & N 617, 638.

(ii) B law merely does not recognise the rights acquired or reserved when the goods were in A since B law requires, for example, that such rights be registered to be effective, and X had not registered his right. This is proposition (ii) above. The registration requirement of the law of B was irrelevant when the goods were in A and X's right is not lost by the goods being removed to B since nothing has occurred there which under B's law would deprive X of his right.

This is illustrated by *Century Credit Corporation* v. *Richard*, with respect to the Ontario registration provision. It is also illustrated by the American case of *Goetschius* v. *Brightman*.[28]

> X let a car on hire purchase to Y in California (A). Title was to remain in X until the price was fully paid. In breach of a promise not to remove the car from California and before the price was paid Y took the car to New York (B) and sold it to Z. By Californian law X's title prevailed; by New York law a reservation of title was invalid unless it was registered in New York.

The New York court held that X's title prevailed; it was reserved when the car was in California, and the New York registration requirement was clearly irrelevant then. Nothing had occurred when the car was in New York which by New York law would deprive X of his right since New York law had no provision like s. 25(1) of the Sale of Goods Act.

Two American decisions are concerned with the converse situation, in which goods are taken from A to B and sold there by Y to Z. By the law of A, such a sale deprives X of his rights, but by the law of B it does not. Nothing has happened in B which under its law would have such an effect. It would seem, also, that the law of A ceases to have effect when the goods leave A.

This conclusion was arrived at in *Marvin Safe Co.* v. *Norton*,[29] where A (Pennsylvania) law provided that although X's reservation of title was valid, it would be overridden by a subsequent sale by Y to Z. By B (New Jersey) law, it would not. The New Jersey court upheld X's title.

This seems correct in principle but in *Dougherty* v. *Krimke*[30] where New York law seems to have been identical to that of Pennsylvania in the previous case, the New Jersey court held that X's rights were overridden by the sale by Y to Z when the goods were brought to New Jersey.

It is not clear whether the English courts would follow this decision. Dr Morris approved it; he distinguished it from and reconciled it with *Marvin Safe Co.* v. *Norton*[31] by suggesting that the New Jersey courts

---

[28] 245 NY 186 (1927).
[29] 48 NJL 410 (1886). See also *Rennie Car Sales* v. *Union Acceptance Corporation* [1955] 4 DLR 822.
[30] 105 NJL 470 (1929).   [31] 48 NJL 410 (1886).

thought that the Pennsylvania law applied only to sales in Pennsylvania, whereas the New York law applied to sales taking place anywhere. If this is true of the New York law, then there was no reason why the New Jersey court should not give it effect, for if the law under which X acquired his title says he has lost it, why should the courts in another country say he has not?

But this can be answered by saying that if New Jersey courts wish to apply New York law to transactions taking place in New Jersey, they are free to do so. But there is no reason why they should; A's law, on principle, ceases to have effect when the goods leave A. And why should Z, the purchaser in B, on discovering he has got no title under its law, be able to rely on the law of A, whose existence, let alone relevance, could not have crossed his mind when he purchased the goods? *Dougherty* v. *Krimke*[32] is arguably wrong on principle.

Possible exceptions to the lex situs *rule*

Some exceptions to the *lex situs* rule were proffered by counsel in *Winkworth* v. *Christie, Manson & Woods*[33] and apparently accepted by Slade J.

(i)   Where the goods are in transit and their *situs* is casual or unknown at the time of the transaction, a transfer valid and effective by its proper law should be valid and effective in England. This may be accepted, though as has already been said,[34] the exception is comparatively unimportant.

(ii) Where the purchaser claiming title did not act in good faith. This is dubious. By English law, in one situation a purchaser can obtain good title though he did not act in good faith, that is, if he buys from an unpaid seller who is exercising his statutory right of resale.[35] There seems, therefore, no good reason for English law to adopt a different stance where a foreign law is in issue.

(iii) Where to recognise the rule of the *lex situs* would be contrary to English public policy. One decision possibly bears this out but is not above criticism.[36]

(iv) Where an English statute prescribes the application of English law. No such statute appears to exist.

---

[32] 105 NJL 470 (1929).   [33] [1980] Ch. 496.
[34] See p. 246 above.   [35] Sale of Goods Act 1979, s. 48.
[36] *The Rose Mary* [1953] 1 WLR 246 (Supreme Court of Aden), as explained in Re *Helbert Wagg & Co. Ltd's Claim* [1956] Ch. 323. These cases are discussed more fully at pp. 364–5 below. The foreign law would have to be very outrageous for this view of it to be taken; see remarks in *Oppenheimer* v. *Cattermole* [1976] AC 249 HL.

(v) General assignments of movables on bankruptcy or succession. This is accepted law. These matters are governed by the law of the domicile of the bankrupt or of the deceased.[37]

Movable property: intangible movables (choses in action)

If the choice of law rule relating to title to tangible movables is now tolerably clear, the same cannot be said of that concerning title to intangibles. A leading international lawyer remarked in the 1930s: 'The decisions on the subject are conflicting, indecisive and obscure, and the writings of the leading authors are equally contradictory and certainly more obscure.'[38] This stricture is, perhaps, rather harsh as far as the writers are concerned, but is still, to a fair extent, true of the decisions, many of which are in any event somewhat old. Since, in commercial matters, the law relating to intangibles in the conflict of laws seems much more important than that concerning tangibles, it is, perhaps, surprising that there are not more recent decisions than in fact do exist.

The difficulty which pervades this topic stems from two sources of confusion. One, which complicates many of the decisions, is the failure to distinguish clearly between questions which are related to the right assigned, and questions related to the assignment itself, and rather old-fashioned views with regard to the latter. The other, which also affects the writings, is the failure to distinguish between proprietary and contractual issues. These will be enlarged upon in due course.

The situs *of intangible movables*

Unlike a piece of tangible property an intangible does not physically exist, and so, obviously, cannot really be situated anywhere. But since it has a legal existence, the law can and does ascribe a *situs* to an intangible.

Specific rules exist for ascertaining the *situs* of certain intangible interests. Thus, intellectual property rights like patents, copyrights and trade marks have their *situs* where, by the law which governs their creation, they can be effectively transferred, and, if they are assigned, where their holder is. A share or other security issued by a company is, if transferable by an entry in the company's share register and represented by a share certificate, situated where the register is kept. If a register is kept in each of two or more countries, the *situs* of a share is the place where a register is kept in which the shares can be effectively

---

[37] See ch. 15 below.
[38] J. G. Foster, 'Some Defects in the English Conflict of Laws' (1935) 16 *BYIL* 84 at 94.

dealt with, or would usually be dealt with. Thus, in *Standard Chartered Bank Ltd* v. *Inland Revenue Commissioners:*[39]

> Shares in certain South African companies were inscribed in registers kept there and in England. But for the refusal of consent by the Treasury they would have been dealt with in the register kept in South Africa.

It was held that they were situated outside the United Kingdom.[40]

If a security is a bearer security represented by a warrant, its *situs* is where the warrant is kept.

The simple case is that of a contract debt (or of an equitable interest under a trust). Generally, its *situs* is where it is properly recoverable or can be enforced. This is where the debtor resides. If X owes a debt under a contract governed by French law but resides in New York, the applicable law of the debt is French law, but its *situs* is New York.

If the debtor has two or more residences or (in the case of a company) places of business, the *situs* is where payment is expressly or implicitly stipulated for. So, in *Kwok Chi Leung Karl* v. *Estate Duty Commissioners,*[41] it was held that when a Liberian company which did business in Hong Kong gave a promissory note to a Hong Kong resident, the debt was situated in Liberia where it was stipulated to be payable. Where there is no such place, then the debt's *situs* is the place where it would be paid in the ordinary course of business. Thus a debt arising under a bank's documentary letter of credit is situated not where the issuing bank is located but where the monies are payable or drafts can be drawn against the documents.[42]

Assignments of intangible movables

As has been said, some confusion is caused by failure properly to distinguish between questions which depend on the transaction which creates the debt and those which depend on the assignment. Moreover, confusion also arises between the contractual and the proprietary effects of an assignment. Although some questions are contractual, and though these are dealt with fully in books on the English law of contract, the assignment of a right to recover a debt has proprietary effects, as does a contract to sell a car, and the tendency to regard the questions as mostly contractual may be thought to lead to an overemphasis on the

---

[39] [1978] 1 WLR 1160. See also *Macmillan Inc.* v. *Bishopsgate Investment Trust plc* (No. 3) [1996] 1 WLR 387, CA.

[40] For the purpose of Finance Act 1949, s. 28(2).

[41] [1988] 1 WLR 1035 PC. See also *New York Life Insurance Co.* v. *Public Trustee* [1924] 2 Ch. 101 CA; *Jabbour* v. *Custodian of Israeli Absentee Property* [1954] 1 WLR 159.

[42] *Power Curber International Ltd* v. *National Bank of Kuwait* [1981] 1 WLR 1233 CA.

law governing the contract rather than on the *lex situs*. Moreover, the interest in question may arise not out of a contract but by law, and there may be no contract for the assignment. It may be either by way of gift, or it may be involuntary, when it is imposed by law.

It is proposed to deal first with voluntary assignments, and to divide the discussion between issues which are connected with the interest assigned and those which depend on the assignment itself.

Issues connected with the interest assigned. Where the interest arises out of a contract, that is, where it is a simple contract debt, Article 12(2) of the Rome Convention on the Law Applicable to Contractual Obligations, 1980, provides that

The law governing the right to which the assignment relates shall determine its assignability, the relationship between the assignee and the debtor, the conditions under which the assignment can be invoked against the debtor and any question whether the debtor's obligations have been discharged.

Thus, English law would presumably govern the question whether the salary of a Crown employee is assignable (which it is not). Or, if an English contract were to provide that rights under it could not be assigned, a purported assignment would seemingly be ineffective.[43] The English courts have held that the law governing the interest determines whether other types of intangibles are assignable. So whether 'renewable copyright' in a popular song, 'The Very Thought of You', was assignable or not was determined by New York law, where the copyright was taken out, under which law it was assignable, and not by English law, the proper law of the assignment, by which it was not.[44] The assignability of an English cause of action was held, in *Trendtex Trading Corporation v. Crédit Suisse*,[45] to be governed by English law and not by Swiss law, the proper law of the assignment. It has been held that the requirements for an assignment of such a right are a matter of English law.[46]

Other questions in this category appear to be whether notice has to be given to the debtor to permit the assignee to sue in his own name[47] or whether he has to join the assignor as a party.[48] These issues concern the debtor and not only the parties to the assignment.

---

[43] See *Helstan Securities Ltd* v. *Hertfordshire* CC [1978] 3 All ER 262.

[44] *Campbell, Connelly & Co.* v. *Noble* [1963] 1 WLR 252.

[45] [1982] AC 679 HL affirming [1980] 3 WLR 367 CA where the point is more fully discussed.

[46] *Cia Colombiana de Seguros* v. *Pacific Steam Navigation Co.* [1965] 1 QB 101, esp. 128–9.

[47] As is required by English law: Law of Property Act 1925, s. 136.

[48] He must do so by English law if the assignment is equitable. If the assignment is of only part of the debt both the assignor and assignee must join the other if either wishes to sue the debtor.

Presumably, 'the law governing the right' means the law applicable to the contract, if any, out of which the interest arises and not the *lex situs* of the interest. If this is so, the applicable law will be determined by the rules laid down in the Rome Convention if the contract out of which the right arises is one which falls within the Convention. If it is not within the Convention being, for example, a right which arises under an insurance policy which covers a risk situated in a member state of the EC,[49] the applicable law will have to be determined by reference to the rules of common law. It is hoped that the English courts will not keep alive any distinctions which may exist between the Convention rules and those of the common law.

Where the right assigned does not arise out of a contract, but is, for example, an intellectual property right or a cause of action as in *Campbell, Connelly & Co.* v. *Noble*,[50] *Cia Colombiana de Seguros* v. *Pacific Steam Navigation Co.*[51] and *Trendtex Trading Corporation* v. *Crédit Suisse*,[52] it is not really possible to talk of the applicable law. It is submitted that, in the case of these types of rights, the governing law should be the *lex situs*. So, for example, a right of action in an English court, whose assignability is clearly a matter for English law, should be deemed to be situated in England, and whether it is assignable should be governed by English law as its *lex situs*.

Issues connected with the assignment. The assignment of an intangible is a transaction between the assignor and the assignee and does not necessarily concern the debtor at all. The rather elderly and confused English cases on the matter did not constitute a coherent body of law and failed to adopt any conceptual position. Article 12(1) of the Rome Convention now makes it clear that, in so far as the assignment is by way of contract (and if it is by way of gift the choice of law rules for contracts can be applied by way of analogy), contractual issues are decided by the law which governs the contract of assignment and not by that which governs the interest assigned. It provides that

The mutual obligations of assignor and assignee under a voluntary assignment against another person ('the debtor') shall be governed by the law which under this Convention applies to the contract between the assignor and the assignee.[53]

Thus, all that is now needed is to refer the reader to the chapter of this book concerned with contract. So for example, the interpretation, material validity and legality of the contract are determined by its

---

[49] Rome Convention, Art. 1(3).   [50] [1963] 1 WLR 252.
[51] [1965] 1 QB 101.   [52] [1982] AC 679 HL.
[53] Logically, the treatment of such matters as assignability should have preceded a provision concerning the assignment. For the explanation of why Art. 12(1) and (2) are the wrong way round and why Art. 12(1) is so inelegantly drafted see the Official Report, p. 34.

applicable law and its formal validity, generally speaking, by either its applicable law or the law of the place of contracting.[54] One matter which is not dealt with in the Convention is the capacity of a natural person to assign or to receive an assignment of an intangible. The common law must, therefore, be referred to. Unfortunately, the two decisions on this matter are remarkable for their lack of clarity. In an old case, *Lee* v. *Abdy*,[55] an assignment between a South African husband and his wife in South Africa of the benefit of an insurance policy taken out there with an English insurer was held void because of their lack of capacity to give or take the assignment by South African law. The grounds for the decision were that South Africa was the place of their domicile and of contracting.

The question was discussed in the confused and indeterminate case, *Republica de Guatemala* v. *Nunez*,[56] whose *ratio decidendi* is almost, if not quite, impossible to discover.

> In 1906, Cabrera, President of Guatemala, deposited sums of money with Lazards Bank in England. By an assignment executed in 1919 in Guatemala and sent to Lazards, he asked the bank to transfer the sums to his illegitimate son, Nunez. In 1920 he was deposed and in 1921 under duress assigned the sums to the Republic. Nunez's claim under the assignment of 1919 was valid by English law but invalid by Guatemalan law, for two reasons: (i) being a minor he lacked capacity to accept otherwise than through a legal representative, (ii) being unsupported by consideration and not effectuated in notarial form it was formally void. Both Nunez and the Republic claimed the debt and Lazards interpleaded.

English law was both the *lex situs* and the proper law of the debt. Guatemalan law was the *lex loci actus* and almost certainly the proper law of the assignment,[57] and the law of the domicile of the parties. The Republic's claim was dismissed, as was its appeal against this dismissal. Nunez's claim was also dismissed. With respect to capacity, Scrutton and Lawrence LJJ both held that this was governed by the law of the domicile or the *lex loci actus*, but since these were both Guatemalan law there was no need to decide between them. (Formal validity, being now governed by Article 9 of the Rome Convention, need not detain us.) The

---

[54] See pp. 210, 212 and 207–8 above. These rules reflect English common law, for example, *Campbell, Connelly & Co.* v. *Noble* [1963] 1 WLR 252 (interpretation governed by English law as the law governing the assignment) and *Re Anziani* [1930] 1 Ch. 407 (validity of the exercise of a power of appointment seemingly governed by Italian law, the proper law of the instrument of appointment).

[55] (1886) 17 QBD 309.　　[56] [1927] 1 KB 669 CA.

[57] Lawrence LJ seems to have thought that English law governed the assignment. This cannot be right.

only possible *ratio decidendi* of the *Guatemala* case is that upon which two members of the Court of Appeal agreed, that is to say that capacity to take (and presumably to give) an assignment is governed by either the law of the domicile or the *lex loci actus*, but this is not very helpful or accurate. It is submitted that, as was suggested in attempting to state the law which governs capacity to contract generally,[58] this should be the applicable law objectively determined. Since, as we have said, in the *Guatemala* case this was almost certainly Guatemalan law, the assignment was void for that reason.

It is submitted that it is still possible to contend that the proprietary effect of an assignment of an intangible movable should be governed by its *lex situs*. The Rome Convention is only concerned with contractual obligations and, as has been explained in connection with tangible movables, it is quite possible to have a contract of sale governed by one law and its effect on title governed by another. So it could be argued that, assuming an assignment is valid by virtue of Article 12(1) of the Convention, it does not operate so as to confer title to the debt on the assignee if by the *lex situs* it does not do so. The Official Report states that 'property rights . . . are not governed by these provisions', that is, the provisions of the Convention as a whole. The same argument can be advanced even more strongly in the case of interests which do not arise under contracts.[59,60] However, the leading English textbooks take the opposing view.[61] The Dutch Supreme Court held that Article 12(1) applies to the proprietary aspects of an assignment.[62] More recently, an English court has applied Article 12(2) in a case in which, it was argued, both contractual and proprietary questions were in issue. In *Raffeisen Zentral Banke Osterreich A/G* v. *Five Star General Trading LLC*[63]

> C was the assignee of a marine insurance policy made with French insurers but governed by English law. By French law (the *lex situs* of

[58] See pp. 208–10 above.

[59] In *Macmillan Inc.* v. *Bishopsgate Investment Trust plc* (No. 3) [1996] 1 WLR 387 CA, the Court of Appeal held that title to shares which had been fraudulently transferred from the original owner should be determined by the law of New York, where the company in question was incorporated.

[60] For a persuasive argument on these lines see R. M. Goode, *Commercial Law*, 2nd edn (Harmondsworth, Penguin Books, 1995) 1126. See also M. Moshinsky, 'The Assignment of Debts in the Conflict of Laws' (1992) 108 *LQR* 591, 615–16.

[61] A. V. Dicey and J. H. C. Morris, *The Conflict of Laws*, 13th edn (London, Stevens, 2000) 980, 983; G. C. Cheshire and P. M. North, *Private International Law*, 13th edn (London, Butterworths, 1999) 957–8.

[62] *Brandsma qq* v. *Hanse Chemie A/G* (Hoge Raad), 16 May 1997. See H. D. Struycken, 'The Proprietary Aspects of International Assignment of Debts and the Rome Convention, Art. 12' [1998] *LMCLQ* 35, who thinks the decision is wrong.

[63] [2000] 2 All ER (Comm.) 897; affd (2001) *The Times*, 21 February, CA.

the debt) the assignee could not recover since notice of the assignment had not been given to the insurers by or through a French bailiff. By English law, the law governing the contract of insurance, he could recover, since notice had been given in writing which was all that was required.

It was held that Article 12(2) applied, since it deals with the conditions under which the assignment can be invoked against the debtor, and English law governed the matter. If Article 12 did apply, it is submitted that the English judgment is correct in holding that Article 12(2) rather than 12(1) is applicable. It must be emphasised that the court found it difficult to say that the claim related to the proprietary effect of the assignment.

It has been suggested that the *lex situs* should be confined to existing debts and that proprietary aspects of assignment of future debts should be governed by the law of the *assignor's* place of residence or business.[64]

Priorities. Priority between successive valid assignments of the same interest[65] is in English law determined by the rule in *Dearle* v. *Hall*,[66] that the first assignee to give notice to the debtor will obtain priority provided that when he took his assignment he knew of none preceding it. Other systems of law may have different rules, as, for example, giving the first assignee in time priority.

The choice of the law to determine this may appear to lie between five possible candidates: (1) the law of the place of the assignments; (2) their applicable law; (3) the applicable law of the debt; (4) its *lex situs*; and (5) English law as *lex fori*. But (1) and (2) may be discarded at once, for the place and the applicable law of the different assignments may differ and there is no reason to prefer one to another. Moreover, who has priority obviously concerns the debtor, since he has to know to whom he must repay the debt. He is a stranger to the assignments themselves.

Only two English cases concern competing *voluntary* assignments. In the old case of *Le Feuvre* v. *Sullivan*,[67] which is actually a Jersey case, the Privy Council seems to have held that priority between two assignments of a life assurance policy with an English insurance company was determined by English law and not that of Jersey, where the assignor and his wife (an assignee) were domiciled and where the assignments took place and whose law was the *lex fori*.

Much store seems to be set upon this case, and Dr Morris relied on it to support his thesis that the applicable law of the 'debt' governs the

---

[64] See Moshinsky, 'Assignment of Debts', at 609. There is no authority in point.
[65] Some intangibles, such as shares, have their own rules.
[66] (1828) 3 Russ. 1. See also Law of Property Act 1925, s. 137.
[67] (1855) 10 Moo. PC 1.

issue. But it was decided before modern theories of the proper law had evolved. English law was also the *lex situs*, so the decision is compatible with that being the governing law. Apart from being conclusive against the *lex fori*, *Le Feuvre* v. *Sullivan* is not, as a precedent, very important or impressive.

The second case is *Kelly* v. *Selwyn*.[68] This is also inconclusive, and is not, probably, entirely in point.

> An estate of an English testator was being administered in England by English trustees and comprised English securities. The testator's son, domiciled in New York, assigned his interest (i) to his wife by deed in New York. She gave no notice to the trustees since this was not required by New York law; (ii) to C in England, who gave notice to the trustees. Under New York law, the wife had priority, under English law, C.

It was held that English law governed and C won. Warrington J said 'The fund is an English trust fund, the English court was the one which would have administered it, the order in which the parties are to be held entitled to the trust fund must be regulated by the court which is administering that fund.'

Although the *lex situs* and the proper law of the fund were also both English law, these remarks clearly suggest that English law was applied as the *lex fori*, as Scrutton LJ recognised in *Republica de Guatemala* v. *Nunez*.[69]

But, though the *lex fori* governs administration of estates, bankruptcy and priority of maritime liens,[70] in all these cases the court is administering a fund and one law must govern priority; moreover administration is for the *lex fori*, being a matter of procedure. *Kelly* v. *Selwyn* is this type of case, and seems to be of little authority when a single debt is in issue. The question cannot be regarded as procedural, for if A can claim all the debt by virtue of his priority, B will get nothing. *Le Feuvre* v. *Sullivan* at least makes clear that the *lex fori* is not applicable.

The choice, therefore, lies between the *lex situs* and the proper law of the debt. Most often these are the same law, for example, English law is both *lex situs* and proper law of a bank account held at the London branch of a New York bank.[71] But if they are not the same, as where a party to a contract governed by French law is resident in New York, is French law or New York law to govern the matter?[72] The proper law

---

[68] (1905) 2 Ch. 117.   [69] [1927] 1 KB 669.
[70] See *The Halcyon Isle* [1981] AC 221 PC, p. 67 above.
[71] *X A/G* v. *A Bank* [1983] 2 All ER 464.
[72] The Rome Convention, 1980, Art. 12 does not deal expressly with priorities, no doubt because they are not a contractual matter.

finds favour. But the *lex situs* may be preferable for several reasons. (i) The issue is a proprietary one, and if the *lex situs* determines competing claims to tangibles, why not also claims to intangibles? (ii) The *lex situs* determines priority between a voluntary and an involuntary assignment and between competing involuntary assignments,[73] so why not between two voluntary ones? (iii) An assignee will wish to know when he is offered an assignment whether he will obtain priority over others and how to do so. Surely, he should be expected to make enquiry in New York where the debtor is, and not somewhere in France. (iv) The proper law of the debt governs the relation of debtor and assignor; it signifies little to a third party who may, if the contract contains no express choice of law, find it difficult to discover what law is the applicable law. (v) Though a debtor may move (and this is said to be a disadvantage of the *lex situs*) most, such as banks, rarely do. (vi) The matter concerns the debtor; the *situs* is where he is. (vii) The applicable law is hardly appropriate if the competing claims are in respect of interests which do not arise out of contracts, such as rights to trace one's property.[74]

Involuntary assignments. An involuntary assignment is one which occurs without the agreement of the assignor and assignee. An example is the effect of the appointment of a receiver by the secured creditors of a company; this operates as an equitable assignment to those creditors of the debts owed to the company.

(a) Garnishee orders. A garnishee order is a method of execution of a judgment, by attachment of a debt.[75] If A owes a debt to B and C obtains judgment against B, C may get an order from the court addressed to A telling him to pay C instead of B. The making of an order is in the court's discretion, which will only usually be exercised if the debt is situated in England, that is, if A (the debtor) is present here[76] or has submitted to the jurisdiction.[77] B (his creditor, who is, in turn, C's judgment debtor) should also be subject to the jurisdiction, so that he can be bound by the order. If he is not, there is a danger that A will have to pay him again abroad, having paid C in England, should the foreign courts not recognise the garnishee order. But even if B is not within the jurisdiction it suffices that the debt is situated in England, as it will be if A is here. Thus in *Swiss Bank Corporation* v. *Boehmische Industrial Bank*[78]

---

[73] See p. 261 below.
[74] Goode, *Commercial Law*, 1127. He points out that an assignee of a right to trace assets would be unlikely to be aware of the existence, let alone the terms, of the agreement under which the debt arose.
[75] See CPR Sched. 1, RSC Order 49.   [76] *Ibid.*, r. 1(1).
[77] *SCF Finance Co.* v. *Masri* (No. 3) [1987] QB 1028 CA.   [78] [1923] 1 KB 673 CA.

> S sued B, a Czech bank, to judgment. B had submitted to the jurisdiction. S got a garnishee order and attached a debt due to B from two English banks. They asked for it to be set aside, arguing that if they paid S they might be liable to pay the debt again to B in Prague.

It was held that since the debt was situated here, and B had submitted to the jurisdiction, there was no more than a theoretical risk that it would have to pay twice over and the order was made absolute. But where the debtor was a bank's German branch, there appeared to be a real risk that it would have to pay the debt in Germany and an order was refused.[79] In *Zoneheath Associates Ltd* v. *China Tianjin International and Technical Cooperative*[80] the Court refused to allow garnishment of the account of the debtor at a branch in China of a Chinese bank merely because it also had a branch in England, there being evidence that the English garnishee order would not be recognised in China.

However, even if the debt is situated in England a garnishee order may be refused if there is a real risk that the debtor will have to pay again, as in *DST* v. *Shell International*,[81] where the foreign court was exercising over the debtor what the House of Lords regarded as exorbitant jurisdiction and indulging in what was looked upon as judicial extortion.

Only three reported decisions concerned the recognition of foreign garnishee orders.[82] If the English court were to give no effect to such an order, then the debtor might have to pay twice, first to the garnishor abroad, then again to his creditor (the foreign judgment debtor) in England. The crucial question appears to be whether or not the debt is situated in the country where the order was made. In *Rossano* v. *Manufacturers Life Insurance Co.*[83]

> An Egyptian order was served in England by the Egyptian revenue authorities. It was in respect of Egyptian taxes due. The debt, which consisted of monies due under maturing insurance policies, was not situated in Egypt, but in Ontario, at the head office of the insurers. (Though the *situs* of the debt was by Egyptian law Egypt, this was, of course, irrelevant.)

The English court refused to give effect to this order.

---

[79] *Martin* v. *Nadel* [1906] 2 KB 26 CA.   [80] [1994] CLC 348.

[81] *Deutsche Schactbau- und Tiefbohrgesellschaft mbH* v. *Shell International Petroleum Co. Ltd* [1990] 1 AC 295.

[82] Re *Queensland Mercantile Agency Co. Ltd* [1891] 1 Ch. 536 CA; *Rossano* v. *Manufacturers Life Insurance Co.* [1963] 2 QB 352; *Power Curber International Ltd* v. *National Bank of Kuwait* [1981] 1 WLR 1233 CA.

[83] [1963] 2 QB 352, especially at 374–83. Other reasons for this were (i) the debtor was not subject to the jurisdiction of the Egyptian courts; (ii) the claim was for taxes; (iii) the order was an administrative, not a judicial, order.

(b) Priorities. Priority between two or more involuntary assignments of the same debt is governed by the *lex situs* of the debt. In Re *Maudslay*[84]

> (i) A receiver of an English company was appointed by the court in an English action by debenture holders. This operated as an assignment of debts due from French debtors to the company to the debenture-holders. (The *situs* was France.) Then (ii) other English creditors of the company got an attachment order against the same French debtors.

It was held that French law, as the *lex situs* of the debts, determined priority between the debenture-holders and the other creditors.

The same rule applies where voluntary and involuntary assignees are in competition. In Re *Queensland Mercantile Agency Co. Ltd*[85]

> A Queensland company charged its uncalled share capital to an Australian bank, but notice of this was not given to its Scottish share-holders. The company called in this capital and created a debt due from the shareholders. Before it was paid, a Scottish creditor of the company got an order for arrestment (or garnishment) of the amount due from the Scottish shareholder. According to Scots law, but not English or Australian law, the creditor got priority over the bank.

It was held that the effect, including priority, of the arrestment order was to be determined by Scots law as the *lex situs* of the debt.

Immovable property

Jurisdiction
Common law. English cases concerning title to foreign immovable property are few, since it is only in exceptional cases that the English courts have jurisdiction. In *British South Africa Co.* v. *Companhia de Moçambique*[86] the House of Lords held, in an action for trespass to land in Africa, that as a general rule the English courts have no jurisdiction to try any action involving the determination of title to or the right to possession of immovable property situated out of England.

Although it has been held that an action for rent for leased premises in Chile was a personal action in contract and not within the rule,[87] it

---

[84] [1900] 1 Ch. 602.   [85] [1891] 1 Ch. 536 affd [1892] 1 Ch. 219 CA.
[86] [1893] AC 602 HL. The rule is therefore known as the *Moçambique* rule. Under the Civil Jurisdiction Act 1982, enacting the Brussels Convention, Art. 16(1), the courts of the EU country which is the *situs* of an immovable have exclusive jurisdiction over actions concerning it; see pp. 264–6 below. In *Tyburn Productions Ltd* v. *Conan Doyle* [1991] Ch. 75, it was held, relying on *Potter* v. *Broken Hill Pty Co. Ltd* (1906) 3 CLR 479 H. Ct Austr., that the rule also applies to bar actions concerning the validity or infringement of rights arising under foreign copyright or other intellectual property laws.
[87] *St Pierre* v. *South American Stores Ltd* [1936] 1 KB 382 CA.

was doubtful whether an action for negligently causing damage to foreign land or buildings could be entertained by the English courts.[88]

Moreover, whilst admitting that this self-denying rule had little or no justification (since if the English court were to take jurisdiction it would usually apply the *lex situs* to the substantive issue), the House of Lords affirmed it and applied it so as to bar an action in respect of an alleged conspiracy in England to trespass upon an hotel in Cyprus. But this case, *Hesperides Hotels* v. *Aegean Turkish Holidays*,[89] was reversed and any lack of jurisdiction over an action in negligence was removed by the Civil Jurisdiction and Judgments Act 1982, section 30 of which provides that the

jurisdiction of any court . . . to entertain proceedings for trespass to, or any other tort affecting immovable property shall extend to cases in which the property in question is situated outside [England] unless the proceedings are principally concerned with a question of title to, or the right to possession of that property.

The general rule is subject to two exceptions, neither of which can be said to be entirely logical. These are as follows.

(i) Where the English court is exercising jurisdiction and administering an English trust or will which consists in whole or in part of foreign land and question of title thereto arises incidentally.[90] In so far as the general principle rests upon the basis of effectiveness, in that an English court could not make its determination effective in the face of a contrary decision by a local court, this does not apply in such a case as the present, where an English court can act upon the person of the trustee or personal representative.

(ii) Equitable jurisdiction *in personam*. This is a somewhat ill-defined exception based on the principle that the English courts can act *in personam* upon a person within their jurisdiction to enforce a personal obligation incumbent on him when the subject matter is land abroad, by making a decree of specific performance against him and dealing with him as being in contempt of court if he disobeys. The basic requirements are (a) that the defendant is within the jurisdiction;[91] (b)

---

[88] It was held in Canada that the court had no jurisdiction in such a case: *Brereton* v. *Canadian Pacific Railway* (1897) 20 OR 57.

[89] [1979] AC 508 HL. See especially the criticisms by Lord Fraser of Tullybelton at pp. 643–4. The absurdity of the rule being applied in the case is heightened by the House permitting the action to go ahead as regards the contents of the hotel.

[90] See, for example, cases on *renvoi* (pp. 22–3 above), such as Re *Ross* [1930] 1 Ch. 377; Re *Duke of Wellington* [1947] Ch. 501, and see *Nelson* v. *Bridport* (1845) 8 Beav. 527.

[91] Or can be served under CPR Rule 6.20: Re *Liddell's Settlement Trusts* [1936] Ch. 365 CA.

that the subject matter of the action arises out of a contract between the parties, or concerns his fraudulent or other unconscionable conduct, or arises from an equitable or fiduciary relationship; and (c) that the act the defendant is ordered to do must not be illegal or impossible by the *lex situs*.[92] The cases in which the English courts have operated in this way are few; this is understandable since they are effectively doing by a roundabout route what they disclaim a right to do directly. Moreover, it is doubtful whether they would themselves, as the courts of the *situs* of English land, take a similar foreign decree into account.[93] Requirement (b) needs further elaboration.

Contract. This is the clearest case. In *Penn v. Baltimore*,[94] a decree of specific performance was made to enforce a contract to fix the boundaries of Pennsylvania and Maryland. The courts have ordered the creation of a legal or equitable mortgage of foreign land in pursuance of an agreement to do so[95] and in *West (Richard) & Partners (Inverness) Ltd v. Dick*[96] specific performance was ordered of a contract of sale of land in Scotland.

Fraud. In *Cranstown v. Johnston*[97] a creditor, ostensibly in order to recoup money owed to him, refused the debtor's tender of payment and put up the debtor's land in St Cristophe at a public sale but bought it himself at a low price. He was ordered to reconvey the land on payment of the debt, otherwise a gross injustice would be perpetrated and perpetuated.

Any other equity or fiduciary relationship. The difficulty is to determine when this arises in cases other than fraud.[98] It requires a privity of obligation between the parties but it is no easier to determine when this exists. Thus if A agrees to sell foreign land to B, A is under the necessary obligation to B, but if A then sells to C, there is no privity of obligation as between C and B.[99] In the absence of privity, knowledge by C of the preceding transaction between A and B is not sufficient for the exercise of this jurisdiction against C. Thus in *Norris v. Chambres*[100]

---

[92] The equitable jurisdiction is not curtailed only by reason of the fact that by the transaction sought to be enforced no interest subsists under the *lex situs*. See Re *Courtney*, ex parte *Pollard* (1840) Mont. & Ch. 239. It suffices that by that law the defendant can carry out the order of the court. If he cannot, the court can only award, e.g., damages for breach of contract.

[93] In *Duke v. Andler* [1932] SCR 734 the Canadian Supreme Court refused to recognise such a decree of a Californian court.

[94] (1756) 2 Ves. Sen. 444.

[95] Re *Smith* [1916] 2 Ch. 206 (legal mortgage of land in Dominica); Re *Courtney*, ex parte *Pollard* (1840) Mont. & Ch. 239 (equitable mortgage of land in Scotland).

[96] [1969] Ch. 424.   [97] (1796) 3 Ves. 170.

[98] See *Cook Industries v. Galliher* [1979] Ch. 439.

[99] Re *Hawthorne* (1883) 23 Ch. D 743; *Deschamps v. Miller* [1908] 1 Ch. 856.

[100] (1861) 3 De GF & J 583.

The chairman of a company agreed to buy mines in Prussia for the company and paid part of the price to the vendor. He then committed suicide, whereupon the vendor repudiated the agreement and conveyed the mines to trustees for another company, who knew of the payments made by the chairman. The latter's administrators brought an action against the trustees who were in England, claiming a lien on the mine for the amount of the payments. Neither the original company nor the vendor were parties to the action.

It was held that the court had no jurisdiction.

This case is difficult to reconcile with *Mercantile Investment & General Trust Co.* v. *River Plate & Co.*[101] where

An American company issued debentures to the plaintiffs secured by an equitable charge on land in Mexico. It then transferred the land to the defendant company, the transfer deed stating that the defendant was to hold the land subject to the charge, but the registration needed to make this condition binding under Mexican law was not effected.

The court held that it had jurisdiction to enforce the charge since the defendants had expressly agreed to respect the claimant's rights when taking a transfer of the land. It is not easy to distinguish this case from *Norris* v. *Chambres*,[102] since the difference between buying a mine with notice of a previous contract and taking property subject to notice of a charge, even when expressly agreeing to be bound by it, seems somewhat tenuous. The *River Plate* case can better be distinguished as a case in which the defendant was accused of fraud or other unconscionable conduct.[103]

Brussels and Lugano Conventions. Article 16(1) of these Conventions confers exclusive jurisdiction over '[p]roceedings having as their object rights in rem or tenancies of immovable property' to the 'courts of the contracting state in which the property is situated'.

This covers two matters. The first is proceedings having as their object rights *in rem*. These include those which involve title to or possession of immovable property, but probably not an action for damage to it.[104] In *Reichert* v. *Dresdner Bank*[105] the European Court held that an action to set aside a gift of land made in fraud of the donor's creditors does not fall within Article 16(1). In *Lieber* v. *Göbel*[106] the same court held that when, under an agreement between two Germans to settle a

---

[101] [1892] 2 Ch. 303.   [102] (1861) 3 De GF & J 583.
[103] The same is certainly true of *Cook Industries* v. *Galliher* [1979] Ch. 439. Moreover, in that case, the third person acted in collusion with the original party. They were, in fact, co-defendants.
[104] Schlosser Report, paras. 169–72.
[105] [1990] ECR I 27.   [106] [1994] ECR I-2358.

dispute, a flat in France was transferred from one (G) to the other (L) and L lived in it for some years, after which the settlement was declared void *ab initio* and the flat reverted to G's ownership, his claim against L for compensation for use of the flat was based on a right *in personam* and not one *in rem*. Moreover, in *Webb* v. *Webb*,[107] the European Court agreed with the English court that, where a father had bought a flat in France in his son's name and later claimed that the son held the flat on constructive trust for the father and should do what he could to transfer the legal title to the father, the proceedings were *in personam* (as Maitland said of the English trust). Article 16(1) does not confer exclusive jurisdiction over actions which are based on rights *in rem* and not merely those which have rights *in rem* as their purpose.

On the other hand, in *Re Hayward*,[108]

> H and X jointly bought property in Spain, which was registered in the Spanish property register as held by them 'in indivisible halves'. H became bankrupt and his assets vested in his trustee in bankruptcy; he then died intestate. H's widow then purported to transfer H's half-share to X, who became registered on the property register as sole owner. The trustee sought an order from an English court declaring that, as trustee, he was entitled to the half-share and that it formed part of H's estate and an order for rectification of the Spanish register.

Rattee J, having held that the action did not concern bankruptcy,[109] held that the trustee's action had as its object a right *in rem* and that the English courts had no jurisdiction.[110]

The second matter covered by Article 16(1) is tenancies of immovables. The European Court stated that the term 'proceedings having as their object . . . tenancies' should be interpreted restrictively, since its application can result in exclusive jurisdiction being vested in the courts of a state in which neither party is domiciled.[111] Thus, although in *Rösler* v. *Rottwinkel*[112] it held that the courts of the *situs* have exclusive jurisdiction in respect of a short lease of a holiday home, in *Sanders* v.

---

[107] [1994] QB 696 ECJ. P. Rogerson, note [1994] *CLJ* 462. It was applied in *Ashurst* v. *Pollard* [2001] 2 WLR 722 CA.
[108] [1997] Ch. 45.　　[109] See p. 135 above.
[110] He also held that since the action was in respect of an entry in a public register it fell within Art. 16(3) and the English courts had no jurisdiction for that reason also.
[111] *Sanders* v. *Van der Putte* [1977] ECR 2383. Moreover, the Court has recently reiterated the need not to give Art. 16 a wider interpretation than is required by its objectives: *Hacker* v. *Euro Relais GmbH* [1992] ILPr. 515 (package holiday).
[112] [1985] ECR 95; [1980] QB 33; applied in *Dansommer A/S* v. *Andreas Götz*, see [2000] ILPr. 127 ECJ to an action claiming damages for taking poor care of property and damage to accommodation rented for a few weeks' holiday. As to cross-border tenancies, see *Scherrens* v. *Maenhout* [1988] ECR 3791.

Van der Putte[113] it earlier held that they did not do so in respect of a business carried on upon leased premises.

> Two Dutchmen, S and V, agreed that S would take over V's flower business in Germany. The shop was in rented premises. S was to pay the main rent to the landlord and additional rent to V. S later disputed the agreement and V sued him in the Dutch court. S argued that the German courts had exclusive jurisdiction.

The European Court of Justice rejected this argument.

In *Jarrett* v. *Barclays Bank plc*,[114] the Court of Appeal held that a timesharing agreement for a flat in Spain did constitute a tenancy. However, the tenants, who had been induced to buy the timeshare by the seller's misrepresentation, had brought an action under the Consumer Credit Act 1974 against the bank, which had financed the deal. The court held that the timeshare agreements were not the object of the proceedings. The action was founded on the debtor–creditor–supplier agreement and the debtor's personal statutory rights under it.

In *Rösler* v. *Rottwinkel*, the European Court held that Article 16 applied to an action for rent of leased premises. This means that:

> If A and B are both domiciled in England and A lets his holiday home in Italy to B for a month at a certain rent by an agreement under which all disputes are to be decided in England, then if B fails to pay the rent, A must sue him in Italy and cannot sue him in England.

By an amendment in 1989, if A and B are natural persons, both domiciled in England, and the letting is for not more than six months, either may be sued in England. The Lugano Convention permits this if A is a company and they are domiciled in different countries (other than Italy).

Choice of law

Here the *lex situs* holds almost complete sway. There are exceptions to this in the case of succession,[115] but none respecting *inter vivos*. The transfer and extinction of interests in immovables and formal and essential validity of transfers are governed by the *lex situs*.[116] Thus, in *Adams* v. *Clutterbuck*,[117]

> Two domiciled Englishmen entered in England into a lease of land in Scotland. The lease was unsealed and it was argued that the shooting rights were not appurtenant to the land, as was true under English law.

---

[113] [1977] ECR 2383.   [114] [1999] QB 1 CA.   [115] As to which see pp. 275–6 below.
[116] The general principle was stated by Lord Langdale MR in a case concerning the validity of a devise of land in Sicily: *Nelson* v. *Bridport* (1845) 8 Beav. 527.
[117] (1883) 10 QBD 403.

It was held that Scots law determined the issue, and since under that law no seal was required, the rights were appurtenant to the land.

It seems that capacity to convey or to take a conveyance of foreign land is governed by the *lex situs*.

In *Bank of Africa Ltd* v. *Cohen*[118]

> A married woman domiciled in England, by a deed executed here, agreed to make a mortgage to a bank here of her land in South Africa to secure the debts of her husband. Under South African law she had no capacity to do so. She was sued for breach of contract.

Even though it was clear that she knew what she was doing, it was held that she could not be liable since she had no capacity to enter into the agreement.

It may be true that any conveyance she might have executed would have been void. That though this means that Mrs Cohen could not have been compelled to execute the mortgage,[119] that provides no reason why she should not have been liable in damages for breach of contract. The case concerned the contract to convey, and this is governed by its applicable law, which is ascertained in the same way as that applicable to any other contract. In the absence of an express or inferred choice under the Rome Convention on the Law Applicable to Contractual Obligations, 1980, Article 3, that law is the law of the country with which the contract has its closest connection. By Article 4(3) this is discovered by the aid of the presumption that the *lex situs* is the applicable law. However, this is only a presumption and can be rebutted.[120] In *British South Africa Co.* v. *de Beers Consolidated Mines Ltd*,[121] a contract concerned with land in Northern and Southern Rhodesia was held to be governed by English law. Arguably, the contract into which Mrs Cohen entered was governed by English law, under which she had capacity, so should have been bound.

The formal validity of a contract concerning immovable property is governed by the law of the place of contracting, or the applicable law (Rome Convention, Article 9). This is, however, subject to the application of mandatory rules of the *lex situs* concerning forms.[122]

---

[118] [1909] 2 Ch. 129 CA.
[119] Thus distinguishing the case from Re *Courtney* ex parte *Pollard* (1840) Mont. & Ch. 239 and Re *Smith* [1916] 2 Ch. 206.
[120] See p. 201 above.   [121] [1910] 2 Ch. 502 CA.   [122] See p. 208 above.

15   Succession

Characterisation

A distinction must be made between the administration of an estate by the personal representatives and its distribution among those entitled to it. Administration includes those matters not concerned with distribution of the estate and which arise before distribution takes place. It includes collection of debts due by[1] the estate and other matters of management, such as the power of English administrators to postpone sale of estate property,[2] and power to make payments out of the estate for the maintenance and advancement of minor beneficiaries.[3]

Administration of estates

Choice of law

Although succession in the sense of distribution is generally governed by the *lex situs* in the case of immovables and the *lex domicilii* of the deceased in the case of movable property,[4] matters of administration are governed by the law of the country where the personal representative obtained his power to act. Thus, if he obtained probate or letters of administration from an English court, English law will govern, as the *lex fori*.[5]

Jurisdiction

The English courts have jurisdiction to make a grant of representation if the deceased left property in England, and such a grant will normally extend to all his property wherever it is situated. Until 1932 no grant could be made unless there was property here,[6] but now such a grant

---

[1] Re *Kloebe* (1884) 28 Ch. D 175.   [2] Re *Wilks* [1935] Ch. 645.
[3] Re *Kehr* [1952] Ch. 26.   [4] See pp. 270–6 below.
[5] See Re *Wilks* [1935] Ch. 645; Re *Kehr* [1952] Ch. 26.
[6] In b. *Tucker* (1864) 3 Sw. & Tr. 585.

(known as a 'nil grant') may be made although there is not.[7] Normally a grant will not be made in such circumstances but a case in which it will is where the court of the country where the property is situated requires an English grant in respect of the estate of a person of English domicile or British nationality.

Foreign personal representatives

Usually, an English grant of representation is needed by a foreign personal representative for him to be able to make title to and administer property here. A foreign grant does not suffice for him to act here or sue here in his representative capacity, nor can he be made liable in that capacity.[8] The procedure for obtaining an English grant is now laid down in the Non-Contentious Probate Rules, 1954.[9] These give preference among claimants to a person who has been appointed personal representative under the law of the deceased's last domicile, but if there is none, preference is given to the one who is entitled to appointment under that law. Nevertheless, this is not automatic, and the court may appoint anyone it thinks fit, especially if no one can prove his rights under the foreign law[10] or if there are special circumstances.[11] If a foreign personal representative seeks an English grant on the strength of his foreign grant, he will normally ask for an ancillary grant and English courts will follow the decision of that of the deceased's last domicile. But they are not bound to do so, and will not make a grant to anyone, such as a minor[12] or where there is a minority or life interest,[13] to whom a grant could not properly be made under English law.[14]

If an English grant is ancillary to a foreign grant of representation, the English representative will normally be allowed to hand over any surplus assets after the creditors have been paid off to the principal

---

[7] Administration of Justice Act 1932, s. 2(1); repealed by Supreme Court Act 1981, s. 152(4); Sched. 7, but kept alive by Supreme Court Act 1981, s. 25(1).

[8] *Ewing* v. *Orr-Ewing* (1885) 10 App. Cas. 453; *Enohin* v. *Wylie* (1862) 10 HCL 1. He may, however, first get a foreign judgment against a debtor and enforce this in his personal capacity: *Vanquelin* v. *Bouard* (1863) 15 CB (NS) 341. A foreign personal representative who, without an English grant, meddles in the estate here may be made liable as an *executor de son tort: New York Breweries Co. Ltd* v. *Attorney-General* [1899] AC 62 HL.

[9] SI 1954 no. 796, especially rule 29. But see Supreme Court Act 1982, s. 114(2).

[10] In b. *Kaufman* [1952] P 325 CA.   [11] Practice Direction [1953] 1 WLR 1237.

[12] In Re *HRH Duchess of Orleans* (1859) 1 Sw. & Tr. 253.

[13] Non-Contentious Probate Rules 1954, rule 29(d). See note 9 above.

[14] For special conditions where probate is granted of a foreign will see *In the Estate of Goenaga* [1949] P 367; In b. *von Linden* [1896] P 148; In b. *Briesemann* [1894] P 260.

administrator appointed under the law of the last domicile if he is a different person.[15] It may, however, restrain this being done if it would result in benefiting persons who have no claim in English law, such as a creditor whose claim is time-barred[16] or a person who would receive under a will void by English law.[17]

Distribution

Movable property

Once administration is completed, the estate must be distributed to those entitled to it. As a general rule, and by way of exception to the principle that title to property is governed by its *lex situs*, succession to movable property is governed by the law of the last domicile of the deceased.

The question which arose in the exotic case of *Lynch* v. *Provisional Government of Paraguay*[18] was, does this mean the law of the country where the deceased was domiciled at the time of his death, whatever its relevant rules may be at the time it falls to be distributed, or that law as it was at that time? If it means the former, changes in the law will be taken into account; if the latter, they will not. The court decided that it meant the latter.[19]

> Lopez, dictator of Paraguay, died in 1867 after defeat in a war against Argentina, Brazil and Uruguay. He left property, including funds in a London bank, to his Irish mistress, Madam Lynch. She sought probate of the will in England, but this was opposed by the Provisional Government which, after Lopez's death, had enacted a decree purporting to invalidate his will and to confiscate his property to the state.

The Government's claim was rejected; it was held that Lopez's will, being valid by Paraguayan law when made and when he died, was not invalidated by the subsequent change in that law. The decision is not a very strong one since the decree was penal and confiscatory.[20] Also, and more significantly, the property was in England and, as Lord Penzance pointed out, the Provisional Government's claim was not a claim by way of succession; it was really making a claim to the property based

---

[15] Re *Achillopoulos* [1928] Ch. 433.   [16] Re *Lorillard* [1922] 2 Ch. 638.

[17] Re *Manifold* [1962] Ch. 1.

[18] (1871) 2 P & D 268 followed by Re *Aganoor's Trust* (1895) LJ Ch. 521, a case arising out of state succession. See also p. 31 above.

[19] This case was distinguished in *Starkowski* v. *Attorney-General* [1954] AC 155 HL, when a decree of a foreign state which validated an invalid marriage was given effect. See pp. 297–8 below.

[20] For a discussion of such decrees see pp. 363–7 below.

upon the confiscatory decree. But Paraguayan law not being the *lex situs*, such a claim must fail.[21]

The law of the last domicile governs intestacy. It ceases to operate, however, when there is, or remains, no one who, under that law, can succeed on intestacy. If the property is in England, then, as with other ownerless property or *bona vacantia* such as treasure trove and wreck, it will, under English law as the *lex situs*, go to the Crown by prerogative right; the law governing the succession to the estate has ceased to be relevant.[22] This is also true, even if someone exists who could succeed by English law, if English law does not govern the succession. If, under the law of the country of the last domicile, the foreign state, government or treasury would take the deceased's property in default of successors, by way of *bona vacantia* or *jus regale* (what are known as 'caduciary' rights), the Crown will take the property. But if it would be entitled under its law to take by way of succession in the absence of anyone else entitled to succeed it will be entitled to claim the property in England. Thus, in *Re Maldonado*,[23]

> Maldonado died domiciled in Spain by whose law, in default of any other successor, the Spanish state was entitled to all the intestate's property as *ultimus heres* and not by caduciary right.

It was held that the Spanish state was entitled to his property here, to the exclusion of the Crown. The decision has been severely criticised as an extreme example of characterisation by the *lex causae* by paying too much attention to the wording and appearance of that law, rather than to its true object and effect. But the decision seems correct; if we regard the issue as being one of succession to movables, we must apply the rules of succession of the law of the last domicile.

Wills of movables

Capacity to make a will is determined by the law of the domicile of the deceased.[24] The unanswered question here is, when the deceased's domicile changed between his making his will and his death, and either he had capacity at the time of making the will but none when he died or *vice versa*, which law is to govern? The question is not really answered by reference to English domestic law, under which capacity is determined

---

[21] As to this see Diplock J in *Adams* v. *National Bank of Greece and Athens SA* [1958] 2 QB 59.

[22] Re *Barnett's Trusts* [1902] 1 Ch. 847 (Austrian law); Re *Musurus* [1936] 2 All ER 1666 (Turkish law).

[23] [1954] P 223 CA.

[24] In b. *Maraver* (1828) 1 Hagg. Ecc. 498; *Re Fuld* (No. 3) [1968] P 675 at 696.

at the time of making, for that is not concerned with a change of domicile. However, it is submitted that if the deceased lacked capacity when he made the will, it is not validated by a change of domicile, for there is nothing to be validated, but if he had capacity at the time of making, the will should not be invalidated in consequence of a change of domicile.

Capacity to take as a legatee is determined by the law of the testator's last domicile or by that of the legatee's domicile, whichever is the more favourable.[25]

Formal validity of wills requires fuller consideration, since it has been the subject of legislation.

This was governed at common law by the law of the testator's last domicile.[26] In *Bremer* v. *Freeman*[27] a will made in France by an English-woman who had died domiciled in France, which was valid by English but not by French law, was held invalid. The inconveniences of this to British subjects were to some extent alleviated by the passing, four years later, of the Wills Act 1861, known as Lord Kingsdown's Act, but this was rather ineptly and inaptly drafted. However, that Act was itself repealed and replaced by the Wills Act 1963.[28]

The 1963 Act provides a selection of seven[29] laws by which the formal validity of a will can be established: the law of the place where the will was made and the law of the domicile, nationality or habitual residence of the testator, at the time he made the will, or when he died.[30] In the application of these laws, *renvoi* is excluded.[31] Any altera-tion in the relevant law after the date of making of the will applies if it validates the will, but not if it invalidates it.[32] Any requirement of a relevant law that a person can only make a will in a certain form is to be treated as a matter of form and not of capacity.[33] Special rules govern the validity of wills made on board merchant ships.[34]

---

[25] Re *Hellman's Will* (1866) LR 2 Eq. 363; Re *Schnapper* [1936] 1 All ER 322.

[26] *Renvoi* has been resorted to in some cases in order to hold a will valid. See, for example, *Collier* v. *Rivaz* (1841) 2 Curt. 855.

[27] (1857) 10 Moo. PC 306.

[28] This enacted into law the Hague Convention on Forms of Testamentary Dispositions, 1958.

[29] The Act applies to wills of immovables also. In the case of immovables, their *lex situs* may be referred to: Wills Act 1963, s. 2(1)(b).

[30] *Ibid.*, s. 1.

[31] *Ibid.*, s. 6(1). For the definition of 'internal law' where a state comprises several law districts see *ibid.*, s. 6(2).

[32] *Ibid.*, s. 6(3).

[33] *Ibid.*, s. 3. This provision was really directed at a rule of Dutch law requiring a Dutch national to make a will in 'authentic' form wherever he makes it.

[34] *Ibid.*, s. 2(1)(a).

The essential validity of a will is governed by the law of the last domicile. This determines whether and to what extent a will is invalid by reason of a requirement that a certain part of the estate must go to a particular person or class of persons (this is sometimes known as the *legitima portio*).[35] *Renvoi* has been applied in such a situation.[36] In Re *Priest*[37] a bequest to a witness of a will of a testator who died domiciled in England was held to be void, as is the case under English law,[38] since the validity of the bequest was regarded as a matter of essential validity and not of form. The decision has been criticised, but seems correct in principle.

Interpretation or construction of wills of movables is governed by the law intended by the testator. In the absence of an express statement that some other law is to govern, or wording which suggests that that was his intention, this is presumed to be the law of his domicile at the time he made the will.[39] The Wills Act 1963 provides that a change of domicile after that time shall not affect the interpretation of the will.[40] It may be added that, by way of exception to the application of the *lex situs*, the same rule applies to wills of immovable property.[41]

Revocation of wills of movable property

There is little case law on this matter, except where the subsequent marriage of the testator was in issue. In principle the question whether a will has been revoked should be answered by the law of the testator's domicile at the date of revocation. In *Velasco* v. *Coney*[42] (a case on the power of appointment under a will) a testator domiciled in Italy purported to revoke an appointment under a will which had been executed in conformity with Italian and English law in a manner effective by Italian law but not by English law. It was held that the appointment was effectively revoked.

But a will may be revoked in several different ways. Under English law, for example, it may be revoked by (a) an act of revocation, such as burning, tearing up or otherwise destroying it; (b) change of circumstances: by the Wills Act 1837, section 18,[43] it is usually revoked *ipso facto* by a subsequent marriage of the testator;[44] (c) the execution of a later will or codicil. These require separate consideration.

---

[35] An example is the Succession Act 1965 of the Republic of Ireland.
[36] Re *Annesley* [1926] Ch. 692; compare Re *Ross* [1930] 1 Ch. 377.
[37] [1944] Ch. 58.   [38] Wills Act 1837, s. 9.
[39] Re *Cunnington* [1924] 1 Ch. 68; *Bradford* v. *Young* (1885) 29 Ch. D 617.
[40] S. 4.   [41] *Philipson-Stow* v. *IRC* [1961] AC 727 HL.   [42] [1934] P 143.
[43] Substituted by Administration of Justice Act 1982, s. 18 (with stated exceptions).
[44] Unless made after 31 December 1925 in contemplation of marriage: Law of Property Act 1925, s. 177; see now Administration of Justice Act 1982, s. 18.

An act of revocation[45]

The problem here is caused by changes of domicile.[46] It may be argued that since a will only operates from death it is the law of the domicile then which should govern the issue, and determine whether the act revoked the will. But if the domicile was different when the act was done and it was by the law of that domicile an effective revocation, there is no instrument for the law of the domicile at death to operate upon. It has been suggested that the following possible cases and consequences may occur: (1) T domiciled in A makes a will. He acquires a domicile in B and burns the will. He dies. By the law of A this burning does not revoke the will, by the law of B it does. The will is *revoked*. (2) T domiciled in A makes a will and burns it. He acquires a domicile in B and dies there. By the law of A the burning revokes the will, by the law of B it does not. At the death in B there exists no will since it was revoked earlier. (3) T domiciled in A makes a will and burns it. He acquires a domicile in B and dies. Under A law the burning does not revoke the will but by B law it does. At first sight one might say the will has been revoked. But as has been suggested it is probably *not revoked*, since when the act was done it was not in law (A law) a revocation, and when it could have been an act of revocation (by B law) no such act occurred.[47]

Subsequent marriage

Again, problems arise if the testator changes his domicile. By the law of Scotland, for example, a will is not revoked by his subsequent marriage. Once again, different permutations of fact require consideration. (1) H, domiciled in England, makes a will. He acquires a Scots domicile and marries an Englishwoman. At his death the validity of the will is governed by Scots law and it is *not revoked*. (2) The same facts, but H marries before changing his domicile. The will is *revoked* by English law and there is no will upon which Scots law can operate. This was decided in Re *Martin*,[48] a case concerning the will of a Frenchman. The rule is said, however, not to be a rule of testamentary law, but of matrimonial law and governed by the law of the parties' domicile immediately after marriage, by which was meant the husband's domicile at that time.[49] (3) H domiciled in Scotland makes a will and marries. He acquires an English domicile and dies in England. The will is *not revoked* since it

---

[45] See F. A. Mann, 'The Time Element in the Conflict of Laws' (1954) 31 *BYIL* 217 at 231.
[46] If the domicile does not change between the act in question and death *cadit quaestio*.
[47] Mann, 'The Time Element'.   [48] [1900] P 211.
[49] Since a married woman may have her own domicile, presumably if it is her will that is in issue, it is the law of her domicile which governs.

was not revoked by the law of the domicile at the time of the marriage. (4) The same facts, but he acquires a domicile in England before marrying. The will is *revoked*.

Testamentary acts

This question really involves the validity or interpretation of a will or other testamentary act. A later will or codicil may expressly revoke an earlier will, or may impliedly do so, as where its provisions are inconsistent with those of the earlier will.

Express revocation. Whether a will is expressly revoked by a later will or codicil depends on whether the later instrument is valid under the law governing the matter, generally that of the testator's last domicile.[50] If it is valid under the latter law, the earlier will is revoked.[51] By the Wills Act 1963[52] the second instrument is effective to revoke the first if the second complies with any law governing the validity of the first, though not so effective by the law governing its own validity.[53]

Implied revocation. When the second instrument does not expressly revoke the first but their provisions are mutually inconsistent, the question is one of interpretation of the second instrument, so whether it was meant to revoke the first is a question answered by the law of the testator's domicile when he created the second one.[54]

Immovable property

This is governed generally by the *lex situs*. *Renvoi* has been applied in this area.[55] The *lex situs* governs intestate succession.[56] With respect to testate succession, though there is no authority, on principle the *lex situs* should govern capacity to make a will,[57] as it clearly governs capacity to take under a will.[58] Whether a will has been revoked depends on the *lex situs*.[59]

Formal validity of a will is governed by the *lex situs*.[60] This rule is preserved by the Wills Act 1963,[61] which, however, extends to wills of immovables the other choice of law rules laid down therein.[62]

---

[50] See p. 271 above. But other laws may be referred to to determine the formal validity of a will under the Wills Act 1963, considered at p. 272 above.

[51] Re *Manifold* [1962] Ch. 1.   [52] S. 2(1)(c).

[53] If the second will contains a revocation clause but only deals with property in A, but the first dealt also or only with property in B, the first will is not necessarily revoked. Re *Wayland* [1951] 2 All ER 1041.

[54] See p. 273 above for the rules governing interpretation of wills.

[55] See Re *Ross* [1930] 1 Ch. 377; Re *Duke of Wellington* [1947] Ch. 406.

[56] *Duncan* v. *Lawson* (1889) 41 Ch. D 394. See also Re *Collens* [1985] Ch. 505.

[57] See for capacity to contract with respect to, and to convey, foreign land *Bank of Africa Ltd* v. *Cohen* [1902] 2 Ch. 129 CA, p. 267 above.

[58] *Birtwhistle* v. *Vardill* (1839) 7 Cl. & F 895.   [59] Re *Alberti* [1955] 1 WLR 1240.

[60] *Pépin* v. *Bruyère* [1902] 1 Ch. 24.   [61] S. 2(1)(b).   [62] See p. 272 above.

The essential validity of a disposition under a will of immovables is also governed by the *lex situs*.[63] In *Nelson* v. *Bridport*[64] a disposition of lands in Sicily by the second Lord Nelson became invalid under that country's law and was for that reason held to have been invalidated.

Interpretation of a will of immovables is governed, as we have seen, by the law intended by the testator. This is usually taken to be the law of his domicile at the time he makes the will.[65]

---

[63] *Duncan* v. *Lawson* (1889) 41 Ch. D 394.

[64] (1845) 8 Beav. 527. With respect to subsequent changes in the relevant law as respect a will of movables, see *Lynch* v. *Provisional Government of Paraguay* (1871) 2 P & D 268 (pp. 270–1 above).

[65] *Philipson-Stow* v. *IRC* [1961] AC 727 HL, p. 273 above.

16   Matrimonial property relations

In any system of law, including English law, it may be possible for spouses to regulate their rights in their property by agreement or settlement. In other countries, but not in England where for over a century there has been, in the absence of such agreement, complete separation of the husband's and wife's property, matrimonial property regimes may be imposed by law or the law may imply an agreement between the parties. There may, for example, be full community of property, where all property is held jointly in undivided shares, or community of property acquired by the parties during marriage. Other laws may impose 'deferred' community of property, by which each is entitled to a certain share in the other spouse's property, but this share can only be claimed on termination of the marriage by death or divorce.

It is essential, though it may be difficult, to distinguish between rules concerning matrimonial property and those which are rules of succession.[1] 'Deferred' community rules are similar in effect to rules of law which are of the kind which were known to Roman law as *legitima portio*. Matrimonial property rules say in effect that half the husband's property was the wife's from the inception of the marriage, but that the wife cannot take her half until the marriage ends; succession rules say that if the husband leaves all his property to someone other than his widow, she can claim part thereof and his will is invalid to the extent of that part of the estate.[2]

Regimes existing by virtue of a contract or settlement

The governing law

Such contract or settlement is, like any other contract, governed by its proper law. The Rome Convention, 1980, does not apply to 'contractual

---

[1] This is a very difficult question of characterisation, and is exemplified by the Maltese Marriage case, decided by a French court at Algiers: *Anton* v. *Bartolo* (1891) Clunet 1171.

[2] As in the law of the Republic of Ireland: Succession Act 1965. The determination of this question may affect assessment to tax. The problem may not arise, however, if the doctrine of mutability (see pp. 282–4 below) is adopted by the English courts.

obligations relating to . . . rights in property arising out of a matrimonial relationship' (Article 1(2)(b)). In the absence of any express choice, the governing law will usually be the law of the matrimonial domicile, which has been taken to mean the law of the husband's domicile at the time of the marriage. For this (and other) reasons English law was held to be the proper law in *Duke of Marlborough* v. *Attorney-General*.[3]

> H, the ninth Duke, domiciled in England, married W, the daughter of a wealthy New Yorker. The marriage took place here and W's father agreed by a settlement executed in England and in English form to settle immediately $2.5 million and covenanted to leave another $2.5 million by will. There was no English property in the settlement; all the property was, and remained, in American securities. One trustee was American and one English. Terms used in the settlement were meaningless under New York law.

It was held that the proper law was English law and that estate duty was payable.

The parties are free, of course, to select another law expressly or impliedly. The presumption of the law of the matrimonial domicile in the sense explained above may be rebutted if, for example, the property in question already belonged to the wife before the marriage and her domicile before marriage differed from her husband's. In *Re Bankes*,[4]

> Before their marriage, a domiciled Italian man and a domiciled Englishwoman executed in Italy a marriage settlement in English form, whereby she settled funds invested in an English mortgage with a direction that, if realised, they should be reinvested in English investments. The settlement was valid by English law but not by Italian law.

It was held that the settlement was valid because the English elements in it gave reason for not applying the law of the matrimonial domicile. Now that a married woman can have her own domicile[5] this may be a more frequent result in future.

A settlement will be formally valid if it is so either by the law of the place where it is executed (*lex loci actus*) or by its proper law.[6]

Capacity

This is a rather confused and obscure matter. Three cases decided between 1887 and 1900 seem to hold that capacity to conclude a

---

[3] [1945] Ch. 78 CA.
[4] [1902] 2 Ch. 333; Re *Fitzgerald* [1904] 1 Ch. 573 CA.   [5] See p. 47 above.
[6] *Guépratte* v. *Young* (1851) De G & Sm. 217; *Van Grutten* v. *Digby* (1862) 31 Beav. 561 (settlement executed in France by an Englishwoman in respect of property in England was held valid since it conformed with its English proper law, though it was not in the form required by French law). See also Re *Bankes* [1902] 2 Ch. 333.

marriage property contract is governed by the laws of the domiciles of the parties at the time of the marriage, so that if the wife, say, is a minor and incapable of contracting under her personal law, the settlement will not be binding on her. In all the three cases to be mentioned, the wife was a minor. One of these cases seems clearly to support this view of the law, though it is not entirely satisfactory; the other two may not really carry the point.

In Re *Cooke's Trusts*:[7]

> A woman domiciled in England and a minor by English law contracted in France in French form prior to her marriage to Vicomte d'Angeval, a domiciled Frenchman. The contract in fact gave her full power of free disposition of her property. There were children of the marriage. After freeing herself of the Vicomte she was married again to one Briggs to whom she left all her property. She died domiciled in New South Wales. The children attacked the gift to Briggs on the ground that the contract gave them vested rights in her property.

Stirling J held that the gift to Briggs was valid. The contract was void, as the wife had no capacity to enter into it by English law. It is difficult to see, however, what difference this made, since the contract gave the woman freedom of disposition of her property and excluded the French regime of community of goods.

Cooper v. *Cooper*,[8] decided by the House of Lords the following year, is much clearer and to the point.

> A minor woman (W) domiciled in Ireland (whose law was taken to be the same as English law) made a contract in Ireland with a domiciled Scotsman whom she proposed to marry. She purported to relinquish property rights to which she would become entitled by Scots law on his death. The marriage took place in Dublin. The parties lived in Scotland during their marriage. The husband died thirty-eight years after the contract was made and thirty-five years after W attained her majority. She then tried to set the contract aside.

The House held that she could do so. By virtue of Irish law she lacked capacity and the contract (apparently) was void. The difficulty perceived by some learned writers[9] is that under English (or Irish) law such a contract was not void but only voidable by the minor within a reasonable time (thirty-five years seems very unreasonable) after attaining majority. This was held to be the law by the House of Lords itself, but only five years after *Cooper* v. *Cooper*.[10] These writers argue that capacity is

---

[7] (1887) 56 LJ Ch. 637.   [8] (1888) LR 13 App. Cas. 88.
[9] See J. H. C. Morris, *Conflict of Laws*, 5th edn (London, Sweet & Maxwell, 2000) 456–7.
[10] *Edwards* v. *Carter* [1893] AC 360. See Goldberg, 'The Assignment of Property on Marriage' (1970) 19 *ICLQ* 557, who believes that this case turned on estoppel.

governed by the proper law, and that this was Scots law. This would have made the contract void as a donation between husband and wife.[11]

But it is difficult to agree wholeheartedly that the House of Lords took into account Scots law in the light of their expressly stated views. It is quite clear that Lords Halsbury and Watson based their judgments on the application of the rules of Irish law, and Lord Macnaghten said:

> It has been doubted whether the personal competency or incompetency of an individual to contract depends on the law of the place where the contract is made[12] or the law of the place where the contracting party is domiciled . . . [the preponderant view is the domiciliary law]. But where the domicile and the *lex loci contractus* are the same, there is no room for dispute. It is difficult to suppose that Mrs Cooper could confer capacity on herself by contemplating a different country as the place where the contract was to be fulfilled . . . or by contracting in view of an alteration of personal status which would bring with it a change of domicile.[13]

In *Viditz* v. *O'Hagan*,[14] the third case:

> H, domiciled in Austria, married in Switzerland W, domiciled in Ireland and a minor. They made a settlement in English form. Twenty-nine years later, H and W, still domiciled in Austria, purported to enter into an agreement in Austrian form to revoke the settlement.

It was held that it was revoked. Again, it has been argued, since this was long after the wife attained majority, it was too late for her to avoid the settlement under English (Irish) law. Therefore it was Austrian law which, as the proper law, governed. But it may be suggested that what was in issue was capacity to revoke, governed by Austrian law.[15]

Change of domicile

It is now settled that if there is a property settlement or the law of the matrimonial domicile implies one, its terms continue to govern movable property, provided that they include property acquired during the marriage, though the spouses acquire a new domicile elsewhere whose law provides differently. This was held in the famous 'Café Royal' case, *De Nicols* v. *Curlier*.[16]

---

[11] Morris, *Conflict of Laws*, 458. This does find some support in the judgment of Lord Watson in *Cooper* v. *Cooper* and in *Viditz* v. *O'Hagan* [1900] 2 Ch. 87 CA. See also G. C. Cheshire and P. M. North, *Private International Law*, 13th edn (London, Butterworths, 1999) 1027.

[12] Lord Watson seems to have had this in mind.

[13] I.e. to Scotland.   [14] [1900] 2 Ch. 87 CA.

[15] As the law of the domicile at the time of revocation. In that case, the decision is not very relevant.

[16] [1900] AC 21 HL. See also *Tezcan* v. *Tezcan* (1992) 87 DLR (4th) 503.

Two domiciled French persons were married in France without making a marriage contract; they had little or nothing in the way of property to contract about. French law deemed that they had contracted under the system of community of property that each should have a half share in all the property that either of them owned or afterwards acquired. Under French law this was not altered by a change of domicile.[17] They acquired an English domicile and a large fortune was made mainly out of the extremely fashionable Café Royal in London.

It was held that the wife was entitled after her husband's death to a half share in the property despite any attempt by him to dispose of it by will. In the subsequent case of Re *De Nicols* (No. 2)[18] the same conclusion was applied to immovable freehold and leasehold property.

The courts have a statutory power on granting a decree of divorce, nullity or judicial separation to vary settlements, including such settlements as these.[19]

Where there is no contract or settlement

The governing law

Where the parties to a marriage have concluded no agreement with respect to their property, the matrimonial property will be subjected to any regime imposed upon it by the law of the matrimonial domicile. In the absence of special circumstances this is the law of the husband's domicile at the time of the marriage, or so said all the writers except the late Professor Cheshire, who argued that if the parties intended the matrimonial home to be somewhere else, the law of the intended matrimonial home should apply.[20] But this difference of opinion was settled by Roxburgh J in Re *Egerton's Will Trusts*.[21]

A domiciled English soldier married a domiciled Frenchwoman in England. They agreed that they should set up home in France 'as soon as possible', but did not do so until more than two years later. On the husband's death his widow claimed that the estate was to be administered in community as under French law.

---

[17] The conclusion would have been different had French law provided otherwise.

[18] [1900] 2 Ch. 410. It is arguable that this case could have been decided on the ground that the immovable property was purchased with movable property (cash).

[19] Matrimonial Causes Act 1973, s. 24(1)(c).

[20] This is consistent with his view that capacity to marry is governed by that law: see p. 301 below.

[21] [1956] Ch. 593. The learned judge was faced with a conflict of views between the two learned Oxford jurists, the late Drs Cheshire and Morris, to his evident delight: 'Mr Wilberforce [counsel for the widow] has propounded an argument which might almost be said to set the professors by the ears.'

The judge rejected this; the presumption that the husband's personal law at the time of marriage was the law of the matrimonial home was not displaced nor did the agreement to set up home in France imply any agreement that French law should govern.

Roxburgh J agreed that in special circumstances this presumption could be rebutted in favour of the intended matrimonial home, provided, for example, that the parties intended to go to country A and do so at once and then possess little property. (Nowadays since the wife now can have her own domicile after marriage the law of the husband's domicile might well be displaced.) But in the slightly earlier case of *Estate Frankel* v. *The Master*[22] a West German and a Czech who had married in Czechoslovakia, having agreed to go to South Africa, went there four months after the marriage. The South African court held that West German law, under which their property was not held in community, rather than South African law under which it was, applied.[23]

Change of domicile

The effect of a change of the matrimonial domicile in such cases is one of the unanswered questions in the English conflict of laws. There are two competing theories, those of 'immutability' and 'mutability'. According to the first, as the word suggests, the parties' property acquired after the change of domicile is subject to the regime (e.g. of community of property) which was established before the change of domicile. Under the latter doctrine, it is not so subject and rights to property acquired after the change are regulated by the law of the parties' domicile at the date of its acquisition.

Mutability is the favoured doctrine in the United States,[24] and one House of Lords decision of respectable antiquity, *Lashley* v. *Hog*,[25] also appears to support it.

> A Scotsman with an English domicile married a domiciled English-woman (W) and then reacquired a domicile in Scotland. Then W died and after H's death their daughter, Mrs Lashley, brought an action in the Scots court claiming a share in H's movable property.

---

[22] (1950) (1) SA 220.

[23] The result was that estate duty was payable. See also *Sperling* v. *Sperling* (1975) (3) SA 707 where it was held that even though East German law imposed community of property upon the husband and wife who were domiciled there when they married only after they had acquired a domicile in South Africa, it applied *there* since it operated retrospectively to the date of marriage.

[24] American Law Institute, *Restatement of the Conflict of Laws* (2nd), s. 258.

[25] (1804) 4 Paton 582 HL (Scot.).

She argued that it was subjected during H's lifetime *after* the change of domicile to community of property and that she was entitled in right of her mother.[26]

The House of Lords held that she was entitled to the share she claimed.

It is not clear, however, that this case is in point, and the House of Lords, which distinguished it in *De Nicols* v. *Curlier*,[27] did so on two grounds, one which does, and one which does not, support mutability. (a) The ground which does do so is that there was a contract, albeit an implied contract, in *De Nicols* v. *Curlier* but none in *Lashley* v. *Hog*. (b) The ground which does not do so is that Scots law gave W a right of succession to H's property on his death, in which case the right was derived from Scottish succession law, and was not a matrimonial property right at all.[28]

A case which seems to favour immutability is *Chiwell* v. *Carlyon*,[29] which involved immovable property, where it was held that land acquired in England after parties domiciled in South Africa had obtained a domicile in England was held in community of property as South African law required, and which by that law applied to property acquired both before and after a change of domicile. It has been suggested, however, that the case is no support for immutability, since the land represented money which was already owned in community before the change of domicile. It was not, therefore, newly acquired after the change of domicile. The question at issue, it has been said, was as to the intention of H and W in making a joint will. Moreover, Dr Morris[30] apparently regarded *Chiwell* v. *Carlyon* as being a case concerning an implied contract, like Re *de Nicols* (No. 2),[31] but it is submitted that the decision did turn on the question being considered here, and does give support to immutability.

It is argued in favour of immutability that if it did not apply the husband could cheat his wife out of property rights by changing their domicile. But since 1973 this is not necessarily true. In favour of mutability it is argued that in the case of some people such as refugees or displaced persons, it is unfair and unrealistic to submit property they

---

[26] If this case was concerned with matrimonial property law, W's rights were enlarged after the change of domicile.

[27] [1900] AC 21 HL.

[28] To this effect see A. E. Anton, *Private International Law*, 2nd edn (Edinburgh, Green, 1990) 584.

[29] (1897) 145 SC 61 (South Africa).

[30] However, Cheshire and North, who make the suggestions referred to (*Private International Law*, 13th edn, 1024 n. 11), treat the case as being one where no contract or settlement of any kind existed.

[31] [1900] 2 Ch. 410.

acquire in, say, England, to a regime which arose under the law of a country from which they are refugees. Moreover, if this doctrine is adopted the difficult question of characterisation between matrimonial property questions and questions of succession referred to earlier[32] does not arise.

A leading textbook proposes a compromise solution which appears to be satisfactory: that is, the doctrine of 'vested rights', by which the rights of husband and wife in each other's movables are governed by the law of their new domicile if they are acquired after the change of domicile, unless rights in the movables have been acquired already under the law of the earlier domiciles.[33] Thus, if H had a win on the football pools after a change of domicile to England, W would not share in this money. On the other hand, if property is acquired in England after the change of domicile with assets acquired before the change, the property will be regulated by the law of the earlier domicile.[34]

With respect to immovable property, *Chiwell* v. *Carlyon*[35] goes some way towards establishing that immutability applies.

> H and W domiciled in the Cape of Good Hope married there. Their property came under a community system. They made a joint will disposing of their joint property. After they apparently acquired a domicile here, the husband bought land in Cornwall and after both had died, the court was asked to decide whether the land was disposed of by the joint will.

The court remitted to the Supreme Court of the Cape two questions, and asked it to answer them according to South African law. The Supreme Court's replies were (i) if H and W had remained domiciled in the Cape, the land would have fallen into the community system; (2) if they had acquired a domicile in England, the position would be the same. On receiving these answers the court held that the land was effectively disposed of by the will.[36]

On the other hand, the House of Lords has held that the *lex situs* must be taken into account.[37]

---

[32] See p. 277 above.

[33] A. V. Dicey and J. H. C. Morris, *The Conflict of Laws*, 13th edn (London, Stevens, 2000) rule 150.

[34] This is a possible explanation of *Chiwell* v. *Carlyon*.

[35] (1897) 14 SC 61 (South Africa).

[36] The question arose, but because of lack of evidence of foreign (Danish) law, the Privy Council did not answer it, in *Callwood* v. *Callwood* [1960] AC 659.

[37] *Welch* v. *Tennent* [1891] AC 639.

The court has power to make any order it thinks fit when any question arises between husband and wife regarding title to, or possession of, property.[38] This is so if property is in England though the spouses are domiciled elsewhere and their property is subjected to a community regime,[39] and also if property is abroad.[40]

[38] Married Women's Property Act 1882, s. 17.
[39] Re *Bettinson's Question* [1956] Ch. 67.
[40] *Razelos* v. *Razelos* (No. 2) [1970] 1 WLR 392.

17 Trusts

Before 1987, the English conflict of laws contained very little clear authority on the choice of law rules governing trusts, or rules for the recognition of foreign trusts, and what authority existed was almost entirely concerned with trusts created by will and matrimonial property settlements. There was virtually nothing about other settlements created *inter vivos*. This state of affairs was not, perhaps, surprising, since the concept of the trust is virtually unknown, at least in its English sense, outside the common law world. The occasions on which conflicts questions concerned with trusts come before the English courts must be relatively few.[1]

However the Hague Conference on Private International Law, at its Fifteen Session, drew up a Convention on the Law Applicable to Trusts and their Recognition, which was signed in 1986. This Convention was given effect in the law of the United Kingdom by the Recognition of Trusts Act 1987.[2] The title of this Act is rather misleading, since most of the Convention is concerned with laying down choice of law rules to govern trusts and only a few articles are concerned with their recognition. It should be said that the main interest of this country in the conclusion of the Convention was not so much in laying down choice of law rules but in securing the recognition of English trusts by other countries' courts.

Application of the Hague Convention

The Convention applies to trusts created voluntarily and evidenced in writing (Article 3).[3] So purely oral trusts, for example, are not within it.

---

[1] Many of those which have come before the courts concerned taxation. Cases have come before the Australian courts more frequently, but that may be because Australia consists of eight separate legal systems.

[2] S. 1(1). The text of the Convention, with some omissions, is scheduled to the Act. The Official Explanatory Report is by Overbeck in *Actes et Documents de la 15e Session* p. 370. More accessible is D. J. Hayton, 'The Hague Convention on the Law Applicabe to Trusts and on their Recognition' (1987) 36 *ICLQ* 260.

[3] The Convention applies to trusts regardless of the date of their creation: art. 22. However the Recognition of Trusts Act 1987, s. 1(5) provides that this does not affect the law to be applied to anything done or omitted before 1 August 1987.

But they and other kinds of trust are not invalid or incapable of recognition; the principles which were applicable before 1987 will continue to apply to them and it is believed that these principles do not differ materially from those of the Convention. Article 3 also excludes trusts created by judicial decision, though Article 20 allows contracting states to extend the Convention to such trusts and this was done by the Recognition of Trusts Act 1987, section 1(2).[4] Nor does the Convention apply to trusts created by statute, but in respect of both those and oral trusts arising 'under the law of any part of the United Kingdom', section 1(2) applies the Convention rules to them.[5]

Many constructive trusts will be included by the extension of the Convention rules to trusts created by judicial decisions, but not when such a trust has been created by way of remedy.[6]

A trust is defined in Article 2(1) as 'the legal relationship created – *inter vivos* or on death – by a person, the settlor, when assets [movable or immovable] have been placed under the control of a trustee for the benefit of a beneficiary or for a specified purpose'. (The last words include a charitable trust.) A lengthy list of the characteristics of a trust then follows. The trust as known to English law possesses these characteristics.

The Convention does not apply to what Article 4 calls 'preliminary issues' but only to questions concerning the validity and operation of the trust provisions themselves. This means that it does not deal with questions which relate to the validity of the instrument which creates the trust. This is governed by the law which governs the validity of wills or contracts generally.[7] Whether the assets have been validly and effectively transferred to the trustees is likewise a preliminary issue. This matter must therefore be determined by the law which governs the transfer of property, that is, the *lex situs* in most cases.[8]

The Convention applies whatever the governing law of the trust might be and to recognition of all trusts and not only where the governing law is that of a contracting state or the trust is established under such law.[9]

---

[4] This was in order for the United Kingdom to comply with its obligations under the Brussels Convention, 1968, Art. 5(6): see p. 140 above. The rules for recognition of such trusts are the rules governing recognition of foreign judgments generally, that is the Civil Jurisdiction and Judgments Acts 1982 and 1991 (pp. 168–73 above) and at common law (ch. 9 above).

[5] For examples of trusts arising under statutory provisions see Law of Property Act 1925, ss. 35–6, Administration of Estates Act 1925, s. 33, and Mental Health Act 1983, s. 96.

[6] See on this and on resulting trusts Hayton, 'The Hague Convention', at 264.

[7] See pp. 272, 275–6 and 207–8 above.   [8] See pp. 244–51 and 265–7 above.

[9] Recognition of Trusts Act 1987, s. 1(4).

Choice of law rules – the governing law

Articles 6 and 7 of the Hague Convention provide[10] that a trust is governed by the law chosen by the settlor. By Article 6, his choice may be *express* or be *implied* from the terms of the instrument which creates or the writing which evidences the trust, interpreted in the light of the circumstances of the case. No further assistance is given as to how the implication is to be made.[11]

The settlor's freedom of choice may be limited to some extent at least by the application of mandatory rules of English law or by the requirements of English public policy.[12]

Article 7 states that, in the absence of an express or implied choice of law, a trust is governed by the law with which it is most closely connected. This is to be ascertained by reference, in particular, to (a) the place of administration designated by the settlor; (b) the *situs* of the assets; (c) the trustee's place of residence or business; and (d) the objects of the trust and the places where these are to be fulfilled.[13] These considerations are not exclusive of others. It might be possible to refer to the settlor's domicile, as was done in *Iveagh* v. *IRC*.[14]

By Article 17, application of *renvoi* is excluded throughout the Convention.

If the chosen law does not provide for trusts or the category of trusts involved, the choice is ineffective and the trust will be governed by the law with which it is most closely connected.[15]

By Article 8, the system of law thus ascertained governs the trust's validity, construction, effects and administration. It governs, in particular, (a) the appointment, resignation and removal of trustees, capacity to act as a trustee and devolution of the office of trustee, (b) the rights and duties of trustees *inter se*, (c) their right to delegate the discharge of their duties or exercise of their powers, (d) their powers to administer, dispose of, create security interests in or to acquire new trust assets, (e) their powers of investment, (f) restrictions on the duration of the trust and on accumulation of its income, (g) the relationship between trustees and beneficiaries including the former's personal liability to the latter,

---

[10] These provisions are, not surprisingly, more or less the same as the basic rules which determine the applicable law of a contract (pp. 192–210 above) and the previous rules of English law.

[11] Perhaps implications could be drawn from such factors as the *situs* of property and the presumed intention of the settlor that the governing law should be one under which the trust is valid.

[12] Arts. 15, 16 and 18 and Art. 13, pp. 290–1 below.

[13] See *Chellaram* v. *Chellaram* [1985] Ch. 409.

[14] [1954] Ch. 364.   [15] Art. 6.

(h) variation and termination of the trust, (i) distribution of the trust assets, and (j) the trustees' duty to account.[16]

Article 9 states that a severable aspect of a trust, in particular its administration, may be governed by a different law from that governing other aspects.[17] By Article 10, the law which governs the validity of the trust determines whether that law itself or the law governing a severable aspect may be replaced by another law.[18]

Recognition of trusts

Article 11(1) of the Hague Convention provides that 'a trust created in accordance with the law specified in the Convention must be recognised as a trust'. In order to indicate what recognition will consist of and what its effects will be, it is further provided that recognition implies, as a minimum, the following consequences: that the trust property is a separate fund, that a trustee may sue and be sued in his capacity as such and may appear or act in this capacity before a notary or any person acting in an official capacity. Moreover, if the trust's applicable law so provides, recognition implies that the trustee's personal creditors have no recourse against the trust assets, that these form no part of his estate on his insolvency nor part of his or his spouse's matrimonial property or estate on his death and that trust assets may be recovered when he has in breach of trust mingled trust assets with his own property or has alienated them.[19] If the trustee desires to register assets or documents of title to them, he may do so in his capacity as trustee or in such a way that the existence of a trust is disclosed, provided that this is not prohibited by or inconsistent with the law of the state where registration is sought.[20]

The least satisfactory aspect of these provisions is that they concentrate almost entirely on the position of the trustee and deal not very satisfactorily with the beneficiary's position.[21]

The effect of recognition is restricted by the provisions on mandatory rules and public policy.

---

[16] This is all similar to the common law. See, for example, *Augustus* v. *Permanent Trustee Co. (Canberra) Ltd* (1971) 124 CLR 245; *Lindsay* v. *Miller* [1949] VLR 13.

[17] So the construction of the terms of a trust instrument might be governed by a law different from that which governs the trust, such as the law of his domicile, even if the settlor has not expressly stipulated this. Cf. *Philipson-Stow* v. *Inland Revenue Commissioners* [1961] AC 727.

[18] For variation of an English settlement in this way see p. 291 below.

[19] Art. 11(2)(3). However, the rights and obligations of a third party who holds trust assets remain subject to the law determined by the rules of the forum (*ibid.*).

[20] Art. 12. So, for example, a trustee could not register himself as trustee of shares in a British company: Companies Act 1985, s. 360.

[21] See Hayton, 'The Hague Convention'.

Restrictions: mandatory rules; public policy

The application of a law selected by a settlor to govern the trust and the recognition by an English court of a foreign trust may both be restricted by the application of mandatory rules and of English public policy. Several articles of the Hague Convention are relevant.

By Article 13, the English courts need not recognise a trust if its significant elements are, but for the choice of the applicable law, the place of administration and the habitual residence of the trustee, more closely connected with a state or states which do not have the institution of the trust or the category of trust involved. The possibility of non-recognition might inhibit the settlor in exercising his freedom to choose a governing law.

The English courts may continue to apply mandatory rules of English law, described in Article 16 as 'provisions of the law of the forum which must be applied even to international situations'.[22] A possible example is the rule against perpetuities.[23]

Article 15, which is very cumbrously drafted, provides that the Convention 'does not prevent' the English court applying provisions of a law designated by its own conflicts rules in so far as such provisions cannot be derogated from by voluntary act, relating to certain matters 'in particular'. These are: (a) the protection of minors and incapable persons; (b) the personal and proprietary effect of marriage; (c) succession rights, especially indefeasible shares of spouses and relatives; (d) transfer of title to property and security interests therein; (e) protection of creditors on an insolvency; and (f) protection of third parties acting in good faith. If recognition of a trust is thereby prevented, the court must try to give effect to the objects of the trust by other means.[24]

The mandatory rules referred to here are not English mandatory rules but those of a system of law other than the one which governs the trust, whose application is determined by the rules of the English conflict of laws. Moreover, the English conflict rules are rules other than those contained in the Convention; that is to say, as the list set out in the last paragraph demonstrates, the rules are those which apply to issues which are not concerned with the validity of a trust itself, or its recognition.

---

[22] Compare the definition of mandatory rules in the Rome Convention, 1980, Art. 7(2), p. 213 above.

[23] Art. 16(2), which would allow a court to apply mandatory rules of the law of a closely connected third state, is not enacted. The United Kingdom, as permitted, (Art. 16(3)) made a reservation with respect to it.

[24] By the 1987 Act, s. 1(3) the English court must apply any such rules.

Article 18 provides that the Convention's provisions may be disregarded if their application would be 'manifestly incompatible' with English public policy.

Variation of trusts

The Variation of Trusts Act 1958 gives the English courts the power to vary the terms of a trust in certain circumstances.[25] This power extends to trusts of both movable and immovable property.

In the case of an *English* settlement, section 1(1) allows the court to approve an arrangement revoking the settlement and substituting for it a foreign settlement and foreign trustees. In Re *Seale's Marriage Settlement*,[26] a settlement governed by Quebec law was substituted. But the court will not approve a substitution if it does not consider the proposed arrangement to be a proper one. Thus, in Re *Weston's Settlements*,[27] the settlor and two of his sons who were beneficiaries emigrated to Jersey three months before the application was made to the court. The parties' uncontradicted evidence was that they intended to remain there permanently, but the Court of Appeal did not believe this. It was convinced that, even though a substitution of a settlement governed by Jersey law would benefit the beneficiaries, the object of the arrangement was solely to avoid taxation, and refused to approve it. On the other hand, in Re *Windeatt's Will Trusts*,[28] the substitution of a Jersey settlement was approved. The life tenant had lived in Jersey for nineteen years and was probably domiciled there and her children were born there.

As to a *foreign* settlement, in Re *Ker's Settlement*,[29] Ungoed Thomas J held that the court had power under the Act to approve a variation of a trust governed by a foreign law. In that case he approved an arrangement which involved a Northern Irish trust. He said that section 2(2), which states that the Act does not extend to Scotland or Northern Ireland, means only that the courts of those countries have no jurisdiction to approve a variation. In Re *Paget's Settlement*,[30] Cross J accepted this, but, having assumed that the settlement was governed by New York law, warned that where there are substantial foreign elements involved, the court must consider carefully whether it is proper to exercise its jurisdiction.

This jurisdiction or power to vary the terms of a foreign trust seems to be unaffected by the Recognition of Trusts Act, but in exercising

---

[25] See also the Hague Convention, 1986, Art. 10, p. 289 above.
[26] [1969] Ch. 574.   [27] [1969] 1 Ch. 223 CA.
[28] [1969] 1 WLR 692.   [29] [1963] Ch. 553.   [30] [1965] 1 WLR 1046.

that jurisdiction, Cross J's caution should be heeded by the court. Moreover, it should only exercise that jurisdiction and vary its terms if the law governing the trust allows it to be varied, since the Hague Convention, by Article 8(2)(h), provides that the variation of a trust is a matter which is regulated by that law.

By the Matrimonial Causes Act 1973, section 24, the court can, on granting a decree of divorce, nullity or judicial separation, vary any ante- or post-nuptial settlement made between the parties to the marriage. This power is exercisable though the settlement is governed by a foreign law and the property is abroad.[31] But any order will only be made in such a case if it would be effective in the foreign country.[32] It seems that the ability of the court to exercise this power is not restricted by the Recognition of Trusts Act 1987. Article 15 of the Hague Convention allows the court to apply its conflict rules (here, leading to the application of English law) to 'the personal and proprietary effects of marriage'.

---

[31] *Nunneley* v. *Nunneley* (1890) 15 PD 186; *Forsyth* v. *Forsyth* [1891] P 363.
[32] *Tallack* v. *Tallack* [1927] P 211; see also *Goff* v. *Goff* [1934] P 107.

Part V

Family law

18   Marriage

The choice of law rules which govern the validity of a marriage, and which, therefore, also govern nullity of marriage, depend on the particular issue which is involved. The old rule of English conflict of laws was to the effect that, whatever the ground of invalidity that was alleged, the conclusion of a marriage was a matter for the law of the place where it was celebrated. But since about 1860 this rule has, generally speaking, been confined to questions of formalities of marriage. There now exist several different choice of law rules for marriage, some of which are disputed or difficult to state with full confidence.

Basically, there are four requirements of a valid marriage: (i) that the requisite formalities are complied with; (ii) that the parties have legal capacity to marry each other; (iii) that they freely and knowingly consent to do so; and (iv) that the marriage is consummated.

These will be discussed in turn; the discussion will be followed by an account of the law relating to polygamous marriages.

Formalities of marriage

Formal requirements of a marriage include such matters as whether a religious or a civil ceremony is necessary, whether banns have to be called or notices published and the form of words which must be used. No rule of the conflict of laws is clearer or longer established than the one which lays down that these matters are regulated by the *lex loci celebrationis*, the law of the place where the ceremony takes place, which reflects the rule *locus regit actum*. Thus a ceremony which takes place in France produces a formally valid marriage if it complies with the formal requirements of French law; it does not do so if it complies with the personal law of the parties but not with French law. This was made clear as early as 1752,[1] and the rule was reaffirmed by the Privy Council

---

[1] *Scrimshire* v. *Scrimshire* (1752) 2 Hagg. Con. 395; also *Dalrymple* v. *Dalrymple* (1811) 2 Hagg. Con. 54.

in *Berthiaume* v. *Dastous*,[2] where a marriage performed by a French curé of two French Canadians in France in the mistaken belief that it had been preceded by a civil ceremony as required by French law was held invalid.

In *Taczanowska* v. *Taczanowski*[3] the Court of Appeal was prepared to apply *renvoi* and to hold that, if a marriage was not celebrated in compliance with the *lex loci celebrationis*, but that law would hold the marriage valid if it accorded with the parties' personal law, it would be valid here.

The *lex loci celebrationis* also determines whether a marriage can be celebrated by proxy. In *Apt* v. *Apt*[4] a ceremony performed in Argentina between a man who was there and a woman in England who was represented there was recognised since representation by proxy was permitted by Argentine, though not by English, law.

Indeed, a marriage may be recognised even though the *lex loci celebrationis* does not require the presence of either party personally or by proxy, if the entertaining case, *McCabe* v. *McCabe*,[5] is correct.

> H was domiciled in the Irish Republic, W in Ghana. They met in London. W became pregnant by H, had an abortion and became pregnant by him again. They lived together in England. W's great uncle Mark, who was visiting England from Ghana, suggested H and W should marry according to the custom of the Akan, a people in Ghana. Over lunch they agreed. Uncle Mark told H that he had to provide a bottle of schnapps and £100 as 'aseda' (earnest). H gave him £100 and a bottle of gin (which would do instead of schnapps), and Uncle Mark took these back to Ghana, where a ceremony was held at W's father's house. H and W were neither present nor represented (nor was Uncle Mark, through illness). The ceremony was performed by W's Uncle Nelson. Eight members of W's family were there. W's father and the rest of the gathering assented to the marriage. They opened the bottle of gin and all drank some of it from a glass. They changed the £100 into Ghanaian cedis and shared some of them out; the rest of the cedis (though not the gin) were taken and given to other members of the family.

W now petitioned for a divorce and H argued that there had never been a valid marriage. The Court of Appeal held that the marriage was valid since it was valid by Akan law, which did not require presence personally or by proxy of the parties and which required H's consent as

---

[2] [1930] AC 79.
[3] [1957] P 301. But, though it would have been recognised by Italian law (the *lex loci*) if it was valid by the personal law (Polish), it was not in fact valid by the latter law. The marriage was upheld on another ground: see p. 300 below.
[4] [1948] P 83, followed in *Ponticelli* v. *Ponticelli* [1958] P 204 (an Italian ceremony).
[5] [1994] 1 FLR 410 CA.

given by him presenting the money and the gin. The difficulty with this conclusion is that the court's judgment is entirely concerned with its assessment of the (very distinguished) expert evidence of Akan law as the *lex loci celebrationis*. It did not consider whether the *locus celebrationis* was Ghana (under whose law, one expert said, no ceremony was necessary at all) or whether it was England, where H and W consented to marry. This, the relevant point of private international law, does not seem to have been argued.

By what is generally regarded as an unsatisfactory exercise in classification, the English courts[6] have treated the question of whether parental consent is required as a matter of formal validity and not of capacity to marry. In *Simonin* v. *Mallac*[7] it was held that a provision of French law which required a person under a certain age to make an 'acte respectueux' and ask his parents' permission to marry, though not complied with, did not render void a ceremony celebrated in England. In fact it probably did not do so under French law either. But in *Ogden* v. *Ogden*,[8] where again the ceremony had taken place here, a different provision of French law requiring parental consent and rendering the child incapable of marrying without it was regarded in the same light and was held to go only to formalities. Thus it was ignored and the marriage held valid. It should be emphasised that the English courts take the view that the English requirement of parental consent to the marriage of a person under eighteen is a matter of form, so that a marriage abroad without such consent is valid if the *lex loci celebrationis* does not require it to be obtained.[9]

With respect to retrospective changes in the law of the country of celebration subsequent to the date of the marriage, the House of Lords held in *Starkowski* v. *Attorney-General*[10] that a marriage which was formally invalid by the local law when it was celebrated was validated by the operation of a law enacted in the foreign country in question at a later date.

> H and W, both domiciled in Poland, married in Austria in May 1945 in a religious ceremony. At that time Austrian law required a civil ceremony. In June 1945 the Provisional Government of Austria

---

[6] Likewise the Scottish and British Columbia courts, *Bliersbach* v. *McEwen* 1959 SC 43; *Reed* v. *Reed* (1969) 6 DLR (3d) 617.

[7] (1860) 2 Sw. & Tr. 67.

[8] [1908] P 46; *Lodge* v. *Lodge* (1963) 107 Sol. Jo. 437. These decisions were concerned with rules of a particular legal system. Such rules of other laws might be regarded differently.

[9] *Compton* v. *Bearcroft* (1769) 2 Hagg. Con. 444n.; *Middleton* v. *Janverin* (1802) 2 Hagg. Con. 437.

[10] [1954] AC 155.

enacted a law which enabled religious ceremonies to be retrospectively validated if they were publicly registered.[11] A child (Barbara) was born of the union. H and W then came to England and acquired a domicile here. W then bore a child (Christopher) by S, another Pole. Then, unknown to W, who had separated from H, H registered the Austrian ceremony in Austria. W then went through a marriage ceremony with S at the Croydon register office. Christopher asked for a declaration that he had been legitimated by the subsequent marriage of his parents.

This was refused; the English marriage of W to S was void since the Austrian marriage had been validated by its registration.

The case exemplifies the general problem of the 'time factor' in the conflict of laws.[12] Three variations of the facts have been propounded, though the House declined to give any decision on them. (1) If the Croydon ceremony had preceded the registration, recognition of the validation would have entailed invalidation a valid English marriage. It is hoped that the 'validation' would not have been recognised.[13] (2) Suppose the Austrian marriage had originally been valid but was later invalidated by an Austrian law.[14] (3) Would the decision have been the same if the Austrian marriage had been annulled by an English court before it was registered? This would have meant that an English court would disregard the effect of an English judgment. There is, as yet, no answer to these questions.

The actual decision has come in for commendation on the ground that it upheld a marriage. But it should be observed that the question of the validity of the marriage arose incidentally in the course of deciding the real question, which was whether Christopher was legitimated. He can hardly have been happy with the result,[15] though no doubt Barbara was, since the decision meant that she was not illegitimate in the eyes of English law.

---

[11] The law which required a civil ceremony was enacted by the Germans after their incorporation of Austria into Germany in 1938. This was repealed in June 1945 and purely religious marriages were permitted once more.

[12] See pp. 29–32 above.

[13] Compare the more or less analogous British Columbia case of *Ambrose* v. *Ambrose* (1961) 25 DLR (2d) 1.

[14] Compare *Lynch* v. *Provisional Government of Paraguay* (1871) 2 P & D 268, where the English court refused to hold that a will was invalidated by such an invalidating law. See further as to this matter pp. 270–1 above.

[15] He was, of course, only a baby at the time. His illegitimacy could not be cured as the law then stood by praying in aid the doctrine of putative marriage since this was only introduced into English law by the Legitimacy Act 1959 (now Legitimacy Act 1976, s. 1(1)); see p. 351 below. Nor could it have been altered by W divorcing H and remarrying S since Christopher was an *adulterinus* who could not thus be legitimated under the Legitimacy Act 1926. This was not altered until the Legitimacy Act 1959.

Exceptions to the lex loci celebrationis

There are several exceptions to the general rule, two of them statutory.

The Foreign Marriage Acts 1892–1947

These (as amended slightly by the Foreign Marriage (Amendment) Act 1988) provide that a marriage celebrated thereunder in a foreign country or place before a marriage officer (generally a British consul) between two parties of whom at least one is a British citizen is valid under English law though invalid under local law.[16]

Military marriages under the Foreign Marriage Act 1892, section 22[17]

This renders valid marriages celebrated by chaplains of HM forces between parties, one of whom must be a member of HM forces (though not necessarily a British citizen). It supersedes the common law rule that a marriage 'within British lines' according to English common law is valid.[18] It does not apply to a marriage of a member of foreign armed forces not operating directly under British command.[19]

Common law marriages

It has been held that where there is no available legal form of ceremony in the foreign place of celebration, or if the local form is unsuitable, a marriage which complies with the requirements of English common law as it existed before 1753 is valid in England. This has had some surprising consequences. Thus a marriage between Canadians in a remote part of China in a ceremony performed by a Church of Scotland clergyman was held valid by English common law,[20] as was a marriage in eclectic form between a Jew and a non-Christian Chinese woman presided over by an elderly Chinese gentleman in Singapore.[21]

In the nineteenth-century decision in *R* v. *Millis*[22] the House of Lords held, controversially, that the common law required not only that the parties should agree in each other's presence (*per verba de praesenti*) to take each other as man and wife, but that their vows should be exchanged

---

[16] The local authorities must not object. For detailed regulations see Foreign Marriage Order-in-Council 1970 (SI 1970 no. 1539 as amended by SI 1990 no. 598).
[17] As substituted by the Foreign Marriage Act 1947. Orders made thereunder are SI 1964 no. 1000; SI 1961 no. 131; SI 1990 no. 2592.
[18] *Ruding* v. *Smith* (1821) 2 Hagg. Con. 371.
[19] *Taczanowska* v. *Taczanowski* [1957] P 301 CA.
[20] *Wolfenden* v. *Wolfenden* [1946] P 61.
[21] *Isaac Penhas* v. *Tan Soo Eng* [1953] AC 304 PC.
[22] (1843–4) 10 Cl. & F 534 (marriage in Ireland by a Presbyterian minister).

before an episcopally ordained clergyman.[23] This may have been historically incorrect, and the decision was on an equality of votes.[24] It has subsequently been held that such a clergyman's presence was not necessary if there was none available[25] or if it should be inappropriate to require it.[26]

By a further benevolent extension of this doctrine, even more surprising decisions were arrived at by the English courts following World War II. In *Taczanowska* v. *Taczanowski*[27] the doctrine was employed so as to render valid in England a marriage in Italy, then under belligerent occupation by Allied armed forces, of two Poles, when the ceremony was invalid by Italian (and by Polish) law. For a marriage to be valid in such a case, one at least of the parties must be a member of the armed forces of a belligerent occupant and, possibly, those forces must be associated with, though not necessarily under the command of, a British army occupying the country in question. Thus, in *Preston* v. *Preston*,[28] the Court of Appeal upheld a marriage which was celebrated in part of a camp at Nordheim in Germany which was occupied by military personnel, the husband being a member of the Polish armed forces which were associated with the Allied belligerent occupants.

The reason that such marriages are valid, in spite of their not being valid by the law of the place of celebration, is said to be that the parties thereto have not intended to submit themselves to the local law. If, however, one party is a national of the country in question, this reason does not apply and in *Lazarewicz* v. *Lazarewicz*[29] where a marriage was celebrated in Italy between a member of the Polish armed forces and an Italian woman, in contravention of Italian requirements, the marriage was held invalid.

Marriages on board merchant ships

It appears that the validity of a marriage celebrated on board a merchant ship would be determined by the law of the ship's flag, if the ship

---

[23] A Roman Catholic priest would, of course, be qualified: *Limerick* v. *Limerick* (1863) 4 Sw. & Tr. 252.

[24] It was a criminal prosecution for bigamy; the case was decided in favour of the defendant who could not be guilty if the ceremony was invalid. The decision was followed by the House of Lords in *Beamish* v. *Beamish* (1861) 9 HL Cas. 274.

[25] *Catterall* v. *Catterall* (1847) 1 Rob. Ecc. 580; also *Wolfenden* v. *Wolfenden* [1946] P 61.

[26] *Isaac Penhas* v. *Tan Soo Eng* [1953] AC 304 PC.   [27] [1957] P 301 CA.

[28] [1965] P 411 CA. The court disapproved the application of *Taczanowska* v. *Taczanowski* to render valid a ceremony between two persons in the displaced (non-military) persons' part of the same camp in *Kochanski* v. *Kochanska* [1958] P 147.

[29] [1962] P 171. This decision was approved in *Preston* v. *Preston* [1965] P 411 CA. The principle clearly does not apply to marriages of civilians in a country by necessity (for example deportation) and not of choice: compare *Starkowski* v. *Attorney-General* [1954] AC 155 HL, p. 297 above.

is then on the high seas. This would be the English common law, if the ship's port of registry was in England, provided it was impracticable to wait until the ship reached port. There is no English authority on the point. A marriage on board a British warship would be valid if it was celebrated in accordance with the Foreign Marriage Acts 1892–1947.[30]

Legal capacity to marry

Although the parties have gone through a ceremony which is formally valid by the *lex loci celebrationis* and so valid in England, the marriage may nevertheless be void if the man and woman do not have legal capacity to marry each other. For example, one or both may be under age, or be already married to a third person, or they may be within the prohibited degrees of relationship (consanguinity). As we have seen, lack of parental consent has been regarded by the English courts as a matter of form and not of capacity,[31] but if a requirement of parental consent under some foreign law were to be classified as being a rule affecting capacity, non-compliance with it might also render a marriage void.[32]

What law governs capacity to marry has been the subject of considerable academic argument and, recently, of differences of judicial opinion. Two rival choice of law rules have been advocated: (1) the dual or antenuptial domicile test, according to which if both parties have capacity to marry each other by the laws of their domiciles at the time of the ceremony, the marriage is valid, but (generally speaking) it is invalid if by either or both of these laws they have no such capacity;[33] (2) the law of the intended matrimonial home, that is, the country where, at the time of the ceremony, the parties intend to, and after the ceremony do, set up home. This was advocated by the late Professor Cheshire.

These two tests are in fact consistent with the facts and to some extent with the decisions in several of the decided cases, but it is now generally thought that the dual domicile test is the correct one, and some decisions proceed upon the basis that it is. However, some judges have apparently preferred the intended matrimonial house test.[34] In a

---

[30] See p. 299 above. A marriage on a British warship of two British subjects domiciled in England celebrated by a chaplain without banns or licence was upheld at common law in *Culling* v. *Culling* [1896] P 116.

[31] See p. 297 above.

[32] This possibility was mentioned in *Ogden* v. *Odgen* [1908] P 46 CA.

[33] This test has been advocated by most writers in modern times; see A. V. Dicey and J. H. C. Morris, *Conflict of Laws*, 13th edn (London, Stevens, 2000) rule 68.

[34] *Radwan* v. *Radwan* (no. 2) [1973] Fam. 35, where, however, Cumming-Bruce J expressly confined his view to capacity to contract a polygamous marriage, as to which see pp. 304–5 below; *Perrini* v. *Perrini* [1979] Fam. 84.

decision at first instance a test of 'the law of the country with which the marriage has a real and substantial connection' has been adopted, apparently in place of the intended matrimonial home doctrine, although these both indicated the application of English law.[35]

However, two further points must be emphasised. (i) Exceptions must be made if the dual domicile test is to be preferred; the whole question is a little more complicated than at first sight appears. (ii) In many, though not of course all, cases the validity of a marriage has only been indirectly in issue, and the real question has been the legitimacy of a child and, or, rights of succession.

The dual domicile test

Before about 1860, the *lex loci celebrationis* was regarded as governing all questions affecting the validity of the marriage, but in two cases decided at that time, the courts clearly distinguished between formal validity, which is governed by the *lex loci*, and essential validity, governed by the parties' personal law.

In *Mette* v. *Mette*,[36] which concerned the revocation of a will by marriage, a German who was domiciled in England married his deceased wife's sister, who was domiciled in Germany, in a ceremony there. Though the marriage was valid by German law it was invalid under English law, whereby the man had no capacity to marry his deceased wife's sister. The marriage was held void. In *Brook* v. *Brook*,[37] which concerned legitimacy and succession, a man married his deceased wife's sister in Denmark, under whose law the marriage was valid. Both were domiciled in England; the House of Lords held that the marriage was void.

These decisions appear to have been based on the fact that one or both of parties was domiciled in England under whose law the incapacity existed, but it must be admitted that the facts and indeed the wording of the judgments are consistent with the intended matrimonial home test.[38]

The decisions in the following cases seem to be inconsistent with the intended matrimonial home test. In the first, *Sottomayor* v. *de Barros* (No. 1),[39] the facts (so it then appeared) were that:

---

[35] *Lawrence* v. *Lawrence*. The Court of Appeal decided the case on different grounds: [1985] Fam. 106, but Purchas LJ was critical of this test.

[36] (1859) 1 Sw. & Tr. 416.

[37] (1861) 9 HL Cas. 193; Re *de Wilton* [1900] 2 Ch. 481.

[38] The House of Lords applied the dual domicile test in *Shaw* v. *Gould* (1868) LR 3 HL 55.

[39] (1877) 3 PD 1 CA.

> A marriage took place in England between two Portuguese cousins domiciled in Portugal. Under Portuguese law they could not marry without Papal consent, which they did not have.

The Court of Appeal held that the marriage was void since their capacity was governed by the law of the antenuptial domicile and not by that of the place of celebration, by which they had capacity to marry.

This case was then re-argued on the footing that the man was already domiciled in England; the decision in the later proceedings will be discussed later.[40]

In Re *Paine*,[41] which involved a question of inheritance, where the facts are consistent with either test, the clearly preferred ground of decision was the antenuptial domicile test. In that case a woman domiciled in England married a man domiciled in Germany. The marriage was valid by German law, but they were within the prohibited degrees of relationship by English law. The marriage was held void.

The dual domicile test is the only one compatible with the clear decision of Sir Jocelyn Simon P in *Padolecchia* v. *Padolecchia*.[42]

> H, domiciled in Italy, married there in 1943 and later obtained a divorce in Mexico. This was not recognised in Italy. He went to live in Denmark and on a one-day visit to England succeeded in 'marrying' W, domiciled in Denmark; they both returned to Denmark. H petitioned for a decree of nullity in respect of this marriage, alleging that at the time he was still married to his first wife. Danish law was unclear as to whether he had capacity.

The court held that since by the law of his Italian domicile the husband lacked capacity, the English ceremony was bigamous and void. The learned President expressly applied the dual domicile test.

In *Pugh* v. *Pugh*,[43] which concerned lack of age, it was held that an English domiciled adult army officer lacked capacity to marry a Hungarian domiciled girl in Austria (she was only fifteen but by Hungarian law could marry) since by the law of his domicile he could neither (i) have married had he been under sixteen nor (ii) though himself over sixteen, marry someone who had not achieved that age.

The dual domicile test seems the only one consistent with the Marriage (Enabling) Act 1960, which permits certain previously forbidden

---

[40] See p. 306 below.   [41] [1940] Ch. 46.
[42] [1968] P 314 and that of the Divisional Court in the *Brentwood Marriage* case (*R* v. *Brentwood Superintendent Registrar of Marriages*, ex parte *Arias* [1968] 2 QB 956) discussed at pp. 28–9 above and p. 307 below.
[43] [1951] P 482. The court pointed out the public policy considerations behind the rule which was in question.

marriages, whether these take place within or out of Great Britain.[44] This provision does not, however, validate a marriage, if either party to it is at the time of the marriage domiciled in a country outside Great Britain and under the law of that country there cannot be a valid marriage between the parties.[45]

Of course, if both parties are domiciled abroad and marry abroad and have capacity to marry each other by their personal laws, their marriage will, within certain possible limits,[46] be regarded as valid by our courts.[47]

The intended matrimonial home test

As has been said already, this test has been preferred in some fairly recent cases.[48] In *Perrini* v. *Perrini*[49] Sir George Baker P evidently preferred it. His reasoning on several points is obscure and the decision could be supported by orthodox arguments.[50]

> An American lady from New Jersey went to Italy and married a domiciled Italian. The marriage was not consummated and she returned to New Jersey where she obtained a decree of nullity. This was not recognised in Italy. The husband came to England and married an Englishwoman. The latter petitioned for a nullity decree on the ground that the man was still married to the American lady, so his marriage to herself was bigamous.

It was held, first, that the court must recognise the New Jersey decree. This meant that the man had capacity to marry in our eyes, since English law regarded him as a single man, even though Italian law regarded him as still married and therefore as having no capacity to marry. The learned President refused to follow *Padolecchia* v. *Padolecchia*[51] where, he pointed out, Sir Jocelyn Simon P had not considered the intended matrimonial home test as propounded in *Radwan* v. *Radwan* (No. 2).[52] This preference is surprising since in the latter case Cumming-Bruce J, who applied this test to determine capacity to contract a

---

[44] These are marriages between a man and his former wife's sister, aunt or niece, or the former wife of his brother, uncle or nephew, whether his former wife or his brother, uncle or nephew is alive or not: s. 1(1).

[45] S. 1(3).   [46] Discussed further at p. 308 below.

[47] Re *Bozzelli's Settlement* [1902] 1 Ch. 751 (marriage of Italians in Italy, within prohibited degrees by English law); *Cheni* v. *Cheni* [1965] P 85 (Jewish uncle and niece domiciled and married in Egypt); also *Mohammed* v. *Knott* [1969] 1 QB 1 (lack of age).

[48] See pp. 301–2 above.   [49] [1979] Fam. 84.

[50] See further p. 306 below.   [51] [1968] P 314.

[52] [1973] Fam. 35. If taken literally, this is curious, since *Radwan* v. *Radwan* (No. 2) was decided five years after *Padolecchia* v. *Padolecchia*.

polygamous marriage, expressly disclaimed any suggestion that he would have applied it to any other questions of capacity.[53] Sir George Baker P also thought that England was the intended matrimonial home. Even this is unclear; the parties did live in England after the marriage, but it is not certain that they so intended at the time of its celebration.

Perrini v. *Perrini* was followed, in effect, by Anthony Lincoln J in *Lawrence* v. *Lawrence*,[54] where

> A woman domiciled in Brazil had married in Nevada a man who was seemingly domiciled at the time somewhere in America. They had immediately acquired a home in England and a domicile here. The learned judge disregarded the wife's lack of capacity by Brazilian law, and applied English law as the law of the intended matrimonial home because England was the country with which the marriage had the closest and most real connection.

Apart from departing from orthodoxy, the learned judge actually turned legislator to achieve this result.[55]

The arguments for and against the two rival theories have been frequently rehearsed. There is one practical consideration which did not occur in most of the cases, but did in one of them.[56] The question of capacity does not always arise only long after the ceremony was performed. It can arise at the time the parties want to get married. If the registrar or clergyman discovers that the parties are domiciled abroad and cannot, by the law of the domicile of either or both, marry each other though they have capacity under English law, what is he to do? Marry them or not? And how is he to discover whether they will set up home in England; is he simply to take them at their word if they say they intend to do so? And if he refuses, is the court to which *mandamus* is applied for to compel him to do so?

Several particular problems are discussed below.

Capacity to marry and the lex loci celebrationis

Though the law of the place of celebration does not, as a general principle, govern capacity to marry, it cannot be entirely ignored. Two converse situations call for examination.

---

[53] Even the application of this test to capacity to contract polygamous marriages is dubious: see pp. 315–17 below.

[54] The Court of Appeal decided the case on different grounds, but Sir David Cairns was willing to support the intended matrimonial home test; Purchas LJ was less sympathetic: [1985] Fam. 106 CA.

[55] See p. 307 below.

[56] *R* v. *Brentwood Superintendent Registrar of Marriages*, ex parte *Arias* [1968] 2 QB 956.

Where the marriage takes place in England

These are two possible combinations of fact.

(i) Both parties have capacity by the law of their foreign domiciles, but not by English law. Though no case so decides, the marriage must be void. It is inconceivable that an uncle and niece could contract a marriage[57] here even if they could do so by their personal laws.

(ii) One party is domiciled here and has capacity to marry the other by English law; the other is domiciled abroad and lacks capacity by the foreign country's laws. In this case, by way of an allegedly illogical exception[58] to the dual domicile test, the marriage is valid, since the incapacity of the foreign domiciled party is ignored. Hannen P decided this in *Sottomayer* v. *de Barros* (No. 2).[59]

After the decision in *Sottomayor* v. *de Barros* (No. 1)[60] the Queen's Proctor showed that at the time of the English ceremony the man was domiciled in England. The judge, influenced perhaps by the *lex loci celebrationis* rule, and by a desire to protect English domiciliaries, held that the incapacity under Portuguese law of the woman to marry her first cousin could, therefore, be ignored and now held that the marriage was valid.[61]

Although this case was cited in argument in *Perrini* v. *Perrini*,[62] Sir George Baker J did not refer to it in his judgment. But he could have reached his decision by applying it, and this exception, to the dual domicile test. Because the court recognised the New Jersey nullity decree, in the eyes of English law the man was unmarried (though he was still married by the law of his domicile). Therefore, the English domiciled woman was, by English law, free to marry him.[63] Since the marriage was celebrated in England, the marriage was valid.

Where the marriage takes place abroad

If both parties have capacity to marry by their personal laws and succeed in going through a ceremony in a country by whose law they lack capacity, is the marriage valid? It has been held valid in two Commonwealth cases,[64] in which incapacity by the *lex loci celebrationis* was ignored.

---

[57] See *Padolecchia* v. *Padolecchia* [1968] P 314 at 335.
[58] The Law Commission (Working Paper no. 89 (1985)) (see p. 312 below) at one time proposed its abolition.
[59] (1879) 5 PD 94.   [60] (1877) 3 PD 1 CA; see p. 302 above.
[61] This was also one ground for the decision in *Ogden* v. *Ogden* [1909] P 46 and was applied in *Chetti* v. *Chetti* [1908] P 67.
[62] [1979] Fam. 84. See p. 304 above.
[63] It would have been otherwise had the New Jersey decree not been recognised.
[64] In *Will of Swan* (1871) 2 VR (IE & M) 7 (Victoria); *Reed* v. *Reed* (note 65 below).

Thus in *Reed* v. *Reed*:[65]

> H and W were first cousins domiciled in British Columbia. They were married in Washington State where first cousins could not marry each other. Thus the marriage was valid by the *lex domicilii*, but invalid by the *lex loci celebrationis*.

The court in British Columbia upheld the validity of the marriage.

This is much more satisfactory than what, so it appears, might have been the decision of Karminski J in *Breen* v. *Breen*.[66] He referred to the law of the Republic of Ireland to determine whether a marriage in that country between two persons domiciled in England was valid. The man's first marriage had previously been dissolved by an English court. Karminski J held that the divorce would be recognised by Irish law.[67] But the inference is that, if it would not have been so recognised, the marriage would have been invalid by both Irish and English law.[68]

Remarriage after English and foreign divorces and annulments

Remarriage after an English or foreign decree which is recognised

The problem to which *Breen* v. *Breen* gives rise and those which arose in the *Brentwood Marriage Case*,[69] *Perrini* v. *Perrini*[70] and *Lawrence* v. *Lawrence*,[71] is that, although an English court has granted a divorce or annulment, or recognises one granted by a foreign court, the parties may not have capacity to remarry by their personal laws (which do not recognise the divorce or annulment). This has been settled by the Family Law Act 1986, section 50, which provides that

Where, in any part of the United Kingdom – (a) a divorce or annulment has been granted by a court of civil jurisdiction, or (b) the validity of a divorce or annulment is recognised . . . the fact that the divorce or annulment would not be recognised elsewhere shall not preclude either party to the marriage from re-marrying in that part of the United Kingdom or cause the remarriage of either party (wherever the marriage takes place) to be treated as invalid in that part.

In other words, the incapacity by the personal law is ignored and the remarriage is valid.

---

[65] [1969] 6 DLR (3d) 617. W, a minor, had not obtained the consent of the parents as required by British Columbia, though not by Washington, law. This was held to be a matter of formalities, governed by the latter law, and not of capacity.

[66] [1964] P 144.

[67] It is now clear that such a divorce would be recognised: Domicile and Recognition of Divorces Act 1986 (Ireland).

[68] This consequence would not now follow.

[69] *R* v. *Brentwood Superintendent Registrar of Marriages*, ex parte *Arias* [1968] 2 QB 951.

[70] [1979] Fam. 84.   [71] [1985] Fam. 106 CA.

Remarriage after a foreign divorce or annulment which is not recognised

This problem, like the previous one, has been discussed in connection with the 'Incidental' question.[72] It arose in the Canadian case of *Schwebel* v. *Ungar*[73] in 1962 in which, it will be recalled, a Canadian court upheld a ceremony which had taken place in Ontario between a man domiciled in Ontario and a woman then domiciled in Israel, who had capacity to marry by Israeli law which recognised her divorce from her first husband. Ontario law did not recognise the divorce and so regarded the woman as still being the wife of her first husband. In so doing, the Ontario court held valid an Ontario ceremony which was bigamous and criminal by Ontario law. The Law Commission in its Report in 1984 thought that this decision was so obviously nonsensical (and indeed it was)[74] that no English court would follow it so no legislation was necessary. One hopes that the Law Commission was not being over-optimistic.

Capacity, incapacity and public policy

Capacity

When a marriage has been celebrated abroad, and is valid by all relevant foreign laws, it will, generally speaking, be regarded as valid in England. But there must be some limit to the extent to which English law would accept the capacity of parties under their personal laws. Cases have already been mentioned in which English courts have accepted the capacity to marry of persons who would not have capacity under English law by reason of con-sanguinity or lack of age. But the closeness of affinity of the parties, or their extreme youth, might lead the English court to conclude that public policy demanded that they should not be regarded as husband and wife here.[75]

Incapacity

Apart from the case regulated by the Family Law Act 1986, section 50,[76] there are other situations in which incapacities imposed by the law

---

[72] See pp. 28–9 above.

[73] (1962) 42 DLR (2d) 622, affd (1964) 48 DLR (2d) 644 (Supreme Court of Canada).

[74] It has been suggested (at p. 306 above) that, even if both parties have capacity to marry by their foreign personal laws, a ceremony in England will be void unless they also have capacity by English law. A ceremony in which one party is domiciled in England and has no capacity to marry the other must be even more obviously invalid.

[75] As to marriages in England see p. 306 above.   [76] See p. 307 above.

of a foreign domicile will, or may be, disregarded. For example, suppose a foreign court has dissolved a marriage, but its country's law imposes a restriction upon the ability of one of them to remarry for a determinate or indeterminate period of time. If both parties are placed under such a prohibition or restriction, this will not be regarded as 'penal'[77] and contrary to English public policy, and their disability will be recognised.[78] But if only one of them is so affected, the incapacity may be stigmatised as 'penal' and he or she will not be regarded as precluded from remarrying.

This was decided in *Scott* v. *Attorney-General*,[79] where a woman placed under such a restriction after being divorced in South Africal later came to England and wished to remarry. It was held that she could do so; the restriction must be disregarded.[80] Of course, if such a person were to acquire a domicile here when she wished to remarry and her divorce was recognised in England, the incapacity under the foreign law would be no impediment to her remarrying, since it does not form part of her domiciliary law.[81]

It is thought that, at any rate, when the marriage is celebrated here, if the parties are domiciled in a foreign country whose law precludes them from marrying on racial or religious grounds, such a restriction would be disregarded.

Royal Marriages Act 1772

This statute warrants only a brief mention. It precludes descendants of King George II from marrying without the Sovereign's consent, or without the marriage being approved by Parliament when that consent is withheld. It was enacted to try to place some control in the hands of King George III over the unsuitably amorous and uxorious proclivities of his sons.[82] It has been held in the only relevant case, the *Sussex Peerage* case,[83] that the Act applies even if the ceremony takes place abroad; the rule is, therefore, one governing capacity to marry. Perhaps

---

[77] For a discussion of 'penal' laws see p. 362 below.
[78] *Warter* v. *Warter* (1890) 15 PD 152; *Miller* v. *Teale* (1954) 92 CLR 406 (Australia).
[79] (1886) 11 PD 128; *Lundgren* v. *O'Brien* (No. 2) [1921] VLR 361. In considering the latter unsatisfactory decision, it should be borne in mind that 'penal status' is a term which has been given a rather wide and curious meaning by English courts: see Re *Langley's Settlement Trusts* [1962] Ch. 541 CA, p. 363 below.
[80] The case was thus explained in *Warter* v. *Warter* (1890) 15 PD 152.
[81] But for the explanation of it given in *Warter* v. *Warter, Scott* v. *Attorney-General* could be explained on this ground.
[82] It was singularly ineffectual in this.   [83] (1844) Cl. & F 85.

it is nowadays more a possible cause of embarrassment to the Sovereign and her relatives than anything else.[84]

Consent of the parties

It is clear that factors which may vitiate the parties' consent to marry each other, as opposed to the method by which they give their consent, are related to the essential, rather than the formal, validity of marriage.[85] It is also now clear that, under English domestic law, a marriage celebrated after 1971, which is vitiated by lack of consent, is voidable only, rather than void.[86] The defect of lack of consent includes the presence of duress or mistake as to the identity of the other party or the nature of the ceremony, and (in English law) mistake as to certain attributes of the other party. These are, ignorance that at the time of the marriage he or she was suffering from mental discorder or venereal disease or, in the case of a woman, that she was pregnant by some other man.[87]

The personal law, as opposed to the *lex loci celebrationis*, should govern this question.[88] In some cases the marriages were celebrated abroad where the parties were domiciled and English law was applied, but these are inconclusive since there appears to have been no evidence of the foreign law.[89]

The only reasonably clear case is *Szechter* v. *Szechter*[90]

> A Polish professor married his secretary to get her out of prison so she might escape to the West where she could obtain urgently needed medical treatment. He and his wife were domiciled in Poland. He divorced her and 'married' his secretary in prison. But they did not

---

[84] It does not apply to the issue of princesses who have married into a foreign royal family. This may restrict the number of persons to whom it applies more than is supposed. See C. Parry, 'Further Considerations upon the Prince of Hanover's Case' (1956) 5 *ICLQ*. 1, replying to C. de O. Farran, 'The Royal Marriages Act 1772' (1951) 14 *MLR* 53. This scholarly contest will not be refereed here.

[85] See *Apt* v. *Apt* [1948] P 83 at 88 CA; *Way* v. *Way* [1950] P 71, 78. In *Parojcic* v. *Parojcic* [1958] 1 WLR 1280, where the parties had a domicile of origin in Yugoslavia but the marriage took place at Oxford, the court seems to have applied English law as the *lex loci*, but by the time the ceremony took place they had acquired a domicile in England.

[86] Matrimonial Causes Act 1973, s. 12(c).   [87] *Ibid.*, s. 12.

[88] *Way* v. *Way* [1950] P 71, 78. But there was no difference between the personal law of the party who allegedly had not consented and the *lex loci* (Soviet law). The decision was approved by the Court of Appeal on the ground of lack of forms: *Kenward* v. *Kenward* [1952] P 124.

[89] *H* v. *H* [1954] P 258; *Buckland* v. *Buckland* [1968] P 296.

[90] [1971] P 286. The case is not entirely clear since the personal law of the parties and the *lex loci celebrationis* were the same. Moreover Sir Jocelyn Simon P. held that the marriage was invalid not only by Polish law but by English law also. But this he may have done only in order to show the (then) similarities between the two systems.

really mean any of this, and the whole thing was a sham; they only did it all because they believed the secretary would die if she stayed in gaol.

Regarding this as 'duress' Sir Jocelyn Simon P held that the marriage was void and granted a decree. This was because it was void by Polish law[91] and Polish law as the parties' personal law applied to the issue. He expressly approved Dicey and Morris's *Conflict of Laws*:[92] 'no marriage is valid if, by the law of either party's domicile one party does not consent to marry the other'.

This is fair enough if the parties are, as in *Szechter* v. *Szechter*,[93] domiciled in the same country. If they are not, it could mean that the marriage might be invalid, though by the law of the party who allegedly lacks consent it is valid. So now Dicey and Morris[94] adopt this view expressed in another leading work[95] and opine that the marriage should only be invalid if it is so by the law of the domicile of the party who allegedly lacks consent.

This seems sensible. It could further be argued (i) that lack of consent would be fatal if the ceremony took place here and is a nullity by English law since it would be surprising if two Arcadians went through a ceremony in a Cambridge church, the husband having a concealed gun held to his back by his prospective father-in-law, and the marriage was held valid because it was valid by Arcadian law,[96] and (ii) that the converse should be true since the foreign *lex loci* has no interest in the matter. There is no authority on the point.

Physical incapacity

A marriage will be voidable by English law if it is not consummated, either because one party cannot consummate it by reason of impotence or because he or she will not do so (wilful refusal).[97]

Impotence is a fairly common ground for nullity in legal systems generally. Wilful refusal to consummate is not. Sometimes it is a ground for divorce, and sometimes it gives no right to matrimonial relief at all.

If the choice of law rule governing consent is now reasonably clear, that governing physical incapacity most certainly is not. Until 1947 no other law than English law was applied.[98] In the inconclusive case of

---

[91] See previous note. As we have seen, lack of consent now renders a marriage voidable, not void, by English law.
[92] Then rule 32. Now (13th edn) rule 69.
[93] [1971] P 286.   [94] *Conflict of Laws*, 13th edn, 690.
[95] G. C. Cheshire and P. M. North, *Private International Law*, 13th edn, 781.
[96] Cf. *Parojcic* v. *Parojcic* [1958] 1 WLR 1280, note 85 above.
[97] Matrimonial Causes Act 1973, s. 12.
[98] *Easterbrook* v. *Easterbrook* [1944] P 10; *Hutter* v. *Hutter* [1944] P 95.

Robert v. *Robert*,[99] in that year, Barnard J expressed preference for the *lex loci celebrationis*. But this cannot be correct; the matter is not one of forms, as was pointed out in *de Reneville* v. *de Reneville*[100] where the law of the husband's domicile or that of the intended matrimonial domicile was favoured. But that case is equally inconclusive. Moreover, it was not concerned with choice of law but with jurisdiction.

In *Ponticelli* v. *Ponticelli*,[101] Sachs J held that English law, preferably as the law of the husband's domicile at the time of the marriage (it was also the *lex fori*), governed the issue. This preference for the law of the husband's domicile at the time of the marriage (which would also usually be both his and his wife's domicile after the marriage) presents a difficulty nowadays since a wife can have a domicile different from that of her husband.

It has been suggested that the law applicable should be that of the petitioner's domicile.[102] It has further been suggested that the problem could be made to disappear if wilful refusal (which is the only post-nuptial defect which affords grounds for a nullity decree) were to be made a ground for divorce.[103]

But for the present, the law remains obscure.

Choice of law rules in marriage: proposals for reform

In 1985, after a far-ranging review of the choice of law rules governing all aspects of marriage, the Law Commission produced some recommendations for discussion.[104] However, after further consultation it dropped the matter, except for making minor recommendations for amendment of the Foreign Marriage Act.[105]

Polygamous marriages

At one time polygamous marriages, that is, marriages in which husbands may have more than one wife at the same time,[106] caused considerable

---

[99] [1947] P 164. But the place of celebration and the husband's domicile at the time of the marriage and the matrimonial domicile were the same (Guernsey). The *lex loci* is supported by the Northern Irish case *Addison* v. *Addison* [1955] NI 1.

[100] [1948] P 100.   [101] [1958] P 204.

[102] W. D. Bishop, 'Choice of Law for Impotence and Wilful Refusal' [1978] 41 *MLR* 512, see also J. H. C. Morris, *Conflict of Laws*, 5th edn (London, Sweet & Maxwell, 2000) 206.

[103] *Ibid.*

[104] Working Paper on Choice of Law in Marriage no. 89 (1985).

[105] Foreign Marriage (Amendment) Act 1988, p. 299 above.

[106] Strictly speaking this is 'polygyny' as opposed to 'polyandry' where one woman has more than one husband. But the latter is so rare that the word 'polygamy', which includes both, is generally used to denote only the former.

difficulties in the conflict of laws. For reasons which will be explained, the difficulties have been considerably reduced in recent years,[107] but may still exist in connection with such matters as taxation, social security and immigration.

The concept of marriage in English law

English law regards marriage as being a 'voluntary union for life of one man and one woman, to the exclusion of all others' since that is how marriage is 'understood in Christendom'. These words were employed by Lord Penzance in *Hyde* v. *Hyde & Woodmansee*[108] in 1866:

> An Englishman joined the Mormon community in Utah and contracted a marriage which, by the Mormon doctrine, was potentially polygamous. He subsequently renounced and preached against that faith,[109] became a missionary in the Sandwich Islands and then a dissenting minister in Derby. Having resumed a domicile in England he petitioned for divorce, because the lady had married another Mormon.

This was refused because his Mormon union was not a marriage as understood by the Divorce Court, which could not, therefore, give matrimonial relief in respect of it.

The law appears to have drawn back from regarding all polygamous unions as not being marriages, since the consequence would have been that a large portion of Queen Victoria's subjects would have been bastards. So this attitude prevailed only in the Divorce Courts and signified only that a polygamous marriage was a marriage in respect of which matrimonial relief was not available.[110]

One other point is nowadays obvious: the words 'for life' must be read as 'potentially for life', otherwise few marriages would exist, in view of the ease and popularity of divorce.[111]

---

[107] One reason is that it has been reduced by being outlawed in several countries in which it was formerly practised.

[108] (1866) LR 1 P & D 130. See also Re *Bethell* (1887) 38 Ch. D 220.

[109] Later, that faith renounced polygamy. Utah would not have become a State of the Union otherwise; faced with a practice commanded by God but banned by the United States Constitution, the Mormons threw in their lot with the latter.

[110] And even this common law restriction has, fairly recently, been removed. See p. 317 below. The decision in *Hyde* v. *Hyde & Woodmansee* may have rested on a misconception. The court seems to have assumed that the Mormon faith was the law of Utah. But see an absorbing article by G. W. Bartholomew: 'Polygamous Marriages' (1952) 15 *MLR* 35. He points out that Utah was federal territory which was annexed from Mexico by the Treaty of Guadeloupe Hidalgo in 1849. The law there was, therefore, either Mexican or the common law, neither of which countenanced polygamy.

[111] *Nachimson* v. *Nachimson* [1930] P 217 CA where a marriage was regarded as a marriage though it could be dissolved merely by a joint declaration which was registered.

Finally, a marriage is polygamous though it is only potentially so and though the husband never takes another wife during the existence of his marriage.[112]

Characterisation

What law determines whether a marriage is monogamous or polygamous? The rule is generally thought to be that this falls to be decided according to the law of the place where it was celebrated, and by its nature and its incidents under that law. But even though that law would not call it polygamous, it is so if in the eyes of English law its incidents give it a polygamous character. Thus in *Lee* v. *Lau*[113] under local Hong Kong Chinese customary law a man was not allowed to take another wife, but he could have a concubine. During the subsistence of his marriage concubinage was regarded as a legal status. The English court regarded this as being, in reality, a polygamous marriage.

It has sometimes been suggested that the personal law should decide this question, but this seems quite inconsistent with the decisions in several cases.[114] In *Hussain* v. *Hussain* in 1982 however, to the surprise of everyone[115] the Court of Appeal held[116] that the question would, if the man were domiciled in England so that the Matrimonial Causes Act 1973[117] governed his capacity to contract a polygamous marriage, be decided to some extent by the Act's provisions.[118] It is clear that a marriage in England is monogamous if it is celebrated in accordance with the Marriage Act 1949 wherever the parties are domiciled,[119] and that a 'ceremony' which takes place in England which, were it celebrated abroad, would produce a polygamous marriage, but is not celebrated in accordance with the Marriage Act, is void.[120]

---

[112] *Hyde* v. *Hyde & Woodmansee* (1866) LR 1 P & D 130. In 1985, the Law Commission (Report no. 147) suggested in effect that a marriage should only be regarded as polygamous if actually such.

[113] [1967] P 14.

[114] Re *Bethell* (1887) 38 Ch. D 220 (marriage of a ne'er-do-well Englishman into the African Baralong tribe); *Risk* v. *Risk* [1951] P 50 (marriage of a Scottish peer's daughter to an Egyptian boxer); *Ohochuku* v. *Ohochuku* [1960] 1 WLR 813 (Nigerian Muslim marriage).

[115] Including the Law Commission: see p. 316 below.

[116] [1983] Fam. 26. Ormrod LJ delivered the judgment of the Court.   [117] S. 11(d).

[118] The decision raises problems respecting capacity to contract a polygamous marriage. See pp. 315–17 below.

[119] *Ohochuku* v. *Ohochuku* [1960] 1 WLR 183 (the second, English, ceremony).

[120] *R* v. *Bham* [1966] QB 159; see also *Qureshi* v. *Qureshi* [1972] Fam. 173 at 186. Some mosques are registered for marriages, but marriages therein are monogamous.

Changes in the character of a marriage

If the marriage was monogamous at its inception it remains so even though it could, in certain circumstances, become polygamous later.[121] The marriage gets the benefit of the doubt, so to speak,[122] since a marriage which is potentially polygamous at its inception can, provided it is not actually polygamous, become monogamous by changes in circumstances. These include conversion to a faith which allows only monogamy,[123] a change in the law of the country where the marriage was celebrated so as to prohibit polygamy,[124] or if that law so provides, by the birth of a child.[125] A change to a monogamous character may also result from a change of domicile to a country which does not permit polygamy. This was decided by the Court of Appeal in *Ali* v. *Ali* (1968).[126] (Had this been known in 1866 the decision in *Hyde* v. *Hyde & Woodmansee*[127] must have been different.)

> H and W were Muslims domiciled in India and married polygamously. H (and, therefore, W) acquired an English domicile in 1961. H then petitioned for a divorce on the ground of W's desertion in 1959. She cross-petitioned on the ground of H's adultery since 1964.

It was held that their potentially polygamous marriage had become monogamous, but only in 1961. Therefore, the court could not (at that time) grant H a decree, but could and would grant one to W.

Two comments may be made on this case. The result would presumably have been different if, before 1961, the man had married a second wife, since his change of domicile to England could hardly have divested him of one or both of his wives.[128] It could have been the same, however, if he had had two wives before 1961, but one had died or been divorced before 1961 or one had died after 1961.[129]

Capacity to contract a polygamous marriage

This has become a rather confused area of the law, quite unnecessarily. Left to oneself one would think that this is a matter governed by the same rule as that which governs capacity to contract any marriage,

---

[121] *Mehta* v. *Mehta* [1945] 2 All ER 690.   [122] *Cheni* v. *Cheni* [1965] P 85.

[123] *The Sinha Peerage Claim* [1946] 1 All ER 348n. (HL Committee of Privileges).

[124] *Parkasho* v. *Singh* [1968] P 233 (effect of Indian Hindu Marriage Act 1955 on a Sikh marriage); *R* v. *Sagoo* [1975] QB 885 (Kenya Sikh Marriage Ordinance 1960).

[125] *Cheni* v. *Cheni* [1965] P 85.   [126] [1968] P 564.   [127] (1866) LR 1 P & D 130.

[128] See *Onobrauche* v. *Onobrauche* (1978) 8 Fam. Law 107.

[129] The decision would have been more difficult if (as nowadays) husband and wife could have had different domiciles. In fact there would now be no problem since the English court would have jurisdiction and is no longer precluded from dissolving a potentially polygamous marriage.

which is generally supposed to be the laws of the ante-nuptial domiciles of the parties (the 'dual domicile' test).[130] Thus, if both or one of the parties to a potentially polygamous marriage which is celebrated abroad be domiciled in England, the marriage should be void. But where capacity to marry is concerned some judges seem almost perversely to take delight in muddying the waters.

Thus in *Radwan* v. *Radwan* (No. 2)[131] Cumming-Bruce J held that capacity to contract a polygamous marriage is governed by the law of the intended matrimonial home which, in that case, was Egypt and the fact that the woman was domiciled here was irrelevant.[132] His Lordship, when informed that Parliament had recently proceeded upon the assumption that the orthodox rule governed, replied that Parliament had acted under a misapprehension![133]

The decision is no longer important, since Parliament's intentions have been enacted as law. According to the Matrimonial Causes Act 1973 (section 11(d)) a marriage is void:

in the case of a polygamous marriage entered into outside England and Wales [if] either party was at the time of the marriage domiciled in England and Wales. For these purposes a marriage may be polygamous although at its inception neither party has any spouse additional to the other.

That, one would have thought, would be that. But another rule for capacity, employing this provision in a way no one had ever thought of before, was propounded in *Hussain* v. *Hussain*.[134] If a Pakistani man was domiciled here and went through a ceremony in Pakistan with a lady domiciled there, the marriage was not polygamous after all. He could not enter into a polygamous marriage and since the lady was not allowed by Pakistani law to contract a polyandrous marriage, the marriage must be monogamous.

The Law Commission, which was about to send off a working paper on this very issue to be printed on the day this judgment appeared, had to rewrite the paper, since it had never crossed its members' minds that this was the law.[135] In its subsequent Report it suggested that the law

---

[130] See pp. 302–4 above. This is clearly consistent with the cases cited at n. 114 above, and see *Crowe* v. *Kader* [1968] WAR 122.

[131] [1973] Fam. 35.

[132] Cumming-Bruce J expressly confined his 'law' to polygamous marriages; that did not deter Baker P from approving of it in the case of a monogamous marriage: *Perrini* v. *Perrini* [1979] Fam. 84, see p. 304 above.

[133] The decision has been condemned by every academic writer who has commented on it.

[134] [1983] Fam. 26 CA.

[135] If the roles had been reversed the marriage would have been void, since W could not have contracted a polygamous marriage but H could. This is the result of Pakistan allowing polygyny but not polyandry.

should be changed so as to restrict incapacity to actually polygamous marriages.[136]

This proposal was enacted in the Private International Law (Miscellaneous Provisions) Act 1995, Part II so that both men and women domiciled in England have capacity to enter into a marriage which, though it is polygamous in form, is in fact monogamous. Section 11 of the Matrimonial Causes Act 1973 is amended so as to apply only to actually polygamous marriages[137] and section 5(1) of the 1995 Act expressly provides that

A marriage entered into outside England and Wales between parties neither of whom is already married is not void on the ground that it is entered into under a law which permits polygamy and that either party is domiciled in England and Wales.[138]

By section 6(1) these changes have retrospective effect so as to validate earlier marriages but not if a party to such a marriage has already entered into a marriage which was valid when celebrated or which is validated by the 1995 Act itself.[139]

Recognition

The significance to English law of the existence of polygamy is nowadays much reduced since the courts will recognise a polygamous union as a marriage for most purposes, unless, that is, there is some strong reason why they should not. Thus the courts are no longer precluded from granting matrimonial relief in respect of such a union;[140] and a polygamous marriage is a bar to a subsequent monogamous marriage here, which will, therefore, be void for bigamy.[141] Whether the man could be convicted of the crime of bigamy is not clear. In one case it was held (at West Bromwich Quarter Sessions) that he could not,[142] but though this case was overruled by the Court of Appeal[143] it was only on the ground that the first marriage had in fact become monogamous under the law of Kenya where it had been celebrated.

---

[136] Working Paper no. 83 (1982); Report no. 146 (1985).

[137] Private International Law (Miscellaneous Provisions) Act 1995, Sched. para. 2.

[138] These two provisions do not affect the determination of the validity of a marriage to which the law of another country is applicable under our rules of private international law: *ibid.*, s. 5(2).

[139] *Ibid.*, s. 6(2) to (5). Nor do they retrospectively affect entitlement under a will or intestacy of a person who died before the provisions came into effect nor any benefits, pensions, allowances or tax or succession to a dignity or title of honour: *ibid.*, s. 6(6).

[140] Matrimonial Causes Act 1973, s. 47(1): see p. 319 below.

[141] *Srini Vasan* v. *Srini Vasan* [1946] P 67; *Baindail* v. *Baindail* [1946] P 122 CA.

[142] *R* v. *Sarwan Singh* [1962] 3 All ER 612.   [143] *R* v. *Sagoo* [1975] QB 885.

For certain statutory purposes, provided that the polygamous marriage is only potentially polygamous and that the husband has in fact only one wife, the marriage is treated as if it were monogamous.[144] And in *Chaudhry* v. *Chaudhry*[145] it was held that a spouse of a polygamous marriage could make an application to the court under the Married Women's Property Act 1882, section 17.[146] A man who maintains a wife of a polygamous marriage was entitled to a deduction of tax under the Income and Corporation Taxes Act 1988, section 257(1) even if he has more than one wife.[147]

With the possible exception of succession to entailed property[148] a child of a polygamous marriage is, it appears, legitimate and entitled to succeed to property on intestacy[149] as can also, it seems, the surviving wife of a polygamous marriage on the death of her husband, whether he had one or more wives and even if he died domiciled here.[150]

---

[144] Social Security and Benefits Act 1992, ss. 121(1)(B), 147(5) as amended by Private International Law (Miscellaneous Provisions) Act 1995, s. 8(2), Sched. para. 4.

[145] [1976] Fam. 148 CA.   [146] See also Matrimonial Homes Act 1983.

[147] *Nabi* v. *Heaton* [1981] 1 WLR 1052 from which appeal was allowed by consent: [1983] 1 WLR 626.

[148] See *The Sinha Peerage Claim* [1946] 1 All ER 348n.

[149] See *Bamgbose* v. *Daniel* [1955] AC 107 PC.

[150] See *Coleman* v. *Shang* [1961] AC 481 PC: one of two surviving widows of a polygamous marriage was held to be a wife within the Inheritance (Provision for Family and Dependants) Act 1975; Re *Sehota* [1978] 1 WLR 1506.

19   Matrimonial causes

Polygamous marriages

As has already been mentioned, at one time the English courts could not grant any kind of matrimonial relief in respect of a polygamous marriage.[1] But this state of affairs could not last, in view of the increased immigration into this country from countries which permit polygamy. The Matrimonial Causes Act 1973, section 47(1), now provides that a court

is not precluded from granting matrimonial relief or making a declaration concerning the validity of a marriage by reason only that the marriage was entered into under a law which permits polygamy.

This applies to both actual and potentially polygamous marriages. 'Matrimonial relief' includes divorce and nullity decrees and maintenance orders.[2]

Divorce and judicial separation[3]

Jurisdiction of the English courts

At common law, the English courts only possessed jurisdiction to grant a divorce if the spouses were domiciled in England. Since at common law a husband and wife were both domiciled in the country of the husband's domicile, this could lead to hardship for a wife whose husband deserted her and acquired a domicile abroad. From 1937 statutory jurisdiction was bestowed upon the courts to entertain a wife's petition when her husband was domiciled abroad.[4] By subsequent extensions of such jurisdiction, wives became unduly favoured over husbands. But the abolition in 1973 of the unity of domicile of married couples from

[1] See p. 313 above.   [2] Matrimonial Causes Act 1973, s. 47(2).
[3] Judicial separation is now assimilated to divorce for jurisdictional purposes and for recognition of legal separations obtained abroad.
[4] Matrimonial Causes Act 1973, s. 13.

1 January 1974 was accompanied by amendment and simplification of the jurisdictional rules and the parties to a marriage were placed on an equal footing.

The Domicile and Matrimonial Proceedings Act 1973, section 5(2), now provides that the court has jurisdiction to entertain a petition for divorce if, and only if, either party is at the date of the commencement of proceedings domiciled in England or has been habitually resident here for one year immediately preceding that date.[5]

If proceedings are started in more than one part of the United Kingdom in respect of the same marriage, provisions exist whereby the English court, in some cases must[6] and in others may[7] stay the proceedings before it. The latter apply also when concurrent proceedings are brought in a court and a country outside the United Kingdom. The provisions in question will not be discussed further here.[8]

Choice of law

Unlike some foreign courts, the English courts have always applied the English law of divorce exclusively.[9] This was obviously bound to be the case when the parties had to be domiciled here, but when the statutory extension of jurisdiction took place, there was room for the application of foreign divorce law, for example, French law if the husband had obtained a domicile in France. But the relevant statutes effectively prescribed the application of English law.[10] The Domicile and Matrimonial Proceedings Act 1973 contains no such provision, but the Law Commission had said that its omission was not intended to change the law. It is difficult to see how it could have done so, since the Matrimonial Causes Act 1973[11] says that a petition for divorce may be presented on the ground that the marriage has irretrievably broken down, and mentions no other ground.

---

[5] For the meaning of habitual residence see *Kapur* v. *Kapur* [1984] 5 FLR 920. Once jurisdiction is established the court can entertain additional proceedings in respect of the same marriage, though it would not otherwise enjoy jurisdiction by s. 5(2): *ibid.*, s. 5(5). This is useful if, after the original proceedings have started, the party to the marriage ceases to be domiciled or habitually resident here, and the other party seeks to cross-petition. See also s. 5(4) for proceedings for death to be presumed.

[6] Domicile and Matrimonial Proceedings Act 1973, s. 5(6) and Sched. 1 para. 8.

[7] *Ibid.*, para. 9. See *De Dampierre* v. *De Dampierre* [1988] AC 92 HL, p. 90 above.

[8] For details see A. V. Dicey and J. H. C. Morris, *The Conflict of Laws*, 13th edn (London, Stevens, 2000) 799–804.

[9] *Zanellli* v. *Zanelli* (1948) 64 TLR 556 CA.

[10] Matrimonial Causes Act 1973, s. 46(2). [11] *Ibid.*, s. 1(1).

Nullity of marriage

Jurisdiction of the English courts

This is now also governed exclusively by statute. It is no longer necessary, as it was at common law, to decide for jurisdictional purposes whether the alleged defect made the marriage void or voidable only.[12] The court has jurisdiction if, and only if, at the date of commencement of proceedings either party is domiciled in England or has at that date been habitually resident here for one year. Further, since the question may arise after the death of one or both spouses, jurisdiction also exists if either party to the marriage died before the date of commencement of proceedings and was, at the date of death, either domiciled in England or had been habitually resident here for one year preceding it.[13]

Choice of law

The relevant choice of law rules here are those which govern the validity of marriage as to formalities, legal capacity, consent of the parties and physical incapacity, which were discussed in the previous chapter. The Matrimonial Causes Act 1973[14] provides that where, apart from the Act, any matter would fall to be determined in accordance with the rules of private international law by the law of a country outside England and Wales, the provisions of sections 11 to 13 of the Act (which state the rules of English domestic law with regard to nullity)[15] shall not either (a) preclude the determination of that matter by the foreign law, or (b) require the application to the marriage of the grounds set forth therein unless these are applicable by the rules of private international law.

---

[12] A marriage is void by English law if (i) the parties are within the prohibited degrees, (ii) either is under sixteen, (iii) certain formalities have been disregarded, (iv) either party was already married, (v) the parties are of the same sex and (vi) either party is domiciled here at the time of the marriage abroad and it is polygamous. A marriage is voidable for (i) impotence, (ii) wilful refusal to consummate, (iii) lack of consent, or if, at the time of the marriage, (iv) one party was suffering from mental disorder or (v) venereal disease, or (vi) (being the wife) was pregnant *per alium* (Matrimonial Causes Act 1973, ss. 11, 12). See also ss. 13 and 16.

[13] Domicile and Matrimonial Proceedings Act 1973, ss. 5(3), 6(5). The provisions regarding stays of proceedings also apply: see note 6 above.

[14] Matrimonial Causes Act 1973, s. 14(1).   [15] See note 12 above.

It has been asked whether the English courts would annul a marriage on a ground unknown to English law.[16] For example, if the parties' domicile is Utopia and under Utopian law an error as to an attribute of the other party, such as the husband's being, unsuspected by the wife, the father of another woman's child, or the wife's not being, contrary to the husband's belief, a virgin is a ground for annulling the marriage, would an English court grant a decree? It is difficult to see why not, subject to the requirements of English public policy. After all, the courts have annulled a marriage because of the absence of foreign formalities which are not required by English law,[17] and there seems nothing out-rageous about determining that mistakes such as those mentioned viti-ate a marriage, just as under English law a mistaken impression that the other party is free from venereal disease renders a marriage voidable. But the question is an open one.

Recognition of divorces, annulments and legal separations

When the recognition of a foreign divorce, annulment or legal separa-tion is an issue then, as with any foreign judgment, the English courts are only concerned with the jurisdiction of the foreign court which granted it (if proceedings took place). They are indifferent to the ground on which it was granted. In the following discussion, 'divorce' includes legal separation, except where indicated.

History

The story of the law in this area is tortuous but can now be briefly stated. With respect to divorces, until 1953, they would only be recog-nised if they were granted by the courts of the country of the parties', that is, the husband's, domicile or recognised by that country's law.[18] From 1953, they would also be recognised if they were granted on a jurisdictional basis which also enabled the English courts to grant a divorce, that is to say on the basis of reciprocity.[19] In 1969 the House of

---

[16] J. H. C. Morris, *Conflict of Laws*, 5th edn (London, Sweet & Maxwell, 2000) 236–8. The reference to *Vervaeke* v. *Smith* [1983] 2 AC 145 HL does not seem wholly relevant. In that case, what was in issue was a foreign nullity decree granted on the ground that a marriage in England was a 'mock marriage'. The English court's refusal to recognise the decree was based on two reasons: (a) it conflicted with English public policy; (b) an English court had previously upheld the validity of the marriage. Reason (b) has nothing to do with the point here under discussion.

[17] See *Berthiaume* v. *Dastous* [1930] AC 79 PC.

[18] *Le Mesurier* v. *Le Mesurier* [1895] AC 517 PC, *Armitage* v. *A. G.* [1906] P 135.

[19] *Travers* v. *Holley* [1953] P 246 CA.

Lords, in *Indyka* v. *Indyka*,[20] replaced the existing rules by an elusive test of the 'real and substantial connection' of the parties with the foreign country in question.

However, matters were put on a statutory basis by the Recognition of Divorces and Legal Separations Act 1971, which was enacted primarily to enable the United Kingdom to become a party to the Hague Convention of the same name of 1970. This Act had to be amended by the Domicile and Matrimonial Proceedings Act 1973. But the legislation was somewhat cumbrous and complex and gave rise to difficult questions about the recognition of Islamic divorces.

As to recognition of foreign annulments, this was still governed by rules of the common law which were unclear. In a Report on the Recognition of Foreign Nullity Decrees and Related Matters (1984)[21] the Law Commission recommended that the law relating to foreign annulments should be placed upon the same statutory basis as that concerning foreign divorces but that the latter should be recast. These and other recommendations for improvement of the 1971 Act were enacted, with certain modifications, into law by Part II of the Family Law Act 1986. This has been a marked improvement on the previous state of affairs and has produced scarcely any litigation. It is, however, a masterpiece of the Parliamentary draftsman's art in the sense that you have to know what it means before you read it, so convoluted is its drafting.

It remains to be pointed out that the legislation is based on the Hague Convention of 1970 but the rules of recognition it contains are more liberal than those to be found in the Convention. There is nothing in the Convention to prevent the domestic law being different from the Conventional Rules, so long as the difference does not consist in the domestic rules being less liberal.

Family Law Act 1986, Part II: Rules for recognition

The scheme of this Act contains three sets of rules concerning respectively (a) divorces and annulments granted in the British Islands, (b) overseas divorces and annulments obtained by proceedings outside the British Islands and (c) overseas divorces and annulments not obtained by proceedings.

Divorces and annulments granted within the British Islands
Section 44(2) provides that if such a divorce or annulment has been granted by a court of civil jurisdiction then, subject to two exceptions

---

[20] [1969] 1 AC 53 HL.   [21] Report no. 137 (1984).

which will be mentioned later,[22] it must be recognised throughout the United Kingdom.

Overseas divorces and annulments obtained by proceedings

According to section 45 of the Act, such must be recognised only if they are entitled to recognition under sections 46 to 49 or by any other enactment.[23] Section 46(1) provides that, if the divorce or annulment is effective (presumably, this means to dissolve the marriage)[24] under the law of the country where it was obtained, it will be recognised if, at the date of commencement of the proceedings,[25] either party (whether petitioner or respondent) was (i) habitually resident or (ii) domiciled according to English law or the law of that country in family matters[26] in, or (iii) a national of, that country.

The divorce or annulment does not need to be recognised by the law of the habitual residence, domicile or nationality of the other party.

In this context 'proceedings' means 'judicial or other proceedings'.[27] This term includes not only a divorce or annulment granted by a court but one granted by administrative proceedings. With respect to 'talaq' divorces, after judicial difference of opinion on the meaning of 'other proceedings' in the 1971 Act it was eventually held in *Chaudhary* v. *Chaudhary*[28] by the Court of Appeal that the words did not include an informal or 'bare' talaq (or the Jewish equivalent, the ghet) which is simply a statement by the husband addressed to his wife, a sample being:

This is to inform you that as irreconcilable differences have arisen between you and myself I have formed an irrevocable intention to divorce you and I am divorcing you under the Pakistani law. I divorce you, I divorce you, I divorce you.[29]

This method of divorce, which is only very rarely available to wives, is the only one which exists in some Islamic countries. In others, notably Pakistan, it has been to some extent formalised by requiring additional proceedings. Thus, under the law of Pakistan, the Muslim Family Law Ordinance 1961, a divorce which is instituted by the pronouncement of a talaq does not take effect unless ninety days have elapsed

---

[22] See p. 328 below.
[23] For such enactments see Family Law Act 1986, s. 52(5) which preserves the validity of divorces obtained under those enactments, which are repealed by the Act.
[24] In *D* v. *D* [1994] 1 FLR 38 a 'divorce' in Ghana was not recognised, since, it appeared, it was not effective under the law of Ghana. The tribunal which had granted it had failed to adjourn for the wife to be told of the proceedings.
[25] Family Law Act 1986, s. 46(3)(a).   [26] *Ibid.*, s. 46(5).
[27] *Ibid.*, s. 54(1).   [28] [1985] Fam. 19.   [29] See *Qureshi* v. *Qureshi* [1972] Fam. 173.

therefrom and a notice has been given to the Chairman of an Arbitration Council in Pakistan.[30] In *Quazi* v. *Quazi*[31] in 1980, the House of Lords held that this procedure is 'proceedings'. Therefore a talaq pronounced in Pakistan and followed by the procedure mentioned can be recognised under section 46(1).

'Transnational' divorces. Suppose that a divorce is obtained by Pakistan law by a Pakistani husband writing a talaq here and sending it to the Chairman of the Arbitration Council there. In ex parte *Minhas*[32] the Divisional Court held that this was not an 'overseas' divorce within sections 2 to 5 of the 1971 Act, but was one obtained here. After the Immigration Appeals Tribunal had twice refused to follow this case, the House of lords held in *R* v. *Secretary of State*, ex parte *Ghulam Fatima*[33] that though ex parte *Minhas* was incorrect, a divorce obtained this way was still not entitled to recognition since, although it was 'effective' in Pakistan, it was not obtained by proceedings instituted there, but in England.[34] The same consequence would follow if the talaq was sent from Saudi Arabia or Dubai to Pakistan. The Law Commission recommended no statutory provision about this matter since the law was now clear, so it seems that such a divorce will not be recognised in England.

In *Berkovits* v. *Grinberg*,[35] Wall J followed ex parte *Ghulam Fatima* with respect to the writing of a Jewish ghet in one country and its delivery in another, and held that the divorce could not be recognised in spite of slight differences in wording between the Acts of 1986 and 1971.

Overseas divorces and annulments not obtained by proceedings
The best-known example of these is the 'bare' talaq described previously. They were not the subject of any recommendation by the Law Commission. However, the Family Law Act, section 46(2) and (3)(b), now provides that an overseas divorce, annulment or legal separation

---

[30] Muslim Family Law Ordinance 1961. The talaq can be revoked by the husband at any time before the ninety days have elapsed. If notice is not given the talaq never takes effect. The law is procedural; neither spouse need take part in proceedings before the Arbitration Council, and if that body's efforts at conciliation are unsuccessful, the divorce still takes effect after ninety days.

[31] [1980] AC 744.

[32] *R* v. *Registrar-General of Births, Deaths and Marriages*, ex parte *Minhas* [1977] QB 1.

[33] [1986] AC 627 HL.

[34] This conclusion seems unavoidable given the wording of the 1971 or 1986 Acts. But it produces an artificial result, for if a husband of Pakistani nationality can afford the fare to that country and pronounce talaq there, the divorce would be recognised, but if he could afford only the postage to Pakistan it would not.

[35] [1995] Fam. 142. Wall J made, in effect, the same criticism of the law as that in the previous note.

obtained otherwise than by means of proceedings can be recognised but only if both parties to the marriage were domiciled in the country in which it was obtained or if one was domiciled there and the other in a country whose law would recognise it when it was obtained. Again, domicile here means domicile under the law of that country in family matters or under English law.

Thus, if in Dubai a man domiciled there either by Dubai law or by English law pronounces a talaq and his wife is domiciled there by either law or she is domiciled in Iraq by Iraqi law but not by English law and Iraqi law recognises the divorce, or if a man domiciled in Iraq divorces by talaq in Dubai his wife who is domiciled in Dubai and Iraqi law recognises the divorce, then it will be recognised here.

A difficulty which arises from this is that if one party is domiciled in Dubai and the other in England, the question is, whether the Dubai divorce is recognised in England. This is, of course, the very question we are asking. Perhaps the divorce would not be recognised. The ineptitude of the drafting is self-evident.

However, such a divorce cannot be recognised if either party had been habitually resident in the United Kingdom for one year before the divorce was obtained. The reason for this restriction, which does not apply to divorces and annulments obtained by proceedings, is to prevent evasion of section 44(1). This states expressly that no divorce, annulment or legal separation obtained in any part of the British Islands shall be regarded as effective in England unless it was granted by a court of competent jurisdiction. Thus a talaq pronounced in an hotel in the Scottish Highlands is not entitled to recognition as a divorce in England.

Annulments – special rule

Since a marriage may be annulled after the death of one or both of the parties to it, section 46(4) provides that if either party was habitually resident or domiciled in or a national of the country where the annulment was obtained at the date of his or her death, it will be recognised in England.

Countries with separate systems of law

Section 45 (and section 47(2)) refers to a divorce or annulment which is effective under the 'law of the country' where it was obtained. Section 49 deals with the case of a country which is composed of several territories, each with its own law and divorce jurisdiction. The obvious example is the United States of America. (Canada and Australia have

federal divorce laws.) In cases where the decree was obtained by proceedings, if the basis of the foreign court's jurisdiction was habitual
residence or domicile, the decree needs only to be effective under the
law of the territory (for example, Nevada); if it was nationality, it must
be effective under the law of the whole country (that is, the United
States). If the divorce or annulment was not obtained by means of
proceedings, it must be effective throughout the entire country in which
it was obtained.

Miscellaneous provisions

Section 47(1) applies the jurisdictional provisions of section 46(1) to
decrees obtained by cross-proceedings. Section 47(2) provides that it a
legal separation which is entitled to recognition under the Act is converted in the country in which it was obtained into a divorce, the latter
is entitled to recognition whether or not it would be otherwise entitled
to recognition under the Act.

Findings of fact

By section 48, where a divorce or annulment is entitled to recognition
under the Act, then any finding of fact made by the foreign court
expressly or by implication in the proceedings before it and on the basis
of which it assumed jurisdiction, including a finding that a spouse was
habitually resident or domiciled under that country's laws in, or was a
national of, that country is conclusive evidence of that fact if both
parties took part in the proceedings, including appearing therein. If one
party did not take part, that finding is sufficient evidence of that fact,
unless this is rebutted.

Finality and effect of divorces

Though a recognised foreign divorce does not necessarily terminate a
party's existing obligations under an English maintenance order,[36] the
English courts had until recently no power to grant financial relief to the
parties to a recognised foreign divorce. This was only the case, however,
if the foreign decree had finally dissolved the marriage, and financial
relief could be awarded if the decree was not absolute, but akin to an
English decree *nisi*. Thus the court could (just) do this in *Torok* v. *Torok*,[37]
a case which also shows how the rules for recognition of foreign divorces
and annulments operate in rather surprising circumstances.

[36] *Wood* v. *Wood* [1957] P 254.   [37] [1973] 1 WLR 1066.

H and W were Hungarian nationals. They came here after the Hungarian rising in 1956, married in 1957 and lived together until 1967. They became British citizens in 1964, but the husband retained his Hungarian nationality also. In 1967 H went to Canada leaving W and their two children in England. In 1972 he petitioned the Hungarian court for divorce.

A Hungarian divorce would have had to be recognised under the 1971 Act (as it would under the 1986 Act) though neither party had been back to Hungary since 1956. To the evident satisfaction of Ormrod J the divorce was not yet final in Hungary, so he could award maintenance to the wife. But he exposed a gap in the law.[38] It took ten years for this to be closed, but now by the Matrimonial and Family Proceedings Act 1984, Part III, the court can, if it thinks the circumstances justify it, give matrimonial relief to either party to the marriage after a final divorce.

Exceptions to recognition

Section 51 deals with non-recognition of a divorce or annulment which would otherwise be entitled to be recognised. It provides an exclusive code of the grounds for non-recognition.[39]

In two cases recognition may be refused, wherever the divorce or annulment was obtained, in or outside the British Islands. First, it may be refused if it is irreconcilable with a decision concerning the subsistence or validity of the marriage of the parties previously given either by a court in the United Kingdom or by a court elsewhere and recognised or entitled to be recognised in England. Thus, if an English or Scottish court has decided that a marriage is valid, a decree of a competent Belgian court annulling it may not be recognised, or if a Belgian court has annulled the marriage and its decree is entitled to be recognised in England, a Scottish divorce may not be recognised.[40]

Secondly, the divorce or annulment may be refused recognition if, at the time it was obtained, there was by English law (including its rules of private international law) no subsisting marriage.[41]

In addition, recognition may be refused, but only if the divorce or annulment was obtained outside the British Islands, if[42]

[38] See also Lord Scarman in *Quazi* v. *Quazi* [1980] AC 744.
[39] *Eroglu* v. *Eroglu* [1994] 2 FLR 287.
[40] S. 51(1) in part is a reflection of *Vervaeke* v. *Smith* [1983] 1 AC 145 HL (non-recognition of a Belgian nullity decree).
[41] Under the 1971 Act the court *must* have refused to recognise a foreign divorce for either of these two reasons.
[42] Family Law Reform Act 1986, s. 51(3)(a) and (c). The following three exceptions are, drafting changes apart, the same as the 1971 Act. The cases referred to in notes 44–6 and 48–51 are decisions under that section or under the previous common law.

(a) It was obtained without such steps being taken as were reasonable to give notice of the proceedings to a party to the marriage.[43] In cases decided at common law, it was held that, even though a spouse did not actually receive notice of the proceedings, provided the foreign court's rules for giving notice were followed the divorce would be recognised.[44] But it would be otherwise if, for example, the husband had misled the foreign court into believing that he did not know where his wife was when in fact he knew this perfectly well.[45]

(b) Apart from lack of notice, a party to the marriage was not given a reasonable opportunity to take part in the proceedings.[46]

(c) Recognition would be manifestly[47] contrary to public policy. In *Kendall* v. *Kendall*[48] the court declined to recognise a Bolivian divorce granted to a wife who did not want it but had been tricked into petitioning for it in Spanish, a language she neither spoke nor understood. In *Eroglu* v. *Eroglu*,[49] on the other hand, it was held that it was not open to the former wife to argue that her Turkish divorce should not be recognised on this ground, since she had joined with her former husband in fraudulently deceiving the Turkish court. In three cases,[50] courts were unwilling to recognise divorces obtained by 'bare' talaqs in Dubai, Iraq and Kashmir because in the circumstances it would have been 'manifestly contrary to public policy' to recognise a divorce obtained by a man without his English wife's knowledge or consent.

Finally, where the divorce or annulment has been obtained otherwise than by proceedings, recognition may not be refused on grounds (a) or (b) since notice to the wife or her non-appearance could not prevent the divorce or annulment being pronounced unilaterally.[51] However, it may be refused if there is no official document which certifies that it is

---

[43] This was an alternative ground on which the Ghanaian divorce was refused recognition in *D* v. *D* [1994] 1 FLR 38 (see n. 24 above).

[44] *Boettcher* v. *Boettcher* [1949] WN 83; *Igra* v. *Igra* [1951] P 404.

[45] *Macalpine* v. *Macalpine* [1958] P 35.

[46] *Joyce* v. *Joyce* [1979] Fam. 93; *Mamdani* v. *Mamdani* [1984] 5 FLR 699 (recognition withheld); *Newmarch* v. *Newmarch* [1978] Fam. 79 (decree recognised).

[47] The word 'manifestly' appears in s. 51 of the Act because it is contained in Art. 10 of the Hague Convention. It was inserted therein in order to discourage courts in some contracting states from relying unduly on public policy.

[48] [1977] Fam. 208; see J. G. Collier, note [1978] 37 *CLJ* 45. Compare *Joyce* v. *Joyce* [1979] Fam. 93.

[49] [1994] 2 FLR 287.

[50] *Zaal* v. *Zaal* [1983] 4 FLR 284 (Dubai); *Sharif* v. *Sharif* (1980) 10 Fam. Law 216 (Iraq); *Chaudhary* v. *Chaudhary* [1985] Fam. 19 CA (Kashmir).

[51] *Boettcher* v. *Boettcher* [1949] WN 83; *Igra* v. *Igra* [1951] P 404.

effective under the law of the country where it was obtained or, if one party only was domiciled there, no official document from the country of the other party's domicile stating that it is recognised by that country's law. The reason for the existence of this discretionary ground is difficult to discern.[52]

EU Council Regulation (2000)

In May 1998, the member states of the European Union concluded a Convention on Jurisdiction and the Recognition of Judgments in Matrimonial Matters, known as 'Brussels II', to complement the Brussels Convention of 1968. However, as it did with the latter Convention, the EU Council converted 'Brussels II' into a Regulation ((EC) No. 1347/ 2000),[53] which it promulgated on 29 May 2000. This Regulation entered into force and became directly applicable in EU member states (except Denmark, which exercised its right to opt out) on 1 March 2001.[54] It replaced, as between EU member states, the Hague Convention on the Recognition of Divorces and Legal Separations, 1978, and, in United Kingdom law, the Family Law Act 1986, Part II.[55]

Scope of the Regulation

The Regulation applies to civil proceedings relating to divorce, legal separation and marriage annulment and to other officially recognised proceedings which are to be regarded as equivalent to judicial proceedings. 'Court' means all authorities having jurisdiction in such matters (Article 1).

Jurisdiction

Article 2 confers jurisdiction on the courts of the member state in whose territory the spouses are habitually resident (or were last habitually resident if one of them still lives there), the respondent is habitually resident (in the event of a joint application), either spouse is habitually resident, the applicant is habitually resident (provided he or she either resided there for at least a year before the application was made or resided there for at least six months immediately before the application

---

[52] Family Law Act 1986, s. 51(3)(b). For the definition of 'official document' see *ibid.*, s. 51(4).
[53] Official Journal of the European Communities L160, 30 June 2000, p. 19.
[54] Regulation (EC) No. 1347/2000, Art. 46.   [55] *Ibid.*, Art. 37. See pp. 322–30 above.

was made and is a national of the member state in question). The courts of the United Kingdom and of Ireland have jurisdiction in the last situation if the applicant is domiciled therein. The courts of the state of the nationality of both spouses (or, in the case of the United Kingdom and of Ireland, if they are domiciled therein) have jurisdiction. 'Domicile' has the meaning it has under United Kingdom or Irish domestic law.

Also, a court in which proceedings have been instituted has jurisdiction over a counterclaim (Article 5) and a court which has ordered a legal separation has jurisdiction to convert it into a divorce (Article 6).

This jurisdiction is exclusive; a spouse who is habitually resident in or is a national of a member state or, in the case of the United Kingdom and of Ireland, is domiciled therein, can only be sued in another member state in accordance with the above provisions (Article 7).

Article 8 makes provision for 'residual' jurisdiction. If no court of a member state has jurisdiction, this is determined in a member state by the law of that state. As against a person who is neither habitually resident in nor a national of (or in the case of the United Kingdom or of Ireland is not domiciled in) a member state, any national of a member state who is habitually resident in another member state may, like nationals of the latter, avail himself of its rules of jurisdiction.

Throughout the Regulation 'the United Kingdom' refers to England, Scotland or Northern Ireland as the case may be (Article 41).

Refusal of jurisdiction and staying proceedings

If, say, the English court is seised of a case over which is has no jurisdiction and over which a court of another member state has jurisdiction it must decline jurisdiction of its own motion (Article 9). Where a respondent is habitually resident in another member state, if the English court has jurisdiction, it must stay the proceedings so long as it is not shown that the respondent has been able to receive the document initiating them in sufficient time for him to arrange for his defence or that steps have been taken to that end.

Lis pendens *and dependent actions*

Article 11, which deals with these matters, is in much the same terms as the Brussels Convention, 1968.[56]

If there are two proceedings, no matter whether they involve the same cause of action and are between the same parties or are merely 'dependent' on each other, the court second seised must stay its

---

[56] See pp. 159–65 above.

proceedings until the jurisdiction of the court first seised is established; when this happens, the court second seised must decline jurisdiction. However, the party who brought the second action may thereupon bring it before the court first seised.

Provisional or protective measures

In urgent cases the courts of any member state may be asked to take provisional measures, including protective measures available under its law, even if the courts have jurisdiction over the case itself (Article 12).

Recognition and enforcement of judgments

Meaning of judgment

'Judgment', according to Article 13, means 'a divorce, legal separation or marriage annulment', including any decree order or decision. Authentic instruments and settlements approved by a court which are enforceable in the member state in which they were concluded must be recognised and are enforceable as if they were judgments.

Recognition

By Article 14 recognition is to be automatic and without any special procedure being required. Any interested party may apply for a decision that a judgment be or not be recognised.

The defences to recognition (Article 15(1)) are the same as those contained in the Brussels Convention as amended by Council Regulation (EC) No. 44/2001:[57] public policy, default judgments (unless the respondent has accepted the judgment unequivocally), irreconcilability with a judgment given in the requested state or with an earlier judgment in another member state or non-member state.

Otherwise, there can be no review of the jurisdiction of the court of origin (Article 17). Recognition may not be refused because the law of the requested state would not allow a divorce, legal separation or marriage annulment on the same facts (Article 18). Article 29 prohibits, under any circumstances, review of the judgment as to its substance.

By Article 20, the court may stay recognition proceedings if an ordinary appeal against a judgment has been made in the state in which it was pronounced. Such proceedings in another member state against a judgment of a United Kingdom or Irish court may be stayed if enforcement has been suspended in either of those states by reason of an appeal.

[57] See pp. 168–73, 177 above.

Declaration of marital status

The Family Law Act 1986 contains exclusive jurisdictional rules for the making of such declarations by the High Court or a county court. Section 55 provides that any person[58] may apply for a declaration that a marriage was at its inception valid, that it subsisted or did not subsist on a certain date, or as to the recognition or non-recognition of a foreign divorce, annulment or legal separation, if either party to the marriage is domiciled or has been habitually resident for one year in England at the date of the application or has died and was domiciled or had been habitually resident here for one year at the date of death. The court must make the declaration if the truth of the proposition is proved to it, unless to do so would be manifestly contrary to public policy.[59]

It is important to note that the court cannot make a declaration that a marriage was void. A decree of nullity must be sought.[60]

---

[58] The court may refuse to hear an application by a person other than a party to the marriage if it considers that he has no sufficient interest in its determination: *Ibid.*, s. 65(3).

[59] Family Law Act 1986, s. 58(1).

[60] *Ibid.*, s. 58(5)(a). The powers of the court to grant a decree of nullity are not affected, *ibid.*, s. 58(6).

20 Children

Guardianship, custody and orders concerning children

Guardianship of and custody of children signify two things which have not always been clearly distinguished. Guardianship denotes the appointment of someone to take care of parentless children. It usually includes custody, which is concerned with the right of parents or a parent or a third party to decide matters relating to the upbringing of a child, and it includes control over the child's property. Custody usually, but not always, includes the right to care and control of the child and to determine his residence.

The English courts have also had an inherent jurisdiction and power to make a child, whether an orphan or not, a ward of court, which means that the court is effectively the custodian of the child. It may, for example, prevent the child from contracting an undesirable marriage or associating with undesirable people.

With respect to these matters, English domestic law was radically altered by the Children Act 1989. The concept of 'custody' was abolished. Wardship was preserved but re-entitled simply the 'inherent' jurisdiction, and its ambit severely curtailed.[1] The method of appointment of a guardian was clearly regulated.

Custody orders are replaced by what are called 'Section 8 orders'. By that section of the Act, the courts can make orders as to (i) residence, (ii) contact (which replaces access), (iii) prohibited steps and (iv) 'specific issues'. These orders may be made in respect of a child under eighteen but only exceptionally if the child is over sixteen. Proceedings in which section 8 orders are sought under various statutes, and proceedings under the inherent jurisdiction, are called 'family proceedings' (though orders made under the inherent jurisdiction are not section 8 orders).

---

[1] Children Act 1989, s. 100. It is expected that the inherent jurisdiction will in practice almost wither away.

As to the method of appointment of guardians, by section 5 of the Children Act the court[2] may order an applicant to be a child's guardian if the child has no parent with parental responsibility for him or if a residence order was made in favour of a parent or guardian who died while it was in force. The court may also of its own motion itself appoint a guardian in any family proceedings. The person appointed guardian has parental responsibility for the child. A guardian may not be appointed in any other way.[3]

The term 'custody' will be used in the following pages where appropriate, since, though it is no longer employed by English law, it is often used in foreign laws and it is also used in international conventions and the United Kingdom legislation implementing them.[4]

Jurisdiction of the English courts

Guardianship

The jurisdiction of the English courts to make guardianship orders is a matter which is still governed, it appears, by the common law, since the statutory rules in the Family Law Act 1986, Part I[5] do not apply.

The English courts have had an inherent jurisdiction to make a child a ward of court, which extended to the appointment of a guardian of him. This jurisdiction was derived from the sovereign as *parens patriae* and concerned with the welfare of her subjects who are minors. Therefore, the court's powers extended over all minors who owe allegiance to the Crown and so are entitled to its protection.[6] This includes anyone living in England, it being immaterial that the child is of foreign nationality or domicile.[7] Further, it includes any child who is physically present within the jurisdiction for however brief a period.[8]

---

[2] A guardian may be appointed by the High Court, a county court or a magistrates' court (*ibid.*, s. 92(7)). The power of the High Court to make a guardianship order under its inherent jurisdiction is abolished (s. 5(3)), though it may appoint a guardian of a child's estate if rules of court so provide.

[3] Though a parent who has parental responsibility or a guardian may appoint another person to be guardian in the event of his own death.

[4] See pp. 339–44 below.   [5] See pp. 336–8 below.

[6] As in constitutional law this means a British national; or an alien other than one who is an enemy and present without leave of the Crown: see *de Jager* v. *Attorney-General of Natal* [1907] AC 36 PC (liability of a foreign friendly alien to conviction for treason) and *Johnstone* v. *Pedlar* [1921] 2 AC 262 HL (his right to protection).

[7] *Johnstone* v. *Beattie* (1843) 10 Cl. & Fin. 42 HL; *Hope* v. *Hope* (1854) 4 De. GM & G 328; *Stuart* v. *Marquess of Bute* (1861) 9 HL Cas. 440; Re *B's Settlement* [1940] Ch. 54; Re *D (An Infant)* [1943] Ch. 305.

[8] See Re *P (GE) (An Infant)* [1965] Ch. 568, 588, 592 CA.

Moreover, an appointment or, at one time, a custody order may be made in England in respect of a child who is a British citizen, even though he is abroad. This was decided in two nineteenth-century cases, *Hope* v. *Hope*[9] and Re *Willoughby*[10] where the children were in France. They were affirmed in two twentieth-century cases,[11] but it was said in the latter of these that nowadays the exercise of jurisdiction in such a situation would only be undertaken in exceptional circumstances.[12] It was sometimes suggested that domicile should replace allegiance as the basis of jurisdiction, but this was rejected as being too artificial and too complicated to apply, in the leading modern case of Re *P (GE) (An Infant)*,[13] which concerned jurisdiction to make a custody order. It was held that the court had jurisdiction in that case, in which a child who had been living in England with his mother had, when on a visit to his father, been taken away by his father to Israel. This was because the child had been and still was ordinarily resident in England when the proceedings were instituted. The child's domicile, which was in Israel, did not affect this, nor did the fact that he was not in England.[14]

Jurisdiction exists in all these situations even though the child owns no property in England. On the other hand, a child's entitlement to property in England does not by itself confer jurisdiction.[15]

It should be added that under section 4 of the Children Act 1989 a court may make an order on the application of the father of a child whose parents are unmarried that he is to have parental responsibility. No statutory jurisdictional rules exist for the making of such orders; they may be the same as those just discussed.

Other orders respecting children

Statutory rules governing jurisdiction to make section 8 orders respecting children were enacted by the Family Law Act 1986, Part I.[16] Identical rules were enacted therein for the English, Scots and Northern Irish courts. They apply *vis-à-vis* all other countries. Jurisdiction of the English courts to make an order in the exercise of the inherent jurisdiction 'so far as it gives care of a child to any person or provides for

---

[9] (1854) 4 De GM & G 328.   [10] (1885) 30 Ch. D 324.
[11] *Harben* v. *Harben* [1957] 1 WLR 261; Re *P (GE) (An Infant)* [1965] Ch. 568 CA.
[12] [1965] Ch. 568 at 582, 587 and 588 CA.   [13] [1965] Ch. 568 CA.
[14] The court was prepared to extend jurisdiction to any case of a stateless infant travelling on a British travel document or of an alien on a British passport unless the court was not a *forum conveniens*. An alien who has been resident in this country and travels abroad under a British passport continues to owe allegiance and may be convicted of treason even though he has obtained the passport by false representations: *Joyce* v. *Director of Public Prosecutions* [1946] AC 347 HL.
[15] *Brown* v. *Collins* (1883) 25 Ch. D 56.   [16] As amended by the Children Act 1989.

contact with, or the education of a child' rests on the same basis. Orders within the scope of the Act are 'Part I orders' (section 1).

The fundamental scheme of Part I is to make the jurisdictions of the courts in the United Kingdom mesh together and to create an order of priority as between them. This order is (1) a court in which matrimonial proceedings are continuing, (2) a court in the country where the child is habitually resident and (3) one in the country in which he is present.[17]

So, an English court can make an order in respect of a child who is not yet eighteen if it is exercising its powers in connection with matrimonial proceedings regarding the parents' marriage, that is, proceedings for divorce, nullity or judicial separation.[18] Otherwise it may do so if and only if the child is habitually resident here[19] or present here and not habitually resident in Scotland or Northern Ireland at the date of commencement of proceedings.[20] The court's jurisdiction is, however, excluded if at that date matrimonial proceedings regarding the parents' marriage are taking place in Scotland or Northern Ireland.[21]

If the court has jurisdiction, it has the power to refuse an application for custody where the matter has already been determined in proceedings outside England and can also stay proceedings if concurrent proceedings are under way in a foreign country and the case can be more conveniently heard there.[22] It has powers to order the disclosure of a child's whereabouts, the recovery of a child and to restrict the removal of a child from the jurisdiction.[23]

In addition, the High Court may make an 'emergency' order in the exercise of its inherent jurisdiction if the child is present in England and the court 'considers that the immediate exercise of its powers is necessary for his protection'.[24] This is so even if the child is habitually resident or matrimonial proceedings are in progress elsewhere in the United Kingdom.[25] But such an order is superseded by one made by a court in the country which has primary jurisdiction.

The Act also makes provision for duration and variation of orders.[26]

---

[17] This legislation followed recommendations by the Law Commission (see Report on Custody of Children in the United Kingdom (no. 138) Cmnd 9419 (1984)). The Law Commission was concerned that an end should be put to the sometimes acrimonious conflicts between the English and Scots courts which arose from the exercise by the English courts of the extensive jurisdiction they claimed to make guardianship and custody orders.

[18] Family Law Act 1986, ss. 2(1), 2(A).

[19] For the habitual residence of a child wrongfully removed from or retained out of or who goes or remains out of England, see *ibid.*, s. 41.

[20] *Ibid.*, ss. 2(2), 3.   [21] *Ibid.*, s. 3(2).   [22] *Ibid.*, s. 5.   [23] *Ibid.*, ss. 33–5.

[24] *Ibid.*, s. 2(3).   [25] *Ibid.*, ss. 1(1)(d), 2(3).   [26] *Ibid.*, s. 6.

Exercise of jurisdiction

In exercising its jurisdiction to make any order respecting children, including the appointment of a guardian, the court applies English law, whose primary rule is stated in the Children Act 1989, section 1(1) to be:

When a court determines any question with respect of
(a) the upbringing of a child; or
(b) the administration of a child's property . . .
the child's welfare shall be the court's paramount consideration.

This 'welfare' principle has also been used in cases which involved foreign orders in respect of the same child, though this is not now the basic principle in many such cases and may not be in any of them, as will now be shown.

Foreign guardianship and custody orders

Until quite recently, the recognition of foreign guardianship and custody orders was entirely a matter for the common law, but in 1986 statutory rules were enacted for the recognition and enforcement of custody orders made by courts in other parts of the United Kingdom and in 1985 other rules were enacted concerning foreign orders made in countries which are parties to either of two international conventions. But as regards orders of other countries outside the United Kingdom, the common law rules still apply. These also apply to guardianship, since this is not covered by the statutory rules about to be discussed.

Orders of other courts in the United Kingdom

The Family Law Act 1986, Part I contains rules for the recognition and enforcement of orders concerning children under the age of sixteen[27] made by courts in Scotland and Northern Ireland. These must be recognised in England, but only if they are registered with the High Court,[28] as having the same effect as if they had been made here. Further, if it is requested to do so, the High Court must enforce such a registered order as if it were its own.[29]

---

[27] Sixteen, not eighteen. This is because Scots law does not allow orders to be made in respect of children who are not under sixteen and English orders in respect of sixteen and seventeen year olds are unusual.

[28] Family Law Act 1986, s. 25. For the method of registration see *ibid.*, s. 27 and for cancellation see s. 28. For the staying of and dismissal of enforcement proceedings see *ibid.*, ss. 30, 31.

[29] *Ibid.*, s. 29(1). Section 29(2) gives the court power to make interim directions.

Child Abduction and Custody Act 1985

This statute was enacted in order to enable this country to become a party to two international conventions which are designed to discourage the 'kidnapping' of children, which has become something of an international scandal in recent times. These are the Hague Convention of 1980 on the Civil Aspects of International Child Abduction, and the Council of Europe Convention (the 'European Convention') of the same year on Recognition and Enforcement of Decisions Concerning Custody of Children and on Restoration of Custody of Children.[30] The former Convention has a broader geographical scope in that all thirty member states of the Hague Conference on Private International Law may be parties to it, and they are drawn from all parts of the world; moreover, other states may accede to it in relation to a state which accepts their accession.[31] The European Convention is only open to those European states which are members of the Council of Europe.[32]

The Conventions have different objectives. The Hague Convention is concerned to secure the restoration of children who have been wrongfully removed from one country to another, whether or not in breach of a custody order. The European Convention is in effect complementary to it and covers cases in which there has been a determination as to the custody of a child and represents an attempt to secure recognition of all custody orders whether or not improper removal is involved. But there is some overlap between them and it is advisable where they do overlap to proceed under the Hague Convention, since its restrictions on return are far fewer than those in the European Convention.

The Conventions and the Act apply to cases of removal of children both to and from the United Kingdom and to the recognition and enforcement of United Kingdom custody orders abroad and of foreign custody orders in the United Kingdom.

The Act sets up 'central authorities', as required by the two Conventions, to ensure these are carried out and for coordinating requests from other countries about child kidnaps. The 'central authority' for England and Wales (and for Northern Ireland) is the Lord Chancellor.[33] The basic idea is that parents should make an application to the central authority in their country which would then be sent to the equivalent

---

[30] Some provisions of the Conventions were enacted into United Kingdom law by the Child Abduction and Custody Act 1985, Schedule 1 (the Hague Convention) and Schedule 2 (the European Convention).

[31] In 2000 the parties to the Convention included the United Kingdom. Among the others are Argentina, Australia and its states, Canada and its provinces, Israel, New Zealand and the United States: see SI 1999 no. 2030 Sched. 1.

[32] In 2000 the parties included the United Kingdom: see *ibid.* Sched. 2.

[33] In Scotland it is the Secretary of State for Scotland.

body in the other country where steps would be taken to find the child and send him back.

The Hague Convention deals not only with custody rights (which are not defined but by Article 5(a) include 'rights relating to the care of the person of the child, and, in particular, the right to determine the child's place of residence') arising from decisions of a court in a contracting state, and also those arising out of an agreement having legal effect under that state's law, or those which arise by operation of law or from an administrative decision.

The Convention applies to a child who was habitually resident[34] in a contracting state immediately before any breach of custody or access rights[35] and is under sixteen.[36] According to Article 3 the removal or retention of such a child is considered wrongful where it is in breach of rights of custody attributed to a person, an institution or any other body (this includes a foreign court[37]), either jointly or alone, under the law of the state in which the child was habitually resident immediately before the removal or retention and at the time of removal or retention those rights were actually being exercised or would have been so exercised but for the removal or retention. In Re *H (Minors) (Abduction) (Custody Rights)*[38] the House of Lords held that 'removal' and 'retention' are single events and are mutually exclusive. The removal must be across international boundaries and not simply removal from the person who has custody rights.[39]

The judicial or administrative authorities must act expeditiously in proceedings for the return of children.[40]

Article 12 provides that where the child has been wrongfully removed or retained and less than one year has elapsed since the date of wrongful removal or retention before the commencement of judicial or administrative proceedings, the court or administrative authority must order the return of the child forthwith unless one or more of three grounds for refusal is or are established under Article 13, when the court has a discretion not to order return.[41] The first is if it is established that whoever had the care of the person of the child was not actually

---

[34] As to the meaning of 'habitual residence' see Re *J (A Minor) (Abduction)* [1990] 2 AC 562 HL, discussed at p. 55 above. There are other English decisions about its meaning: see pp. 55–7 above.

[35] See Art. 5(b). See also Art. 21 for the securing of effective rights of access.

[36] Art. 4.

[37] As to this see Re *H (A Child: Abduction: Rights of Custody)* [2000] 2 WLR 337 CA.

[38] [1991] 2 AC 476 HL.   [39] *Ibid.*   [40] Art. 11.

[41] See *B* v. *B (Abduction: Custody Rights)* [1993] Fam. 32 CA. Proceedings may be stayed or the application for return dismissed if there is reason to believe that the child has been taken to another state.

exercising custody rights at the time of removal or retention or has consented to or subsequently acquiesced in the retention. Consent must be given before or at the relevant time and needs to be established by firm and unequivocal evidence[42] and if it was obtained by deception it will be disregarded.[43] Acquiescence can be passive and can be inferred from, for example, lapse of a period of time without objection,[44] and it was said by Lord Browne-Wilkinson in Re *H (Abduction: Acquiescence)*[45] to be a question of fact and the actual subjective intention of the 'wronged' parent and not of the outside world's perception of his or her intentions.

The second ground is that there is a 'grave risk that his or her return would expose the child to physical or psychological harm or otherwise place the child in an intolerable situation'. The English courts have held that the harm in question must be substantial[46] and that the risk must be grave.[47] They have interpreted this exception strictly and narrowly.[48] They have held that the 'intolerable situation' must be something 'extreme and compelling'[49] and have emphasised that the court is not here concerned with the paramount consideration of the child's welfare, but with whether the child should be speedily returned to the country whose courts or authorities are the most suitable for the determination of what is for the child's welfare.[50] In *C v. C (Abduction) (Rights of Custody)*,[51] for example, it was held that a parent who has wrongfully removed the child cannot argue that the separation by the child's return from him or her will cause the child grave psychological harm.

The third ground is that the child's return may be refused if he objects and is old and mature enough to have his views taken into account.[52]

---

[42] Re *C (Abduction: Consent)* [1996] 1 FLR 414.
[43] Re *B (A Minor) (Abduction)* [1994] 2 FLR 249.
[44] Re *A (Minors) (Abduction: Custody Rights)* [1992] Fam. 106 CA.
[45] [1998] AC 72 at 88 HL. However, the wronged parent may be estopped if he or she leads the other to believe that the former does not intend to insist on his or her rights.
[46] See Re *Gsponer's Marriage* (1988) 94 FLR 164.
[47] Re *A (A Minor) (Abduction)* [1988] 1 FLR 365; *E v. E (Child Abduction: Intolerable Situation)* [1998] 2 FLR 980. This need not be considered if there has been acquiescence: Re *A (Minors) (Abduction: Custody Rights)* (No. 2) [1993] Fam. 1 CA.
[48] Re *A (A Minor) (Wrongful Removal of Child)* [1988] Fam. Law. 383.
[49] Re *N (Minors) (Abduction)* [1991] 1 FLR 413; *B v. B (Abduction: Custody Rights)* [1993] Fam. 32.
[50] See, for example, Re *L (Abduction: Pending Criminal Proceedings)* [1999] 1 FLR 433; Re *S (Abduction: Return into Care)* [1999] 1 FLR 843.
[51] [1989] 1 WLR 654 CA.
[52] Re *G (A Minor) (Abduction)* [1989] 2 FLR 473; Re *S (A Minor) (Abduction)* [1991] 2 FLR 1 CA; Re *R (A Minor) (Abduction)* [1992] 1 FLR 105; Re *S (A Minor) (Abduction: Custody Rights)* [1993] Fam. 242 CA.

For example, in Re *T (Minors) (Abduction: Custody Rights)*,[53] the objections of a girl aged eleven, mature beyond her years and subject to emotional abuse by her warring parents, persuaded the Court of Appeal to reverse an order for her return to Spain. Where the application is made after a year has elapsed since the wrongful removal or retention, return may also be refused if it is shown that the child is now settled in his new environment.[54]

The fact that a decision relating to custody has been given or is entitled to recognition in the requested state is not a ground for refusing to return a child but the reasons for that decision may be taken into account in deciding whether to apply the rules of the Convention.[55]

A decision concerning the return of the child is not to be taken as a determination of a custody issue on its merits.[56]

The European Convention provides that the central authority's duty is to take steps to discover the whereabouts of the child (who is a person of any nationality aged under sixteen who has not the right to decide on his own residence under the law of his habitual residence or nationality or the internal law of the state addressed),[57] to secure recognition and enforcement of the foreign custody decision[58] and deliver the child to the applicant if enforcement is granted.[59]

A 'decision relating to custody' means a decision of a judicial or administrative authority which relates to the care of the person of the child, including the right to decide on the place of his residence, or to the right of access to him.[60] An 'improper removal' means removal of the child across an international frontier in breach of a custody decision in a contracting state and which is enforceable there. It includes failure to return a child across such frontier at the end of a period of the exercise of the right of access to him or of any other temporary stay in a territory other than that in which the custody is exercised, and a removal subsequently declared unlawful by a custody decision.[61]

---

[53] (2000) *The Times*, 24 April. The court emphasised that the case was an extreme one. In another case the views of a child aged thirteen were discounted: Re *HB (Abduction: Children's Objection)* [1997] 1 FLR 392.

[54] Art. 12. 'Settlement' means being established in a community in security and stability: Re *N (Minors) (Abduction)* [1991] 1 FLR 413; Re *S (A Minor) (Abduction)* [1991] 2 FLR 1 at 23–4.

[55] Art. 17. By Art. 18 the power of a judicial or administrative authority to order the return of the child at any time is not limited by Chapter III (Arts. 8–19) of the Convention.

[56] *Ibid.*, Art. 19.   [57] Art. 1(a).

[58] The Convention also applies to decisions on rights of access: Art. 11. See Re *A (Foreign Access Order: Enforcement)* [1996] 1 FLR 561.

[59] Art. 5(1). If the central authority in the state addressed has reason to believe the child is in another contracting state it must send the relevant documents to that state's central authority: Art. 5(2).

[60] Art. 1(b)(c).   [61] Arts. 1(d) and 12.

Article 7 provides that a decision relating to custody given in a contracting state 'shall be recognised and, where it is enforceable' there, 'made enforceable in every other contracting state'. It cannot be enforced here unless it has been registered here; once registered, the foreign decision can be enforced as if it were an English one.[62] Articles 8 and 9 provide that in certain cases of 'improper removal' steps must be taken to restore the custody of the child and in other cases must be taken subject to limited exceptions. But the United Kingdom exercised its right of reservation under Article 17 not to apply Article 8 and to apply to Article 9 the exceptions stated in Article 10 (which deals with where removal or retention is not improper).

The result is that the authorities and courts of the United Kingdom may refuse to recognise or enforce any custody decision, whether the removal or retention is or is not proper, on seven grounds. These are: (i) that the decision was taken in the absence of the defendant, if his rights of defence had not been observed; (ii) in such a case, the foreign court had exceeded its international competence; (iii) the decision was incompatible with a decision which became enforceable in the state addressed before the improper removal[63] of the child, unless he had been habitually resident in the territory of the requesting state for one year before the removal; (iv) the effects of the decision are manifestly incompatible with the fundamental principles of the law relating to the family and children in the state addressed;[64] (v) by reason of a change in the circumstances (including the passage of time, but not a change in the child's residence after improper removal) the effects of the decision are manifestly no longer in accordance with the welfare of the child (whose views, where practicable, are to be sought);[65] (vi) because the child's nationality is that of the requested state or because he has his habitual residence there or has the nationality of both states but is habitually resident in the United Kingdom; and (vii) if the decision is incompatible with a decision in the state requested or a third state pursuant to proceedings begun before the request for recognition or enforcement and if the refusal is in accordance with the child's welfare.[66]

Although Article 9(3) provides specifically that 'in no circumstances may the foreign decision be reviewed as to its substance', the fifth ground for refusal seems to come very close to admitting the possibility of such review. For example, an English court refused to return young

---

[62] Child Abduction and Custody Act 1985, ss. 15, 18.   [63] Defined in Art. 1(d).
[64] This, in England, may include the 'welfare of the child' principle: Re *G (A Minor) (Child Abduction) (Enforcement)* [1990] 2 FLR 325.
[65] Art. 15. Re *A (Foreign Access Order: Enforcement)* [1996] 1 FLR 561.
[66] Proceedings may be adjourned for three reasons set out in Art. 10(2).

children who had lived for a year in England after the foreign order was made.[67] But in more recent cases, such a child's return was ordered.[68]

Parental responsibility for Children (EU Council Regulation, 2000)

EU Council Regulation No. 134/2000 on Jurisdiction and the Recognition and Enforcement of Judgments in Matrimonial Matters,[69] which was discussed in the previous chapter,[70] extends also to 'matters of parental responsibility for children of both spouses on the occasion of matrimonial proceedings, for divorce, legal separation and marriage annulment'.[71] It takes precedence, between EU member states (except Denmark), over the European Convention of 1980[72] in so far as the latter concerns matters governed by the Regulation. The Regulation entered into force on 1 March 2001.[73]

Jurisdiction. Jurisdiction over a case relating to these matters is conferred by Article 3 of the Regulation on the courts of the member state which is exercising jurisdiction over an application for divorce, legal separation or marriage annulment, provided the child is habitually resident in that state. If the child is not habitually resident in that state, its courts nevertheless have jurisdiction if the child is habitually resident in another member state and at least one of the spouses has parental responsibility in relation to the child, provided that their jurisdiction has been accepted by the spouses and is in the interests of the child. A court which has jurisdiction also has jurisdiction over a counterclaim.

Jurisdiction ceases when the judgment in the matrimonial proceedings (for example, a divorce) has become final, or, if the parental responsibility proceedings are still pending at that time, when the judgment in the latter proceedings have become final or when either the matrimonial or parental responsibility proceedings have come to an end for another reason. Jurisdiction under these provisions excludes that of the courts of other member states (Article 7).

It is important to observe that Article 4 provides for a situation where international child abduction is involved; it requires the relevant court to exercise its jurisdiction in conformity with the Hague Convention of

---

[67] *F* v. *F (A Minor) (Custody: Foreign Order)* [1989] Fam. 1; see J. C. Hall, note [1989] 48 *CLJ* 189.
[68] Re *K (A Minor) (Abduction)* [1990] 1 FLR 387; Re *G (A Minor) (Child Abduction: Enforcement)* [1990] 2 FLR 325.
[69] Official Journal of the European Communities L160, 30 June 2000.
[70] See pp. 330–2 above.   [71] Regulation (EC) No. 1347/2000, Art. 1(1)(b).
[72] *Ibid.*, Art. 37. As to the European Convention see pp. 342–4 above.
[73] Regulation (EC) No. 1347/2000, Art. 46.

1980 (and, in the United Kingdom, the Child Abduction and Custody Act 1985).

Other jurisdictional provisions (Articles 8, 9, 10 and 11 of the Regulation), which deal with residual jurisdiction, scrutiny of jurisdiction, *lis pendens* and dependent actions and with provisional measures, apply to parental responsibility as they apply to matrimonial proceedings, and were discussed in the last chapter.[74]

Recognition and enforcement of judgments. The provisions of the Regulation (Articles 13, 14, 16, 18 and 20) which define 'judgment' and provide for, *inter alia*, prohibition of review of jurisdiction, differences between domestic laws, non-review of the substance and stays of proceedings, apply as they apply to matrimonial proceedings.[75]

The grounds of non-recognition laid down in Article 15(1) for judgments in matrimonial proceedings are applied by Article 15(2) to judgments about parental responsibility.[76] However, the best interests of the child must be taken into account in deciding whether recognition would contravene public policy. Also, there are two further grounds for non-recognition.

Article 15(2)(b) precludes recognition if the judgment was given (except in case of urgency) without the child having been given an opportunity to be heard, in violation of fundamental rules of procedure of the requested state, and Article 15(2)(d) provides that the judgment may not be recognised on the request of any person who claims that the judgment infringes his or her parental responsibility without his or her having been given an opportunity to be heard.

As to *enforcement* of judgments, Articles 21 to 31 of the Regulation contain provisions as to which judgments are enforceable, the jurisdiction of local courts in requested states, the procedure for enforcement, the decision of the court, notice thereof and appeal therefrom, stay of proceedings pending appeal, partial enforcement, legal aid and non-requirement of security. Articles 32 to 35 deal with the documents required from a party to recognition or enforcement proceedings.

Common law

The English courts appear never to have had to decide what foreign court has jurisdiction to appoint a guardian of, or make a custody or other order in respect of, a child. It is arguable that they would recognise and enforce an appointment or order of a court which has jurisdiction on the basis upon which the English court possesses it, but at present no clear rules exist.

---

[74] See pp. 331–2 above.   [75] See p. 332 above.   [76] See p. 332 above.

In *Johnstone* v. *Beattie*[77] guardians appointed under Scots law for a child in England were not recognised by the English courts as entitled to exercise the guardianship in England, but in *Stuart* v. *Marquess of Bute*,[78] the House of Lords said that the earlier decision did not mean that the foreign guardian is to be entirely ignored and emphasised that the prime question for the court is what the benefit of the child demands.

It appears from two nineteenth-century cases[79] that so long as the foreign guardian is not challenged, he can exercise his powers in respect of the child here. If he is challenged, then even if the English court has appointed a guardian for the child over him whilst he is in England, as in *Nugent* v. *Vetzera*,[80] the foreign guardian may still be allowed to have custody and to remove the child from this country in conformity with an order of a foreign court. It may be doubted, however, whether these cases would be decided in the same way nowadays, when the courts are even more insistent than they were when the decisions were made that the interests of the child are what matter.[81]

With respect to the recognition and enforcement of foreign custody orders, it is clear that, even if such an order has been made, it is nevertheless the task of the English court to decide whether to comply with it is in the best interests of the child, and this is true even though the child has been brought here in violation of the foreign order[82] or has been 'kidnapped', that is, removed from the custody of the person having lawful custody of him against that person's will (whether or not he or she has custody under a court order).[83]

Thus, in the leading case, *McKee* v. *McKee*,[84] which was not a 'kidnapping' case, since the child was lawfully with the parent who removed him,

---

[77] (1843) 10 Cl. & Fin. 42. The Scots guardian had been appointed in the will of the child's father and not by a court.

[78] (1869) 9 HL Cas. 440, where the Scots court appeared to be unwilling to recognise a guardian appointed by the Court of Chancery.

[79] *Nugent* v. *Vetzera* (1866) LR 2 Eq. 704; *Di Savini* v. *Lousada* (1870) 18 WR 425.

[80] (1866) LR 2 Eq. 704.

[81] But see more recently *Monaco* v. *Monaco* (1937) 157 LT 231. The court merely ascertained whether the Reigning Prince of Monaco had been validly appointed guardian and awarded custody of his grandson, Prince Rainier, under Monégasque law. But he wished to keep Prince Rainier at school in England and to prevent his son-in-law, who had been divorced from his daughter, the Prince's mother, from removing the boy from England.

[82] *Re B's Settlement* [1940] Ch. 54: the refusal to send the child back to Belgium was fortunate; Belgium was soon occupied by the Nazis.

[83] No order existed in *Re T* [1968] Ch. 704 (child returned); *Re A* [1970] Ch. 665 (not returned); *Re L* [1974] 1 WLR 250 CA (child returned).

[84] [1951] AC 352 PC approving *Re B's Settlement* [1940] Ch. 54.

A valid Californian order gave custody to the mother, but allowed the father access to the child. When he was with the father the child was removed to Ontario in violation of an agreement with the mother not to take him out of California.

At a hearing in Ontario two years later, the court held that he should stay in Ontario; the Supreme Court of Canada reversed this, but the Privy Council restored the finding of the Ontario court and said that the judge should not take a foreign custody order for granted but must inquire what is best for the child. He might thus be justified in effectively reversing the foreign order. The welfare of the child is the paramount consideration.

This governs all cases, and obviously does so where there is no foreign custody order or kidnapping.[85] Where the child has been kidnapped, the English courts will express disapproval of such conduct and may be prepared to send the child back without a full investigation of the merits of the case, but will only take this course if it is thought to be in the best interests of the child.[86] However, the Court of Appeal, in Re F (A Minor) (Abduction) (Custody Rights)[87] (where there was no existing foreign custody order) emphasised the importance of speedy return to the country of the child's habitual residence where he had been abducted. In that case the father, who had joint guardianship and custody under Israeli law of the child, abducted him to England. Though Israel was not at that time a party to the Hague Convention of 1980, so the Child Abduction and Custody Act 1985 did not apply to it, the court in effect applied the principles of the Convention. Although the court must treat the welfare of the child as the paramount consideration, this, it was held, would usually be best promoted by the speedy return of the child to the country of his habitual residence. The welfare of the child has to be considered by the English court once it has decided that it, rather than the foreign court, should decide what orders should be made concerning the child. However, before that, the child's welfare has to be considered in the context of deciding whether the English court or the foreign court should consider what the child's best interests require. Only if the child's return is not ordered will the English court decide whether, and what, order should be made under section 8 of the Children Act 1989.

---

[85] J v. C [1970] AC 668 HL.

[86] These principles have been applied in cases where the kidnapping has involved a violation of a custody order: see Re H [1966] 1 WLR 381 (child returned); Re E(D) [1967] Ch. 761 CA (not returned); Re R (1981) 2 FLR 416 (not returned).

[87] [1991] Fam. 23. See also Re P (Abduction: Non-Convention Country) (1997) 1 FLR 780; Re JA (A Minor) (Child Abduction: Non-Convention Country) [1998] 1 FLR 231 CR; and Re E (Children) (Abduction: Non-Convention Country) (1999) The Times, 7 July CA.

Legitimacy and legitimation

General

Legitimacy means the status which a child acquires at the time of birth; it denotes a legal relationship with his father. Legitimation means that an illegitimate child becomes legitimate by reason of an event subsequent to his birth. In English law the only event which has this consequence is the subsequent marriage of his parents; in other systems other events may have it, such as recognition by the father that the child is his, or the enactment of a statute. Adoption means the creation of the relationship of parent and child between persons who are usually not (though they may be) related to each other by nature.

Most of the cases in the English conflict of laws in which the question of whether a child was legitimate, legitimated or adopted arose concerned succession to property. This is the most important, but not the only, area in which the question is involved. But the question of whether a child is legitimate, legitimated or adopted may only be a preliminary issue; if he is, the law governing the succession (which may differ from that which determines his personal status) should govern the issue of whether he can succeed, or whether his father or mother or other relatives can succeed.

It should be noted that the Family Law Reform Act 1987 seeks to remove as far as possible the disadvantages in English law of illegitimacy so far as they affect the illegitimate child.

Legitimacy

All persons who are born in what English law regards as lawful wedlock, or conceived therein, are prima facie legitimate in England.[88] Difficulty arises, however, if a child is not born in what English law regards as lawful wedlock, but is legitimate by some other system of law.

In many cases concerning nullity of marriage for want of legal capacity to marry the legitimacy of children of the union and their right of succession to property was the real point at issue.[89] In most of these, either both or one of the parties to the marriage were or was domiciled here and had no capacity to marry by English law, but married abroad. The marriage was invalid by English law and the 'children' could not succeed.

---

[88] Re *Bozzelli's Settlement* [1902] 1 Ch. 751.
[89] For example, *Brook* v. *Brook* (1861) 9 HL Cas. 193; Re *de Wilton* [1900] 2 Ch. 481; *Shaw* v. *Gould* (1868) LR 3 HL 55; Re *Bischoffsheim* [1948] Ch. 79; Re *Paine* [1940] Ch. 46.

Is, then, the test of birth in lawful wedlock exclusive? It is suggested by most writers,[90] and has been stated by courts,[91] that even if a child is not born in lawful wedlock, but is regarded by the law of his parents' domicile at the time of his birth as legitimate, then he is legitimate in the view of English law.

In favour of the exclusivity of the test of birth in lawful wedlock are the cases referred to on nullity of marriage, and in particular the decision of the House of Lords in *Shaw* v. *Gould*,[92] a succession case, in which the preliminary question of the legitimacy of those claiming to be entitled to succeed was the paramount concern of the House.

> Funds were bequeathed by a domiciled Englishman in trust for Elizabeth Hickson for life, and after her death for her 'children'. English land was also devised after her death to the 'first or other sons lawfully begotten'. At the age of sixteen, Elizabeth was induced to marry one Buxton, a domiciled Englishman, but she never lived with him. Sixteen years later she met Shaw, who acquired a Scots domicile. Buxton was paid £250 to go and live in Scotland for forty days. Thereafter, Buxton's marriage to Elizabeth was dissolved by the Scots courts and she then married Shaw in Scotland. This divorce and remarriage were valid by Scots law, but since the English court did not recognise the divorce (Buxton not being domiciled in Scotland in our eyes) the marriage was invalid by English law.
>
> Elizabeth bore Shaw two daughters and a son during Buxton's lifetime, then Elizabeth, Shaw and Buxton all died. Many years later the English court was asked whether the children could take under the settlement.
>
> By Scots law, the domicile of their father at the time of the marriage, they were legitimate, by English law they were not.

The House of Lords decided that they were illegitimate and could not take under the settlement: that is, the question of the validity of the Scots divorce determined that of the validity of the marriage, which in turn determined the status of the children, which determined their right to succeed.

However, in 1948, Romer J in Re *Bischoffsheim*[93] purported to distinguish *Shaw* v. *Gould*[94] and determined the status of a child by the law of

---

[90] Dr Morris was an exception: see J. H. C. Morris, *Conflict of Laws*, 5th edn (London, Sweet & Maxwell, 2000), 299–300 and A. V. Dicey and J. H. C. Morris, *Conflict of Laws*, 13th edn (London, Stevens, 2000) 857–63.

[91] Re *Bischoffsheim* [1948] Ch. 79; *Bamgbose* v. *Daniel* [1955] AC 107 PC; *Hashmi* v. *Hashmi* [1972] Fam. 36; *Motala* v. *Attorney-General* [1992] 2 FLR 261, *revd* on another point [1992] 1 AC 281 HL.

[92] (1868) LR 3 HL 55.   [93] [1948] Ch. 79.

[94] This decision was expressly followed in Re *Paine* [1940] Ch. 46.

his domicile of origin, a matter which was never regarded as relevant, apparently, in the earlier case.

> In 1919 Nesta married in New York, George, a brother of her deceased husband. After, it seems, both parties acquired a domicile in New York, a child was born of the union. Later the question was raised, was the child legitimate so as to take a share in the residue of an estate bequeathed to Nesta for life, then to 'her children'? According to English law a woman could not marry her deceased husband's brother, though she could by the law of New York.

Thus the marriage of Nesta and George was void by English law and the child was born out of lawful wedlock and, therefore, illegitimate. By New York law, the marriage was valid and the child legitimate. Romer J held him to be legitimate. Re *Bischoffsheim* and *Shaw* v. *Gould* are really irreconcilable. The latter, being a decision of the House of Lords, must, therefore, be correct, and the former wrong, in spite of its subsequent acceptance.

Romer J attempted to distinguish *Shaw* v. *Gould* on four grounds which Morris showed[95] are highly unconvincing.

(1) He said that it was decided on peculiar facts and soon after the introduction of a general divorce law in England, which concentrated their Lordships' minds on the proceedings in Scotland. This does not seem much to the point.

(2) He said that since the divorce was invalid the domicile of origin of the children was English. But the fallacy of this is obvious. Quite apart from the fact that the House never mentioned this, it could not have held that their domicile of origin was English until it had decided that the children were illegitimate and the domicile of origin was, therefore, that of the mother. Whether they were illegitimate or not was the very point at issue.

(3) He said that the invalidity of the divorce was a matter of assumption rather than decision, but since Lord Cranworth, for example, said 'the whole, therefore, turns on the validity of the divorce', Romer J's point is rather out of court.

(4) He said the question of heirship to land in England was in issue. It was not.

The decision has also been criticised on the ground that Romer J regarded the domicile of origin of the child as that of his parents at the time of his birth. Given that both Nesta and George were domiciled in

---

[95] Morris, *Conflict of Laws* (5th edn) 300.

New York at that time, no problem arose, since New York was the child's domicile of origin whether he were legitimate or illegitimate. But suppose the father is domiciled in A at the child's birth, but the mother in B, and he is legitimate by one law but illegitimate by the other, what is his domicile of origin? The answer[96] is that of his father if he is legitimate, but of his mother if he is illegitimate. However, this is a vicious circle and question-begging. But Re *Bischoffsheim* was approved by the Privy Council in 1954.[97]

Arguments in favour of the test of the domicile of origin, at least where both parents were domiciled in the foreign country at the time of birth, are as follows.

(1) *Shaw* v. *Gould* is a very old case as these things go.

(2) The notion that legitimacy is, as a matter of English law, exclusively determined by the test of birth in lawful wedlock is not now true, for the Legitimacy Act 1976, section 1(1)[98] provides for the case of a child of a 'putative' marriage, stating that:

> The child of a void marriage, whenever born, shall . . . be treated as the legitimate child of his parents if at the time of the act of intercourse resulting in the birth (or at the time of the celebration of the marriage if later) both or either of the parties reasonably believed that the marriage was valid.

(3) The choice of law clause for this is framed in terms of the Re *Bischoffsheim* principle. Section 1(2) of the same Act continues:

> This section only applies where the *father of the child* was *domiciled in England* at the time of the birth, or if he died before the birth, was so domiciled immediately before his death.[99]

(4) Acceptance of the Re *Bischoffsheim* test would reconcile the choice of law rule governing legitimacy to that governing legitimation, where the law of the father's domicile at the relevant times both at common law and by statute determines whether a child is legitimated in English eyes. Perhaps then, the rule should be that a child is legitimate if he is born in lawful wedlock, but if he is not, he is legitimate if he is so by the law of his father's domicile at the time of his birth.

---

[96] See p. 39 above.
[97] *Bamgbose* v. *Daniel* [1955] AC 107, 120 PC and see *Hashmi* v. *Hashmi* [1972] Fam. 36 and *Motala* v. *Attorney-General* [1992] 2 FLR 261, revd on another point [1992] 1 AC 281 HL.
[98] Replacing the Legitimacy Act 1959.
[99] Thus, this would not affect *Shaw* v. *Gould*, Shaw being then domiciled in Scotland.

Legitimation

At common law

Legitimation was not permitted by English law until the Legitimacy Act 1926. But the English courts had, before then, been asked to recognise foreign legitimations. Over the years, they had evolved the rule that if the father was domiciled both at the time of the child's birth and at the time of his subsequent marriage in a foreign country (such as Scotland) whose law permitted legitimation by subsequent marriage, the child would be recognised in England as having been legitimated by that marriage. Thus, in Re *Goodman's Trusts*:[100]

> A domiciled Englishwoman died intestate, and the question arose as to which of her brother's children were next of kin to her. (i) While domiciled in England he sired three children by CS to whom he was not married. (ii) He acquired a Dutch domicile and had a child H by CS. He then married her. (iii) They had a fifth child, A. Legitimation by subsequent marriage was part of Dutch law.

It was held that since the father was domiciled in the Netherlands at H's birth and at the time of the marriage, H as well as A was legitimate and so next-of-kin. But the children born when he was domiciled in England were not.

This rule has been superseded by the statutory rule since 1 January 1927, but only in respect of legitimation by subsequent marriage. However, it has survived and may be relied upon in three cases, one of which is obviously of diminishing importance. These are: (1) where the individual is not still alive at the time of determination;[101] (2) where it falls to be determined whether a person was legitimated before 1927, since the legislation is not retrospective; and (3) where the legitimation took effect by way of parental recognition rather than by the subsequent marriage of his parents, as was held, Scott LJ vigorously dissenting, in Re *Luck's Settlement Trusts*.[102]

If the child was legitimated by a foreign statute permitting legitimation by subsequent marriage, but his parents were married before the statute came into operation, it is probable, if an Irish decision on the English Legitimacy Act 1926 were to be followed,[103] that it would suffice if the

---

[100] (1881) 17 Ch. D 266; followed in Re *Andros* (1883) 24 Ch. D 637; Re *Grey's Trusts* [1892] 3 Ch. 88; Re *Grove* (1887) 40 Ch. D 216. It was suggested earlier in Re *Wright's Trusts* (1856) 2 K & J 595. *Renvoi* has been applied: Re *Askew* [1930] 2 Ch. 259.

[101] See Legitimacy Act 1976, s. 3.   [102] [1940] Ch. 864.

[103] In Re *Hagerbaum* [1933] IR 198 it was impossible to prove that he was domiciled in England on 1 January 1927. Australian and New Zealand cases seem to suggest that the father must be domiciled in the foreign country on that date also.

father were domiciled in the foreign country when the child was born and at the date of the subsequent marriage. It should not be necessary that he was domiciled there when the statute came into operation (he might be dead by then).[104]

Statute

Under the Legitimacy Act 1976, this 'dual' test is abandoned, and only the father's domicile at the date of the subsequent marriage matters. Section 2 provides for English legitimations, stating that if the father is domiciled in England at the date of the marriage, the child, if living, is legitimated from that date. Section 3 states that where the father is not so domiciled, but is domiciled at that date in a country by whose law the child was legitimated by the marriage, then the child, if living, is recognised in England as being legitimated from the date of the marriage, notwithstanding that the father was domiciled at the time of the child's birth in a country which did not permit legitimation.

Succession by and to legitimate and legitimated persons

Where the succession is governed by English law, in respect of deeds or wills executed or intestacies occurring on or after 1 January 1976 a legitimated and any other person is entitled to take any interest in property as if the legitimated person had been born legitimate.[105] This applies to persons legitimated under both sections 2 and 3 of the Legitimacy Act 1976[106] or recognised as legitimated at common law.[107]

If the succession is governed by foreign, for example Brazilian, law, it would seem that that law would determine the succession rights by and to a legitimate person and possible whether a person had or had not been legitimated for that purpose. There is no English authority in point.

Adoption

English adoptions

Adoption was first made possible by the Adoption of Children Act 1926. Adoption in England and Scotland is now regulated by the Adoption Act 1976.[108]

---

[104] Re *Hagerbaum* [1933] IR 198.   [105] Legitimacy Act 1976, s. 5.
[106] Or under ss. 1 and 8 of the Legitimacy Act 1926, which correspond thereto.
[107] Legitimacy Act 1976, s. 10(1).   [108] As amended by the Children Act 1989.

An adoption order may be made in England by the High Court, a county court or a magistrates' court[109] in respect of a child under eighteen who is not and has not been married, if the applicant, or in the case of a married couple, on of them, is domiciled in a part of the United Kingdom or the Channel Islands or the Isle of Man, and the child is here when the application is made.[110] If the child is not is Great Britain only the High Court may make an order,[111] if he is in Scotland only the Scots court may do so.

It will be observed that the domicile of the adopter(s) is the sole jurisdictional basis; this seems a retrograde step to have taken. A person may be domiciled in the United Kingdom without living here; it is a pity that habitual residence, which is more frequently employed than domicile in personal matters nowadays, should not have been employed. However, unless the adopter has a home in the United Kingdom he can hardly comply with the requirements that the local authority must have seen him and the child in their home environment and that the adopter has to give notice to the local authority.[112]

The court can make an order even though the child is neither domiciled nor resident here.

It appears that English law alone determines whether an adoption order should be made. The Adoption Act 1976, section 6, requires that the courts must give first consideration to the need to safeguard and promote the welfare of the child. Since his domicile or residence is immaterial to the court's jurisdiction, one might suppose that its law is irrelevant to the consideration of whether the order should be made. But in Re *SB (an Infant)*[113] the court seemed to think, in a roundabout way, that regard should be had to the law of the domicile.

> The child was resident in England, but his parents had been domiciled in Spain. Since they were divorced his mother, who had custody of him, might have resumed her domicile in England, so the child might be domiciled here.

The court had jurisdiction and made the order, but stated that it should consider whether the order would be recognised in a country where the child is or may be domiciled, or of which he is a national or a resident. But this was not a vital consideration if adoption would otherwise be for his welfare.

This is questionable. When Parliament has conferred jurisdiction on the English courts to make orders or grant decrees, the courts do not normally ask whether such orders or decrees would be recognised abroad.

---

[109] Adoption Act 1976, s. 62(2).   [110] *Ibid.*, ss. 15(2)(a), 14(2)(a).
[111] *Ibid.*, s. 62(3).   [112] *Ibid.*, ss. 13(3), 22(1).   [113] [1968] Ch. 204.

By the Adoption Act 1976, section 17 the High Court alone has an extended jurisdiction to make adoption orders in certain cases. These are called 'Convention adoptions'.[114] In this respect the Act is only in force *vis-à-vis* Austria and Switzerland.

Recognition of foreign adoptions

Statute
Adoption orders made in Scotland, Northern Ireland, the Channel Islands or the Isle of Man will be recognised automatically in England.[115]

The Adoption Act 1976 empowers the Secretary of State to specify for recognition certain adoptions under the law of any country outside Great Britain as 'overseas adoptions' provided they are made under statutory law of such country.[116] The countries concerned are not only those party to the Hague Convention of 1965, but others whose adoption law is similar to ours. An order has been made specifying most Commonwealth countries (not including India, Pakistan and Bangladesh), Western European countries, the former Yugoslavia, Greece, Turkey, Israel, South Africa and the United States.[117] The adopted person must not have attained eighteen or have been married and recognition must not be contrary to public policy.

Common law
Adoptions other than 'overseas adoptions' may be recognised at common law. The conditions for recognition were discussed in Re *Valentine's Settlement*.[118]

> The adopters were domiciled and resident in southern Rhodesia, the children in South Africa. The adoption was in South Africa, but this was not recognised in Southern Rhodesia. At the time, South African law, but not English law, recognised an adopted child as the legitimate child of the adoptive parents. The settlement was governed by English law, and the question was whether these were children of the adoptive father.

Lord Denning MR and Danckwerts LJ held that the adoption could not be recognised. This was because the parents were not domiciled

---

[114] After the Hague Convention on International Adoptions, 1965, Cmnd 2615. In May 1993 the Hague Conference adopted a Convention on Protection of Children and Co-operation in respect of Inter-Country Adoptions. This was enacted into United Kingdom law by the Adoption (Inter-Country Aspects) Act 1999.
[115] Adoption Act 1976, s. 38(1)(c).   [116] S. 72(2). See also s. 38(1)(d).
[117] SI 1973 no. 19, SI 1978 nos. 1431, 1432.   [118] [1965] Ch. 831 CA.

and resident (then requirements for English adoptions) in South Africa, but in Southern Rhodesia. Lord Denning MR also thought that the child must be resident in the country where the order was made (as in the then English law), though Danckwerts LJ doubted this. Salmon LJ, dissenting, thought that an adoption could be recognised if the country where the order was made had jurisdiction under its own rules and applied safeguards like our own,[119] subject to recognition being withheld on the ground of public policy.

In the light of present English adoption rules, the rule for recognition of foreign adoptions is probably that they will be recognised here if made where the adopter is domiciled, subject to English public policy (for example if the adoption were undertaken in order to promote the White Slave Traffic), or if it recognised by the law of the adopter's domicile should it not be made thereunder.[120]

Succession by and to adopted children

This should depend upon the law governing the succession. If this is English law, the position is now clear.[121] Part IV of the Adoption Act 1976 provides that a foreign adoption has the same effect as an English adoption, so that, for example, an adopted child shall be treated in law as if he had been born, where the adopters are a married couple, in wedlock, and shall be treated as if he were not the child of his natural parents. This applies to both testate and intestate succession and dispositions of property from 1976 onwards.[122] The rule applies to adoptions in the British Isles, 'overseas adoption' and other foreign adoptions recognised at common law.[123]

Presumably if the succession if governed by some foreign law, for example Brazilian law, that law would apply. There is no authority on the point.

---

[119] This would mean that few foreign adoptions would be recognised since few foreign laws have safeguards as stringent as ours.

[120] The latter is suggested by way of analogy with *Armitage* v. *Attorney-General* [1906] P 135. This case was concerned with recognition of foreign divorces. The principle no longer applies to these, having been abolished by statute.

[121] Before 1976 it was exceedingly unclear since English law was changed more than once: see Re *Wilson* [1954] Ch. 733; Re *Wilby* [1956] P 174; Re *Marshall* [1957] Ch. 263, 507 CA; Re *Valentine's Settlement* [1965] Ch. 831 CA.

[122] Adoption Act 1976, s. 39(5). It includes the disposition of entailed interests (*ibid.*, s. 46(5)) but not, in the absence of a contrary intention, of property limited to devolve with a title of honour (*ibid.*, s. 44).

[123] *Ibid.*, s. 38.

Declarations as to status

By the Family Law Act 1986, section 56,[124] any person can apply for a declaration that someone is or was his parent or that he is legitimate or has or has not been legitimated, by English or foreign law, provided that he is domiciled or has been habitually resident for one year in England at the date of the application. No declaration may be made that a person is illegitimate.

On the same jurisdictional basis, section 57 provides that a person whose status as an adopted child of any person under an overseas adoption or other foreign adoption may ask for a declaration that he is or is not the adopted child of that person for the purposes of English adoption law.

The court must make the declaration if the truth of the proposition is proved to it unless to do so would be manifestly contrary to public policy.[125]

---

[124] As substituted by the Family Law Reform Act 1987, s. 22.   [125] *Ibid.*, s. 58(1).

Part VI

Exclusion of foreign laws

21   Public policy

Sometimes the rules of foreign law which would normally be applied by the English courts are disregarded. The reason for this is that to apply these rules would lead to a result which is contrary to English public policy. Public policy, of course, covers a multitude of sins, but English public policy is of narrower scope than the French doctrine of *ordre public*.[1] One reason for its comparatively rare application is that in relation to such matters as divorce or guardianship and adoption of children, in which the public interest looms large, the English courts apply English law in any case. Moreover, in tort cases the basic choice of law rule is the *lex fori*, which is English law also. It is mainly in connection with recognition of foreign legal statutes, capacities and incapacities, the law of contract, and questions of title to property that public policy can be at stake.

Moreover, some of the cases, particularly with regard to title to property, appear to be explicable on grounds other than the application of English public policy, which may have a smaller role to play even than it appears to have.

It must be strongly emphasised that it is not normally the foreign law itself which is obnoxious, nor, usually, the recognition of its effects,[2] but its enforcement by the English courts.

The discussion can be divided into three parts dealing respectively with (a) penal laws, (b) revenue laws and (c) a possible category of other public laws. Foreign exchange control laws require separate consideration.

---

[1] There have been some signs in recent years of a perhaps too willing resort to public policy on the part of the courts: see *Vervaeke* v. *Smith* [1983] 1 AC 145 (where it seems to have been unnecessary). See also the cases on the former Recognition of Divorces and Legal Separations Act 1971, s. 8(2)(b), p. 329 above, and *Gray* v. *Formosa* [1963] P 259 CA where the term used is denial of 'substantial justice'. As to this term see also *Adams* v. *Cape Industries plc* [1990] Ch. 433 CA, p. 121 above.

[2] See the cases on non-recognition of incapacities or legal disabilities, pp. 362–3 below.

Penal laws

A penal law, strictly defined, is one which is intended to have a punitive effect. A penalty, including a penal sum of money, is, therefore, imposed by way of punishment.[3] The adjective 'penal' is also applied to legal disabilities or incapacities which are imposed on someone, not in order to punish him for a criminal offence, but because they are imposed upon one of two persons, or upon a group of people merely because they form a distinct group, such as slaves or Jews. This rather loose usage of the term 'penal' is really being employed when what is meant is 'discriminatory', and may be justified on the ground that the person who is subjected to the disability is in effect being punished for being the sort of person he is.

The English courts will not enforce penalties such as fines for criminal offences,[4] nor will they enforce foreign judgments for sums imposed by way of penalty.[5] Other classes of laws (i) dealing with status and incapacity and (ii) affecting title to property, will be discussed in turn, and then (iii) recognition of penal laws which are relied on by way of defence, will be considered.

Apart from laws concerned with status and incapacity, foreign penal laws will be given effect, as where an action to enforce a contract is resisted in reliance upon such a law; for example, as has already been explained, the English courts will not enforce a contract which contemplates the doing of an act in a foreign friendly country which is illegal under its law, even if that law can be described as 'penal'.[6] This entails, however, only recognition, not enforcement, of the law in question. But the English courts will not entertain a cause of action which is based on such a law. The same distinction between recognition and enforcement to some extent underlies the cases concerned with foreign laws affecting title to property.[7]

Status and legal incapacities

In several cases it has been held that a particular status or legal incapacity imposed on a person is penal because it is discriminatory and, therefore, should be ignored. Apart from cases connected with prohibitions on remarriage of divorced persons or sometimes the survivor of a deceased

---

[3] See Lord Denning MR in *SA Consortium General Textiles* v. *Sun and Sand Agencies* [1978] 2 QB 279 CA.
[4] See *Folliott* v. *Ogden* (1790) 3 Term. Rep. 726 HL.   [5] See pp. 125–6 above.
[6] *Foster* v. *Driscoll* [1929] 1 KB 470 CA; *Regazzoni* v. *KC Sethia (1944) Ltd* [1958] AC 301 HL: see pp. 216–18 above. See also p. 374 below.
[7] See pp. 363–7 below.

marriage partner (which it is difficult to describe accurately as 'penal'),[8] two English decisions are concerned with disabilities imposed by French law upon 'prodigals' or 'spendthrifts' in order to prevent them dissipating their wealth.[9] In both cases the court appears to have disregarded the disability. But these cases are unsatisfactory for two reasons: (i) the issues in question were governed by English law, not French law, and (ii) it is difficult to understand why a disability imposed on a person in order to protect him or his property is to be regarded as penal, since its object is certainly not punishment. This second consideration makes even less satisfactory Re *Langley's Settlement Trusts*,[10] in which an order of a Californian court declaring a person suffering from multiple sclerosis incompetent to execute documents and allowing his wife to do so on his behalf was regarded as penal.[11]

It cannot be doubted that, nowadays, the consequences of slavery would be disregarded[12] and that a law which forbade blacks to marry whites would, it is thought, be regarded as so obnoxious that it would be ignored.

Effect on title to property

A great deal of unnecessary difficulty or confusion has been generated when English courts have been called upon to consider the applicability, effectiveness or enforcement of laws which purport to confiscate property. The basic issues involved, which have sometimes been obfuscated by the unnecessary use of words like 'confiscatory' or 'penal', are proprietary and so, in principle, governed by the *lex situs*, which normally governs title to property. Further discussion may be divided into two parts: (a) cases in which the property is situated outside the foreign country whose laws are in issue (usually in England) and (b) where it is in that foreign country at the time the law is enacted or enforced.

Where the property is in England

If the property is in England at the relevant time and the foreign law does not purport to apply extra-territorially, that law is obviously irrelevant. The fact that it is confiscatory may induce the English court

---

[8] See pp. 308–9 above.
[9] *Worms* v. *de Valdor* (1880) 49 LR Ch. 261 CA; Re *Selot's Trusts* [1902] 1 Ch. 488.
[10] [1962] Ch. 541 CA.
[11] It is possible that this holding was unnecessary anyway.
[12] Since *Somersett's* case (1771) 20 St. Tr. 1 the status of slave has been unknown in England. It is inconceivable that *Santos* v. *Illidge* (1860) 8 CB (NS) 861, where a contract for slavery was enforced in England, would be decided in the same way today.

to hold that it was not intended to affect property outside the foreign country, as did the House of Lords in *Lecouturier* v. *Rey*,[13] a case which concerned a French law which purported to expropriate the property of the expelled monks of the Carthusian order, including the patent of making Chartreuse.

Where it does purport to have this effect then, it has been held, as with a law of the Spanish Republic confiscating the property of ex-King Alfonso XIII,[14] or with Nazi laws confiscating the property of Austrian or German Jews,[15] that it should not be enforced because it was confiscatory and penal since it was intended to discriminate against one person or a class of person.

But the terms 'confiscatory', 'penal' and 'discriminatory' seem to be surplus epithets in this context. Since the property was here, the *lex situs* was English law and no Spanish, German or Austrian law could affect the original owner's continued title to the property.

That this is the case is confirmed by the English court's refusal also to enforce a foreign law which is not only not penal, but meritorious, in English eyes. In *Bank voor Handel en Scheepvaart NV* v. *Slatford*,[16] Devlin J decided that a decree of the Dutch government in exile in London in 1940 requisitioning property of Dutch residents in the Netherlands to prevent it falling under the control of the German occupant did not affect title to certain gold deposited in England. The English court, he said, could not invent a new 'positive' rule of public policy so as to give effect to the decrees of an allied government which was engaged in war against the common enemy over property in England.

Where the property is in the foreign country

If, when the foreign country enacts a law which deprives the owner of title to the property, the property is there, that effect will be recognised in England, even if the law is confiscatory, provided the foreign state or

---

[13] [1910] AC 262 HL.

[14] *Banco de Vizcaya* v. *don Alfonso de Borbon y Austria* [1935] 1 KB 140.

[15] *Frankfurther* v. *WL Exner Ltd* [1947] Ch. 629; *Novello & Co.* v. *Hinrichsen Edition Ltd* [1951] Ch. 595.

[16] [1951] 1 QB 248. Devlin J refused to follow the judgment of Atkinson J in *Lorentzen* v. *Lydden & Co.* [1942] 2 KB 202, where he gave effect to a similar Norwegian decree. Devlin J had been counsel for the Norwegian Government. See also Diplock J in *Adams* v. *National Bank of Greece and Athens SA* [1958] 2 QB 59 discussing *Lynch* v. *Provisional Government of Paraguay* (1871) 2 P & D 268. Whether a foreign law was or was not 'penal' and so unenforceable here, when relied upon to claim property, was, however, discussed at length in *Attorney-General for New Zealand* v. *Ortiz* [1982] QB 349; [1984] AC 1 CA. The House of Lords did not discuss the question. See pp. 366–7 below. See also *Williams & Humbert Ltd* v. *W & H Trademarks (Jersey) Ltd* [1986] AC 368.

government is recognised by the Crown.[17] This effect follows from principle, and it is once again simply an application of the *lex situs* rule.[18] The only case in which a foreign law which affected property in the relevant state at the time it was enacted was not applied (in time of peace) was *The Rose Mary*,[19] in which the Supreme Court of Aden refused to give effect to an Iranian law which deprived the Anglo-Iranian Oil Company, a British company, of its title to oil in Iran by nationalising its concession. This was because it was held that the Iranian law was contrary to public international law, which distinguished it from laws in earlier cases[20] where the property belonged to nationals of the confiscating state. This reason was, however, doubted by Upjohn J in Re *Helbert Wagg & Co. Ltd's Claim.*[21] He explained *The Rose Mary* on the ground that the decree was penal as discriminating against one company. This is not very satisfactory, either, since in *Frankfurther* v. *WL Exner Ltd*[22] it was said that a Nazi law which discriminated against Austrian Jewish property would be effective as regards property in Austria.[23] The case stands on its own, and appears to be a departure from principle.[24]

The House of Lords has now made clear that if a foreign confiscatory law does not require enforcement here, it will in general be recognised and given effect by the English courts. In *Williams & Humbert Ltd* v. *WH Trademarks (Jersey) Ltd*[25]

> The Spanish state had confiscated a Spanish company, Rumasa, by expropriating all its shares and the shares in its subsidiaries, which included the claimants. (Rumasa itself was claimant in a second action, together with two other subsidiaries.) The claimants sued to recover assets in the form of trade marks and property allegedly misappropriated in breach of fiduciary duty by the controller. This was done at the instigation of the Spanish state, the shareholder.

[17] A decree of an unrecognised government was not given effect in *Luther* v. *Sagor* [1921] 1 KB 436 and see *Carl Zeiss Stiftung* v. *Rayner & Keeler Ltd* (No. 2) [1965] Ch. 525 CA reversed [1967] 1 AC 853 HL.

[18] *Luther* v. *Sagor* [1921] 3 KB 532 CA; *Princess Paley Olga* v. *Weisz* [1929] 1 KB 18; *Jabbour* v. *Custodian of Israeli Absentee Property* [1954] 1 WLR 139; *Bank Saderat Iran* v. *Farsneshani* (1982) Comm. LR 111.

[19] *Anglo-Iranian Oil Co.* v. *Jaffrate* [1953] 1 WLR 246. In time of war such a law enacted by an enemy state will not be recognised: *Wolff* v. *Oxholm* (1817) 6 M & S 92.

[20] For example, *Luther* v. *Sagor* [1921] 3 KB 532 CA.

[21] [1956] Ch. 323, but see note 26 below.   [22] [1947] Ch. 629.

[23] In *Oppenheimer* v. *Cattermole* [1976] AC 249 HL there were strong suggestions that Nazi anti-Jewish laws were so contrary to humanity as arguably not to be regarded as laws at all: see p. 250 note 36 above.

[24] Unless there is something more odious about discriminating against a British company than against a national of or section of the population of the foreign state, e.g. Jews. It is hard to see the justice of a distinction between the two situations.

[25] [1986] AC 368 at 414 affirming Nourse J (at 377) and CA (at 387).

The defendants sought to argue that the proceedings were an attempt indirectly to enforce Spanish penal or other public laws. The House disagreed with this. The rights asserted by the claimants were independent rights to recover their own assets which arose before the Spanish laws came into effect. Moreover, the object of those laws was to acquire the ownership and control of the companies and this had been attained by the perfection of the Spanish state's title to the shares in Rumasa in Spain. Thus there was nothing left to enforce by means of the assistance of the English court.[26]

To summarise, (i) if the property is in England when the foreign law is enacted, that law is irrelevant and cannot affect title since it is not part of the *lex situs*; (ii) if the property is in the relevant foreign country at that time, it will, in principle, be given effect since it is part of the *lex situs*. Also, (iii) proposition (ii) is true, it seems, even if the foreign law is 'confiscatory' or 'penal' in the sense explained above.

The only question which remains is whether, if the law in question is part of the foreign legal system or is enacted there at a time when the property is in the foreign country, but the property is then brought to England, that law will only operate to divest the owner of his title if the foreign state or public authority has reduced the property into its possession before it has been brought out of that country. If this has not been done will the English court nevertheless regard title as having been divested by that law? That it will seems compatible with the course of events in *Attorney-General for New Zealand* v. *Ortiz.*[27] It appears to be implicit in this litigation that the foreign state, or someone who has acquired rights from it, could rely on the title derived from the expropriatory law without needing to have reduced the property in question into its possession.

> The Attorney-General of New Zealand brought an action to restrain the sale in London of a Maori artefact and asked the court to order that it should be returned to New Zealand. It had been illegally exported from New Zealand in violation of local legislation which provided for the forfeiture to the Crown of historic articles which were, or were sought to be, illegally exported from New Zealand.[28]

---

[26] This, in the view of the House, distinguished the case from *Government of India* v. *Taylor* [1955] AC 491 HL, *Peter Buchanan Ltd* v. *McVey* [1955] AC 516n. (see on this case Lord Mackay) and such cases as *Banco de Vizcaya* v. *don Alfonso de Borbon y Austria* [1935] 1 KB 140, since in those cases an attempt was being made directly or indirectly to enforce a foreign revenue or confiscatory law. Nourse J at first instance criticised the views expressed by Upjohn J in Re *Helbert Wagg & Co. Ltd's Claim* [1956] Ch. 323 as unsupported by authority and contrary to *Princess Paley Olga* v. *Weisz* [1929] 1 KB 718.

[27] [1984] AC 1 HL.   [28] Historic Articles Act 1962; Customs Acts 1913, 1966.

The first question before the courts, and the only one argued before the House of Lords, was whether the legislation provided for automatic forfeiture of such articles, or merely that the Crown could take proceedings to forfeit them. If it meant the former, title had passed to the Crown when the article was in New Zealand. If the latter, the Attorney-General had to rely on the legislation in order to recover the article when it was in England. Staughton J, the Court of Appeal and the House of Lords held that it meant the latter.[29]

The second question at first instance and before the Court of Appeal was whether the New Zealand legislation could be enforced here. Staughton J held that though it was a public law, it was not penal. It was meritorious, and public policy and comity required its enforcement. But this argument is the very one which Devlin J rejected in *Bank voor Handel en Scheepvaart NV* v. *Slatford*,[30] and violates the *lex situs* rule. Though its members gave slightly different reasons, the judgment was reversed by the Court of Appeal. The fact that the only question before the House of Lords was the meaning of the legislation suggests that had it provided for automatic forfeiture the Crown could and would have won, though it had not reduced the property into possession.

Defence to an action for breach of contract

Apart from cases in which a penal law has been the reason for refusal by the English court to enforce a contract on the ground of public policy,[31] it seems that the enactment of such a law can be a frustrating event. In such a case, the court will allow the penal law to be pleaded as a defence, for it will not be enforcing that law.

In *The Playa Larga*[32]

> Contracts to sell sugar by C, a Cuban state trading enterprise with separate legal personality and not part of the Cuban state, were entered into with I, a Chilean corporation, a majority of whose shares were held by a Chilean state trading concern. C failed to deliver parts of the cargoes of sugar. I claimed in arbitration in England damages for non-delivery. C's defence was that the contracts were frustrated by the enactment by Cuba twelve days after the coup against President Allende in Chile in 1973, of a law purporting to freeze all property of or demandable or claimable by Chilean bodies such as I.

[29] *Attorney-General for New Zealand* v. *Ortiz* [1982] 2 QB 349 (Staughton J); [1984] AC 1 (CA and HL).
[30] [1953] 1 QB 248.   [31] See p. 374 below.
[32] *Empresa Exportadora de Azucar* v. *Industria Azucerera Nacional SA, The Playa Larga* [1983] 2 Ll.R 171. See P. B. Carter, note (1983) 54 *BYIL* 297.

The arbitrators found that the enactment of this law rendered further performance illegal under Cuban law. They, Mustill J and the Court of Appeal all held that it constituted a frustrating event and a defence for C. I contended that the Cuban law was penal and discriminatory. The arbitrators and Mustill J agreed, but thought that since the law did not require enforcement, it could not, though it was penal, be disregarded. Ackner LJ, who gave the judgment of the Court of Appeal, seemed to believe the law was not penal, since it was not intended to punish anyone, but was meant to be a means of helping to secure compensation from Chile for Cuban property damaged in the coup.[33] He thought it did not contravene public policy. This, with respect, seems the more correct approach.

Revenue laws

The English courts will not enforce claims which are based on foreign revenue laws, and will not act as tax collectors for foreign governments and public authorities.[34] This principle was clearly reaffirmed by the House of Lords in *Government of India* v. *Taylor*,[35] where it held that the rejection of a claim by the Indian Government to prove in an English bankruptcy as a creditor for unpaid tax was correct. Nor will the courts enforce such claims indirectly, as when a liquidator of a company sues to enforce debts due to the company, but it is shown that he will have to pay all the proceeds of his action to a foreign revenue authority.[36] A foreign judgment for a claim for taxes will not be enforced in England.[37] A foreign government cannot evade this principle by claiming under some other law if it is really claiming to recover taxes.[38] If the foreign revenue authority makes a claim for possession of goods in order to enforce its claim for payment of tax, then, it was held in *Brokaw* v. *Seatrain UK Ltd*,[39] it will fail.

---

[33] Compare his analysis of the New Zealand Legislation in *Attorney-General for New Zealand* v. *Ortiz* [1984] AC 1, p. 366 above.

[34] Re *Visser* [1928] Ch. 877 (Dutch estate duty); *Municipal Council of Sydney* v. *Bull* [1909] 1 KB 7.

[35] [1955] AC 491.

[36] See the decision of the Supreme Court of Ireland in *Peter Buchanan Ltd* v. *McVey* [1955] AC 516n. which was approved by the House of Lords in *Taylor*'s case and applied in *QRS 1 Aps* v. *Frandsen* [1999] 1 WLR 2159 CA.

[37] See *United States of America* v. *Harden* (1963) 41 DLR (2d) 721; *Rossano* v. *Manufacturers Life Insurance Co.* [1963] 2 QB 352; Foreign Judgments (Reciprocal Enforcement) Act 1933, s. 1(2)(b).

[38] Re *Lord Cable* [1977] 1 WLR 7, where the Indian Government made an avowed claim under the Indian Exchange Control Act. But it seems clear that such a claim would fail also for the same reason.

[39] [1971] 2 QB 476.

In that case, in which the United States Government served notice of a levy in respect of unpaid taxes, on goods on board a ship when it was on its way to England, Lord Denning MR pointed out that had the United States Government reduced the goods into its actual possession in a warehouse or had the matter of the ship attorned in respect of the goods to an officer of that Government, the latter would have obtained a possessory title to them. If it had then lost possession of them, it could have claimed the goods in reliance upon its possessory title. It would not need to have recourse for this purpose to its revenue laws.

Quite so, but such technicalities and distinctions cast doubt upon the merits of a rule which, in fact, countenances the avoidance of payment of non-penal tax lawfully imposed. No real reason for the existence of the rule (and the House of Lords in *Government of India* v. *Taylor*[40] gave none beyond the statements in the first sentence of this section, which are only statements, not reasons) has been given except that a foreign revenue law is a public law. The rule hardly serves the interests of international comity and seems to have no merit whatever.

In any case, a further limitation on the ambit of the rule is that, although Lord Mansfield once said that 'no country ever takes notice of the revenue laws of another',[41] the courts will, though refusing to enforce such a law, recognise it by declining to enforce an agreement designed to avoid its incidence.[42]

Not every sum payable to a state or public authority is payable by way of tax. If it is owed for particular services rendered, such as airport landing charges or a contribution to a state legal aid fund,[43] it is not payable as tax.

The House of Lords very sensibly held in Re *State of Norway's Application*[44] that a request for evidence to be taken in England for use in tax proceedings in Norway was not an attempt to enforce that country's tax laws either directly or indirectly. Their only enforcement would take place in Norway.

Other public laws

A law of a foreign state may be a public law though it is neither penal, in the sense of being intended as a punishment, nor a revenue law. Whether there is a residuary class of public laws which the courts will not enforce is unclear. Examples of such laws, variously described as assertions of the authority of central or local government[45] or as

---

[40] [1955] AC 491.   [41] *Holman* v. *Johnson* (1775) 1 Cowp. 341 at 343.
[42] Re *Emery's Investment Trusts* [1959] Ch. 410.
[43] *Connor* v. *Connor* [1974] 1 NZLR 632.   [44] [1990] 1 AC 723 HL.
[45] A. V. Dicey and J. H. C. Morris, *Conflict of Laws*, 13th edn (London, Stevens, 2000) 94.

manifestations of the 'prerogative' of a foreign state,[46] are import and export regulations[47] or those forbidding trade with the enemy.[48] But it is arguable that these are penal[49] or revenue laws anyway. If, of course, it is sought to enforce such laws against property here, then, as has already been argued, they should be regarded as irrelevant as not forming part of the *lex situs*. In *The Playa Larga*,[50] as we have seen, Ackner LJ in the Court of Appeal did not appear to regard the Cuban law in question as a penal law, but rather viewed it in the light of general English public policy. However, in that case, there was no question of enforcement, only one of recognition.

Obiter dicta of members of the Court of Appeal in *Camdex International Ltd* v. *Bank of Zambia* (No. 2)[51] suggest that there exists this category of public laws, such as exchange control laws, but although Simon Brown LJ thought that it does exist Phillips LJ also thought so but without complete confidence. In *US* v. *Ivey*[52] a Canadian court was very doubtful as to whether such a category does exist.

In the *Spycatcher* litigation in the Antipodes, the High Court of Australia, in 1988,[53] refused to permit an action by the United Kingdom Government to restrain publication of that book. The Government had claimed that publication would amount to a breach of fiduciary duty or of the duty of confidence or breach of contract. The High Court held, somewhat dubiously, that the action was an attempt to enforce the public interests of a foreign sovereign state which arose from the exercise of certain powers peculiar to government, these being, in effect, the protection of national security. The difficulty with this is that 'interests' are not the same as 'laws' and it is the enforcement of laws which is supposed to be prohibited. The laws in question were not public laws

---

[46] F. A. Mann, *Studies in International Law* (Oxford University Press, 1973) 492–514.

[47] *King of Italy* v. *de Medici* (1918) 34 TLR 623; *King of the Hellenes* v. *Brostrom* (1923) 16 Ll.R 167.

[48] *Jabbour* v. *Custodian of Israeli Absentee Property* [1954] 1 WLR 139.

[49] In *Attorney-General for New Zealand* v. *Ortiz* [1982] QB 349, Staughton J thought that the Italian law in the *de Medici* case *was* a penal law. He denied that there was a separate category of unenforceable public laws, but, wrongly, it is submitted (see p. 367 above), concluded that a non-penal or non-revenue public law could be enforced. But see Lord Denning MR in the same case [1984] AC 1.

[50] *Empresa Exportadora de Azucar* v. *Industria Azucerera Nacional SA* [1983] 2 Ll.R 171. See p. 367 above.

[51] [1997] CLC 714 CA.

[52] (1995) 130 DLR (4th) 674. It was held that even if the category of 'other public laws' did exist, the prohibitory rule did not apply in that case. The Ontario Court of Appeal agreed and said that the action, for reimbursement of costs of remedial measures undertaken by the US Environmental Protection Agency respecting a waste disposal site operated by the defendants in Michigan, was in substance of a commercial and private law nature.

[53] *HM Attorney-General for the United Kingdom* v. *Heinemann Publishers Australia Pty Ltd* (No. 2) (1988) 165 CLR 30.

but were those which govern the relationship between any employer and his employee.[54] This was pointed out by the New Zealand Court of Appeal in the same year.[55] It held that the action was not barred by any such rule and dismissed the action on quite different grounds which have nothing to do with the conflict of laws.

Foreign exchange control laws

These require separate consideration, chiefly because of British legislation concerning such laws. At present, there are no British exchange control laws in operation.[56] However, foreign countries continue to operate them. Several propositions can be stated.

(i)   The English courts will not enforce foreign exchange control laws, in the sense of allowing a foreign state to bring proceedings here to recover moneys due under them. In Re *Lord Cable*[57] the court refused to accede to India's request to be joined as a party to proceedings in which English trustees of the estate of a domiciled Indian attempted to restrain an Indian bank which had a branch here from remitting sums to India.

(ii) They will, however, take notice of such laws in so far as they will not prevent a person here from complying with them. In the case just mentioned, the bank was not restrained from remitting the sums to India.

(iii) They will not enforce a contract which is contrary to the exchange control laws of a state whose laws is the applicable law of the contract.[58]

(iv) A contractual obligation is discharged by the operation of such laws if they form part of the applicable law,[59] or where, if that law is English, they have come into force at the stipulated place of performance.[60]

---

[54] See F. A. Mann, note (1988) 104 *LQR* 497, J. G. Collier, note [1989] 48 *CLJ* 33.

[55] *HM Attorney-General* v. *Wellington Newspapers Ltd* [1988] 1 NZLR 129 at 166. The grounds on which the action failed were that the information was already public and that New Zealand national interests required publication in that country.

[56] The Exchange Control Act 1947 was repealed by the Finance Act 1987.

[57] [1977] 1 WLR 7. India was probably really trying to recover unpaid taxes, claims to which are certainly barred by this rule: see pp. 368–9 above.

[58] *Kahler* v. *Midland Bank Ltd* [1950] AC 24 HL; *Zivnostenka Banka* v. *Frankman* [1950] AC 57 HL. Nor, whatever the applicable law, would such a contract be enforced if it violated the Exchange Control Act 1947 were it operative: *Boissevain* v. *Weil* [1950] AC 327 HL.

[59] Re *Helbert Wagg & Co. Ltd's Claim* [1956] Ch. 323.

[60] *Ralli Brothers Ltd* v. *Compania Naviera Sota y Aznar* [1920] 2 KB 287 CA; *De Béeche* v. *South America Stores Ltd* [1935] AC 148 HL (though the proper law in that case is not stated).

(v)   Such an obligation is not, however, discharged if the laws in question do not form part of the applicable law or of the law at the place of performance but only that of the place where the debtor resides or carries on business.[61]

(vi) In addition to these rules, the courts will not enforce an exchange contract which is contrary to the Bretton Woods Agreement Act 1945 (now International Monetary Fund Act 1979) and Order-in-Council, 1946, to which is scheduled the Bretton Woods Agreement, 1944, which established the International Monetary Fund.[62] Article VIII(2)(b) of the Agreement provides that:

> Exchange contracts which involve the currency of any Member [of the IMF] and which are contrary to the exchange control regulations of that Member maintained or imposed consistently with this Agreement shall be unenforceable in the territories of any Member.

This Article has given rise to several problems of interpretation, only some of which will be discussed here.[63]

(a)   It appears that the words 'of any Member' mean that the foreign country must be a Member at the time of the English judgment.

(b)   The transaction must be contrary to the foreign exchange control laws when the contract is concluded. It does not matter if it subsequently contravenes them.

(c)   The main problem has been to decide what is an 'exchange contract'. This was not settled by an Interpretative Decision of the Executive Directors of the IMF of 14 June 1949. There were two main views. One may be expressed by saying that it is any contract whereby the consideration for goods or services is money, or more widely, that it is a contract which in any way affects a country's exchange resources.[64] The other view is that it is only a contract to exchange the currency of one country for that of another.[65] After considerable fluctuations

---

[61] *Kleinwort Sons & Co.* v. *Ungarische Baumwolle A/G* [1939] 2 KB 678 CA; *Toprak Mahuselleri Ofisi* v. *Finagrain* [1979] 2 Ll.R 98.

[62] See *Singh Batra* v. *Ebrahim* [1982] 2 Ll.R 11 CA approved by the House of Lords in *United City Merchants* v. *Royal Bank of Canada* [1983] 1 AC 168.

[63] See generally F. A. Mann, *Legal Aspect of Money*, 5th edn (Oxford, Clarendon Press, 1992) ch. 13; A. Nussbaum 'Exchange Control and the International Monetary Fund' (1949–50) 59 *Yale Law Journal* 426, and, for a critical appraisal of English decisions, J. Gold, '"Exchange Contracts" and the IMF' (1984) 33 *ICLQ* 777–810.

[64] This was advocated by Dr F. A. Mann and adopted by the courts of some countries and by other writers: see Gold, '"Exchange Contracts"'. It was adopted by Lord Denning in *Sharif* v. *Azad* [1967] 1 QB 605 CA. He later recanted: *Wilson, Smithett & Cope Ltd* v. *Terruzzi* [1976] QB 683 CA.

[65] See Nussbaum, 'Exchange Control'. It was adopted by Lord Radcliffe in *Tomkinson* v. *First Pennsylvania Banking & Trust Co.* [1961] AC 1007 HL.

of judicial opinion, the Court of Appeal, in *Wilson, Smithett & Cope Ltd* v. *Terruzzi*,[66] adopted the second view; this has since been confirmed by the House of Lords.[67] In the *Terruzzi* case:

> The claimants were dealers in metals and metal futures on the London Metal Exchange and the defendant was a dealer with whom they had contracted, who speculated in differences in commodities on the Milan Exchange. In so doing he committed breaches of the Italian exchange control laws. His account with the claimants was in sterling and on standard forms of the London Metal Exchange. When sued for the differences or for damages for failure to take delivery of metals, he argued that the contracts were not enforceable.

It was held that the contracts were genuine contracts for the sale and purchase of commodities and not currency exchanges and were, therefore, enforceable.

(d) The Court of Appeal agreed that they would have refused to enforce an exchange contract 'in disguise', that is, one which appears on its face to be a contract for goods or services in exchange for money, but in which the price of the goods or services is not the real consideration. The House of Lords applied this in *United City Merchants* v. *Royal Bank of Canada*.[68]

> An English company agreed to sell goods to buyers in Peru. At the request of the buyers, who wished to evade Peruvian exchange control laws, it agreed to double the price and to transmit half the total when received to the buyers' associates in Miami. Payment was by a letter of credit confirmed by the respondent bank in London.

It was held that, to the extent of one half of the price, the contract was a disguised exchange contract and unenforceable against the bank.[69]

---

[66] [1976] QB 683 CA.
[67] *United City Merchants* v. *Royal Bank of Canada* [1983] 1 AC 168 HL.
[68] *Ibid.*; see also *Mansouri* v. *Singh* [1986] 2 All ER 619 CA (air tickets).
[69] It is open to doubt whether Lord Diplock, who gave the only judgment, was correct in this. The contract of sale could certainly be viewed in this light. But inasmuch as it was held that the letter of credit was, as between the sellers and the bank, such a contract, this appears to be inconsistent with the basis of the decision on the main point at issue and with the New York case of *J. Zeevi & Sons Ltd* v. *Grindlay's Bank (Uganda) Ltd* 37 NY 2d 320 (1975). It is difficult to reconcile this case with the decision of the Court of Appeal in *Sharif* v. *Azad* [1967] 1 QB 605, to which Diplock LJ (as he then was) was a party. For criticism see F. A. Mann, note (1982) 98 *LQR* 526, and see J. G. Collier, note [1982] 42 *CLJ* 49.

(e) A contract which contravenes these rules is not illegal, but only unenforceable. So a collateral contract is enforceable though the main contract is not; it would be otherwise if the main contract was illegal.[70]

(f) If the relevant exchange control regulations are used by the foreign Member as an instrument of discrimination or oppression, the contract might be enforced. A United States court held that it could be enforced.[71]

Contracts contrary to public policy

The English courts will not enforce a contract, whatever its applicable law, if it contravenes English public policy. This is a rule of English domestic law and is fully dealt with in standard works on the law of contract. Examples of such contracts are: a champertous contract,[72] an agreement to stifle a prosecution,[73] an agreement in restraint of trade (trade in this country at any rate),[74] a contract which involves trading with the enemy[75] or an agreement to defraud a foreign revenue authority.[76] One particular kind of contract which falls foul of this rule was dealt with earlier,[77] that is, a contract the parties to which intend the doing or the procuring of the doing by a third party of an act in a foreign friendly state which is an offence by the law of that state. In the cases in which such a contract was refused enforcement,[78] the applicable law was English law, but it is beyond doubt that the result would have been the same had it been another system of law.[79]

---

[70] *Sharif* v. *Azad* [1967] 1 QB 605 (see, however, the *United City Merchants* case). *Sharif* v. *Azad* is also authority that foreign exchange control regulations cannot, in consequence of the Bretton Woods Agreement, affect an English contract between English residents which is to be performed here.

[71] *Perutz* v. *Boehmische Discount Bank* 304 NY 533 (1953) and see Re *Helbert Wagg & Co. Ltd's Claim* [1956] Ch. 323.

[72] *Grell* v. *Levy* (1804) 16 CB (NS) 73.

[73] This is the best explanation of *Kaufman* v. *Gerson* [1904] 1 KB 591 CA.

[74] See *Rousillon* v. *Rousillon* (1880) 14 Ch. D 351.

[75] *Dynamit A/G* v. *Rio Tinto Co.* [1918] AC 292 HL.

[76] See Re *Emery's Investment Trusts* [1959] Ch. 410.   [77] See pp. 216–18 above.

[78] *De Wütz* v. *Hendricks* (1824) 2 Bing. 314; *Foster* v. *Driscoll* [1929] 1 KB 470 CA; *Regazzoni* v. *KC Sethia (1944) Ltd* [1958] AC 301 HL.

[79] The Rome Convention, 1980, allows the English court to refuse to apply a rule of foreign law if to apply it would contravene English public policy (Art. 16).

Part VII

Theoretical considerations

22   Reasons for and basis of the conflict of laws

One might ask, why does private international law exist at all? Why should not an English court assume jurisdiction over any case which is referred to it? There are two answers to this. First, a great injustice might be done to a foreigner, who is abroad and who has not agreed to submit to the English court a dispute arising from a transaction which is unconnected with England, by summoning him before that court and so placing him in the dilemma that either he has to incur the inconvenience and expense of coming here to defend his interests or he has to run the risk of a judgment being given against him in his absence and so putting in peril assets he may posses here.[1] The second is that the assumption of jurisdiction and determination of rights might well be a waste of effort, in particular if it results in making orders affecting property abroad which the court has no means of enforcing.[2]

A more difficult question to answer is, why should an English court ever apply foreign laws? Why should it not always apply English law? After all, the parties have come before an English, not a foreign, court. English lawyers and judges know English law; at any rate they know it better than they know foreign laws. It may be difficult for the English court to discover satisfactorily what the relevant rule of foreign law is.[3] The answer is that the application of English law might work a grave injustice. If the parties to a contract have selected French law to govern their rights and liabilities under it, and have regulated their positions on the assumption that it does govern, it would in most cases be wholly wrong for an English court to impose different rights and duties on them by applying English law. Or if, for example, two persons have gone through a ceremony in France which makes them man and wife,

---

[1] See the remarks of Lord Diplock in *Amin Rasheed Shipping Corporation* v. *Kuwait Insurance Co.* [1984] AC 50 at 67–8.

[2] This is the reason for the rule that the court will not take jurisdiction over a case which requires it to determine title to foreign land. (There are exceptions to this however.) See pp. 262–4 above.

[3] See, for example, Wynn-Parry J in Re *Duke of Wellington* [1948] Ch. 118, p. 23 above.

it would be unjust for English law to step in and say that they are not man and wife and that their children are illegitimate, because they did not marry by a ceremony known to English law, which it may have been impossible to do in France.

It is submitted that these simple examples afford ample justification for the application of foreign law in cases which possess a foreign element. But jurists have not found this enough. They have searched for theories to explain the application by the courts of one country of the laws of other countries, and since these have had some influence on the doctrines and evolution of the English conflict of laws they require a brief discussion.

The most influential theory is the 'territorial' theory of law, propounded in the seventeenth century by the Dutch jurist Huber (1636–94).[4] He put forward three propositions, which influenced later theorists. (1) The laws of each state have authority within its frontiers; they obligate all its subjects there, but not beyond. (2) A state's subjects must be taken to be all those who are to be found within its frontiers, whether residing there permanently or merely for a time. (3) Those who govern the state must act with comity so that the laws of another state which have been applied within its frontiers maintain their force everywhere, so long as no prejudice results to the power or rights of another sovereign or his citizens.[5] Huber based his propositions on the law of nations.[6]

But if law is territorial, the question arises, why should the law of one territory be applied by the courts of another? Three theories which purport to answer this question, though in different ways, will be mentioned here.

The theory of comity

This theory, which was propounded by Story J (1779–1845), the distinguished American jurist and judge, who wrote the first comprehensive treatise on the conflict of laws in the English-speaking world,[7] derives

---

[4] For earlier doctrines, especially that of the medieval post-glossators, mainly Italian scholars, and that of the statutists, mainly French, see G. C. Cheshire and P. M. North, *Private International Law*, 12th edn, 14–27 (omitted from 13th edn).

[5] *De Conflictu Legum* (1689). This is translated by J. L. Davies, 'Influence of Huber's *de Conflictu Legum* on English Private International Law' (1937) 18 *BYIL* 149 and E. G. Lorenzen, *Selected Articles on the Conflict of Laws* (New Haven, Yale University Press, 1947), 136.

[6] Huber's propositions are discussed critically and at length with great learning by F. A. Mann, from the point of view of both private and public international law: *Studies in International Law* (Oxford University Press, 1973) ch. 1.

[7] *Commentaries on the Conflict of Laws*, 8th edn by G. Melville Bigelow (Boston, Little, Brown & Co., 1883).

from the third of Huber's propositions. It is said that it is necessary to apply foreign laws in cases involving a foreign element because not to do so would constitute a disregard of the sovereignty of another state within its territory and thus show a lack of comity towards it. The word 'comity' sometimes appears in English judgments. Comity itself has a part to play in some situations, such as a refusal to enforce an English contract whose performance would involve a criminal breach of a foreign law in the foreign country.[8] However, it is not always clear what 'comity' means in the context in which it is used (it is not obvious what Huber himself meant by it). It may mean 'courtesy' in the sense of lack of rudeness, or reciprocity, in the sense of do as you would be done by, or friendship, or as 'comity of nations' to mean public international law.[9] Moreover, there seems to be no example of a state complaining that another's court has not applied the first state's law in an appropriate case, though the parties to the action or one of them might well complain that the court has been unjust.[10] In any case, 'comity' is far too vague and shifting a notion to serve as a satisfactory theoretical underpinning for a sophisticated system of private international law.

The theory of vested rights

This derives from another of Huber's statements, which he employs to justify the application of foreign laws: 'the laws of another state which have been applied within its frontiers maintain their force everywhere'. The theory runs that justice demands that rights acquired in one country must be recognised in other countries and be protected by recognition and enforcement there. This theory's chief protagonist in England was A. V. Dicey,[11] and in the United States J. H. Beale.[12] The First US Restatement of the Conflict of Laws (1934) bears his imprint,[13] and very distinguished American judges, such as O. W. Holmes Jr[14] and

---

[8] *Foster* v. *Driscoll* [1929] 2 KB 470 CA; *Regazzoni* v. *KC Sethia (1944) Ltd* [1958] AC 301 HL discussed at pp. 216–18 and 374 above. But this involves merely recognition, not enforcement, of the law.

[9] English judges have a curious tendency to employ the term 'comity of nations' apparently in this sense, since their unfamiliarity with international law may lead them to employ a vaguer term.

[10] Should the parties fail to prove the rules of foreign law, the English courts will apply English law. A foreign state could hardly complain at this. For proof of foreign law see ch. 4 above.

[11] See *Conflict of Laws*, 5th edn (London, Sweet & Maxwell, 1932), p. 17.

[12] *The Conflict of Laws* (New York, Baker, Voorhis, 1935).

[13] Compiled by the American Law Institute, an unofficial organisation whose work possesses, by reason of the reputation of its authors, great influence.

[14] *Slater* v. *Mexican National Railway* 194 US 120, 124 (1904).

Benjamin Cardozo,[15] espoused the theory. It was responsible for the American courts being wedded, for example, to the rule that the law of the place where the tort was committed governs liability in tort. It has been abandoned in more recent times,[16] as has the tort liability rule.[17] In English law, the chief influence of the theory seems to have been on the principles regarding recognition and enforcement of foreign judgments in the guise of the doctrine of 'obligation' as expounded by Blackburn J in *Schibsby* v. *Westenholz* in 1870.[18]

There is, however, some logical difficulty in squaring this with the doctrine of the territoriality of law. How can it be said that the law of country A must be applied in B because a right has been vested in X under the law of A? A state's law, it is said (see Huber's first proposition), only applies within its territory. The way out of this is to say that B's courts do not enforce A's law, but only rights acquired thereunder. But this seems to be a figment of the legal imagination; a right does not exist *in vacuo*, apart from the law from which it is derived. If I say I have a right I am making an inference from a rule of law.

There are other serious problems about this theory. The doctrine of vested or acquired rights was first adopted as an argument against retroactivity of laws. If the law of state A gives X a right, it would be unjust to take it from him without compensating him for his loss. This is satisfactory if it is confined to the law of A, but it has been imported, without logical reason, into private international law, so that state B must not, it is argued, deprive him of his right. There is no justification for thus shifting from time to space, and there may be good reason for not doing so, as where the particular right, such as a right granted in A to Madame X to keep a brothel consisting of Mlles O, P and Q, is contrary to basic moral precepts obtaining in B. B would have every justification in using its own doctrine of public policy to refuse to compel those ladies to serve Mme X in such a way.

Secondly, not all rights acquired under one system of law can be thus protected. If X has a right under the law of A and Y an inconsistent right under the law of C, B's courts have to make a choice. If they select X for protection, this cannot be explained on the ground that X has a vested right, since so has Y.

---

[15] *Loucks* v. *Standard Oil Co. of New York* 224 NY 99 (1918).
[16] See American Law Institute, *Restatement of the Conflict of Laws*, 2nd edn (Washington DC, 1971).
[17] Since *Babcock* v. *Jackson* (1963) 2 NY 2d 473; [1963] 2 Ll.R 286.
[18] (1870) LR 6 QB 155 at 159. It is not entirely clear that the doctrine is derived from the theory.

Thirdly, the question before a court is often not whether a right is to be recognised, but whether a disability or non-right is to be maintained; the English courts have been asked to give effect to restrictions placed by a foreign law upon persons remarrying,[19] or dealing with their own property by reason of prodigality[20] or sickness.[21]

Fourthly, some English rules cannot possibly be fitted into the theory. For example, the rule governing liability in tort at common law is, as has been shown, a combination of English law (the primary law) and the law of the place where the tort was committed.[22] The law which governs a contract is its applicable law, which is in theory and often in practice chosen by the parties and not imposed by law; the vested rights theory presumably would dictate that the law of the place of contracting should always govern. But the idea that it does so disappeared more than a century ago.[23]

The really conclusive argument against this theory is that put by the German jurist, Savigny,[24] long ago. It begs the question. That is, what law is to govern the case? Once this is ascertained its application may produce a right to be recognised. The question cannot be answered by positing a right granted by a foreign law and then supposing it must be enforced. If we do this, we have not even started, let alone finished, answering the question we began with.

The local law theory

The English-speaking jurist who did most to demolish the vested rights theory was the American, Walter Wheeler Cook.[25] He was influenced by pragmatism and by the jurisprudential school of American Realists. So he sought to construct a theory out of observable fact by concentrating upon what, in fact, courts do; and not necessarily upon what they say. He contended that a country's courts never apply foreign law as such, but only their own law. If there is a foreign element in the case

---

[19] *Scott* v. *Attorney-General* (1886) 11 PD 128; *Warter* v. *Warter* (1890) 15 PD 152.

[20] *Worms* v. *de Valdor* (1880) 49 LJ Ch. 261; Re *Selot's Trusts* [1902] 1 Ch. 488.

[21] Re *Langley's Settlement Trusts* [1962] Ch. 541 CA. The cases mentioned in notes 19–21 are discussed at pp. 362–3 above.

[22] See ch. 13 above.

[23] For a discussion of the proper (or applicable) law of the contract and its identification see pp. 192–206 above.

[24] For a brief account of Savigny's theories, see pp. 387–8 below.

[25] *Logical and Legal Bases of the Conflict of Laws,* 2nd edn (Cambridge, Mass., Harvard University Press, 1942), first published 1924. The vested rights theory had already been discredited by the Frenchman, P. Arminjon, in (1933–I) *Recueil des Cours,* vol. 44, 1–108.

the rule of law applied will not be that which is employed in a purely domestic case, but will be one modelled upon the appropriate foreign rule; it will, however, be a rule of the law of the court which decides the case.[26] The great Austro-American jurist, Kelsen, said much the same thing:

> The true meaning of the rules of so-called private international law is: that the law of a state directs its organs to apply in certain cases norms which are the norms of the state's own law, but which have the same contents as corresponding norms of another state's law.[27]

Cook said himself that a plain man would find his explanation 'needlessly complex', but as Anton has said, 'this complexity would not be a defect if it were an accurate and helpful explanation of the facts'. He adds that the explanation seems implausible and certainly unnecessary.[28]

Although Cook's work was of considerable value in clearing away a great deal of theoretical dead wood, it is itself open to several objections. First, it is unrealistic. Although it is quite as important to discover what judges, like anyone else, do as well as what they say, all the evidence is that English judges look to the foreign law directly rather than transform it into a temporary rule of English law, invented for the occasion. Secondly, it seems untrue as an explanation of English conflict of laws. In one case,[29] for example, the court treated an Italian agreement which was unsupported by consideration as a contract. It is difficult to argue that the result was attained by creating a new rule of English law to the effect that an agreement not under seal and having no consideration is a contract, since this would be a flat contradiction of English law. Thirdly, the local law theory is really pointless. Cook, in particular, was concerned that the application of foreign law implies subordination to a foreign sovereign and legislator (this concern is shared by proponents of the vested rights theory). But this concern is baseless; it is perhaps connected with Austinian theories of sovereignty and with views such as Kelsen's that rules of law are built on sanctions. But not all rules of law are of this kind; they are not all imperative. An English court does not, therefore, apply a foreign rule because it is bound by the foreign sovereign to do so, but because it is constrained to do so by English law to achieve justice and a satisfactory solution to the problem before it.

---

[26] Judge Learned Hand said something very like this in *Guinness* v. *Miller* 291 Fed. 768 at 770 (1923).
[27] G. Kelsen, *General Theory of Law and State*, 2nd edn (Cambridge, Mass., Harvard University Press, 1961) 244–5.
[28] A. E. Anton, *Private International Law*, 2nd edn (Edinburgh, Green, 1990) 30.
[29] Re *Bonacina* [1912] 2 Ch. 394 CA.

Policy evaluation methods

Something must be said about these 'methodological' approaches to the conflict of laws, which emanate from and abound in the United States, since failure to do so would result in being charged with insularity. But not much will be said, not only because they are discussed at length and with great erudition in other works on the subject,[30] but also because they have had limited appeal on this side of the Atlantic.

These theories vary somewhat in their approaches and in the degree to which they show a departure from orthodox discussions of the rules and principles of the conflict of laws. But they all, it seems, stem from a revulsion from the somewhat mechanical jurisprudence of the 'vested rights' theories as espoused by J. H. Beale, and reflected particularly in the First US Restatement previously alluded to.[31]

The names of the prime movers, though they might not have wished to be listed together, are Cavers, Cheatham, Currie, Ehrenzweig, Hancock, Reese, A. T. von Mehren and Trautmann.[32] They all tend to concentrate upon the policies behind rules of law, and complain that the existing choice of law rules are territorially oriented and that they simply point to the system of law which is to furnish the appropriate rules of decision. These are alleged to be applied mechanistically quite irrespective of their material content. Further, the concepts of choice of law are too rigid and artificial and cause the courts to reach decisions repugnant to commonsense and ideas of justice or to use transparent devices to arrive at a more satisfactory result, by avoiding their application.

These can be illustrated from the law of torts, where American courts applied the *lex loci delicti* to questions of liability,[33] until they first, somewhat artificially, began to characterise the issue before them as in some way concerned with some other branch of the law,[34] before they abandoned the *lex loci* altogether.[35]

---

[30] J. H. C. Morris, *Conflict of Laws*, 5th edn (London, Sweet & Maxwell, 2000) 542–65; Anton, *Private International Law*, ch. 2 has a characteristically balanced and judicious account. A. V. Dicey and J. H. C. Morris, *The Conflict of Laws*, 13th edn (London, Stevens, 2000), scarcely mentions this, or even any other theories. G. C. Cheshire and P. M. North, *Private International Law*, 13th edn (London, Butterworths, 1999) 23–31 devotes rather more space to them.

[31] See p. 379 above.

[32] These are all highly distinguished academic lawyers; this brief account of their work does not do them justice. But the works mentioned in note 30 above make up for this.

[33] An example of this from this side of the Atlantic is the Scots decision in *MacKinnon* v. *Iberia Shipping Co.* [1954] 2 Ll.R 372: see p. 239 above.

[34] See pp. 233–4 above.

[35] In *Babcock* v. *Jackson* (1963) 12 NY 2d 473, [1963] 2 Ll.R 286. A conflict rule, akin to a 'proper law' of the tort test, began to be evolved and applied.

These jurists therefore concentrate on the material content of the potentially applicable laws, and recommend adoption or rejection of one or other in order to achieve the prime objective, which is to arrive at a 'just solution' of the case. They follow a result-selective approach, therefore. These writers would have the court indulge in value judgments explicitly; and among the values which are up for judgment are what are the respective interests of the states whose laws are in contention (sometimes called 'governmental interests' analysis). Further, they suggest that the courts should look for the legislative policy behind the adoption of a particular rule of law, and make an evaluation of those policies to determine what is the 'better law'.

The difficulties about all this are formidable. The search for the 'just solution' on these lines may be entirely chimerical. There may be no particular policies behind, say, some of the rules of the law of tort of a country, and no legislation either. For example, though the general inability of spouses to sue each other in tort has been abolished in some common law jurisdictions,[36] it has not been abolished in others. Those which have abolished it have done so primarily to get rid of an antiquated relic; those which have not have probably simply not yet got round to it. It is, further, one thing for a court to seek the policies behind the domestic rules of its own law, quite another to seek those behind the laws of other countries. Such a task is one which the court in question is not particularly fitted for and it may be time-consuming and therefore expensive to say the least.

The fairly predictable result of such a search is that the *lex fori* would most probably be applied. This is understandable; there is a tendency to regard one's own law as best.[37] This is what has happened to a large extent in the United States, in tort cases at any rate.[38] Some of the writers mentioned earlier are frank about it, and advocate the application of the *lex fori* unless it can be shown very cogently that there is a very good reason for applying another system as the better law.[39] Currie, in a famous phrase, went so far as to say that 'We should be better off without choice of law rules.'[40]

---

[36] It was abolished in England in 1962. The inter-spousal immunity rule's survival has caused problems in the conflict of laws in Australia.

[37] The court is placed in an invidious position. Once it has discovered the policies behind the competing rules of law, by what criteria is it to determine which is the better policy or the better rule?

[38] This has been pointed out by other American writers.

[39] A. A. Erhrenzweig (see his *Treatise on the Conflict of Laws* (St Paul, Minn., West, 1962)) regards reference to such laws as the *lex loci delicti, lex situs* or *lex domicilii* only as possible exceptions to the application of the *lex fori*.

[40] B. Currie, *Selected Essays on the Conflict of Laws* (Durham, N. C., Duke University Press, 1963) 183.

Two other considerations are either overlooked or minimised by these theorists. First, the object of the conflict of laws, as of any other branch of private law, is to advance the interests of private persons, not the state or government. Secondly, one of the interests that private persons (and corporations) have is in some measure of certainty about the law: whether their contract will be enforceable or not and what are their rights and duties under it, whether they will be or are validly married (or divorced), or whether their testamentary dispositions will be upheld or not, to give some examples of what they wish to know.

Moreover, the adoption of fairly clear basic rules is by no means incompatible with their being based on sound policy.[41] If they are found wanting in this respect they should be changed and sometimes are.[42] Also, it is usually possible in the law to apply what are easily ascertainable and well-defined rules with some degree of flexibility, by, for example, making exceptions to them. This was the approach adopted, in effect, by the House of Lords in *Chaplin* v. *Boys*,[43] the leading English case on torts in the conflict of laws. Although it has to be admitted that the way in which their Lordships did this is rather unsatisfactory, it is difficult to criticise the actual result of the case.

One last point. It may not be too difficult for a court in the United States to proceed on the lines suggested by these American writers. That country's conflict of laws is in practice very much concerned with conflicts between the laws of the states of the union. But those laws differ in detail rather than in substance, for they are all but one[44] derived from the common law. Where they do differ their policies may be ascertainable, as may the respective interests of the states concerned. But in England, as with most countries, the main concern is with conflicts between the laws of independent sovereign states, with quite different legal systems in many cases. It is obvious that the task of an English court in following these doctrines would be very much more difficult, if not impossible.

In any event, the House of Lords, when pressed to adopt the 'new' tort conflict rule as propounded in the United States, proved singularly unwilling to do so.[45]

---

[41] This may be true of such rules as that the parties' choice of law governs their liability in contract, and those which to some extent restrict this.
[42] An example of this being done is the Foreign Limitation Periods Act 1984.
[43] [1971] AC 356 HL.   [44] Louisiana.
[45] See *Chaplin* v. *Boys*, especially the speech of Lord Wilberforce.

23   Public international law and the conflict of laws

The distinctions between the fields of operation and the sources of public international law on the one hand and private international law (or conflict of laws) on the other have already been briefly mentioned. But further discussion is called for, since some doctrinal writers have put forward arguments saying that in some way private international law is regulated by overriding rules of public international law, that there are rules of the latter bearing on the former or that the latter is a source of the former.

A tribunal which exercised jurisdiction in the field of public international law, and whose authority was paramount in the enunciation of the rules of that system, clearly drew the distinctions between the two disciplines. In the *Serbian and Brazilian Loans* cases (1929)[1] the Permanent Court of International Justice[2] said with respect to a dispute between France, on behalf of French holders of Serbian state loans, and Yugoslavia, that

[a]ny contract which is not a contract between states in their capacity as subjects of international law is based on the municipal law of some country. The question as to which this law is forms the subject of that branch of law which is at the present day usually described as private international law or the doctrine of the conflict of laws. The rules thereof may be common to several states and may even be established by international conventions or customs, and in the latter case may possess the character of true international law governing the relations between states. But apart from this, it has to be considered that these rules form part of municipal law.

Nevertheless, some writers,[3] sometimes referred to as 'internationalists', have explored the relationship between the two systems further, in an

---

[1] *France v. Yugoslavia* PCIJ Ser. A, no. 20 (1929) at 41. See also *France v. Brazil ibid.* no. 21. These cases are commonly cited as the *Serbian and Brazilian Loans* cases. They were (rarely for a decision of the International Court) relied on by the House of Lords in *Feist* v. *Société Intercommunale Belge d'Electricité* [1934] AC 161.
[2] Forerunner of the present International Court of Justice.
[3] These are mainly continental jurists, of which Zitelman and Lévy-Ullman are the best known. Anglo-American support for this view is singularly lacking.

attempt to show that public international law at least provides principles upon which domestic courts of states may rely in their creation and application of rules of the conflict of laws. A brief discussion of their views is, perhaps, useful.

The universalists

Before examining these theories, a word should be said of other jurists, called 'universalists', whose views do not go so far and who have had more influence, on the English courts at any rate. The leading 'universalist' was the great German jurist, Savigny.[4] He tried to derive principles from the existence of a community of nations and thought it advisable for the courts of the different countries to model their choice of law rules thereon so as to produce approximate uniformity in accordance with them. The common interests of both nations and of individuals indicate that there should be reciprocity in disposing of cases containing a foreign element and equality in adjudicating between the inhabitants of a country and foreigners.

Savigny contended that every legal relationship could be connected logically and rationally with a given legal system; each relationship has a 'definite seat' that is 'a legal territory to which in its proper nature, it belongs or is subject'. The centre of a legal relationship is the person who has a right or interest in it, so a conflicts lawyer should have regard to a person's domicile in preference to the *situs* of property, to the country where an act takes place, or to that in which the court sits. By the 'seat' of a legal relationship Savigny meant its 'centre of gravity', the territory with which it is most closely connected. There is, of course, a great deal in this; the search for the appropriate system in this sense has been and still is characteristic of Anglo-American private international law. Westlake was the English writer who was perhaps most influenced by Savigny.[5]

But there are serious objections. The 'seat' of a legal relationship cannot be discovered by logic, it is dictated by informed choice. It has been jeeringly pointed out that a bilateral contract cannot, on Savigny's

---

[4] He should be well known to those who have studied Roman law: his writings on the conflict of laws are contained in volume 8 (published in 1849) of his *System des heutigen Römanischen Rechts*, translated as *A Treatise on the Conflict of Laws* by W. Guthrie, 2nd edn (Edinburgh, Clarke, 1880).

[5] J. J. Westlake, *A Treatise on Private International Law*, 7th edn by N. Bentwich (London, Sweet & Maxwell, 1925). Westlake was Whewell Professor of International Law at the University of Cambridge. He was the author also of a leading treatise on public international law, and was thus one of the few English jurists who have been an authority on both public and private international law.

hypothesis, sit at all, or if it does, it sits on two chairs. Some of Savigny's own examples have a rather antiquated appearance nowadays. For instance, he thought that the true seat of a marriage relationship is the husband's domicile, since according to all laws of all nations and at all times he is regarded as the head of the family. This thesis would not find very much favour today.[6]

Another jurist of this school was the Italian, Mancini, who became Professor of International Law at the University of Turin in 1851, and gave an impassioned inaugural lecture called 'On nationality as the foundation of the law of nations'. He said that the real force behind the unity of a people is their consciousness of their nationality; the preservation of nationality is a legal duty, and the law of nations is founded on the recognition of the coexistence of different nationalities.[7] These ideas were later applied to private international law by his followers[8] and, later, Mancini himself argued that the concept of nationality must be the starting point of private international law. A person takes his national law with him, and for another state to refuse to apply this in a case concerning him violates the sovereignty of that person's state. The 'nationality' rule (with exceptions) he regarded as sanctioned by public international law.

Mancini's beneficial influence, like that of Savigny, came from his recognition of the need for harmonisation of private international law rules, and he provided the impetus for the First Hague Conference on the subject. But the emphasis on the law of the nationality led to the failure of the first four conventions which the Conference produced in the early years of the twentieth century and precluded the United Kingdom's participation. It is only since World War II, when the Hague Conferences have moderated the insistence on the law of the nationality, that this country has participated and has become a party to some of its conventions.[9]

The internationalists

'Internationalist' jurists have not, in modern times at any rate, sought to argue that public international law is a source of authority for private international law, in that it is by virtue of the former that a state's

---

[6] Since 1973 a married woman has had her own domicile, separate from that of her husband. Their children's domicile may sometimes follow hers rather than his.

[7] Published in P. S. Mancini's *Diritto Internazionale* (Turin, 1873).

[8] A Scots jurist who accepted Mancini's views was Lorimer, *Institutes of the Law of Nations* (Edinburgh and London, Blackwood, 1883). No English writer appears to have followed suit.

[9] See pp. 393–4 below.

domestic courts enjoy jurisdiction and apply rules of the conflict of laws. Domestic courts apply conflicts rules, both of jurisdiction and choice of law, by the same authority as they apply the rest of municipal law, that is, by authority bestowed by the state in which they sit. This is true of English courts and, even in cases in which the English courts have applied rules of public international law, such as those relating to the immunity of foreign states from their jurisdiction,[10] or those concerned with the expropriation of foreign-owned property,[11] this is because public international law is part of the law of England.[12]

Public international law does contain rules governing the jurisdiction of states' domestic courts to apply their criminal laws[13] and such of their public laws as may be assimilated thereto, and these are of great importance when it is claimed by another state that application of such laws amounts to a violation of its sovereignty.[14] It also contains rules which limit the jurisdiction of domestic courts over foreign states and their instrumentalities, diplomatic and consular agents and international organisations. These are given statutory effect in England.[15]

It is, furthermore, clear that from the point of view of public international law, a failure by a state to ensure that its domestic law conforms with its international obligations may result in a denial of justice and so cause it to commit a breach of international law, for which the rules of its domestic law provide no defence.[16] However, this appears to have little consequence when the relevant rules of domestic law are rules of the conflict of laws such as those discussed in this book. The English rules for the jurisdiction of our courts and those for recognition of foreign judgments do not seem to contravene any prohibitory rules of

[10] See *Trendtex Trading Corporation* v. *Central Bank of Nigeria* [1977] QB 529 CA. The rules regarding state immunity are now statutory: State Immunity Act 1978.

[11] *The Rose Mary* [1953] 1 WLR 246. For criticisms and explanations of this decision of the Supreme Court of Aden see p. 365 above.

[12] This is not, of course, true of international obligations contained in treaties. If these require an alteration of English law, this must be effected by legislation: *The Parlement Belge* (1879) 4 PD 179 affd on different grounds (1880) 5 PD 197 CA; *Cheney* v. *Conn* [1968] 1 WLR 242.

[13] Conflict of laws is not concerned with the application of criminal law or with jurisdiction to try alleged criminal offenders.

[14] The most important example of this is the application by United States courts of the United States' anti-trust and other trade laws. The views of the United Kingdom Government on this are epitomised by the Protection of Trading Interests Act 1980. For a discussion of ss. 5 and 6 thereof see p. 126 above. The literature on this is enormous. See D. W. Bowett, 'Jurisdiction: Changing Patterns of Authority over Activities and Resources' (1982) 53 *BYIL* 1.

[15] See State Immunity Act 1978, Diplomatic Privileges Act 1964, Consular Relations Act 1968, International Organisations Acts 1968 and 1981.

[16] *Alabama Claims* Arbitration (1872) Moore, International Arbitrations, 653; *Jurisdiction of the Courts of Danzig* case PCIJ Ser. B, no. 15 (1928), exemplify this point.

public international law.[17] More significantly, public international law does not, apparently, contain any rules prohibiting the adoption of any particular choice of law rule, nor does it seem to possess any positive choice of law rules which a domestic court must apply, apart from those laid down in treaties to which its state is a party.[18] It seems, therefore, that it is only through failure to comply with its treaty obligations, either through neglect to adopt into its law or through omission by its courts to apply those choice of law rules contained in treaties to which it is a party, that the state will incur international legal responsibility in this way.[19]

The 'internationalists' have argued, however, that there is an international consensus on certain rules of private international law, in the sense that domestic systems adopt and apply them, so that they may be said to be general principles of law and thus of public international law. Two jurists, who are highly critical of this approach, have between them identified several such alleged principles or rules from among the writings of the internationalist school.[20] These include: (1) every state must have a system of the conflict of laws; (2) states must not altogether exclude the application of foreign laws and must respect rights acquired thereunder;[21] (3) but states may exclude the application of otherwise relevant rules of foreign law on the ground of public policy;[22] (4) status bestowed on a person by his personal law must be respected in other states in which he is transiently present; (5) the *lex situs* governs immovables; (6) *mobilia sequuntur personam*, that is, title to movables, is governed by the personal law; (7) the *lex loci actus* governs the form of a transaction; (8) the parties have a free choice of the law to govern their contractual obligations.[23]

It has been rightly said[24] that the first four of these, even if they are accepted, do not actually prescribe any rule to govern anything, and

---

[17] No protest against their application by another state seems to have been made.

[18] For such conventions to which this country is a party see pp. 392–4 below.

[19] For a case in which a state was accused of a breach of a treaty concerned with conflict of laws, unsuccessfully as it happens, see *Guardianship of an Infant* case (*Netherlands* v. *Sweden*) ICJ 1968, 55.

[20] K. Lipstein, 'The General Principles of Private International Law' (1972–I) *Recueil des Cours*, vol. 135, 97 at 168; O. Kahn-Freund, 'General Principles of Private International Law' (1974–III) *ibid.*, vol. 143, 20 ff.

[21] For a discussion of the doctrine of vested rights and the difficulties produced by it see pp. 379–80 above.

[22] See the judgment of Judge Lauterpacht in the *Guardianship of an Infant* case ICJ 1968 at 55 for an espousal of the application of public policy by way of exception to a treaty obligation. As to this see K. Lipstein, 'The Hague Conventions on Private International Law, Public Law and Public Policy' (1968) 8 *ICLQ* 506.

[23] See *Serbian and Brazilian Loans* cases PCIJ Ser. A, nos. 20, 21 (1929).

[24] Lipstein, 'General Principles', 169.

that the almost universal tendency to apply domestic public policy as a means of excluding foreign law which is normally applicable by the conflicts rule of the *forum* shows the inability of states to agree on any desirable particular choice of law rules. The possession by practically all countries of systems of private international law at most shows that they wish to observe minimum standards of justice.

The rules numbered (5) to (8) are specific choice of law rules. Of these it has been observed[25] that they are a very poor collection, for they cover only a small part of the ground covered by private international law. Some, such as (6), are ambiguous.[26] Some are not applied by every state: for example Italian courts do not apply the *lex situs* to govern succession to immovables.[27] English courts, as have been seen, do apply these rules, but in the case of each, either to certain aspects of the subject-matter only[28] or with some exceptions[29] or as an alternative to other choice of law rules[30] or with restrictions placed upon them.[31]

Moreover, even if all these eight principles or rules constitute general principles of law, they are principles of private international law, not public international law. They are not, therefore, sources of the conflict of laws as applied by domestic courts, derived from or ordained by public international law, but general principles of law applicable by international tribunals and in that sense sources of public international law.[32]

It may be added that, in some case, an international tribunal or a quasi-international tribunal, such as one created to arbitrate a dispute between a state and a foreign corporation which arises out of an agreement between them, may select a choice of law rule to govern, either with reference to the conflicts rules of one or both of the states which are parties to the proceedings,[33] or by avoiding the problem of choice of

---

[25] Kahn-Freund, 'General Principles', 28.

[26] This also applies to principle (4). The personal law in some systems is the law of the person's nationality, in others the law of his domicile. Resort to the 'personal law' without saying what that actually means is of little assistance in deciding a case.

[27] See Re *Ross* [1930] 1 Ch. 377.

[28] This is true of the brocard *mobilia sequuntur personam*. It governs most aspects of succession on death or bankruptcy, but not all. It is not relevant to questions of title *inter vivos* as was shown at pp. 244–5 above. Nor does the *lex situs* govern all questions relating to immovables: see pp. 267, 275–6 above.

[29] For example, the application of the *lex loci actus* (called *lex loci celebrationis*) to govern the formal validity of marriage: see pp. 295–8 above.

[30] Again, the formal validity of contracts or marriage settlements is governed by either the *lex loci actus* or the proper law of the transaction: see pp. 207–8 and 278 above.

[31] For restrictions placed upon the operation of the parties' freedom of choice in the selection of the applicable law of a contract see pp. 213–18 above.

[32] See Statute of the International Court of Justice, Art. 38(1)(c).

[33] *Serbian and Brazilian Loans* cases PCIJ Ser. A, nos. 20, 21 (1929).

law rather than solving it, by resorting to something like 'principles rooted in good sense and the common practice of civilised states' or 'general principles of law' to find a special rule to decide a case instead of choosing a rule from an existing system of domestic private international law.[34] Sometimes these techniques may be combined, as in the World Bank Convention for the Settlement of Investment Disputes between States and Nationals of other States, 1965.[35] Under this treaty the parties to a dispute may select the rules of law which the tribunal is to apply. Failing any such selection, it is to apply the law of the contracting state which is a party to the dispute, including its conflict rules, and such rules of international law as may be applicable.

However, it seems that public international law, or those parts of it which derive from the practice of states (that is, customary international law)[36] or from general principles of domestic law, is a somewhat infertile producer of rules of the conflict of laws. More promising in this respect is conventional international law, that is, treaties, on the subject of private international law. To these we now turn.

International conventions

The impact of public international law upon the rules of English conflict of laws is of increasing importance because of the number of international conventions relating to private international law to which the United Kingdom has in relatively recent times become a party, which has necessitated legislative amendment of the rules of English domestic law.

A few of these are bilateral treaties, but they are all concerned with the mutual recognition and enforcement of the judgments of the courts of the contracting states.[37] More important are multilateral conventions. These, or the legislation which implements them, have been discussed in detail in the appropriate places, but some example will be given here.

Three conventions deal with arbitration.[38] The United Kingdom is a party to the Protocol on Arbitration Clauses (1923) and the General

---

[34] An example is the *Abu Dhabi Arbitration* (1952) 18 ILR no. 37. Much literature exists on this subject. See, in particular, F. A. Mann, 'The Proper Law of Contracts concluded by International Persons' (1959) 35 *BYIL* 34 and 'State Contracts and International Arbitration' (1967) 42 *BYIL* 1; Lord McNair, 'General Principles of Law recognised by Civilised Nations' (1975) 33 *BYIL* 1–19.

[35] Cmnd 3255.

[36] Statute of the International Court of Justice, Art. 38(1)(b).

[37] These form part of English law by the Foreign Judgments (Reciprocal Enforcement) Act 1933, discussed at pp. 127–8 above.

[38] For details, see A. V. Dicey and J. H. C. Morris, *Conflict of Laws*, 13th edn (London, Stevens, 2000) ch. 16.

Convention on the Execution of Foreign Arbitral Awards (1927), which are implemented by the Arbitration Act 1950, Part II; these are concerned with the mutual recognition and enforcement of arbitral awards. However, these are, to a large extent, superseded by the New York Convention on the Recognition and Enforcement of Foreign Arbitral Awards (1958), which is implemented by the Arbitration Act 1996.[39]

These conventions were concluded under the auspices of the League of Nations and its successor, the United Nations, but they do not deal with choice of law rules.

More significant has been the contribution of conventions concluded by the Hague Conference on Private International Law. This drew up certain conventions in the early years of the twentieth century, but without the participation of the United Kingdom.[40] But the seventh conference was held in 1951 (the statute of the conference entered into force on 15 July 1955), and this country has been able to participate in its work. So far it has produced over thirty conventions; these include that concerning the law applicable to the International Sales of Movable Goods (1955) and that concerning Transfer of Property in such Goods (1958), the Convention on the Law Applicable to Traffic Accidents (1971) and that on the Law Applicable to Products Liability (1973). The success rate, as far as the United Kingdom is concerned, has been relatively slight; we have become parties to but few of them. The United Kingdom has been recommended not to ratify at least two of them, the Convention Governing Conflicts between the Law of Nationality and the Law of the Domicile of 1955 (the so-called *renvoi* convention) and, more recently, the Convention on Celebration and Recognition of the Validity of Marriages (1978).

The United Kingdom has become a party to some Hague Conventions. These are (with their implementing statutes): the Conventions on the Forms of Testamentary Dispositions, 1961 (Wills Act 1963);[41] Adoption, 1965 (Adoption Act 1976);[42] Taking of Evidence Abroad, 1970 (Evidence (Proceedings in Other Jurisdictions) Act 1975); Recognition of Divorces and Legal Separations, 1970 (Family Law Act 1986, Part II); and International Child Abduction, 1980. The last, together with the Council of Europe's Convention of the same year on recognition and enforcement of foreign custody orders, was enacted into English law by the Child Abduction and Custody Act 1985.[43] The Convention

---

[39] See also the Arbitration (International Investment Disputes) Act 1966 implementing the World Bank's Convention for settlement of such disputes, 1965.
[40] For the reasons for this see p. 336 above.   [41] See p. 272 above.
[42] As amended by the Children Act 1989: see p. 355 above.
[43] See pp. 339–44 above.

on the law applicable to trusts and their recognition is enacted into English law by the Recognition of Trusts Act 1987. Only the first and last of these contain choice of law rules. All the others are concerned with procedure or with jurisdiction and recognition or enforcement of judgments or orders of foreign tribunals.

Some impact has been made upon English conflict of laws by membership of the European Union, one of whose objectives is the harmonisation of the laws of the member states. A convention which is in force in respect of this country is the 1968 Convention on Jurisdiction and Judgments in Civil and Commercial Matters, known as the Brussels Convention, implemented by the Civil Jurisdiction and Judgments Act 1982.[44] The United Kingdom was obliged to become a party to this Convention, and did so, with modifications to it, by the Accession Convention of 1978. It was not obliged to become a party to the EC Convention, 1980, on Contractual Obligations. However, it became a party to it in 1991 and it became part of United Kingdom law by the Contracts (Applicable Law) Act 1990.[45]

In conclusion, a brief mention should be made of international conventions which seek to suppress conflicts of laws, not by harmonisation of the rules of the conflict of laws, but by laying down uniform rules of domestic law governing certain matters. A prime example of this type of convention, which has been met with in this book, concerns the carriage of goods by sea. A convention signed at Brussels in 1924 laid down the Hague Rules governing the rights and liabilities of shipowners and cargo owners under bills of lading. It was implemented by the Carriage of Goods by Sea Act 1924.[46] This was repealed by the Carriage of Goods by Sea Act 1971 which gives effect to the Hague Rules as amended by the Brussels Protocol of 1968, called the Hague-Visby Rules, by providing that the latter have the force of law in the United Kingdom.[47]

---

[44] See ch. 10 above. It is also a party to the parallel Lugano Convention, 1989 with EFTA countries, implemented by the Civil Jurisdiction and Judgments Act 1991: see *ibid.*

[45] See ch. 12.

[46] See *Vita Food Products Inc.* v. *Unus Shipping Co.* [1939] AC 277 PC.

[47] See *The Hollandia* [1983] 1 AC 565 HL: p. 215 above.

Index

actions *in personam*, jurisdiction in, 71–83
actions *in rem*, jurisdiction in, 83
administration of estates, 268–70
  choice of law, 268
  distribution, distinguished from, 268
  English grant of representation,
    jurisdiction to make, 266–7; to
    whom made, 267–8
  see also personal representatives;
    succession
Admiralty action, 83
adoption, 353–6
  Adoption Act 1976, 353–5
  British Isles, in, recognition of, 354
  declaration of, 357
  domicile, and, 39
  English, 353–5
  foreign, recognition of, 355–6
  Hague Conventions, 355
  overseas, recognition of, 355
  public policy, and, 356
  succession, and, 356
applicable law
  see contract
arbitration, 179–85
  Administration of Justice Act 1920, 179
  agreement, 180–1
  Arbitration Act 1950, 179, 182
  Arbitration Act 1996, 182–5
  Civil Jurisdiction and Judgments Act
    1982, 136, 180
  common law, and, 180–2
  finality of award, 181–2
  foreign award, defences to action on,
    181, 183–4
  Foreign Judgments (Reciprocal
    Enforcement) Act 1933, 180
  Geneva Convention of Execution of
    Foreign Arbitral Awards, 179–82
  International Investment Disputes, 185
  judgment of foreign court, and, 179,
    181

  law governing proceedings, 181
  law of agreement, 180
  methods of enforcement of award, 179
  New York Convention, 1958, 179, 183
  Protocol on Arbitration Clauses, 179
  recognition of award as defence, 183
  validity of agreement, 180
  validity of award, 180
arbitration clause:
  applicable law of contract, and, 194–5
  restraining foreign proceedings, and,
    106–8
  staying of actions, and, 184–5
armed forces:
  domicile of choice and, 46
  members serving abroad, marriages of,
    299
assignment:
  intangible movables, of, 252–61
association, domicile of, 139

belligerent occupation, marriages in
  countries under, 300
branch or agency, claims arising out of
  running of, 147–9
Brussels Convention on jurisdiction and
  enforcement of judgments, 1968:
  actions *in rem*, and, 160–2
  characteristics of, 133–4
  domicile, under, 138–9
  enforcement of judgments, and,
    167–74
  exclusive jurisdiction under, 153–4,
    264–6
  interpretation of, 132–3
  jurisdiction, under, 136–67
  jurisdiction agreements under, 154–8
  objectives of, 133–4
  protective measures under, 167, 168
  provisional measures under, 167, 168
  reciprocal enforcement within United
    Kingdom, 175

Brussels Convention (*cont.*):
  recognition of judgments, and, 167–74
  refusal of enforcement under, 168–73
  refusal of jurisdiction under, 159
  refusal of recognition under, 168–73
  relationship to other Conventions,
    171–4
  scope of, 134–6
  special jurisdiction under, 140–52
  staying of proceedings under, 159–66
  submission under, 154–9

capacity:
  contract, to, 208–9
  foreign, when disregarded, 308
  immovables, to transfer, 266–7
  intangible movables, to assign, 255–6
  marriage settlement, to create, 277–80
  marry, to, *see* marriage
  will, to make, 271, 273
characterisation:
  analytical jurisprudence and
    comparative law, 17
  English courts and, 17–19
  Falconbridge's views, 17
  lex causae, and, 16
  lex fori, and, 15
  nature of the problem, 13–15
children, *see* adoption; custody; domicile;
    guardianship; legitimacy;
    legitimation; minor; orders
    respecting; polygamous marriage
choice of law rules, analysis, 11–12
Civil Jurisdiction and Judgments Act
    1982, 131–75
Civil Jurisdiction and Judgments Act
    1991, 131
Civil Procedure Rules, service out of the
    jurisdiction under, 74–82
claim form
  service with permission, 74–82
  service without permission, 74–183
co-defendants, jurisdiction over, 149–50
comity, theory of, 378–9
common law marriage, 299–300
companies:
  amalgamation of, 57
  dissolution of, 57
  domicile of, 57–8, 139
  exclusive jurisdiction, and, 153–4
  foreign court, jurisdiction over,
    112–13
  jurisdiction, and, 82–3
  nationality of, 59
  residence of, 58–9
  status of, 57

conflict of laws:
  basis of, 377–85
  characteristics of, 8–10
  late development of, 8–9
  name, 5–6
  reasons for, 377–85
  subject-matter, 3–4
connecting factors, 12–13
consent:
  parental to marriage, 297
  parties to marriage, of, 310–11
consideration, contract, and, 206
consumer contract:
  applicable law of, 202–3
  jurisdiction over, 152–3
contract:
  applicable law, ascertainment of,
    192–205
  breach of, 211–12
  Brussels Convention and, 140–4
  capacity to, 208–9
  carriage of goods, for, 201
  Carriage of Goods by Sea Act 1971,
    215
  characterisation, and, 192
  characteristic performance, 198–201;
    closest connection, 201; express
    choice of, 193; imputed choice of,
    197–201; inferred choice of, 194–5;
    mandatory rules and, 197; *renvoi*
    and, 27, 204; presumptions as to,
    198–203; time at which ascertained,
    204–5
  consideration, 206
  consumer, 202–3
  Contracts (Applicable Law) Act 1991,
    189–219
  defendant out of the jurisdiction when,
    77–80
  discharge of, 212
  employment, of, 63, 203
  exemption clause in, 214, 235–7
  existence of, 206
  extinction of obligations, 212
  formal validity of, 207–8
  formation of, 206
  illegality, and, 212
  immovables, for, 201
  interpretation of, 210
  limitation and, 212
  mandatory rules and, 213–15
  misrepresentation, 206
  mistake, 206
  performance, 211
  place of contracting, law of, 207–8
  place of performance, law of, 211

public policy and, 215–19, 374
putative applicable law, 205–6
scission of, 195–6
statutes and, 213–15
Rome Convention, 1980, application,
    191–2; interpretation, 190–1
termination of, 212
tort and, 235–7
conventions, international, 392–4
Cook, theory of, 381–2
corporations, see companies
country, meaning of, 6–7
criminal proceedings, civil claims in,
    jurisdiction, 140
custody, 336–44
    Child Abduction and Custody Act
        1985, 339–44
    foreign order, effect in England,
        339–44
    international conventions, 339–44
    see also orders respecting children

damages, 65–6
debts:
    assignability of, 253
    assignment of, 252–61; capacity, and,
        255–6; essential validity of, 254;
        formal validity of, 254; priorities,
        257–61
    garnishment of, 259–61
    situs of, 251–2
declarations as to status:
    adopted status, 357
    legitimate or legitimated status, 357
    marital status, 333
    parentage, of, 357
deportation: persons liable to, domicile of
    choice of, 45
divorce, 319–33
    choice of law, 320
    domicile, and, 320
    foreign, see foreign divorce
    granted in British Isles, recognition of,
        323–4, 328
    habitual residence, and, 320
    jurisdiction in, 319–20
domicile, 40–54
    adoption, and, 39
    association, of, 139
    capacity to make will, and, 271
    capacity to marry, and, 302–4
    change of, 39–47
    company, of, 57–8
    construction of wills, and, 273–6
    criticism of, 51–3
    definition of, 37–8

divorce, and, 320
foreign annulment, and, 324, 325–6
foreign divorce, and, 324, 325–6
general principles, 37–8
habitual residence, and, 53, 56
individual, of, 138–9
interpretation of wills, and, 273–6
intestate succession, and, 271
matrimonial, meaning, 281–2
nullity of marriage, and, 321
proposals for reform of law, 53–64
social bond, as, 44–5
transfer of movables, and, 245
trust, of, 139
domicile of choice, 39–47
    abandonment of, 46–7
    acquisition of, 40–5
    domicile of origin, compared with,
        39–40
    intention, and, 40–4; declarations of,
        44; evidence of, 44; motive, and,
        45–6
    proof of, burden of, 42–4, 51; standard
        of, 42, 51
    residence, and, 40
domicile of dependence, 47–50
    married women, 47–8
    mental patients, 50
    minors, 48–50
domicile of origin, 38–9
    acquisition of, 38–9
    domicile of choice, compared with, 39
    legitimacy, and, 351
    revival of, 40, 47, 51, 52–3

EC judgment, method of enforcement of,
    173
EFTA countries, jurisdiction and
    judgments of, 132
employees, domicile of choice of, 46
employment contracts:
    applicable law of, 203
    jurisdiction over, 142–3
equitable jurisdiction, immovables, and,
    262–4
EU countries:
    jurisdiction within, 136–67
    recognition and enforcement of
        judgments of, 167–73
evidence, 60–3
    admissibility, 63
    burden of proof, 61–2
    extrinsic, 63
    manner of proof, 61–3
    presumptions, 61
    written, requirement of, 62–3

exclusion of foreign law, *see* foreign
    exchange control laws; governmental
    taking of property; penal law; public
    policy; revenue law
exemplary damages, foreign judgment,
    for, 126
exemption clause, contract, in, 214,
    235–7
expert evidence, proof of foreign law by,
    34–5
extrinsic evidence, 63

foreign annulment, 322–30
    domicile, and, 324, 325–6
    EU, and, 330–2
    Family Law Act 1986, 323–30
    grounds for attacking, 328–30
    habitual residence, and, 324
    nationality, and, 324
    obtained by means of proceedings,
        324–5
    obtained otherwise than by
        proceedings, 325–6
    recognition manifestly contrary to
        public policy, 329
    recognition of, 323–30
    valid, remarriage after, 307
    void, remarriage after, 308
    want of notice to respondent, 329
    want of opportunity to take part, 329
foreign arbitration award, debtor outside
    England, 81
foreign arbitration clause, staying of
    English actions, and, 96–7
foreign court, jurisdiction of, 110–17
foreign currency:
    judgments in, 65–6
foreign divorce, 322–30
    domicile, and, 324, 325–6
    EU, and, 330–2
    Family Law Act 1986, 323
    grounds for attacking, 328–30
    habitual residence, and, 324
    nationality, and, 324
    obtained by means of proceedings,
        324–5
    obtained otherwise than by
        proceedings, 325–6
    recognition manifestly contrary to
        public policy, 329
    recognition of, 323–30
    Recognition of Divorces and Legal
        Separations Act 1971, 323
    transnational divorces, 325
    valid, remarriage after, 307
    void, remarriage after, 308

    want of notice to respondent, 329
    want of opportunity to take part, 329
foreign exchange control laws, 371–4
foreign judgments, 109–30
    Brussels Convention, 1968, 168–74,
        175
    common law and statute, 109
    debtor outside England, 81
    defence, as, 128–30
    discovery of fresh evidence, and, 118
    doctrine of obligation, 109–10
    enforcement of, Administration of
        Justice Act 1920, 109, 127; bases of
        jurisdiction, 110–16; basis of, 109;
        common law, 109; debt or fixed sum
        for, 125; error of fact or law, 118;
        estoppel, and, 128–30; exemplary
        damages, for, 126; final and
        conclusive, 127; Foreign Judgments
        (Reciprocal Enforcement) Act 1933,
        109, 120, 127
    fraud, and, 119–20, 128, 130
    jurisdiction of foreign court, 110–17;
        domicile, and, 116; nationality, and,
        110, 116; office or place of business,
        and, 115; possession of property,
        and, 116; presence or residence, and,
        111, companies of, 112–13; presence
        when cause of action arose, and,
        111; reciprocity, and, 116–17;
        submission, and, 113–15
    lack of internal competence, and, 118
    merits of, 117–18
    multiple damages, for, 126
    natural justice, and, 120–1
    non-defences to, 117–18
    non-merger rule, abolition of, 123
    penalties, for, 125–6
    public policy, contrary to, 121–3
    punitive damages, for, 125–6
    reciprocal enforcement within United
        Kingdom, 175
    recognition, 109
    recognition and enforcement
        distinguished, 109
    rendered by courts inside EU, 168–74,
        175
    rendered by courts outside EU, 109–30
    statute, under, 109, 127–8
    taxes, for, 125
foreign jurisdiction clause, staying of
    English actions, and, 96–7
foreign law:
    exchange control, 371–4
    exclusion of, 361–71
    penal, 362–8

proof of, *see* proof of foreign law
public, 369–71
public policy, and, 361–74
revenue, 368–9
foreign territorial waters, torts in, 239
formalities of marriage, *see* marriage
forum non conveniens:
　service out of the jurisdiction, and, 75
　staying of English actions, and, 84–100
freezing injunction, 77, 168
fugitives, domicile of choice of, 45–6

garnishment, debt, of, 259–61
geographical considerations, 6–7
governmental taking of property:
　foreign, 363–7; property brought to
　　England, 364–7; property outside
　　territory of foreign state, 363–4
　penal law, whether, 345–6, 363
guardianship, 335–6
　foreign order, effect in England,
　　345–6
　international conventions, 339–44
　jurisdiction of English courts, 335–6
　see also custody

habitual residence:
　contracts and, 198–9
　domicile, comparison with, 53, 56
　divorce, and, 320
　foreign annulment, and, 321
　foreign divorce, and, 324
　formal validity of a will and, 272
　meaning, 55–7
　nullity of marriage, and, 324
Hague conventions, 393–4
high seas, torts on, 238–9
Huber, territorial theory, 378

illegality, contract, of, 212
immovables:
　Brussels Convention, under, 264–6
　capacity to transfer, 267
　choice of law, 266–7
　contract, and, 201
　equitable jurisdiction, 261–4
　exclusive jurisdiction over, 264–6
　jurisdiction, 261–6
　lex situs, and, 266–7
　matrimonial property, and, 284
　movables, and, 243–4
　succession to, 275–6; time factor, and,
　　30
　transfer of, 266–7
immutability, doctrine of, 282–4
impotence, 321

incapacity, foreign, when disregarded,
　308–9, 363
incidental question, 12–13
injunction:
　defendant out of jurisdiction, when, 76
　freezing, 77
　to restrain proceedings abroad, 100–8
insurance contracts, jurisdiction over, 152
intangible movables, 251–61
　assignment of, 252–61
　situs, of, 251–2
international conventions, 392–4
internationalists, the, 388–92
intestate succession:
　immovables, to, 275
　movables, to, 271
invalids, domicile of choice of, 46

joint tortfeasors, 65, 129
jurisdiction of the English court
　actions *in personam*, 71–83
　actions *in rem*, 83
　companies, over, 82–3
　defendant domiciled in EU, when, *see*
　　Brussels Convention, 1968;
　　exclusive, 153–4, 264–6; general
　　rule, the, 136–7; review of, 172–3;
　　special, 140–52; submission, 154–9
　defendant not domiciled in EU, 72–83;
　　extended, Civil Procedure Rules,
　　under, 74–82; presence, 72–3;
　　submission, 73–4
　divorce and judicial separation, 321
　foreign court, of, 116–17
　nullity of marriage, 321
　United Kingdom, within, 174–5

kidnapping, custody, and, 339, 346–7

land, *see* immovables
leaseholds, 244
legal separation, *see* divorce, foreign
　divorce
legislation, conflict of laws, and, 9–10
legitimacy, 348–51
　choice of law rule for, 348–51
　declaration of, 357
　domicile of origin, and, 350–1
　domicile of parents, and, 350–1
　lawful marriage, birth in, and, 349–50
　recognition of status, 348–51
　void marriage, and, 351
legitimation:
　declaration of, 357
　foreign statute, by, 352–3
　Legitimacy Act 1976, 353

legitimation (*cont.*):
  parental recognition, by, 352
  recognition of foreign, 352–3
  subsequent marriage, and, 352–3
  succession, and, 353
lex actus, meaning, 7
lex causae, meaning, 7
lex domicilii, meaning, 7
lex fori, meaning, 7
lex loci actus, meaning, 7
lex loci celebrationis, meaning, 7
lex loci contractus, meaning, 7
lex loci delicti commissi, meaning, 7
lex loci solutionis, meaning, 7
lex situs, meaning, 7
limitation of actions, 63–4
lis alibi pendens, 94–5, 159–63
local law theory, 381–2
Lugano Convention, 1989, 132

marital status, declaration of, 353
maritime lien, 67
marriage, 295–318
  antenuptial domicile, and, 302–4
  capacity, legal, 301–10
  capacity, physical, 311–12
  choice of law rules, proposals for
    reform, 312
  common law, 299–300
  consent of parties, 310–11
  countries under belligerent occupation,
    300
  dual domicile test, 302–4
  effect on property, 280–1
  Foreign Marriage Acts 1892–1947, 299
  formalities of, 295–301
  immovables, effects upon, 284
  impotence, and, 321
  intended matrimonial home test, 304–6
  lack of age, 321
  lack of parental consent, 297; foreign
    requirement, 297
  lex loci celebrationis, 295–9, 305–7
  locus regit actum, 295
  members of armed forces serving
    abroad, of, 299
  mental disorder, and, 321
  merchant ship on high seas, on board,
    300–1
  movables, effect upon, 277–85
  non-consummation, 321
  nullity of, *see* nullity of marriage
  polygamous, *see* polygamous marriage
  pregnancy *per alium*, and, 321
  previous, 321
  proxy marriage, 296

putative, 351
remarriage, *see* remarriage
renvoi, and, 26
Royal, 309–10
subsequent, legitimation by, 352–3;
  revocation of will by, 274–5
validity of, time factor, and, 30, 297–8
venereal disease, and, 321
void, 321; legitimacy, and, 351
voidable, 321
wilful refusal to consummate, 321
marriage settlement:
  capacity to create, 278–80
  capacity to revoke, 280
  effect on property, 380–1
  formal validity of, 277
  law governing, 277–8
  matrimonial domicile, and, 281
  variation of, 285
matrimonial causes, *see* divorce; foreign
  divorce; nullity of marriage;
  polygamous marriage
matrimonial domicile, meaning of, 281
matrimonial proceedings, staying of, 320
matrimonial property, 277–85
  regimes, 281–4
  see also immutability; marriage
    settlement; mutability
mental disorder, party to marriage
  suffering from, 321
mental patients, domicile of, 50
minor:
  capacity to contract, 208–9
  custody and guardianship of, 334–47;
    see also custody; guardianship
  domicile of dependence of, 48–50
misrepresentation, contract, and, 206
mistake, contract, and, 20
mobilia sequuntur personam, 245
movables:
  displacement of title to, 247–50
  immovables, and, 243–4
  intangible, *see* intangible movables;
    assignment of, 256–61
  law of domicile, and, 245
  lex actus, and, 245–6
  lex loci actus, and, 245
  lex situs, and, changing, 247–51;
    constant, 247
  proper law of transfer, 246
  succession to, *see* succession
  tangible, transfer of, 244–51
  title to, 245–51
multiple damages, foreign judgment for,
  126
mutability, doctrine of, 282–4

nationality:
  ascertainment of, 13
  company, of, 59
  foreign judgment, and, 110–16
natural justice, foreign judgment, and,
  120–1
nullity of marriage, 321–2
  choice of law, 321–2
  domicile, and, 321
  foreign, *see* foreign annulment
  habitual residence, and, 321
  jurisdiction in, 321
  void and voidable marriage, 321

offer and acceptance, contract, and,
  206
orders respecting children:
  English, 336–7, 338
  United Kingdom, recognition of,
  338
ordinary residence, 54–5

parental consent, marriage, and, 297
parental responsibility, EU, and, 344–5
parties, 68
  proper defendant, 68
  proper plaintiff, 68
penal law, foreign, 362–8
  contract, and, 367–8
penalty, foreign judgment for, 125–6
personal representatives:
  English, 268–9
  foreign, grant of representation to,
  269–70
policy evaluation methods, 383–5
polygamous marriage, 312–18
  bar to subsequent monogamous
  marriage, 317
  bigamy, and, 317
  capacity to contract, 315–17
  celebrated in England, validity of, 314,
  317
  change in character, 315
  concubinage, and, 314
  immigration law, and, 314
  income tax, and, 318
  legitimacy, and, 318
  married women's property, and,
  318
  matrimonial causes, and, 319
  meaning of, 313–14
  monogamous, becoming, 315
  nature of ceremony, 314–15
  potential, 314
  recognition of, 317–18
  significance of, 317

social security benefits, and, 318
succession by children, and, 318
succession by wives, and, 318
wife as dependant, 318
pregnancy of wife *per alium*, marriage,
  and, 321
presence:
  jurisdiction of the English court, and,
  72–3
  jurisdiction of the foreign court, and, 398
priorities, 67
  assignment of debts, and, 257–61
private international law:
  name, 5–6
  public international law, and, 386–94
procedure:
  execution of judgments, 66
  lex fori, and, 60
  parties, 68
  priorities, 67
  remedies, 64–6
  substance, and, 60–8
prodigals, 363
proof of foreign law, 33–6
  duty of the court, 35–6
  expert witnesses and, 34–5
  method of proof, 34–5
  status of rules of foreign law, 33–4
property, 244–67
  characterisation, 19, 244
  see also governmental taking of
  property; immovables; intangible
  movables; marriage settlement;
  matrimonial property
proxy marriage, 296
public international law, 386–94
  see also Hague conventions;
  international conventions;
  internationalists, the; Universalists,
  the
public law, foreign, 369–71
public policy:
  adoption, and, 356
  contracts contrary to, 21
  exclusion of foreign law, 361–74
  foreign judgment, and, 121–3
  recognition of foreign divorces and
  annulments manifestly contrary to,
  329
  torts, and, 235
punitive damages, foreign judgment for,
  125–6

reciprocity, foreign judgment, and,
  116–17
refugees, domicile of choice of, 45

remarriage:
  foreign divorce or annulment after,
    307–8
  restrictions on, 308–9
remedies, 64–6
renvoi, 20–7
  application of, 26–7
  arguments against, 23–4
  arguments for, 25
  capacity to marry, and, 26–7
  contract, and, 27, 204
  development of, 20–3
  double, 21
  'English', 21
  essential validity of wills, and, 26
  formal validity of marriage, and, 26
  formal validity of wills, and, 26
  immovables, and, 26
  internal law solution, 21
  legitimation of children, and, 26
  limitation of actions, and, 64
  meaning of, 20–3
  movables, and, 28
  national law of a British citizen, and,
    23–4
  origin of, 20
  partial, 21
  succession, and, 26
  tort, and, 27, 229
  total, 21
  transmission, 21
  trusts, and, 288
residence
  habitual, 55–7
  ordinary, 54–5
restraining foreign proceedings, 100–8
  submission to English arbitration or
    court, 106–8
revenue law, foreign, 368–9

Savigny, theory of, 387–8
sea, tort on, 238–9
search order, 168
separation, legal, *see* divorce; foreign
    divorce
shares, *situs* of, 251–2
ship:
  action against, 83
  marriage celebrated on board, 300–1
  tort on, 239
  will made on board, 272
social security benefits, polygamous
    marriage, and, 318
status:
  declaration as to, 357
  penal, 363

Statutes of Limitation, 63
staying of actions, 84–100
  Brussels Convention and, 159–66
  forum non conveniens, and, 84–100
  lis alibi pendens, 94–5, 159–66
  matrimonial proceedings, in, 90, 320
  submission to foreign arbitration or
    court, 96–8
succession, 268–71
  adoption, and, 356
  immovables, to, 275–6; time factor,
    and, 30
  intestate, *see* intestate succession
  legitimation, and, 353
  movables, to, 275; time factor, and, 28
  renvoi, and, 26
  see also administration of estates;
    personal representatives

talaq divorces, 324–6
taxes, foreign judgment for, 125
territorial theory, 378
third parties, jurisdiction in relation to,
    150–1
time factor, 29–32
  changes in conflict rule, and, 29
  changes in connecting factor, and, 30
  discharge of contract, and, 30–1
  illegitimacy, and, 32
  lex causae, changes in, and, 30–2
  succession to immovables, and, 30
  succession to movables, and, 31
  torts, and, 30–2
  validity of marriage, and, 30
title:
  immovables, to, 266–7
  movables, to, 245–51
  renvoi, and, 26, 28
tort, 220–39
  aircraft, on, 239
  Brussels Convention and, 144–7
  common law, 241–8
  contract, and, 235–7
  defamation, 237
  defendant outside jurisdiction, when,
    81
  England, committed in, 233
  exemption clause, and, 235–7
  general choice of law rule, 22;
    avoidance of, 233–5; exclusion or
    displacement of, 225–6, 227, 231–3
  lex fori, and, 222, 226
  lex fori theory, 220–1
  lex loci delicti, and, 222–5
  lex loci delicti theory, 220
  maritime torts, 238–9

place where harmful event occurred, 80–1, 145–7
place where tort committed, 227–8, 229–30
proper law theory, 221
public policy, and, 235
time factor, and, 235
United States, in, 221
trustee outside jurisdiction, 81
trusts, 286–92
  administration of, 288
  choice of law and, 288–9
  construction of, 288
  constructive, 287
  governing law of, 288–9
  Hague Convention, 1986, 286–7
  mandatory rules and, 288, 289–90
  marriage settlement, under, 278
  public policy and, 291
  recognition of foreign, 289–91
  Recognition of Trusts Act 1987, 286
  renvoi and, 288
  validity of, 288
  variation of, 291–2

United Kingdom:
  jurisdiction between different parts, 174–5
  recognition and enforcement of judgments within, 175
Universalists, the, 387–8

venereal disease, party to marriage
    suffering from, 321
vested rights, theory of, 379–80
void marriage, 321
  legitimacy and, 351
voidable marriage, 321

wardship, 335
wilful refusal to consummate marriage, 321
wills
  authentic form, Dutch, 272
  capacity to make, 271, 275
  construction of, 273, 276
  domicile, and, 272
  essential validity of, 273, 276
  family provision, 318
  formal validity of, 272, 275
  habitual residence, and, 272
  immovables of, 275–6
  interpretation of, 273, 276
  legatee, capacity to take as, 272
  lex situs, and, 272, 275
  movables, of, 271–5
  nationality, and, 272
  renvoi, and, 275
  revocation of, 273–5
  vessel, made on board, 272
  Wills Act 1963, 272
writ, service outside jurisdiction, 81–8